191630/3000

15.00
H112

D1788785

IMPORTED PUBLICATIONS, INC.
320 W. OHIO ST.
CHICAGO, ILL. 60610

HUNGARIAN
FOREIGN POLICY
1919—1945

HUNGARIAN FOREIGN POLICY 1919–1945

by
GYULA JUHÁSZ

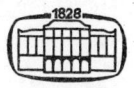

AKADÉMIAI KIADÓ · BUDAPEST 1979

Revised Edition of the Hungarian Original:

MAGYARORSZÁG KÜLPOLITIKÁJA
1919—1945
KOSSUTH KÖNYVKIADÓ, BUDAPEST 1975

Translated
by
Sándor Simon

Translation revised
by
Mária Kovács

ISBN 963 05 1882 1

© Akadémiai Kiadó, Budapest 1979

Printed in Hungary

CONTENTS

CHAPTER I

HUNGARIAN FOREIGN POLICY AT THE TIME OF THE RISE TO POWER AND CONSOLIDATION OF THE COUNTER-REVOLUTIONARY RÉGIME, 1919–1926

1. Antecedents 7
2. International circumstances at the time of the counter-revolutionary take-over   27
3. The peace treaty. Scheming and experimenting in foreign politics from the peace negotiations to admission to the League of Nations 41
4. Foreign politics in the consolidation period 67

CHAPTER II

CONSOLIDATION OF THE FOREIGN POLICY OF COUNTER-REVOLUTIONARY HUNGARY

1. The 'active' foreign policy of the Bethlen Government, 1926–1930 81
2. The effect of the world economic crisis on Hungary's international position and on her foreign policy 93

CHAPTER III

THE BERLIN–ROME AXIS AND HUNGARY, 1933–1939

1. Hungarian foreign policy from 1933 to 1936 107
2. The foreign policy of the Darányi Government 125
3. The Munich Pact and the first Vienna Award 136
4. Hungary's participation in the complete dismemberment of Czechoslovakia . 145

CHAPTER IV

HUNGARY'S FOREIGN POLICY IN THE FIRST STAGE OF THE SECOND WORLD WAR, 1939–1941

1. The foreign policy of the Teleki Government at the outbreak of the Second World War 157
2. The 'funny war' and Hungary 165
3. The second Vienna Award and its consequences 172
4. Hungary's participation in the aggression against Yugoslavia 177
5. Hungary's entry into the Second World War 188
6. The functions of foreign policy in counter-revolutionary Hungary. The road to war 190

CHAPTER V

HUNGARIAN FOREIGN POLICY IN THE SECOND STAGE OF THE WORLD WAR

1. Hungary's more active participation in the war against the Soviet Union. Declaration of war on Hungary by Great Britain and the United States 199
2. The Kállay Government's foreign political ambitions and half-hearted attempts to withdraw from the war 208
3. The German occupation of Hungary 284
4. Horthy's attempt at defection. The 15th of October, 1944 299
5. Formation of the Provisional Government at Debrecen. Signing of the armistice 330

Sources and references 339
Index of names 351

CHAPTER I

HUNGARIAN FOREIGN POLICY AT THE TIME OF THE RISE TO POWER AND CONSOLIDATION OF THE COUNTER-REVOLUTIONARY RÉGIME, 1919–1926

1. Antecedents

In August 1919 the great attempt at a democratic and socialist transformation of Hungarian society ended in failure. The intervention of the Entente Powers, the superiority of the forces of intervention, and the activity of domestic reaction, all acted to bring about the collapse of the Soviet government. The new trend of Hungarian foreign policy for the next 25 years of counter-revolutionary government already began to take shape after the collapse.

The foreign policy of a country is determined by both its social system and international relations. These not being static, renders the examination of certain antecedents necessary, which should also be complemented by a careful consideration of how they were conceived by the different groups of the state-forming nation.

After the fall of the Hungarian Republic of Councils, the political attitude of the Hungarian ruling classes returning to power was indelibly marked by two staggering experiences within barely a year: 1. The revolutions of 1918/1919 which, during the spring of 1919, had culminated in the establishment of soviet power, in an attempt to achieve a radical, socialist transformation of Hungarian society. 2. The disintegration of 'historical' Hungary as a result of the collapse of the Austro-Hungarian Monarchy. After four years of the world war which ended with the defeat of the Central Powers, an entirely new international situation had been created. A revolutionary wave swept all over Europe under the influence of the successful socialist revolution in Russia. The revolution and the disintegration, having taken place simultaneously, shocked the Hungarian ruling classes as catastrophes that followed from one another, and were conceived, falsely — as it happens when political fear predominates — as events in causal relation. We may not be far from the truth if we say that public opinion in Hungary coincided with this view.

When reviewing the foreign policy of the counter-revolutionary period, therefore, we cannot omit to make a brief survey of the preceding war years.

Having been defeated in the war, the Monarchy collapsed and fell apart. The Allied Powers signed an armistice with Austria–Hungary in Padua on November 3, 1918. The agreement provided for the cessation of hostilities and the evacuation of the territories which troops of the Monarchy had occupied during the war. The line of demarcation was only drawn on the south-western front, the armistice line for Hungary was thus left to coincide with the historical boundaries of the country (without Croatia). It was the irony of fate that the signatories on behalf of Austro—Hungary no longer represented any country: the Monarchy had practically ceased to exist by then.

On October 28, 1918, the Czech National Council announced the formation of an independent Czechoslovak Republic. On October 30 the Slovak National Council proclaimed the independence of Slovakia and her union with the Czech state. On October 29 the Croatian regional assembly announced secession from the Kingdom of Hungary and from the Austro—Hungarian Empire, and joined the Serb—Croat—Slovene state. On October 27 the Rumanians living in the Monarchy proclaimed secession and on the 31st the Ukrainians did the same. On the 30th the Austrian National Assembly adopted a new, provisional constitution for Austria. And finally, on October 31, 1918, the bourgeois democratic revolution was launched in Hungary; the Károlyi Government, proclaiming the independent Republic of Hungary, took office.

The Monarchy was torn to pieces by its own nations. The declarations of independence, the formation of autonomous Governments and National Councils only aggravated the crisis of the Monarchy's dualist system that had been gradually unfolding and deepening long since. Dualism itself was a product of the crisis of the Habsburg empire, in which five historical nations and six nationalities were forced into a single frame by the international and military power of the dynasty, without any one of those nations or nationalities identifying themselves with the Monarchy.

Even the Austrian Germans denied to identify themselves with the Monarchy, because to them the Compromise of 1867 meant abandoning their status as the leading people in the entire Monarchy; what is more, after the establishment of German unity under Prussian leadership, they even lost the hope to regain the leading role they had once played within the German Empire. The Dualist Compromise was opposed by several nationalities, among them by the Slavs, constituting the majority of the population. It became more and more difficult to explain to them why they could not be granted the rights of statehood Hungary enjoyed.

In a few decades after 1867, Dualism was heavily opposed by ever growing national aspirations and the feeling against those in power became stronger in Hungary too. The Magyar supporters of Dualism rigidly guarded the edifice erected in 1867, in an effort to protect their class interests, and out of an ingrained fear of the national movements and the dynasty's — already diminishing — international and military weight. They guarded it as a form of constitutionality, although it was nothing of the sort; and as a token of independence, although essentially, it was far from being that; as a guarantee of the continuity of historical Hungary, although it was no longer that.

True, the half century of Dualism provided opportunity for a more rapid economic development all over the Monarchy even though territorial inequalities and phase lags in economy persisited. This development, however, couldn't be fully realized, because the advantages of belonging to a greater community were paired by the disadvantages of the rigid political structure of the Austrian Empire, of its social and political backwardness and the national conflicts it couldn't avoid. The immense energies spent for decades on reforming and developing the 1867 settlement were to no avail, and could do little to prevent its becoming politically and morally discredited by the first decade of the twentieth century. Serious problems became manifest in Hungarian society and political life and in the intellectual development of the country. National and ethnic conflicts grew into irreconcilable contradictions. Political development came to an impasse, because from 1867 onward the independent Hungarian Ministry, responsible to the Parliament, depended on a solid parliamentary majority which had to accept the Compromise under all circumstances and, with it, everything the Compromise could and did imply: the rejection of a democratic political government; an extremely restricted suffrage and the practice of electoral fraud, political mudslinging and corruption; counterselection in filling political, administrative and other public functions; backwardness in public education; and, if the need arose, the use of brute force. thus paralysing the advocates of complete independence, social revolution and national self-determination from gaining a majority. In Hungary, this state of affairs was not only accepted by the ruling classes, by the main body of political leaders, but also by the bulk of the intelligentsia, which in this country, as in all of Central Europe, played an outstandingly significant role in formulating public opinion. The demand for an entirely independent constitutional Hungary was tantamount to the dissolution of the Monarchy, and the consistent implementation of democratic freedoms would also have implied the right of nations to self-determination, and this would have entailed the risk of historical Hungary's falling to pieces. The intelligentsia did not dare to face such dangers. They were afraid of the military power of the dynasty behind which, remembering the catastrophe of 1849 and the era of absolutism, they saw the support of the European Great Powers; and they were also afraid of the secessionist aspirations of the nationalities, not forgetting their attitude towards the revolution and the War of Independence of 1848/1849. (It may not be needless to point out here that the dismantlement of the 'historical' framework was reckoned with neither by the Hungarian progressives nor by the working-class movement.)

This is how the nationalist ideology which basically determined the views and social attitude of the Hungarian ruling classes had, by the turn of the century, evolved into a pervasive chauvinism. It came to influence the great masses of Hungarian society: the middle classes, the intelligentsia, the petty-bourgeoisie, and even a considerable part of the labouring classes. The more so, since the promoters of this ideology, primarily the landed gentry, coupled it demagogically with the anti-Habsburg aspirations of the masses, although this nationalism had long departed from the progressive democratic political and ideological aspirations endorsed by the bourgeois forces at the time of the revolution of 1848 and the subsequent War of Independence.

During the half century of Dualism, social development came to a standstill. The feudal vestiges had not disappeared. In point of fact, the immobility of power relations in Hungarian society persisted.

The stagnation in the policy towards the nationalities now became absolute; the same fear that had dragged Hungary into the Compromise, now induced the holders of power to avert the danger of the disintegration of historical Hungary by forcibly assimilating the national minorities. But the coercive political methods, the repressive cultural measures and the frequently brutal police actions against the nationalities only resulted in provoking an unprecedented hostility towards the Hungarian state by the turn of the century, while the linguistic and ethnic boundaries within Hungary remained unchanged.

The crisis of Dualism meant not only an internal but also an international crisis of the Monarchy. The international relations, which made the creation and the survival of the Dualist Monarchy possible, changed radically by the first decade of the twentieth century. The rivalry between the imperialist powers for the repartition of the spheres of influence led to certain shifts in the Alliances. Austria–Hungary allied with Germany and turned against Great Britain, Czarist Russia and France. The disintegration of the Turkish Empire, a protracted process, completed by the Balkan wars, inspired the newly free Balkan peoples to ever more energetic efforts to achieve nationhood, which in turn, gave further impetus to the national movements inside the Monarchy.

And so, when under the pressure of a growing war weariness and the senseless losses, of the increasingly unbearable privations and the peoples' desire for peace, the Governments, at the turn of 1916 to 1917, began seeking a way out of the imperialist war towards an imperialist peace; when the oppressed classes of the belligerent countries, encouraged partly by the victory of the 1917 Socialist Revolution in Russia, began to demand a democratic peace settlement, there was but little doubt that before long the Monarchy would also meet its fate.

Coupled with the aspirations for national independence, the revolutionary movements led by the working classes opened up new prospects for social and national emancipation to the peoples of the Monarchy too. The decree of the Leninist Soviet Government on peace, the repudiation of the power ambitions of Czarist Russia and the Soviet proclamations on nationalities all worked to the same effect as the unambiguous signs of the defeat of the Central Powers did. Even those weak ties that previously had, to some extent, bound the peoples under Habsburg rule to the Monarchy on the basis of certain national interests, had been dissolved by this time. The relatively long survival of the obsolete Dualist Empire was not only made possible by the international balance of power, or by its own military strength and oppressive apparatus, and by the power and influence of the ruling classes, but it was also aided by the fact that the nations living within its boundaries saw a lesser evil in keeping up the Monarchy than in the dangers they were to face in case of its dissolution: the Poles and Rumanians were threatened by Czarist Russia, the Czechs and Slovenes by pan-Germanism, and the South Slavs of the Adriatic coast by Italian irredentism. This may have been one of the reasons why the oppressed nations of the Monarchy were initially in support of the war, although disappointment and hidden opposition were soon to be faced.

The fall of Czarist Russia and the victory of the Socialist Revolution practically thwarted these threats and influenced the Entente Powers in favour of the right of peoples to self-determination and made it, at least in principle, the basis of settlement in Eastern Europe.

At the outbreak of the World War the Entente Powers had not yet thought of the dissolution of the Monarchy. And although their concept as to the fate of the Monarchy underwent certain alterations when seen required to win the war, they did not question the survival of the Monarchy until 1918, and spoke only of certain territorial losses. The strategy of the Entente Powers was to win over new allies by diplomatic means, to weaken the enemy camp. To this end, they took advantage of the national and ethnic problems, just as the other belligerent bloc did. In the Monarchy, for example, special army corps were organized on a national basis to demonstrate the government's respect for national self-determination (these subsequently gave significant support to the efforts at secession and achieving independent statehood). Both Germany and the Entente made territorial promises. In the Treaty of London (April 1915), for example, the Entente Powers promised Italy the Italian-inhabited parts of Austria (later Tyrol as well), Trieste and a part of Dalmatia. Their note of August 18, 1915, promised to let Serbia have Bosnia—Herzegovina, Slavonia, Croatia and Fiume (now Rijeka, Yugoslavia). The Bucharest Treaty of Alliance and Military Convention with the Allies signed on August 17, 1916, provided that Rumania should have Transylvania, the Banat as far as the Tisza river, and Bukovina. But these treaties were not intended to change the structure of the Monarchy fundamentally, and even the Entente peace terms offered in January 1917 spoke only of a settlement on a national basis. At the same time, certain influential Entente circles emphasized the necessity to dismember the Monarchy.

At the same time, the émigré politicians of the oppressed nations of the Monarchy meant to achieve their aims by currying favour with the Entente. As early as May 1915, Croatian émigrés established the Yugoslav Committee with the rallying cry for a united Yugoslav state. Serbia agreed to the programme of establishing the Kingdom of Serbs, Croats and Slovenes united under the Karageorgevich dynasty only much later, in July 1917. At that time, the Entente Powers did not yet recognize the Southern Slav Kingdom.

The Czechoslovak émigrés were active in Paris under the leadership of Thomas G. Masaryk and Eduard Beneš. The Czech Committee was formed in November 1915, followed in February 1916 by the Czechoslovak National Council which announced the programme of an independent Czecho—Slovak state.

The Entente Powers gave the émigré committees political support but denied their official recognition. For a long time the bourgeois émigré politicians had no effective national movements behind them, because the genuine political activity of the oppressed nations only began to take shape after the turn in world politics. The revolutionary agitation reached the areas inhabited by the nationalities in the spring of 1918.

The national committees functioning abroad could now justify their aims in the eyes of their Western protectors by pointing to the manifestations of democratic national public opinion and could argue that, in view of the apparent danger of revolution, the bourgeois leaders should receive support to strengthen their influence. Their efforts were crowned with success; the Entente Powers, led by military considerations of an earliest possible total victory — especially after the failure of the attempts at a separate peace — deemed the partition of the Monarhy advisable.

The change in the attitude of the Entente Powers was primarily due to the new power relations in Europe. Although there were British and even some French political circles which saw no point in the dismemberment of the Monarchy, nevertheless by 1918 they lost their importance in France, while the British acknowledged the dissolution as an unalterable fact. With Germany's defeat, it was thought that German pressure would ease for some time. And the victory of the October Revolution rendered it likely that Czarist pan-Slavism no longer represented a danger and this in turn weakened the argument that the Monarchy might serve as a stronghold against Russian expansionism. The revolution seemed to eliminate Russia as a power factor from European politics for a long time to come. On the other hand, leading Western, especially French, politicians expected to strengthen the defence against a renewal of the German peril and against Bolshevist advance in Central Europe by the dissolution of the Monarchy. The general view was that the continued existence of the Monarchy would only further provide Germany with its traditional potential ally, while the new national states with feelings of fresh successes and nationalism could counterbalance Germany better, and what is more, they could resist 'Communist contagion' more efficiently than the multinational Central European Empire with its built in conflicts. Instrumental in the change of the Entente's attitude was the hostility of Western public opinion towards the Monarchy's reactionary system, especially concerning the treatment of the nationalities in Hungary. This was what enabled the bourgeois leaders of the ethnic movements to combine their national efforts with the cause of freedom, democracy and enlightenment.

Under the combined effect of these factors the Entente Powers gave up their position regarding the integrity of the Monarchy. In the summer of 1918 they recognized the Czechoslovak National Council as a belligerent ally, and promised support to the leaders of other nationalities too. The dissolution of the Monarchy resulted in a revolutionary crisis in the summer and autumn of 1918.

In the autumn of 1918 the Monarchy fell to pieces. The formation of the new states led by the nationalist bourgeoisie was in the line of progress as compared to the Dualist system, but did not, and could not, solve the problems of the peoples of the Danube Basin. The question of the dissolution of the Monarchy has widely been discussed since the First World War. Arguments have been set forward by politicians and diplomats, publicists and historians. According to some, the dissolution of the Monarchy was merely due to the unfortunate great-power policy of the Entente. Others — mainly in counter-revolutionary Hungary — blamed the revolutions of 1918/1919. And even many of those who understood that the failure of the Dualist system, the disappearance of the Habsburgs from the European political scene, had been a long maturing historical necessity, raised the question whether it had been impossible to replace the old structure with a modern federation of states which, besides the full implementation of national self-determination, could have provided opportunities for the Danubian peoples to find new forms of co-existence, and to modernize their social and economic life.

Although questions like 'What would have been if...' and 'How would it have happened if...?' are unhistorical, these debates did in fact stimulate the scholars of history by provoking them to enter into a comprehensive research of the Dualist era, to analyse its economic, socio-political and ethnic problems. Their results have shown that the requisites were not given at that time for a federative transformation of the Monarchy, for a radical reorganization of the political structure, for the liquidation of the feudal vestiges, for successfully balancing national forces (which would have been vital for a more favourable economic development). Nor was there to be found the goodwill necessary to dispel the mutual prejudices and habitual fears which set the peoples of the area against one another. The political boundaries of the nations within the Monarchy did not even roughly follow the ethnic dividing lines, and no effort was made to set the boundaries more satisfactorily.

And although the nations and nationalities within the Monarchy shared the same fate end underwent similar development in history, they weren't unified by such historical experiences which would have brought them together, unlike in the case of the Soviet Union where the peoples of the historical Russian empire were long fused together by a succession of staggering historical events: the Socialist Revolution, the civil war, then the heroic struggle for a new society, and the Great Patriotic War.

Revolutionary forces in the Danube Basin were strong enough to destroy the Monarchy, and they were able to meet the national demands, but at the same time, they were incapable of carrying out an overall social reform, so much so that most of the new states didn't even succeed in forming a democratic republic. In 1918/1919 the newly won national independence of the respective areas was already exploited to back an expansionist great-power policy. Justified national aspirations were confused with expansionism, and both were, for the most part, fulfilled by the good offices of the Great Powers. The ethnic and national conflicts persisted within the particular countries; what is more, they grew all the more acute as the nationality problem became regarded as an issue of foreign policy. New grievances, fears and emotions were added to the old ones, because the frontiers of the newly independent countries did not coincide with the 'historically' conceived national borderlines; because national independence did not necessarily bring about a bourgeois democratic transformation; and because wherever such a transformation or revolution did succeed, it either resulted in the establishment of some multinational state completely lacking any kind of historical tradition, or in the destruction of the traditional frameworks of statehood. Economic difficulties were accumulating, due not only to the disintegration of the traditional economic unit of the Monarchy, but also because political differences and territorial aspirations stood in the way of efficient cooperation between the new states. Furthermore, the region as a whole fell a prey to the struggle for great-power influences. The Great Powers, especially France, were soon to realize that their efforts to adjust the new Central Europe to their security policy and their interests had been unsuccessful. The sense of failure reached some of the far-sighted Western politicians in no time, but there was no way of undoing the accomplished facts.

When, in the autumn of 1918, the revolution brought the National Council to power, most Hungarians hoped that the victorious Powers would sympathize with the Károlyi Government's bourgeois democratic and Wilsonian principles, and would, to show their approval, define Hungary's new frontiers favourably.

These hopes were only enhanced by illusions about the Fourteen Points which President Wilson of the United States proposed in January 1918 urging "The settlement of every question ... upon the basis of the free acceptance of that settlement by the people immediately concerned, and not upon the basis of the material interest or advantage of any other nation or people", and by Wilson's message of November 5, 1915, calling for the consolidation of the national and social movements under a bourgeois democratic system.

International realities, however, left no room for illusions. The Entente Powers were much less concerned with the bourgeois democratic character of the Government than with the fact that Hungary was one of the losers of the war. Károlyi's bourgeois democratic régime was thus, from the beginning, crippled by being the successor to a morally bankrupt system. The Great Powers, fearing revolution and Communism, supported the formation of strong Czech, Rumanian and South Slav states at Hungary's expense. Although there was no consensus among the Entente Powers on a Central European settlement, jockeying as they all were for economic positions in the region, they all basically agreed that no conflict among them should interfere with their concerted action against the Communist peril.

Disagreements were thus overcome to give way to the Poincaré—Clemenceau line, which intended to create a chain of strong successor states — covering as vast an area as possible, regardless of ethnic considerations — on the territory of the former Monarchy as a protective belt against Germany and Soviet Russia and as a dividing zone between these two Powers. At the same time, the leaders of the states emerging on the territory of the Monarchy or obtaining part of it also tried to secure the biggest possible share of the loot, primarily to consolidate their position against the popular revolutionary movements.

So the Padua armistice failed to fulfil the territorial promises which the Entente Powers had made to the Czech émigré Government, to the representatives of the South Slav peoples and to the Rumanian Government. It was evident that the Czechs, Yugoslavs and Rumanians would do their best still before the peace conference to take possession of the territories they had been promised. And indeed, the turn of events in this direction was not long to come. Composed mostly of Serbian armed units, the Entente forces in the East, under the command of French General Franchet d'Esperey, marched up into the Balkans in preparation to push forward against Germany who was still fighting. Advanced guards crossed the river Save on November 5, 1918. It seemed almost certain that the Balkan army would not respect the Padua armistice provisions concerning the Hungarian frontiers.

In this situation the Hungarian Government, since it could not think of armed resistance, decided to send a delegation to Belgrade to negotiate with General Franchet d'Esperey about the application of the Padua armistice agreement to Hungary. At the same time the delegates wished to propose that the National Councils should present their territorial demands to the Peace Conference, and abstain from the use of arms until its decision had been taken. The Government thought that direct connection with Franchet d'Esperey would sufficiently document its break with the former policy and its orientation towards the Entente.

In Belgrade on November 13, 1918, the Hungarian delegation led by Károlyi signed the military convention proposed by Franchet d'Esperey giving effect to the armistice agreement in relation to Hungary. The main provisions were as follows: the Hungarian troops should be withdrawn to the line running from the upper Szamos valley, through Beszterce (now Bistrita, Rumania), along the river Maros, Baja and Pécs down to the river Drava. Evacuation was to take place within eight days. The evacuated territory would be occupied by Allied forces, but its civil administration would be controlled by the Hungarian Government. The Hungarian army should be reduced to six infantry and two cavalry divisions. The Allies would have the right to make use of all means of transport and communication in the country, to occupy all localities and strategic points indicated by the Allied High Command. Hungary would be obliged to sever all relations with Germany. Finally it was provided that the Allies would not interfere in Hungary's internal affairs.

Franchet d'Esperey did not recognize the general validity of the Padua armistice which designated Hungary's historical frontiers as the line of demarcation. The convention failed to make mention of Northern Hungary.

Though unfriendly, Franchet d'Esperey was in fact a correct and understanding negotiating partner, but his standpoint was contrary to the Entente policy concerning these parts of Europe, contrary to the promises made by the Great Powers to their Czechoslovak, Rumanian and Yugoslav allies, and this is why the terms he dictated to the Hungarians were 'unrealistic'.

Clemenceau angrily called Franchet d'Esperey to account for the conclusion of the Belgrade military convention implying the *de facto* recognition of the Károlyi Government, and for the fact that the Slovak-inhabited areas had been left under Hungarian administration. In his letter of December 1 he wrote that the armistice had been concluded with representatives of 'an alleged Hungarian state', a state which the Allies did not recognize and which was not even existing internationally. He would have most gladly declared the convention null and void, but for practical reasons he assented to the implementation, "as an arrangement made with the local authorities", of those provisions which did not run counter to the Padua armistice. Accordingly, he instructed Franchet d'Esperey to take steps to get the Hungarian troops withdrawn from Slovakia.

The Belgrade military convention satisfied neither the Hungarian Government nor the Governments of the neighbouring countries. Even the small Allies were quarrelling among themselves. Rumania and Yugoslavia, for example, were rivalling for the possession of the Banat, and their conflict led to the involvement of French forces in the occupation of the Banat. The provisions of the Belgrade convention were not carried out. On December 5th Rumanian troops crossed the demarcation line. The Czech Government got things moving in Paris and succeeded in occupying Slovakia in defiance of the convention. In the occupied territories the provision on the maintenance of Hungarian administration was not observed. The danger of all Hungary's military occupation had become imminent.

The conclusion of the Belgrade military convention, or rather its violation on the part of the Allied Powers, fundamentally affected the position of the Károlyi Government, which was unable and unwilling to use force. Not even after the violation of the convention did it take action against the intruders, because it was afraid that engagement in armed conflicts with the neighbouring countries enjoying Allied support might jeopardize Hungary's chances at the Peace Conference.

In reality the Hungarian government could not have been able to deploy any considerable military force; this had already been precluded in advance by the discharge of the army, speeded up by the Government's pacifist policy. The Government saw the only chance in convincing the Great Powers of how intolerable the situation was, and in working out a compromise with the nationalities. But the conception underlying this attempt — built upon Oszkár Jászi's ideas of preserving the integrity of Hungary proper by granting broad autonomy to the nationalities, with the transformation of the country into a kind of 'Eastern Switzerland' — was already anachronistic. Nor did the negotiations with the nationality leaders bring any result. Dozens of protests and proclamations were addressed to the Entente military representative in Hungary, Lieutenant-Colonel Vix, who had arrived in Budapest as the head of a 57-member delegation on November 26 with the intention of enforcing the implementation of the Belgrade military convention. The proclamations pointed out that occupation was contrary to the Wilsonian principles and inconsistent with international law, that it arbitrarily anticipated the decisions of the peace conference, and even disregarded the Belgrade convention. The protests proved ineffectual, for from December 1918 onward Paris adopted an expressly hostile attitude towards the Hungarian 'sham Government'.

By the end of November the Foreign Minister of France had already informed his diplomatic representatives in London, Rome and Washington of the situation with regard to Hungary. He qualified the appointment of Róza Bédy-Schwimmer to head the Hungarian Legation in Switzerland as a tactical move on the Hungarian part, and asked the envoys to warn the respective Governments of "the perfidious and sly policy of the Hungarians, especially Count Károlyi", whose ultra-democratic façade he interpreted only to serve the purpose of continuing the oppression of non-Hungarian nationalities.

The Hungarian Government tried everything, both through official and non-official channels, to enter into contact with the Entente Powers, but, up to the end of 1918, its attempts were of no avail.

On December 3 Lieutenant-Colonel Vix informed Károlyi of the French Government's decision: France did not recognize Károlyi's Government. Shortly London and Washington endorsed the French position. Yet, even Vix was embarrassed by the successive violations of the Belgrade military convention. In this report of December 23 he wrote: "In summary, the Convention of November 13 is no more than a scrap of paper. The attitude taken by our small Allies and by ourselves, the absence of authority capable of redressing the abuses, seem to show well that now there is one authority: the right of the strongest." When at last a change nevertheless occurred in this respect, it was not due to efforts of the Hungarian Government, but to the work of the Peace Conference.

The Allied attitude towards the extinct Austro–Hungarian Monarchy, inclusive of Hungary, was again determined by power interests and conflicts at the Peace Conference that opened in January 1919. The United States and Great Britain — concentrating primarily on the colonial question and on strengthening and extending their naval forces — were not directly interested in this part of Europe, but they did not wish to see French influence grow too strong. Britain did not wish to see the total destruction of Germany's continental position, which the French were intent on carrying out. On the other hand, both the French and the Italians tried to win parts of the former Monarchy under their influence. Owing to her great-power status, to her good relations with the Czechs, Rumanians and South Slavs, France was in a better position and was able to take advantage of it to the detriment of Italy at the peace conference. In order to secure stability and equilibrium as soon as possible, President Wilson and British Prime Minister Lloyd George spoke out against the French excesses and the greed of the new states, but this was of little consequence to Hungary, because their common interests — primarily the demonstration of unity against the danger of revolution — overcame the disagreements between the Allies.

One of the main problems of the Entente Powers was the 'Russian question'. The debates in connection with the intervention naturally led to the question as to which states could be counted upon to act against Soviet Russia, how could they prevent the spread of the revolution, particularly in the Danube Basin where the revolutionary wave was still rising. The staunchest to advocate destroying Soviet Russia and overcoming the danger of revolution by force of arms was France, and this was also why French policy-makers attained a decisive influence in any matter concerning Central Europe, including the question of Hungary's frontiers.

The Peace Conference, or rather its member Powers, appointed special committees to investigate the political and economic situation in Austria, Hungary and the neighbouring countries. The American political mission headed by A. C. Coolidge and the economic mission under A. E. Taylor arrived in Budapest in January 1919. Having studied the state of affairs in Hungary, and on the basis of their consultations with the Government, they informed the Peace Conference that the position of the Hungarian Government was extremely unstable, the influence of Communists in turn was considerable and the soldiers' councils under Communist direction already constituted effective power. The domestic difficulties were only added by failures in foreign policy. The Government was powerless against the Czech, Rumanian and Serbian actions taken in violation of the armistice. In conclusion, with a view to avoiding a debacle, the committees found it necessary to render the Hungarian Government economic, political and possibly military assistance.

Simultaneously with the organization of the Entente missions the Peace Conference dealt with the armed and political conflicts raging in Hungary and in other parts of the former Monarchy. On January 24, 1919, the Council of Ten, upon British initiative, issued a communiqué censuring the internecine struggles and denouncing the efforts to influence the decisions of the Peace Conference by occupying certain territories. But the communiqué did not bring too great a result. When, towards the end of January, 1919, the Peace Conference began to discuss the territorial problems of former Monarchy areas, sharp conflicts developed between Rumania and Yugoslavia, between Italy and Yugoslavia, as well as between Czechoslovakia and Poland. Finally, on February 13, 1919, the Council of Ten requested the military committee chaired by Marshal Foch to work out proposals for the cessation of the hostilities in the territory of the former Monarchy.

The visits to Budapest by the Taylor and Coolidge missions and the communiqué of January 24 inspired the Hungarian Government with the hope that Hungary had at last been integrated into the Great Powers' sphere of interest, and that this would surely mean their effective political and economic assistance. But this hope soon collapsed. In reality, every Hungarian effort came up against a definitively adverse policy and proved to be of no avail.

The Hungarian Government received no political or economic assistance from the Great Powers. Domestic difficulties grew from day to day and finally led to a Government crisis in January 1919. By that time the Allies had also realized that the Hungarian Government was extremely unstable domestically and was unable to display enough strength to control the Communist movement. Berinkey's Government tried to refute this conclusion; on February 20 it had leaders of the Communist Party of Hungary arrested, after a demonstration in front of the Népszava editorial offices. They expected that, as a repercussion, Hungary would be treated less severely in Paris.

The Government's foreign and domestic policy, which, by February 1919, had been entirely suited to the Entente demands, failed to bring the desired results. In mid-March the Government could no more rely on any serious force to back it up; its position could have been improved only if armed assistance had come from the Entente. Instead of giving assistance, however, the Peace Conference took measures which directly caused the fall of the bourgeois democratic Government.

As mentioned before, the Council of Ten dealt with the conflicts in the territory of the former Monarchy in the second half of January 1919. The committee in charge of Rumanian affairs proposed the creation of a neutral zone between Rumania and Hungary, by withdrawing the armed forces ten kilometres deep on both sides, and called for an Entente occupation of the evacuated area. The proposal was accepted on February 26, 1919. The decision was intended to bolster Marshal Foch's plan of intervention against Soviet Russia. It would have, on the one hand, given new territories to the Rumanians as a reward for fighting against the Soviet state (the demarcation line it indicated was by and large fulfilling the promises made to Rumania in the London Treaty of 1916) and, on the other hand, the neutral zone was meant to secure the rear of the Rumanian troops of intervention. In addition, it would have ensured the northward railway connection in case of an intervention. Intervention was the sole objective, for there had been no effective incidents between Rumanian and Hungarian forces up till then. The neutral zone would have run north-west of Vásárosnamény, west of Debrecen, Dévaványa, Gyoma, Hódmezővásárhely and Szeged, reaching the southern demarcation line below Szeged.

Lieutenant-Colonel Vix presented the note on the neutral zone to Mihály Károlyi on March 20, 1919, fixing March 21 as the deadline for a reply.

That note produced conclusive evidence as to the fact that the Peace Conference, or more precisely, the French political and military circles attributed no significance to the bourgeois democratic nature of the Hungarian government. It thus became evident that the acceptance of the ultimatum would bring about the downfall of the Government already on the verge of collapse. At the Cabinet meeting held on the evening of March 20, Károlyi stated that the Government's pro-Entente policy meant failure, its position was untenable in domestic and foreign relations alike. He proposed that power should be transmitted to those who were enjoying the support of the working classes, the single organized force in the country, and who, with their program of a radical social transformation were able to draw a mass support by which they could prevent any further dismemberment of the country. At the Cabinet meeting the Government unanimously decided to resign.

On March 21, 1919, as a result of negotiations held in the Budapest City Prison, Communist and Social Democratic leaders agreed to merge their parties and to assume power, proclaiming a Republic of Councils in Hungary.

With the proclamation of the Hungarian Republic of Councils the Hungarian foreign policy changed radically. Its new principles were determined by the proletarian character of power. It followed that the Government should seek alliance with Soviet Russia instead of the Entente. The Socialist Party of Hungary and the Revolutionary Governing Council declared 'complete ideological and spiritual community' with the Government of Soviet Russia and proposed a military alliance with the Russian proletariat.

The proletarian character of the Hungarian Republic of Councils made it possible to establish the relationships with the neighbouring peoples on an entirely new basis. Leaders of the Hungarian proletarian state repeatedly stressed that the Republic of Councils did not insist upon the principle of territorial integrity and would not use force to bring non-Magyar people under its sway, that it would scrupulously respect the right of peoples to self-determination.

The Hungarian Republic of Councils was determined to maintain peaceful relations with all peoples and all states. The Government had no expansionist designs in any direction whatever, but having set itself against the Great Powers, it had to face the consequences from the very outset.

News of the events in Budapest took the participants in the Paris Peace Conference by surprise. The formation of a Socialist Republic in Hungary was like a bombshell in Paris, where it was understood that the most significant among the aims of the Republic of Councils was not the protection of Hungarian national interests but the spread of Communism. The Entente Powers were fearing that the Hungarian example would soon be followed in Rumania, Czechoslovakia and elsewhere. It seemed that the efforts made to contain the advance of Communism proved futile. The establishment of the Republic of Councils in Hungary thus created a new source of conflicts between the Great Powers. American and British politicians had already expressed their disagreement with the general line of overt armed intervention which was primarily represented by the French High Command and the French Foreign Minister. After March 21, 1919, Great Britain, the United States and Italy emphasized more and more that they blamed the unreasonably rigid anti-Communist policy of France for the situation in Central Europe, and that the idea of a neutral zone also originated from the French, namely from Marshal Foch. Even Clemenceau himself didn't share the opinion of his generals, he was for a policy of wait and see, for the blockade, that is, for indirect methods. On March 29 he gave Franchet d'Esperey instruction to content himself with 'checking the Bolshevist advance', because the occupation of Budapest was out of the question.

Until early April the Great Powers participating in the Peace Conference had been unable to reach an agreement and this greatly influenced the situation of the Republic of Councils. As the Entente policy at the outset was not focussed on intervention, on an 'immediate overthrow', the Revolutionary Governing Council of Hungary could set about the solution of its tasks in domestic and foreign politics under relatively peaceful conditions.

In this situation the foreign policy of the Republic of Councils was aimed at taking advantage of the differences between the Entente Powers. It was beyond doubt that the Entente Powers felt a deep antipathy to the proletarian dictatorship, yet they deemed it reasonable to normalize relations, because the peaceful declarations of the Governing Council and its appropriate practical measures could not be construed as a pretext for intervention.

On March 24, 1919, the People's Commissariat of Foreign Affairs sent the Entente Powers a note which was taken to Paris by the Italian Duke Borghese staying in Budapest. The note pointed out: 1. The Revolutionary Governing Council recognized the validity of the armistice signed by the preceding Government, and was of the opinion that rejection of the Vix note did not mean a violation of the agreement. 2. When the Governing Council entered into an alliance with Russia, it did not think that this step could be interpreted as the severance of diplomatic relations with the Entente Powers or as a declaration of war upon the Entente. Its alliance with Soviet Russia was no formal diplomatic alliance but a tie of natural friendship which followed from the identical constitutional structure of the two countries and could have nothing in common with an aggressive combination. It was the firm desire of the new Hungarian Republic to live in peace with all other nations. 3. The Socialist Party of Hungary wished to organize a new kind of 'socialist state' in which all men lived by their own labour, but this state would not be hostile to other nations; on the contrary, it wanted to co-operate with them. 4. The Government of the Hungarian Republic of Councils declared itself ready to discuss the territorial questions on the basis of the principle of self-determination, and it viewed territorial integrity accordingly. Finally, the note stated that the Governing Council would gladly welcome to Budapest a civil and diplomatic mission of the Entente, would guarantee it extraterritoriality and provide for its absolute safety.

When the note was introduced to the Council of Four by Prime Minister Orlando of Italy on March 29, it raised quite a storm. At the meeting of March 31, the Great Powers, with the exception of France, condemned the way in which the Peace Conference had treated Hungary until then. British Prime Minister Lloyd George expressed doubts as to whether the Vix note had made it sufficiently clear that the neutral zone would have no effect upon the definition of new frontiers. Wilson thought that the decision on the neutral zone was unwise, and that the Allies should avoid treating the states of the area harshly, because this might drive them into the arms of Bolshevism.

He proposed that a mission should be sent to Budapest. Lloyd George and the Italian Prime Minister were of the same view, while the French became isolated for the time being. The Council of Four decided to send an Entente mission headed by General Smuts to Budapest to make inquiries.

Although the delegation of Smuts did not mean the recognition of the Governing Council, it was an outstanding diplomatic success of the young Hungarian Republic of Councils: the preparations for intervention were to be suspended for the time being, even though considerable Allied forces had been concentrated both in the north and in the south.

The General's special train arrived at the Eastern Station in Budapest on April 4, 1919. The new proposal made by Smuts on behalf of the Great Powers was more favourable than that of the Vix note: 1. the Hungarian Government should withdraw its troops to a newly drawn line of demarcation, which was more advantageous to Hungary than that designated in the Vix note; 2. the Rumanian troops would be forbidden to advance further from their actual positions; 3. the neutral zone thus established would be occupied by British, French, Italian and possibly American troops; 4. the Hungarian Government should accept the armistice of November 3 and the convention of November 13.

In return, Smuts promised that the new demarcation line would not affect the future Hungarian frontiers, and that in Paris he would propose the termination of the blockade and the invitation of Hungarian representatives to the Peace Conference. He didn't, however, propose any secure guarantee of these promises. Therefore the Governing Council presented a counterproposal according to which it would agree to the establishment of a neutral zone on the basis of the lines drawn in the Belgrade military convention, provided that the forces of occupation would not interfere in domestic economic and social affairs, and that the constitution of the Hungarian

Republic of Councils would be given effect in Szeged and Arad. Besides several stipulations and proposals of an economic nature, it demanded that the Entente Powers should put an end to the persecution of the labour movement in the occupied territories.

The Governing Council expected that its counterproposals would be followed by further negotiations. But Smuts was in no position to accept anything but a reply with no reservations. Receiving the reply, he declared the talks ended and left Hungary that same day.

Practically simultaneously with Smuts's visit to Hungary, Franchet d'Esperey was busy organizing a joint Rumanian, Serbian and Czech attack on the Hungarian Republic of Councils. Preparations went on at a rapid pace. Although Franchet d'Esperey had no official permission for armed intervention, he enjoyed tacit support from military quarters. Clemenceau, in a sharply worded telegram on April 8, took the General to task about his preparations for attack, and at the same time ordered him to remain on the defensive.

On April 16, however, the Royal Rumanian army crossed the demarcation line and set out to invade the territory of the Hungarian Republic of Councils. Aiming at the overthrow of the dictatorship of the Hungarian proletariat, the Rumanians were joined by troops of the Czecho-Slovak Republic towards the end of the month. The Yugoslav Government declined to take part in the intervention.

The beginning of the armed intervention created a new situation in Hungary. In addition to efforts made to strengthen the army, the Governing Council was compelled to find additional means to check the advance of the numerically superior Rumanian troops.

On April 26 the question of the intervention was raised at the Peace Conference in connection with the treaty of peace with Austria and Hungary, and President Wilson succeeded in having his proposal adopted for the Peace Conference to call upon Rumania to stop the advance of her army. But the letter containing this appeal was not forwarded until days later when the new situation, resulting from the intervention, made it necessary to implement the decision.

At the end of April the Governing Council appealed to President Wilson to take steps in order to end the military operations, and declared that the Hungarian Republic of Councils had no intention of interfering in the domestic affairs of other countries. On April 30 it addressed a note to the Czech, Rumanian and Serbian Governments, emphasizing its unconditional acceptance of the national territorial demands and that it was not insistent on the principle of territorial integrity. Stressing that no national interest of any kind could justify the war any longer, it demanded the immediate cessation of hostilities, a stop to interference in Hungary's domestic affairs and it gave guarantees for the protection of ethnic minorities in Hungary.

The Rumanian army stopped advancing before the delivery of the Governing Council's note. This, of course, was not due to the benevolence of the Rumanian High Command but to the combined effect of significant international events. Of considerable help were the steps taken by Soviet Russia coming to the rescue of the Hungarian Republic of Councils. On April 26 the Red Army General Staff at Kiev was given orders to advance and establish direct contact with the Hungarian Red Army. The Soviet People's Commissariat of Foreign Affairs sent the Rumanian Government an ultimatum demanding the military and administrative evacuation of occupied Bessarabia by the 3rd of May, or else the Soviet Government would reserve the right to act freely against Rumania. The letter from the Peace Conference arrived in Bucharest simultaneously.

Early in May however, the Revolutionary Governing Council knew nothing about the step taken by Soviet Russia nor about the decision of the Peace Conference. The military situation was extremely grave. The Rumanian interventionists reached the river Tisza. The French marched into Makó and Hódmezővásárhely. Attacking from the north, Czechoslovak troops under the command of Italian and French officers occupied Ruthenia (Carpatho–Ukraine) and established contact with the Rumanians. On May 2 the Czech interventionists took Miskolc and came immediately below Salgótarján.

Simultaneously with the reorganization of the Hungarian Red Army the Governing Council concentrated its forces on the northern, the Slovakian, front. Late in May the northern campaign began. By June 10 Red Army units moved on as far as 60 to 150 kilometres.

Despite the victories it scored, the Governing Council was in a very difficult situation. The forces of international revolution were suffering serious defeat. Early in May the counter-revolution succeeded in overthrowing the Bavarian Soviet Republic. Soviet Russia was waging a life-and-death struggle against Russian counter-revolutionary forces and intervention. This made it impossible for her to establish contact with the Hungarian Republic of Councils. The revolutionary struggles took an unfavourable turn in Western Europe as well. At the same time the forces of counter-revolution in Hungary stepped up their activity and strengthened their connections with the Entente Powers: in Vienna the so-called Anti-Bolshevist Committee headed by Count István Bethlen and Count Pál Teleki was formed. This Committee established contact, among others, with representatives of the British, U. S. and Italian Governments. It sent the Peace Conference appeals one after another urging the start of intervention, the invasion of Hungary by Entente troops.

On May 5 another group of counter-revolutionaries formed a Government under Count Gyula Károlyi in Rumanian occupied Arad with the aid of bourgeois politicians. Upon the insistence of the Rumanian authorities, this counter-revolutionary Government was compelled to move to Szeged. Although the Rumanians supported the overthrow of the Republic of Councils, they did not sympathize with the Arad Government because the accession to power of such a Government would have made their intervention purposeless in the eyes of the Great Powers, and furthermore the nationalist-irredentist programme of Count Gyula Károlyi's government might have put obstacles in the way of Rumanian expansionism. The counter-revolutionary Government in Szeged was reshuffled. It was headed by Dezső Ábrahám as Prime

Minister, with Pál Teleki, delegated by the Viennese Committee, as Foreign Minister. Teleki had already set about creating the foreign service apparatus of the counter-revolutionary régime. The diplomatic staff he recruited was made up almost exclusively of aristocrats and ex-diplomats of the Monarchy, and it was later to supply the backbone of the Ministry of Foreign Affairs during the entire period of the Horthy régime. It was at this point that Miklós Horthy appeared as Minister of War. It was him, who, together with Gyula Gömbös, organized the armed forces of the counter-revolution, the officers' detachments and the 'national army'.

The Entente Powers, especially France, supported the counter-revolutionary Government but did not recognize it officially. Their co-operation, however, was far from harmonious. They held the government's program to be unduly reactionary, but since their main goal was to put down the proletarian revolution, they felt compelled to support these circles disregarding even the fact that they aimed at restoring territorial integrity.

The unfavourable turn in European revolutionary wave made it easier for the Peace Conference 'to settle the Hungarian question'. Incidentally, Paris worried about the defeat of the Czechoslovak troops. The fact is that the Great Powers were afraid of Germany's reaction to the stringent terms of peace. They found it necessary to prepare for taking appropriate military measures forcing the Germans to accept the peace terms. The Czechoslovak army was planned to have a role in the operation. This influenced the Peace Conference to include in its agenda the consideration of the situation in Hungary early in June 1919.

For the time being, intervention did not prove to be a suitable means to suppress the Republic of Councils. Emphasis was again placed on the overthrow of the proletarian dictatorship by diplomatic means. On June 7, 1919, the Council of Four, upon a proposal of Clemenceau, sent a note to Budapest, promising to summon leaders of the Hungarian Government to the peace negotiations, and stressing at the same time that the Entente was "decided to have immediate recourse to extreme measures to oblige Hungary ... to put an end without delay to its attacks on the Czecho-Slovaks ..."

Béla Kun replied in the name of the Governing Council on June 9. He welcomed the willingness to invite Hungary to the Peace Conference. He emphasized the peaceful intentions of the Republic of Councils; that the attack had been started by the troops of Czechoslovakia and the Kingdom of Rumania; and that the Republic of Councils was only fighting in self-defence. The Revolutionary Governing Council was ready to stop its military operations and to discuss any controversial questions, both military and economic, provided that these were taken up without delay by a committee composed of representatives of the states concerned under Allied chairmanship. With its reply, the Governing Council gained time, and Paris was compelled to seek further ways of action against the Hungarian Republic of Councils.

At the Peace Conference the Hungarian question was in the focus of heated debates. The Great Powers, particularly the United States and Great Britain, intended to make Rumania and Czechoslovakia responsible for the untoward situation. Wilson said that the advance of Rumanian troops to the line of the Tisza was a greater help to the survival of Bolshevism in Hungary than any propaganda. At long last, the Great Powers agreed that the designation of an armistice line was insufficient to settle the question. Therefore it would be necessary to mark the definitive Czechoslovak–Hungarian and Rumanian–Hungarian boundaries, to explain this to the interested Governments, stressing at the same time that the frontiers should be respected under all circumstances. As a matter of fact, the boundaries had already been marked out by that time. The committees charged with drawing the Czechoslovak, the Rumanian and the Yugoslav frontiers had submitted their reports as early as between March 3 and 13, that is, before the proclamation of the Hungarian Republic of Councils. The draft was approved by the Peace Conference. Minor modifications were only made at the Hungarian–Yugoslav frontier, where the 'Baranya triangle' and the Muraköz sector were ceded to Yugoslavia.

On June 15 Clemenceau sent a new telegram, presenting an ultimatum. The French Prime Minister designated the definitive frontiers which might only slightly be modified, according to local considerations; he then stated that recent military occupations did not influence these boundary lines. (These lines were to become final in the Trianon Treaty of Hungary except for some minor modifications.) He demanded that the armed forces of the Hungarian Republic of Councils should be withdrawn behind these frontiers within four days.

He promised that "the Rumanian troops will be withdrawn from Hungarian territory as soon as the Hungarian troops have evacuated Czecho-Slovakia." Notes of similar content were sent to the Rumanian and Czechoslovak Governments too.

The leading bodies of the Hungarian Republic of Councils accepted the ultimatum of the Peace Conference and informed Paris accordingly on June 16.

To Clemenceau the acceptance of the ultimatum meant the justification of his conception. That which could not be achieved by force of arms could be attained by diplomatic means. The Czech High Command, on its part, noted with satisfaction that the Red Army had evacuated the northern areas. On the other hand, the Rumanian High Command, after two weeks' silence declared that it would consent to order its troops back from the Tisza line only after the demobilization of the Hungarian Red Army, since the Budapest Government "had ordered a mobilization threatening the security of Rumania".

By July 1919 international power relations had considerably changed. On June 28, representatives of Germany accepted the treaty of peace. The Peace Conference succeeded in solving its most difficult task. The United States became resolved that from then on it would only participate in the work of the conference and in the settlement of European disputes to a limited extent. Wilson sailed for home. Lloyd George also left Paris. In July the Council of Four was replaced by the Council of Plenipotentiaries. Thus control passed into the hands of Clemenceau and other French political and military leaders foreboding an overt intervention and the overthrow of the Hungarian Republic of Councils.

After the Great Powers had been relieved of the burden of their most burning problems, they paid greater attention to Central European settlement. Early in June the French succeeded in convincing the Peace Conference that the Hungarian proletarian dictatorship should be overthrown by an intervention of the armed forces of the neighbouring countries: Czechoslovakia, Rumania and Yugoslavia. The plan was mapped out and presented to the Peace Conference by Marshal Foch. He couldn't, however, win the consent of the British and the U. S. Governments, and Italy's stand was not unequivocal either. Czechoslovakia and Yugoslavia were reluctant to join in the aggression unless they were given a considerable recompense. Only the Rumanians endorsed the plan for the occupation of Budapest without reservation. Ultimately the Peace Conference rejected the plan of intervention, but the debates continued until events outrun the Foch plan. Hungarian Social Democratic politicians went to Vienna to seek contact with emissaries of the Allies. Their talks assumed an official character towards the end of July, when Vilmos Böhm was appointed to head the Hungarian Legation in Vienna. Contrary to the intentions of the Governing Council, the talks were already about the formation of a new provisional Government without Communist participation. The Szeged counter-revolutionary Government, too, wanted to have a major share in the overthrow of the Republic of Councils, but the Great Powers and especially the neighbouring states, prevented their participation.

The course of events speeded up when, early in July 1919, the Governing Council decided, upon a suggestion of military leaders, to launch a new offensive to liberate the region east of the Tisza. On July 11 Béla Kun sent Clemenceau a telegram demanding fulfilment of the promise concerning the withdrawal of Rumanian troops. The reply of the Peace Conference arrived on July 14: negotiations were out of question until the armistice agreement had been executed on the Hungarian side. Since it was obvious that the Allied Powers had not the slightest intention of keeping their promise, the Red Army was ordered to open military operations against the Rumanians on July 20. But the attack was soon subdued by the Rumanian forces.

In the meanwhile, as a result of the Vienna negotiations, the Entente missions elaborated their proposals for the removal of the Governing Council and forwarded them to Paris. The supreme council of the Peace Conference dealt with the Hungarian question on July 25/26, and issued a declaration in support of the removal of the Governing Council. The declaration stated that the Allied Powers were intent to send food supplies, lift the blockade and conclude peace only after the Government in power had been replaced by a Government to their liking.

In the hopeless international, domestic and military situation, the Rumanian troops having already crossed the Tisza line and moving rapidly towards Budapest, a joint meeting of the party leadership and the Government on August 1 decided that the Governing Council should resign and give all power to a Government to be composed of trade-union functionaries headed by Gyula Peidl.

The Allied Powers attained their aim: the Hungarian Republic of Councils was no longer a threat to the 'order' in Central Europe. But the influence of the Peace Conference did not stop at supporting the overthrow of the Governing Council. The

Allies also refused to support the Peidl Government (the so-called 'trade-union government') thus promoting the establishment of a counter-revolutionary régime.

After taking office, the Peidl Government immediately contacted the sole Entente representative in Budapest, Colonel Guido Romanelli of Italy. It informed him of the change of government and presented a request for the Rumanian troops to halt their advance and to sign an armistice agreement until the terms of peace would be worked out. The 'trade-union government' would have been ready to recognize the Tisza line as a line of demarcation. Romanelli immediately sent word to Paris from where he received an answer to the effect that there was no reason for the Peace Conference to intervene in the domestic affairs of Hungary. No other basis was acceptable for the negotiations than the military convention of November 13, 1918, and the conference decision of June 13, 1919. "The Allied Council will only ask the Rumanian Government to stop its troops in the positions they now occupy," they wrote. There is no doubt that such a request would have been of no avail. The reply definitively demonstrated that the Peidl government could not count upon support from the Great Powers.

On August 3, 1919, the Rumanian troops arrived in Budapest and marched into the capital in the afternoon.

2. International circumstances at the time of the counter-revolutionary take-over

In the midst of the Rumanian occupation the Peidl Government tried to survive by rapidly shifting to the right. It definitely disassociated itself from the policy of the Republic of Councils and began to liquidate its achievements. But its fate was sealed. Peidl was unable to do anything to break isolation; the Allied Powers reacted at his efforts with indifference. True, on August 5 the Peace Conference resolved to send an official military mission to Budapest in order to establish contact with the Government and to supervise the execution of the armistice agreement.

Even the withdrawal of the Rumanian troops to the frontiers fixed in the note of June 13 was decided. But the decision came too late. The Rumanian Government denied its execution and instead, it voiced further territorial aspirations ensuring by all possible means that the Great Powers did not prevent their realization. Simultaneously with the Peace Conference decisions, on August 5, the Rumanians issued an ultimatum, dictating new terms of armistice by the right of the victor. Those terms — surrender of the entire supply of arms and ammunition, 50 per cent of the rolling-stock, 30 per cent of all agricultural machines and of the cattle-stock, 30 000 wagonloads of wheat and maize, the payment of all costs of occupation, etc., — were tantamount to the total economic depredation of the country.

On August 6, a day after the delivery of the ultimatum, a group of counter-revolutionaries headed by István Friedrich—having realized that the Allies did not support the Peidl Government — with the assistance of a body of mounted police, army officers and Rumanian soldiers, made a coup forcing the Peidl government to resign.

Archduke Joseph of Habsburg — who was appointed *homo regius* by King Charles IV in October 1918, and whom Friedrich already summoned to Budapest — declared that he took over as Regent of the country and appointed Friedrich Prime Minister.

The formation of the Friedrich Government failed to reassure the Allies. They still feared that the restoration of the bourgeois order would be less than thorough, and that the concluding of the peace treaty would thus be forestalled. No agreement was likely to be reached until the Rumanian occupation continued, and it was rightly to be feared that procrastination only bolstered nationalism and stepped up resistance to the terms of peace. Moreover, the restoration of state sovereignty was a formal requisite for the peace treaty to be signed. Rumanian withdrawal, on the other hand, seemed feasible only after the formation of a Government strong enough to consolidate the bourgeois order.

The Great Powers of the Peace Conference wished to see the advent of a Hungarian Government which enjoyed relatively broad mass support and had an appropriate police force, but which would not be extremely reactionary and nationalistic, acceptable thus to western public opinion as well.

They saw the chief guarantee for Hungary to accept — and to observe — the peace treaty in a relatively democratic Government free of chauvinism and aggressive ambitions.

Even when the danger of revolution in Europe was no longer an immediate threat, conservative British and French circles continued to support the liberal forces and the moderate left wing in Germany and in Hungary, all the more so, as the peace achieved at Versailles became increasingly unstable. They thus hoped to create equilibrium against the forces of revanche.

In the autumn of 1919, however, the principal aim of the Entente Powers was to conclude the peace treaties as soon as possible, even if this meant an acceptance of the unfavourable situation following the defeat of the proletarian dictatorship. Though having wished for a relatively democratic political power, the Allies, reluctantly as they did, were forced to neglect this aspect and concentrate on the creation of a Government coalition which would include both the parties that had survived and those that were formed after the overthrow under the Republic of Councils, and which would have the support of the influential political groups. It was required that such a Government guaranteed certain civil rights at least formally, and that it saw to the easing of terror. These parties and groups, however, were anything but democratic.

The forces of the left became disorganized in the atmosphere of fear and treachery created by *revanchism* and the white terror. A nationalist and anti-Semitic hysteria was sweeping over the country — among the upper and lower classes as well, as a reaction to the revolutions of 1918 and 1919. It was only by a *renouncement* of the political aims of both 1918 and 1919 that any party (including the liberals) could hope to survive.

After August 1919, the right wing became dominant in the leadership of the Socialist Democratic Party, the only working class party that survived the collapse of the Republic of Councils. But even this position was very unstable. The Friedrich

Government seemed unfit to fulfil the requirements of the Entente Powers. The Great Powers feared that such a reactionary government might bring with it the danger of revolution. Nor did the government have any real authority since its basis was narrow even among the ruling classes.

The counter-revolutionary groups that had been organized under the Republic of Councils and that were seeking connections with the Entente Powers stood in opposition to the Friedrich Government. True, on August 19, the Szeged counter-revolutionary Government resigned and yielded to the Budapest Government. Horthy, however, refused to recognize the competence of the latter. Early in August, Horthy moved to Transdanubia with French permission. He set up his headquarters at Siófok and, with the assistance of army officers grouped around him, began preparing for a take-over. He extended his influence all over Transdanubia where he exercised sovereign rights, counteracting the efforts of the Friedrich Government.

Besides, all of the counter-revolutionary groups around István Bethlen, Pál Teleki or István Nagyatádi Szabó — were inclined to co-operate with the Rumanians; they in fact presented the most diverse offers and plans to the Rumanian Government. In order to defend his power, Friedrich, too, started talks with the Rumanian military authorities about the conclusion of a separate peace which would prolong the occupation for a year. But neither Friedrich nor the other negotiating groups were able to reach any agreement, because the Rumanian condition for any agreement was the annexation of the entire Hungarian territory east of the Tísza to Rumania; moreover, their terms included the recognition of the King of Rumania as ruler of Hungary, as can be read in the report of August 19 sent to the British Government by Admiral Troubridge, head of the inter-Allied commission established to supervise navigation on the Danube.

The Entente Powers were not at all impressed by the pro-Habsburg tint of the Friedrich Government, which immediately provoked a protest on the part of the neighbouring countries. In a memorandum to the Peace Conference the Czechoslovak Government pointed out that Habsburg restoration posed a threat to Czechoslovakia and the Kingdom of Serbs, Croats and Slovenes, so they would regard the election of any member of the House of Habsburg as head of state in Hungary as an act of aggression, and they would be ready to take military precautions to avert the danger. Yet, in the given situation, the withdrawal of the Rumanian troops, urged first of all by the British Government would have strengthened the position of the Habsburgs.

All things considered, in August 1919, the Entente Powers thought that while Rumanian occupation was the only guarantee of capitalist restoration and of order in Hungary, a continued occupation would prevent genuine consolidation. The Rumanians were also aware of this dilemma. They openly claimed that the Entente Powers were in no position to make them evacuate the Hungarian territories. The Rumanian troops would stay in Hungary as long as they thought it fit, even if it meant the rejection of Allied demands. To the Allied notes demanding a stop to requisitioning, the elimination of abuses, the abandonment of attempts at a separate peace, and the withdrawal of troops, the Rumanian Government gave evasive replies. It referred to the services it had rendered in defeating Bolshevism, and pointed out that the occupation could only be safely terminated after the establishment of properly equipped Hungarian police forces (whereas the Rumanian authorities had confiscated all kinds of weapons and were delaying the organization of the police and the gendarmerie). Finally, it argued that the reactionary Hungarian Government threatened the neighbouring countries, making the occupation necessary. Thus the Rumanian Government was intent to continue the looting of Hungary and to acquire further (not only Hungarian) territories by bargaining with the Entente. Bessarabia's status, for instance, was not definitively settled, and Rumania had not given up the plan of the annexation of the entire Banat.

The Hungarian question was further complicated by the conflicting interests of the Great Powers. The French supported the Rumanian demands in order to realize their plan of a Danubian settlement which would have strengthened their influence in Central Europe. They helped the Rumanian Government to prolong the occupation, especially by diluting the decisions of the Peace Conference and by delaying their dispatching to Bucharest. Italy rather supported the Rumanian plan because this seemed to harmonize with her own demands. The British showed a growing dislike for the growth of French influence in Central Europe. A rival of France for economic positions in the area, Britain shaped her Hungarian policy to back that of the United States which, in fact, had no immediate interests in the Danubian Basin. Britain thus demanded the termination of Rumanian occupation with growing decisiveness.

The Hungarian counter-revolutionary politicians were well aware of the British position. They thought that Great Britain was the only Power able to enforce the termination of occupation and to help Hungary obtain more favourable terms of peace.

If this were so, Britain was likely to have a say in the establishment of a Hungarian Government acceptable to the Peace Conference too. For these reasons, all of the counter-revolutionary groups wished to secure Britain's goodwill in advance. As early as August 8, Count István Bethlen, head of the Viennese Committee and a representative of the Szeged Government, sent Lloyd George a letter requesting the head of the British Government to use his influence in the fixing of Hungary's definitive frontiers. Bethlen brought forth every possible argument, from reference to resemblances in British and Hungarian history to the demonstration of intentions of a really democratic reconstruction policy. "We have the stern will," he wrote, "to lead (our people) to a happy future by the way of an honest democracy being in accordance with the ruling spirit of the age and guaranteeing to all classes of the population an equal form of influence on the shaping of their fate."

Soon thereafter, on August 30, Prime Minister Friedrich — true to his political narrow-mindedness — in his letter to Admiral Troubridge, asked no more for intercession but downright for a protectorate régime. Claming that he had the backing of 95 per cent of the country's population until the elections, he wrote:

"The Government assure Your Excellency, that this wish is a long-felt wish of every genuine, true Hungarian, that Great Britain is the only Power to maintain order and discipline in this country, to develop the country's natural resources and to raise the cultural level of its inhabitants."

As will be seen below, Horthy also donned the cloak of democracy during his negotiations with Sir George Russel Clerk.

In August 1919, the Peace Conference was practically unable to reach a settlement in Hungary. Its only achievement was to force Archduke Joseph to resign from the regency on August 23. The reshuffled Friedrich Government, however, was just as legitimist as its predecessor. Its notes addressed to Rumania had no effect whatsoever. The British and the Americans insisted that Hungary send an ultimatum to the Rumanian Government, which was eventually forwarded by a personal emissary early in September.

The Commission was given to a British diplomat, Sir George Russel Clerk, who had earlier been head of the Central European Department in the Foreign Office. The ultimatum which, in fact, had been worded by British Foreign Secretary Balfour, pointed out that the Rumanian policy could no longer be considered defensive. It denounced the looting and despoiling of Hungary and requested a clear answer to whether Rumania was willing to withdraw her troops from Hungary at a date to be appointed by the Peace Conference and to surrender the requisitioned goods to the Reparations Commission; whether she was ready to co-operate with the Allies to ensure the restoration in Hungary and the establishment of a Government with which the peace could be concluded.

Clerk arrived in Bucharest on September 12, 1919. His mission turned out to be a long one because the Allied action provoked a Government crisis in Rumania. Bucharest replied as late as September 20, and even then it formulated new conditions. It demanded the formation of a Hungarian Government to the liking of Rumania and voiced further territorial demands: the town of Békéscsaba, the Maros estuary, and the shifting of the frontier farther to the west. After his lengthy stay in Bucharest, on October 1, Clerk travelled to the Hungarian capital to obtain information personally. He conducted negotiations with the Rumanian authorities of occupation, with representatives of the Friedrich Government and various political groups, as well as with members of the Entente military mission. His personal experiences convinced him that the prolongation of occupation was not only leading to an economic catastrophe but deteriorated the political situation as well, because the extreme reactionary forces thus gained time to get reorganized and increasingly control the situation.

And, as he pointed out in his report, Rumania shrewdly exploited the differences between the Great Powers, and therefore he urged them to arrive at a uniform standpoint. The majority of the negotiators on the Hungarian side tried to convince Rumania that the Friedrich Government enjoyed a support which made the continuance of occupation unnecessary and could, at the same time, furnish a basis for the formation of a new Coalition Government. The Social Democrat Ernő Garami, on the other hand, argued that, as long as Friedrich was the head of the government, every way towards a coalition was barred. He claimed that Friedrich's removal could be achieved only by an energetic step of the Peace Conference. Garami added that until the formation of a Coalition Government, and before the retreat of the Rumanian troops, Entente forces should be stationed in Budapest, or else Horthy's armed units would march in, and the capital would see a repetition, on a mass scale, of the bloody massacres that had taken place in Transdanubia, and this might again lead to revolution and anarchy.

Garami's practical proposal was for representatives of the political parties to call on the Entente mission and present a list of the Coalition Government designed in accordance with the Allied demands. A requisite for this was, however, that the Entente Powers should unambiguously lay down their demands and the ways of their fulfilment as soon as possible, for otherwise everybody would be fishing in troubled waters. And when the Supreme Council assented to the formation of the provisional Government, it should immediately take office and hold it as long as the Rumanian occupation lasted. Clerk consented to most of Garami's proposals, except for the one about the maintenance of Rumanian occupation until the establishment of the Government.

Clerk's suggestions were discussed by the Peace Conference on October 10. As a result, the Supreme Council prepared two notes to be sent to the Rumanian and the Hungarian Government respectively. The note to Rumania, which was forwarded on the 12th, stated that there was no way of fulfilling the new Rumanian territorial demands. It said that Rumania should support the establishment of a new Coalition Government in Hungary and withdraw her troops simultaneously with the organization of a Hungarian police force; entrust the confiscated goods to the Allied Control Commission and stop requisitioning. The note meant for Hungary was not dispatched because it was realized that this might mean recognition of the Friedrich Government. Teherefore, as an expedient, Clerk was sent to Budapest on behalf of the Entente Powers with the oral commission to enforce the Peace Conference decisions through negotiations with representatives of the political parties. He was to insist on the resignation of the Government appointed by Archduke Joseph and on the formation of a Coalition Government which would rely on a broad political support and would thus be able to maintain order within the boundaries fixed by the Allied Powers, to conduct a democratic election and to sign the peace treaty.

Clerk arrived in Budapest on October 23. What he saw was that the delay and procrastination further deteriorated the Hungarian political situation. It was especially Horthy and his gentry and military followers who managed to strengthen their position, because the supreme command could freely exercise its influence in Transdanubia, which was not under Rumanian occupation. There Horthy could continue retaliation and freely organize the armed forces. By the time Clerk began negotiating in Budapest, this supreme command had become the only force that possessed a relatively strong armed body. This influenced Clerk to emphasize that the leading role in the new Government should be entrusted to the Christian National Unity Party and the maintenance of order should be entrusted to Horthy who, as Clerk wrote in his first report, impressed him as a person of capacities.

On the basis of the reports received, the Peace Conference took up the Hungarian question on November 3 once more. Several proposals were submitted, each of which reflected the conflicts of interests. The French proposal was based on the report of the French member of the Entente military mission in Budapest, who saw only one feasible solution: to get the Friedrich Government to resign before the Rumanian withdrawal, then to replace the Rumanian troops by Allied armed forces; to organize the police under the surveillance of these forces, simultaneously with the disarming of Horthy's white terrorist commandos, which would finally lead to the elections. In November the international situation was disfavourable to such a proposal especially as the Italians opposed it, because they saw in Horthy a future ally against the South Slav state. Finally, the Peace Conference gave up the idea of sending an Allied armed force to Hungary (Clerk also protested against this plan), and decided that the withdrawal of the Rumanians and the formation of a new Government would be sufficient even if this Government had a conservative majority. The only condition was the preclusion of a Habsburg restoration.

Meanwhile Clerk indicated that he now saw better chances to form a Coalition Government than previously, therefore he asked for patience in forcing the Friedrich Cabinet to resign. The Peace Conference accepted Clerk's suggestion, and having ordered the Governments of Yugoslavia and Czechoslovakia to evacuate the territories occupied by them beyond the boundaries of June 13, it concentrated its attention on the termination of Rumanian occupation. The fact is that the Government of Rumania, in its reply of November 1 to the earlier note, only promised that the Rumanian forces would start retreating to the Tisza line on November 10.

At the meeting of November 12, the mood in the council of the Peace Conference turned against Rumania. The British demanded energetic steps; as a result, a strongly worded ultimatum was sent to Bucharest on November 15. It demanded retreat behind the definitive frontier, and surrender of the looted goods to the Allied Control Commission; should Rumania fail to fulfil these demands, the Entente Powers would sever diplomatic relations with her, and Rumania could no more count upon their goodwill with regard to the still undecided territorial questions.

In the meanwhile, on November 14, the Rumanian troops had evacuated Budapest, so Clerk could concentrate upon the forming of the new Government. Early in November he had already told Horthy that after the Rumanian withdrawal, his troops could take possession of the capital if he was willing to guarantee that his armed units would keep order and refrain from atrocities. On November 5, Horthy gave his guarantee in writing, since he saw that his power ambitions could only be fulfilled with British aid (and this aspect is not to be overlooked with regard to his later attitude either). In exchange, the Peace Conference gave its assent to Horthy's march into Budapest. Two days later, on the 7th, Clerk arranged a consultation between Horthy and leaders of the liberal parties and the Social Democratic Party. There, the representatives of the political parties conceded that the Entente Powers deemed it desirable for the 'national army' to march into Budapest. Horthy in turn signed a declaration to the effect that the army would put itself under the authority of the Government to be set up with the approval of the Entente.

On November 16, the army, with Horthy at its head, marched into Budapest, 'the sinful city', and in spite of the promise made to the Entente, immediately launched a campaign of terror. The officer's commandos acted so brutally that even the British and the U. S. Governments felt compelled to protest, especially, against the arrest of Social Democrats.

The problem of the armed forces was thus solved, but new difficulties arose in the way of forming a Government. Friedrich was not inclined for a compromise and hindered any agreement. Finally, on November 17, at an inter-party conference convened with much difficulty and attended by twelve independent politicians and Horthy himself, Clerk declared that in case no decision was made in a few days, he would leave Budapest, and Hungary would have to face serious consequences in respect of the peace treaty. He said he did not object to a Government with a Christian National Unity Party majority under the leadership of Friedrich, but could not accept a Government built exclusively upon this party. After a debate that was adjourned several times and in which Horthy also gave a speech, emphasizing that "it would be adventurous to stand up against the Entente" a decision was finally reached. On November 22, a Cabinet called 'Government of Concentration' was formed under Károly Huszár. On November 25, Clerk recognized it on behalf of the Peace Conference as a Provisional Government pending the forthcoming elections. In his related note Clerk stated: "This recognition is subject, naturally, to the conditions that the Provisional Government undertakes to hold the elections without delay, to maintain law and order in the country, to commit no aggressive action, to respect the provisional frontiers of Hungary pending their final definition in the Treaty of Peace, and to guarantee to every Hungarian national full civil rights, including those of a free Press, free right of meeting, freedom to express political opinions and a free, secret, impartial and democratic election based on universal suffrage."

From the point of view of the Peace Conference the Hungarian question was thus settled. The way was open to the peace treaty to be signed. On December 1, 1919, Clemenceau, in the name of the Great Powers, invited the Hungarian Government to send its plenipotentiaries to the Peace Conference.

Little was realized out of the agreements which Horthy and the Hungarian politicians concluded with the Entente regarding the political system and the policies of the country. Right from the moment of taking office, the Government used every possible means to destroy the guarantees. On November 25, in reply to the Entente's note of recognition dated the same day, Prime Minister Huszár already informed Clerk that although the Government accepted the conditions it would still maintain a certain degree of censure of the press "in order to make impossible all kinds of agitation of Bolshevik tendency, and this way to ensure the order of justice, the social peace and the force of the State power." The agreement itself was the result of a compromise in which the Entente Powers abandoned a good part of their reservations, to have bourgeois order restored and the peace treaty accepted. The recognition of the Huszár

Government was also made dependent on this aim. This was reflected in the international and domestic political implications of the elctions as well.

The elections that were called according to the agreements, and conducted in an atmosphere of unbridled terror, were likely to lead to Friedrich's party attaining majority in Parliament, together with the Habsburg legitimists, thus making it possible to restore the Habsburgs to the Hungarian throne. In Entente quarters there was a strong demand to stop this, if need be, even by helping Horthy's military dictatorship into power. In January 1920, Horthy had several talks with Thomas Hohler, the new British chief representative (and later head of the British Legation) in Budapest, and with General Reginald Gorton, the British member of the Entente military mission. In his report of January 9, 1920, Gorton wrote that Horthy had told him it was to be feared that the elections would bring about a legislature that might install Friedrich as Prime Minister and elect Archduke Joseph to be head of state. Horthy, with his habitual turn of mind, added that the new Parliament which probably would have 'many peasant members', would demand the distribution of the large estates, although these constituted the pivot on which Hungary's prosperity hinged. Would it not be wiser, he asked, to establish a military dictatorship still before the elections?

A formal military dictatorship was not set up, but Horthy succeeded in having himself elected Regent of Hungary with considerable assistance from the Entente Powers, mainly from Great Britain. Hungary's form of Government, or rather the issue of a head of state, was a topic of discussion at that time. There was no doubt that all groups of the ruling classes wanted kingdom as a constitutional form, because for them a republic would have been equivalent to the revolutions of 1918/1919 and the dissolution of historical Hungary. Without describing in detail the internal political and power aspirations involved in the struggle between the Habsburg legitimists and the free royalists, we can state that the maintenance of kingdom became a symbol hindering any kind of democratic development of the country and at the same time impeded the efforts to restore its territorial integrity. The talks with Entente representatives in January, touched upon the question of the constitution and the head of state in connection with the coming elections. The subject was discussed by Horthy just as well as by Albert Apponyi or Károly Huszár.

Gorton and Hohler appealed to their Government for advice. The Entente had committed itself to a Provisional Government and general elections, so it could hardly accept a military dictatorship or refuse to recognize a Government formed on the basis of the election results, which in turn might incur the danger of Habsburg restoration. What was to be done?

Finally on January 29, 1920, the British Foreign Office, cutting the Gordian knot, instructed its representative in Budapest to inform the Prime Minister and the leading politicians of Hungary that the British Government maintained its protest against the election of Archduke Joseph or any other members of the House of Habsburg as head of state. Otherwise it had no comment to make on the constitutional form of Hungary. The British were ready to agree to have some prominent Hungarian aristocrat elected head of state, and to a modification of the constitution, if necessary. It was immaterial to the British Government whether the head of state was called king or palatine or bore any other title, if that person assumed powers by lawful and constitutional means. And with regard to the earlier reservations to the domestic policies of the country, the Foreign Office authorized Hohler to declare also that " ... the internal affairs of Hungary are not a matter in which His Majesty's Government desire to intervene so long as the policy of the Hungarian Government towards the Powers and towards their neighbours peaceful in character." On February 3, the Council of Ambassadors, on behalf of the Entente Powers, issued a joint declaration stating that although the Allied Powers did not intend, as they did not think it was their business, to interfere in Hungary's internal affairs or to dictate to the Hungarian people what kind of Government or constitution they should choose, but since Habsburg restoration affected countries outside of Hungary, they could neither recognize nor tolerate such a restoration.

The international situation was favourable for Horthy's ambitions. The Entente representatives in Budapest had practically unanimous confidence in Horthy, and the British were especially favourably impressed by him. This was mainly due to his part in the negotiations with the Entente representatives from the autumn of 1919 onwards, by successfully posing as a politician who, in addition to being a champion of anti-Bolshevism and a competent advocate of law and order, was also trying to suppress all kinds of extremism, to allay the terror, consistently observing the agreements concluded with the Entente. As mentioned earlier, he played an important part in setting up a coalition Government at the time of the Clerk mission. He had no particular scruples about signing the declaration of November 7. When, after his march into Budapest, the white terror spread over the capital too, Horthy shifted the responsibility upon the officers' detachments. In the early days of January 1920, speaking of the internal difficulties of the country, he told the British chief representative that even in the most difficult situations in recent months, he had not only been able to prevent a new outbreak of Bolshevism but he also managed to restrain violence and anti-Semitism. Hohler forwarded Horthy's statements to his Government without comments. It is worthwhile noting that the good impression Horthy made was also the result of a coincidence: he was an old and intimate friend of the British chief representative, whose reports considerably influenced the opinion of his Government, and who wrote in his report of January 20, 1920: " ... Horthy ... happens to have been an old and very intimate friend of mine before the war, so that I think he is probably ready to talk more openly with me than with most people. I have every personal reason for believing in his complete sincerity."

Since the Entente protest had eliminated Archduke Joseph from the candidates, only two persons remained eligible for the functions of head of state: Count Albert Apponyi and Miklós Horthy. The British Foreign Office would have regarded Apponyi, in spite of his pro-Habsburg disposition, as an ideal candidate even for the throne of Hungary, yet it refrained from supporting him because of his advanced age and mainly because of feared protests by the French and Czechoslovaks (Apponyi's estates were situated on the territory annexed to Czechoslovakia). So the only person left was Horthy, whom the British chief representative in his telegram of February 4, described as perfectly qualified for the post of Regent, because " . . . (he is) absolutely honest, reliable and vigorous. He has nothing of the character of an adventurer or a military chauvinist." (!)

As soon as Horthy convinced himself that he did not have to fear from international complications, he took steps to seize the supreme power with the help of the army officers loyal to him. And when the Entente Powers insisted on constitutionality, he found a constitutional precedent to his case in the story of Napoleon's election as First Consul. He acted accordingly. First, he had to prevent the new Parliament from electing Friedrich Prime Minister which was a step that pleased the Great Powers as well. On January 30, 1920, as commander-in-chief of the army, Horthy published a declaration stating that the agreement concluded in November 1919 with the Entente Powers regarding a provisional Government and the holding of elections could only be interpreted to mean that the new National Assembly should elect a head of state, to whom the Provisional Government would transfer power and who would appoint the new Prime Minister. Horthy did not hesitate to refer to the army as a means of stopping any 'breach of order'. On the other hand, the Parliament, in which the Smallholders' Party and the Christian National Unity Party were in the majority, was reluctant to elect Horthy as head of state. Eventually on March 1, 1920, the House of Representatives, with the threatening attendance of officers making their way into the Parliament building, elected Miklós Horthy to the post of Regent, concentrating large powers in his hands.

The parliamentary elections of January 1920 and Horthy's election as Regent closed the period of transition which began at the end of the World War. This transition period was marked by the fact that international events played a decisive role in internal politics, and the victorious Powers could exercise open and indirect influence over the shaping of the country's domestic affairs. In the spring of 1920, the consolidation of the counter-revolutionary régime was still far from being completed, but the way towards consolidation, the structure of the new régime and the main course of its internal and external policies were already determined by the landmarks of the transition period: the fall of the revolution and the victory of the counter-revolutionary régime, the composition of the counter-revolutionary groups and the political complexion of the new parties, the conclusion of the peace treaty, the political fears and falsely conceived historical lessons that came to determine the mentality of the Hungarian gentry and middle classes.

Thus, after the overthrow of the Hungarian Republic of Councils, the reactionary and conservative forces came into power at the price of an agreement with the Entente which they, once in possession of power, endeavoured to violate, but which nevertheless acted upon the structure of the counter-revolutionary régime, in so far as it contributed to the enforcement of a few indefinitely implemented civil rights, to the renouncement of the military dictatorship, and to the maintenance of a parliamentary system of government.

But parliamentarism as realized in Hungary hardly resembled the parliamentary system taken in a bourgeois democratic sense. The political parties participating in the elections (in January 1920 the Social Democratic Party withdrew from the Government and did not enter the electoral campaign) were, all without exception, parties which committed themselves both politically and socially to counter-revolutionary politics. Of course, this does not mean that there were no differences between the ideas and the political and social programmes of the conservative-reactionary, fascistoid or liberal-bourgeois political formations or parties, which all had a different social basis, and the interests represented various different classes, strata or social groups. But there was one thing in which all the parliamentary parties were alike: they were all counter-revolutionary in the sense that they accepted the fundamental principles of the régime. (By the way, the qualifier 'counter-revolutionary' was not derogatory at the time, it rather implied justification, even vainglory, and was claimed by political and social organizations, politicians and public figures alike.) That is, all of them were against everything that the 1918/1919 revolutions signified on the political, social and ideological plane; they repudiated not only socialism but also bourgeois democracy, accepted the basically static structure of the counter-revolution. The only difference was that the conservative-reactionary wing — which represented the latifundia and big capital — was altogether united in opposing any kind of even partial social reform, while the racialist, fascistoid and fascist groups — which primarily represented the gentry, the officers and the civil servants striving for an effective, if not maximal share in political power — wanted to enforce their aspirations by introducing sham reforms and pseudo-revolutionary measures. But even the liberal-bourgeois parties, which essentially represented no more than a wing of the Hungarian bourgeoisie, constituted an opposition only in the sense that they stood on the left of the conservative-reactionary parties, while their political and social platform could not be extended to include genuine bourgeois democratic demands.

Of course the various political tendencies could not be clearly distinguished merely on the basis of the political complexion of the various parties especially in the early years of the counter-revolutionary period. The class support of the various parties was still indistinct. Group interests and individual ambitions confused the picture. There were conflicts between Habsburg legitimists and free royalists, between racialists and conservatives, between 'small-holders' and agrarians. Parties merged, fused and were reorganized, but all this took place within the closed system of the political régime.

An important component of the construction and consolidation of the counter-revolutionary régime was the psychological and ideological impact of the great national, political and social upheavals of 1918/1919, and this factor played no small part in shaping the social basis of the régime, in strengthening its closed nature. The Hungarian gentry classes rejected the 1918/1919 revolutions. But the bourgeois democratic revolution of 1918 and the Hungarian Republic of Councils of 1919, and the subsequent decomposition of historical Hungary, resulted in conceiving these events in a false causality, not only among the bourgeoisie and the petty bourgeoisie but also among the intelligentsia, who, for the most part, had strong nationalist feelings and who, at the same time, were unprepared for reacting to such social upheavals as the revolution of 1918 to which, in fact, they weren't in opposition.

According to them the revolution of 1918 was to be blamed for the dissolution of historical Hungary because first, it had a share in the collapse of the Monarchy and secondly, it was responsible for the rise of the Hungarian Republic of Councils, because it led straight to the dictatorship of the proletariat, which not only attacked middle-class property but was responsible also for the new frontiers drawn in the peace treaty. The conclusion was practically self-evident: bourgeois democracy was to be rejected because it had led to Bolshevism, because it had resulted in the partition of the national territory, so it was the principal cause of all misery. The ideologico-political construction of Dualism was thus justified retrospectively by the argument that the free play of democratism led to a national catastrophe.

The propaganda machinery of the counter-revolutionary régime spared no effort to spread these lies counting on the fears and false conclusions among the privileged classes in order to cover up its embarrassing inherent defect — namely that the Entente had helped the counter-revolutionary groups come into power on condition that they accepted the peace treaty. Well, this is how the counter-revolutionary ideology branded the entire working class, revolution and democracy as 'antinational', and every advocate of progress as a 'traitor to the nation'. This was an appealing and easily adaptable ideology, because it could do without painful national self-examination, because it could be used for concealing the enormous lag of social development, the domination of the privileged classes, the deprivation and poverty of the oppressed classes. This led to a situation where all attempts to alter the class structure of society, or to change its counter-revolutionary character would be discredited on the basis of these being 'attempts leading to a national catastrophe' in the eyes of many of those who had no interest in the maintenance either of the régime or even of class rule. This myth was good for obscuring the obvious facts: that the blame for the dissolution of historical Hungary was to be cast not on the revolution — which only, followed the collapse of the Monarchy — but on the unbalance of national forces prevailing in the Monarchy, on the Dualist policy towards the national minorities; that it was precisely the bourgeois democratic Government which had refused to accept the terms of peace; that it was the Republic of Councils which had fought with arms against the Entente Powers and their allies; that responsibility for the frontiers drawn at Trianon could not be laid upon the Republic of Councils because they had been dictated by the victorious Powers' interests, by their relations with their allies, and that those frontiers had already been decided before the birth of the proletarian dictatorship.

This ideology was accepted not only by the bourgeoisie and petty bourgeoisie, afraid of losing their property, existence and social standing, but it also seemed to be a reliable life-belt to those intellectuals who could not, or did not dare, face the facts of history, who did not understand the great prospects of development inherent in revolutions, to whom the Hungarian Republic of Councils only symbolized dictatorship and social failures (e.g. the default of the distribution of land). And those who accepted these false political evaluations were driven to accept its consequences as well, whether of a political, social, national or ideological nature. This is how more and more of the bourgeoisie and the intellectuals were assimilated, in outlook and attitudes, by that lower stratum of the Hungarian gentry whose nationalism and unyielding feudal view of society became even more desperate and aggressive after the proletarian revolution. This is how effective class interests, existential fears, false patriotism, racialism, nationalism, anxiety for social rank, and gentry pride drove all those, who were to form the social basis of the counter-revolutionary régime, to accept the counter-revolutionary world of ideas which shaped them into a mass called the 'Christian Hungarian middle classes'.

The political platform of the counter-revolutionary system was, by its very nature, restricted: it could not 'open' to the left. The suffrage at the 1920 elections and the form of parliamentarism that resulted from those elections did not yet preclude a future formal shift towards democracy. The political consolidation of the régime therefore had to be accomplished so as to make any such shift impossible. A precedent could easily be found by those who, from the experiences of 1918/1919, concluded that they should restore the Dualist political construction: the methods of Dualism had to be used as much as possible. A world resembling that of 1867 should be rebuilt even if there was no dynasty and historical Hungary any more. The political structure of the Dualist system rested on two pillars: the power of the dynasty and a legislature which supported the policy of the king-appointed Government under any circumstances; and when, in exceptional cases, this failed, the sovereign's authority could be used for an adjournment or the dissolution of Parliament and, if necessary, to set the military or the police in motion.

One of the pillars of the counter-revolutionary system was created by Horthy's election to the regency, which meant that the head of state became a great authority, essentially identical with the royal authority of the era of Dualism. But something was still lacking. The counter-revolution found in Count István Bethlen a politician who was able, cunning and aggressive enough to fill in the gap. He brought into existence a single Government party, called the United Party, which attained such an overwhelming majority in Parliament that it could never be outvoted, thus being able to carry through the adoption of any draft bill presented by the Government. To preserve this situation and to prevent the Government from ever being left in the minority, the elective franchise had to be 'reformed' too. Relying on the United Party, Bethlen abolished universal suffrage and the secret ballot, and introduced a suffrage restricted by property qualifications and the open ballot. There was only one party which remained outside the closed political construction, namely the Social Democratic Party, but an agreement — called the Bethlen—Peyer pact — was reached with the social Democratic Party's leader, as a security measure. The Government was thus in a position to stabilize the power construction of the counter-revolution. There was a legislature, but there was no real suffrage, there was constitutionality, but there were no constitutional guarantees of the civil rights. There was no dictator, but there was a dictatorial Government, and there was a 'supreme warlord' invested with special powers: the Regent. This was what remained of the agreements of November 25, 1919.

3. The peace treaty. Scheming and experimenting in foreign politics from the peace negotiations to admission to the League of Nations

The foreign policy of the counter-revolution was not difficult to predict. A uniform, well considered political line was out of the question, but the main contours were already visible. The practical tasks of foreign and internal politics were determined by the composition and political complexion of the counter-revolutionary groups and by the circumstances under which they came into power. They were also influenced by the imminent consequences of the new frontiers and the unfavourable terms of peace, by the fact that the peace treaty was not yet signed and that the international situation was still extremely unstable.

Europe, especially Central Europe, remained in a chaotic state for a long time to come. The great transformations, which the war, the Socialist Revolution in Russia, and the terms of peace dictated by the victors had caused in European affairs, still involved many factors of uncertainty. Few believed that the new relations would be lasting. Soviet Russia was engaged in heavy fights against internal counter-revolution and outside intervention. The principal concern of the Western Powers was to overthrow the Soviet power. The difference between victors and vanquished was not yet so sharp as it was to become, since even the victors were still quarrelling among themselves about their gains. And it was not only the Great Powers who fought for spheres of influence, but conflicts also broke out between small countries siding with the Entente. Poland was squabbling with Czechoslovakia, and Rumania with Yugoslavia, about territorial questions. Relations between the Great Powers and the small countries were also to be settled. France was still far from deciding what system of alliance would best promote her great-power ambitions, she just began to surmise what she had bungled. Both at home and internationally, Italy was in too precarious a position to be able to map out a consistent policy concerning Europe and Central Europe. She changed views and partners on the spur of the moment, depending on where she hoped her grievances might be remedied. It is quite understandable that under such circumstances in the defeated countries — where internal power relations were in a state of constant change and ferment — there were rising currents the advocates of which represented extreme reaction at home and were unwilling, even for a short time, to resign themselves to the consequences of the defeat, to accept the new territorial settlement; clamouring for a war of revenge, they took every opportunity to establish good connections between one another, and devised many adventurist schemes which today would seem to be products of wild fantasy.

It could come as a surprise to no one — the least of all to the Entente Powers — that the foreign policy of the counter-revolutionary Government of Hungary exhibited, right from the outset, strong nationalist-irredentist tendencies, and that efforts were exerted to use any means to get the terms of peace changed. The memorandum of October 1919 on the Hungarian foreign political issues was very remarkable from this point of view. It was hallmarked by Horthy's name. The document, drafted at the time of the negotiations conducted with Clerk (reminiscent of these talks are a few passages recommending tolerance in a tone that was utterly alien from the spirit of the Siófok supreme command), analysed the foreign political situation in connection with the tasks of the army. Horthy and the gentry officers rallying round him were seized with the desire for a prompt war of revenge. From the circumstances of the defeat of the Hungarian Republic of Councils, and from the Rumanian occupation, they at once drew a lesson fitting in well with their political views and ambitions: reward is due to the states which had rendered the Great Powers services in defeating Bolshevism, in preserving (or restoring) bourgeois order; the size of this reward would not be proportionate to the role played in the war by the state concerned; such policing services could be expected first of all from a state which had spared its military energies up to the end of the war. Thus they would, to a certain extent, be able, regardless even of the intentions of the Great Powers, to acquire or to retain what they wanted. Horthy's argumentation boiled down to this:

— Hungary's number one enemy is Rumania, because the greatest territorial claim is made against her, and because she is the strongest of all the neighbouring states. The principal aim of foreign policy is therefore to get square with the Rumanians by recourse to arms. The international situation is shaping favourably to this end, since Rumania, owing to her greed and the protraction of occupation, will gradually lose the sympathy of the Entente, especially that of the British and the Americans; she also has conflicts with Bulgaria, Serbia and Russia over territorial issues; she has increasing difficulties in home politics and with the nationalities. Until the appropriate time of attack (in Horthy's estimation it would be 1921), a semblance of peaceful relations ought to be maintained with Rumania, but every opportunity must be grabbed to isolate her diplomatically, and an active irredentist organization must continue in Transylvania.

— Despite territorial disputes, normal or, for the time being, even friendly relations must be entertained with Yugoslavia, since she can be expected to play a major part in the diplomatic encirclement of Rumania. At the same time, Hungary must make use of Yugoslavia's internal conflicts, giving secret assistance to the Croatian separatists, without jeopardizing a future anti-Rumanian alliance with the Serbian ruling quarters.

— The Hungarian army must be made fit to carry out acts of war. The armament limitations imposed by the peace terms must be circumvented and can even be expected to become less effectual.

— Hungary must acquire an appropriate international standing, which she can do first of all by keeping order in Central Europe. "The Entente States, primarily Great Britain and the United States, are by all means interested to see normal relations along the middle reaches of the Danube in order to preserve peace on this important trade route. Through our own inner regeneration we have to prove that Hungary alone, among the Danubian states (including the Balkan countries), . . . is able to earn respect as a safe prop of the maintenance of order, and that Rumania is no match for us in this respect." With this in view (a) we have to thwart "any new Bolshevist outbreak"; (b) we have to refrain "from any act which, by dint of its too reactionary nature, would create confusion and from any extravagances in whatever direction"; (c) we have to lay stress on the rearmament, equipment and dependability of the army.

— When Hungary's standing will be upgraded in this way, "then we shall be entitled to take action as defenders of order outside our territory as well." This should primarily concern Austria, where the 'Red' movement is strengthening. The outbreak of a revolution in Austria would be favourable for Hungary, because she could undertake to crush it by joining the Austrian right-wing forces; thus, in addition to relieving militarily pressure from the Austrian side, she might possibly retain Burgenland, which the Saint-Germain peace treaty has awarded to Austria and which is still under Hungarian control. (That the main issue was the retention of Burgenland, is best demonstrated by the fact that late in 1919, and early in 1920, both the Austrian and Hungarian Governments addressed a series of notes and aide-mémoires in the matter of Burgenland to the Great Powers, particularly to Great Britain. The Austrian Government, demanding the invalidation of the peace treaty with regard to Burgenland, never forgot to point to the reactionary, chauvinistic nature of the Hungarian Government. On the Hungarian side, however, efforts were made to convince the British Government that a 'Bolshevist outbreak' was threatening in Austria. In January 1920, Horthy was explaining to the British chief representative in Budapest that socialism in Austria was so powerful that it practically meant the advent of Bolshevism, and therefore Austria was no less en enemy of Hungary than the rest of the neighbouring countries.)

Before taking action against Rumania, territorial gains were to be enforced against Czechoslovakia. Horthy raised the idea of a common Polish—Hungarian frontier and planned to establish connections with the Sudeten German movement and with Hlinka's Slovak autonomists.

Horthy's memorandum — although clearly based on an entirely unrealistic view of Hungary's strength and the chance of a war of revenge — was to have a definitive bearing on some of the foreign policy issues throughout the coming decades of counter-revolutionary rule.

A conception applied consistently throughout the memorandum was that connections were to be sought by all possible means with the counter-revolutionary, reactionary forces of the neighbouring countries. Supporting these, did not remain merely a requirement of principle; in fact, it was realized in the Hungarian—Austrian, the Hungarian—Croatian, and the Hungarian—Slovakian relations from 1920 onward. At that time, counter-revolutionary Hungarian politicians began to approach all kinds of German extreme-right revanchist groups and organizations. The Hungarian ruling circles took a share in the activities aimed at the overthrow of the Renner Government in Austria and promoted the schemes of Ludendorff and of the Bavarian Kahr Government. Establishing connections with, and providing assistance to the Croatian and Slovakian separatist movements were important methods of Hungarian secret diplomacy. Ways and means were easy to detect in these countries, because the ethnic problems of the new states, their aspirations to achieve (or at least to demonstrate) nationhood provoked the national minorities to increasingly desperate resistance. The ethnic groups and organizations naturally sought points of contact with those states which were opposed to the Versailles peace settlement, unable to reconcile themselves to the existing status quo. The political practice of these groups developed the methods — from mere subversion through pogroms to terrorism — which later became part and parcel to the arsenal of Fascism. These methods were more and more often enforced by the leaders of the national and ethnic movements and gained active support from various Hungarian irredentist organizations as well as from official Hungarian Government circles.

Headed by Count Albert Apponyi, the Hungarian delegation invited by the Entente Powers to be handed the terms of peace, left for Paris early in January 1920, and presented its credentials on the 14th. At the same time, the Hungarian delegation tendered eight notes, with enclosures running into volumes, trying to disclaim Hungary's responsibility for the war and adducing historical, ethnic, political and economic reasons to justify her demands for the possession not only of areas with homogeneous Magyar populations beyond the new frontiers, but also of territories inhabited by national minorities and disannexed already in 1918, for domination over the whole of 'historical Hungary'. This introduced the activity of the Hungarian delegation to cunteract the intentions of the Entente Powers.

The Hungarian peace delegation was practically ignored by representatives of the Great Powers, but it had some formal opportunities to set forth its views. On January 16, Apponyi, in his address to the Peace Conference in reply to the terms of peace, proposed that a plebiscite should decide the question of all disputed areas, and on February 12, he presented the Hungarian observations in writing to the Council of Four. On February 6, the representatives of Rumania, Czechoslovakia and Yugoslavia, with reference to Apponyi's statement, sent the Peace Conference a joint memorandum in which they formulated their claims on Hungary, and protested against the proposed plebiscite. They also prepared a joint reply to the Hungarian Government's observations on the peace terms. This action indicated the coincidence of the interests of Czechoslovakia, Rumania and Yugoslavia in respect of their anti-Hungarian policies. This common defence against the Hungarian revisionist ambitions became the basis of the existence of the Little Entente.

As appears from Horthy's memorandum, the lesson underlying the counter-revolutionary politicians' immediate political action was that, if there was any hope at all for a change in the territorial clauses of the peace treaty before it was signed, it could be effected only if the Hungarian Government was able to convince the Great Powers of its ability not only to maintain order at home but to do services in overcoming the revolutionary danger abroad, either by joining in the intervention against Soviet Russia or by crushing the left-wing movements in other countries. It seemed that they could expect success in foreign politics from the slogan of 'order'. Therefore, they availed themselves of every opportunity that offered the faintest hope to obtain a more favourable peace or to win the Great Powers over to support action against the anti-Hungarian unity of the neighbouring countries.

A direct consequence of the British diplomacy's role in helping the counter-revolutionary system into power was that the attention of Hungarian politicians primarily turned towards Great Britain. Hungary had nothing to expect from France, except during a short transition period which will be discussed later on. Italy was too weak, her international positions were too unstable to support Hungary as a partner in foreign politics, although the zigzag line of Italy's diplomacy did not preclude the possibility of contemplating co-operation with Hungary. In January 1920, Horthy conferred with the British chief representative about Hungary's internal and international position. He explained that the Hungarian Government was compelled to look for some 'new orientation', and asked for the British Government's advice, saying that Great Britain was the only Power in which he and his country had full confidence. When Hohler requested him to expound his conception of a new orientation, Horthy replied that the Italians, wishing to counteract Yugoslavia, were seeking connections with Hungary, but they could not be trusted. Nor did he entertain great hopes concerning the Peace Conference, for this was unable even to get the Rumanian Government to evacuate the territories east of the Tisza. Eventually, the Hungarian Government might feel compelled to turn to the Germans, no matter how unpopular they might be in Hungary, because some kind of new orientation must be developed sooner or later.

Horthy's disquisitions made it clear that, in fact, he would have expected more substantial support from Britain. Members of the British diplomatic and military mission in Budapest were ready to use their influence in London. On January 24, 1920, Hohler wrote a letter to the Foreign Office, raising the question: " ... are our interests exactly identical with those of our Allies? ... You cannot get away from the fact that the Hungarians are the strongest race in South Eastern Europe, and that they must, at the present time, turn for assistance, moral and material, to some great power, and ... if that power is not England, it is going quite inevitably to be Germany ... I am very strongly of the opinion that the peace of Europe in the next few years is directly dependent on the treatment of and state of affairs in Hungary." Hohler and his colleagues built their argument on the Bolshevist peril. They started from the assumption that in the spring of 1920, the Soviet army was expected to move against Rumania, and that such a contingency, considering the condition of the nationalities in that country, would entail catastrophic consequences. Hohler agreed with General Gorton that Hungary seemed to be the chief protection in South Eastern Europe against Bolshevism. On this account, Hohler sent long reports to Lord Curzon, in which he emphasized how unjust he found the territorial decisions of the peace treaty. Hohler pledged Lord Curzon to step up in Hungary's favour before the treaty would be signed.

But the Foreign Office did not think it probable that the Soviet army would enter upon action in South Eastern Europe. And although the Foreign Office's reply emphasized that the British fully realized the importance of Hungarian friendship to Britain, it stated that it was too late to revise the terms of the Hungarian peace treaty. As to Germany, the British thought that Czechoslovakia, Rumania and Yugoslavia, being on good terms with one another, could form a bloc of forty million and be a more reliable barrier against Germany than seven or even ten million Hungarians.

The conceptions built upon Great Britain thus failed to materialize. At that time, however, new hopes were suddenly inspired by the policy of the French Government.

France, especially after the most extreme wing of French imperialism gained power early in 1920, gave priority, over everything, to anti-Soviet intervention in order to establish French hegemony in Central and Eastern Europe. The Hungarian counter-revolutionary régime willingly offered its services. Leading French politicians at the time, Premier and Foreign Minister A. Millerand, and Maurice Paléologue, general secretary in the Foreign Ministry, were ready for a rapprochement with Hungary. This found considerable response in Budapest, mainly because it was known that certain French quarters would not feel antipathetic to a Habsburg restoration. At the same time, French business circles tried to expand their sphere of influence in Hungary, for they thought that Hungary's central position might enable them to pave the way for French economic hegemony over the whole of South Eastern Europe. From this point of view, it would have been especially important to gain control over the Hungarian railway network. To strengthen French influence in Central Europe, it was desirable that Hungary should sign the peace treaty at the earliest possible date. This is why it seems right to suppose that the covert aim of French foreign policy in those negotiations was nothing more than to have the peace treaty accepted.

The Paléologue—Halmos negotiations which, in fact, were proposed by the Schneider—Creusot financial group towards the end of March 1920, started after the formation of the Simonyi-Semadam Government in Hungary. One of the authorities behind the negotiations on the Hungarian side was Foreign Minister Pál Teleki, while direct negotiations were carried on by Károly Halmos. The talks held in the French capital were joined in by Count Imre Csáky as special representative of the Hungarian Government, by Kornél Tolnay, the general manager of the Hungarian State Railways, and by Count István Bethlen. Csáky, in his account of the first meetings, stated on March 29, that the whole discussion "made the impression that concealed behind it, was a well considered and highly important plan, and this impression only became stronger when the negotiations went on. . . . Saint-Sauveur, who is the representative of Creusot, stressed how big interests this concern controlled in Czechoslovakia, Rumania and Poland, and pointed out that, should Hungary come into this sphere of interests, the huge concern would set up its headquarters in Budapest. As a result, Hungary would become the main pillar of France's eastern policy." Paléologue followed the same train of thought.

The representatives of the French Government set forth their demands as follows: 1. the Hungarian State Railways and the State Machine Works should pass into French hands in the form of a lease; 2. French participation should be secured in the Hungarian Credit Bank which controlled the majority of the most important industrial enterprises; 3. a concession should be granted for the construction of a commercial free port on the Danube in Budapest.

In compensation for compliance with the French demands, the Hungarian Government would have liked to obtain a modification of the territorial provisions of the peace treaty. Simultaneously with the Paris negotiations, the head of the French mission in Budapest, Maurice Fouchet, also talked with representatives of the Hungarian Government, and in exchange for the acceptance of the French demands he promised a change in the French policy towards Hungary. On April 23, 1920, Teleki sent detailed directives to the Hungarian negotiators in Paris. In return for the economic concessions, 1. he asked for assistance in the equipment of the Hungarian army, in the military rehabilitation of Hungary; 2. he wished to obtain modifications in the territorial clauses of the peace treaty, in such a way that the areas inhabited dominantly by Magyars along the frontiers (the minimum demand) as well as Eastern Slovakia, Ruthenia, in Bácska (Bachka) as far as the Francis Joseph Canal and the entire Banat region should belong to Hungary, and the Magyar and Saxon population in Transylvania should be given autonomy. The Foreign Minister also pointed out that great caution should be exercised at the negotiations because France's international position was weakening and a pro-French line in Hungarian foreign policy would set Hungary against her potential allies Germany and Italy.

The demands of the Hungarian Government were entirely unrealistic in the given situation. Even if France had been willing to support certain Hungarian territorial demands in exchange for economic penetration, any attempt to modify the peace treaty would have come up against the most resolute opposition of the successor states. And although it were the British, who had the largest number of reservations concerning the 1919 frontiers before they were accepted, they were most reluctant to support their alteration at this point only to let French influence become dominant in Hungary.

And indeed, the Supreme Council of the Peace Conference on May 6, 1920, declared the treaty of peace with Hungary final.

The covering letter, which the chairman of the conference, A. Millerand, handed the Hungarian delegation together with the text of the treaty of peace, reflected to a certain extent the result of the Franco—Hungarian negotiations, yet it also became clear that any change in the frontiers could only mean minor rectifications, even in principle. Millerand gave detailed reasons why the arguments of the Hungarian peace delegation were unacceptable, and stated that the Allied and Associated Powers would, in no respect, modify the territorial clauses of the peace treaty, because any breach of the established frontiers would entail serious consequences. The Hungarian ruling classes, living in a dream of overheated expectations, still saw certain gleams of hope appear from the passages of the covering letter in which the Allied and Associated Powers admitted that the frontiers defined in the treaty might not always follow the ethnic and economic requirements, and that if during the implementation, the frontier commissions should recommend to redress certain injustices, the Allied Council might, at request from an interested party, offer its good offices to carry out some rectifications. The letter stressed however, that any such changes were impossible to be made promptly, since that would have delayed the signing of the peace treaty against the will of all of Europe.

The hopes that it might be possible to obtain territorial adjustment in exchange for major economic concessions before the signing of the peace treaty, were thus destroyed on May 6. But the Franco—Hungarian negotiations continued, partly in view of the expectations regarding the above passage of the Millerand letter, but mainly because the Polish—Russian war seemed to provide new possibilities of a territorial revision.

The Polish troops supported by the French attacked Soviet Russia on April 25, 1920. After considerable initial successes of the interventionists (who took Kiev on May 7) the Red Army started a counteroffensive and broke through the front early in June. The Polish forces retreated. In this situation it seemed that counter-revolutionary Hungary might become an important support for an anti-Soviet intervention, chiefly because the Czechoslovak Government displayed no special enthusiasm for the affair; not that it felt any sort of sympathy for Soviet Russia, but because it had differences with Poland.

In the beginning, at the time of Polish successes, the French gave no particular attention to the Hungarian offer. After the collapse of the Polish front, however, the idea arose of making use of Hungarian military force in addition to the fulfilment of economic demands.

A step forward in the Franco—Hungarian negotiations was Fouchet's consultation with Horthy on May 18, 1920. France's chief representative, in the presence of Horthy and several members of the Hungarian Government, read out a declaration by the French Government laying down the directives to be followed in relation to Hungary. Without making any concrete promise, the declaration stated that the French Government interpreted the Millerand letter as meaning that France offered her good offices in order to make amends for the ethnic and economic injustices of the terms of peace. Fouchet said that the French Government would facilitate any move of the Hungarian Government in the matter of transport and the railways, financial questions, etc. At the same time he named the economic and financial concessions which the French expected to receive on behalf of the Schneider—Creusot group in return for French support. Ten days later, the Hungarian Government issued the letter of option on the lease of the Hungarian State Railways, which, upon French insistence, Horthy approved in a special note on June 9 (after the signing of the peace treaty).

In the spring of 1920, the signing of the treaty of peace with Hungary could not be postponed any longer for several reasons. The Hungarian ruling circles, although they had found the terms of peace extremely injurious, decided to sign it, primarily because they had no alternative, while, at the same time, they hoped that acceptance of the peace arrangements would bring recognition of the counter-revolutionary régime and international support for it. They also wished to promote the consolidation of the régime at home. Instrumental in the decision were the unfounded hopes they pinned on the Franco—Hungarian negotiations, with the assumption of the possibility of a certain territorial revision of the peace treaty.

The representatives of Hungary signed the peace treaty at Trianon Palace on June 4, 1920. The document consisted of fourteen parts. Part I contained the Covenant of the League of Nations. Part II described the new frontiers of Hungary. The territory of Hungary, which, before the war had been 282,000 sq.km. (without Croatia), was cut to 93,000 sq.km., her population was reduced from 18 million to 7.6 million. The treaty sanctioned the separation from Hungary of areas where the majority of the population was made up of nationalities (Slovakia, Ruthenia, Transylvania and Croatia), but it even gave the neighbouring countries territories where all of the inhabitants or their majority were Hungarians. One million Hungarians were added to the population of Czechoslovakia, one and a half million to that of Rumania, and about half a million to that of the Kingdom of Serbs, Croats and Slovenes. Nearly one and a half million out of the three million Magyars, annexed to the three neighbouring countries, lived in the frontier regions, in areas with a homogeneous Hungarian population. Part III of the peace treaty defined the obligations of Hungary towards the neighbouring and other European countries. It enumerated the provisions concerning the protection of national minorities and those concerning citizenship. It obliged Hungary not to give up her independence without the consent of the Council of the League of Nations. Consequently, she would have to refrain — especially pending her admission to membership of the League — from any act that might directly or in any other manner jeopardize her independence through participation in the affairs of another Power (Art. 73). This provision was primarily meant to prevent a possible union with Austria. Article 74 obliged Hungary to recognize all the new frontiers as they had been fixed by the Allied and Associated Powers (the frontier commissions began working on the site after the signing of the peace treaty) as well as all conventions concluded or to be concluded with Powers who had fought on the side of the Austro—Hungarian Monarchy.

Part IV dealt with Hungary's interests outside Europe, and Part V contained the military, naval and air clauses. It was laid down that universal conscription should be stopped in Hungary; the strength of the armed forces, organized on a voluntary basis, could not surpass 35,000 men and this army could be used only for the maintenance of order and for frontier guard duties; the importation to Hungary of all kinds of arms, ammunition and war material was prohibited; it was forbidden for Hungarians to manufacture and to import armoured vehicles, tanks or any other facilities that might be used for military purposes; all monitors, torpedo-boats belonging to the Danube flotilla and other vessels equipped with arms — except for three reconnoitring gunboats — had to be surrendered to the Principal Allied and Associated Powers; Hungary was not allowed to maintain military or naval air services in the army; and finally, it was stipulated that these provisions should be enforced by Hungary under the supervision of the Inter-Allied Commission or a military control commission specially delegated to Hungary.

Part VI provided for the prisoners of war and military graves. Part VII defined the penalties and provided for the extradition of persons found guilty of war crimes. Part VIII dealt with the question of war reparations. Hungary had to undertake to pay for the war damage an amount to be fixed by the Reparations Commission. It was stipulated, among other things, that Hungary was bound to deliver to each of the interested Allied and Associated Governments its respective share of all those official papers, documents and historical notes which were directly related to the history of the ceded territories and which had been removed from there since January 1, 1868. Part IX containing the financial clauses stipulated that the Reparations Commission should have all property and revenue of the Hungarian state pledged as security for reparations payments. Part X summed up the economic clauses. In it, the victor Powers obliged Hungary to grant them, without being requested to do so and without any compensation, all those facilities in goods traffic (for imports, exports, transit and accounting) which she had accorded to other countries except those stipulated in such trade agreements to be concluded in the next five years with Austria and Czechoslovakia which would ensure preferential terms for the importation of certain raw materials and industrial goods.

Part XI of the peace treaty laid down that pending Hungary's admission to the League of Nations, the Allied and Associated Powers' aircraft would be free to fly over Hungary and to land on its territory. Part XII dealt with the questions of ports, waterways and railways, Part XIII with matters concerning the International Labour Organization, and Part XIV contained miscellaneous provisions. The peace of Trianon, like all other such treaties concluded in Versailles, closed the war — an imperialist and unjust war on both sides — in an imperialist and unjust manner. The designation of the frontiers eventually settled — without dispute — all controversial questions at Hungary's expense and to the benefit of the victors. This resulted not only from the greedy expansionism of the bourgeois governments of the new states (the unreasonable demands of the Rumanian Government even induced the Great Powers to give Rumania less than they had promised in the Bucharest treaty of 1916). The drawing of the new frontiers was fundamentally decided to serve the imperialist Powers' interests in redesigning the map of Central Europe.

Towards the end of the First World War, the victorious Great Powers, especially France, concentrated on two main purposes: to prevent Germany from attaining predominance again, and to contain the spread of the Russian proletarian revolution, i.e. to isolate Soviet Russia. After the dismemberment of the Monarchy, which the Great Powers had been ready to break up because they thought it was not equal to the task, this role could only be assigned to the new states or to those in Central Europe which became strong after the war: Poland, Czechoslovakia, Yugoslavia and Rumania. Hungary as a defeated country did not at all fit in with this conception. For this reason, in order for Czechoslovakia to fill the role she was expected to play against Germany, her frontiers were to be fixed so as possibly to be strategic frontiers, to secure her from Hungary. The Danube, as such, was fit to serve as a natural frontier, therefore the Peace Conference, yielding to the arguments of the Prague Government, cared little about ethnic considerations in drawing the Czechoslovak—Hungarian frontier. Rumania also wanted her western frontier to run along a defensible line in order to make it a section of the anti-Soviet *cordon sanitaire*. Therefore the Paris Peace

Conference, whenever considerations of strategy and communications arose (mostly fictitious points of view, since e.g. insignificant rivulets were made to appear as navigable streams) in marking out Hungary's new frontiers in the spring of 1919, unhesitatingly cut off Magyar-inhabited areas. And not much care was given to the simple truth that with a modern technique of warfare it was very little probable for 'natural' frontiers, namely those running along rivers and mountain ranges, to acquire strategic importance in an armed conflict, but it was almost certain that the territorial demands justified by national grievances might lead to war conflicts.

The nearly eighteen months from the collapse of the Monarchy to the signing of the peace treaty, was, by historical standards, too short a time for the events to be rationalized and accepted as final; the Trianon Peace Treaty, at one stroke, made Hungary the smallest country in Eastern Europe in respect of area and population and the weakest in terms of economic resources and military strength. The Hungarian ruling classes, although accepting the peace treaty in the interest of consolidating their power, did not, for a moment, give up the hope of regaining, in case of a favourable international constellation, control over the lost territories inhabited, as they were, mostly by nationalities.

This endeavour was further enhanced by the classes of landowners and big capitalists as well as by the oversized middle classes, since a good number of the magistrates of the county and local apparatus of public administration, army officers and all kinds of office holders, teachers, etc. had, by the turn of events, lost their means of subsistence. These strata crowded now in one-third of the traditional territory of Hungary, threatened to brust asunder the whole societal framework.

The principal aim of counter-revolutionary Hungarian foreign policy had, from the very outset, been to achieve the total revision of the peace treaty, and not merely to obtain mitigation of the damage done to the ethnic principle. The national exasperation provoked by the unjust territorial clauses of the Trianon peace treaty was thus used as a mass support for the programme of the restoration of Greater Hungary.

And this effort was not futile: the fact that such a disregard of the ethnic principle had separated three million Hungarians from their proper country was enough to prove unacceptability of the new frontiers to the broad masses. The circumstances in which the peace treaty had been drawn up only strengthened the illusion — harboured not only by the gentry classes but by the country's entire public — that the secession of the nationalities, the disintegration of historical Hungary, was not the outcome of a long overdue historical process, but a result of brutal foreign violence due to a mere coincidence of internal turmoils and new international power relations at the end of the war. The contradiction between the Wilsonian principles and the terms of the peace treaty contributed to the growth of the public sentiment, inspired by counter-revolutionary propaganda, that the principle of self-determination was only a humbug, that it had been proclaimed with the only purpose of being a basis of reference for the victors to carry out their expansionist designs. Thus the peace treaty was considered to have been an arbitrary act of the victors, and people forgot about the fact — self-contradictory, as it was, in the dictated peace — that the aspirations of the oppressed peoples for independence could eventually be realized through the collapse of the Monarchy. A large part of the population thus became exposed to the revisionist propaganda, lining up with nationalist incitement to hatred for the neighbouring peoples, and accepting the principle of a total revision.

Failure to understand the real historical processes, and confusing them with the effective national grievances caused by the peace treaty created a situation in which the antidemocratic nationalism of the era of Dualism could live on and penetrate the deepest layers of society. This nationalism, firmly antidemocratic from the Dualist beginnings, became even more reactionary, aggressive and militarist after the war. From then on it formed the most important component of the ideology of the counter-revolutionary régime. The revisionist argument was seemingly, though falsely, justified: If the disintegration of historical Hungary has merely been a consequence of the arbitrary doings of the victors, it should then be evident that the Dualist system's policy towards the nationalities played no part in the catastrophe; the secession of the nationalities then, is not final, not irrevocable, and the restoration of Hungary's pre-1918 frontiers depends only on a change in power relations. And, as the status quo created by the peace treaty compels masses of Hungarians to live under Czechoslovak, Rumanian and Yugoslav rule, the new power relations will then open the way to the reestablishment of the old system, and so Slovaks, Ukrainians, Rumanians and Croats will again live under Hungarian rule.

The acceptance of grievance-generated irredentism promoted the formation of a hysterical social frame of mind which furthered the crystallization of the view based on one-sided interpretations of the tragic set-backs in Hungarian history, a view according to which the principal cause of all national misery was that Europe had always let down Hungary when she was fighting for freedom and in defence of European civilization; that Hungary had suffered many injustices which she might rightly expect the world to remedy, and if this was not to happen, she might feel relieved of the responsibility for the peace of Europe.

However, even the exploitation of national despair and confusion for the purposes of revisionism, a strong public sentiment suited to these purposes would still have been insufficient basis for pursuing a foreign policy centered on the issue of revision from the position of a non-existent Great Power in anticipation of a paramount role in the Danubian basin. It was Horthy's system that was needed to carry on such a conception, based on the hope that the serious tensions arising from the faults of the Versailles peace settlement might lead to a radical change in the international situation.

It sounds like a commonplace to say that the foreign policy of a country adequately complements its domestic policy, yet we know of but a few instances where this truth was so clearly and directly manifested as in the counter-revolutionary régime of Hungary. The closed nature of the political construction interwoven with conservative, Fascist elements — the fact that the forces of progress, and even those of bourgeois democracy, were debarred from political life — led to a paralysation of all sensible foreign political aspirations. Silence was imposed on those who could and would have distinguished between the secession of territories historically ripe for secession, and the loss of the unjustly disannexed territories; who could see that Hungary's extrication from the Dualist system was to her advantage by abolishing the bonds of both the Dualist aggressors and of those suppressed by Magyar nationalism. For this very reason, under the counter-revolutionary régime the ideology of a total revision meant that all means and methods to bring revision closer were a priori considered proper and justified. Any retrograde international force was a potential ally of Hungarian foreign policy whose irresponsibility towards the peace and fate of Europe was striking from the period when the changes in the international situation had given revision a chance.

How foreign and internal policies supplemented one another will all the more be clear if we understand that the foreign policy of revisionism in fact served to divert attention from the social backwardness of the system, from the reactionary character of its political construction, to make sure that the working masses did not expect a favourable change from effective national emancipation, but believed that the nation's prosperity could be realized in proportion to the size of recovered territories. We might even say that this was the primary function of foreign policy till the period when it reached a really active stage. When the territorial issue became the only guiding principle of foreign policy, it was inevitable to render every issue in the service of this one aim; no one could, without having been accused of high treason, venture to call attention to the effective social evils, to propose a more reasonable course in foreign politics; any progressive idea could be stifled with reference to law and order, and to national, unity which were said to have been the prerequisites of the realization of the 'great national aim'.

The fact that these became the main principles of the counter-revolutionary foreign policy was, to a certain extent, undeniably due to the serious faults of the Versailles peace settlement: before long the peace arrangements proved to contain a great many factors of uncertainty. It is commonly known that Soviet Russia did not recognize the peace achieved at Versailles, including the Trianon treaty. Lenin called the Versailles system an imperialist, unjust peace of marauders. But not even the leading political quarters of the Entente Powers were of the same attitude, although the differences of opinion were not due to a sense of justice, but to power interests. When, especially because of the failure of the Wilsonian foreign political endeavours, the positions of the isolationists had been strengthened, the United States Congress refused to ratify the peace treaties. The United States concluded separate treaties of peace with the vanquished countries. The peace treaty between the United States and Hungary was signed in Budapest on August 29, 1921. The treaty upheld the rights and privileges guaranteed to the United States by the Trianon treaty, but at the same time, it was stipulated that the United States accepted no kind of obligation whatever in relation to the clauses contained in, or connected with, Parts III, IV and XIII of the Trianon Treaty of Peace, and did not recognize itself bound by Part I of the treaty either — the provisions of the League of Nations Covenant.

Apparently the Versailles peace system did not suit the security aspirations and aims of France either. The independent states created on the eastern frontiers of Germany – Czechoslovakia, Poland (and the Baltic republics) – could not seriously counterbalance Germany, since from the first moment they had been engaged in border conflicts and their internal, primarily ethnic, difficulties were too great not to come to the light. There was not much hope of creating a united and firm system of alliance to offset the weaknesses of those countries. And the system of alliance known as the Little Entente, which had been established in the early twenties in order to prevent a Habsburg restoration, and to which France eventually committed herself, was only an illusory factor against rising Germany, because the only real common interest of the three Little Entente states was their opposition to Hungary's revisionist aspirations. Moreover, their interests differed even in this respect. The differences Hungary had with Yugoslavia were insignificant as compared to those with Czechoslovakia and Rumania, therefore Yugoslavia was, from the outset, potentially the weakest member of the Little Entente, where the alliance could have been weakened, especially when – from the late twenties onward – the danger of Habsburg restoration was gradually subsiding and, compared to other looming dangers, was only an illusion or a political bogey rather than a real possibility.

All this led to a situation in which, peculiarly enough, the Little Entente, created to check Germany and Soviet Russia, was no guarantee, for example, for the French against the Germans. A dynamic German foreign policy could easily drive a wedge into this system of alliance, and for the German military strategists, the idea of a speedy victory over the eastern neighbours was a traditional and a plausible one, given the relative weakness of these countries when compared to Germany. The Little Entente was worth only as much as France was able to provide it with, and its existence was assured only as long as it could count upon military assistance from France. But there was little prospect of such an assistance, since the French changed their military strategy from offensive to defensive after the First World War (Maginot line). All this was still aggravated by the fact that the rectification of the mistakes came up against serious difficulties. When, during the world's great economic crisis, the big changes in the international situation in Europe began, and the danger of a new war became imminent owing to the Fascist break-through in Germany, when a few Western politicians recognized that it was impossible to stop German aggression without the co-operation of the Soviet Union, then, paradoxically, the attempts to establish an Eastern security pact failed mainly because of the reluctancy of those states which, at the time of their birth, were meant by the Entente to isolate the Soviet Union.

The grave faults of the Versailles system, the weaknesses of the postwar alignment in Central Europe were not as manifest in the twenties as they became ten years later, but were already, at the start, obvious enough to support a prediction of a radical change in European relations within a short time. For Hungary, this meant that, from the moment of signing the peace treaty, she based her foreign policy on an expected shift in the European situation which might enable her to recover the lost territories. Total revision, principal among all issues of foreign policy, thus fundamentally determined the foreign political orientation of the Horthy era and Hungary's relationships with the neighbouring countries. This is why, while waiting for the favourable moment, the Hungarian Government did not specify its demands and spoke only in general terms about the necessity of revision. This is why neither amidst the chaotic conditions following the war nor at the time of a relative stabilization of the international situation in Europe, did Hungary seriously contemplate seeking an understanding with her neighbours. True, these neighbours did not offer to make an agreement either, because while Hungarian diplomacy was hamstrung by the secret hope of 'getting everything back', the scarce initiatives coming from the neighbouring countries were restricted by their determination 'to keep everything they gained'.

After the conclusion of the peace treaty, on July 19, 1920, a new Government was formed by Count Pál Teleki, one of the Hungarian big landowners making up the traditional political leading class. The conservative-reactionary gentry then came to dominate in the composition of the Government and began to 'legitimize' the counter-revolutionary terror which, however, did not really succeed until 1923.

The establishment of the Teleki Government brought no change in the foreign policy announced by Horthy.

The Franco–Hungarian negotiations continued after the conclusion of the Trianon treaty, but it became increasingly clear that France would not undertake to give open support to the Hungarian territorial demands. On June 7, Count Csáky already reported from Paris that no greater political concessions than those previously outlined could be expected from the French. The most that might be expected is some concession in the matter of Burgenland (which was still under Hungarian military occupation). The Hungarian Government sent the French Government an aide-mémoire dealing with this question and with problems concerning army organization, the Danube Commission and reparations. The French, however, were only willing to transmit to the Hungarian Government, in the form of a verbal note of June 24, the general declaration read out by Fouchet on May 18. Two days earlier, the Hungarian plenipotentiaries in Paris had already presented the requested letter of option.

In June 1920, the Franco–Hungarian negotiations were interfered by the British Government, which could not tolerate a French monopoly position in Hungary. On June 30, a secretary of the British Legation in Budapest called on Teleki and read out to him a letter from Foreign Secretary Lord Curzon. Curzon stated that the agreement concluded with the French was unacceptable because it violated the peace treaty, and he warned the Hungarian Government that the political promises, especially those concerning territorial advantages, which French statesmen or officials might have made to Hungary were not at all in harmony with the real intentions of the French Government. On June 9, Gusztáv Gratz reported from Vienna that according to British chief representative Lindley, the Franco–Hungarian negotiations could not lead to any essential result either politically or economically. "Politically, because the French are not in a position to keep any promise they may have made in the matter of the frontiers; and economically, because the Reparations Commission still may have a say in the issue of the lease of the railways, and Lindley does not think that the

Commission would approve the lease." The head of the Hungarian Legation in Rome informed his Government that the Foreign Minister of Italy, Count Sforza, held the Franco–Hungarian negotiations to be dangerous and said that Hungary was mistaken if she believed that her relationships with the Entente would thus be improved.

Inspite of the British and Italian protests, the Franco–Hungarian negotiations were carried on, primarily because of the Soviet–Polish war. The Soviet Red Army, pursuing the Polish interventionist troops, was approaching the heart of Poland. When this war broke out, Horthy and the Hungarian Government already made efforts to join in the campaign of intervention and to occupy a part of Slovakia and Ruthenia under the pretext of defence against the 'Soviet peril'. Poland was ready to accept the help offered by Horthy and to press for a 'common Polish–Hungarian frontier'.

By mid-June, 1920, the Polish–Hungarian talks led to the conclusion of an agreement. Under the secret military pact, Hungary undertook to provide as much assistance as was possible to Poland in her struggle against Bolshevism and supply her with war equipment. The Hungarian Government, in addition to the war material supply, proposed two ways of helping Poland: 1. should Czechoslovakia attack Poland while the latter was fighting against Soviet Russia, Hungary would start an attack on Czechoslovakia; 2. Hungary would place a legion of 30,000 volunteers at the disposal of Poland. To launch the latter action and to gain free passage through Czechoslovak and Rumanian territory, Poland was to win the assent of the Entente Powers.

Negotiations were also conducted with the French Government to the effect that Hungary would deploy a force of four divisions (to be equipped by France) for the occupation of Eastern Slovakia and Ruthenia 'threatened by the Russians'. On June 19, 1920, the French Government informed Prague that the Hungarian Government would address such a request to the Supreme Council and possibly to the Czechoslovak Government. This plan was upset by the energetic joint protest of the Czechoslovak, Rumanian and Yugoslav Governments and by the Czechoslovak military countermeasures. Hungarian war supplies nevertheless reached Poland through Rumania; Hungary sent the Polish army about sixty million infantry cartridges.

As long as the war went on between Poland and Soviet Russia, the French Government carried on its diplomatic, political and military negotiations with Hungary, but avoided making concrete promises in respect of territorial questions. There was no other alternative, because already by July 22, 1920, the Council of Ambassadors sent secret instructions to the frontier commissions to disregard the Millerand letter and to observe strictly the territorial clauses of the peace treaty. On October 12, 1920, Poland concluded a preliminary peace with the Soviet Government. Millerand and Paléologue retired from the French Foreign Ministry; the new French Government openly rejected the territorial demands of the Hungarian Government and, with reference to protests from London, refused to give assistance in the equipment of the army. In November 1920, the Hungarian representatives left Paris.

The experiments in Hungarian foreign policy aiming to break out of international isolation by joining in the intervention and continuing the related negotiations with the French, and thus to obtain a revision of the territorial clauses of the peace treaty, were of no avail. What Teleki was afraid of, namely that a Franco–Hungarian rapprochement would impair Hungary's position with the other Great Powers of the Entente and would create difficulties in her relations with Germany and especially Italy, came true.

On August 14, 1920, a pact of alliance was concluded between Czechoslovakia and the Kingdom of Serbs, Croats and Slovenes, providing in Article 1 that, in case of an unprovoked attack from Hungary, the contracting parties should come to each other's rescue. This pact was the first among the so-called Little Entente treaties. A still more serious development from the point of view of Hungary's foreign political ambitions was that on November 12, 1920, Italy and Yugoslavia signed a treaty which formally closed the frontier disputes between the two countries. In complementary agreements, Italy and Yugoslavia undertook to observe the peace treaties with Austria and Hungary, to oppose Habsburg restoration (Italy accepted on obligation only to manifest diplomatic opposition) and to inform each other in case their security was threatened by Austria or Hungary. Finally the Italian Government specially expressed its satisfaction with the conclusion of the Czechoslovak–Yugoslav pact. The Rapallo treaty resulted in a rapprochement between Italy and Czechoslovakia, too. In January 1921, Foreign Minister Beneš of Czechoslovakia went to Rome where the two Governments exchanged notes stressing the identity of their views on issues of foreign politics. About the turn of 1920 to 1921, Italy seemed to be momentarily far from becoming a help for Hungary to break through her international isolation.

The shaping of the international events made it increasingly evident to the Hungarian Government that it could not hope for a modification of the peace treaty in the near future. Although in the vanquished countries, first of all in Germany, there were considerable forces which did not, for a moment, wish to resign themselves to the consequences of defeat, and were making adventurous plans which only very few believed ever to succeed. It had to be expected that for the time being, they had to accommodate themselves within the boundaries established by the peace treaties and would have to seek new ways to break their isolation in international affairs. But opportunities of finding such ways hardly presented themselves at the time. The international relations in the early twenties provided neither possibilities nor partners for shaping foreign policies to the detriment of peace. Italy's position had already been mentioned above. In Hungarian foreign policy Germany had, from the beginning, been regarded as a potential ally, yet in the years following the conclusion of the peace treaties, the establishment of official German–Hungarian relations was not contemplated. The spirit of the Weimar Republic was too alien to the counter-revolutionary, reactionary Hungarian régime which, at that time, chose to seek contact with underground forces of the extremist nationalist and militarist circles. Neither did Weimar Germany sympathize with the Horthy régime. Closer co-operation with Austria was barred as yet, among other things, by the question of Burgenland.

The other way out of international isolation would have been an agreement with the neighbours, but this was not considered seriously in Hungary's foreign policy. And when early in 1921 the Teleki Government nevertheless made approaches to Czechoslovakia these were more motivated economically than politically. The postwar difficulties were experienced by all countries in the Danubian basin. Efforts to reestablish commercial contacts were made in every country. The Teleki Government also wished to seek an economic rapprochement between Hungary and the successor states, but thought it possible only if it could avoid a simultaneous political rapprochement.

Czechoslovak–Hungarian negotiations began at Bruck on March 14, 1921. Participating in the talks were Prime Minister Teleki and the new Foreign Minister appointed in January, Gusztáv Gratz, on the Hungarian side and Foreign Minister Beneš on behalf of Czechoslovakia. The main topic of discussion was an economic rapprochement between the two countries on the basis of a preferential tariff system. According to some sources the Czechoslovak Government was willing, in exchange for an agreement and economic co-operation with Hungary, to negotiate the transfer of Magyar-inhabited border regions. Relying on statements by Beneš, French sources definitely denied that any serious offer of this kind had been made. There were certain hints, but all that was rather a diplomatic manoeuvre than a serious intention to rectify the frontiers. It is evident that an attempt to modify the status quo established at Versailles would have met the opposition not only of Rumania and Yugoslavia but also of the Great Powers, because it involved the danger of a chain reaction. It is difficult to believe in the seriousness of such an offer because it does not seem probable that the Czechoslovak Government which, at the Paris Peace Conference, had most persistently clamoured for the new frontiers, would have changed its mind after a few months, when no pressure was brought to bear on it. Nor was it a secret that the Hungarian Government was not only striving for a mere partial frontier revision. So Beneš could safely show readiness to consent to a frontier adjustment, because he didn't have to fear from its practical realization. In the Hungarian policy, demanding total revision, there was no inclination to accept such offers, if only for tactical reasons, and a probable refusal might have enhanced the moral prestige of the Czechoslovak Government.

The Bruck negotiations were interrupted by the first royalist putsch. In the spring of 1921, the legitimists made an attempt to restore the House of Habsburg in Hungary. They drew some encouragement from the attitude of certain members of the French Government, although already on February 2, 1920, the Entente Powers had protested, in an official note, against the possible restoration of the Habsburg dynasty to the throne of Hungary. Responsible French quarters, however, sympathized with the idea of averting the danger of the *Anschluss* by resuscitating the Habsburg Monarchy as a counterbalance to Germany in Central Europe. The first step in this direction would have been the restoration of the House of Habsburg in Hungary. At the time of the attempted putsch, the French Government behaved rather ambiguously. Rumours were spread in diplomatic circles that French politicians had taken part in the preparation of the attempt, and that Briand himself endorsed the action of Charles IV, or rather he took the position that in case of success he would put up with the accomplished fact. The Hungarian Ministry of Foreign Affairs received similar information about the position of certain British quarters.

On March 26, 1921, Charles IV, the ex-Emperor of Austria and ex-King of Hungary, arrived at Szombathely and was accommodated in the palace of Bishop Count János Mikes. Prime Minister Teleki and Minister of Education József Vass, who happened to stay at Szombathely as guests of legitimist leader Count Antal Sigray, immediately entered into negotiations with the ex-King about his accession to the throne. The next day, on the 27th, Charles decided to go to Budapest in order to meet Horthy. Teleki and Vass, who had earlier left Szombathely to prepare the meeting, had engine trouble with their car and arrived too late in the capital. Is it possible that the engine ran down because no one could foresee the outcome of the talk between the Regent and the King and because the two Ministers did not wish to side openly with any one of them? Charles IV met Horthy in the royal palace. The Regent, who was sure of having strong support in the country and could also rely on British support, did not adopt a negative attitude formally, but the terms to which he subjected his resignation (a title of duke and the supreme command of the army) indicated that he had no intention of surrendering power to Charles. Since the several hours of heated debate failed to bring any result, Charles IV, in company with Teleki and Sigray, and one of Horthy's *aide-de-camps* returned to Szombathely the same day.

While negotiations continued in Szombathely, Horthy hastened to take military precautions. The majority of the staff of officers were behind him. "The national army," he wrote later in his order of the day dated March 30, "has kept its oath according to my expectations, uniformly and faithfully, even in these tense days." Representatives of the Smallholders' Party took a stand against Charles IV on the 31st. All this made it obvious that the Charlists could not count upon the unanimous support of the army and the administrative authorities.

On March 28 and 29, the diplomatic envoys of the neighbouring countries presented to the Hungarian Government protests of their Governments against the attempt at restoration. Representatives of the Entente Powers only protested unofficially on March 29. As no energetic step was taken in the following days either, and Charles IV did not leave the territory of Hungary, Czechoslovakia and Yugoslavia declared the incident a *casus belli* and ordered partial mobilization. The relations between Hungary and the neighbouring countries became extremely strained and threatened to grow into an armed conflict. Seeing the danger, and that the ruling authorities in Hungary were evidently against the return of Charles to Hungary, the Entente Powers started to take action. On April 3, they presented a note to the Hungarian Government, declaring again that they could neither recognize nor tolerate the restoration of members of the Habsburg family. At the same time, they took measures to stop the military preparations of Czechoslovakia and Yugoslavia.

The first attempt of Charles IV at a restoration failed because of the power relations at home and abroad. On April 6, the ex-King was compelled to leave Hungary. The failure of the attempted putsch brought with it the fall of the compromised Teleki Government. Gusztáv Gratz, the legitimist Foreign Minister, had already resigned on April 4. On April 13, Count Teleki tendered the resignation of his Government. The next day, a new Government was formed under Count István Bethlen.

The attempted putsch further deteriorated the international position of Hungary. On April 23, 1921, a Rumanian—Czechoslovak treaty of alliance was signed. It provided not only for mutual assistance in case of an attack from Hungary but also for the co-ordination of policies towards Hungary. Six weeks later, on June 7, 1921, a Rumanian—Yugoslav treaty was concluded, extending defensive alliance and co-operation in foreign politics against Bulgaria with a view to upholding the peace of Neuilly.

In this situation, the Bethlen Government, having recognized that the Hungarian ruling classes would have to accommodate themselves to the territorial clauses of the peace treaty for the time being, did better than its predecessor in understanding that it had to accept the given European constellation in order to be able to break Hungary's isolation by pursuing a long-range foreign policy. In his first speech on April 19, 1921, Bethlen said that 'the raising of the foreign policy horizon of the nation' was a foremost task of his Government. As a first step in the realization of this programme, Foreign Minister Count Miklós Bánffy applied for Hungary's admission to membership of the League of Nations on May 23, 1921. With this application, the Government incurred bitter attacks from those who were unwilling even provisionally to resign themselves to the status quo. Those opposing Hungary's entry into the League of Nations primarily argued that Hungary would thereby acknowledge an obligation to comply with the Treaty of Trianon. (The Covenant obliged Member States to respect all treaty obligations as well as the territorial integrity and political independence of all Members of the League.) On the other hand, the Hungarian Government argued that even since the conclusion of the peace treaties the principal scene of international life had been the League of Nations, and therefore Hungary could only get out of her international isolation by participating in the work of the League of Nations as an independent state and an equal Member. Besides, it argued that by signing the peace treaty, Hungary had already once undertaken to keep the peace of Trianon, and this obligation would in no way be greater by a second acceptance. In addition, it made reference to Article XIX of the Covenant providing for the periodical reconsideration of treaties which had become inapplicable and whose continuance might endanger the peace of the world. Thereby, the Government alluded to the possibility of a peaceful revision.

Nevertheless, Hungary's accession to the League of Nations did not take place in 1921. At that time it was opposed by Czechoslovakia, Rumania and Yugoslavia. In view of the Burgenland events, the support of the Great Powers could not be taken for granted either. The Western Powers could not afford to qualify Hungary's refusal to cede Burgenland to Austria as a breach of treaty and at the same time to claim in the League that Hungary was complying with her international obligations.

In this situation the Hungarian Government, wishing to avoid repudiation while unwilling to acknowledge defeat openly, chose a compromise solution. On September 24, 1921, Hungary's chief representative at the League, Count Albert Apponyi, requested the League Assembly that, because of the wrangling about the implementation of Article 71 of the Trianon treaty (in the question of Burgenland), consideration of Hungary's application for admission be postponed until the next session.

The Bethlen Government resumed the negotiations started earlier with Czechoslovakia: From June 10 to 23, 1921, Foreign Minister Bánffy, ex-Prime Minister Teleki and Eduard Beneš held talks in Marienbad. After the failure of the legitimist coup, Czechoslovakia showed readiness to establish a kind of economic co-operation with Hungary that might develop into an alliance. The Czechoslovak delegation proposed a Czechoslovak–Hungarian–Austrian customs union. Britain, evidently with an anti-French bias, supported the Czechoslovak idea. In June 1921, Hohler, the British chief representative in Budapest, said that Great Britain would be pleased to see better neighbourly relations develop between the two countries. He added that it would be regrettable if the Hungarian political quarters would, at the outset, adopt a negative attitude towards Beneš's plan of alliance.

At the beginning of the negotiations, the Hungarian side was more willing to come to an agreement than before. A circular telegram from the Czechoslovak Foreign Ministry stated that, in political matters, the Hungarians had come considerably closer to the Czechoslovak position regarding the acceptance of the given situation. The differences nevertheless proved to be insurmountable. No agreement was reached on the important questions, and the faltering negotiations were ultimately interrupted by the aggravation of the Burgenland issue.

As is well known, under the Saint-Germain Peace Treaty, the region called Burgenland with the town of Sopron and environs was awarded to Austria, and the Treaty of Trianon obliged Hungary to cede this mostly German-inhabited territory, but she was not expected to carry out the evacuation until the ratification of the treaty. The Trianon Peace Treaty was ratified in July 1921, but Burgenland was still not evacuated. The Hungarian Government tried to take advantage of the uneasiness and concern of the Entente Powers about the *Anschluss* tendencies coming to the fore in Germany and Austria. On June 5, 1921, Foreign Minister Bánffy instructed the Hungarian Minister in Paris to warn the French Government that a vigorous pan-German agitation was going on in Burgenland, coupling the cession of the territory with the annexation of Austria to Germany. France and the other Allied Powers were looking for guarantees against the *Anschluss;* this might be facilitated if Burgenland continued to be under Hungarian administration until the definitive settlement of the *Anschluss* question. These arguments hardly convinced the Entente Powers. On August 1, after repeated Austrian demands, Hungary was called upon to withdraw her police and administrative organs from Burgenland. The Hungarian Government refused to comply, and declared that it was unwilling to evacuate the territory until Serbian troops had been withdrawn from the city of Pécs and Baranya County which had been awarded to Hungary by the peace treaty. Upon a repeated energetic demand of the Entente Powers, the Serbian troops began retreating from Pécs and the Baranya districts in the middle of August. At the same time, the Hungarian Government undertook to deliver, as part of the reparations, a considerable amount of coal to Yugoslavia and to transfer the Burgenland territory to Austria.

In the second half of August, the regular troops were withdrawn from Western Hungary, with the exception of Sopron and environs, which were occupied by the

Ostenburg detachments of officers. The justification for this was that Yugoslavia had not evacuated all the occupied territories, and that Austria had given no kind of guarantee to compensate the Hungarian owners for the loss of their landed estates and industrial enterprises in Burgenland. Simultaneously with the retreat of the regular troops, however, semi-regular armed bands — detachments commanded by Pál Prónay and Iván Héjjas — marched into Burgenland with the consent of the Government and committed atrocities on the pretence of 'insurrection'. In explaining the affair to the Western Powers, the Hungarian Government, in the hope of obtaining concessions in the question of Burgenland in return for the suppression of the banditry, claimed to be against the doings of the officers' detachments.

The Czechoslovak Government, especially after the successful Austro—Czechoslovak negotiations in August, saw with anxiety the events in Eastern Hungary which threatened to upset the equilibrium on the point of being consolidated. On September 12, Beneš addressed a note to the Council of Ambassadors and demanded energetic action. At the same time, in an effort to reach a compromise, he offered to mediate between Austria and Hungary. He met Bánffy at Brno on September 26. At the talks, he supported the Hungarian demand for Sopron and environs to remain part of Hungarian territory.

On October 3, the Entente Powers again called upon the Hungarian Government to surrender Burgenland. The next day, however, Prónay at the head of the officers' detachments called a 'constituent' assembly at Felsőőr and proclaimed Western Hungary an autonomous province called the 'Leitha Banate'.

The situation had thus become extremely complicated. Upon an Italian initiative, Bethlen proposed to the representatives of the Principal Allied Powers that they should try to solve the Burgenland question through the intercession of Italy. The Italian suggestion was that the Governments of Austria and Hungary should hold a conference in Venice, with Italian participation. On October 7, the representatives of the Great Powers in Budapest informed Bethlen that their Governments accepted the proposal.

The negotiations in Venice started on October 11, 1921. Austria was represented by Chancellor Schober, Hungary by Bethlen and Bánffy. The conference chairman was Foreign Minister Torretta of Italy. The negotiations were concluded on October 13 with an understanding that 1. Hungary would soon put an end to the bandits' atrocities and 2. a plebiscite should decide the status of Sopron and environs.

The Venice conference was the first success of the Bethlen Government's foreign policy. Contrary to the provision of the peace treaty, a compromise settlement was reached on the territorial issue. The Great Powers consented to the holding of a plebiscite, an idea which had been rejected most categorically by the Millerand letter a year before. Later the Hungarian Government often used the Sopron plebiscite for a long time as a precedent to show that international law supported Hungary's demand for a peace revision. At the same time, the way of closing the entire Burgenland affair, the frontier commission's compliance with Hungarian interests, threw light upon the anomalies of the frontier lines drawn at Trianon. Hungary succeeded in obtaining a frontier rectification at a point where her demands were much less substantiated from the strict ethnic angle than elsewhere. Of course, in this case the Great Powers had to decide between two vanquished countries, so they could put on the cloak of impartiality.

The Bethlen Government could register as an international success that Italy undertook to mediate by supporting the Hungarian demands and to render services to Hungary. At the time of the Venice negotiations, Torretta came to a secret agreement with Bánffy to the effect that in designating the boundary line, the Italian Government would use its influence to satisfy the Hungarian demands, and would instruct the Italian member of the frontier commission accordingly. Moreover, Torretta also mentioned that Italy would like to conclude a commercial agreement with Hungary at the earliest possible time. The Italian behaviour was a promising indication of the favourable future development of relationships between the two countries.

The Hungarian Government prepared the Sopron plebiscite — which was held between December 14 and 16, 1921 — so as to be secured against surprises. Thus 15,343 votes were cast for Hungary, and only 8,227 for Austria. On December 31, 1921, the Entente commission announced that Sopron and environs belonged to Hungary. The Sopron plebiscite pointed beyond its local importance as against the whole of the Versailles system. The new Austro–Hungarian frontier became the calmest section of the Trianon frontiers. Austria accepted the result of the plebiscite, Hungary resigned herself to the loss of Burgenland. Except for a certain right-wing agitation which took place in the second half of the thirties, the question of Burgenland was never again raised seriously as an issue of revision either on Government level or in public opinion.

The closing of the Burgenland affair had a favourable influence on the relationships between Austria and Hungary although for the time being Austria seemed to be approaching the Little Entente. Bethlen made the best of this situation in order not to return to the 'spirit of Bruck and Marienbad' in relation to Czechoslovakia.

The confusion around Burgenland drove the legitimist elements of the Hungarian ruling classes to make another attempt, in the autumn of 1921, to restore the House of Habsburg. This time, the action was also supported by French royalist politicians, and was also encouraged by unofficial British and Austrian circles.

On October 20, 1921, Charles IV. together with his wife, took a plane in Switzerland and landed at Dénesfa, on the estate of József Cziráky in Vas County. Having learned from the failure of the earlier attempt, this time the ex-King didn't intend to seize power by negotiating with Horthy but by resorting to military force. The next day, on the 21st, he flew to Sopron and appointed István Rakovszky Prime Minister. At the same time, he chose the other members of his Government as well: Count Andrássy became Minister of Foreign Affairs, Gusztáv Gratz was appointed Minister of Finance, Baron Antal Lehár, commander of the Szombathely garrison, was made Minister of Defence, etc. The Ostenburg detachment stationed at Sopron and the Szombathely garrison swore an oath of allegiance to the King. On October 22, Charles IV, together with his Government and the military who had joined him, took a train heading for the capital. On the way the garrisons of Győr, Komárom and Tatabánya also pledged allegiance to him.

Horthy and Bethlen were now less willing to let the legitimists assume power than in April. Therefore, they immediately took measures to thwart the attempt through force of arms. The formations hurriedly recruited from army units, the various groups of armed bands, the members of student fraternities and the Association of Vigilant Hungarians seemed strong enough for them to rely on. It was also evident that, in the tense political atmosphere created by the Burgenland affair, a foreign intervention could be reckoned with. Already on the 22nd, Bethlen called upon the authorities to obstruct the ex-King's travel to Budapest, and tried to dissuade Rakovszky from taking Charles to the capital. Charles IV's newly appointed Prime Minister replied with threats. He declared that if the Regent and the Government refrained from hindering "His Majesty's troops from marching into Budapest" they might count upon a favourable deal, otherwise the King's troops would be given a free hand to square accounts with them. Thus the negotiations were to no avail. On October 23, the ex-King's troops arrived at Budaörs. Following another round of talks, on the 24th, after Charles IV and Queen Zita had attended a mass celebrated by the local parish priest at the Biatorbágy railway station, the 'battle' started. The armed forces, supported by artillery, under the command of Gyula Gömbös, soon dispersed the 'royal' troops; Charles and his retinue took shelter in the Esterházy castle of Tata. Upon instructions from the Bethlen Government the ex-King, his wife and leaders of the putsch were taken prisoners and escorted to Tihany.

Already on October 22, the Entente Powers sent the Hungarian Government a note expressing the hope that it would do its utmost to prevent the ex-King's attempt, because a putsch would entail fatal consequences upon Hungary. The note of the Great Powers contained a very cautious warning, but the action of the Little Entente states was all the more energetic. These were afraid that a Habsburg restoration in Hungary might serve as a starting-point for the reconstitution of the Monarchy, which primarily endangered the existence of Czechoslovakia and Yugoslavia. In his circular telegram of October 22, Beneš declared that Charles IV's stay in Hungary was a *casus belli* and stated: "We shall not hesitate resorting to the most energetic precautions in concert with the other Members of the Little Entente. Even in case Charles of Habsburg will be removed from Hungary, we shall use every means, the strongest diplomatic and — if need be — military pressure, to dispose of the Habsburg question in Hungary and to eliminate the Habsburg danger from Central Europe." The diplomatic representatives of Rumania, Czechoslovakia and Yugoslavia called on Foreign Minister Bánffy, and told him that, in case the Hungarian Government was not in a position to protect the peace of Central Europe, their Governments themselves would take the measures necessary to preserve the peace. On October 23, Czechoslovakia and Yugoslavia ordered partial mobilization and massed considerable forces on the Hungarian frontier. On the 24th, the Little Entente states addressed a note to the Council of Ambassadors, stating that they were resolved to take the most drastic steps in the hope of support from the Allied Powers.

After the Charlists' military defeat, the countries of the Little Entente started a vigorous campaign to obtain the removal of the ex-King from Hungary and the dethronement of the House of Habsburg. On October 26, Beneš declared that Czechoslovakia and Yugoslavia were determined to issue an ultimatum on November 1, demanding that Hungary should proclaim the dethronement of the Habsburg dynasty. The Entente Powers were against Czechoslovak and Yugoslav mobilization (Britain raised an especially strong protest) but demanded that Hungary should proclaim the dethronement. To avoid this, the Hungarian Government did everything it could to bring Charles of Habsburg to announce his voluntary abdication, but without any success.

On October 29, the representatives of the Entente Powers in Budapest demanded in a note that the Bethlen Government should proclaim the deposition of Charles IV without delay. The same day, the Czechoslovak, Rumanian and Yugoslav envoys in Budapest already demanded the dethronment of the entire House of Habsburg. Another note, dated October 31, from the Allied Powers demanded likewise the dethronement of ex-King Charles and the entire House of Habsburg in such a way that the related bill should be passed by the National Assembly within eight days.

In the evening hours of October 31, Foreign Minister Bánffy already informed the representatives of the Great Powers that the Government accepted the demands without delay. The next day, the Cabinet adopted the text of the dethronement bill. The same day, in accordance with a decision of the Council of Ambassadors, the Hungarian Government delivered Charles of Habsburg and his wife to the commander of the British Danubian flotilla. Charles IV, on board of the gunboat *Glowworm,* left Hungary. The Allied Powers deported them to the island of Madeira. There, King Charles IV died on April 1, 1922.

On November 3, 1921, the Bethlen Government tabled the dethronement bill in the National Assembly. The bill, while maintaining the institution of kingdom, proclaimed the dethronement of the House of Habsburg, but did not expressly provide that the Habsburgs should be excluded from a free election of the King of Hungary. The subsequent démarche of the Little Entente and of the Great Powers had, as the only result, that November 5 Bánffy, in a note signed by members of the Government, informed the Great Powers that the Hungarian Government would comply with the Council of Ambassadors' decisions of February 2, 1920, and April 3, 1921, and promised that before raising the issue of the election of a king, it would ask for the opinion of the Powers represented at the Conference of Ambassadors, and would not make any arrangement without their consent.

The failure of the second royalist putsch made the defeat of the legitimists complete. The Habsburg question was dropped, and this move improved the international position and the possibilities of the Hungarian Government.

After the fiasco of the second attempt at a Habsburg restoration, and after the settlement of the Burgenland question, one of the main aims of the Bethlen Government's foreign policy was to achieve Hungary's admission to the League of Nations. This seemed all the more necessary, since towards the end of 1921, the Little Entente states made efforts to strengthen and broaden their system of alliance which threatened to close the ring around Hungary. A Polish–Czechoslovak political convention was signed on November 6, 1921. It recognized the frontier between the two states as definitive, provided for benevolent neutrality in the case of an attack on one of the contracting parties by a neighbouring country, and obliged the parties not to conclude with third states any agreement that was inconsistent with their convention. This pact, especially its last provision, made the Hungarian Government feel quite uncomfortable. (The Polish–Czechoslovak convention was not put into force, but this could not be foreseen at the end of 1921.) On December 16, 1921, President Hainisch of Austria and Foreign Minister Beneš of Czechoslovakia, on the basis of preliminary negotiations between the two states, concluded a convention for the period of five years. They undertook to observe strictly the provisions of the peace treaties of Saint-Germain and Trianon, mutually guaranteed each other's frontiers, and declared that in the interest of their security, they would support each other diplomatically and politically, and would take action against any plan or attempt to reestablish the old régime. (The convention remained in force until March 1927 and was not prolonged.)

Since the Hungarian Government did not withdraw its application for admission in September 1921, but only asked for the postponement of its consideration, it didn't have to present a new application to the League of Nations. In 1922, the chances of success were better than a year before. Since the Habsburg problem had been settled by the dethronement of the Habsburg dynasty, and since it appeared that the Hungarian counter-revolutionary régime became relatively firm, there could be no serious objections to Hungary's accession to the League. Nor did any new conflicts arise in 1922, although there were serious differences of opinion with the Reparations Commission in the matter of reparations because the Hungarian Government refused to deliver the prescribed amount of living cattle. This controversy was, however, eclipsed by the International Economic Conference held in Genoa (April 10 to May 19, 1922).

On August 27, 1922, representatives of the Little Entente states assembled in Prague decided not to oppose Hungary's admission to the League, but they resolved to demand as many guarantees as possible from the Hungarian Government for the observance of the peace treaty.

The Secretary-General of the League of Nations informed the Hungarian Government on August 2 that its application for admission would be considered by the next, the third, Assembly. Foreign Minister Bánffy, as representative of the Government, arrived at Geneva early in September. The League Assembly opened on September 4, 1922. Bánffy was given a courteous welcome, and he conferred with British, Austrian, Czech and Yugoslav statesmen.

The competent League committee took up the question of Hungary on September 11. There, Bánffy made a statement to the effect that Hungary entirely met the requirement of membership in the League. Hungary's admission was passed practically without debate. Although Osuský, the Minister of Czechoslovakia in Paris, on behalf of his Government, proposed that Hungary should only be admitted if she expressly acknowledged her obligation to pay the reparations, this suggestion was dismissed, and, upon a motion from Poland, Hungary's accession to membership of the League was adopted by acclamation.

Thus the Hungarian Government attained its aim, and subsequently it endeavoured to make the best it could of the resulting advantages. Membership in the League enabled Hungary, first of all, to improve the possibility of gathering information and to build up her relations with the various Powers. In fact, admission meant a sort of political rehabilitation. Hungary became an equal member among the capitalist countries, at least, formally. At the same time, the Hungarian political circles hoped that, with the aid of the League of Nations, they would be able to make better use of the rights guaranteed in the peace treaty, and were also confident that they might obtain some reduction of the obligations (in respect of reparations, military control, etc.). The Hungarian ruling quarters regarded the Covenant as a source of law in respect of disarmament (or equality in rearmament as interpreted by the defeated countries) and the national minorities, and hoped that they could demand certain frontier rectifications. These issues fell within the competence of the League of Nations.

The principal motive of the counter-revolutionary régime for obtaining Hungary's accession to the League was the desire to consolidate its rule at home and make itself acceptable internationally. Like all states with revanche ambitions, Hungary too, could not regard the League as a genuine protector of her interests, for the main task of the League was to maintain the existing system of peace. Even though there was some hope for concessions to be obtained with the League's aid, the Hungarian ruling classes could only expect satisfaction of their revisionist demands from an alliance of revanchist states, from the use of force to change the status quo. So already in the nineteen twenties, it was obvious that the foreign policy of Hungary would sooner or later depart openly from the spirit of the League of Nations. At the time of preparations and the concentration of its energies, however, it could profitably make use of the League's assistance.

4. Foreign politics in the consolidation period

The consolidation of the counter-revolutionary régime was completed by 1922/1923. It was based on a society in an increasingly difficult economic situation. The growth of economic anarchy, which already began to exert an adverse effect on the immediate economic interests of the Hungarian ruling classes, threatened to undermine the stability of Bethlen's political establishment. It was evident that the political consolidation was a function of economic consolidation. From the character of the régime, from the postwar situation in Hungary and the peace provisions it followed that the only way the Government found to create economic stability was to take sizable foreign loans. But for the time being, the raising of foreign loans was made difficult by the reparations obligation, the amount of which was not yet fixed in 1922, while all state property had been pledged as security for the payment of reparations.

Minor reparations (shipments of coal to Yugoslavia, cattle and animal products, etc.) were already under way, but amidst a mounting inflation and the troubled financial conditions of the country, there was not much hope for the payment of sizable indemnity. People in the Government knew, however, that the amount of reparations would soon be fixed. Therefore the Bethlen Government wished to link the matter of a foreign loan with the settlement of the reparations liability, arguing that Hungary could not pay reparations because of the inflation, which in turn could be stopped only by means of foreign loans. And loans were impossible to raise as long as all state revenue was pledged as security for reparations.

The Hungarian Government found it essential to solve the problem of reparations. While general economic interests demanded that the amount of reparations be fixed at the lowest possible figure, it was essential for the Government to be informed on the amount, if it wanted to secure stabilization and prepare a balanced budget.

Since the issue of reparations was not confined to Hungary alone, but was connected with the whole problem of the postwar European settlement, with the relationships between victorious and defeated countries, with the power shifts among the Great Powers, the realization of economic consolidation in Hungary became a problem closely related to the shaping of the international situation in Europe.

In 1922/1923, it was precisely in the question of reparations that Great Britain's endeavour to secure the balance of power on the Continent conflicted most violently with the French ambitions for European hegemony. The conference of the Reparations Commission in December 1922 and January 1923 reached no agreement in the question of German reparations. Ever since the end of the war, it had been a source of discord that the French wanted to exact the payment of an enormous indemnity from Germany while the British were against Germany's being totally exploited because this might have led to an immoderate strengthening of France and to a shift in European power relations in favour of the French. This is why the British Government, though it did not oppose the principle of reparations in general, if only because of its own active debts owed by France, tried to moderate the French claims in respect of German reparations.

The problem of the German reparations led to the Ruhr conflict: on January 11, 1923, with reference to a decision of the Reparations Commission concerning Germany's default in reparations, French and Belgian troops marched into the Ruhr valley. This incident sharpened the Franco–British differences.

The British Government obtained the support of the United States in restraining the French aspirations, although Washington did not give up entirely its isolationist position with regard to European questions yet. In return for U. S. support, the British had to pay their war debts, for which they depended on France's solvency, which in turn was influenced by the state of German reparations. Therefore, the Anglo–Saxon Powers connected the question of German reparations with Germany's economic reconstruction in such a way that, simultaneously with the payment of a reduced amount of reparations, Germany should receive large investment credits and access to wider markets.

The Ruhr conflict greatly disturbed the situation in Central Europe, which had just begun to come to a stability. The Little Entente accused Hungary of preparing for war. Border clashes occurred every day. The Hungarian Government feared that the neighbouring countries would compel Hungary to pay reparations by resorting to methods similar to the Ruhr occupation. In this situation, the settlement of the reparations issue was an urging necessity in connection with the raising of foreign loan. In respect of Hungarian reparations, France supported the Little Entente states in insisting on the imposition of a high levy. She thus wished to sustain her own debts owed by Germany. And with reference to the Ruhr conflict, she proceeded to build up her relations with the Little Entente states, an endeavour which had temporarily been disturbed in 1920 by France's growing political interest in Hungary and by the attitude of certain French statesmen at the time of the attempted coup of Habsburg legitimists.

Italy also supported the French claims to a certain extent, exactly because of her own demands for war indemnity from Hungary. True, especially after Mussolini's rise to power in the autumn of 1922, the Italians began to approach Austria and Hungary, which was all the more clear after Mussolini refused to join in a possible application of the 'Ruhr policy' against Hungary. But the Italian foreign policy was not yet crystallized at that time. The interest she took in Hungary and Austria could still be brought consistent with her relationships with the Little Entente, especially with Rumania. The Italian position regarding the question of reparations did not yet promise any radical changes, Mussolini brought the reduction of Hungarian reparations into connection with the remission of Italy's war debts.

The Hungarian Government could only expect support from London. Faithful to Britain's aims and economic interests on the Continent, the British Government opposed the French and the Little Entente's plans, but did not object to the imposition of a fair amount of war reparations upon Hungary. The British members of the Reparations Commission declared as early as November 1922, that Hungary was bound to pay reparations in accordance with her liabilities under the peace treaty, but she would have to pay as moderate an amount as possible.

From the early twenties onward, it was primarily the Anglo–American capital which played the most significant role in Hungary's economy. It was only natural therefore that, when the need for foreign loans arose, the Government should first turn to the Anglo–Saxon Powers. It was also evident that the raising of loans was not merely an economic affair; the Hungarian Government expected the Anglo–Saxon loans to bring political support as well, mainly against the Little Entente states and France. Thus the strengthening of the relations with the Anglo–Saxon group of the victorious Powers was an organic part of Bethlen's scheme of consolidation.

Delegates of the Hungarian Government started negotiations in London in March 1923. British financial circles were not against granting a loan but they wanted the deal transacted under the supervision of the League of Nations and made the loan subject to suspension of the right of pledge. On April 6, 1923, the Council of Ministers accepted, on the basis of the British proposal, such a supervision by the League, and approved of a Government memorandum to the Reparations Commission. The memorandum contained an application for a short-term and a long-term loan (40 million gold crowns and 550 million gold crowns, respectively) and for the cancellation of the right of pledge with a view to procuring the loan. Towards the end of April 1923, Prime Minister Bethlen and Finance Minister Tibor Kállay went on a tour of Europe to win support for the request. During their negotiations, they achieved full success in London, only partial success in Rome, but accomplished little result in Paris because of certain French reservations.

In May 1923, the Reparations Commission — which was composed of representatives of France, Britain, Italy, the Little Entente states, Poland, Greece and (as observers) those of the United States — discussed two draft projects of a loan to Hungary. The draft submitted by Britain and Italy proposed the suspension of the right of pledge and the use of the loan under the supervision of the League of Nations. The French proposal on the other hand, while it did not oppose suspension, was intended to execute the loan transaction under the supervision of the Reparations Commission (this meant French control guaranteed by the votes of the Little Entente states), and stipulated that a part of the loan should be used for the payment of reparations. On May 23, the Commission accepted the French proposal by a majority of votes, with the proviso that Hungary was obliged to proceed with the current deliveries of coal and cattle.

Since the Hungarian Government was unwilling to accept these terms, it asked for a modification of the decision of the Reparations Commissions on British advice. At first, France and the Little Entente states flatly refused. To break the Little Entente opposition, the British made it public that the Czechoslovakians — applying for loans precisely at that time — could only hope support from the British financial circles in case she stopped obstructing the Hungarian request's being met in the spirit of the British project. The Czechoslovak Government eventually reconsidered its opinion.

Owing to the British pressure, the Sinaia Conference of the Little Entente states in July 1923, adopted a somewhat more favourable position regarding the Hungarian loan. The conference consented to the cancellation of the right of pledge and agreed that from the first instalment of the loan, nothing should be deducted for the purposes of reparations. In return for this, however, it demanded that the utilization of the loan should be supervised by the Reparations Commission and that the Little Entente states should be included in the arms control commission in Hungary. To counteract an expected strengthening of Hungary, the participants of the conference continued to consolidate their system of military alliances.

After the Sinaia Conference the question of supervision was still a considerable obstacle to the raising of the loan. In fact, Hungary demanded that supervision should be exercised by the League of Nations to the exclusion of the Little Entente states. The British Government supported the Hungarian position and practically rejected the Sinaia decisions. It insisted that the loan to Hungary should be accorded through the mediation of the League of Nations, and therefore, control should be entrusted to a neutral body appointed by the League, and stated that the Little Entente had no right to take part in the military control of Hungary.

In the summer of 1923, it seemed that in spite of the Sinaia Conference, the loan project had come to a deadlock. In this situation, Bethlen decided to enter into personal talks with the Foreign Ministers of the Little Entente states. The opportunity presented itself in September 1923, when the statesmen arrived one after another to attend the League Assembly in Geneva. There, Bethlen and his recently appointed Foreign Minister, Géza Daruváry, succeeded in getting the Little Entente states to accept a conciliatory proposal of the Assistant Secretary-General of the League of Nations according to which the loan should be granted through a joint procedure of the League and the Reparations Commission. And in return for the promise that Hungary would refrain from pursuing an open revisionist policy and would strive for the normalization of trade and other relationships, it was agreed that the loan would not be encumbered with the payment of reparations.

The Reparations Commission received this agreement favourably; the main obstacles to the loan transaction were thus removed. In November 1923, a League of Nations delegation arrived in Budapest to study the economic situation. At the same time the details of the loan project were worked out. On the basis of this project, the financial committee of the League of Nations fixed the amount of the loan at 250 million gold crowns for a period of thirty months.

The question of reparations arose again in connection with the loan negotiations. The British Government could enforce its conception to some extent; so reparations were reduced in general, the reduction being rather considerable in the case of Hungary.

By virtue of the Reparations Commission decision of December 18, 1923, Hungary had to pay 200 million gold crowns during a term of twenty years. The Hungarian Government accepted this decision. And in January 1924, at the request of the Little Entente states, it undertook to deliver to Yugoslavia 880 tons of coal every day up to September 1926, and railway rolling stock worth 13 million gold crowns from 1926 to 1929. The Little Entente, in turn, withdrew its demand for participation in the arms control commission.

On February 21, 1924, the Reparations Commission freed the way for the loan to be raised. This closed the first stage of the project for the acquisition of foreign loans. The loan of the League of Nations was floated in July 1924. To supervise the fulfilment of the loan terms and the conduct of public finances, the League sent a chief delegate, the American jurist Jeremiah Smith, to Hungary. A considerable part of Hungary's state revenue — the excise on tobacco, salt, sugar, etc. — was pledged as security for the loan.

The stabilization plan was put on the statute book as Act IV of 1924; furthermore, Act V brought into life the National Bank of Hungary, whose gold and foreign exchange reserves were complemented by a Bank of England loan to the sum of £4 million (82 million gold crowns) and by the obligation to pay any amount of pounds sterling in exchange for Hungarian crowns.

Inflation was finally stopped in June 1924. The stabilization rate of the Hungarian crown was linked to the pound sterling (£1 = 346,000 crowns; 1 gold crown = 17,000 paper crowns). The new currency (pengő) was only introduced in 1927, when the value of 1 gold crown was fixed at 1.16 pengő

The terms of the League of Nations' loan meant that Hungary became financially dependent on the Western Powers, Britain in the first place. But the basic significance of the loan was that it stabilized the conservative counter-revolutionary régime at home, under the Bethlen establishment. It consolidated the régime against the working-class movement and the bourgeois democratic forces, and contributed to the suppression of the extreme-right forces. And, on the international plane, it gave absolution to the Horthy régime born in the bloody white terror, so much the more as their capital investments made the Western Powers interested in the maintenance of the régime. The League of Nations loan paved the way for further and still bigger investment loans in the form of short-term and long-term credits extended to municipalities, to large estates and to various industries. The sum of these loans had risen to over $96 million by 1929.

By 1931, Hungary's foreign debts, including the loans raised in the crisis years, and previous credits, soared up to P 4,300 million.

The troubled postwar relations slowly calmed down by 1923/1924. After nearly ten years of chaos, Europe began to show signs of political consolidation in international affairs. The revolutionary wave was over by the end of 1923, the revolutionary movements having suffered defeat in the European countries outside the Soviet Union. The 1922 victory of Fascism in Italy and Hitler's attempted Munich putsch in 1923 expressed tendencies to resort to the most reactionary methods in order to suppress the revolutionary working-class movement. But the political stabilization of the capitalist system was only relative, since the Soviet military power had succeeded in crushing the forces of counter-revolution at home and foreign intervention. In respect of foreign politics, the Soviet Union — although it did not yet take an active part in international affairs — succeeded in breaking out of isolation. In addition to a number of agreements with neighbouring countries, this trend could also be observed in the Rapallo treaty concluded with Germany in 1922, which opened the way for the further improvement of German–Soviet relations. The capitalist Powers were compelled to recognize the Soviet state. By 1924/1925, all the Great Powers, except the United States of America, had established diplomatic relations with the Soviet Union, and so did a number of small countries: Norway, Sweden, Greece, Austria, etc. Several capitalist states, including the states of the Little Entente, still hesitated to recognize the Soviet Union.

Following the failure of the adventurous plans for immediate revanche, the differences between the victors and the losers were temporarily relegated to the background. The forces seeking agreement with the victorious Powers and advocating the provisional acceptance of the status quo consolidated their positions in the defeated countries. Stresemann's policy in Germany was in favour of reconciliation with the Western Powers. Germany's reconstruction began under the Dawes plan; the implementation of some provisions of the peace treaty resulted in the conclusion of the Locarno Pact in which Germany recognized, while Britain and Italy guaranteed, the German—French and German—Belgian frontiers drawn by the Versailles treaty. The Locarno Pact made it possible for Germany to gain admission to membership of the League of Nations. But Locarno was not much help in promoting the cause of European security; those arrangements only guaranteed Germany's western frontiers and thus potentially opened the way for the German drive eastward (with Poland and Czechoslovakia, Germany only signed agreements on arbitration for the peaceful settlement of disputed questions, without any international guarantee). Locarno brought to the surface the serious defects of the new Central European settlement, although in the twenties, this did not involve any danger since Weimar Germany pursued its policies in the spirit of temporary appeasement. To counteract the policy of Locarno a Soviet—German treaty of friendship and neutrality was concluded in 1926.

The relative strength of each of the victorious Powers also became clear. The British effort to ensure a balance of power on the Continent seemed to succeed with the aid of the United States. The U. S. and Great Britain intended to create a sort of capitalist equilibrium that would be stable enough to resist any revolutionary influence and would still not imply the European hegemony of any one of the continental Powers. France, although her attempts at hegemony failed, became powerful enough to remain an important political factor in Europe, in the latter half of the twenties. From 1924 onward, Paris built a network of alliances in Central Europe upon interrelated pacts of alliance. In January 1924, a Franco—Czechoslovak pact of alliance and friendship was concluded. After Locarno, this was complemented by a guarantee treaty. France signed another such treaty with Poland. Treaties of friendship were concluded between France and Rumania in June, and between France and Yugoslavia in November 1927.

France's system of alliances in Central Europe appeared to be a solid affair. The states of the Little Entente seemed to have been assigned an important role in the maintenance of the status quo.

The consolidation of international relations could not fail to make its influence felt on the foreign policy of the Bethlen Government either. There were indications that Hungary would not only feel compelled but also be willing to accommodate herself, for the time being, to the consolidated conditions of Europe. Already by the time the loan project was started, Bethlen was forced to put restraint on Hungarian irredentist propaganda activities, a fact which — although there was no substantial improvement in Hungary's relations with the neighbouring countries — still acted towards the normalization of relations. This became manifest in the settlement of a number of disputes, and in the conclusion of various trade agreements. Basically, however, in spite of its more active foreign policy, the country was still in an international isolation. Moreover, Hungary was financially and militarily under League of Nations control.

In this situation, it became a vital problem for Hungary to make use of the opportunity which the normalization of relations with the Soviet Union might offer for an international breakthrough.

Her best interests could have moved Hungary to establish relations with the Soviet Union. The Soviet Union was the only Power that did not recognize the treaty of Trianon; the establishment of contacts could have strengthened Hungary's international position against the Little Entente and would have opened up considerable prospects for trade. The Association of Hungarian Manufacturers (GYOSZ) pressed for the establishment of diplomatic relations in the hope of obtaining important Soviet orders.

As early as 1922, an exchange of views started, on Soviet initiative, about the normalization of relations between the two countries. The Genoa conference — which had been convened by Great Britain to ease postwar economic difficulties of Europe, to promote international trade, with the participation of Germany, Soviet Russia and the defeated small states — found no solution to the economic problems and thus dealt mainly with the 'Russian question'. While the main object of the Entente Powers and especially of France was to induce the Soviet Government to agree to their financial demands, Count Bethlen, at the head of the Hungarian delegation, sought contacts with representatives of the Great Powers in order to expedite the issue of national minorities. A secret talk took place between the Soviet People's Commissar for Foreign Affairs, G. V. Chicherin, and Foreign Minister Bánffy about the establishment of trade and possibly diplomatic relations, an aim to which the Hungarian statesmen probably drew inspiration from the Rapallo treaty between Germany and Soviet Russia. For a long time, no further contact was made on the diplomatic plane, the question of Soviet–Hungarian relations was again raised only in the spring of 1924.

On May 24, 1924, Foreign Minister Daruváry called an interdepartmental conference where he said that he was strongly in favour of diplomatic relations with the Soviet Union, because the Soviet state was becoming an increasingly important international factor, and because Hungary could thus enter into contact with a Power which was outside the coalition grown out of the odious peace treaties. He pointed out that "this would put an end to the impression of our present total impotence". Members of the Government expressed various misgivings about Daruváry's suggestion. They conceded that the establishment of diplomatic relations might secure serious economic advantages, but feared that this step might undermine the moral and political credibility of Hungary's anti-Communist propaganda at home. The conference discussed in detail the Hungarian reservations to diplomatic recognition, reservations which in fact expressed discrimination against the Soviet Union.

Official negotiations between the two states started in Berlin on August 26, 1924. The Hungarian Government was represented by Deputy Foreign Minister Kálmán Kánya and Councillor of Legation M. Jungerth-Arnóthy; Moscow's representative was Nikolai Krestinsky, the Soviet Ambassador in Berlin. The talks were later joined in by Deputy People's Commissar for Foreign Affairs M. M. Litvinov.

In exchange for the recognition of the Soviet Union, the Hungarian Government wished to obtain commercial advantages: the setting up of Russo—Hungarian mixed companies and trade concessions. The Soviet side took the position that the issue of trade agreements did not belong in a treaty on the establishment of diplomatic relations. But Kánya and Jungerth wanted to connect the trade agreement with a treaty on diplomatic relations.

On August 28, Kánya asked his Foreign Minister for instructions whether to maintain the Hungarian position and force the creation of mixed companies, because in this case it was probably impossible to reach an understanding. Daruváry replied that the connection of the two issues should be insisted upon but the demand for mixed companies could be dropped.

The Soviet Government adopted a position against granting Hungary the favours which earlier, in an extremely serious economic and foreign political situation, it had conceded to states that had seceded from Russia or had already recognized the Soviet Union; its interpretation of the most-favoured-nation principle was that it would grant Hungary only the favours to be conceded to other states from that time onward.

Early in September 1924, the negotiations were about to yield a result. Daruváry then authorized the Hungarian plenipotentiaries to sign the agreement, on condition that this was not to be published pending Horthy's approval. The diplomatic agreement was dated September 5, 1924, and the trade agreement bore the date of September 12, 1924, on the understanding that they should be published and ratified within three months.

In spite of all precautions, information about the Hungarian—Soviet deal leaked out through the international press and thus to the Hungarian newspapers. The Hungarian Government could not avoid making a statement. Already on September 16, Kánya was instructed to agree with Krestinsky that they should issue a communiqué; Kánya did as he was instructed, but the publication of the communiqué was also subjected to Horthy's previous approval. Horthy was the most vehement opponent of the establishment of relations with the Soviet Union. He declared that he was unwilling to give his formal consent, because this preliminary gesture would be embarrassing to him later, at the time of ratification, although he could not even for a moment imagine the content of the agreements as being able to move him to give his approval. Thus Horthy was from the outset against ratification. Although he did not stop the communiqué from being published — "in so far as the Government considered it necessary for diplomatic reasons" — he reserved himself a free hand.

On October 10, 1924, the Council of Ministers discussed a proposal concerning the agreeements on the establishment of diplomatic and trade relations with the Soviet Union. The proposal pointed out that the Soviet Union must also be reckoned with in the settlement of European affairs, and that "no change is likely to take place in the internal life of Russia for a long time to come", a realization of which had so far prompted many states in Europe to enter into official contact with the Soviet Union, and emphasized that trade relationships with Soviet Russia would have considerable advantages. The Council of Ministers adopted the proposal.

Still no ratification followed. Horthy and other opponents of the proposed step received unexpected encouragement from the events in Britain. The Labour Government of MacDonald, which had reestablished British—Soviet diplomatic relations and concluded a trade agreement with the Soviet Union, fell in October 1924. The Baldwin—Austen Chamberlain Government represented the most aggressive anti-Soviet line of British conservatism. Right after taking office the new Government denounced the trade agreement signed three months earlier.

Hungarian foreign policy, which at that time followed a British orientation, did not fail to react to the change in British—Soviet relations. Already on November 13, the Ministry of Foreign Affairs instructed the Hungarian Minister in Berlin to ask for the Soviet Government's consent to the extension of the deadline of ratification for another four months. The Soviet Union accepted a delay of two months, but in January 1925, the Hungarian Government demanded another extension for three months and then again for six months.

All this made it evident that the Hungarian Government had no intention to carry through the ratification of the agreements. Therefore the Soviet representative declared, towards the end of March 1925, that the Soviet Union would give another six months' delay only in condition that the most-favoured-nation treatment provided for in the trade agreement should be relinquished.

Apparently, the Hungarian Government only waited for an appropriate pretext for cancelling the agreements. On April 11, the new Foreign Minister, Lajos Walkó, instructed the Hungarian Minister in Berlin to bring to the notice of Krestinsky that the Hungarian Government considered the most-favoured-nation clause to be the most important provision of the Soviet—Hungarian agreements and that, this having been dropped, it was in no position to ratify them. Thereupon the Soviet Ambassador declared that his Government would consider the negotiations closed and the agreements null and void.

Owing to the stiffening of the Hungarian Government's anti-Soviet policy, the question of the establishment of relations with the Soviet Union was dropped from the agenda to be taken up again much later, in a different international situation, early in 1934.

In the middle of the twenties, Hungary made attempts at a rapprochement with Yugoslavia, too. The relations between the two countries were gradually improving from 1924 onward, during the economic reconstruction of Hungary. Direct negotiations started on Yugoslav initiative in 1925. Characteristically, this move of the Hungarian counter-revolutionary régime was motivated by the leakage of the secret that it harboured contacts with Croatian separatists. Upon the arrest of Radić, the leader of the Croatian Peasant Party, the Yugoslav authorities discovered facts which compromised the Hungarian Government, and they took advantage of this situation to bring pressure to bear upon Hungary in the interest of a rapprochement. The negotiations began with an offer to conclude an agreement on arbitration.

In spite of membership in the Little Entente and alliance with France, Yugoslavia's international position was not quite secure. Her relations with the neighbouring countries had been worsened by territorial disputes; she apparently had irreconcilable differences with Bulgaria on account of Macedonia, with Greece because of Salonika, and with Italy, in addition to their dispute over Fiume, because of the Italian aspiration after hegemony over the Adriatic and influence in the Balkans. The mere existence of Yugoslavia was an obstacle in the way of Italy's great-power aspirations. The division of the ex-Hungarian Banat carried the germs of the deterioration of Hungarian–Yugoslav relations, although common interests still overshadowed the differences for a long time. Yugoslavia was in an unpleasant situation because she could not rely for support against Italy on the two other states of the Little Entente and could co-operate only with Rumania in defeating the territorial claims of Bulgaria.

In seeking a Yugoslav–Hungarian rapprochement, the Bethlen Government was primarily guided by its aim to disrupt the Little Entente. The Hungarian experts in foreign politics and, it seems, Bethlen himself thought that they might be able to act successfully against one of the Little Entente states, provided that some agreement could be reached with another of them while the third one was pinned down by one of the Great Powers. All this had to be done before the Germans would actively claim revanche. Horthy later described this project as follows: "Since we wanted to break the iron ring closing around us, I tried to make approaches to the Serbs. . . . In our difficult position, in order to be able to breathe, I tried to find a sort of *modus vivendi*." Horthy, however, conceived this *modus vivendi* as something to take advantage of without making even the slightest concession.

While staying in Geneva in March 1926, Bethlen had a talk with Italy's Secretary of State for Foreign Affairs, Count Dino Grandi. There he mentioned that the termination of financial and military control might enable Hungary to pursue a more active foreign policy, and asked how Italy would react to a Yugoslav–Hungarian rapprochement. Grandi's reply, although rather uncertain, did not seem entirely negative. A few days later Bethlen started negotiations with Yugoslav Foreign Minister Nincic, who also happened to stay in Geneva. Ninčić said that there would be no reason why Hungary should not temporarily enter into some agreement exclusively with Yugoslavia of all her neighbours.

After this meeting, the Yugoslav–Hungarian negotiations were resumed. In a speech delivered in August, to commemorate the 400th anniversary of the battle of Mohács, Horthy took a stand in favour of the Yugoslav–Hungarian rapprochement.

During the negotiations, it appeared that Yugoslavia would like to conclude a treaty of non-aggression in a way that it would not be contrary to her existing obligations laid down in the Little Entente pacts. Bethlen, on the other hand, wanted to make an agreement that would guarantee neutrality in case of a conflict with a third state without reference to mutual guarantees of the Yugoslav–Hungarian frontier. Even the Hungarian Ministry of Foreign Affairs saw clearly that the idea was unrealistic, as it would have nullified the Little Entente pacts, and was unacceptable to Yugoslavia in the given circumstances. On the other hand, a neutrality pact would have incurred Italy's displeasure. Therefore, the Foreign Ministry abided by the idea of a treaty of arbitration 'and possibly of friendship', which would help to weaken 'the impression of Hungary's isolation' and might, still later, result in the loosening of the Little Entente.

Walkó and Ninčić opened concrete negotiations in Geneva on September 13, 1926. Then, however, Italy intervened, and consequently the Hungarian counter-revolutionary régime started a genuinely active foreign policy to play down the peace treaty.

To follow a more active foreign policy in the service of revisionist aims, it was essential to develop the army. However, in all the defeated states, this was prohibited by the limitations provided for in the peace treaties, and it was made difficult by the victorious Powers' permanent military control. Towards the middle of the twenties, therefore, the Bethlen Government launched an action with the view of obtaining the termination of permanent military control over Hungary.

In June 1924, Great Britain proposed to include in the League of Nations' agenda the issue of modifying military control over the Central Powers. The Council accepted the British proposal and instructed the Permanent Advisory Committee to prepare a practical plan for the modification of military control, and invited the legal committee to make a proposal as to which states, in addition to Members of the Council, should be invited to the substantive discussion of the question.

To the 1924 Council session in Geneva, the Hungarian Government delegated a military expert in the person of Lieutenant-Colonel Géza Siegler, whose report then served as a basis for a tactical plan to obtain the termination of military control. The plan contained the following provisions: 1. The Hungarian Government should make an effort to secure the participation of Austria, Bulgaria and Hungary in the debates of the League Council, and if this proved unfeasible, to attempt to exclude the Little Entente from the negotiations. 2. It should be ensured that military control by the League ceased to be permanent, was exercised only from time to time, in virtue of special Council decisions, and was confined to the *ad hoc* examination of serious complaints which seemed to threaten the peace of Europe. 3. Half of the members of the control commission, and its chairman should always belong to states which had been neutral in the World War. Representatives of the Little Entente states should not serve on the *ad hoc* committees.

The plan envisaged the launching of intense diplomatic action towards all Governments from which Hungary could expect support, or at least goodwill, in respect of the termination of permanent military control. The Hungarian Government wished to make sure that the former Central Powers took concerted action, but it did not succeed in this effort. On the other hand, the diplomatic action launched for support to be won from the Great Powers brought some result. On August 2, the Hungarian Minister in London reported that Lord Parmoor, the British representative, had promised to support the Hungarian proposals. The Italian Government promised only to give a favourable consideration to Hungarian interests.

In August 1924, the legal committee of the League of Nations decided that representatives of the interested states should not be summoned to the substantive debates.The Permanent Advisory Committee presented its proposal in September. According to this, permanent military control would be replaced by occasional control. This would be ordered by the Council of the League of Nations if a Government sent a written notification to the Secretary-General of the League or if the Permanent Advisory Committee found an on-the-spot inquiry to be necessary. The Council should appoint the members of the committee of inquiry to include representatives of all member states of the Council and of the states neighbouring the country which was to be subjected to inquiry.

The League Council approved of the proposal of the legal committee and the Permanent Advisory Committee, but could not fix a time-limit. Ultimately, the Council of Ambassadors dissolved the Military Control Commission as of March 31, 1927, and introduced a system of occasional inspections.

The talks concerning the termination of permanent military control were still in progress when the franc forgery affair erupted. The counterfeiting of French franc banknotes was part of the political adventurism which went along with the counter-revolutionary régime's revisionist plans: this was how the policy-makers wanted to 'acquire' foreign currency to finance their irredentist activities carried on in the neighbour countries. The plan of counterfeiting French franc notes was worked out in the summer of 1923, with the knowledge and under the direction of Prime Minister Bethlen, Prince Lajos Windischgraetz and Chief Commissioner of Police Imre Nádosy. In the summer, Windischgraetz went to Germany and discussed the matter with Ludendorff and Hitler, both of whom approved the Hungarian plan and sent engineer Arthur Schulze to Budapest to serve with expert advice. It was with his help that the counterfeiters purchased machines in Leipzig and paper in Munich. At home, Pál Teleki placed the necessary premises and expert personnel at their disposal in the Cartographical Institute. Broad strata of the Hungarian ruling quarters, from the Bethlen—Teleki group through the racialist Gyula Gömbös to the legitimist Windischgraetz, compromised themselves in the franc forgery affair.

After careful preparations, the counterfeiting of banknotes began in 1924, and 30 to 35 thousand forged 1,000-franc notes were ready by the end of 1925. But the more difficult part of the venture was still to come: the putting of counterfeit money into circulation abroad. On December 14, 1925, ex-Colonel Arisztid Jankovich, in possession of a diplomatic courier's passport issued by the Hungarian Ministry of Foreign Affairs, arrived at The Hague with a package containing ten million French francs in counterfeit notes. He was exposed the same day, when he tried to cash his first 1,000-franc banknote.

The Dutch authorities immediately transmitted the facts of investigation to the competent French services, which at once joined in clearing up the case, all the more so, because ever since 1924, they had been informed about franc forgery being afoot in Hungary. French detectives arrived in Hungary in December 1925.

The exposure of the franc forgery affair created an international scandal which even threatened to lead to the fall of Bethlen, if joined by domestic opposition. This might have led to the formation of a more progressive or, at least, more liberal Government.

But Bethlen managed to ride out the storm raised at home and abroad by the franc scandal, and to this end he even found support in Britain's loyalty.

The waves of the franc scandal calmed down, which was favourable to the Hungarian Government's plan to request, in the spring of 1926, the termination of financial control by the League of Nations, a plan the financial and political foundation of which had been laid by the success of stabilization. The financial committee of the League was willing to ease control but demanded that the state finances should first be taken over by the National Bank of Hungary. The Bethlen Government consented, and the Council of the League of Nations on June 7, 1926, declared the control functions of the League chief commissioner terminated with effect from July 1, 1926. Foreign financial control still continued, but only in a less stringent form, so that confidential agents appointed by the League Council to represent the interests of the holders of loan titles, together with Royall Tyler, financial adviser of the National Bank, remained in Hungary for a long time.

The termination of permanent financial and military control and thereby the formal restoration of state sovereignty created an internal situation favourable for a genuine break-through in Hungary's international isolation. It was only an appropriate partner who still had to be found. And late in 1926, this partner presented himself in the person of Mussolini.

CHAPTER II

CONSOLIDATION OF THE FOREIGN POLICY OF COUNTER-REVOLUTIONARY HUNGARY

1. The 'active' foreign policy of the Bethlen Government, 1926—1930

Internal political and economic consolidation was on its way, but Hungary's international position was still rather unstable. For Bethlen's work to become complete, it was necessary to improve the foreign relations as well. This required a more active foreign policy, an increased stressing of the revisionist aspirations. And this was made possible by the growing differences between European countries in the latter half of the twenties when attempts were made to bring about new political combinations. It was precisely Italy, one of the victorious Powers, that gave expression to her dissatisfaction with the Versailles peace settlement. Thus the Hungarian Government was impelled to seek the Italian alliance not only by its ideological affinity to Italian Fascism but also by practical considerations.

On earlier occasions, Hungary had already obtained Italy's support, in more or less concrete forms, at different international forums. The first major act of co-operation between the two states, however, took place as late as 1926, in connection with the Hungarian Government's rapprochement with Yugoslavia.

When, in September 1926, Walkó and Ninčić started negotiations in Geneva about a rapprochement between Hungary and Yugoslavia, Walkó met Italy's Secretary of State for Foreign Affairs, Dino Grandi, who then offered the good offices of the Italian Government. In other words, he stated in the language of diplomacy that Italy was not against the Yugoslav—Hungarian parley — with Italian participation. A month later, the Italian Minister in Budapest called on Bethlen and took him to task for having failed to provide the Italian Government with detailed information about the Yugoslav—Hungarian negotiations, and for ignoring the Italian offers. He then told Bethlen that the Duce wished to discuss with him, as soon as possible, the matter of the Yugoslav—Hungarian rapprochement and to broach the idea of a far-extending Italo—Yugoslav—Hungarian tripartite agreement. Bethlen's reply was this: "I'm glad to be at Signor Mussolini's service."

Although, in his message, Mussolini did not yet take an open stand against the rapprochement with Yugoslavia, his aim could hardly be misinterpreted. Italian foreign policy had, for years, been trying to gain a footing in South Eastern Europe. In the beginning, it intended to secure a position in the Little Entente states. The Rapallo treaty, concluded between Italy and Yugoslavia in 1920, was complemented with a treaty of friendship and cordial co-operation in January 1924. An Italo—Czechoslovak treaty of co-operation was signed on June 5, 1924. In it, the parties pledged 'mutual assistance and cordial co-operation' in upholding the peace treaties of Trianon, Saint-Germain and Versailles. Since the pacts between Paris and the Little Entente frustrated this endeavour, Italy, just like Hungary, set herself the task of disrupting the Little Entente. But, in striving to encircle Yugoslavia, the Italians made approaches to Rumania. In 1926, they signed the Italo—Rumanian treaty, a secret clause of which provided that, should one of the contracting parties make war on a third state, the other party should remain neutral. Shortly thereafter, Italy recognized the annexation of Bessarabia by Rumania in a protocol, and the two states concluded a secret neutrality agreement. That same year, the Italian Government signed a treaty of friendship and security with Albania, providing for mutual assistance in the preservation of Albania's political, legal and territorial status quo. This treaty laid the foundations of an agreement on defensive alliance which was forced upon Albania a year later, and which placed Albania under Italy's 'protection' for a period of twenty years. There was no doubt that this treaty was directed against Yugoslavia.

Mussolini wanted Hungary to take part in his plans to change the power relations in Central Europe and to help establish Italian hegemony in South Eastern Europe. Ten days after his above-mentioned message, on October 23, 1926, he sent the Hungarian Government, through Hungary's Minister in Rome, another message which made it clear that he was not in favour of the Yugoslav—Hungarian rapprochement and that he had not been quite serious about the idea of a tripartite agreement. Mussolini informed Count Nemes that he vould not put a spoke in Hungary's wheel in respect of the Yugoslav—Hungarian treaty, but Italy intended to conclude 'a far-reaching political convention' with Hungary, which would include a treaty of friendship, co-operation and arbitration, and would be more advantageous than any treaty Hungary might conclude with Yugoslavia.

There was no doubt as to which of the two options would be chosen by Hungarian foreign policy, which concentrated on a territorial revision of the peace treaty. With Italy, the Bethlen Government could gain the support of a Power which, dissatisfied as it was with the postwar territorial divisions, intended to bring about changes in the status quo. As a result of Mussolini's intervention, the Hungarian—Yugoslav negotiations soon came to an impasse, and preparatory consultations to an Italo—Hungarian treaty began. In March 1927, Minister of Public Education Count Kunó Klebelsberg went to Italy in order to prepare the treaty and Bethlen's meeting with the Duce.

Bethlen arrived at Rome in April 4, 1927, and immediately paid a visit to the Italian head of Government. He explained to Mussolini Hungary's foreign political position, pointing out that "the factors which determine our scope of action are our present frontiers, our being disarmed and encircled by the Little Entente". He declared that at this point, after the termination of financial and military control, the Hungarian Government found it opportune to launch an active foreign policy and informed Mussolini of his conception of a Central European 'realignment'. Realignment was conditional upon the upsetting of the current situation, Bethlen said: "The situation in Central Europe is not definitive. The only question is, which of the Great Powers will have its influence prevail in the new settlement." The Hungarian Government rejected the French plans for a Danubian confederation, and also rejected the recurring idea of the French ruling quarters about a Habsburg restoration resulting in a Hungarian–Austro–Czechoslovak combination which would bar the way of the Austrian *Anschluss* efforts and Germany's strengthening, and would counterbalance Italy. Bethlen said he was convinced that the realignment of Central Europe would be influenced either by an increasingly strong Germany or by the Soviet Union.

The negotiating parties paid much attention to the question of the *Anschluss*. Bethlen explained that, although it was a greater comfort to be a neighbour of a small state than that of a powerful Germany, yet the *Anschluss* had to be reckoned with indeed, and Hungary could not really prevent it in any way. Mussolini agreed that the annexation of Austria to Germany should sooner or later be reckoned with. What he said, however, made it clear that he wanted to make Germany pay for his acquiescence.

Bethlen then mentioned Hungary's principal problem in the field of foreign politics – the Little Entente. He stated that the negotiating sides were both interested in the dissolution of the Little Entente, but this could only be achieved if one or another of the Little Entente states changed its attitude toward Hungary, if they came closer to her and reached an agreement with her.

After Mussolini emphasized that a Yugoslav–Hungarian understanding would be contrary to Italy's interests, Bethlen began explaining Hungary's relationship with Czechoslovakia. "Hungary is unable to act," he said, "as long as the Czechoslovak frontier is only thirty kilometres away from Budapest." Thereupon the Italian Prime Minister immediately noted that he agreed that the first problem for Hungary to settle was the Czechoslovak question. Bethlen agreed, but added that it was an essential condition that an agreement should be reached with another state of the Little Entente, and the third should have its hands tied in a different direction.

Mussolini suggested a rapprochement with Rumania. Bethlen pointed out that he saw hardly any possibility of a Rumanian–Hungarian rapprochement, mainly because of the grievances of the minorities and the optants' case (an action in court for indemnification against the loss of Hungarian proprietors' estates expropriated in Transylvania). Mussolini promised to use his influence with the Rumanian Government in the interest of an agreement with Hungary. For the event of a possible Hungarian action against Czechoslovakia he would prevail upon Rumania to remain neutral. Chances were to grow substantially if the Hungarian Government could persuade Poland to adopt a similar stand.

The first step for Hungary to be able to pursue an active foreign policy was her rearmament. It was chiefly with this end in view that Bethlen wanted to obtain Mussolini's support. So two days later, at another meeting with the Duce, Bethlen asked him for the delivery of the Austro–Hungarian stock of arms left in Italy after the war. Mussolini was willing to grant the request but saw difficulties in carrying the plan into execution. Finally, on Bethlen's proposal, it was agreed that – on the basis of a preliminary arrangement with the Polish Government – the considerable stock of arms would be consigned to Poland. The delivery would be *via* Austria, and Hungary would pass on only a token part of the consignment.

Bethlen told Mussolini that the question of the royal power was not a topical issue any more. Mussolini noted this with satisfaction, and Italy promised Hungary the use of the port of Fiume.

During the talks, the definitive text of the Italo–Hungarian treaty was agreed upon and signed on April 5, 1927. Article 1 provided for 'permanent peace and eternal friendship' between the two countries; Articles 2, 3 and 4 defined the methods of settling by arbitration the disputes that could not be solved through diplomatic channels; and Article 5 provided for the ratification of the treaty. The treaty was concluded for a period of ten years to be prolonged for another ten years unless denounced six months before expiry.

The treaty was complemented by a secret agreement; in an exchange of notes the two heads of Government undertook to practise closer political co-operation and to conduct negotiations about questions that might, in any form, affect the cordial relationship between the two Governments.

Back from Rome, Bethlen presented the Italo–Hungarian treaty to the public as a great success of his active foreign policy. With this treaty, Hungary surely broke out of her international isolation, but made her relations with the Little Entente more strained without gaining any major advantage, despite all Bethlen's expectations. Most of all, he expected an enforcement of splitting the Little Entente. Though there were many indications of internal differences within the Little Entente, the cohesive force which kept it together against Hungary did not diminish, on the contrary, it increased. In August 1927, Foreign Minister Walkó stated in a circular telegram that Hungarian foreign policy rejected every possibility of a rapprochement with the countries of the Little Entente, including initiatives of an economic character, because this kind of economic integration "would politically strengthen enormously the position of our neighbours against us, and would lessen every chance of a revision of the Trianon frontiers even by peaceful means".

From that time on, Italian orientation was prominent in Hungary's foreign policy until, in the flaming light of the world conflagration, it became clear that only in the distorting mirror of European power relations in the interwar years did Italy seem to be a serious power factor, and that Mussolini's strength was just like that of a circus athlete who cheated his spectators by lifting *papier-mâché* dumbbells made to appear solid iron weights. With the Italo–Hungarian treaty, the Hungarian ruling quarters set out to create new alliances, on which they could build their revisionist plans, and which linked Hungary's foreign policy to the most aggressive Powers in Europe.

At the end of the twenties, however, this did not yet mean that the Bethlen Government was giving up its British orientation or that it was turning against France. The reasons for this were primarily of an economic nature, but tactical considerations of foreign policy also made it necessary to maintain and improve Hungary's international relations. Hungary was financially dependent on Great Britain; and

Bethlen, in spite of Mussolini's pathetic promises, could not seriously rely upon Italy for material aid. Thus in 1927/1928, he again took up the idea of a major investment loan, expecting to make use not only of Anglo—American but also of French capital. And since there were no signs of a radical change in the European situation, nor were the attempts at an Italo—German rapprochement successful for the time being, Hungarian foreign policy was compelled to continue concentrating on Great Britain and France as the Great Powers that invariably dominated the European constellation. All the more so, since in the planning of French policies, the nationalist groups that had played a decisive role in the postwar European settlement, were relegated to the background, and the new liberal leading quarters agreed more and more that the peace settlement did not in fact solve the general problems, just as it did not promote the ultimate attainment of the French goals. And the British, opposing the French ambitions from the beginnings, were also sympathizing with the idea of a territorial adjustment in favour of Hungary, although towards the end of the twenties this was not yet realistically feasible. To expect a radical change in the status quo with Anglo—French help was beyond hope even in the perspective, and the Hungarian policy-makers were aware of this fact, but they thought that it would still be of advantage to exploit the uneasy conscience of the Western world for popularizing the cause of a Hungarian revision and to keep it up as an issue of international public opinion. All the more so, since the real aim, total revision, could thus be concealed behind the smokescreen of effective national grievances.

Following the Italo—Hungarian treaty, an open campaign of revisionist propaganda was launched in Hungary. It pervaded all fields, and was greatly facilitated by the so-called Rothermere action. Not long after the signing of the Italo—Hungarian treaty, Mussolini met the owner of the British paper *Daily Mail*, the conservative British press magnate Lord Rothermere, who undertook to launch in his paper a campaign for the revision of the Trianon Treaty of Peace. The Lord, who received no serious support from his own country, was not so much guided by a desire to remedy an injustice as rather by the interest he showed in the vacant throne of Hungary. Rothermere met Bethlen, and promised him to launch the revisionist campaign. His first article was published in the *Daily Mail* of June 21, 1927, under the title "Hungary's Place under the Sun". In it, he emphasized that only a rectification of the Trianon frontiers could guarantee security in Central Europe, and spoke up for returning the border areas of Czechoslovakia, Rumania and Yugoslavia to Hungary, which would have involved about two million people.

Rothermere's action met with wide international response, provoked large-scale counter-propaganda in France and the Little Entente states, stimulated the latter to better co-operation and resulted in the strengthening of French influence. The British Government disliked Rothermere's activity and dissociated itself from him. In December 1927, Foreign Secretary Austen Chamberlain let the Hungarian Prime Minister know that the Rothermere action "was harmful as it further irritated Europe, already in an agitated situation, without leading to any practical consequence". Therefore, he recommended the Hungarian Government to keep clear of this action. The fact that a part of the public opinion overestimated the power and weight of Lord Rothermere even caused anxiety to the Hungarian Government. So, Foreign Minister Walkó instructed the Hungarian Minister in London to try, with great caution though, to cut down the number of Rothermere interviews dispatched to Budapest.

In 1927, on Rothermere's initiative, the Hungarian Revisionist League was formed under the presidency of Ferenc Herczeg. Its aim was to establish non-official relations abroad, to influence international public opinion through various propaganda publications, and to enforce chauvinism and nationalism in Hungary. Concomitant with revisionist propaganda were anti-Communism and anti-Sovietism, the pretension that Hungary was the only bulwark of the West against the 'Soviet peril'.

Official government policy already began to clamour for the rectification of the frontiers. In a speech at Debrecen in March 1928, Bethlen said that his foremost aim was a revision of the Trianon frontiers. "On the point of the Danubian basin where the Hungarians stand, peace is not definitively ensured by the peace treaties in force today. . . . What we need is not a revision of the peace, we need different frontiers," he declared. He was the first to stress: "The frontier questions are not merely a matter of justice and law, they are usually questions of power." Bethlen's claim was given great support by the Italian Government's official and open stand in favour of a revision of Hungary's frontiers. In a speech on June 5, 1928, Mussolini pointed out: "Hungary can have trust in Italy's friendship. It can be said that she has been deeply hurt by the territorial provisions of the treaty of Trianon. . . . It will be well, not only from the point of view of general justice but also in the interests of Italy, for Hungary's fate to shape more favourably".

When Bethlen advocated the cause of peaceful revision, he was aware that he used contradictory notions which excluded each other. He had not changed his mind, he still believed that only a rearrangement in European relations could help realize Hungary's revisionist aspirations. After the propaganda campaign had started in Hungary, seeing that domestic political public opinion began to acquiesce in the idea of a revision limited to the ethnic frontiers, the Government hastened to speak up against this misconception. In May 1929, Bethlen expounded in a general order that the primary aim of the Government's foreign policy was invariably to restore the integrity of Hungary, and added that those who wished to limit the revisionist movement to the ethnic frontiers, on the assumption that there would be better chances of a revision in this way, "forget that this assumption precludes in advance any serious prospect of revision if occasion arises in an unforeseeable political constellation".

It was with the view of 'unforeseeable political constellations' that, simultaneously with the high-gear propaganda campaign, steps were taken to get ready for rearmament. The Government made a 15-year contract for the promotion of aircraft manufacture with the Weiss Manfred Works and the Hungarian State Machine Works (Magyar Állami Gépgyár). The manufacture of ammunition was also stepped up and new barracks were built.

The Italo—Hungarian treaty of friendship and co-operation was followed by steps aimed at immediate collaboration in the military field as well. The principal goal was to expedite Hungarian rearmament. Under the agreement between Mussolini and Bethlen, Italy dispatched the first consignment of arms to Hungary towards the end of 1927. The consignment — five waggonloads of machine-guns and spare parts disguised as agricultural machinery — arrived at Szentgotthárd *via* Austria on January 1, 1928. The Austrian custom-house officers, who, as usual, performed the customs formalities at the Hungarian frontier station, found out that the waggons contained arms and other war equipment. They demanded that the train should be shunted back to Austrian territory, but the Hungarian authorities refused. The case was given publicity in Austria and grew into an international scandal. The Little Entente states requested the League of Nations to appoint a commission to investigate the rearmament of Hungary.

However, it was only on March 7, 1928, that the League of Nations Council decided to set up a three-member neutral commission. After an examination by arms experts, the commission presented its report on May 7. The report noted with regret that an attempt had been made to forward a secret consignment of arms, but it found that the equipment was of no great military value. This mild condemnation was also given expression by the Council of the League of Nations on June 5, when — chiefly upon the insistence of British Foreign Secretary Austen Chamberlain — it was agreed to close the matter. The consignment was indeed unimportant from the military point of view (the subsequent supplies of arms from Italy were also devoid of any serious military value, this being a true reflection of the gap between Mussolini's promises and his real possibilities), but the incident contributed to the revival of suspicions about Hungary and to motivating the Little Entente states for better military collaboration.

At their Bucharest conference in June 1928, the states of the Little Entente reacted to the Italo—Hungarian co-operation and the general intensification of revisionist propaganda by passing a decision on the prolongation of their previous agreements. A year later, the Little Entente block took a definite form. The provisions of the basic conventions were co-ordinated, and the military concert of the three states against Hungary became closer.

Bethlen knew full well that the consolidation of Hungary's foreign relations and the foundations of her revisionist plans were not firm enough if she depended solely on her Italian ally. Moreover, Italy could not do much to help Hungary economically, especially in respect of her grain problem. Germany was more important as a market. Therefore the Government, simultaneously with the Italo—Hungarian treaty, made an attempt to build up relations with Germany as well. Of outstanding significance was the promotion of a rapprochement and an alliance between Italy and Germany. This coincided with the aim of the Italian foreign policy to alter Stresemann's moderate German foreign policy towards France. So, the Italian Government was pleased with the Hungarian Prime Minister's co-operation in this endeavour. Bethlen said that he saw a possibility of improving German—Italian relations, since Italy would be ready to consent to Austria's *Anschluss* on condition that Germany would openly recognize and guarantee the Austro—Italian frontier running through the Brenner pass and dividing the Tyrol. Though Stresemann showed interest in the communication, he did not regard the *Anschluss* as a topical issue, and was especially unwilling to give any kind of guarantee against anybody for any section of the frontiers. Recognition of the Brenner frontier might have given rise to a similar Polish claim with regard to the Polish—German border. And, as Stresemann pointed out, the kind of German statesman who would be ready to guarantee the eastern frontiers was not yet born. The German Foreign Minister did not want to take the risk of deteriorating Franco—German relations either; his main goal was precisely to have an end put to the French occupation of the Rhineland and to obtain a reduction of war reparations, but this endeavour ran counter to the plan of an Italo—German rapprochement directed against France. This is why he refused to accept the Italian orientation and paid no special attention to Bethlen's mediating efforts. It seemed that a change of course in Germany's foreign policy could not be expected for a long time yet. In July 1928, after the formation of the Müller Government, the Hungarian Minister in Berlin, K. Kánya, stated his opinion as follows: "If since the initiation of the Locarno programme the Reich has taken only little interest politically in the Danubian states and notably in Hungary, with the accession to power of the new Government the situation certainly cannot be expected to change for the better in this respect." Bethlen gained a similar impression when, in December 1928, he resumed his negotiations with Stresemann.

In 1930, the Bethlen Government had another try at improving German—Hungarian relations. The chances of success seemed to improve when the Brüning Government took office and German revanchism was visibly gaining ground. On November 21, 1930, Bethlen arrived at Berlin, had talks with Chancellor Brüning and Foreign Minister Curtius, and saw also President Hindenburg. The immediate aim of his journey was the preparation of a trade agreement making it possible to increase Hungary's agricultural exports to Germany. At the same time, Bethlen wished to attain far-reaching political results and to promote the Italo—German rapprochement.

The Hungarian Prime Minister was given a cordial welcome in Berlin, but no result of political significance was reached, the negotiations did not go beyond mutual inquiries. Germany still had an aversion to alliance with Italy. As was stated in the confidential bulletin of the Hungarian Ministry of Foreign Affairs, Bethlen's impression was that the German Government intended to follow its cautious foreign policy towards France and would only intensify the propaganda of revanche.

The Italian—German—Hungarian alliance urged by Bethlen could not be realized at that time, but the plan served as a basis for a later political conception.

After the conclusion of the Italo—Hungarian treaty of friendship, the Hungarian Government sought the ways of widening its international relations and enhancing the significance of Italo—Hungarian friendship until the eagerly expected German—Italian rapprochement became a reality. During the Mussolini—Bethlen negotiations in April 1927, it had already been suggested that the normalization of Rumanian—Hungarian relations, and with it, the weakening of the Little Entente, would greatly be promoted by a Polish—Hungarian rapprochement, as a result of which Poland might also mediate between Rumania and Hungary.

Fraternization with Poland had been a promising feature of Hungarian foreign policy since 1919. In case of a favourable constellation, the rapprochement might be facilitated, not only through coinciding foreign political interests and the previously established relationships, but also by the similarity of the internal political systems of the two countries as well. Poland was headed by a marshal, Hungary by an admiral, and both claimed to be champions of the struggle against Bolshevism. In 1927, there were indications that certain conditions of co-operation between them had been created, despite the fact that the Franco—Polish accord linked Poland to France's East European network of alliances. In spite of French efforts, the Polish Government was unwilling to enter into an agreement with the Little Entente bloc in general, or rather with Czechoslovakia in particular. Poland only concluded a treaty with Rumania which was primarily directed against the Soviet Union; and the Czechoslovak—Polish treaty signed at the end of 1921 was never ratified.

From 1927 onward, the Hungarian Government pressed for a rapprochement with Poland. In May 1928, Polish Foreign Minister Zaleski made a visit to Budapest and undertook to mediate between Rumania and Hungary. Late in November, 1928, Foreign Minister Walkó went to Warsaw to return the visit. He signed a Polish—Hungarian treaty of arbitration and conducted negotiations with Marshal Piłsudski. Piłsudski expressed the hope that friendly relations between Poland and Hungary would gradually develop, and he confirmed his agreement with Hungary's foreign policy. He thought that even though Hungary insisted on a revision of the peace treaty, this only meant a revision at some later date without creating serious complications at the given moment. He added that in the present state of European affairs he did not find it possible to accomplish any major change.

German response to the Polish—Hungarian rapprochement and to their treaty of arbitration indicated, as early as 1928, the weakest point of this fraternization. This weak point was the connection with Germany. Already on December 1, 1928, the German Minister in Budapest remarked to Deputy Foreign Minister Khuen-Hédervára that Walkó's trip to Warsaw had awakened mixed feelings in Berlin. Two weeks later, during a talk with Bethlen, Stresemann also brought up the question of the Polish—Hungarian treaty. He expressed his doubt that the treaty could, in a given case, prevented Poland from joining the Little Entente. Bethlen tried to convince the German Foreign Minister that Polish—Hungarian friendship was not inconsistent with the desire to strengthen German—Hungarian relations; moreover, Hungary did services also to Germany by trying to hold Poland off the Little Entente. Although Stresemann's scepticism was not justified — as in the following decade Poland came closer to Germany and co-operated with the Hitlerite establishment — the party who was to be disappointed turned out to be Bethlen, who had to learn by experience that lasting friendship with Poland was inconsistent with German—Hungarian co-operation.

Towards the end of the twenties, new opportunities presented themselves for the establishment of Turkish—Hungarian relations. France and Italy were competing with each other for the favours of Turkey; Turkey seemed to be the state whose attitude might determine which of the Great Powers would succeed in wielding its influence on the Balkans. Renewed under the leadership of Kemal Pasha and grown into an important international factor, Turkey had not yet decided what policy to adopt towards the plan of a Balkan pact. (One thing was certain: a Balkan pact under the aegis of any one of the Great Powers and without the active participation of Turkey was contrary to the interests of the Turkish Government.) Considering the earlier conflicts which Turkey had with the Entente Powers, as well as the 1923 Lausanne Treaty and, last but not least, the Soviet—Turkish relations — which had been established by a treaty of friendship and fraternity in 1921 and cemented by the 1925 treaty of neutrality and non-aggression — it seemed probable that the Turkish Government would be agreeable to a rapprochement with Italy in case it received guarantees that Italy did not harbour hostile intentions towards Turkey.

In 1927, the Turkish Government made approaches to Hungary with a view to building up closer relationships. In December, Foreign Minister Tevfik Rüstü informed the Hungarian Minister in Ankara that he would be pleased if Hungary concluded a treaty with Turkey, similar to that signed with Italy, because this might be to the advantage of both countries: through Turkey Hungary might establish at least some indirect contacts with the Soviet Union and thus strengthen her position against Rumania, while through Hungary Turkey could work towards a rapprochement with Italy and thus counteract French influence in Greece. At a secret conference with Mussolini in Milan, in April 1928, Bethlen brought up the Turkish suggestion. Mussolini said that he just had discussions with the Turkish and Greek Governments about a chain of bilateral treaties of neutrality, so he would like the Hungarian—Turkish negotiations to take place after the Turco—Italian talks.

Bethlen had a secret meeting in Milan with Tevfik Rüstü, and they agreed that following the Italo—Turkish talks, the Hungarian Government would initiate Turco—Hungarian negotiations. On January 5, 1929, Hungary and Turkey concluded a treaty of neutrality, conciliation and arbitration, in which each contracting party undertook not to enter any kind of political or economic alliance directed against the other party, and they pledged neutrality for the event of an unprovoked attack from third states on either one of them. As a result, the relations between the two countries improved. In March 1930, Foreign Minister Walkó went to Turkey, and this was followed by Prime Minister Bethlen's visit in November. Bethlen and the Turkish negotiators agreed to adopt a negative attitude against the Little Entente as well as against a Balkan Union and Briand's plan for a 'United States of Europe'. (In 1934, in a different international situation, the Balkan pact was nevertheless brought into existence as a regional security organization, to preserve the Balkan status quo, with the participation of Greece, Rumania, Yugoslavia and Turkey.)

In the late twenties, one of the most important features in Turco—Hungarian relations was that the Turkish Government proposed over and over again that Hungary should establish diplomatic relations with the Soviet Union and offered to mediate between them. The Hungarians declined the initiative every time. True, Bethlen pointed out to the Turkish Prime Minister that he saw no conflict between the Soviet Union and Hungary in respect of foreign politics, they might as well be allies for that matter; moreover, he admitted that the establishment of diplomatic relations would sooner or later become inevitable, but with reference to internal political reasons, he refused to take steps in this direction.

Both for the stabilization of Italian influence in Central Europe and for the revisionist plans of Hungary it was essential to divert Austria from the Franco–Czechoslovak orientation. These efforts were rendered extremely difficult by the internal conditions of Austria, first of all by the fact that the Social Democratic Party held strong positions both in and outside Parliament (it had an armed organization of its own, called the Republikanischer Schutzbund, and exercised considerable influence over the regular army as well). Therefore, Mussolini sought to contact the Austrian Heimwehr movement, which was striving to effect radical changes in the republican constitution and ultimately to establish a rightist dictatorship.

After the conclusion of the Italo–Hungarian treaty, the Hungarian Government, which had earlier entered into contact with the Heimwehr leaders soliciting its assistance, was ready to come to Italy's rescue. Close co-operation was developed between the two Governments in preparing for a 'right turn' in Austria.

The principles of the policy to be pursued towards Austria were laid down during secret talks between Mussolini and Bethlen at Milan in April 1928.

Bethlen spoke of his conceptions as follows: "One aim ought to be to make sure that in Austria a right-wing Government, with the aid of the Heimwehr, takes over from the present Government. Their foreign political goals are not quite congruous with ours, and they consequently have embarked on a policy which, being friendly with Czechoslovakia in particular and with the Little Entente in general, is rather unpleasant to the Hungarian Government. ... A rightist régime that would rise to power with the help of Italy and Hungary, and which would lean upon these two countries, would be to Italy's advantage inasmuch as it would not harp so much on the Tyrol question and would postpone also the issue of the *Anschluss* because it would adopt an internal policy different from that of the present, or rather the next, Government of Germany shifting more to the left after the elections. Thus the *Anschluss* would be put off by the internal political conflicts. The advantage which Hungary might have would be that traffic between Italy and Hungary and the importation of arms would be secured." At the same time, Bethlen made a request for a loan of three million pengős and 400 Italian airplanes for the rearmament of Hungary.

On the basis of information received from Austrian right-wing politicians, Bethlen explained that the plan could be carried out in a short time because the development of the Heimwehr military organization was about to be completed, and that since secret co-operation existed between the Heimwehr and the official Austrian armed forces, support from the latter could also be counted upon. The Heimwehr needed three hundred thousand schillings for the completion of its development, and the Hungarian Government was ready to offer its good offices. On the last day of the negotiations, Mussolini declared that he was willing to accept the Hungarian offer and place one million Italian lire at the disposal of the Heimwehr leaders if these accepted the obligation to take over the power at the earliest possible date.

After the Milan agreements, the Hungarian Government assigned General Béla Jánky to a diplomatic post in Vienna with the secret mission to maintain contact with the Heimwehr. Jánky managed to arrange meetings between Bethlen and Heimwehr leader Richard Steidle at Budapest in June and July 1928. As a result of these talks, leaders of the Heimwehr made a written declaration to the effect that in case they came into power they would regard the question of the South Tyrol as non-existent in the Austro–Italian relations. After the declaration had been forwarded to Mussolini, the Italian Government paid part of the promised money to the Hungarian Ministry of Foreign Affairs.

The execution of a rightist putsch was, however, put off by the formation of the Schober government in September 1929, because Mussolini found in the person of Schober a suitable guarantee for a turn to the right and for the development of Italo–Austro–Hungarian co-operation. Therefore, the Italian Government dropped the plan for a Heimwehr rising and stopped providing material support. This turn of events, however, did not quite please the Hungarian Government; it urged Schober (who had earlier been in contact with the Heimwehr) to carry out the turn to the right. The Chancellor, with reference to his effort to obtain loans abroad, promised only to execute a slow, gradual change of course. But in accordance with Mussolini's hope, he freed the way for a rapprochement with Italy and Hungary.

In the first half of April 1930, Bethlen had talks in Rome with Mussolini. They found the Schober Government's activity to be propitious to Italy and Hungary. Therefore, they agreed to have a stop put to the antigovernment plans of the Heimwehr, but to remain ready to provide effective assistance again, if necessary. Bethlen also indicated his intention to invite the Austrian Chancellor to make an official visit to Budapest. Mussolini suggested to Bethlen that he should make use of Schober's stay in Budapest for the conclusion of an Austro–Hungarian treaty of friendship, for in this way, the combination of three treaties (inclusive of the Italo–Austrian treaty signed in February 1930) would, though only indirectly, sketch the outlines of the proposed political bloc.

Schober arrived at Budapest on July 8, 1930. The talks only lasted one day but were sufficient to lead to complementing the arbitration treaty of 1923 by a treaty of friendship and a secret protocol on the co-ordination of policies to be followed towards the Little Entente. The documents were signed during Bethlen's visit in Vienna on January 25, 1931. The text of the secret protocol read as follows:

"The High Contracting Parties are agreed that, in virtue to the preamble to the treaty of arbitration signed at Budapest on April 10, 1923, they will maintain constant contact, through their diplomatic representatives, with regard to all political questions of interest to both parties, especially those concerning their common neighbours."

2. The effect of the world economic crisis on Hungary's international position and on her foreign policy

The economic boom of the entire capitalist world came to an end in 1929, and the gravest overproduction crisis in the history of capitalism broke out. The general crisis of world economy added to an agrarian crisis that had previously shaken the world, meant a crisis of trade and industry and a complete crush in the world of finance, including the international credit system. The general crisis violently shook the economy of the entire capitalist world, thus setting sweeping processes in the foreign and domestic policies of many countries in motion. It thus became the starting-point of radical changes in international relations. Dissension was growing between the victorious Powers of the First World War, and the conflicts between the victors and Germany were sharpening. In the first years of the general crisis, however, these conflicts did not fully develop into open clashes because the crisis in the various countries began, mounted and wore off at different times. The crisis attacked the international power relations with ever increasing violence, and seemed to be wrecking the Versailles system of peace; nevertheless, up to 1931/1932, it appeared that the European status quo of the twenties would withstand the storm, and the main framework of power relations would be left intact. Moreover, since the crisis reached France, the leading Power on the Continent, later than the other Great Powers, it seemed that she would be able not only to retain but even to strengthen her positions in Europe, especially in Central Europe. However, it gradually became obvious that France's superiority had only been an illusion created by the time lag in the crisis.

The world economic crisis dealt a particularly heavy blow on the economies of Central and South Eastern Europe. The one-sidedness of the economic structure of the countries in South Eastern Europe did not change during the twenties; what is more, the domestic and foreign policies of the successor states only added to the initial difficulties. Financial reconstruction and economic investments in these countries were essentially carried out by means of foreign loans. The loans, which were for the most part disproportionate to the economic strength of the respective countries, were to be heavily paid for when it came to the serious international credit crisis and financial collapse. What still added to these problems was that for the South Eastern European countries struggling with a sales crisis, the nearest markets were the German and the Italian, while the loans, charged mostly against the state treasuries, came from Anglo—American and French sources. On top of all this came the political difficulties of the region. Even at the time of consolidation, there were enormous political tensions dormant in Central and South Eastern Europe; under the influence of the crisis the embers of enmity started to glow again. The economic crisis increasingly polarized the internal antagonisms in these countries, thus enforcing their economic and political dependence on foreign factors. Dissension among the successor states was growing, decomposing the Versailles peace system, and becoming another source of preparations for a new world war.

The grave problems in Central Europe gave occasion for intervention on the part of the rivalling Great Powers. It was evident that decisive influence would be wielded by the Power capable of rendering assistance in coping with the crisis. This gave a major impetus to French foreign policy to stabilize the system of defence against German revanchism, to organize the Danubian basin under French supremacy. On the one hand, France used her loan transactions for trying to dominate the countries of the Danube basin, granting financial aid with political strings attached; on the other hand, she proposed plans for economic co-operation among the countries of the Danube basin.

From 1929 onward, various projects were formulated in order to create a kind of loose economic co-operation by building up a system of preferences. In 1930, talks began about the establishment of a so-called agrarian bloc with Hungary, Rumania and Yugoslavia as members. The talks were soon joined in by Czechoslovakia, Poland and the Baltic states. But these plans failed to realize partly because of the British, Italian and German opposition, and partly owing to the intricate web of differences between the states concerned.

From 1930/1931 onward, Germany followed the French example in procuring markets in South Eastern Europe and expanding her economic influence in these agrarian countries. Although among the Great Powers it was Germany who was hit hardest by the crisis, her prospects for an active trade policy were shaping more favourably from several points of view. As early as 1929, the German Government already demanded a reduction or the settlement of her reparations debt, because the amount of the war indemnity had not been definitely fixed at the time of Germany's reconstruction under the Dawes plan, only the sum of annuities had been named. The success of the German diplomatic action was reflected by the so-called Young Plan and the related Hague Convention, which fixed the total of reparations at 113.9 thousand million gold marks to be paid in 57 years. (The reparation payments were suspended by the Hoover moratorium in 1931, and the indemnity from Germany was definitely cancelled by the Lausanne treaty of 1932 against a lump-sum payment of three thousand million marks.) After the Hague convention, financial control over Germany was terminated. France, on Britain's initiative, already consented to the evacuation of the Rhineland before the scheduled date at the first Hague conference.

From this time onward, German commercial policies were more strongly influenced by political considerations, by efforts at penetration into South Eastern Europe. Penetration was facilitated by the fact that Germany did not impose political conditions on the countries wishing to sell their products on the German markets. Especially after the failure of the plans for economic co-operation, the crisis drove the agrarian countries to turn increasingly to the German markets which provided practically unlimited opportunities for the sale of agricultural products. This is why Germany could begin to acquire economic positions in South Eastern Europe, which she subsequently used to enhance her political influence, to disrupt the Little Entente.

In the summer of 1929, the Entente Powers extended the negotiations about the indemnity due from Germany to deal with the question of the so-called Eastern reparations, in order to arrive at definitive agreement on Austria's, Bulgaria's and Hungary's reparation liabilities and the terms of payment. They convened the Eastern Reparations Conference in Paris in September 1929 and summoned the indebted states to attend it. The representatives of the Entente Powers at the Paris Conference connected the issue of Hungarian reparations with the so-called optants' law-suits, going on for a number of years. The optants' case arose when, after the war, the Governments of Rumania, Czechoslovakia and Yugoslavia expropriated for the purpose of a land reform some of the big estates, including those of Hungarian landowners who had opted to retain their Hungarian nationality and moved to Hungarian territory. These landowners, with reference to related clauses of the Trianon Treaty of Peace, demanded the return of their estates or indemnification.

Since the mixed arbitration court could not reach a decision, in 1927, the Hungarian Government submitted the case of the optant landowners to the League of Nations Council, which proposed that the Hungarian and Rumanian Governments should enter into negotiations with each other. The two Governments complied, but the negotiations, in spite of Poland's intercession, led to no result. At the Eastern Reparations Conference, the committee dealing with Hungary's case made the suggestion that, inasmuch as the Hungarian Government insisted on the optant landowners' being indemnified, Hungary should continue to pay reparations after 1943, which should then be used in part for indemnification purposes.

The Hungarian Government rejected this suggestion in October 1929, and so the Paris negotiations ended without result. The Bethlen Government found itself in a very complicated situation: should it insist on indemnification, it would be compelled to connect the optants' case with the question of reparations and to accept the augmentation of Hungary's liabilities. Bethlen first wanted to rid himself of the dilemma by resigning his post for the time being, because his class standing and his personal interests kept him from waiving his claim to indemnification, but he was unwilling to face the internal political consequences of an increase in Hungary's reparations debts. On Mussolini's advice, however, he dropped his intention to resign, and in January 1930, he himself went to the Hague to attend the negotiations about reparations.

In the matter of Hungarian reparations, the Hague conference set up a special committee which then worked out a new proposal. Accordingly, the optant landowners would be indemnified from a special fund of 219.5 million gold crowns. The receipts of this fund would consist of half the amounts to be paid by Hungary after 1944 as 'special debts', the total amount to be paid by the Little Entente states to the expropriated landowners, the annuities due to the Great Powers from Hungarian and Bulgarian reparations, as well as certain sums assigned to the fund by the Entente Powers.

On January 20, 1930, the second Hague conference approved of the agreements under which Hungary was to pay from 1944 to 1966, that is over 23 years, a yearly sum of 13.5 million gold crowns as 'special debts' arising from the peace treaty. The

Funds A and B (this latter was to satisfy the demands other than those occasioned by the land reform) amounted to 310.5 million gold crowns.

The newly imposed debt thus came to 310.5 million gold crowns which, together with the reparations liability fixed at 200 million in 1924, totalled 510.5 million gold crowns. (Up to 1930, Hungary had paid off 23 million gold crowns.) The Hague conference appointed a committee to draw up the final text of the agreements. The committee working in Paris concluded its work on April 28, 1930. The agreements, known as the Paris Accords, were signed the same day. In virtue of the Paris Accords, the general pledge was definitively cancelled, and the Reparations Commission ceased to function.

The Bethlen Government tried to make the dissolution of the Reparations Commission appear as a great diplomatic success, thereby wishing to cover up the failure it suffered from its way of closing the question of war reparations and the optants' case. It wanted to obscure the fact that it had insisted on the indemnification of the optant landowners even at the price of a tremendous increase in the heavy liabilities imposed on Hungary; that it practically obliged the Hungarian state to indemnify at its own expense the Hungarian landed gentry against the loss of their estates confiscated in the neighbouring countries. This is a characteristic documentation of Bethlen's policy, of the class content of the counter-revolutionary system, and it is not in the least altered by the fact that with the suspension of Hungarian reparations in 1931, and with their *de facto* cancellation in 1932, the indemnification fund ceased to exist practically before it was set up.

In 1930, the deepening economic crisis prompted Hungary's policy-makers to concentrate their efforts on obtaining foreign loans. For the event of Hungary's assuming the new reparations debt and ratifying the Paris Accords, British financial circles had earlier promised to grant the major loan solicited by Bethlen ever since 1928. Therefore, the Government rushed ratification through Parliament (May 1930), and Bethlen went to London. The journey was announced as a courtesy visit of the Prime Minister who wished to thank the British Government for its favourable attitude adopted at the Hague and Paris conferences, but in reality it was a loan-raising tour.

Bethlen arrived at London on June 15, 1930, and had talks with members of the British Government and other politicians. The official talks did not touch the financial issues; the real aim of these talks was to prepare a better political atmosphere for the loan transaction. During the talks, MacDonald's Labour Government, although it deemed it desirable for Hungary to improve her relations with the Little Entente states, and deplored the oppression of the Hungarian leftist opposition, practically assured the Hungarian Government of its goodwill. Of decisive importance were, on the other hand, the discussions with London financiers, Rothschild and other bankers. Although even after his London meetings, Bethlen told a *Financial Times* reporter that Hungary intended to contract a loan of £12 to £13 million, it became known that Great Britain was not in a position to grant the proposed big loan.

What Bethlen was able to obtain was very little for the Government to stabilize its financial position; in November 1930, the banking group of Rothschild, together with a number of American banks, extended to the Hungarian state a one-year credit of 87 million pengős secured by bills of exchange.

A few months later, as a sign of Germany's rise in the international arena, European politics was burst into by the idea of an Austro—German customs union, which created a considerable stir in Hungary, too. The plan, made public on March 21, 1931, raised violent objection, especially in France and Czechoslovakia, but even the Italians objected to it, seeing their plan to create an Italo—Austro—Hungarian bloc in danger. The Italian objection to the customs union was not motivated by unconditional opposition. Even at this point, Mussolini regarded the *Anschluss* question as a sales transaction (because from the outset, he considered the customs union as a means of camouflaging the plan of the *Anschluss*): Let the spheres of influence be divided between Germany and Italy, and the German Government should recognize the Brenner frontier. But the Germans were not inclined to do so, therefore Italy took a more inflexible stand and came closer to the French position. Ultimately, on Britain's compromise proposal, the case of the customs union was submitted to the Council of the League of Nations. The French Government not only tried to foil the customs union scheme by exerting financial pressure on Austria, but it immediately proposed a counterplan. This plan, advanced by Briand, boiled down to the establishment of a system of preferential tariffs and credits to be granted to the agrarian-industrial countries of the Danubian basin.

The plan for the German—Austrian customs union confronted the Hungarian Government with a difficult problem, all the more so, since the situation evolving amidst the deepening crisis awakened the Hungarian ruling classes to the necessity of reconsidering foreign policy and orientation. On the one hand, the Bethlen Government saw its revisionist conceptions justified, inasmuch as with the strengthening of German revanchism, the chances of developing a new system of alliance were growing. On the other hand, as a result of the crisis, Hungarian foreign policy once more began to concentrate on loan-raising actions in the years of 1930/1931, and this required efforts to improve Franco—Hungarian relations. Economic interests and political considerations divided the ruling classes. Some groups, especially from among the agrarian quarters, emphasized the prime importance of German orientation and broached the idea of joining the Austro—German customs union. Other groups, representing mainly the finance capital, were in favour of a French orientation, supported by the Anglo—French sympathies of the left-wing opposition aroused by the rightist shift in Germany, by the dynamism of the National Socialists. Amidst the given conditions of the crisis, French orientation seemed more advantageous, but this would have meant temporary silence imposed upon the revisionist aspirations. Under the influence of the customs union controversy, France turned towards Hungary with growing attention to counterbalance Austria's conduct. At this point the French were in a key position to enforce economic co-operation and political rapprochement between the Danubian countries. For this reason, in addition to granting Hungary a minor loan as immediate aid, France urged the resumption of Czechoslovak–Hungarian trade relationships and was not reluctant to voice encouraging political views. At the end of March 1931, the French Minister in Budapest told the new Hungarian Foreign Minister, Count Gyula Károlyi, that "they in France already comprehend that they have thus far followed the wrong policy. They regret that after the war they failed to support the drive for a strong Hungary in order to seek the mainstay against German expansionism there; they made a mistake when they based their policy upon the Little Entente at the expense of Hungary, because, as they can now see, they cannot safely rely on the Little Entente." France promised to grant Hungary a loan of 500 million francs but connected it with the issue of the customs union.

Although adopting a neutral attitude, the Bethlen Government in fact opposed the customs union. Over and above all this, it was of decisive significance that an Austro–German customs union to the exclusion of Hungary threatened Bethlen's entire foreign political conception: at once it would have exposed Hungary to German pressure, precluding the possibility of Hungary's enforcing her claims even by way of negotiations.

The policy towards the Austro–German customs union was ultimately defined by a conference of diplomatic envoys on April 10, 1931, as a result of which the Hungarian Government addressed a memorandum to the Italian government on April 17. It proposed that Rome should join in the talks about the interpretation of accession to the customs union, and enter into contact with France in order to find out the French plans and to have the Brocchi scheme accepted. (The Brocchi scheme was meant to establish the economic co-operation of Italy, Austria and Hungary on the basis of mutual preferences in the form of export bonuses.) It expressed the view that open action against the customs union and definite turn to France would not be advisable. Until the details of the plan would come to light, greater pressure ought to be exerted on Germany. Finally, it was stressed in the document that Hungary could not take the initiative, so the first move ought to be made by Italy.

At the same time, the Government made an effort to exploit the issue of the customs union for the purposes of its own actual aims. It tried to get the Italians to advance the secret military loan which they had promised in 1928, but which had remained unrealized, and to bring the Brocchi scheme into effect. To the Germans, an offer was made according to which Hungary would refrain from opposing the customs union if Germany should pay more respect to Hungarian commercial interests. To the French, it was intimated that Hungary could safeguard her economic independence only if she received the necessary aid from France. The result — except for French goodwill — was not too encouraging. Germany only made promises, and Italy, being suspicious of the manoeuvres of Hungarian foreign policy, repeatedly put off granting the loan. The Brocchi scheme was further deferred, first by the customs union affair, then by the suspicion, growing into absolute distrust, about the foreign policy of the new Hungarian Government that took office after the fall of Bethlen.

On May 29, 1931, the Council of the League of Nations referred the case of the Austro–German customs union to the Permanent Court of International Justice in the Hague. This move made it clear that the plan had failed and could thus be removed from the agenda of Hungarian foreign policy as well.

The plan for the customs union raised the issue of Habsburg restoration again. In May 1931, the Italian and the French press repeatedly dealt with the restoration of the Habsburg dynasty, or the reestablishment of Austro–Hungarian federation. Already prior to this, French 'private circles' close to the Quai d'Orsay gave voice to the opinion that a Habsburg restoration would be less dangerous than the *Anschluss*. On April 1931, a senior diplomat of the Italian Ministry of Foreign Affairs told Miklós Kozma, director-general of the Hungarian Telegraphic Agency, that Italy would be pleased with an Austro–Hungarian rapprochement, or even union, maybe under Habsburg rule, to prevent the establishment of the customs union and the subsequent *Anschluss*.

The Italian conception seemed even more probable when the news spread in diplomatic quarters that young Otto of Habsburg was about to marry Duchess Mary of Savoy, that the ex-Empress had consulted the Pope about a possible journey to Hungary and had paid a call to Mussolini as well. The information was not confirmed, but neither Paris nor London nor Vienna found it impossible that Mussolini was playing with the idea of restoration, probably only in order to make the Austrian and Hungarian Governments more pliable and more lenient towards a triple alliance.

In 1930/1931, London was seriously concerned with the Habsburg question too, mainly about the nature of obligations Great Britain had assumed under the agreement of November 1921, which entitled the Entente Powers to have a say in the question of the vacant Hungarian throne. Already in December 1930, the Foreign Office prepared a detailed study of this problem. The view it adopted was indicated by its decision made in November 1931 which, with reference to recent occurrences, stated that the Council of Ambassadors was no longer competent in the matter, and the whole question came within the province of the League of Nations. (And by that time the world had already begun to form an idea of how effective the measures taken by the League could be.)

Following the reaction of the French and Italian press and the news of the dynastic marriage, the legitimist agitation in Hungary was kindled. This was facilitated by the fact that the new Foreign Minister (and later Prime Minister), Count Gyula Károlyi, was not a consistent anti-Habsburg politician. The legitimists saw the last chances of a Habsburg restoration in the apparent leniency of the French and the Italians. The Bethlen Government, however, was not more disposed towards restoration now than it had been before. Its principal aims besides the Italo–Austrian line continued to be based, despite all difficulties, on the hope of a rapprochement between Germany and Italy. Bethlen did not give up the idea of a total revision of the frontiers either. The French connections were strengthening, but this was nothing more than part of the inevitable tactics. Short term tactics played a growing role in the foreign policy of the counter-revolutionary régime at grips with the economic crisis; its essence was formulated by the Foreign Minister in the Upper House as follows: Hungary must take care not to commit herself too soon, because thereby she would forfeit "her diplomatic weight superior to her physical strength".

Bethlen was aware of the saying that diplomacy is the art of possibilities, so he tried to direct foreign policy accordingly. But he seemed not to have learnt another basic tenet, namely that politics is the science of exigencies, so he was bound to fall.

The outbreak of the finance crisis in the summer of 1931 made it extremely urgent to procure a foreign loan. The Government could obtain only bits of immediate aid. Owing to the difficulties caused by the crisis, the London house of Rothschild was unable to help, but it did not wish to let Hungary go bankrupt either, for it had the monopoly of Hungarian state loans. Therefore it agreed to the Hungarian Government's entering into negotiations with France, and the French — as we have seen — promised to grant a loan. On July 22, 1931, the Hungarian Ministry of Foreign Affairs instructed the Legations in London, Paris, Rome and Washington by telegram, to start talks immediately with the respective Foreign Ministers in the matter of a loan. It was stated in the telegram: "The Hungarian Government, by applying certain measures, can uphold the stability of the currency for one more week, but after this it will be inevitable to depart from gold parity, a measure that would lead to the collapse of the financial reconstruction effected with the aid of the League of Nations. The situation in Hungary can still be saved today if we obtain a loan of at least £5 million immediately."

On August 15, 1931, the first official communiqué on the signing of an agreement for a loan of £5 million in Paris was published in Hungary. Four days later, on August 19, the Bethlen Government resigned, and the Regent accepted the resignation.

It is beyond doubt that internal problems were highly instrumental in the fall of the Bethlen Government, but its foreign policy contributed to it as well. (Since the victory of the counter-revolutionary régime and its consolidation, internal affairs had never been so much interrelated with the international situation as in the years of the crisis, when not only foreign orientation but also the tactical moves of foreign policy directly influenced internal power relations.) The strengthening of French connections — even if it did not imply any change of orientation, and even if it remained on the tactical plane — had necessarily to lead, at least provisionally, to certain concessions to the Little Entente, and to the eclipse of revisionist endeavours. Let us not forget that the £5-million loan was still a kind of emergency relief, while the greater loan was to come in the autumn. The French Government certainly did not stipulate conditions requiring a regular agreement, but the entire French loan policy indicated that there must have been political considerations and plans behind it. (Similar information reached London through the diplomatic corps.) And in the eyes of France and her allies Bethlen seemed to be unfit to carry out those ideas.

The new Government was formed by one of Horthy's close associates, Count Gyula Károlyi. In his appointment, the Paris newspapers welcomed the strengthening of French orientation. The new Prime Minister made a programme declaration on August 24, 1931. As to his foreign political conception, he said that his aim was to cultivate the steadily strengthening relations established with Italy in such a way that good relations with Germany should not be disturbed and "our relations with France should not be prevented from improving". He made no mention of the revisionist claims, and in connection with the neighbour countries, he stated that political differences still existed, "but since no one contemplates eliminating them otherwise than peacefully and by mutual agreement, it can be hoped that the existing impediments will be removed by and by".

The Károlyi Government, appointed to settle the crisis, primarily had to solve the economic problems, including first of all the selling of agricultural products. Since the German market was not yet sufficiently open to Hungarian grain, and since for the above-mentioned reasons trade relationships with Italy did not develop to the desired extent, the Hungarian Government had to think of other expedients, without making any change in the general line of Bethlen's foreign policy. In the winter of 1931, Czechoslovak Foreign Minister Beneš proposed the economic co-operation and customs union of Czechoslovakia, Austria and Hungary. His proposal was heeded by Hungary alone, and in this case, Hungary refrained from making economic co-operation subject to the satisfaction of the revisionist demands. This was enough for the Italian Government to become suspicious and launch a counteraction. If we add that the Hungarian Government did not officially respond to Prague's proposal it can be supposed with good reason that Hungary wanted to use the Czechoslovak proposal as a pretext for giving effect to the long overdue Semmering arrangements (the Brocchi scheme). In the beginning, the Italian government only wished an understanding between Austria and Hungary, but when, in January 1932, Bethlen went to Rome and broached the plan for a customs union of Hungary, Italy and Austria — provided that a system of preferences would be established as a first step — Mussolini's suspicion was dispelled and he accepted the Brocchi agreement. This was signed on February 20, 1932, but was not put into force because of controversies regarding minor questions.

France made another attempt to counteract Germany's growing expansionism by creating a Central European economic bloc. Early in March, 1932, French Prime Minister Tardieu came out with a plan to unite Austria, Hungary, Czechoslovakia, Rumania and Yugoslavia in a customs union and a common economic organization.

The Italian Government, becoming aware of the danger to its influence and expansionist effort in Central and South Eastern Europe, decided to act immediately in order to torpedo the Tardieu plan. Mussolini redoubled his efforts to press for closer relations between Austria, Hungary and Italy and to have the Brocchi scheme put into force. Besides, he took steps to set up the customs union suggested by Bethlen. But neither Austria nor Hungary believed in its feasibility, and Foreign Minister Walkó informed Rome accordingly on March 21. Since Italy was unable to agree with Austria and Hungary about the rejection of the Tardieu plan, she offered co-operation to Germany with a view to thwarting the French initiative.

Hungary's stand regarding the Tardieu plan was not completely negative. Walkó's view became crystallized after his talks with the French Prime Minister, in March 1932, and his visit to Rome on two occasions. He summed up his view in the so-called Committee of 33 as follows: "As I understand this collaboration, we have to make the best possible commercial agreements among the five of us, and to make them in such a way that, even if we concede certain benefits to one another, no one else can refer to these benefits, and that we ensure that turnover among these countries increases considerably." Walkó's view regarding the Tardieu plan and the related problems was indicative of a departure from Bethlen's foreign policy line. It seemed that Germany had been removed from the focus of foreign policy; the rapprochement and economic co-operation with the neighbouring countries were not automatically brought into connection with political requisites, that is, with insistence on the necessity of revision; and the tone adopted towards the Little Entente countries was unusually moderate. But in Hungary's foreign policy this was only a brief episode possibly interrelated with the French plan to settle the crisis. When the crisis in France deepened, this plan of reconstruction crashed, and moderation in foreign policy, together with the first buds of an economic rapprochement, vanished into thin air.

In 1932, when the suffocating smoke of the general economic crisis began to dissolve, the emerging unhealthy look of Europe revealed how badly Europe was wounded by the crisis. The safeguards of the international status quo established during the twenties, and the ramparts of the Versailles peace system were battered by the heavy waves of international economic and political life. The economic and political consequences of the crisis exercised an especially profound effect on the states of Central and South Eastern Europe. The collapse of the postwar international monetary and credit system and, as part of it, the suspension and subsequent cancellation of reparations (by virtue of a decision of the Lausanne conference in the summer of 1932) not only compelled these states to reform their whole economic policy, but also gave a larger scope to revisionist-revanchist policies within the vanquished countries, with the support of the extreme right. Loss of the Western loans in fact atrophied the umbilical cord connecting these countries with the Western Powers.

At the same time, France was unable to maintain, by economic methods, her previous influence in the East Central European countries. And since from 1932 onward, Britain showed increasing indifference towards the problems of Central Europe, France was gradually left alone, with the handicaps of the Versailles system, in the face of a Germany growing into an economic and political power factor. France's security policy and her network of alliances brought out more and more factors of uncertainty, and this compelled her to look for new powerful partners in the interest of her own security. The only eligible Power was the Soviet Union, which the Western Powers had earlier tried to keep out of European politics. Of course, it cannot be left out of account that in the early thirties, new elements began to appear in the Soviet foreign policy. Even before Hitler's rise to power, the strengthening of the Nazi Party shook the Soviet Government's confidence in the durability of German–Soviet friendly relations based upon the Rapallo Treaty. The first step in the new direction was the Franco–Soviet treaty of non-aggression concluded as early as 1932.

The economic crisis further deepened the internal conflicts in the East Central European countries, increased their economic and political dependence on other Powers, and sharpened their conflicts. What is more, this was precisely the time when signs of an intention to change the status quo began to appear in the foreign policy of the Great Powers, first of all in that of Great Britain. All this gradually led to the weakening of British and French influence in East Central Europe, giving way to German and Italian penetration, thus making the area a source of changes in the status quo which ultimately led to the preparation of the new world war.

The Károlyi Government, which was utterly unstable in its home politics, fell in the changed international situation in September 1932. On October 1, 1932, Gyula Gömbös was appointed Prime Minister. The Gömbös Government actually entered the arena with the programme of foreign policy formulated by Bethlen: close friendship with Italy, stronger relations with Germany. But while friendship with Italy was based on more than five years of co-operation, the practicability of the German orientation was questioned because of the internal chaos culminating precisely at the time of Gömbös's taking office. For the time being, therefore, Gömbös had no other option than to follow the traditional path. Yet, what was completely new in Gömbös's policy was the confused and inconsistent tactics ensuing from the personality of the newly appointed Prime Minister, and from the accelerated pace of international developments. In the autumn of 1932, Gömbös considered it his most immediate duty to consolidate friendship with Italy. For this reason, he wrote a letter to Mussolini on October 4, emphasizing that he wished Hungary's foreign policy towards Italy and Germany to continue where Bethlen had left off. He wished to rely on Italy in the first place, and counted upon her assistance in the marketing of grain, in the question of disarmament, etc.

After announcing his pretentious domestic programme, Gömbös would have liked to score a rapid and spectacular success in foreign politics, so he started out in various directions at the same time. He launched a violent revisionist campaign — referring to immediate possibilities of change — and addressed to Czechoslovakia an unofficial message in which he offered an economic agreement and a political truce for a period of several years. In his notorious '95 points' he promised better 'protection for the minorities' and harangued about sincere co-operation with the neighbouring states.

The protection of national minorities, in the policy of Gömbös just as in that of all earlier Goverments, was in reality a factor subordinated to revisionist aims. None of the counter-revolutionary Governments seriously sought to improve the situation of the Magyar minorities living in the neighbouring countries, because this would have weakened the argument for the necessity of revision. True, the neighboruing countries did not offer too many chances for improvement, partly because the problem of the protection of minorities fell within the competence of the League of Nations under the Versailles system. Measures for the protection of minorities were of two basic kinds. Either the Entente Powers concluded conventions on the protection of minorities with the countries concerned (as did Czechoslovakia, the Serb–Croat–

Slovene Kingdom and Rumania in the autumn of 1919) or the countries with minorities made unilateral declarations to the League of Nations on the measures they took. In virtue of Article 18 of the Covenant, it was the League of Nations which, after the registration of the conventions, assumed responsibility for the fulfilment of such international engagements. This meant that the Eastern European countries did not conclude conventions on protection for the minorities living in their territory with the state to which the respective minorities belonged, but the rights of the minorities were guaranteed by international forums. In practice, however, this guarantee consisted merely in that the grievances of minorities could be submitted to the League of Nations; however, the remedies for grievances, in the vast majority of cases, stuck in the labyrinth of complicated League procedures.

Although the possibility existed for any two countries to enter into a bilateral agreement providing mutual protection for their national minorities, the respective Hungarian Governments would not even hear of such engagements, because the League system of the protection of minorities very well suited the revisionist aspirations of the counter-revolutionary system. The Hungarian Governments' policy on the protection of minorities was merely to collect the facts of grievances and submit them to the League of Nations, which meant an incessant agitation at the supreme international forum against the territorial clauses of the Trianon Treaty of Peace.

On November 10, 1932, Gömbös, setting out on his first journey abroad, left for Rome. His talks with Mussolini covered a broad range of problems, under the slogan that Italo–Hungarian co-operation should be filled with concrete meaning, that inaction should be replaced by dynamism. Gömbös and Mussolini agreed to revive the plan for the Italo–Austro–Hungarian customs union to be followed by an appropriate political convention, in which the Austrians, if they so desired, would be assisted in carrying out a turn to the right. They talked about the ways of accelerating 'the process of disintegration in Yugoslavia' and agreed to provide the Croatian separatist movement and the Macedonian terrorists with regular and systematic assistance, as they had continually done since the conclusion of the Italo–Hungarian treaty during the tenure of Bethlen. They resolved, pending the creation of the customs union, to grant each other additional commercial preferences. Finally, Mussolini promised to give help in having Hungary's right to rearm recognized and in promoting her rearmament.

Gömbös's desultory actions only entailed negative consequences. In January 1933, there erupted the scandal of the so-called Hirtenberg arms delivery. A Social Democratic newspaper of Vienna reported that a consignment of 6,500 rifles and 200 machine-guns from Italy had arrived in the Hirtenberg armaments factory to be repaired and then forwarded to Hungary. In the wake of the newspaper report, the question was brought up by interpellations in the French National Assembly, and the affair grew into a diplomatic incident. The British and the French Governments, through their diplomatic representatives, demanded explanation in Budapest, Vienna and Rome. The Italian Government pointed out that there was no convention in force to prescribe where Italy should send her old arms for repairs. In Vienna, the answer was that the peace treaty did not prohibit the repair of the arms of other states, and the Hungarian Ministry of Foreign Affairs denied that the arms had been intended for Hungary. The British and French Governments — chiefly on the suggestion of the Little Entente states — found the replies unsatisfactory, and the incident was not closed until in February 1933, when Italy declared herself ready to transport the arms back.

The Hirtenberg affair and the Gömbös Government's diplomatic actions were also instrumental in that in February 1933 the Little Entente changed the system of alliance based on bilateral conventions into a multilateral alliance. When, however, this pact was concluded, the Chancellor's post in Germany was already occupied by Adolf Hitler.

CHAPTER III

THE BERLIN–ROME AXIS AND HUNGARY, 1933–1939

1. Hungarian foreign policy from 1933 to 1936

In January 1933, Hitler and his National Socialist Party rose to power in Germany. It was only little by little that the world became aware of the possible international consequences of the German Fascists' advent to power. Many of the European statesmen who were trained in the school of classical bourgeois diplomacy could not realize that Nazi Germany was an utterly aggressive Power of a new type which wanted to take revenge for the defeat suffered in the First World War by aspiring after European hegemony, and whose aggressiveness was fired not by the mere desire to grow into a Great Power equal in rank to the others but by the ambition for exclusiveness in this respect.

In 1933, the Powers which were defending the status quo they had established felt only that the forces taking over the Government in Germany were of the revanchist kind which, once militarily prepared, were ready to assert their claims, for want of other options, even through war. So for a long time, their main problem was how to divert the German demands into acceptable channels, how to check the expansive forces by giving up certain positions in defence of presumably essential power positions in the interest of avoiding a new world war, but failing to realize that thereby, instead of contributing to the maintenance of peace, they promoted the preparation of war and jeopardized their own power positions as well.

The small states of East Central Europe clinging to the status quo only felt that the realization of the Hungarian (and Bulgarian) revisionist aspirations and the Italian designs in the Balkans might be enforced with the assistance of Germany. That is why they grew more and more inclined to thwart those aspirations by making approaches to Germany in case the Powers which had framed the status quo would no longer be able to provide assurances.

The nations which opposed the status quo or were discontented with it only felt that their endeavours might receive support in an alliance with Germany which had a population of sixty million. Therefore, they strove to create such an alliance, but they failed to understand that Germany was aiming at exclusiveness, and not at the division of spheres of interest; that, in relation to the particular countries, what guided Germany's foreign policy was not her view of the status quo, but the Moloch of power interests ready to swallow up other peoples.

In January 1933, Prime Minister Gyula Gömbös also felt that Hitler's rise to power actually brought within reach the realization of the original aim: Italian friendship combined with German friendship. The conception was based on the expectation that the two Great Powers would conclude an alliance and divide the spheres of interest, with the idea that at the meeting-points of the divided spheres of interest Hungary might rely on the balance of power for receiving free hand in the Carpathian basin. Or, as Gömbös put it: Hungarian revisionist demands should be asserted through reliance on Germany in the north and on Italy in the south.

German intransigence regarding the question of the *Anschluss* seemed to be an insuperable obstacle. Besides, it was not in the least clear what attitude Hitler's Germany would adopt in respect of the Hungarian revisionist demands, how she would be ready at a given moment to help Hungary with her most burning problem, the placing of her surplus of agricultural goods. Internationally, Hungary's general position was not exactly rosy either. True, relationships with Italy had been on the upgrade since Gömbös's taking office, but this process coincided with Italy's diplomatic approaches to France, a fact that was not likely to be promising to the aims of Hungary's foreign policy, as was indicated by the quadripartite pact which was arrived at after lengthy discussions (but which ultimately petered out), and which, in respect of equality, mentioned only Germany and left Hungarian revision unmentioned.

Gömbös was thus prompted by the given international position of the country to try to find out what possibilities he could have with regard to Germany. However, he could not entirely leave out of account the moods which dominated a considerable section of political public opinion at home. The brutal retaliation of the Nazi Government against the forces of opposition, including representatives of the bourgeois parties, too; the explosive outburst of German *völkisch* agitation, which made no distinction between 'friendly' and 'hostile' nations; the political practice adopted towards Austria — all this roused deep anxiety not only in left-wing and liberal intellectual circles but also in important groups of the Hungarian bourgeoisie and of the conservative-reactionary forces. On the other hand, many members of leading political quarters were pleased with the course of events in Germany.

The trend of the international situation created a favourable ground for the forces of Fascism in Hungary and encouraged them to try to establish a totalitarian dictatorship in an effort to eliminate the economic, political and social difficulties which had arisen in the years of crisis and had shaken the pillars of the Bethlen type of consolidation internally and internationally alike. In the crisis years, there came again to the fore, under the slogan of salvaging and stabilizing the system, the strata of the gentry, army officers and civil servants which in the twenties had lost their importance for independent aspirations, these strata which constituted the main trustee of what the extreme right represented, and which now, under the guidance of a Prime Minister grown out of their ranks, were looking forward to reaching the summit of power. Gömbös wished to achieve the stabilization of the system by establishing a totalitarian state, by initiating a rightist mass movement relying on the middle classes, by destroying the legitimate organizations of the working-class movement, and by introducing a resounding 'reform programme' resorting to social demagogy. In the first years of Gömbös's premiership, his experiment seemed to go off well, because the ruling classes as a whole stood in shuddering fear of the radical left-wing mass movement during the crisis, and most of them intended to get out of the political and economic misery and chaos by transforming the system of government, even though, in respect of the extent the form and the pace of change, there was a substantial difference of conception between various groups of the ruling classes.

At the same time, Gömbös set his hopes on the good many people — especially intellectuals whose opposition to Bethlen's system implied opposition to the counter-revolution, to the putrefying air of its social immobility, to everything which this system meant on the plane of public life and public morals; opposition to the social injustices, to the poverty of the toiling masses, mainly to the distress of the poor peasantry. These, unaware of the pitfall, were inclined, for a time and for different reasons, to believe that Gömbös's reform programme was not mere social demagogy but a realistic and well-intentioned attempt to carry out social reforms.

Those in the decisive political and economic power positions were well aware of the dangers of such a situation, so much so that they even opposed sham reforms in order to stem the danger, because the real evils in Hungary were rooted so deep that sham reforms could not even create an illusion of alleviating them. In view of the unjust distribution of landed property, and of the great number of destitute and semi-proletarian peasants, genuine social reform in Hungary would have to begin with the solution of the land question. The right-wing tendencies were unable to evade the agrarian question, but the idea of land distribution was contrary to the fundamental interests of the landowning classes. Added to this, the antecedents and circumstances of the victory of the counter-revolutionary system conditioned the ruling classes to oppose political reforms too; and they were against the use of those methods of the arsenal of Fascism which involved 'mass mobilization', no matter how retrograde their motivation was. For this reason, from Gömbös's entry onward, the conservative-reactionary wing of power tried to curb the afore-said tendencies.

Gömbös intended to reinforce his domestic political aspirations by reshaping his foreign policy orientation. Already on the day following Hitler's appointment as Chancellor, the Hungarian Prime Minister, who was in charge of Foreign Affairs for a few weeks early in 1933, instructed his Minister in Berlin to make a formal call on the new Chancellor of Germany and inform him that the Hungarian Government wished to establish co-operation between the two countries on the economic and diplomatic plane, and that the disarmament conference would present a favourable opportunity for such co-operation. Gömbös also referred to the necessity of close co-operation between the Magyar and German national minorities living in the successor states.

The Hungarian Minister in Berlin conveyed Gömbös's message on February 6, 1933. During the conversation, Hitler explained that his main task in foreign policy was to lay the foundations of friendship between Germany and Italy, which, he believed, would create the possibility of German—Hungarian co-operation as well. The establishment of closer relations was, for the time being, hindered by the difficulties of the crisis, but the new German Government intended to let political interests dominate the shaping of Germany's economic relationships. The new Chancellor made no secret of his view that economic expansion was a means of promoting his political aims and he wished to use it for exerting pressure to that end.

Hitler's disquisitions made it clear that he gave the building of German–Italian relations priority over the development of German–Hungarian relations, and so, early in 1933, Gömbös was seeking to promote the rapprochement between the two Fascist Great Powers, an issue in which a key role was played by the *Anschluss* question. Highly instrumental in the new mediating efforts of the Hungarian Government was Bethlen's visit to Germany from March 6 to 18, 1933. The ex-Prime Minister's trip was announced as a lecture tour by a private individual, but the role he played in Hungarian political life left no doubt that his journey served important political purposes. His mission was to give the new German leaders unofficial information about Hungary's foreign and internal policies; by reason of its close co-operation with Italy the Hungarian Government did not want the informative talks to take an official form.

Bethlen conferred with Hitler, Papen, Neurath and Blomberg. He acquainted them with the Hungarian revisionist aims in full detail. He emphasized that Germany could count upon Hungary's support in her confrontation with the Little Entente. In addition to problems of an economic nature, he dwelt mainly on the question of Austria, for this was the main obstacle to the German–Italian rapprochement. The ex-Prime Minister called attention to the fact that, in consequence of the growing activity of Austrian Nazis, Chancellor Dollfuss was compelled to approach the Little Entente, and this should be prevented in the interest of both Germany and Hungary.

In June 1933, Gömbös, first among the heads of Government in Europe to do so, suddenly arrived in Germany on an official visit.

The main topics of his talks with Hitler were the co-ordination of Germany's policy towards Central Europe and of the Hungarian revisionist claims, the *Anschluss* issue and, in this connection, the potentialities of German–Hungarian economic relations.

Hitler approved the Hungarian designs against the Little Entente. He stressed that Germany's foremost foreign political aim was to disrupt the Little Entente and to drive France out of Central Europe, but that he could not support Hungary's revisionist policy in every respect. The Hungarians might count upon German assistance only against Czechoslovakia, because Germany wished to draw Yugoslavia and Rumania, by means of economic penetration, into the orbit of German capital, and at the same time to isolate them from France and Czechoslovakia.

With regard to the *Anschluss,* the Hungarian Prime Minister made the point that Hungary was prompted to think of it mainly for economic reasons, since Austria was one of the most important markets for Hungarian agricultural exports, while the Hungarian–Italian relations could not be left out of consideration either. Gömbös clearly indicated that the Hungarian Government was not really against the *Anschluss,* and that its future attitude would depend not only on the development of German–Hungarian political and economic relationships but on the shaping of the German–Italian relations as well. Hitler replied that Germany did not insist on the immediate annexation of Austria but demanded the granting of rights to the Austrian National Socialists. Hitler felt no great enthusiasm for Bethlen's proposals for a German–Italo–Austrian–Hungarian alliance, for broad-based economic co-operation, for the co-ordination of foreign policies and of the work of General Staffs. The Hungarian Prime Minister offered to mediate between Italy and Germany, and promised to hold back Dollfuss from Franco–Czechoslovak orientation.

The Gömbös–Hitler meeting found unfavourable response in Italy. Mussolini looked at the unfolding of German–Hungarian relations with anxiety; he was for the establishment of closer Italo–Austro–Hungarian relations before Germany could upset his apple-cart by winning Hungary over to her side. At the bottom of Mussolini's plans there was already the idea of a rapprochement with France. In the summer of 1933, there was no serious prospect of an agreement with Germany concerning Central Europe. On the other hand, France – intending to guarantee the independence of Austria in league with Italy and to thus barr Germany's way to the countries of the Danubian basin – was more and more definitely approaching Italy, offering her the settlement of Franco–Italian controversies and certain concessions in Africa; all this in exchange for leaving Austria under Italian influence.

In his letter of July 1 to Gömbös, Mussolini described his conception of the development of Italo–Austro–Hungarian relations in detail. He emphasized that the rapprochement between Austria and Hungary with the effective assistance of Italy would put both states in a position to start negotiations with their neighbours on the footing of equality. "This might serve," he wrote, "to create a whole network of treaties with the states of the Little Entente on the one hand and with Germany on the other, while Austria and Hungary, thanks to their very close relations with Italy, would be secured from both the overt and the covert danger of being swallowed up."

In the summer of 1933, barely half a year after Hitler's accession to power, the Government was confronted with serious problems:

A considerable gap separated the Hungarian political conception from the German aspirations, so the German–Hungarian rapprochement could not, for the time being, be expected to win recognition and support for the Hungarian revisionist demands. On the other hand, Italy, the old partner – seeing that Hitler was opposed to the division of the Central European spheres of interest between Germany and Italy – had a leaning towards an agreement with France, a fact that threatened to be disadvantageous to the Hungarian revisionist aspirations. So the idea of building Hungary's diplomacy on a sort of pendulum policy between German and Italian orientation held out no promises for the time being.

In this situation, the Hungarian policy-makers, for want of anything better, took the view that it was to Hungary's best interest to remain 'in good strength' until revision became feasible. According to papers of the Ministry of Foreign Affairs, dating from 1933, political security was expected to be ensured by the Italian armed forces, all the more so since it was held to take at least ten years to build up a powerful German army. At the same time, continued efforts should be made at the rapprochement with Germany, primarily because Italy could be only of little help in solving Hungary's economic problems. So the German market should be secured. Over and above this, Germany could be counted upon to help — if in nothing else, with regard to the Little Entente — at least in counterbalancing Czechoslovakia. These considerations should determine Hungary's conduct in the *Anschluss* question, too. The tactical idea was first to pretend to be cautious opponents to the *Anschluss,* thus manoeuvring for position in the negotiations with the Germans.

As can be seen, the Hungarian conception of foreign policy in 1933 still rested upon the foundations laid by Bethlen. The professional representative of this policy was Kálmán Kánya, who had occupied leading posts in the Ministry of Foreign Affairs since 1920 and was made Foreign Minister in February 1933. In his conception the 'pendulum policy' meant seeking the combined support of all Powers opposing the Versailles status quo. He not only expected this to enforce revision but possibly to counteract extreme German pressure.

One might ask: What did Gömbös really mean by this conception, how did he make it tally with his foreign political aims? Gömbös certainly had his own point of view: he would have liked to score spectacular, prompt successes in the issue of revision and use them for the promotion of his domestic policy. And since it was increasingly evident that he could rely for success upon the aid of Germany's dynamic foreign policy, he was for the establishment of closer ties between Hungary and Germany. But this effort of his was hindered by obstacles in the way of a German—Italian rapprochement. Thus he also had to try to overcome this hindrance. Therefore, in concert with the Ministry of Foreign Affairs, Gömbös broached the idea of a German—Austro—Hungarian alliance in reply to Mussolini's letter proposing an Italo—Austro—Hungarian alliance. He stressed that his journey to Berlin had not made him change his mind, but in his opinion, Hungary had to foster friendship with Germany in additon to Austria, and this was made necessary not only by economic but by political considerations, notably by the aim of co-operation against Czechoslovakia. The struggle against the Little Entente was a requisite for the Austro—Hungarian rapprochement. Hungary would not be ready for co-operation with the Little Entente beyond normal economic relations until her political demands had been satisfied.

Although Gömbös knew that the Austrians as well as the Italians were only pressing for the rapprochement with Hungary in order to secure protection from the predominance of Germany, he nevertheless maintained that in opposition to the defenders of the status quo, Germany and Italy had generally identical international interests, so they would sooner of later have to come to terms on the basis of the division of the spheres of influence. (By the way, the Italians also fell in with this view.) Therefore Gömbös conceived the Italo—Austro—Hungarian bloc proposed by Mussolini to be a formation that might in the future become Germany's Central European ally.

This conception was given expression during Gömbös's official visit to Vienna on July 9—10, 1933. As the result of negotiations with Dollfuss about the Austro—Hungarian rapprochement proposed by the Duce, the following agreement was entered into between Hungary and Austria: 1. In any question concerning both countries neither side shall decide without consulting the other side. 2. The foreign policy of both states shall be based on friendship with Italy. 3. Both countries shall endeavour to improve relations with Germany, but this must be conditional on Germany's recognition of Austrian and Hungarian independence. 4. Aware of Hungary's special position towards the Little Entente, Austria "is ready to support Hungary's defence against the hegemonic policies of the Little Entente".

This agreement, Articles 3 and 4 of which were based on a mutual compromise, practically laid the foundations of the Rome protocol of 1934. Shortly after the Austro–Hungarian negotiations, on July 26, 1933, Italo–Hungarian talks started in Rome with the participation of the Prime Ministers and Foreign Ministers about questions of closer Italo–Austro–Hungarian co-operation. The guiding principle of Gömbös's view was that the three countries should establish friendly relations with Germany, and since the main obstacle to this was constituted by the differences between Germany and Austria, the Italian Government ought to take steps in Berlin with a view to settling this problem. Mussolini, on the other hand, not being against German–Italian rapprochement, laid emphasis on the preservation of Austrian independence and the necessity of a triple alliance. Albeit in his note made of the negotiations, he yielded to the Hungarian position, during the discussions, the Duce did not conceal that he would give up neither the French line nor his plans regarding the Little Entente. At the same time, he assured the Hungarian Prime Minister that he continued to uphold Hungary's revisionist claims. In the matter of Italo–Austro–Hungarian economic relations, it was stressed that both negotiating parties were ready in principle to establish a customs union of the three countries; and until the conditions became ripe for this, they would continue developing their economic contacts on the basis of the Semmering convention of 1931 providing for mutual preferences. Finally, they agreed that they would endeavour to establish closer relations between Austria and Hungary so as to preclude the possibility of a Habsburg restoration and of a personal union in general.

From the angle of Hungary's foreign political aspirations, the Rome talks took place at an auspicious time. In view of the possibility of a German–Hungarian rapprochement, the Italian Government treated the Hungarian interests with the utmost care, being afraid of losing an ally who might secure Italy's power influence in the Danubian basin. It showed appreciation of Hungary's German connections and took notice of her terms concerning relations to be established with the Little Entente. The reason for this was that Mussolini did not drop the issue of German–Italo–French relations either. After the Rome negotiations the Hungarian Ministry of Foreign Affairs was of the opinion that the further shaping of these relations depended on the behaviour of Germany, namely on whether the Nazi Government would be willing to accede to the Italian demands. The conclusion it arrived at, was that Budapest might in a certain sense play the role of mediator between Berlin and Rome, and this might, for a short time, give Hungary's foreign policy some momentum and a free play.

Since Germany persisted in refusing to enter into any South Eastern European agreement based on concessions and continued her policy of interference in Austrian affairs, Mussolini speeded up his activity aimed at the extension and reinforcement of the Italian sphere of influence. In January and February 1934, Austro–Italian, Austro–Hungarian and Italo–Hungarian negotiations took place in Vienna and Budapest, respectively, about the creation of a triple alliance. At the end of these talks, Gömbös summed up his position stating that the most urging issue of Hungary's foreign policy was to connect Austria with the Italo–Hungarian political line, but this should, by no means, be pointed against Germany.

German leading quarters looked at the Italo–Austro–Hungarian negotiations with displeasure; they feared that the alliance of the three states might take a form which could render it very difficult to achieve their aims concerning Central Europe. To prevent this, they wanted to rely upon Hungary in the first place, and with good reason. The Hungarian Government also found it necessary to reassure the Germans. On February 26, 1934, Foreign Minister Kánya told the German Minister in Budapest that in the Austrian question Hungary desired a solution which was not directed against Germany, and that in the future he would further let Italy understand that friendship with Germany was indispensable to Hungary.

Indeed, in a Rome conversation between Gömbös and Mussolini, on the day before the three-Power negotiations, the Hungarian Prime Minister set forth that this conference should bring concrete results on which to build a policy in the long run. Mussolini invariably put emphasis on Austrian independence, stating that it might be to the advantage of Hungary, too. Gömbös, on the other hand, arguing that in the given international situation Germany could by no means make an attempt at the *Anschluss,* took the position that it was needless for Hungary to take an explicit stand.

The official negotiations between Italy, Austria and Hungary started in Rome on March 14, 1934. They began with the discussion of political questions. The negotiating parties accepted as a general starting-point that the broadest possible political and economic co-operation of the three countries was necessary. The political questions of direct concern to the three countries centred on the relations between Germany and Austria. So, in the interest of 'peace and high policy' those relations should be improved. Here, however, each party stated its own position. Dollfuss insisted that such improvement was feasible only if Germany recognized the independence of Austria, and stopped interfering in Austrian internal affairs. Gömbös, on the other hand, did not fail to point out that in the interest of a territorial revision, Hungary could not do without Germany's assistance. Mussolini and Dollfuss even conceded that Hungary was in a special position regarding the development of German–Hungarian relationships. In the end, all three countries admitted that understanding with Germany was necessary.

The agenda of the first day included a number of other important questions. Dollfuss said that both internal and foreign political reasons militated against a Habsburg restoration. Gömbös again stated that Hungary was only willing to negotiate with the Little Entente after the satisfaction of her revisionist claims. Finally, it came to the drawing up of the communiqué. Gömbös wished to interpret the paragraph concerning the possible joining of other states as being applicable to Germany in the first place and to the Little Entente states only in the second place, that is, only after the satisfaction of the Hungarian demands.

The economic questions came up for discussion on the second day. Hungary succeeded in making contracts for the delivery of a considerable amount of grain to Italy and Austria.

The Rome Protocol was signed on March 17, 1934. To be precise, the agreements were framed in three documents. The first was about political co-operation between the three states, the second was about economic co-operation, and the third about the development of Italo—Austrian economic contacts. The text of the political agreement ran as follows: "The Royal Hungarian Prime Minister, the Federal Chancellor of the Republic of Austria and the Head of the Government of His Majesty the King of Italy, in an effort to contribute to the maintenance of peace and to the economic reconstruction of Europe on the basis of respect for the independence and rights of all states, in the belief that joint action to this effect on the part of the three Governments will create the objective conditions for more extensive co-operation with other states, and with a view to attaining the above aims, undertake to consult one another about any question of special interest to them, as well as about questions of a general character, in order that, in the spirit of the treaties of friendship in force between Hungary and Austria, between Hungary and Italy, and between Austria and Italy, treaties which are based on awareness of the existence of many common interests, they shall co-ordinate their policies aimed at the fostering of genuine co-operation between European states, and in particular between Hungary, Austria and Italy. With this end in view the three Governments shall meet in conference whenever at least one of them deems it necessary."

From Italy's endeavours and from the events related to the Rome agreements it appears that the political aspect of the pact was meant to strengthen Italy's influence and to weaken Germany's position in Central Europe. On the other hand, one of the main problems of the Hungarian Government was invariably how to dispel the German suspicions and to prevent the accord from being extended to apply to the Little Entente states.

Immediately after the Rome negotiations, Gömbös had a discussion with the German Ambassador in Rome and explained to him that the agreements were not directed against Germany. In the spring of 1934, he made further attempts at mediation in this spirit in order to iron out the Italo—German differences. Barely a few weeks after the signing of the Rome agreements, early in May 1934, in connection with rumours of a Habsburg restoration, Horthy sent Hitler a message in which he proposed the improvement of German—Austrian relations and thus some sort of accommodation with Austria. Of course, Horthy and his men were bothered by the rumours of restoration not only for reasons of internal policy; they were also afraid that the intensification of such efforts might lead to closer German—Yugoslav collaboration. The Hungarian Ministry of Foreign Affairs, in the course of 1934, received information, through various channels, about preparations to this effect.

The German Minister in Budapest, Mackensen, brought the reply to Horthy's message on May 29, 1934. Hitler intimated to Horthy that, since Dollfuss was stubbornly against satisfying the demands of the National Socialists, it was highly improbable that the talks proposed by the Regent could yield any result. Germany would start negotiations with the Austrian Government only if this consented to a plebiscite in Austria. Neither the Hungarian attempts at mediation nor the Hitler–Mussolini meeting brought any success. Hitler did not renounce the use of force against Austria. This is how in July 1934, it came to the putsch of Austrian National Socialists, in the course of which Chancellor Dollfuss was assassinated.

The Hungarian Government viewed the events in Austria with anxiety; it was afraid of a German–Italian conflict which would have ruined the hopes pinned on a combination of the Fascist Powers. Beset with this nightmare, Gömbös, on July 27, sent Mussolini a message in which he argued that the Austrians were capable of liquidating the uprising by themselves, and expounded his view that military intervention on the part of Italy was unnecessary even in case the restoration of order would take a longer time. Mussolini's answer conveyed through the Hungarian Minister in Rome, allayed the tension. He said that he did not seriously contemplate any act of intervention, that he would intervene only in case of an emergency and at the express request of the Austrian Government. This reply confirmed the Hungarian Government circles in the belief that the idea of a German–Italian understanding must not be abandoned, that the policy of reconcilement must be continued.

The events which took place in Austria in the summer of 1934 were highly responsible for the reshufflement of international relations in Europe. One of the most important new features was the entry of the Soviet Union on the scene of world politics. The reason for this can be found in the peace efforts of Soviet policy as well as in the fact that the French ruling classes realized that the existing network of alliances provided no sufficient protection to France against reviving and increasingly powerful German imperialism, and that new guarantees should be sought. In spite of repeated French demands, England was unwilling to commit herself to the maintenance of the Eastern status quo. French Foreign Minister Barthou, recognizing the impending danger, wished to change the French policy built solely on British orientation and on the exclusion of the Soviet Union from European affairs. The steps taken towards an Eastern pact correlated with the continued strengthening of the international position of the Soviet Union. The Gömbös Government could not evade the impact of this process. In February 1934, mainly upon Italian insistence, it came at last to the establishment of Soviet–Hungarian diplomatic relations. Instrumental in this decision was also the fact that, with reference to the growing German peril, the Zagreb Conference of the Little Entente decided in January 1934, for the member countries to take up diplomatic relations with the Soviet Union, and that Czechoslovakia and Rumania shortly thereafter carried out this recommendation. In September 1934, members of the League of Nations invited the Soviet Union to join the international organization.

Thus in the latter half of 1934, the general international situation was shaping favourably from the point of view of the maintenance of peace. A defensive system based on the Franco—Soviet alliance was taking shape, and the idea of collective security gained ground with the growing diplomatic activity of the Soviet Union.

The attempted Nazi putsch in Austria also strengthened the Franco—Italian rapprochement; Mussolini, through looking askance at Barthou's efforts to 'rigidify' the Central European system, still sought France's friendship, with an eye to protecting Italy's interests in the Danubian basin and furthering her African aspirations.

These developments, and especially the French orientation of Italian foreign policy made the Hungarian Government pretty uncomfortable. The Italo—French rapprochement involved the danger of efforts being made to have Hungary adhere to pro-French policy or to compel her to choose between Italy and Germany. The solution of the problem was made difficult by the fact that the Hungarian Government did not believe in the feasibility of a revision with France's consent, which Italy had promised to procure, while the Germans visibly showed growing interests in Yugoslavia and Rumania, thus frustrating again the Hungarian revisionist |plans.

The Nazi leaders even uttered threats against the Hungarian Government. Through András Mecsér, a Hungarian Nazi who had attended the Nuremberg party rally in September 1934, they sent word to Budapest that they expected Hungary to take a definite stand, or else Germany would build her Central European policy on Yugoslavia and Rumania. And this would imply priority given to the interests of these countries. This time, the Germans expected Hungary to mediate more effectively between Berlin and Rome. At that time, this meant first of all keeping Italy back from the French orientation.

The Italian orientation of Hungarian foreign policy was still strengthened for a time by the intensifying rapprochement of Germany with Yugoslavia and Rumania and by the international situation after the regicide at Marseilles. On October 9, 1934, a Macedonian terrorist assassinated King Alexander of Yugoslavia and French Foreign Minister Louis Barthou at Marseilles. The assassin was hacked to pieces on the spot, but his four accomplices, who belonged to the Croatian Ustashi organization, were arrested by the French police. The plot which roused furious international indignation could be traced back in part to Budapest; the four Ustashi had been trained in Hungary, at Jankapuszta in the vicinity of the Yugoslav frontier. From the early twenties the Hungarian Government, as mentioned above, gave every possible material and other support to the Croatian separatist movement. After 1929, the year of dictatorial change in Yugoslavia, it kept in touch with émigré leaders of the Law Party, the founders of the Ustashi organizations, and, in 1932, it allowed them to take the Jankapuszta estate on lease for camping and training purposes.

As regards the assassination proper, it seems probable that the Hungarian Government, though having no share in its execution, knew about the preparations, even if it had no information about the details. In any case, Hungary's complicity in the Marseilles affair could hardly have been denied, and this put the Government in an awkward position internationally, all the more so, since the Western Powers did not wish — and the Little Entente states did not dare — to pry into the responsibility of Italy and Germany. Thus it could be expected that all responsibility would be shifted on to Hungary.

The assassinations at Marseilles causing immense infuriation all over the world temporarily plunged Hungary into almost complete international isolation. This was peculiarly to the advantage of Gömbös's domestic policy, because the appeal for 'internal unity' in the state of 'national aggravation' found response in part of the opposition as well, and this fact was given expression in the opposition's gradual reconciliation with the Government, but the prospects of Hungary's international relations underwent an unprecedented deterioration. The international isolation resulted not only from the impeachment of Hungary by the League of Nations, and from the extremely incisive tone adopted towards Hungary by the states of the Little Entente, Yugoslavia in particular, but also from the fact that Germany — seeing a possibility of rapprochement with Yugoslavia — denied the Hungarian Government every kind of support. (This found an expression in Goering's ostentatious appearance at the funeral of the King of Yugoslavia, as well as in German pronouncements against Hungary's revisionist ambitions.)

In this situation, some support could be obtained from Poland: Gömbös left for Warsaw on October 19, 1934. By that time Piłsudski had already brought off an agreement with Hitler, and now Gömbös offered to conclude a treaty between the two countries. But Piłsudski, referring to his allies, did not accept the offer. On the other hand, it is a fact that he solemnly declared that Poland would never make war on Hungary and would do everything possible to keep back Rumania from taking such a step.

The Hungarian Government could expect support from Mussolini in the first place considering that he, as chief protector of the Ustashi, was also interested in glossing over the affair. On November 4, 1934, Gömbös left for Rome to discuss, among other things, the tactics to be applied in the Marseilles issue. The talks also covered the question of extending the triple accord of Rome. After the conclusion of the negotiations, Gömbös made a statement in which, in connection with the conditions of co-operation with Germany, he laid special emphasis on the necessity of safeguarding the independence of Austria. And on November 8, he met Chancellor Schuschnigg of Austria at the Semmering, and assured him of Hungary's full solidarity, demanding, in exchange, Austrian support against the assaults by the Little Entente in the matter of the Marseilles assassination case.

With regard to the plan of extending the triple accord of Rome and the issue of the Franco–Italian rapprochement, Gömbös managed to persuade Mussolini to accept the Hungarian terms, including the demand for revision. And in the Marseilles affair, by pointing out that in case of continued attacks against her, Hungary would appeal to the League of Nations to institute a thorough inquiry into the matter, Gömbös succeeded in securing the Duce's absolute support.

In a special meeting on December 10, 1934, the Council of the League considered Yugoslavia's petition exposing the responsibility of the Hungarian Government regarding the regicide at Marseilles. But the Council, under pressure from Great Britain, Italy and France (at that time French external affairs were already in the hands of Laval), adopted a resolution leaving it to the Hungarian state to decide what responsibility rested on its inferior organs and what penalty to impose on them.

The League of Nations resolution relieved the Hungarian Government of the oppressive burden of the Marseilles affair, thus enabling it to increase its activity in preparing the rapprochement with Germany and to carry out its domestic political plans.

Towards the end of 1934, Mussolini's flirtation with France brought a concrete result, a draft political agreement called the Danube Pact. Early in January, Hungarian Foreign Minister Kánya received the text of the chapter of the Franco–Italian draft agreement dealing with Central Europe. This stated that a survey of the situation in Central Europe and especially in Austria had convinced France and Italy of the necessity that the interested states should, under the auspices of the League of Nations, conclude a convention placing them under the obligation not to interfere in one another's internal affairs and not to promote any propaganda directed against the territorial integrity of another contracting state or aimed at effecting a drastic change in its political and social system. It was contemplated that the convention should be concluded by Austria, Czechoslovakia, Germany, Hungary, Italy and Yugoslavia and acceded to by Great Britain, France, Poland, Rumania and later by other states as well.

The draft gave no preferences to Hungary, since it not only contained the guarantees of Austrian independence, as had originally been envisaged, but provided for non-intervention in one another's affairs and respect for the territorial integrity of the states concerned.

On January 3, Kánya informed the Italians that the Hungarian Government could accept the provisions on non-intervention and on the prohibition of propaganda only in case of appropriate guarantees being stipulated for the observance of the treaties on the protection of national minorities, and that Hungary would accede only to the pact together with Germany. The following day, Gömbös sent Mussolini a message requesting the exclusion of the Little Entente, because Hungary could not sign a document which recognized the integrity of the Little Entente states; this, he stated in conclusion, would have an adverse effect on the cogency of the triple accord of Rome.

At that time, however, Mussolini could hardly be inconvenienced by the negative attitude of the Hungarians. In his plans, he gave priority to Italian expansion in Africa. During his talks with Laval in January 1935, therefore, in order to win France's consent to his African scheme, he accepted the original draft of the Danube Pact. At the same time, he tried to break Gömbös's obstinacy. On January 11, Italy's representative at the League in Geneva reproved Kánya for Hungary's negative attitude, which, "after what Italy has done in order to gloss over the Marseilles affair, can rightly be qualified as disloyalty". He then expounded that France would gradually drop her Little Entente allies for the sake of the more important Italian alliance, and this would open up better possibilities to Hungary too. The Hungarian Foreign Minister received this argument sceptically and declared that his Government would only be ready to adhere to the pact in case of the recognition of Hungary's right to rearm and in exchange for extensive concessions in the minority question.

At the same time, Hungary, as mentioned before, made approaches to Germany. Already on New Year's Eve, Gömbös had written a letter to Minister of War Blomberg: he emphasized the importance of German–Hungarian co-operation north of the Danube. He concluded his letter by saying how pleased he would be if he, or Horthy in person, could discuss the possibilities of further developing German–Hungarian relations with Blomberg in Berlin.

In January 1935, Kánya instructed the Hungarian Minister in Berlin to make the Franco–Italian draft known to the German Government and to explain that in the opinion of the Hungarian Government the pact was certainly directed against Germany but would become unnecessary – and this view was apparently shared by Italy – if Germany should openly declare that she would respect the independence of Austria.

The building of German–Hungarian relations reached the next stage when Goering made a honeymoon trip to Hungary on May 24–25, 1935. It was Goering's intention to get a clear picture of the main lines of Hungary's foreign policy and, beyond that, to make the revisionist policy subject to German interests. Still in Berlin, he had told Masirevich, the Hungarian Minister, that the Hungarians would never succeed in their revisionist schemes if they persisted in pursuing their hostile policy towards the Little Entente states. It would be well for them to understand the German aspirations and to try to disrupt the Little Entente by coming to terms with Yugoslavia and concentrating their forces against Czechoslovakia. With respect to Hungary's foreign policy in general, Horthy and his men sought to reassure Goering, but still took no clear position regarding the latter subject. Early in 1935, the efforts of Hungarian foreign policy thus proved to be of no avail in relation to Germany either.

In the meantime, France and Italy had attempted, on the basis of previous information from the Governments concerned, to give effect to the Danube Pact. This was a matter of great urgency because on March 16, 1935, Germany unilaterally declared the military clauses of the Versailles treaty null and void and introduced universal conscription. In reply to this step England, France and Italy, assembled at the Stresa conference, adopted a declaration protesting against the unilateral repudiation of international treaties.

On May 6, 1935, the Hungarian Government stated its definitive position at the Foreign Ministers' conference of the states signatories to the Rome Protocol. Kánya repeated the terms, insisting that the Central European pact should provide for the continuance of revisionist propaganda. In fact, this incurred flat refusal. Since Germany and Yugoslavia also made their accession subject to unacceptable conditions, the plan of the Danube Pact was removed from the agenda. This, however, brought only temporary improvement in Hungary's international position, although it fortunately coincided with Gömbös's successes in domestic politics.

In the summer of 1935, Mussolini started immediate preparations for the realization of his scheme of conquest in Africa. The preparations for aggression on Ethiopia were the prelude to further changes in the international situation and consequently to the reorganization of Italy's foreign relations. The 'Stresa front', just created, began to break up. Estrangement came about first of all in Anglo–Italian relations. At the same time, a slow hidden process of improvement in German—Italian relations began, since Mussolini, to protect his rear on the march into Africa, would have liked to reduce his differences with Germany.

Indications of a change in the relations between Germany and Italy became visible from May 1935. Negotiations were started about the Austrian question, an agreement was reached for the mutual suppression of the use of abusive language in the press, and so forth. All this encouraged the Duce, in spite of increasing pressure from Britain, to embark on his Abyssinian adventure. War started in October 1935.

The Hungarian Government was the first to congratulate the Italian dictator. Later it voted 'no' to the economic sanctions proposed against Italy in the League of Nations. Mussolini's war in Africa came in handy for Hungarian foreign policy, in so far as it brought Italy closer to Germany. On the other hand, since it weakened the Italian position militarily and internationally, it brought no comfort to the foreign policy of Hungary. In the general international situation created by the Italo—Abyssinian war the Hungarian Government had reason to be afraid that Italy and Germany might arrive at an agreement from which Hungary would be excluded and in which Italy, instead of being an equal partner, might play a subordinate role.

Gömbös therefore sought to strengthen the Hungarian positions in Germany. Already prior to the commencement of the African campaign by Italy he, and his Foreign Minister went to Berlin, where he again set forth his view of an Italo—German—Austro—Hungarian alliance, but cautiously began to sell the position of the Hungarian Government regarding the *Anschluss* question. In private, Hitler promised Gömbös that Hungary would receive back Burgenland if she should render Germany effective assistance in her effort to take possession of Austria, but he also let him understand that the Hungarian Government had to abandon its hostile attitude towards Yugoslavia and Rumania.

According to some sources, the Hungarian Prime Minister had an exchange of views with Goering about a change in Hungary's internal power policies, and they reached a secret agreement on mutual support for the future totalitarian systems in the two countries.

This time Gömbös made effective promises, but Berlin did not yet commit itself. The main goal which the German Government wished to attain through these negotiations, as appears from the preparatory papers of the German Foreign Ministry, was to make it clear to Gömbös that "the primacy of German leadership must definitely be acknowledged by the Hungarians in case of political collaboration"; moreover, that "... the results of friendly relations between Germany and Hungary shall certainly depend — last but not least — also on Hungary's attitude, for it stands to reason that Hungary cannot expect Germany to pay regard to Hungarian interests if she herself fails to make allowance for German interests." Towards the end of 1935, Gömbös appointed General Döme Sztójay, a leading figure of the extremist revisionist officers' groups closely bound to the German General Staff, to head the Hungarian Legation in Berlin, and from that time onward, Sztójay conveyed the German wishes not only faithfully but in terms of profound sympathy.

In the months following the start of the war on Ethiopia, Mussolini made the decisive steps towards Germany, as could be expected. In January 1936, he sent Hitler a message stating that he would no more go back to the Stresa policy and had no objection to Austria's adopting a policy 'parallel' with Germany or even concluding an alliance with her. Two months later, he submitted a written declaration to the effect that he would not support England and France against Germany if the latter should denounce the Locarno treaty; this implied, at the same time, approval of Germany's schemes against Austria and Czechoslovakia.

Now the formal establishment of the 'Axis' was only a matter of time. In this situation Hitler — encouraged also by the Western Great Powers' hesitation to apply severe sanctions against Italy — on March 7, 1937, occupied the demilitarized left bank of the Rhine, thus violating the Locarno treaty.

The Italian aggression and the arbitrary move of Germany indicated the coming of tragic changes in international relations. The changes began to cast dark shadows on the peoples of Central Europe. The Italian and German blows dealt at the League of Nations, and the fact that in the matter of Abyssinia Mussolini did not get the assistance he had expected on the basis of the agreement of January 1935 from France, gradually brought the two Fascist Powers closer together. At the same time, in part as a result of Italy's preoccupation in Africa, German influence over Central Europe increased. After the occupation of the Rhineland, France was no longer in a position to march into the Rhine zone in case of a German aggression in the East; consequently France's allies in Central Europe lost some of their importance for French interests, and even France's importance diminished from the point of view of the Little Entente states and Poland. Of still more serious consequence was England's increasingly pronounced retirement from the problems of Central Europe. In January 1936, seizing the occasion when leading European statesmen arrived in London to attend the funeral of King George V, the British Government made another attempt to clarify the Central European questions by means of multilateral negotiations and British mediation.

On May 16, 1936, Horthy, afraid that the British attempts or a conference of the Great Powers might lead to the stabilization of the status quo, wrote a long letter to the new King of England, Edward VIII, who, as Prince of Wales, had several times visited Hungary. Horthy pointed out that if a treaty should again be of wrong construction and the suffering peoples should gain no hearing, then it would surely build the foundations of a disaster. His letter contained passionate outbursts against the Soviet Union and Bolshevism. Horthy's letter was shelved in London with the remark that it was a rather wild comment upon the international situation, a document of the erroneous line of Hungarian foreign policy.

The attempt failed mainly because the British were unwilling to assure guarantees. From then on, the British Government showed growing unconcern for Central European affairs. Sir Robert Vansittart, Under-Secretary of State for Foreign Affairs, explained his Government's position to the Hungarian chargé d'affaires in London, stressing that the British public opinion was little concerned with the fate of Central

Europe; in this situation the Government was in no position to make commitments for smoothing out the differences of the Danubian basin and securing its future; Central Europe and the Balkans did not present any considerable openings for the British economy, and future prospects were not promising either.

Indeed, the prospects were not promising, especially not for the peoples of Central Europe. The situation was tellingly described by a telegram which, on July 12, 1936, the French Ambassador in Bucharest, d'Ormesson, sent to the Quai d'Orsay from the Little Entente conference held in Bucharest: "The Little Entente, which was originally directed against Hungary and has preserved its unity in this relation, does not want now to take action against Germany unless under circumstances in which the Western Powers themselves are willing to do so. The attitude of Paris and London thus becomes more and more the key of defence against German politico-military expansion in the direction of Central Europe and the Balkans." At the time, however, this key was too unwieldy to be used.

But even under such circumstances, attempts were made chiefly upon Czechoslovak initiative, to stabilize the situation in the Danubian basin and — even though in a vague and contradictory manner — to contain the German advance by bringing Czechoslovakia, Austria and Hungary closer together (such an experiment was, e.g., the Hodža plan). But these attempts were wrecked in the labyrinth of conflicting interests. In Rumania, Titulescu, who wanted to strengthen relations with the Soviet Union, was dismissed. Rumanian foreign policy increasingly stressed that the Little Entente states must not work against Germany, with whom they wished to come to terms. Yugoslavia concluded an agreement with Germany. The German Government stated that it refused to support the Hungarian revisionist claims and, if requested, would willingly guarantee the frontiers of Yugoslavia; in return, the Yugoslav leaders declared that they did not and would not commit themselves to any anti-German combination. Poland renewed her relations of alliance with France and Rumania, but she underlined her opposition to the principle of collective security. To prevent the stabilization of relations in the Danubian basin, counter-revolutionary Hungary had — already from the moment of Hitler's victory — endeavoured, even against Italy, to play into the hands of the Germans.

This was reflected in the Austro–Hungarian negotiations held in Budapest on March 13–14, 1936, prior to the conference of the states signatory to the Rome Pact. The Hungarian Foreign Minister managed to convince Chancellor Schuschnigg that, until the Italo–Abyssinian conflict was settled, the Rome Pact states should carefully avoid any Central European combination and refrain from making any statement which Germany might regard as harmful to her interests.

The Prime Ministers and Foreign Ministers of the states of the Rome Pact met in conference in the Italian capital from March 21 to 23, 1936. Mussolini suggested that the Rome agreements should gradually be developed into an alliance and the parties should establish a customs union. Gömbös approved of Mussolini's idea, mainly because he expected, and with reason, to keep Austria back from a rapprochement with the Little Entente. He proposed at the same time that the Rome bloc be extended to include, first of all, Germany and Poland. However, he did not succeed in having this put on record as he also failed in the object of having the records support the Hungarian territorial claims. The idea of having the Little Entente states accede to the Rome bloc was ultimately rejected by resolution.

Finally, the resolutions of the 1934 protocol were confirmed, and the participants adopted complementary protocols to the Rome Pact, providing as follows:

1. A permanent consultative body composed of the Foreign Ministers of Member states shall be set up.

2. Negotiations about Danubian problems which may lead to the conclusion of a treaty of a political character shall be started by any one of the Member states only with the approval of the other two Members.

3. Agreements for the expansion of trade with the Little Entente states shall be concluded only in the form of bilateral treaties.

The unfolding of German—Italian political co-operation was given a new impulse by the outbreak, in July 1936, of the Spanish civil war, in which an important part was played by the intervention of the two Fascist Powers.

At the outbreak of the Spanish civil war the Hungarian Government evaded its contractual economic obligations towards republican Spain and promised to supply arms to General Franco. It used every means at international forums to support the rebels, in spite of the fact that it maintained diplomatic relations with the Madrid Republican Government until the autumn of 1937

In September 1937, Horthy's Hungary recognized Franco's régime and established diplomatic relations with it.

Simultaneously with the improvement of German—Italian relations, Italy's influence was declining and her positions in Central Europe were weakening. There is no doupt that this was the main reason for the first meeting between Hitler and Horthy on August 22, 1936, at Salzburg where the Regent of Hungary had occasion to listen to the Führer's monologue about the dangers of Communism, about the Italo—German rapprochement and his designs against Czechoslovakia. What he heard then was pleasing to Horthy, who emphasized the necessity of Anglo—German understanding, but the meeting brought no concrete results for the time being.

From the point of view of the German advance, the visit to Berlin, in October 1936, by the new Italian Foreign Minister, Count Galeazzo Ciano was of great significance. Ciano's negotiations in Berlin laid the foundations for the Fascist Berlin—Rome Axis. A German—Italian secret protocol, signed on October 25, stated in its paragraph concerning Central Europe that "the two Governments shall deal with the political and economic problems of the Danubian basin in the spirit of amicable collaboration."

The 'Axis' was thus established, but Gömbös, who — with no little self-conceit — believed he was the creator of the Axis, did not live to see its birth. He died of nephrosclerosis in October 1936. And Hungarian foreign policy had to face the failure of the conception intended to build upon a balance of forces within the alliance of the two Fascist Powers. This equilibrium was non-existent, because Italy had, from the outset, been oppressed by the overwhelming superiority of Germany. No mutual concessions were made, nor did Germany commit herself in any respect to support the Hungarian revisionist demands. The *Anschluss* was also decided, Hungary's consent could not be made subject to conditions. Now Hungary had to pay for German assistance.

With the birth of the Berlin–Rome Axis, Hungarian foreign policy reached the end of a nearly ten-year period which had begun with Bethlen's 'active foreign policy' to switch over to Gömbös's pendulum policy of balancing between the two Fascist Powers, a policy which, with the given international power relations, enabled Hungarian foreign policy to enjoy some influence and independence for a certain time.

Bethlen's conception of Hungarian foreign policy had, from the moment of the régime's birth, built all hopes for a revision of the peace treaty upon a radical change in the international situation owing to the revival of Germany. The expected changes in the international power relations did, in fact, happen within a decade and a half, but the conception of Hungarian foreign policy failed precisely at a time when it seemed to succeed, because, while the counter-revolutionary régime could pull its feet out of the pillory of the Versailles peace system, its neck got stuck in the tight squeeze of German power supremacy. Once the 'Axis' came into existence, German pressure could no longer be counteracted. And the search for new possibilities was, until the final collapse, hamstrung by the web of revisionist endeavours and internal political power relations.

2. The foreign policy of the Darányi Government

On November 11–12, 1936, barely a few weeks after the appointment of Prime Minister Kálmán Darányi, the representatives of the Rome Pact states again met in conference at Vienna. The conference was already dominated by the spirit of the Berlin–Rome Axis. The participants took note of the German–Italian accords approvingly. They agreed that if Italy should quit the League of Nations they would jointly decide what step Hungary and Austria should take. Hungary and Austria recognized the Italian Empire of Ethiopia. And finally they all confirmed the Rome Pact and the complementary protocols.

After the Vienna meeting, Ciano spent two days conferring in Budapest. What he said indicated that Italy was no longer willing to support Austria at the risk of forfeiting her good relations with Germany. At the same time, Ciano emphatically recommended the Hungarian Government to improve relations with Yugoslavia. He stressed that Italy had the same intention and had even stopped supporting the Croatian separatists for the time being. Behind the Italian Foreign Minister's suggestion it is easy to discover two seemingly opposite but actually interdependent factors. On the one hand, the rapprochement with Yugoslavia tallied with Germany's efforts to disrupt the Little Entente and to pave the way for German power influence in South Eastern Europe. On the other hand, the Italians, who had willy-nilly given up trying to prevent the *Anschluss,* secretly contemplated a scheme, in case of the elimination of Austria, to maintain the balance by a Rome—Belgrade—Budapest line; this 'second line of defence' was intended later to include Poland, too.

The idea of the Italian—Yugoslav—Hungarian—Polish 'horizontal axis' did not pass unheeded in Hungary either due especially to the failure of Gömbös's efforts.

As the storm of the world economic crisis was abating, the conservative-reactionary wing of the Hungarian ruling classes — first of all the aristocratic and finance-capitalist circles — had gradually turned against Gömbös, whose social demagogy and dictatorial ambitions they found dangerous, so they eventually stood up for the preservation of the constitutional rules established by Bethlen. This opposition took a definite shape when Gömbös, on the occasion of the elections in January 1935, disclosed his conception of the creation of a Fascist dictatorship and set about reorganizing the Government Party into a Fascist mass party, and when, as a result of the elections, representatives of the gentry, army officers and civil servants gained the upper hand in the Government Party, and substantial changes were made in the personnel of the state administration to the advantage of the extreme right. The moment the elections were called, the Government Party split: Bethlen with a few of this followers withdrew from the party and formed an independent group. Gömbös's ambitions were opposed also by another faction which, though following Bethlen, remained in the ranks of the Government Party. The alliance between Gömbös and the Smallholders' Party headed by Tibor Eckhardt broke up during the elections. From that time on, the Smallholders' Party became increasingly 'constitutionalist' and liberal in both foreign and domestic policy. And last but not least, the opponents of the experiments in totalitarianism received strong support from the liberal parties and the Social Democratic Party. The concerted action of these forces seemed sufficient to bring about the fall of Gömbös; the Prime Minister was saved from a formal fall only by his sudden death.

The pro-Bethlen groups of the ruling classes were also prompted to turn against Gömbös's ambitions by the shift in the international power relations: there was uneasiness because the balance between Germany and Italy was tipping, the German superiority within the Fascist Axis was growing, and because they saw the consolidation of German orientation in Hungarian foreign policy. In domestic policy, the German orientation was increasingly helpful to the forces of the extreme right, which, by applying more and more consistently the German-type Fascist methods, endangered the economic and political influence and positions of the finance capitalists — composed mostly of Jews — and of the aristocratic, mainly legitimist, big landowners. Of course, these groups were not against German orientation proper but only wished German—Hungarian co-operation to remain on the plane of foreign politics and not to lead — in Bethlen's words — to "the regimenting of political life to the taste of the extreme right."

In 1935/1936, there were many signs on an international scale indicating the growth of opposition to Fascism and war: the victory of the Popular Front in France and Spain, the Spanish people's courageous and stout resistance to the Fascist forces, the growing diplomatic activity of the Soviet Union, certain positive elements in the policy of the Little Entente towards the Soviet state. As a result of all this, the Western Powers, especially France, intensified their diplomatic activity in Eastern Europe, and beside the policy of 'appeasement' there were half-hearted efforts at collective security, which were given expression particularly in the Franco–Soviet treaty and the Czechoslovak–Soviet mutual assistance pact.

In the beginning, these circumstances induced the Darányi Government to adopt, even though for a short time only, a more moderate line of internal and foreign policy. In the first half of 1937, Darányi was rather influenced by the conservative wing of the ruling classes which had helped him to power than by the extreme right. In order to return to Bethlen's system of government, the Prime Minister restored the old forms of organization in the Government Party, ousted the pro-Gömbös politicians from leading positions (Minister of the Interior Miklós Kozma resigned) and drafted a bill on the extension of the power of the Regent and the Upper House. In foreign policy, while entertaining the German connections, the Government planned a more categoric reliance on Italy. (This was manifested by the Italian royal couple's visit to Hungary in May 1937.) On the other hand, it took steps to renew the relations with the Western Powers, England in the first place. In his speech Darányi gave expression to these efforts when he said: "The Hungarian nation, in undivided unity, wishes to secure the friendship of England and would welcome the creation of amicable relationships with France through the recognition of each other's interests." A social upshot of this course was the formation of an Anglo–Hungarian Friendship Society.

The German chargé d'affaires in Budapest, Werkmeister, even found it necessary to call this fact to the notice of his Government, summing up his report as follows: "On the Hungarian side contacts with England are sought in all fields." Seeking contacts with England certainly did not mean that the Hungarian Government believed that the Western Powers would serve as a counterbalance to the overwhelming superiority of Germany as Italy could no longer outbalance her. So, there was no question of any kind of British orientation, for the realization of the revisionist ambitions seemed to depend on German assistance. What was behind British orientation was rather that the Hungarian foreign politicians were highly interested how far the British Government would be tolerant of Hitler's aspirations, how far Hungary could go in co-operating with Germany without taking the risk of a general European conflict which might jeopardize the survival of the régime. From 1937 till the time Hungary was dragged into the Second World War, this was the basic posture of Hungarian foreign policy, encumbered, of course, with a number of domestic problems (the activity of the extreme right) and international ones (German pressure coupled also with the former issue).

All these had an irritating effect on Berlin, and this nervousness was given expression in criticism and in the support of the extreme right in Hungary. The Germans began to pry into the situation of the German minority in Hungary, and used — as a most effective weapon — double talk about the German support of the Hungarian revisionist endeavours. On November 15, 1936, the *Völkischer Beobachter* carried an article by Alfred Rosenberg on the problems of South Eastern Europe. It was emphasized in the article that Germany was striving to build a 'new Europe' and not to restore the prewar conditions; that Germany could not support far-reaching revisionist ambitions — though a certain readjustment of the frontiers was necessary. In Budapest, it was not for a moment doubted that the hint was addressed to Hungary. In this way there was a perceptible freeze in German–Hungarian relations after Gömbös's death.

In the first half of 1937, the Government was not so much against taking a more sensible view of the relationships with the neighbouring countries as previously. Late in 1936 and early in 1937, the other two states parties to the Rome Pact, Italy and Austria, guided by different motives, were seeking the way of approach to one or another of the Little Entente states. In March 1937, on the occasion of his negotiations in Budapest, Chancellor Schuschnigg again broached the idea of co-operation with Czechoslovakia. Although the Hungarian Government stubbornly rejected the suggestion, the communiqué on the talks stated the following: "As regards the question of the Danubian states, there is full agreement between Austrian and Hungarian statesmen to the effect that the establishment of correct relationships with the neighbouring states is to the interest of all and could even be gradually achieved through the proper accommodation of all parties concerned."

There was an unbridgeable gap between Hungarian and Austrian aspirations. Austria, being afraid of the *Anschluss,* invariably had an eye to Czechoslovakia in the first place, while Hungary tried to normalize her relations mainly with Yugoslavia, and this coincided with the German and Italian aims.

Under the Soviet, English and French influence, negotiations between Hungary and the Little Entente states began upon the initiative of the latter. In January 1937, the Czechoslovak, Rumanian and Yugoslav Ministers in Budapest, each separately, called on Foreign Minister Kánya and proposed the opening of negotiations about the settlement of relations between the Little Entente states and Hungary. Essentially, though with some differences in their wording, the three proposals boiled down to this: The three states would acknowledge Hungary's right to rearm in exchange for a non-aggression pact. The proposal presented by the Yugoslav Minister went one step further by offering the conclusion of an agreement very much like a treaty of friendship, too.

Hungarian foreign policy reacted to the Little Entente initiative in two ways: on the one hand, it tried to make use of this move for getting Germany to support Hungary's revisionist demand more effectively; on the other hand, in conformity with the Germany conceptions, it adopted different attitudes towards each of the proposals of the three states which were practically identical. The rapprochement between Hungary and the Little Entente states thus partly came about as a result of the Little Entente's initiative and partly because of the Hungarian Government's anxiety about the strength of the Germans. The reason why all this took place in the year 1937, was obviously the anxiety concerning the Germans which was apparent in the foreign policy of the Hungarian Government.

The Foreign Minister received the calls of the envoys of the neighbour states on January 20 and 21, and on the 23rd Kánya already conferred with Mackensen, the German Minister in Budapest. He intimated unmistakably that the Little Entente states were trying to exploit the cool atmosphere that had come about in Hungarian—German relations as a consequence of the Rosenberg article; that the Little Entente representatives in Budapest eagerly sought the ways of approach towards Hungary and argued that, as a result of the deterioration of Hungarian—German relations, the time had come for the Danubian states to join forces against the German peril. Kánya pointed out to Mackensen that Hungary and Germany had invariably common interests and their co-operation seemed to be secured for the future.

The Germans of course tried to dispel the Hungarian anxieties. They admitted that Germany's designs indeed required tolerance towards Yugoslavia and Rumania, but they added that this did not mean that revision would be out of the question there. Goering told Döme Sztójay, the Hungarian Minister in Berlin, that the Rosenberg article was meant only to win the favour of the Rumanian right wing. He tried to make the Hungarian Government understand that in case of a conflict Hungary could, with a wise policy, keep Rumania from supporting Czechoslovakia without recognizing the Rumanian frontiers.

The Hungarian reply to the initiative of the Little Entente states was as follows. Kánya flatly refused the Czechoslovak offer with the remark that Hungary's right to rearm was not an object of bargaining. He did not accept the Rumanian proposal either, but there, he pointed to the necessity of a rapprochement between the two countries. With Yugoslavia, on the other hand, he entered into negotiations and, moreover, he endeavoured to conclude an agreement as early as possible. The Ministry of Foreign Affairs emphasized that the proposed agreement applied only to Yugoslavia and did not concern the other two Little Entente states.

The quick reaction of the Hungarian Government could be accounted for by the desire to get ahead of an Italo—Yugoslav agreement, supposing that in the new situation created by such an agreement, Yugoslavia would be less tractable in the Hungarian question. In virtue of the Rome protocol, Kánya even asked Rome for information about the state of the Italo—Yugoslav negotiations and expressed the hope that the Italian Government would take the Hungarian interests in consideration, and would not agree with Yugoslavia before Hungary did.

The Italian Government promised to take these wishes into consideration, and the Hungarian Ministry of Foreign Affairs hastened to prepare the Hungarian—Yugoslav agreement. On March 23, 1937, the Hungarian Minister in Belgrade handed the Yugoslav head of Government a draft declaration which, in the spirit of the Briand—Kellogg pact, stated that Hungary did not wish to resort to force as a means of national policy and would, in the future, abstain from any act that might disturb the good relations in the making between Hungary and Yugoslavia. In return for this declaration the Hungarian Government asked for recognition of Hungary's right to rearm and for guarantees of certain rights of the Hungarian minority in Yugoslavia. A special aide-mémoire dealing with this latter question was enclosed.

Prime Minister Stojadinović found the Hungarian proposal significant and adequate and only asked for a few days' time to study the documents. On March 25, 1937, however, there came a bolt from the blue – the Italo–Yugoslav agreement was signed. Kánya's fears had materialized. The agreement, which, as an eloquent sign of the crumbling of the Little Entente, Yugoslavia concluded without the knowledge and consent of the partner states, caused great alarm in Czechoslovakia and Rumania. The reaction of the Allies put the Yugoslav Government on guard against negotiating with Hungary. That was why on March 31, Stojadinović, contrary to his earlier position, gave an essentially negative reply to the Hungarian proposals. He said that the draft declaration did not seem satisfactory since it contained nothing more than what Hungary had already undertaken in the Briand–Kellogg pact. The Prime Minister refused to say anything concrete about the gestures to be made to the Hungarian minority. After all this, Kánya instructed the Hungarian Minister in Belgrade to desist from pressing for the acceptance of the Hungarian proposals.

Thus Czechoslovakia and Rumania succeeded in keeping Yugoslavia back from striking a unilateral bargain with Hungary, but they thought that an agreement between Hungary and all the three Little Entente states was invariably necessary. The resolutions of the Little Entente conference held at Belgrade in April 1937 laid down that in the matter of negotiating an agreement with Hungary the three states should hold preliminary consultations; if any one of them wished to enter into a bilateral agreement with Hungary, it had to obtain the consent of the other two allies. Finally it was decided that they would be ready to acknowledge Hungary's right to rearm only if Hungary concluded a non-aggression treaty with the Little Entente or with each of the three countries at the same time. The idea of a collective agreement with the Hungarian Government was most forcibly proposed by Czechoslovakia under the immediate threat of German agression.

At the end of May and early in June, the envoys of the Little Entente states again went to see the Hungarian Foreign Minister in order to propose an agreement in the spirit of the Belgrade resolutions. This time, however, the three proposals differed widely from one another. The only identical feature in them was that they offered to acknowledge Hungary's right to rearm in exchange for a non-aggression pact. But while the Czechoslovak Government stated this in plain terms, the Yugoslav proposal was confined to generalities with the remark that by submitting the proposal the Yugoslav Government wished to do a favour mainly to Czechoslovakia; and Rumania simply declared that she had no objection to the restoration of Hungary's right to rearm, but expected the Hungarian Government to offer the conclusion of a non-aggression pact shortly after making a declaration to this effect.

The Hungarian Government tried to profit by the differences in the three notes, saying it did not know which of the proposals was 'authentic'. Finally, since Czechoslovakia did not want to miss the opportunity, she agreed with her allies that negotiations with the representatives of Hungary would start, subject to no preliminary conditions, at the next conference of the Little Entente.

The Sinaia Conference of the Little Entente states met on August 30, 1937. László Bárdossy, the Hungarian Minister in Bucharest, made an appearance there in behalf of his Government in order to enter into negotiations with the participants of the conference. The Hungarian Government had not the slightest intention to come to an agreement with the three Little Entente states simultaneously, therefore it insisted first of all on the solution of the minority question, being aware that this was the best way to prevent the adoption of a uniform position. In the name of his Government Bárdossy suggested the signing of three identical protocols on the following subjects: 1. Czechoslovakia, Rumania and Yugoslavia voluntarily decide to recognize Hungary's right to rearm. 2. The three states voluntarily decide to introduce certain administrative measures in favour of the Hungarian minorities. 3. Hungary voluntarily decides to make a declaration on non-aggression, and the three Little Entente states shall reciprocate. 4. The Governments of Yugoslavia, Czechoslovakia and Rumania undertake to enter into communication with the local leaders of the Hungarian minorities and to start negotiations for radical changes in the situation of the minorities.

The Little Entente states found the Hungarian proposals unacceptable. Although they did not reject them in a point-blank manner, their reply was delayed and the chance of an agreement seemed to be more and more remote. It was only in the summer of 1938 that the talks brought result — this time not only with Yugoslavia but with all three states of the Little Entente. The further shaping of the policy of the Darányi Government was perceptibly influenced by the fact that the year 1937 brought a further strengthening of Nazi Germany.

To promote the aims of Axis policy, the Italian Government definitively gave up supporting Austrian independence and even assumed an active role in spreading German influence in Austria. Indicative of the invigoration of Axis policy was that in November 1937, Italy joined the Anti-Comintern Pact and then withdrew from the League of Nations. In British foreign policy, the line aimed at 'appeasement' towards Hitler eventually became dominant. In the interest of improving German–British relations, the Chamberlain Government which had come into power in May 1937, displayed growing indifference to Central Europe and reiterated that it was not firmly against a revision of the peace system. Under-Secretary of State for Foreign Affairs Lord Halifax (who was named Foreign Secretary in February 1938, after Eden had resigned in protest against the 'policy of non-intervention') paid a visit to Hitler in November 1937, and gave him to understand that Britain recognized the necessity of a change in the order of Central Europe in accordance with the German demands. The talks with Halifax convinced Hitler that in a given case Great Britain would not move a finger against the annexation of Austria and Czechoslovakia. The realization of the *Anschluss* and the attack on Czechoslovakia were now on the horizon.

Before taking these steps of great consequence Hitler wished to see clearly what attitude his allies would adopt. This gave Prime Minister Darányi and Foreign Minister Kánya occasion to make a journey to Germany towards the end of November. The Germans pursued a twofold aim with regard to Hungary: she should remain indifferent to the annexation of Austria and take an active part in the attack on Czechoslovakia.

The first discussion between Darányi, Kánya and Goering took place on November 22. To intimidate the Hungarian statesmen, Goering struck a rather inimical tone, accusing Hungary of having failed to stand up resolutely enough against the attempts to create a Vienna—Prague—Budapest bloc and against contemplating the provision of armed Hungarian assistance to Austria in case of a German—Austrian conflict. Kánya vigorously protested against the accusations and indirectly let Goering know that Hungary would create no obstacle in the case of the occupation of Austria.

Goering noted the pronouncements of the Hungarian statesmen with satisfaction and then took up the Czechoslovak question. He stressed that in Hitler's conception " ... Hungary's present generation has to content itself with taking the offensive in only one direction and recovering thereby the Hungarian territories annexed to Czechoslovakia." For this reason, he said, Hungarian—Yugoslav understanding must be restored at whatever cost (at the price of recognizing the actual frontiers), and at least a sort of *modus vivendi* must be created between Hungary and Rumania. True, Hitler did not disapprove of the Hungarian revisionist claims on Rumania but was convinced that this objective should be put off for a time.

Kánya explained that Hungary's foreign policy had so far respected the German standpoints and could not be blamed for the failure to reach an agreement with Yugoslavia and Rumania. He would gladly accept Goering's good offices in regard to Yugoslavia if his mediation should have as a result that in exchange for the recognition of the Trianon frontiers between Hungary and Yugoslavia, the Yugoslav Government would undertake to remain neutral in any conflict that might arise between Hungary and 'one of her neighbours'.

Darányi and Kánya also conferred with Foreign Minister Neurath, who emphatically referred to the result of the talks he had had with Halifax in Berlin. On November 25, the Hungarian delegation was received by Hitler. Hitler again requested Hungary not to fritter away her energies in different directions but to concentrate her attention on Czechoslovakia alone.

The results of the Hungarian statesmen's visit to Berlin boiled down, in principle, to an agreement for an action against Czechoslovakia. In the hope of a successful revision the emphasis was put on the complete identity of views with the Germans in respect of the main objectives of Hungarian foreign policy. Finally it was decided to co-ordinate the plans of the General Staffs for an aggression on Czechoslovakia. (Rearmament against Czechoslovakia was the aim of the Győr programme announced in February 1938, the realization of which was promoted by the fact that on January 27, 1938, the League of Nations exempted Hungary from every kind of financial control.)

A few weeks after the talks, in December 1937, Horthy sent Hitler a message in which he disclosed that for the event of an Austro—German conflict there existed no Austro—Hungarian and no Austro—Hungarian—Czechoslovak agreement, and that as long as he remained Regent of Hungary he would not tolerate any such policy, and he conceded that Austria should belong to Germany. This stand was then reiterated by the Ministry of Foreign Affairs early in 1938.

Either owing to the growth of Nazi Germany's strength or to the strengthening of German—Hungarian diplomatic co-operation or to the increased influence of Fascist ideas in Hungary, the foreign political events inevitably had consequences in Hungarian internal policy as well. We are not only thinking about the strengthening of the National Socialist parties, or the exploitation of the mass discontent for Fascist propaganda, but also about the growing political influence of military quarters who regarded themselves as agents of a German—Hungarian military alliance. The highest positions in the Ministry of National Defence and in the army (particularly in its General Staff) were then already in the hands of generals appointed by Gömbös. They thought that totalitarian military leadership was easy to reconcile with Fascist rule, and were ardent advocates of the suppression of political tendencies opposed to their views, be it even among the ruling circles.

Nevertheless, non-official or unofficial quarters of Hungarian political life were seriously alarmed and scared by the possibility of the *Anschluss,* by the drastic measures the Germans took against Austria during the early months of 1938. This alarm made itself felt in the attitude of Foreign Minister Kánya who, seeing the danger coming from Germany, again took up the idea of a 'horizontal axis'. On March 2, 1938, in a non-official message sent to Foreign Minister Beck of Poland through the Hungarian Minister in Warsaw, he wrote: "... we should prefer the maintenance of Austria's independence rather than the neighbourhood of an eighty-million strong Germany. Being familiar with the related very resolute intentions of the German National Socialist Government, however, we have to be prepared for the event that the union of the two German states will sooner or later be consummated." Kánya explained that in his wiev, the Western Powers would not throw obstacles in the way of the *Anschluss,* and that good relations between Germany and Hungary would make agreement with Germany possible even in case of the *Anschluss.* But he added: "Considering the awfully strong dynamism of the National Socialists, however, other contingencies must also be reckoned with." And for this reason it would be well to start negotiations between their respective two countries. According to Kánya's information "Italy already takes in to account the danger of a shift in the balance of power in Central Europe and is contemplating the necessary preventive measures. It is in this context that the idea of an Italo—Yugoslav—Hungarian—Polish line had arisen." (Related to the 'horizontal axis' idea was, in part at least, Horthy's official visit to Warsaw in February 1938.) This repeatedly emerging idea, however, was made illusory by the fact that the participants of the 'horizontal axis' were firmly bound to Nazi Germany by various interests, and any sort of union could be imagined only on a pro-German line.

On March 13, 1938, German troops marched into Austria. The Hungarian Government was the first to congratulate Germany on the 'bloodless execution' of the *Anschluss.* In addition to the telegram of congratulation, the Hungarian Government hastened to recognize also *de jure* the annexation of Austria by closing down the Hungarian Legation in Vienna.

Broad strata of Hungarian society, including influential quarters, were alarmed at the appearance of the Nazi Great Power on the frontiers of the country. Another cause of the alarm was the fact that the German Government made no declaration on the recognition of the actual frontiers of Hungary, although it did so in relation to Italy, Yugoslavia and Switzerland. With reference to this anxiety, strongest in economic quarters, Kánya asked the Germany Government for a public recognition of the frontiers in relation to Hungary as well.

Typically of those times, he at once offered that in exchange, his Government would agree to the Budapest local group of the National Socialist Party being renamed 'Landesgruppe der NSDAP'.

Eventually the Germans complied with Kánya's request: they let him know that they did not object to the publication of a declaration on the recognition of the frontiers. On April 3, 1938, Horthy went on a radio broadcast in an effort to calm down the excitement and fear aroused by the *Anschluss*. "In the past few days," he said in his speech, "a peculiar feeling of uncertainty, nay a sort of anxiety, has seized the souls of many. . . . He who judges the events with a clear mind and seeing eyes has to know that the union of Austria with Germany means nothing else than the union of an old and good friend of ours, whom the peace treaties had involved in an impossible position, with another old and good friend and companion-in-arms of ours. . . . That is all, nothing else has happened from our point of view." The mere denial of the dangers that had created the anxiety could not have a particularly convincing tone. To make his words more emphatic, Horthy expressed his discontent about the extreme-right tendencies in Hungary (the Arrow-Cross movement) and promised to take energetic steps in defence of the existing form of government.

The alarm fomented by the *Anschluss,* however, could not overpower the revisionist desires of the Hungarian ruling quarters. In the days following the occupation of Austria, unofficial steps were taken in an effort to recover Burgenland or at least part of it. This was urged especially by the extreme-right circles which expected that a possible success would strengthen their domestic position. András Mecsér, one of the leaders of the extreme right, called on German envoy Erdmannsdorff on March 16. He pointed out that, in the autumn of 1935, Hitler had promised Gömbös to return Burgenland to Hungary. He said that this gesture, even if confined merely to Hungarian-inhabited areas, would make a profound impression and enable Hungary to fall into line with Germany's political interests. With the knowledge of the Government, Baron Béla Malcomes, an ex-Counsellor of Legation, started soundings in Berlin. Secretary of State for Foreign Affairs Weizsäcker noted down in a document related to the affair that an official suggestion on the part of the Hungarian Government would be resented because, quoth he, Hitler would hardly intend to present such an undeserved gift to Hungary. On April 13, the Secretary of State informed the German Minister in Budapest that Hitler regarded the German–Hungarian frontier as definitive and the frontier revision suggested by Mecsér was out of the question. Moreover, he wrote, the question could not be settled on an ethnic basis, because in such a way

Hungary, who had a German minority living along her frontier, would lose more than gain. Thus the Burgenland question was definitively scrapped.

The fact of the *Anschluss,* which caused serious alarm in the Hungarian ruling quarters, mainly among finance capitalists and aristocratic landowners, continued to strengthen in Hungary the out-and-out pro-German elements. These included certain sections of the gentroid strata of the upper bureaucracy and the civil servants, the General Staff and army officers, who saw the best support of their power aspirations in a firm pro-German policy already back in Gömbös's time. The activity of the Arrow-Cross (Nazi) parties and groups recruited from among petty-bourgeois and lumpen elements also got an impetus. The forces of the extreme right had already started vehement actions in 1937, and in the second half of the year, this activity accelerated the rightist shift in the internal policy of the Darányi Government. (Darányi gave free play to the Arrow-Cross organization. In the spring of 1938 he introduced the Bill on the first anti-Jewish Act and the notorious press law which resulted in the banning of 400 liberal and left-wing papers.) This process ultimately moved the ruling circles rallying round Bethlen to turn the Darányi Government out of office in May 1938, and to raise to power a Government headed by Béla Imrédy whom they expected to put a stop to the further shift to the right and to counteract the German influence, or at least to make better use of the shuttlecock policy.

From the second half of the thirties, as the international balance of power was tilting in favour of Germany and the superiority of German influence got consolidated in Central Europe, a particular regularity could be observed in Hungary's foreign and domestic policy. The essence of it was that every new Hungarian Government started, in foreign and domestic policy alike, with a programme more moderate than that of its predecessor, but then, in the course of time, each went much farther than the predecessor had in the field of co-operation with Germany, thus bringing a further shift to the right at home. In this process a decisive role was played – in addition to German expansion and the actions of the extreme right – by the consistent aim of the *whole* of the Hungarian ruling classes: the aspiration for a territorial revision, which could be conceived of only in league with Germany. Consequently the conservative-reactionary groups of the ruling classes never turned resolutely against pro-German policy and the extreme right, but, when the policy of the Government had shifted too far to the right and was already threatening with the collapse of the traditional forms of government, with the extreme right's victory, they confined themselves to an effort to divert the events in a more auspicious direction by appointing a new Prime Minister who seemed more dependable to them and more pliable to their interests. Each new Government, however, since it could find its basis only within the closed framework of the system, under a growing pressure from Germany and from the domestic extreme-right wing, made concession after concession to try to take the wind out of the sails of the extreme right. Determined opposition to pro-German policy would have meant co-operation with and reliance on the left-wing, democratic forces, but this was unthinkable to any group of the ruling classes.

3. The Munich Pact and the first Vienna Award

The new head of Government, Béla Imrédy, took office in an extremely difficult international situation. After the annexation of Austria, Czechoslovakia became the direct target of Nazi aggression. Long before the *Anschluss,* Germany had already begun diplomatic and military preparations for an attack on Czechoslovakia. Hitler intended Hungary to play an important part in this operation. In the wake of Darányi's visit to Germany, in November 1937, consultations between the German and Hungarian General Staffs ensued and were interrupted only by the events in Austria. On the very day of the *Anschluss,* Minister Sztójay asked Goering about the proposed date of attack on Czechoslovakia and the resumption of negotiations in the matter of collaboration. In April 1938, Hitler discussed with his generals the details of the planned aggression on Czechoslovakia. In May, they agreed on the definitive version of the project known as 'Fall Grün' that laid down the political and military directives. The project also dealt with the role which Hungary and Poland were expected to play, starting from the principle that the prospective allies should be won over to the case by promises of territorial gains.

While the first phase of preparation laid stress mainly on the use of diplomatic pressure and subversive actions inside Czechoslovakia, the Hungarian Government was not by any special consideration inhibited from co-operation with the Germans, including e.g. co-ordination of the demands and doings of the German and Magyar minorities living in Czechoslovakia through the minority leaders. Now, however, the question was the possibility of an armed conflict. In this situation the substantial changes in Anglo–Hungarian relations were of fundamental importance.

As we have seen above, the Powers which had inspired the talks between Hungary and the Little Entente, first of all the Soviet Union, regarded the rapprochement between Hungary and her neighbours as an important factor in their policy aimed at containing Germany's advance into South Eastern Europe. In March 1937, Litvinov sent word to Foreign Minister Kánya through the Hungarian Minister in Moscow: "Try to come to terms and co-operate with the Little Entente states; such a plan may count upon Soviet assistance."

For a time the British also pinned such hopes on the Bled conference, but as the policy of appeasement was gaining the upper hand, the British approach to the negotiations between Hungary and the Little Entente became a 'function' of the general line of British foreign policy. Moreover, when the talks had started it became more and more obvious that there was very little hope that the conflicts of interests between the states of the Danubian basin could be adjusted so as to create a political bloc raising a barrier to German aggression. First of all, because Hungary was unwilling to renounce her demands for a treaty revision. In reality, however, the anti-German foreign policies of the Little Entente countries also could not be reconciled.

In March 1938, a confidential memo originating from the British Foreign Office stated: "As it has been part of our policy during the last 12 months to encourage these negotiations between Hungary and the Little Entente, it would be as well to consider, in the light of the latest information, what the value of their successful conclusion is likely to be to us. From the outset it must be recognized that the formation of a political block capable of resisting aggression or attraction on the part of Germany is out of the question. Hungarian timidity in view of her newly acquired position *vis a vis* the Reich, Yugoslavia's determination to pursue a policy of neutrality, and the general impression that Roumania will not go to the aid of Czechoslovakia, show that any combination which may be achieved will not effect the great Powers. . . ." The memo revealed recent information that Germany strongly recommended the Hungarians to define their territorial claims on Czechoslovakia. And, on April 2, Deputy Under-Secretary of State for Foreign Affairs Sargent stated: "We are not working for an anti-German bloc in Central Europe."

What then did British foreign policy work for when Hitler who, in line with his tactics of small steps, raised the Sudetenland question as 'the last demand'? The essence of Chamberlain's appeasement tendency was to make Germany formulate its demands concerning South Eastern Europe in a way that it could be fulfilled, in England's opinion, without recourse to war.

What mattered for Great Britain was Germany, the aim was to 'save the peace' by satisfying the German demands, but the trouble was that the status quo was not merely a German question but, among others, a Hungarian one. Hungary did not renounce her territorial claims, and England could not help in this respect. The British could not choose to insist on the satisfaction of all territorial demands, because this might have triggered a chain reaction aggravating all the problems related to the status quo in South Eastern Europe; because the main pillar of the British arguments — namely that the issue was not a correction of the Versailles peace system but the curbing of Hitlerite aggression — would have fallen.

A single solution was left: to give Hungary something that might at least loosen the Trianon-dictated obligations, primarily, with regard to the military sanctions. For if Hungary renounced the use of force in exchange for recognition of her right to rearm, it would eventually be easier to force Czechoslovakia into concessions towards Germany, that is, to avoid armed conflicts.

At that time, however, Hungary was — both in this connection and in other respects — a preoccupation of British policy-makers. In the spring of 1938, it was in fact suggested from different sides and on several occasions that England should render Hungary active assistance, mainly in the economic field, and thus save her from falling into Germany's arms. In April and May, the Foreign Office received several memoranda on this subject, among others, from Hamilton Bruce, governor of the Bank of England, Royall Tyler, financial adviser to the National Bank of Hungary and League of Nations financial adviser to the Hungarian Government, as well as from representatives of various Hungarian economic and political circles.

After the *Anschluss,* the opinion prevailed in the Foreign Office that Hungary was becoming more and more closely linked to Germany, and Britain was unable to counterbalance this process by economic measures. They interpreted Horthy's radio address of April 4 as wise talk, but then what could Hungary do against German pressure? They did not place much hope in Imrédy's appointment as Prime Minister which was welcomed with sympathy by the above-mentioned British economic circles. Commenting upon Imrédy's policy speech, leading officials of the Foreign Office expressed strong doubts whether the new Prime Minister would be capable of protecting Hungary from the advent to power of the extreme right. In May, the British Minister in Budapest stated: "Hungary is lost to us...", and Sir Orme Sargent concurred in this opinion. Sargent wrote in a confidential note on May 29, 1938:

"I am sure there are lots of unhappy Hungarians who would like Great Britain to protect them from being 'absorbed' by Germany, and who hope that this may be effected by Great Britain's economic intervention. But all our past experience, and all our present evidence, goes to show that Hungary cannot be rendered independent of Germany by any economic action that we can take. Even if we could buy the whole of Hungarian wheat crop we would have no guarantee that German political pressure and power of attraction would not continue as before. There are other countries where British interests are definitely more important and where moreover we have got the means of reinforcing our position, such as Greece in the first place and possibly also Roumania. Don't therefore let us be tempted to waste our energy or our money in trying to salvage countries like Hungary, where the game is already up."

And he added that if Hungary could be salvaged at all it was dependent not on British intervention but (a) on the maintenance of Czechoslovakia's independence, (b) on assistance from Italy, (c) on a radical change in Hungary's foreign policy towards the Little Entente. (Permanent Under-Secretary of State Cadogan agreed with this view.)

Even the British were far from believing in the probability of the first condition, and their general line of foreign policy acted against it. The value of Italian assistance was very questionable because in the Axis, unbalanced already at its birth, Italy fell under overwhelming German superiority. And the possibility of a radical change in Hungary's foreign policy towards the Little Entente had already definitively been blown away by the wind of the revision that could be attained with German help.

The Foreign Office people saw this quite well and had drawn the conclusions. In connection with the Bled negotiations they only wished to achieve a minimum goal, an agreement which would preclude the possibility of a Hungarian armed action. It was with this understanding that they encouraged the four interested Governments, and this is how the Bled agreement was reached at the very moment when Hitler launched the last assault to take possession of the Sudetenland. And their general attitude was determined by the fact that they regarded Hungary as lost to them, a territory under German influence, and they defined the British interests as being in the more remote countries of South Eastern Europe. They wished to give assistance to these latter.

True, there were British politicians and diplomats who thought differently, such as O'Malley, the new British Minister in Budapest. Attempts were made to change the British attitude, but the basic stand regarding Hungary remained the same from the summer of 1938 onward. Up to 1941, this remained unchanged except for temporary improvements at times when the respective Hungarian Governments voiced reservations about German friendship or were opposed to German demands. These changes, however, never reached the state of active assistance, except in the months of the 'funny war' when the delivery to Hungary of raw materials of a strategic character was made possible. The improvement in relations was manifest not in the form of promises for the future, but in the maintenance, in the *non-severance,* of relations.

In the spring and summer of 1938, the Imrédy Government deemed the power relations unfavourable to successfully launch an invasion. It did not find Germany strong enough to carry out a successful military operation in the case of intervention by the Western Powers — a contingency to be reckoned with especially after the so-called May crisis. The pacts of Czechoslovakia with France and the Soviet Union were in force. True, these pacts made Soviet assistance to Czechoslovakia dependent on military aid from France, but in the summer of 1938, it could not yet be taken for certain that France would opt for submission to Germany, thus making her whole network of alliances ineffectual. Nor could neutrality on the part of Yugoslavia and Rumania be taken for granted. Under such circumstances, Hungary's military intervention seemed a risky undertaking. Not to mention that the Hungarian army was not yet in a position to engage in a battle in the hope of success, should the Czechoslovak armed forces resolve upon putting up resistance.

Undoubtedly, the Hungarian Government had no faith in the feasibility of military action against Czechoslovakia in the summer of 1938. Nevertheless it wanted to profit from the international tension. Kálmán Kánya thought that the Little Entente and especially Czechoslovakia, being in a quandary, would perhaps be willing to make concessions to Hungary, if not in the form of the return of some territory to her, at least in the question of the Magyar minorities and Hungarian rearmament. Beneš thought that in exchange for such concessions he could bring Hungary to renounce the use of force. This is how the Bled agreement was arrived at, as an example characteristic of the provincialism prevailing in the foreign policies of the small states of East Central Europe. Budapest was happy to have succeeded, after nearly twenty years' time, in getting the Little Entente to acknowledge Hungary's right to rearm, although this was already beside the point. What mattered was territorial acquisition, which now seemed to have been made possible by the use of force, but this was renounced in Bled. Prague was happy to see Hungary rest content, for the time being, with the recognition of her right to rearm and with some improvement in the situation of the minorities, although the very existence of the Czechoslovak state was already in extreme danger; for it was true that Hungary renounced the use of force, but Germany did not, and military force was represented by powerful Germany, not by little Hungary.

This was how the Bled agreement became worthless the moment it was signed, because what most of the Hungarian statesmen and the experienced German diplomats and generals did not believe in, was indeed taken seriously by the dilettante diplomat and soldier Hitler, who in the summer of 1938, decided to bring the Czechoslovak matter to a head by autumn that year.

In August 1938, Regent Horthy, Prime Minister Imrédy and Foreign Minister Kánya were summoned to a parley in Germany. As the Bled agreement was made public simultaneously with the Hungarian delegation's arrival in Germany, the German–Hungarian negotiations about the Czechoslovak question had inevitably to deal with the recent agreement between the Little Entente and Hungary.

The first discussion between Ribbentrop, Imrédy and Kánya took place on August 23, 1938. The German Foreign Minister fulminated against the Bled agreement. He qualified it as Hungary's renouncement of territorial revision: "the one who gives no help shall go away empty-handed", he said and went on to ask what Hungary intended to do if Germany resorted to arms against Czechoslovakia. Kánya gave no definite answer. He emphasized that Hungary's participation was dependent upon Yugoslavia's neutrality, and said that it would take the Hungarian Government two more years to make the army combat-worthy. Ribbentrop tried to reassure the Hungarian statesmen about the attitude of Yugoslavia but stressed that some risk must be assumed for the sake of revision.

In the meantime, Horthy had a separate conference with Hitler. He, too, expressed his concern about the probable attitude of the Western Powers, but spoke in plain terms about Hungary's intention to co-operate. The same afternoon, Hitler received Imrédy and declared resentfully that in the given situation he requested nothing of Hungary but "he who wants to sit at the table must at least help in the kitchen."

Imrédy who, as Prime Minister, now made his first visit to Germany, having gone through bitter hours of humiliation and being fascinated by the German parade under arms, soon became willing to come closer to the German standpoint.

The fear of missing the opportunity for a revision presently made the Hungarian delegation more tractable. On August 25, Kánya again had a talk with Ribbentrop. This time he already said that the Bled agreement could eventually be invalidated if, for example, Hungary voiced excessive demands in the question of the minorities. He did not speak about the two years needed for the purposes of rearmament either; 'correcting' his earlier remark, he declared that by October 1, 1938, Hungary would be in a position militarily to join in an action.

The Hungarian statesmen, however, refrained from making concrete promises. They were prompted to do so also by the experience they gained at the Kiel and Berlin negotiations, namely that not even leading generals of the Wehrmacht believed that a Czechoslovak–German war might remain an isolated conflict. This had been explained by General Beck to Minister of Defence Jenő Rátz. And this was referred to by Hitler who, according to Rátz's notes, "does not listen to his generals because they always claim to be unprepared and always have scruples". This was obviously what also influenced Horthy, the military man, when, back from Berlin, he told the German Minister in Budapest that the peculiar situation arose that he, who for years had had no more burning desire than to fulfil the Hungarian revisionist aims as soon as possible, was now compelled, owing to the pressure of world politics, to sound a note of caution. But when, in September 1938, it appeared clearly — especially from the attitude taken by the British Government — that no serious consequences were to be feared, Horthy already embarked more resolutely on the road of co-operation with the Germans.

Hitler's speech at the Nazi party rally on September 12, 1938, preluded the direct preparation of the action against Czechoslovakia. Two days later, on the 14th, Sztójay showed up at the Wilhelmstrasse and declared that his Government had the same claims on Czechoslovakia as the Sudeten Germans did. And another forty-eight hours later, when Goering demanded more vigorous action from Hungary, the envoy could already refer to concrete measures taken by his Government, including the call-up of 100,000 soldiers.

On September 20, when it became known that British Prime Minister Neville Chamberlain and Hitler would shortly meet again, Imrédy, in company with his Foreign Minister, made a hurried trip to Berlin with the intention of trying to amend what they had bungled in August. They wished to make their claims known to Hitler, lest some distinction should be made between the Hungarian and the Sudeten German demands. When the talks began, however, Hitler — who, from the favourable position he was in, wanted to hit back for the irresolute attitude the Hungarians had shown in August — as Imrédy wrote in his report, " . . . gave expression to his astonishment at the Hungarian conduct which he did not find to be firm enough"; sometimes he tended to believe, quoth Hitler, that Hungary was unconcerned with the Czech question; he could not know if Hungary might even be willing to guarantee the frontiers of Czechoslovakia. He said he thought it possible to arrange a settlement in which, plebiscite or no plebiscite, the area inhabited by Sudeten German population would be annexed into Germany without any mention being made of the other minorities. "If he receives a proposal," Imrédy went on, "which satisfies his demand for the annexation of the Germans, he will have no moral title to raise further demands either before the world or before himself, and cannot make his standpoint subject to the treatment of other nationalities."

Thereupon Hitler suggested to a shocked Imrédy that the Hungarian Government should immediately demand a plebiscite and not guarantee any frontiers proposed to Czechoslovakia. Imrédy agreed. But his position regarding the further demands was less clear. Hitler would have liked Hungary to start a military action against Czechoslovakia while he was conferring with Chamberlain. He then could break off the negotiations, intervene in the fighting, and so "the question would be settled" not on an ethnic but on a territorial basis — that is, through the complete dismemberment of Czechoslovakia.

Imrédy referred to the immense responsibility, to the fact that the Hungarian army was unprepared and was to face a force five times as great in number. No agreement was reached on this point.

It was evident that in case of a Hungarian onslaught on Czechoslovakia at a time when Hitler was negotiating with the Western Powers, Hungary would obviously be the sole aggressor, and thereby she would unequivocally become obligated to Germany and turn against the Western Powers. Let alone that, should Hitler back down for all that, Hungary would be left to herself facing a total diplomatic, political and military defeat.

The Hungarian Government could not assume such a tremendous risk, however much it was inflamed with the desire to see the nearly twenty-year-old revisionist dream come true. But it was afraid also of incurring Hitler's wrath again. So it chose an intermediate solution. It launched a sweeping diplomatic action against Czechoslovakia in accordance with the German wishes. On September 22, and again on the 28th, it dispatched to Prague an energetic note, demanding the return of the Magyar-inhabited areas and the granting of autonomy to Slovakia and the Carpatho–Ukraine (Ruthenia). It decided to employ irregular so-called free-troops instead of the regular army. These armed bands, under the command of Miklós Kozma, were dropped behind the Czechoslovak frontier, but only belatedly, after the Munich decision had been made. And this was no help to the German conceptions. Hitler could not "laugh in Chamberlain's face".

Although Horthy did not entirely fulfil Hitler's wishes, he would have liked to attain the fulfilment of the Hungarian territorial demands to the greatest extent possible. When it became known that London and Paris were ready to seek the solution of the Czechoslovak crisis by means of a conference of the Great Powers, that they were ready to satisfy the German demands, Sztójay called on Goering on September 28, to sound him whether the Hungarian issue was included in the agenda of the Munich conference. Goering, although aware of the fact that the Hungarian question was not officially among the agenda items, unscrupulously assured the Hungarian envoy of Germany's most substantial support. Relying on this assurance, Sztójay immediately put through a phone call to Budapest and requested that Chief Secretary Count István Csáky, equipped with maps indicating the Hungarian territorial demands, should leave for Munich at once. On the 29th, at Munich Csáky was received by Mussolini in audience and outlined the Hungarian claims. The Duce replied with an oratorical panegyric stating that, as soon as the Sudeten German question was settled, he would instantly raise the issue and demand a similar solution to the Hungarian question. But his dynamism slackened at the conference table. Hitler did not find it desirable for the four-Power conference to decide the case of the Hungarian and Polish territorial demands. He himself wanted to say the decisive word with a view to fixing a price for his decision himself. Mussolini did not contradict Hitler.

Under the Munich Pact concluded on September 29, 1938, the Western Powers consented to Hitlerite Germany's annexing the Sudetenland. The Hungarian and Polish demands were mentioned only in a rider to the agreement. According to this, Hungary and Poland should try to solve their territorial problems by means of bilateral negotiations with the Czechoslovak Government, and in case no understanding ensued in three months' time, the case should be referred to the participants of the conference.

When the decision of the Munich conference was made public, it first caused disappointment to the Hungarian Government quarters: Hitler and Mussolini had not kept their promise. Germany received the Sudetenland, but Hungary had to submit herself to the torture of a doubtful outcome of bilateral negotiations. For all the misty veil of bitterness, however, Horthy and his men soon awakened to the real significance of Munich. They understood that the Munich Pact was a turning-point in postwar Europe, that with the disintegration of Czechoslovakia the collapse of the Versailles peace system had irresistibly begun, and this would also ripen the fruits of Hungary's revisionist policy. On October 1, 1938, Horthy and Imrédy congratulated Berlin and Rome by letter, expressing their gratitude for the steps taken in the interest of Hungarian revisionism.

After Munich the Hungarian Government engaged in feverish activity. On October 3, it sent a strongly worded note to the Czechoslovak Foreign Minister. It proposed to start bilateral negotiations at Komárom on the 6th, and demanded that, in order to create a 'peaceful atomosphere' for the negotiations, the Czechoslovak Government should immediately effect the following measures: 1. It should forthwith release the political prisoners of Hungarian nationality. 2. It should immediately demobilize the soldiers of Hungarian nationality. 3. Local police units under mixed command should be set up with the task of ensuring the protection of life and property. 4. As a token of the transfer of territories, two or three Czechoslovak frontier towns to be ceded to Hungary were to be occupied by Hungarian troops.

On October 5, the infiltration of irregular troops started. The armed bands carried out subversive acts, assaulted smaller Czechoslovak military formations. Care was also taken to co-ordinate the actions of the irregulars with the parallel activity of Polish forces.

Although the Hungarian Government knew just too well that, by virtue of the Munich Pact, its official demands to be raised at the forthcoming negotiations might apply only to Magyar-inhabited areas, it nevertheless made preparations for taking possession of the whole of Slovakia and the Carpatho–Ukraine, because it counted upon Hitler's earlier promises concerning those territories. However, after Munich, co-operation with Hungary lost much of its importance for Germany. Hitler had already had schemes of his own regarding Slovakia and the Carpatho–Ukraine. For this reason, with reference to ethnic principles, he advised the Hungarians to confine their claims merely to Magyar-inhabited territories.

The Czechoslovak–Hungarian talks, which began at Komárom on October 9, 1938, were conducted in a very tense atmosphere. Plenipotentiaries of the Czechoslovak Government, headed by the leader of Slovak separatists, Monsignor Tiso, who obviously built upon Hitler's plans concerning Slovakia, stunned the Hungarian delegation by offering only autonomy for the territories with Magyar population. Although territorial concessions were also hinted at, these did not make up even one-tenth of the Hungarian demands. Thus the negotiations were broken off four days later without bringing any result.

Now again the Hungarian Government turned to the Axis Powers. On October 14, Kálmán Darányi went to Germany, where he conferred with Hitler in the presence of Keitel and Erdmannsdorff. At that time, Darányi was no longer a member of the Government — he was speaker of the House of Representatives — but in Budapest they considered him to have won Hitler's sympathy with his policy during his office as Prime Minister, and considered him capable of restoring co-operation between the two Governments.

Darányi first tried to obtain Hitler's agreement to Hungary's launching an armed attack on Czechoslovakia. But Hitler firmly opposed this idea, he even allowed himself to inveigh violently against Foreign Minister Kánya, who, he thought, had obstructed German—Hungarian collaboration prior to the Munich Pact. Then Darányi, to reason Hitler into willingness, offered Hungary's more categorical espousal of Axis policy (including maybe Kánya's dismissal), accession to the Anti-Comintern Pact, and withdrawal from the League of Nations, as well as the conclusion of an economic agreement with Germany for a period of ten years.

But Hitler did not give in: Hungary ought to have decided to take military steps when he had asked her to do so. The Hungarian Government had to understand, he said, that the Munich decision was made on an ethnic basis, and Hungary's demands must remain within the same bounds. Finally, Darányi drew forth the maps showing Hungary's minimum territorial claims and bid for Germany's support.

Simultaneously with Darányi's journey, Count Csáky went to Italy to secure Mussolini's support. The Italians, as was their wont, were lavish of promises this time, too, and assured Hungary of their far-reaching political, military and diplomatic support. Csáky and Mussolini agreed that the two Governments would jointly suggest to Hitler the convening of a four-Power conference.

Setting its mind on arbitral procedure, the German Government rejected the Italo—Hungarian suggestion but declared itself ready to mediate between Czechoslovakia and Hungary. The wrangling, mainly about where the towns of Ungvár and Munkács (now Uzhgorod and Mukachevo, in the Soviet Union) should belong, went on for a time, because the Germans — striving to fix as high a price as possible for the revision — constantly shifted their ground. When, for example, the Czechoslovaks and the Hungarians were ready to accept the procedure of arbitration, Berlin again began harping on the idea of the four-Power conference. Of course, this was good only for blackmailing, since the Germans knew that England and France did not wish to continue dealing with the Czechoslovak problem.

On October 27, 1938, at last, Ribbentrop went to Rome, and after a few days of negotiations agreed with Ciano on arbitration by the Axis Powers and on the annexation of Kassa (now Kosice, in Czechoslovakia), Ungvár and Munkács to Hungary.

The first Vienna Award was pronounced in the golden hall of Belvedere Castle on November 2, 1938. The arbitral decision returned to Hungary a territory of 12,400 sq.km. with a mostly Magyar population of 1,100,000. The Horthy régime arranged celebrations to congratulate itself on the first fruit of twenty years of revisionist policy. Undoubtedly the Vienna Award signified a momentary success of Hungarian diplomacy, as most of the demands submitted to the Komárom conference were fulfilled without recourse to war. But those who saw clearly, understood that Hungary had to make considerable economic and political concessions in exchange for German assistance. The triumphant celebrations could not conceal the ruling classes' dissatisfaction with the Vienna Award, because the seizure of the Carpatho—Ukraine would have been at least as important as, if not more important than, the reannexation of the Hungarian-inhabited zones of Upper Hungary.

4. Hungary's participation in the complete dismemberment of Czechoslovakia

The acquisition of the Carphatho—Ukraine seemed indispensable to the foreign policy of counter-revolutionary Hungary, not only and not even primarily because of the raw material resources of the territory, but mainly in order to extend the scope of foreign political manoeuvres. Many leading politicians of the régime were of the opinion that the reannexation of the Carpatho—Ukraine, the establishment of a common Polish—Hungarian frontier, would not only toll the death knell of the Little Entente as a political structure opposed to the Hungarian revisionist endeavours, but could make this unbroken 'horizontal axis' act as a certain counterbalance to German pressure, thus creating a more favourable possibility of enforcing Hungary's revisionist claims within the bounds of pro-German policy. This idea was perhaps most clearly expounded by Miklós Kozma in his diary: "Nine million Magyars are living cooped up in the cage of Trianon Hungary, surrounded on three sides by the Little Entente, the fourth side being barred by Germany since the accomplishment of the *Anschluss*. If in the future, either peacefully or at the price of blood, we recover the lost Hungarian territories — which nobody can doubt any longer — it will only mean that a little more Hungarians will live in a little larger cage. On the other hand, Ruthenia means that we shall have cut through the Little Entente ring at a section between Rumania and Czechoslovakia so that we shall have a common frontier with Poland. It is unquestionable that even then we must invariably pursue our friendly policy towards Germany, but it is beyond question that we shall be able to pursue it as a country of greater value in quite different circumstances. The Warsaw—Budapest—Belgrade—Rome line is not inconsistent with the policy of the Rome—Berlin Axis, but it is a relief to us." In other words, many were of the opinion that, even without the Carphatho—Ukraine or by bringing this territory under her control, Germany would preclude the possibility of Hungarian foreign policy departing in any respect from the Berlin-dictated line. Some ruling quarters, with Prime Minister Imrédy at their head, considered the reannexation of Ruthenia important for a quite different reason. Imrédy, in whose policy a pronounced shift took place in the summer of 1938, wanted to score spectacular successes in foreign policy in order to surmount the difficulties accumulating in the way of a Fascist transformation of the country's internal political life.

Thus in the autumn of 1938, following the first Vienna Award, the question of an operation against the Carphatho—Ukraine was put on the agenda. The Hungarian political and military leaders found the international situation by and large suitable for the purpose. On the one hand, they expected that, after the Munich Pact, and the blows of the Vienna Award, Czechoslovakia was incapable of serious resistance;

on the other hand, they supposed — and not without reason — that in the given situation, the Western Powers and the Soviet Union would tolerate the Carpatho—Ukraine's being returned to Hungary rather than its annexation by Germany.

In the autumn of 1938, the greatest obstacle to the occupation of the Carpatho—Ukraine was Germany herself. It was at that time that, in connection with anti-Soviet schemes, Nazi leading quarters set forth the conception of the formation of an 'independent' Ukrainian state, the basis of which would have been furnished by Ruthenia under German control. They saw clearly that Hungary's aim, with the establishment of a Polish—Hungarian frontier, was to seek a freer scope of movement in opposition to growing German influence. On the other hand, an independent Hungarian military action could seriously impair the prestige of the arbitrating Axis Powers. By the way, the Nazi leaders had long entertained a definite idea regarding the Hungarian territorial demands. Notably, the objective they wanted to achieve was that Hungary should recover territories only with German help, out of Germany's hands, at a time convenient to the German aspirations of the day, because only in this way could they increase Hungary's economic and political subjection to German interests, and because they could make good use of the Hungarian revisionist endeavours for the strengthening of Germany's influence over the countries of the Danubian basin.

The occupation of the Carpatho-Ukraine was preceded by rather complicated preparations and called for fast diplomatic action. The Hungarian Government intended to carry it out with the participation of Poland. But already the organization of Polish—Hungarian collaboration was encumbered with difficulties. On November 9, 1938, Kánya requested the Polish Government to join in the Hungarian campaign with at least four divisions. The Polish Ministry of Foreign Affairs, however, declined the request; it promised only to dispatch irregular troops to promote the Hungarian military operations and to do everything in its power to keep Rumania back from intervention.

It was again Kálmán Darányi who was commissioned to obtain Hitler's consent, or at least his tacit approval, by renewing earlier promises. On November 7, Darányi wrote the Führer a letter offering to carry out the promises made in October in exchange for German approval. But the Germans did not yield, all the less since they regarded the fulfilment of those promises as payment for the Vienna Award. As concerns the Italian Government, Ciano, on November 11, warned the Hungarian Minister in Rome that Berlin regarded Ruthenia as belonging to Germany's sphere of interests. He went on explaining that Italy could not support the Hungarian ambitions, and should the Reich so demand, she would be compelled to make protestations to Budapest in common with Germany. As information about the Hungarian preparations was accumulating, the German warning became more and more emphatic. The attack was scheduled to start on November 18. That day, Erdmannsdorff presented his Government's note qualifying the proposed Hungarian action as a risky step, and stated that Germany could not render assistance to Hungary. The Hungarian Government reacted to the note as if it had forgotten how to read a diplomatic text correctly. It construed the warning as something that was not against the Hungarian conceptions but, on the contrary, was pointing to the possibility of obtaining Germany's approval. So the only consequence was that the start of the attack was put off until November 20 and then until the 21st.

During the delay, the Germans managed to come to an agreement with the Italians, and on November 21, the two Governments, in sharply worded parallel notes, protested against any military step on the part of Hungary: "The frontiers between Hungary and the Carpatho-Ukraine have been designated by the arbitral award which the German and Italian Governments have recently pronounced in Vienna at the request of the Czechoslovak and Hungarian Governments. With signing the award in Vienna, Hungary has recognized before the world those frontiers as definitive. If now Hungary makes an armed attack upon Czechoslovak parts in the Carpatho-Ukraine, the Royal Hungarian Government puts itself in a morally serious situation. Furthermore, such a course of action may have, as a consequence, that the Vienna Award becomes worthless and thus causes injury to the reputation of the Arbitrating Powers." The note stressed that the Axis Powers were not currently in a position to support Hungary in any form whatever.

Upon receipt of the notes, the Council of Ministers held an emergency meeting and resolved that, by officially confirming the promises made through Darányi, it would try to induce the Nazi leaders to change their minds. On November 22, Sztójay presented an aide-mémoire to the German Ministry of Foreign Affairs:

"Ever since the creation of the Berlin—Rome Axis, co-operation with it has been the main objective of Hungary's foreign policy, and this co-operation has been made still more complete by the Vienna Award.

"Out of this consideration the Hungarian Government finds it necessary, with a view to strengthening relationships with the German Reich in both the political and the economic field, to start negotiations with the German Government.

"As regards the political issues, the Hungarian Government thinks of the common struggle against Bolshevism in the first place. Hungary is perhaps the first state that has never departed from the line of the struggle against Communism, and she has never been disposed to enter into any agreement or compromise with Bolshevism.

"The anti-Bolshevist conduct of the Axis Powers has always met with understanding and approval on the part of the Hungarian Government, and if the Axis Powers deem it necessary, we are ready to prepare our accession to the Anti-Comintern Pact.

"New possibilities exist also in the economic field, and Hungary, who has in the past, transacted a considerable part of her foreign trade with the Axis Powers, wishes to prepare the further extension and intensification of economic relationships, and is ready to stabilize and develop them in practice through reciprocal additions. We think that in this way we can come closer to the objective of strengthening our relations with the Axis Powers and create a situation which will be apt to promote the interests of the Axis Powers and Hungary alike."

It was unreasonable to believe that these offers might do something to make amends for the fiasco in the matter of the Carpatho-Ukraine. Ribbentrop's only reaction was to reproach Hungary for having failed to offer to quit the League of Nations (as

Darányi had promised), and he gave Sztójay to understand that Germany had no intention of changing her mind.

The idea of taking possession of the Carpatho-Ukraine had thus to be put aside for a time. The retreat and demobilization of the troops deployed on the frontier began. Those among the ruling quarters who worried about growing German influence and were opposed to the introduction of totalitarian Fascism, and who, at the time, had helped Imrédy to power by removing Darányi, now were busy trying to turn Imrédy out of office. And on November 23, at last, Béla Imrédy tendered his resignation. But Horthy again appointed him Prime Minister, for fear lest the dismissal of Imrédy should further deteriorate the relations with the German Reich. He was of the opinion that although it would be desirable to dismiss Imrédy and replace him with a politician who would be able to eliminate the confusion in the Government's work, to overcome its pliancy to external and domestic pressure, and to abide by the constitutional methods of government by repressing right- and left-wing opposition alike, this would only be possible at a later, more convenient date, when German pressure diminished. Imrédy, on the other hand, understanding that he was dependent upon German help, began with what every previous Government had thus far refused to do: on November 26 he authorized the legitimate formation of the Volksbund, making it possible thereby for the German minority in Hungary to organize in accordance with the interests and wishes of Nazi Germany.

Thus Imrédy remained. The only change in the composition of the Government was the dismissal of Kálmán Kánya, whose attitude during the Munich days definitively made him a *persona non grata* to the Germans. Kánya was replaced by Count István Csáky. The new Foreign Minister, in complete agreement with the Prime Minister, made it his first task to restore good German—Hungarian relations.

The foreign policy of the new Imrédy Government concentrated on the establishment of the closest possible co-operation with the Axis Powers. Accordingly, the closing weeks of 1938 and the beginning of 1939 witnessed the fulfilment of earlier promises. The impulse to this was given by Ribbentrop's message of December 5, 1938. In it the German Foreign Minister pointed out that in the interest of promoting the friendly relations between the two countries it would be expedient to start a thorough and all-comprehensive exchange of views in order to iron out the misunderstandings which had arisen in recent times. The tone and purport of Ribbentrop's message indicated that the Germans did not intend to increase tension. The anti-German mood growing in the wake of the autumn events and the efforts to unite the opposition left of the Imrédy Government, had, as a consequence, that it became important for the Germans to reassure and strengthen the Imrédy Government which showed readiness for a rapprochement. The Germans thus became intent on easing the overpowering political and economic pressure exerted upon Hungary. Instrumental in this process were Germany's farther plans concerning Eastern Europe. Difficulties also arose unexpectedly in German—Rumanian relations, after the assassination of Iron Guard leader Codreanu and his companions.

Imrédy, who wanted to demonstrate his 'dependability', was pleased with the German offer and let Ribbentrop know that the new Foreign Minister would answer the invitation in January 1939.

It was a decade-old tradition in Hungarian foreign policy to discuss the problems at negotiations with Italy before major diplomatic decisions. This is how it came to Count Ciano's visit to Budapest at the end of December 1938. The Italian Foreign Minister was given the promise that Hungary not only would give effect to her promise to accede to the Anti-Comintern Pact but would also withdraw from the League of Nations, a step that had not been referred to in the Hungarian Government's note of November 22.

Csáky promised to act promptly but did not act as fast as Berlin and Rome had expected him to do; first he wanted to find out how the Western Powers would react, and second, he wished Germany to make some preliminary promise concerning the Hungarian revisionist claims, especially in respect of the Carpatho-Ukraine or, at least, to disclose where and to what extent he might reckon with German support. On December 27 he sent the Hungarian Ministers in Paris, London and Washington the following telegram: "We are immensely interested in joining the Anti-Comintern Pact. We hope to receive in return considerable political support from the German Reich. ... Nevertheless, before taking this step, I wish to obtain confidential information about what reaction it might produce and to see whether the chance we take in this way would anyway be commensurate with the disadvantage our decision might incur in the face of political circles and public opinion there."

The promt answers from London and Washington were clearly reassuring to the Hungarian Government. According to the impressions gained by the chargé d'affaires in London, "in the British relation there are no considerations of decisive importance to speak against the proposed step called for by Hungarian political interests." The report from London enlarged upon the question of withdrawal from the League of Nations, pointing out that, in the personal opinion of an informant, Chamberlain would not be bothered by a further weakening of the League, because this would confirm him, over against the opposition, in his opinion of the uselessness of the League of Nations. On the other hand, as reported by Minister Khuen-Héderváry from Paris, the French would remain indifferent to the Hungarian move only in case they could make sure that it was designed merely as an anti-Soviet and anti-Communist demonstration and would not lead to any kind of secret convention directed against the Western Powers.

While Csáky waited for the requested information to come in, the Italians demanded more and more insistently that Hungary should sign the pact. The Hungarian Foreign Minister was playing for time, claiming that Hungary's accession had been first proposed in the German relation, so what would be needed in the first place was Germany's official consent or a formal invitation from the Axis Powers. On January 3, 1939, Vinci Gigliucci, the Italian Minister in Budapest, conveyed Germany's consent on condition that Hungary should quit the League of Nations not later than the opening of the League Council session in May. For want of further subterfuges Csáky had to promise that on January 12 he would publicly announce in Parliament Hungary's intention to accede to the pact. The next day he informed the German Minister in Budapest that he accepted the time-limit of May for withdrawal from the League.

In the talks about accession to the Anti-Comintern Pact there were only a few formal questions left to decide when, on January 9, People's Commissar for Foreign Affairs Litvinov made the Soviet view known to the Hungarian Minister in Moscow. Litvinov stated that he had been informed by 'reliable sources' about the Hungarian intentions, and stressed that the pact was a political convention in the service of aggressive designs against certain peace-loving nations, including the Soviet Union. Consequently Hungary's accession would be entirely incomprehensible to the Soviet Government, especially because the Soviet Union had no controversy with Hungary and had never acted against Hungarian interests, and Hungary's accession to the Anti-Comintern pact would very gravely affect relations between the two countries. In his reply written in an unusually rude tone, on January 10, Csáky, misrepresenting the facts, made things appear as if nothing had been done in the interest of Hungary's accession, and stated that he did not intend to let his decision be influenced by Soviet pressure.

On January 12, the Foreign Minister, true to his promise, made an official statement to the effect that Hungary would willingly join the Anti-Comintern Pact if she received an invitation to do so. The next day the Italian, German and Japanese Ministers in Budapest put in an appearance in the Ministry of Foreign Affairs to invite Hungary to sign the pact. Although the pact was to be signed only later, on February 24, the Axis Powers' invitation and Csáky's positive statement made Hungary's joining the Anti-Comintern Pact an accomplished fact on January 13. On February 2, therefore, the Soviet Government declared that, since with her accession Hungary had forfeited much of her independence, the Soviet Government considered it unnecessary to maintain direct diplomatic contact with her and closed down the Soviet Legation in Budapest. The maintenance of diplomatic contact would in the future be through the Legation of a third state. On February 5, 1939, the Hungarian Government also recalled the staff of its Legation in Moscow.

As Hungary had joined the Anti-Comintern Pact and made a definite promise to quit the League of Nations (this step was taken on April 11, 1939, already under the Teleki Government), it was believed in Budapest that the balance of German—Hungarian relations had shifted in favour of Hungary, and this might make it possible to persuade the Nazi leaders to adopt a positive attitude towards further revisions. Before leaving for Berlin, Csáky announced in the Council of Ministers that during the talks he would raise the question of the Carpatho-Ukraine's annexation to Hungary.

The Berlin negotiations started on January 16. The newly appointed Foreign Minister, on whose letter of appointment the ink had hardly become dry as yet, could not feel quite at ease when Hitler, in the presence of the German Minister in Budapest, the Hungarian Minister in Berlin and Foreign Minister Ribbentrop, began his monologue. He had to realize that the Führer introduced an altogether unusual tone in international negotiations, that not even in front of representatives of friendly states was he sparing of savage invectives, of humiliating and abusive outbursts. Hitler began his rhetoric with accusations. He enlarged upon the Hungarian foreign policy previous to the Munich Pact, reproached his guest for the Bled agreement and for the 'impotence' betrayed by the Hungarian Government during the Czechoslovak crisis. He blamed the Hungarians for the autumn events related to the Carpatho-Ukraine, stating that their importunate behaviour was all the more incomprehensible since they alone were responsible for the fact that the Czechoslovak crisis the year before had been closed on an ethnic basis and not with a territorial settlement. He called Hungary ungrateful, for it was Germany who had enabled her to score her first success in respect to revision. He branded the standpoint of Hungarian politicians and Csáky's opinion 'idiotic' and 'stupid'.

In reply to this diatribe the conceited little Count Csáky could say only that "Germany's essential demands will be met. Hungary is aware that she can do nothing without Germany, that all by herself she could never have coped with her enemies". Hitler then changed his tone and began to speak of the future in which "great successes can be attained only by mutually co-ordinated action". He said that Germany was not in the least interested in certain territories, and if the ethnic course must be departed from and the territorial principle must be accepted, it might be done only through common efforts: "The solution of the question must be sought through territorial policy, and both Poland and Hungary shall take part in it." He said that the complete dismemberment of Czechoslovakia must be scheduled for the most appropriate hour, and that before March no military steps might possibly be taken in Europe.

Csáky promised everything that was to Hitler's liking: 'frenzied armament' and a new law of national defence, the establishment of good relations with Rumania and Yugoslavia, withdrawal from the League of Nations; he pointed out that his Government had given up the idea of complete revision, because since Munich, Hungary had learned to think differently and would be satisfied with uniting the Hungarians; moreover, he stressed the need to solve the Jewish question on an international scale. But expect for vague hints, he was given no concrete promise of aid in respect of revision. Thereafter he did not even dare to raise the question of the Carpatho-Ukraine.

On January 16 Csáky had a separate discussion with Ribbentrop. The German Foreign Minister practically repeated the Führer's discourse. He again warned his Hungarian counterpart that for the moment, Germany, for a number of reasons, did not intend to become embroiled in any conflict. Therefore, he most categorically advised the Hungarian Government against any individual action in Czechoslovakia. The disturbances along the frontier should stop because "Germany can never allow the Hungarian–Czechoslovak boundary problems to be solved by unilateral action". The only concrete 'result' which Csáky drew from his talk with the German Foreign Minister was Ribbentrop's promise that Hitler in his speeches would hereafter mention

Hungary first among the small countries. Csáky, on the other hand — hoping that Hitler's allusions to Czechoslovakia would once manifest themselves in permitting Hungary to take possession of the Carpatho-Ukraine — undertook much more concrete obligations. Again he offered an economic agreement for ten years and accepted the German point of view that Hungary should stop industrializing. He spoke about the pro-German commitment of Hungarian foreign policy not only in general terms, but he emphasized also that "Hungary's rapprochement with Germany is at the present time proceeding on the ideological plane as well", and that he on his part endeavoured to promote progress in that direction. He promised even to authorize the functioning of the Volksbund in Hungary.

Thus Csáky could not take home in his baggage Hitler's permission to occupy the Carpatho-Ukraine, and his visit resulted merely in another unilateral commitment, yet he had, against his will, a certain share in the fact that his negotiations initiated new developments, if not in foreign policy, but at least in internal affairs. He managed to 'settle' the differences which had arisen in German–Hungarian relations, to reassure the Nazi leaders about Hungary's friendship for Germany, and since those were willing "to start a new era in the history of Hungarian–German relations", German pressure on Hungary began to ease off. This made it practically possible to bring about the fall of Béla Imrédy by finding a pretext satisfactory from the German point of view: Imrédy's Jewish descent in the grandparental line. On February 16, 1939, Regent Horthy appointed a new Prime Minister in the person of Count Pál Teleki.

After Teleki's appointment the only change in Hungary's policy regarding the Carpatho-Ukraine was that the new Government tried to broaden the horizon for the diplomatic preparation of the action by taking advantage of the given international situation so as to make the future occupation of the territory appear as an independent Hungarian move. These efforts were facilitated by the fact that Teleki's appointment was received with sympathy in the West, and that he himself had good Western connections, especially in England. The new Prime Minister changed the argument in support of that territory's annexation to Hungary. He well knew that reasoning on the ethnic line could hardly be made acceptable in the case of the Carpatho-Ukraine, historical references were not satisfying either, and even the phrases vilifying Bolshevism and pan-Slavism were flimsy arguments. Therefore Teleki, the geographer, produced economic, geoeconomic and geopolitical motives. In a voluminous memorandum forwarded to the Governments of the Great Powers he explained that the Great Hungarian Plain is connected by the Tisza river in a geographic and hydrogeographic unity with the Carpatho-Ukraine; that the Government of the Carpatho-Ukraine was ruthlessly wasting the forest resources, involving the danger that the heavy rainfall might change the disafforested areas into barren karstland, and the mass of water running down the Tisza might make the Great Plain a swampy country. Consequently Hungary, if she was to prevent a catastrophe, had to act, namely to take possession of the territory. This reasoning seemed more convenient even to the Germans, since it did not lay emphasis on the importance of a common Polish–Hungarian frontier for Hungary.

In February 1939 it was already certain that Hitler was planning to violate the Munich Pact, and the days of independent Czechoslovakia were numbered. The Hungarian Government felt that the imminent German action might at last bring the historic moment for the acquisition of the Carpatho-Ukraine. In Budapest, however, one could only vaguely surmise what solution Hitler would choose and what part would he assign to Hungary. Nor could one know precisely what territories Germany would lay claim to and in what form, and what she intended to let Hungary take. Teleki did not wish to procrastinate as his predecessor had; he was intent on taking possession of the Carpatho-Ukraine. He wanted to act, as far as possible, one instant before the Germans did, or at least simultaneously with them, lest the delay should let Hitler have a head start, assume the right of arbitration, and fix a price for his decision as he pleased, or bar definitively Hungary's way to the 'northern gate'.

From February 1939 onward, the Hungarian Government did not stop plying the German Foreign Minister with questions about when the prohibition of the occupation of the Carpatho-Ukraine would be lifted. The Germans evaded a straight answer, advised the Hungarians to be patient, promising to inform the Government as soon as there was some relevant development. In the meantime reports on German preparations were received. Rumour had it that Germany was preparing to occupy Slovakia, particularly after the news came that, on March 10, the power in Slovakia had been taken over by the army and practically all members of the separatist Tiso Government had been dismissed. The uncertainty, the fear of missing the golden opportunity prompted Teleki to get the Council of Ministers, on March 10, to adopt the decision that, in case the German armed forces marched into Czechoslovakia or Slovakia proclaimed her independence, the Hungarian army should occupy the Carpatho-Ukraine even if the Government failed to obtain the Germans' consent. Teleki immediately notified Rome and Warsaw of the Government's decision, making a point of emphasizing that should Slovakia "slip under the sway of the German Reich" without a common Polish—Hungarian frontier being established, this would enable Germany to wield such superiority which would endanger not only Hungarian but Polish and Italian interests as well.

When this telegram was dispatched, there was already no need to worry. Under the impact of the events in Slovakia, the Nazi leaders decided to give Hungary a free hand in the Carpatho-Ukraine. On March 11 the German Minister in Budapest presented a note to the Hungarian Ministry of Foreign Affairs. In it, the Wilhelmstrasse, "anticipating certain Hungarian actions to be taken in the territory of the Carpatho-Ukraine", specified Germany's economic and political demands. These were as follows: during and after the occupation of the Carpatho-Ukraine full consideration should be given to German transport requirements; the Hungarian Government should recognize the treaties and agreements of an economic nature which the Government of the Carpatho-Ukraine had concluded with German official or private persons; it should recognize the existing rights of the *Volksdeutsche* living in the territory; members of the Carpatho-Ukraine Government and its leading politicians should not be persecuted on any pretext.

In the afternoon of March 12, Hitler received the Hungarian Minister in Berlin, Döme Sztójay, and requested him to inform his Government that the break-up of Czechoslovakia was imminent. Germany would recognize the independence of Slovakia, but would not grant recognition to the Carpatho-Ukraine for 24 hours' time. Hungary would thus have 24 hours in which to solve the Ruthenian question. In the evening hours Sztójay, in company with Altenburg, the official in charge of Czechoslovak affairs in the political department of the German Foreign Ministry, flew by a special aircraft to Budapest and immediately reported to his superiors. The following day Altenburg, accompanied by the German Minister in Budapest, made a call to Horthy and had talks with the Prime Minister, the Chief of Staff and the Deputy Foreign Minister. These talks resulted in an agreement. It was agreed that Hungary would provoke a border incident on March 16 and launch an attack on the 18th. Reference was also made to the note of March 11. Teleki, in the presence of Altenburg, acceded to the German demands, though later he denied having given his consent, which resulted in a nearly six-month-long dispute between the two Governments.

Horthy hastened to express his thanks to Hitler. In his telegram of March 13 he wrote that "notwithstanding our volunteers of five-weeks, we set about this affair with the greatest enthusiasm", and emphasized that he would never forget "this token of friendship" and that the Führer "can always firmly rely" on his gratitude. From that moment the events followed so rapidly that the originally scheduled date had to be changed. On March 14, in accordance with an agreement with the Germans, Slovakia proclaimed her independence. At early dawn on the same day, the Voloshin Government of the Carpatho-Ukraine also proclaimed the territory independent and asked for the protection of the German Reich. This unexpected interlude, in spite of Hitler's promise concerning the 24 hours' delay, caused alarm in Budapest. They did not know whether Voloshin's move had not been suggested by the Germans in violation of previous agreements. The moment of action had come. On March 14 several large-scale border incidents were provoked at Munkács and Ungvár, and in the morning hours of the 15th the Hungarian army, only partly deployed, started the attack.

The German troops marched into Prague at the same hour, after Hitler, during the night, had forced the aged President of Czechoslovakia, Emil Hácha, to sign a proclamation placing the fate of the Czech people in Hitler's hands and asking for German protection. The German troops occupied the Czech territories without firing a shot. Resistance was only put up in the Carpatho-Ukraine, where the Sitch Guardists, in the hope that Hitler would comply with the request of the Voloshin Government and provide protection against the Hungarians, joined battle with the Hungarian forces. This hope, however, was a wild one. Hitler did not want to intercede, and the Hungarian troops reached the Polish frontier in a short time, and thus took possession of the Carpatho-Ukraine.

The dismemberment of Czechoslovakia was complete. Horthy's army had performed its first 'feat of arms'. The Government's propaganda machinery started to glorify the Hungarian armed forces which stood guard along the ridge of the Carpathian Mountains.

Teleki was satisfied because he could avoid living through the bitter hours of an arbitral procedure and facing its consequences, and because he could make a good part of the public believe that the latest territorial gain was a result of the Government's alertness and determination, of independent Hungarian action, against the Germans' will. Teleki had the feeling that he had consolidated his position both internally and internationally. But disappointment was bound to come soon. The dismemberment of Czechoslovakia, accomplished with Hungarian assistance, shifted the balance of power in the Danubian basin entirely to the advantage of Nazi Germany, and had resulted in significant changes in the whole European situation as well. The outbreak of a new world war was looming on the horizon. The consequences had now to be faced.

CHAPTER IV

HUNGARY'S FOREIGN POLICY IN THE FIRST STAGE OF THE SECOND WORLD WAR, 1939–1941

1. The foreign policy of the Teleki Government at the outbreak of the Second World War

Barely a week after the Wehrmacht divisions had occupied what had been left of Czechoslovakia after the Munich Pact, Hitler, whose audacity was heightened by the attitude of the Western Powers with regard to the subjugation of Austria and Czechoslovakia, brought all Germany's diplomatic and military pressure to bear upon Poland.

In the spring of 1939, however, a gradual turn occurred in the international situation. Following the dismemberment of Czechoslovakia, the anger of democratic public opinion throughout the world was perceptibly growing at the sight of Nazi aggression and this clearly made its effect felt on the policy of the Western Powers. At the same time some political leaders in the West realized that phrase-mongering about an 'anti-Bolshevist crusade' only served to conceal Germany's aspirations for world hegemony. Chamberlain's policy of appeasement was faced with a mounting opposition which, in the interest of maintaining the British Empire, found it necessary for England to break with the policy of compromise towards Germany. On April 6, 1939, Great Britain and Poland signed a mutual assistance treaty. France ratified the Franco–Polish pact. On April 13 the British and the French Government concluded guarantee treaties with Rumania and Greece.

These changes could not remain without effect on Hungarian foreign policy either. From 1939 onward the ruling classes had to face the possible consequence that further political co-operation with Germany (a trend that previously seemed to have been justified by Chamberlain's policy of appeasement towards Germany) might eventually involve Hungary's participation in the German–Polish conflict threatening to grow into a world war, and might result in an open break with the Western Powers. The Hungarian Government continuously received information through its Minister in London, György Barcza, about the relevant views of the influential politicians in England.

It is doubtless then that in 1939 the foreign policy pursued by the Hungarian ruling quarters was strongly influenced by the factors which pointed to the possibility of an outbreak of war between Germany and the Western Powers. On the other hand, Hungarian policy-makers did not overlook the fact that England and France, while securing their own frontiers, were still attempting to come to terms with Germany, first of all at the expense of the Soviet Union. Should such an agreement lead Great

Britain and France to give up their policy of guarantees, it would not only prove the main line of Hungarian foreign policy right, but it might even facilitate the realization of revisionist objectives.

Following the Munich Pact and the first Vienna Award, German economic expansion towards Hungary was getting ever stronger, clearly to make the country a raw material and food supply base of the German national economy. This economic expansion, coupled with great-power aspirations, was increasingly hurtful to the interests, to the independent imperialist goals of Hungarian finance capitalists and big landowners.

To growing German economic and political pressure was added a substantial invigoration of the pro-German groups of the domestic political scene. Prime Minister Imrédy himself had taken sides with the extreme-right groups and wished to carry through his line of unconditional German orientation in foreign politics and to introduce the methods of German Fascism in domestic politics. This turn of events, as we have seen above, had prompted representatives of the interests of big landowners and finance capitalists to bring about the downfall of the Imrédy Government. This is how Count Pál Teleki, and old politician of the counter-revolutionary régime, took the office of Prime Minister in February 1939. To protect the economic, political and power influence of the finance capitalists and the landlords of the latifundia who in fact improved their connections with the Germans, thus altering their previous aspirations for independence, Teleki was to cultivate the ties with Germany, while checking any further German encroachment. At the same time he was expected to frustrate the political ambitions of the extreme right. In this way, besides the endorsement of revision, the traditional aim of the counter-revolutionary régime's foreign policy, the Government came to intensify its activity to 'protect the régime'.

The Government, however, could fulfil this function only partially, primarily because it was simultaneously trying to crush those democratic and progressive forces on which it could have relied against the ultra-right. Although it managed to preserve the traditional structure of government and to avoid a change in favour of the extreme right-wingers, the political weight of the pro-German rightist opposition did not diminish, it rather grew. At the parliamentary elections held towards the end of May, 1939, the Arrow-Cross parties, partly subventioned with German money, obtained 900,000 votes and won over 40 seats in Parliament, and thus constituted the second strongest political force in the country. Thus the followers of unconditional pro-German policy gained considerable strength in the legislature and kept exerting pressure upon the foreign policy of the Government for further concessions to be made to Germany.

All these factors taken together determined the Teleki Government's more cautious foreign policy from the spring of 1939 onward. The basis of this policy continued to be collaboration with Nazi Germany. This policy was built on adherence to the Berlin–Rome Axis, but it wished to strengthen the southern part of the Axis as a counterbalance to growing German pressure. Close friendship with Italy, the emphasis on the common Italo–Hungarian interests again came to the fore. The gist of this conception was determined at the Italo—Hungarian talks of April 21, 1939, as follows: The only policy conceivable in Central Europe is the Axis policy, but "a strong Hungary is of paramount interest to Italy, and a strong Italy is a matter of almost vital interest to Hungary . . . There is need for a balance within the Axis policy itself, since only this makes it a lasting affair. The balance can be ensured only if the greatest possible number of small and middle-size states join the Axis, for it is obvious that, owing to the given power relations, the accession of these states will strengthen Italy in the first place."

The Teleki Government was also cautious to keep pro-German policy from leading to a definitive break with the Western Powers, should the German—Polish conflict grow into a world war. Teleki and other far-sighted members of the ruling classes not only did not believe that a German—Polish clash could remain an isolated conflict, but they were convinced that an armed conflict between Germany and the Western Powers — which had behind them the United States as a natural ally — would not be a short *Blitzkrieg* but a long, exhausting war that might end in the defeat of Germany or in her considerable weakening. Consequently, they thought that Hungary should, if possible, stay away from the war; she should guard against getting entangled in an open armed conflict with the Western Powers; she should take care not to be pushed into international isolation as she had been in the period following the First World War; so, by relying on her essentially intact armed forces, she had to ensure that the régime survived through the great world conflagration which would presumably bring about a political and power vacuum in Central Europe. The lesson drawn from the 1919 experiences and the effects of Rumanian occupation was that in a vacuum of this kind the decisive say in the Danubian basin would be had by the country which possessed an intact and combat-worthy army.

Thus, in the summer of 1939, Hungary was to observe neutrality in the Polish—German conflict. This was also justified by the state of Hungarian—Polish relations, these having been determined by the fact that the foreign political interests of the two countries were not basically contrary and even coincided at certain points. This coincidence followed not only from the territorial claim on Czechoslovakia raised by the two Governments, but also from shared fear of German expansion parallel with the rise of Nazi Germany. The attitude of the Hungarian Government was also influenced by the general sympathy which Hungarian public opinion felt for the Poles.

The above-outlined foreign political endeavours of the Teleki Government did not of course mean that it had given up its main objective, the continued revision of the territorial clauses of the Trianon treaty of peace. Indeed, from 1939 onward, the Hungarian Government concentrated on the recovery of Transylvania. From the point of view of the revisionist demands, German friedship was becoming a two-edged weapon: the German dynamism continued to support the efforts to change the status quo, but simultaneously, after the Munich Pact, the German aspirations ran counter to the Hungarian claims. The tug-of-war prior to the occupation of the Carpatho-Ukraine, as well as the fact that, when Czechoslovakia was carved up, Slovakia had not been annexed to Hungary but had been constituted an 'independent state' under German protectorate, are examples to the point. After the conclusion of the Rumanian—German economic pact of March 1939 it became increasingly evident that — for the time being at least — active support from Germany could not be counted upon in the matter of Transylvania either. Nazi foreign policy tried to lessen the Hungarian—Rumanian differences and exerted pressure on the Hungarian Government in order to normalize its relationship with Rumania. For this reason, from the spring of 1939 onward, Hungarian Government quarters placed emphasis on the conception that the revisionist claims on Rumania should be enforced without active support from Germany, by relying on Hungary's own armed force, as soon as it was made possible by the development of international power relations in Central Europe. Part of this conception was that should the differences between Germany and the Western Powers turn into a war, the revision concerning Transylvania was to be carried out by all means, by exploiting the chaos produced by the wartime conditions, before the war was ended. The Teleki Government obviously calculated upon the possibility that it would be easier to have the status of recovered territories recognized *de jure* by the victorious Powers — especially if Hungary did not enter the war on Germany's side — than to achieve a modification of the Rumanian—Hungarian frontier at a peace conference. The connection between the Teleki Government's effort to preserve armed neutrality and the principle of a separate solution of the revision at Rumania's expense could also be seen in other respects. The Germans exacted great economic and political concessions from Hungary in return for the first Vienna Award. Besides, the successes of revisionism attained with German help broadened the basis of those ultra-right elements which were for an unreserved pro-German domestic and foreign policy, under the slogan of the possibility of further 'territorial aggrandizement'. Teleki and his political adherents knew that another territorial revision achieved with the active co-operation of the Germans, or possibly through another arbitral award, would have to be paid for with concessions which would inevitably lead to Hungary's giving up her armed neutrality, to her joining the war on the side of Germany.

The foreign political conception developed by the Teleki Government on the threshold of the Second World War, although it certainly scored some temporary successes, was in fact, built on such irreconcilable contradictions which were bound to bring about the failure and collapse of this policy. The contradictions already became manifest in May 1939. The desire to satisfy the Hungarian territorial aspirations was far too strong to let the Government adhere to the principle of armed neutrality.

Military preparations against Rumania began already in May 1939. But the Hungarian Government knew full well that it could not launch a separate action without Hitler's consent, therefore the scheming against Rumania had to be built on the conceptions of the Axis Powers. At the same time the Government did not at all know what role the Germans ascribed to Hungary in their war plans, although it was pretty well informed that a German attack on Poland was scheduled for late August or early September.

In July 1939, Teleky and Csáky received a personal message from Mussolini to the effect that, since Hungary could not remain neutral in a general conflict, and since there were to be negotiations prior to the impending war, Hungary was required to sign a written declaration stating that, should the Axis Powers get entangled in war with a group of democratic states, Hungary would follow the policy of the Axis.

On July 24, 1939, in compliance with this appeal, Teleki addressed identical letters to Hitler and Mussolini. The letters contained the requested declaration, but Teleki also wrote a second letter to notify the German Government of his reservations and to allude to his revisionist demands.

In the first letter Teleki stressed that: "guided by profound faith in the moral and material strength of the Berlin—Rome Axis . . . in the event of a general conflict, Hungary will make her policy conform to the policy of the Axis." He proposed the convening of German—Italo—Hungrian three-Power consultations to discuss "all the problems that may arise from the closest co-operation of the three Powers". To this he added: "There should be no doubt, however, that our accommodation to this policy can in no way impair our sovereignty, which is embodied in our constitution, and must not bar the way to the realization of our national goals." In the second letter, to avoid any misinterpretation of his first letter, he stated that "if no serious change occurs in the given circumstances, Hungary cannot, on moral grounds, be in a position to take armed action against Poland".

Teleki's message — of which Ciano wrote in his diary that "I strongly suspect that he wrote the first letter for the sake of presenting the other" — was received in Berlin with indignation and was answered during Csáky's next visit.

The Hungarian Foreign Minister went to Berchtesgaden on August 8, where Hitler received him in the presence of Ribbentrop. The Führer cast angry reproaches upon the Hungarian Government. He declared that Poland presented no military problem at all to Germany, and Hungary's military participation in the war aginst Poland was not reckoned with. He qualified Teleki's letter as inexplicable after Hungary had been able to recover part of her lost territories only with Germany's assistance. Then he made Csáky understand that in the given military situation there was no possibility of continuing to support Hungary's revisionist demands.

Frightened by Hitler's harangue, Csáky ultimately requested, without being authorized to do so, that both letters of Teleki should be regarded as not having been written. The next day Minister Sztójay stated in an official note that the Hungarian Government was revoking the two letters.

Neither the revocation of the letters of July 24 nor the proposals Csáky made in Rome a few days later — in connection with the establishment of an alliance of the Axis Powers with Hungary — meant that the Government had abandoned its foreign political ambitions; on the contrary, these were rather justified by the international events that took place in the middle of August 1939. On the one hand, after the German—Italian talks at Salzburg it appeared that Italy was also unwilling to enter the war in connection with the German—Polish conflict and was striving for the status of a 'non-belligerent' power. On the other hand, on August 23, 1939, a non-aggression treaty was concluded between Germany and the Soviet Union. By accepting the German offer of a pact, the Soviet Government thwarted, or rather delayed, the danger of a German assault upon the Soviet Union. This also crushed the secret hopes of the Hungarian ruling classes for a compromise between Germany and the Western Powers to the detriment of the Soviet Union. It became evident that the German–Polish conflict would lead to the outbreak of war between Germany and the Western Powers.

Having estimated the probable course of international power relationships — and doubting the certainty of Germany's victory — Teleki thought that, as a result of the Soviet–German pact, the Soviet Union would, in any case, come out of the war a substantially more important power factor in East Central Europe than before, regardless of whether the pact remained in force or if Hitler attacked the Soviet Union, which in turn, would bring about an anti-Fascist coalition of the Great Powers. This, he thought, would involve a mortal danger to the Hungarian régime which he deemed it his foremost duty to defend and salvage, in case Hungary could not avoid entering the war on Germany's side. Thus Teleki saw himself justified in his cautious attitude.

To make his position known to the British Government, Teleki, at the end of August, sent an unofficial message to Foreign Secretary Halifax informing him that the Hungarian Government would not co-operate with Germany in her conflict with Poland; that Hungary was striving for neutrality but, in view of her geographical location, she abstained from making a declaration of neutrality. He emphasized that the Government's intention not to declare neutrality was not merely conform to Germany's request; the other reason why he did not wish to commit himself to strict neutrality was that he might thus be free to enforce Hungary's revisionist demands at the proper moment.

An Italian attempt to mediate between Germany and the Western Powers opened up new prospects for the revisionist ambitions of the Hungarian ruling quarters. In fact, in the last days of August, the Italian Government proposed that the Great Powers should create the possibility of convening, by September 5, an international conference "to revise those clauses of the Versailles treaty disturbing life in Europe". The Hungarian Government began to meditate on the outlines of a new Munich that might possibly solve the question of a Transylvanian revision. Its hope to this effect was substantiated by the fact that, although the German army began the invasion of Poland on September 1, 1939, neither on the day of aggression nor the day after did Great Britain and France declare war on Germany.

Teleki, on September 2, wrote Mussolini a letter, requesting that the proposed international conference should take up the issue of Hungary's revisionist demands. And he declared that, should it be impossible to comply with his request, the Hungarian Government would continue making military preparations in silence but with the determination that, by taking any risk, it might "set the Rumanian–Hungarian territorial dispute at rest for a long time". Teleki asked the Duce to prepare the international public for the impending events and to give Hungary every possible diplomatic assistance.

The hopes of the Teleki Government, however, soon faded away. On September 3 Great Britain and France declared war on Germany. The illusions about a 'second

Munich' vanished. An attack on Rumania would have brought with it the consequences of the Anglo—French guarantees.

At the same time the pressure of German diplomacy again weighed on Hungary in order to exact her consent to making use of the Polish—Hungarian frontier zone for an attack on Poland from the rear.

On September 3 Deputy Under-Secretary of State for Foreign Affairs Ernst Woermann and the next day Ribbentrop himself said to Sztójay that Germany was absolutely interested in the maintenance of peace in South Eastern Europe, so Hungary could by no means start an attack on Rumania. Ribbentrop requested that Csáky should call on the German General Headquarters on September 7 in order to talk over 'special questions'.

The indication was that this time the Germans would demand permission for the Wehrmacht to pass through the territory of Hungary. This involved a great danger to the independence of the country but did not deter members of the Hungarian Government, in their obsession with revision, from ignoring all the 'moral considerations' of the Polish question, if this was the price of the Nazi leaders' consent to an attack on Rumania. On September 6, Csáky sent Ciano a message stating that he would be inclined to comply with the German demand in exchange for Germany's consent to Hungary's opening military operations against Rumania. But the Italian Foreign Minister dissuaded Csáky from his plans and reminded him that such an operation would invite a declaration of war from the Western Powers.

On September 7, the Hungarian Foreign Minister flew to the German General Headquarters. Ribbentrop again warned him categorically that an attack on Rumania would not be tolerated. Csáky promised not to take action against Rumania until an agreement was arrived at with Germany on this matter, and even declared that the Hungarian Government would be willing to conclude a non-aggression treaty with Rumania. The issue of German troops crossing Hungary was not brought up on this occasion, since to Ribbentrop's question whether Hungary had any territorial claims on Poland, Csáky gave an answer in the negative.

But already on September 9 Minister Erdmannsdorff showed up at the Hungarian Ministry of Foreign Affairs and presented Ribbentrop's message: In view of future contingencies, he does not deem it opportune for Hungary to conclude a non-aggression treaty with Rumania. And after this vague hint of the possibility of a Transylvanian revision, the German Foreign Minister phoned Csáky the same day, asking him to make the Kassa railway line immediately available to the German armed forces for the transport of troops into Poland.

Fulfilment of this demand would have meant that Hungary has openly identified herself with Nazi Germany. It was also beyond doubt that this concession would have incurred an Anglo—Franco—Polish declaration of war, that is, Hungary's entry into the war, which in turn would have meant the failure of Teleki's foreign policy in a situation unfavourable for the revisionist demands. On September 10 the Cabinet meeting, presided by Teleki, rejected the German demand. The reasons were that first, it could count upon diplomatic support from Italy; and second, it could take it for granted that in the very midst of the German—Polish war there was no reason to fear a German assault, or a German attempt to march through the country without Hungarian consent. All the more so, since of all European countries Hungary had the strongest ties binding her to Germany. Even if she did not participate in armed action, she still provided economic assistance to the Germans and was pursuing a pro-Axis policy.

Csáky at once gave the Hungarian Government's reply to Ribbentrop, who took notice of it but asked for permission to transport war material on the previously designated railway line. On September 11 the Foreign Ministry informed Erdmannsdorff that the Hungarian Government only allowed the transport of war materials, in locked-up waggons, without military escort.

This time the refusal was thus really not followed by reprisals, although from then onward, whenever German diplomacy wished to exert pressure on the Hungarian Government, it referred to the refusal of troop transport. Ciano even made a note in his diary in this connection: "The Hungarians will have to pay for this once." At the given moment anyway, Teleki indeed managed to strengthen Hungary's armed neutrality, to avoid being entangled in the war.

Another intermezzo in this affair came when the Slovak Government, on the 11th, also requested for its troops the right of passage through the Kassa railway line. This request was denied in a form far from polite, in an angry and menacing tone.

The position of the Teleki Government was of little military consequence to Poland, because the Polish Government and army already stood on the verge of total collapse. This, however, does not lessen the significance of the refusal of the German request. As a consequence of this measure, the common Polish—Hungarian frontier section remained under Hungarian control (this is exactly what the Germans intended to prevent by their request for passage), and this made it possible for more than 70,000 Poles to flee to Hungary in the days of the débâcle. Their majority were soldiers; many of them crossed the frontier fully armed. Thus, among others, the 10th armoured brigade, the 3rd mountain riflemen's brigade, the 3rd heavy artillery regiment, and 9th and 2nd lancers' regiments, etc.; 10 per cent of the Polish refugees were officers, 86.6 per cent warrant officers and enlisted men, 1.4 per cent policemen and custom-house officers.

The attitude of the Government towards Poland during the September war and thereafter can be defined as one of benevolent neutrality. After September 1939 the Hungarian Government kept recognizing Poland as a state. It failed to recognize the Polish Government newly constituted at London, but it authorized and ensured the functioning of the Polish Legation in Budapest until November 1940 — in spite of repeated German protests — and the Legation was only closed after Hungary's accession to the Tripartite Pact. The Government created opportunities, from the autumn of 1939, for Polish soldiers to find their way, at a more or less rapid pace depending on the momentary strength of German pressure, into Western Europe. This involved a regular recruitment or conscription, under the direction or the military attaché of the Polish Legation in Budapest, with the help of the Hungarian Ministries of National

Defence and Foreign Affairs. The number of Polish refugees who had left Hungary for the West by 1941 was 50,000.

The Polish refugees who had remained behind in Hungary were placed in the charge of a specially appointed Government commisioner. Their subsistence was ensured through regular state subsidies. Polish-language schools were opened for their children, a Polish secondary school functioned at Balatonboglár.

2. The 'funny war' and Hungary

Since the factors instrumental in the shaping of the foreign policy of the Teleki Government continued to be effective at the time of the 'funny war', the aim of Teleki's foreign policy also remained the same. At the outbreak of war, neither Germany nor the Allied Powers wished to change Eastern and South Eastern Europe into a theatre of war. This was a favourable situation from Teleki's point of view.

Although Hitler did not immediately take the offensive on the Western front following the subjugation of Poland, Germany was invariably interested in the maintenance of peace in South Eastern Europe because, in view of the gradually imposed British economic blockade, it was vitally important for the German war machinery to continue the increasing exploitation of the economic resources of the area, first of all the crude oil of Rumania, but of no lesser importance was ore mining in Yugoslavia. This is why Rumania, and Yugoslavia were more prominent targets of German diplomacy than Hungary which
more so since the Germans had much stronger positions in Hungary than in Rumania protected by Anglo—French guarantees, or in Yugoslavia. In the few months following the outbreak of war there was hardly any official demonstration of German 'friendship' for Hungary. Although in the autumn of 1939 the German Government did not voice any major political demands, it reacted most violently to any minor Hungarian move considered to be hurtful to German interests. Any Hungarian diplomatic move or political statement directed against Rumania came up against resolute opposition on the part of Germany. Charging the Hungarian Government with the violation of neutrality the Germans especially criticized Hungary's loyal attitude towards the Polish refugees.

At the time of the 'funny war' German foreign policy was mainly intent on securing the fullest possible satisfaction of German economic needs. To this end, it made use of the most diverse methods of diplomatic blackmail. From the autumn of 1939 onward, Sztójay, in his reports to Budapest, repeated time and again that German political quarters were dissatisfied with the situation in Hungary. On November 3, at last, Horthy wrote Hitler, giving him his assurances that Hungary stood firmly by Germany.

During the German—Hungarian economic negotiations opened in September 1939, the German representative, Ambassador Clodius, put forward important demands, which the Hungarian Government fulfilled only in part. This resistance, however, did not last long; the German Government had its own way to make its economic needs fully satisfied. The prohibition of certain military transports introduced in the early days of the war was upheld. The restriction of German arms transports was a serious blow to the armaments programme of Hungary preparing for an attack on Rumania. For this reason, during the negotiations in December 1939 and January 1940, the Hungarian Government complied with the German demands and promised to do all in its power to assist Germany economically in every respect.

In the months following the outbreak of war Hungarian foreign policy endeavoured to lean upon Italy within the Axis alliance, but it could not count upon Italian support to the extent it did before the outbreak of war. Not only because Italy played second fiddle to Germany within the alliance, but also because she exerted herself as a 'non-belligerent party' to increase her influence in the neutral countries of South Eastern Europe conforming to pro-Axis policy. Therefore, at least until the summer of 1940, Italy supported the German effort at the preservation of peace in South Eastern Europe in every way. So, the Hungarian Government could not reckon with Italy's co-operation and support either; moreover, from the beginning of the war, Ciano repeatedly advised Hungary to exercise patience and moderation.

After the outbreak of war the attitude of England and France evinced a certain goodwill towards Hungary in spite of her continued pro-Axis policy. The fact that, in September 1939, Hungary had observed neutrality induced the Western Powers to try, by showing tact towards Hungary's official policy and making certain economic concessions (which concerned chiefly the import of raw materials and were fairly considerable under the blockade), to keep the Hungarian Government back from drawing closer to Germany and joining the war. They also showed cautiousness in the matter of the revisionist policy. At that time Hungary displayed intense diplomatic activity in London and Paris in an effort to prevent a postwar reestablishment of the Versailles frontiers and the independence of Czechoslovakia. British and French official quarters kept reassuring the Hungarian Government on these questions, though they refused to make any promises or commitments in return for Hungary's neutrality. They — especially the French — dealt all the more thoroughly with various plans for the war; they also discussed these plans with Hungarian diplomats and politicians.

The attitude of the Soviet Union towards Hungary was essentially determined by the Soviet—German non-aggression treaty. In the second half of 1939, when formations of the Red Army marching into the Western Ukraine and Western Byelorussia, which had belonged to Poland since the First World War, reached the Hungarian frontier, Moscow sent the Hungarian Government a message informing it that the Soviet Union respected the frontiers of Hungary and wished to live in peace with all neighbouring countries. On September 24, 1939, the Soviet Union reestablished diplomatic relations with Hungary. When the new Hungarian Minister in Moscow, József Kristóffy, presented his credentials, the Chairman of the Presidium of the Supreme Soviet, M. I. Kalinin, emphasized that no conflict of interests existed between the two countries, and that the Soviet Union intended to develop political, economic and cultural contacts with Hungary.

Under the impact of German—Soviet relations the Hungarian Government's anti-Soviet attitude became more moderate as reflected by official manifestations. Some half-hearted attempts were made to establish economic contacts. But on the whole, the Hungarian Government had not the slightest genuine intention to maintain good neighbourly relations with the Soviet Union. In this period of the war Hungary's foreign policy was pivoted on anti-Sovietism. In the peculiar international situation created by the German—Soviet non-agression treaty, Teleki wanted to exploit this in order to broaden the basis of his domestic and foreign policy, and he even had some success. Beyond the hopes of revision, it was anti-Sovietism that always sustained the German orientation of the Hungarian ruling quarters. For this very reason the non-aggression treaty, as well as the fact that, in the light of both German and Soviet manifestations, the state of neutrality seemed to be a lasting affair, spread confusion and 'disenchantment' in the Hungarian ruling classes and also in the bourgeois and petty-bourgeois strata trained in an anti-Soviet spirit. This situation lessened the influence of the extreme-right and strengthened the support for Teleki within the ruling quarters. Towards the Western Powers, the Government emphatically held to anti-Sovietism as one of the principles of its foreign policy during the 'funny war'. This conduct was even supported by certain politicians in the West — mainly adherents of Chamberlain — who tried hard to convert the war between Germany and the Allies, by opening new theatres of war in Eastern Europe and making a compromise with the Germans, into a war against the Soviet Union. (Hungary's envoy in London, György Barcza, wrote a number of reports on the related ideas of Chamberlain and Halifax.) These politicians pursued the same aim of extending the conflict in connection with the Soviet—Finnish war that broke out at the end of November 1939. Teleki — who pinned his hope on the sharpening of the differences between the Soviet Union and the Western Powers — was practically the first among the European statesmen to openly espouse, in Parliament on December 5, the idea of a united anti-Soviet front. The Hungarian Government got busy demonstrating its readiness to take an active part in 'a vast anti-Bolshevist European front'. Teleki personally took charge of the dispatch of volunteer units to Finland. Hungary delivered considerable amounts of war material to the Finnish forces.

As to Transylvania, the Teleki Government concentrated on achieving the revision at a time preceding the termination of the current war conflict. This programme determined Hungary's relations with the neighbouring countries and the Government's decisions regarding the problems of Central Europe and the Balkans. In practice this meant that the Hungarian Government, by subordinating every one of its moves to the realization of revision, lessened the chances which, in the first period of the war, might have promoted solidarity with the neighbouring countries and thereby the success of the efforts to preserve neutrality. Thus, this policy in fact increased the probability of Hungary's becoming a tool in the service of Germany's imperialist plans concerning South Eastern Europe.

It was the Italian Government that first raised the idea of a Central European neutral bloc, but it soon backed out, because this might have temporarily tied Italy's hands in case she entered the war. Furthermore, the Germans also received the Italian idea with antipathy. The plan of a neutral bloc was again broached by the Rumanian Government in November 1939, after a preliminary consultation with the Balkan pact states. The related agreement was planned to include the following provisions: a declaration of neutrality in the face of the existing conflicts; a non-aggression pact among the contracting states; an obligation to observe benevolent neutrality in case one of the parties fell victim to aggression; the development of economic co-operation among the parties to the agreement. Out of consideration for Hungary and Bulgaria the draft contained no guarantees for the status quo. The idea was that Hungary and Bulgaria would be invited to accede after the Balkan pact states had agreed, and then all interested states would ask for Italy's support.

The plan met with lively response in the interested states as well as among the Great Powers. The creation of a neutral bloc might have served, to a certain extent, to settle the mutual differences of the small states of South Eastern Europe, offering better chances of protection against the German peril, against increasing German pressure and menace.

Of course, the conception of a neutral bloc entailed some hidden motives as well. The originator, Rumania, expected to obtain support in the question of Bessarabia against the Soviet Union and for the maintenance of the status quo in general, and this was practically the point over which the plan eventually failed. The plan stimulated the hopes of those Western quarters which were striving to establish a common anti-Soviet front. On this score Barcza wrote in one of his reports: "The British are of the opinion that it is tremendously important to uphold Italy's neutrality and the neutrality of the states of South Eastern Europe not only at present, but also later, in order to keep the Soviets in check."

On the other hand, the Germans resolutely opposed the plan. In this stage of the war, Germany wanted the states of South Eastern Europe and the Balkan peninsula to maintain their neutrality, counting upon the deepening conflicts to eventually lead to the growth of German influence in these countries.

In November 1939 the Hungarian Government, through diplomatic channels, received word about the plan of the neutral bloc and the related discussions. Without waiting for official information, the Government made its refusal public, pointing out that until the differences between Hungary and the states intending to co-operate were settled, accession was out of the question, because Hungary was not willing to make one-sided sacrifices or to give any promises with regard to this issue. By insisting on territorial revision as a price for Hungary's joining the proposed bloc, the Teleki Government ruled out any further progress in the case. Three days after the publication of this statement, the German Foreign Ministry informed Sztójay that Hungary's negative attitude was noted with satisfaction.

The Hungarian Government tried to make use of every little stir for the purposes of its revisionist claims on Rumania, and when, in the autumn of 1939, it heard rumours that the Soviet Union was supposed to take steps to recapture Bessarabia, which had been occupied and annexed by Rumania at the time of the war of intervention, it instantly engaged in feverish diplomatic and military preparations. Government quarters, especially the military chiefs, proposed that in case of a supposed Soviet–Rumanian conflict Hungary should capture Transylvania by force. Colonel-General Werth submitted to the Supreme Defence Council a number of memoranda in which he demanded the conclusion of a military convention with the Soviet Union for the co-ordination of the time of attack. True, Prime Minister Teleki and Interior Minister Keresztes-Fischer tried to restrain the military chiefs, but since Teleki himself did not wish to miss this opportunity, a detailed plan was worked out specifying the Hungarian claims on Rumania and the conditions of intervention, with the purpose of obtaining the approval of the Great Powers, first of all that of England and France who were bound to Rumania by guarantee treaties, or at least their tacit consent to a possible military action. The maximum claim on Rumania was a demand for the reannexation of an area of 78,000 sq. km. with over four million inhabitants, the minimum version spoke of 50,000 sq. km. Intended first of all for the Western Powers, the reason adduced for this demand was that Hungary alone was capable of forming a 'defence' against the Soviet Union in the Danubian basin.

The diplomatic action did not bring much success. Italy, to whom Rumania had appealed for support against the Hungarian ambitions, advised the Teleki Government to restrain itself, and informed it that in case of a Soviet–Rumanian armed conflict she would come to Rumania's rescue. At the time when the Balkan Pact states held their conference in February 1940, Berlin stated repeatedly that it would not even touch a subject that might open, either directly or indirectly, the possibility of a conflict in South Eastern Europe. The Western Powers, though having tacitly recognized the necessity of a readjustment of the Rumanian–Hungarian frontier, considered it possible to take up the question only after the war, under the auspices of the peace conference.

In February 1940 all this induced Teleki, by making considerable concessions, to change the decisions on the prerequisites of an armed attack on Rumania. According to this, Hungary did not renounce her territorial claims on Rumania but would not attempt to enforce them during the war, unless a war broke out between the Soviet Union and Rumania resulting in the collapse of the Balkan status quo, or unless Rumania ceded Dobrudja to Bulgaria. But Hungary did not intend to intervene if Rumania put up a successful resistance, or if the Near East forces of the Allies joined battle on Rumania's side. Bessarabia's peaceful transfer to the Soviet Union would not be regarded as a vindication of intervention. The position taken by the Hungarian government was put down in an aide-mémoire which was forwarded to London and Paris, and which the Budapest correspondent of *The Times* was authorized to make public in his paper.

Hungary's envoys in Paris and London were commissioned to present the aide-mémoire and at the same time to convey the following oral message: Hungary had no aggressive designs against anybody; she was ready to defend her independence, by force of arms if necessary, against foreign aggression; in no circumstances was she disposed to co-operate with the Soviet Union. Sargent, whom Barcza handed the note, talked in fairly plain terms replying: "Since Hungary can render us no service in the war, it is not worth our while to make any sacrifices on her behalf."

From January 1940 onward, however, the Hungarian Government received information from several sides indicating that Germany contemplated the military occupation of Rumania in order to seize her oilfields for the event of an armed conflict on account of the Bessarabia affair. Since the way of the Germans to Rumania could lead only through Hungary, the Teleki Government was faced with a new problem: the passage of the Wehrmacht. It was beyond doubt that such a contingency might bring satisfaction to Hungarian territorial demands, but it also seemed certain that co-operation with the Germans in an anti-Rumanian campaign might turn Hungary against the Western Powers, bringing with it the collapse of Teleki's entire foreign political conception.

Early in May the Council of Ministers held a meeting to decide how to reply to the expected German appeal. A scheme drawn up in the Ministry of Foreign Affairs proposed that participation in a German attack on Rumania be made subject to possible Soviet troop movements, on the grounds that Hungary's action in this way might be backed up by the Anti-Comintern Pact provisions.

Before consulting the Germans, Teleki sent an emissary to Rome to find out what support the Hungarian Government might obtain from Italy if it parried the German demand. This time, however, Mussolini's answer was a categorical denial. Teleki wished to know the British Government's view as well, so he drew up an aide-mémoire describing in detail the catastrophic consequences which Hungary would have to face if she refused to permit the Germans' passage through her territory.

Teleki's arguments found no response in London and caused further stiffening and estrangement in Hungarian—British relations. When Chamberlain's policy definitively failed (on May 10, 1940, Chamberlain resigned, and Churchill formed a Coalition Government), the British revised their policy towards Hungary. Minister Barcza summed up his experiences as follows: "The British attitude towards Hungary has recently begun to become sceptical, because the English anticipate that the Germans would advance in the south-eastern direction, in which case Hungary will not be in a position to resist, so it would be a mistake to supply raw materials or arms to Hungary." The information Barcza had sent was reliable. When, for example, on February 22, 1940, the Belgrade conference of the Balkan alliance gave occasion for the revival of the idea of a neutral bloc in South Eastern Europe, Sargent again made it clear that "from the beginning of the war we have all along recognized that it would be impossible to establish any 'front' in South East Europe which could include Hungary. For this reason there was never any question of guaranteeing her against Germany as we did Rumania. In other words, we have recognized Hungary to be in the German sphere, and nothing we can *say* will change this."

In May 1940 — in connection with the plan of the German occupation of Rumania — the British Government stated its position in principle. On behalf of his Government the British Minister in Budapest let Csáky know that the British could not remain indifferent to rumours according to which, under certain circumstances, the Hungarian

Government would authorize the passage of German troops through the territory of its country, because this was inconsistent with Hungarian neutrality. At the same time he outlined the consequences that might affect Anglo–Hungarian relations in case of its submissiveness to the German demands. Through other channels, Teleki was given to understand that, should the actual Hungarian Government resist the Germans and survive either at home or abroad, the British Government would officially recognize it as the only lawful Government of Hungary and treat it accordingly at the postwar peace conference.

The idea of an émigré Government already preoccupied Teleki and his men on the eve of the outbreak of war, on the assumption that it was imperative to avoid the repetition of the situation at the end of the First World War, when Hungary had been left without any Western representation acceptable to the Entente. The proposal was first made by János Pelényi, the Hungarian Minister in Washington, in the spring of 1939, and a year later Teleki saw the time ripe for taking steps with a view to realizing the plan for the event that Germany's march into Rumania would entail the occupation of Hungary. In concert with Regent Horthy, Prime Minister Teleki instructed Pelényi to deposit in the United States five million dollars for the purpose of a future émigré Government. In his letter to Pelényi dated March 17, 1940, he made arrangements for the conditions under which the fund might be used. He wrote: "The persons to whom Your Excellency shall be entitled and bound to surrender the money in question are, in addition to His Highness the Regent, the following gentlemen designated by the Regent himself as leaders of a possible Hungarian emigration: in the first place Count Gyula Károlyi or Count Pál Teleki, who are singly and exclusively entitled to take over the fund and to dispose of the money in the interest of our national freedom; in the second place Count Sándor Khuen-Héderváry, Mr. György Barcza, Mr. Lipót Baranyai, Count István Bethlen and Mr. Ferenc Keresztes-Fischer, any two of whom are entitled to receive the fund in conjunction with you ... If ... only one of those named in the second place, in conjunction with Your Excellency, that is only two Hungarians could be present, then the third person entitled to receive the fund shall be Mr. Royall Tyler, an American citizen and a friend of our Country."

At the same time there had been a considerable swing to the right inside Hungary. The right wing of the Government Party, the pro-German General Staff and the Arrow-Cross M.P.s attacked the foreign policy of the Government, demanding entry into the war by the side of Germany instead of mere pro-German neutrality. German economic and political pressure was simultaneously growing. All this was instrumental in pushing Teleki to abandon step by step his foreign policy platform. Since the Hungarian Government did not receive information about the proposed move against Rumania, Teleki on April 17, 1940, in order to find out the German plans, wrote Hitler a letter proposing German-–Italo–Hungarian consultation with the view of an attack on Rumania. He again raised the idea of three-Power negotiations, expressing his willingness to co-operate in an alliance with the Axis Powers, but he demanded equal partnership rights for Hungary, at least with regard to questions concerning South Eastern Europe.

Although the German General Staff had indeed planned to attack Rumania, this did not happen in the spring of 1940. At that time Germany was already preparing to launch the offensive in the West, so she was rather interested in maintaining peace in South Eastern Europe and the Balkan peninsula. Therefore, four days after the start of the offensive in the West, on May 14, Hitler in his reply to Teleki rejected the idea of three-Power negotiations and thus left the Hungarian Government in the lurch. A policy trying to initiate 'new development' in the Balkans, he wrote in his letter, would entail incalculable consequences, therefore Germany — in concert with Italy — would undertake nothing in the Balkan peninsula. Hitler did not fail to point out that, when advising Hungary to keep quiet, he was not asking the Hungarians to make sacrifices, since the Hungarian Government ought to know that friendly collaboration with Germany and Italy was "immensely advantageous to Hungary."

Teleki, in his letter of May 20 to Hitler, acknowledged the Führer's communications. The next day he wrote a letter to Pelényi in Washington and let him know that the idea of the formation of an émigré Government, or rather the appointment of a Western plenipotentiary, had been dropped for the time being. A few months later Pelényi was instructed to repay the five million dollars into the account of the National Bank of Hungary. This is how the plan for an émigré Government was cancelled.

So in the spring of 1940 Hungary could preserve her armed neutrality, but the price was the failure of the revisionist endeavours...

3. The second Vienna Award and its consequences

The possibility of recovering part of Transylvania was finally brought about by the new situation created by the German offensive resulting in the successful subjugation of Western Europe. This, however, put an end to Hungary's armed neutrality as well.

The triumphal progress of Nazi aggression, Italy's entry into the war, and France's capitulation made a double impact on Hungary's foreign policy. In the ruling classes the prevailing view was that the Germans could not be defeated and the end of war was in fact within reach. On the other hand, just as a consequence of this conception, the question of taking action against Rumania was again brought up.

As already mentioned, the Hungarian Government was of the opinion that the Transylvanian revision should be carried out before the end of the war in Europe. In June 1940, therefore, the matter already seemed pressing. When, on June 26, the Soviet Union called upon Rumania to cede Bessarabia and Northern Bukovina, Hungary's Government, diplomatic and military machinery got moving. On June 27 the Cabinet meeting put down in a decision that the Government would not tolerate discrimination, and if Rumania complied with the Soviet demands, she should also be forced to satisfy Hungary's territorial claims. At the same time the Supreme Defence Council of Hungary decided on the mobilization of the army and its gradual deployment on the Rumanian frontier.

These moves were obviously inconsistent with the Government's principles adopted in February. But Teleki, under the influence of the German successes at the Western front, was now of the opinion that the fast conclusion of the war was still possible, so a decision had to be enforced with regard to Transylvania. He was further impelled by the fact that, on July 1, Rumania renounced the British guarantee, and thus the danger of British intervention was eliminated. Teleki stuck to his earlier position on a single point: he was against co-operation with the Soviet Union. True, he did not need to deal seriously with this problem, since Rumania had complied with the Soviet demands.

It seemed to be a greater problem to clarify the German attitude. On June 28 Foreign Minister Csáky told Ambassador Clodius, who was staying in Budapest, to inform Ribbentrop that, if Germany consented to the attack on Rumania, the Hungarian Government would be willing to introduce further economic restrictions and to supply Germany with more grain. He also promised that Germany would be granted the right of free passage through Hungary in the south eastern direction, in which the German Government was specially interested.

In spite of these offers, the Hungarian move met with unsympathetic response in Berlin. At that time Hitler still contemplated launching the invasion of England, and he was sorely in need of Rumania's petroleum for the purpose. In the given moment, peace in South Eastern Europe and the Balkans was indispensable to Germany's war in the West. In addition, Rumanian foreign policy was geared to an unreserved pro-Axis line. At the news of Hungary's mobilization, Ribbentrop sent a note energetically pointing out to Csáky that a Balkan war that might ensue from the Hungarian military move was diametrically opposed to Germany's current interests, and Hungary could not count upon any kind of assistance from Germany. At the same time he invited Teleki and Csáky to go to Munich in order to clear the issues.

As a consequence of the German warnings the Hungarian attack was cancelled but the situation remained tense. At Munich, in the presence of Ribbentrop and Ciano, Hitler cautioned Teleki and Csáky not to start an action against Rumania. He suggested a settlement of the conflict through negotiations and made the promise that, in agreement with Mussolini, he would write to the King of Rumania and call upon him to try to come to an agreement with Hungary. Then he declared that Germany did not wish to attend those negotiations.

The Hungarian statesmen left Munich in a discontented mood. The possibility existed, though, that they would open negotiations about the territorial questions with the Rumanian Government, but, at the negotiating table, they could neither employ military pressure nor refer to the overt support of the Axis Powers. All this meant that the satisfaction of the Hungarian territorial claims on Rumania again depended on the goodwill of Germany. Hitler would decide how much Hungary should receive of the territory of Transylvania and what she should pay for it.

A few days after the Munich talks Hitler sent a letter to King Carol of Rumania, and on July 26 he conferred with the Prime Minister and the Foreign Minister of Rumania. On that occasion, resorting to threats and promises alike, he urged the earliest possible solution of the problems through negotiations. He even pointed to the practical aspects of a solution. All this indicated that, in July 1940, Hitler's position regarding the territorial problems of the states of South Eastern Europe underwent considerable changes. Until then Germany had flatly refused to satisfy the Hungarian and Bulgarian territorial claims on Rumania, and now she sat down to the conference table, asserting that the time had come to change the South Eastern European status quo established by the Paris treaties of peace.

The main reason for Germany's change of position was that the Nazi leaders, in July 1940, began preparations for an aggression upon the Soviet Union. At a conference with military leaders in the Berghof on July 31, 1940, Hitler mapped out his plans for an attack on the Soviet Union, and in this connection he spoke of the problems of a Balkan settlement, declaring that after the solution of the Hungarian–Rumanian territorial problems he would guarantee the frontiers of Rumania. In order to ensure the deployment of the southern flank of the armed force attacking the Soviet Union, he had first of all to eliminate from South Eastern Europe those factors which might hinder the troop movements. Such annoying factors might be the territorial disputes between Hungary and Rumania, between Bulgaria and Rumania.

Hitler well knew that the price to be paid for the use of railway lines in Hungary might only be the satisfaction, at least in part, of the Hungarian revisionist demands. On the other hand, Rumania was of prime importance to him from both the strategic and the economic point of view. Therefore he intended to settle the Hungarian–Rumanian territorial dispute in such a way that: 1. the arrangement should give Hungary sufficiently sizable areas for the Hungarian Government to be willing to authorize the transit of German troops and to fulfil other wishes of Germany with the least reluctance possible; 2. it should not discourage Rumania by causing her to renounce unduly large areas of her territory; 3. it should not satisfy the demands of either the Hungarian or the Rumanian ruling classes and should make sure that in the hope of further revision, or counter-revision, both countries placed themselves at the service of the German war machinery. All this was feasible only if both Governments were compelled to accept Germany's arbitration.

This is why Hitler suggested bilateral talks, presuming that these would become deadlocked because of excessive Hungarian demands and the absence of Rumanian willingness. And if, in this situation, the Hungarian Government still resorted to the threat of force, and Rumania again turned to Germany, in the utterly tense situation he could, through arbitration, set such conditions as he pleased.

The Hungarian–Rumanian negotiations started at Turnu Severin on August 16 and, as was to be expected, brought no result. What is more, both sides took new military measures. The talks were broken off on August 24. The Hungarian Government again contemplated a settlement through force of arms, while Rumania asked the Axis Powers to decide the question by arbitration. Hitler was confirmed in his calculations. On August 27, the German Ministers in Bucharest and Budapest were recalled for reporting. On the basis of their reports Hitler, with the participation of Ribbentrop and Ciano, drew a map of the partition of Transylvania. Then the Foreign Ministers of

Hungary and Rumania, as well as Prime Minister Teleki as an observer, were summoned to appear at Vienna on August 30.

Teleki and Csáky went to Vienna on August 28, and were received by Ribbentrop and Ciano. After Ribbentrop had taken the Hungarian statesmen to task for the situation that had arisen, declaring that the most energetic steps would follow if the Hungarian Government decided to take armed action, Csáky accepted Germany's arbitration in the question of Transylvania and recognized in advance that the arbitral decision should be binding upon Hungary without reservation. The Rumanian Foreign Minister was accorded the same treatment and, having been given promises of guarantees for the Rumanian frontiers, also accepted the proposed arbitration.

The protocol and the arbitral award were signed at Vienna's Belvedere Castle on August 30, 1940. In accordance with the decision, an area of 43,000 sq. km. with a population of 2.5 million, including more than a million Rumanians, were returned to Hungary. Approximately 400,000 Magyars had remained in Rumania. Simultaneously with the pronouncement of the award, a document was issued guaranteeing the frontiers of Rumania, and a Hungarian–German and a Rumanian–German agreement on minority question were signed.

The second Vienna Award brought partial satisfaction to the Hungarian revisionist demands, but Hungary had to pay a stiff price for it. The agreement signed at Vienna already provided for the granting of special rights to the German minority in Hungary; recognizing the Volksbund as an exclusive party of the Germans in Hungary and investing it with powers the like of which were granted to no other party or association in Hungary.

On September 10, the Hungarian Minister in Berlin handed Hitler a letter from Horthy expressing the Regent's gratitude for the second Vienna Award. Sztójay had a talk of an hour and a half with the Führer, and then, in his report to Foreign Minister Csáky, he outlined the German wishes and a programme which he thought would be an adequate expression of 'gratitude' in the hope of further revisions. This programme provided for the following: Hungary's firm espousal of the German cause; aid to Germany by supplying her with raw material and food in excess of the provisions of the economic agreements in force, even to the detriment of Hungary's internal needs (possibly the introduction of ration cards for flour and bread); free political organization for the German minority in Hungary; radical internal reforms and measures concerning the Jewish question; personal changes in the state apparatus; and finally Hungary's accession by treaty to the Axis alliance.

It did not take long for Teleki to fulfil these requirements, which mostly coincided with the demands of the ultra-rightists who were attacking the policy of the Government. In the middle of September the Arrow-Cross leader, Ferenc Szálasi, was set at liberty. On September 29, it came to the suspension of Decree No. 3400: civil servants were again free to join any political party. On October 10, the Government concluded with Germany an economic agreement in which it undertook to increase the production and deliveries of industrial crops and fodder plants in accordance with the German requirements. At the same time it promised to frame and put into force a third anti-Jewish law, following the two anti-Jewish laws of 1938 and 1939. On top of it all came two essentially interrelated moves which were to entail serious consequences: the passage of German 'task forces' through Hungarian territory into Rumania, and Hungary's accession to the Tripartite Pact.

The Tripartite Pact was concluded by Germany, Italy and Japan on September 27, 1940. This agreement, which in Article 1 recognized German and Italian hegemony in Europe and Japanese hegemony in the Far East, was a military convention of an overtly aggressive character. The very day of the signing of the pact Sztójay, without being authorized to do so, offered to the German Foreign Ministry that Hungary would join it. Shortly thereafter he repeated the offer upon instructions from the Government. The Hungarian Government expected that, if it was the first to join of its own accord, Hungary would be assigned a distinguished place in the alliance system of Germany.

The German Government first rejected the offer on the grounds that the contracting parties did not consider desirable the accession of other states; that they had addressed only a general appeal to sympathizing states, the declarations of which they regarded as mere gestures in support of the pact. On receipt of the unexpected German answer, the Hungarian Government, for want of a different solution, made a hurried statement on its 'spiritual accession' to the Tripartite Pact.

On September 28 the German Minister in Budapest requested the Hungarian Government to consent to the transport of German 'task forces' through Hungarian territory into Rumania. Two days later Erdmannsdorff could already forward to Berlin the Hungarian Government's positive answer. The real aim of the transport of German troops into Rumania was to prepare the attack on the Soviet Union. This was the beginning of the deployment of the German army for the war against the Soviet Union on the southern flank of a prospective front. From October 1940 the Hungarian railways were reorganized to serve the war purposes of Germany. From that time until the end of the war, the passage of German troops continued practically without interruption. Thus the territory of Hungary had become an effective military springboard for the German war machine.

The only diplomatic 'success' which compliance with the German demands brought Hungary was that, when Hitler decided to let the pro-Axis countries join the Tripartite Pact, Hungary was the first to sign it ahead of Rumania and Slovakia. The protocol of accession was signed at Vienna on November 20, 1940. Thereby Hungary recognized the European hegemony of Germany and Italy and pledged solidarity with the Axis Powers for the event of an attack upon the Fascist Powers from any Power that was non-belligerent until then. In return for this, the Hungarian Government was entitled by the agreement to appoint its representative to attend any conference of the three Powers dealing with questions concerning Hungary. But Germany never observed this provision.

Following the second Vienna Award the international position of Hungary was rapidly deteriorating. Estrangement in Anglo–Hungarian relations became more and more pronounced, but Anglo–Rumanian relations were also at their all-time low.

Foreign Secretary Eden pointed out that the British Government distinguished between the Rumanian—Bulgarian territorial settlement (which it recognized as an agreement) and the Hungarian—Rumanian territorial readjustment resulting from an Axis diktat. Britain would not recognize the territorial changes which had taken place after September 1, 1939. In December 1940, after the Teleki Government had granted the passage of German troops through Hungary into Rumania, Eden stated: "... the question did not immediately concern Great Britain, since Roumania was not that country's ally: but if Hungary allowed German troops to cross her territory against a country allied or in friendly relations with Britain, Great Britain would regard this as an unfriendly act, and would break off diplomatic relations with her. If she allowed those forces to remain on her territory, and to utilize her military installations, still more if she herself participated in the attack, this would be a casus belli."

In the autumn of 1940 the German-occupied countries practically encircled Hungary. On the West, owing to the accomplishment of the *Anschluss,* Hungary was bordering on the German Reich. Slovakia and Rumania were teeming with German soldiers. After Antonescu's rise to power in Rumania, the Hungarian—Rumanian relations became viciously hostile. Relations between Slovakia and Hungary were characterized by mutual hatred. Slovakia and Rumania came potentially closer to each other in their hostility towards Hungary.

There was one more lesson which the Hungarian ruling classes were compelled to draw. The events of 1940 definitively demonstrated that the idea of counterbalancing German predominance by relying on Italy had completely failed, for Italy took, even in questions of detail, the same position as Germany did. Horthy's letter to Mussolini dated October 23, 1940, reflected this realization. The Regent stated that he had witnessed a number of things which gave him the impression that the Duce was "shaken in the sympathy which was for over a decade the carefully guarded and most cherished pillar of Hungarian foreign policy".

4. Hungary's participation in the aggression against Yugoslavia

The Teleki Government, in order to strengthen its increasingly weak positions in South Eastern Europe and to rescue the remainders of its degraded and discredited conception of foreign policy, sought the ways of understanding with Yugoslavia. The fact was that through her north-eastern frontier, Hungary was in direct communication with the Soviet Union, and a rapprochement between the two countries was a reasonable possibility. The Soviet Government had repeatedly stated that it had no differences and no problems with Hungary. In the summer of 1940 it emphasized on several occasions that it regarded certain Hungarian demands in connection with Transylvania as warranted. In September 1940, the first Hungarian—Soviet trade agreement was signed. The Soviet Government intended this agreement to strengthen the basis of expanding contacts between the two countries. But the Hungarian Government did not mean to develop a lasting relationship with the Soviet Union, not only because of its ingrained anti-Sovietism but also because it thought that, owing to the superficially still undisturbed neutrality in German–Soviet relations, any progress in this respect might do harm to Hungary's connections with the Western Powers.

Yugoslavia, relatively independent, thus remained the 'only window' on the outside world. Of course, when seeking the way of a rapprochement with Yugoslavia, the Hungarian Government did not think of joining forces with her against Germany. More than ever before, it clung to its pro-Axis foreign policy. Yet, through Yugoslavia, it might have been able to sustain its weakening contacts with the Western Powers and to strengthen its positions, mainly against Slovakia and Rumania.

On October 3, 1940, Count Csáky sent the Hungarian Minister in Belgrade, György Bakach-Bessenyey, written instructions to suggest bilateral talks for the settlement of undecided issues between Hungary and Yugoslavia, including territorial questions. This approach thus indicated that the Hungarian Government had not given up its revisionist demands. All the less so, since after the second Vienna Award, prominent representatives of the Hungarian ruling classes were of the opinion that, having succeeded in enforcing, even though only in part, the revisionist claims on Czechoslovakia and Rumania, they were now to turn towards Yugoslavia, whose international positions in South Eastern Europe had melted into thin air. On October 3, 1940, Rumania repudiated all her obligations arising from the Little Entente and Balkan pacts. Yugoslavia was faced with territorial demands raised by her neighbours – Italy, Bulgaria and Hungary.

The Teleki Government, although it did not give up its revisionist ambitions, now would have been willing to reduce its demands (the Baranya triangle; the Muraköz sector; the zone of the Danube–Tisza interfluve down to the Francis Joseph canal and, if necessary, to postpone their satisfaction, in the hope that Yugoslavia, being in a diplomatic quandary, would be disposed to recognize in principle her obligation to make some territorial concessions in the interest of establishing friendly relations with Hungary.

Barely a few weeks after the opening of the Hungarian–Yugoslav diplomatic parley, on October 28, 1940, Italy launched an attack on Greece. The unexpected Italian action, which was soon followed by successive defeats suffered by the aggressor, threatened to offset all Germany's plans concerning the Balkan and South Eastern European area. The opening of the new front in those parts jeopardized Germany's military preparations for her war against the Soviet Union, and it was to be feared that under the influence of the Italian fiasco the surrounding states would step up their resistance to German encroachment. It became still more urgent for Hitler to bring the Balkan peninsula completely under control before the start of the attack on the Soviet Union. Filling the gap opened by Italy's fiasco seemed to be a matter of the greatest urgency: on November 12 Hitler issued orders to start preparing an attack on Greece.

A prerequisite of the German offensive against Greece was to 'find out' the probable reaction of Yugoslavia, to force her to adopt a resolutely pro-Axis stand. Although the German High Command had, from the outset, pondered the chances of armed intervention as well, Hitler found it better to force Yugoslavia by diplomatic means into Germany's fold of vassals. On November 18 Hitler and Ciano came to an agreement to the effect that if, in case of a German attack, Yugoslavia refrained from intervention in support of Greece, demilitarized the Adriatic coast and joined the Tripartite Pact, the Axis Powers would in return guarantee her territorial integrity and cede to her the port of Salonika.

Under such circumstances Hitler did not oppose the Yugoslav—Hungarian rapprochement and even regarded it as an important element of the diplomatic action aimed at ensnaring Yugoslavia. Therefore, when talking to Teleki and Csáky at Vienna on the occasion of Hungary's accession to the Tripartite Pact, he expressly invited the Hungarian statesmen to create peaceable contacts with Yugoslavia which might make it possible for Hungary not to waive definitively her revisionist claims, but which would provide guarantees for seeking a solution to their satisfaction by common agreement with the Yugoslav Government.

The Yugoslav—Hungarian negotiations were resumed towards the end of November, this time with German sanction. The terms of an agreement now seemed secured, since, there being no insistence on revisionist demands, it was easier for Yugoslavia to accept the rapprochement, and the resistance of the extreme right was also broken down by the circumstance that all this was also to Hitler's liking. But this agreement served different purposes from those originally intended by Teleki. The Hungarian Government knew full well that after Hungary had joined the Tripartite Pact, this new agreement might become a means of forcing Yugoslavia into the Axis camp. But owing to the coincidence of circumstances Teleki's only hope to salvage what had been left of his foreign political conception, and to avoid a definitive break with England, was precisely that Yugoslavia — the only small state among Hungary's neighbours that might have been indicated by the hint in the above-mentioned message of the British Government — should join the Axis Powers, thus precluding the possibility of Germany's attack on Yugoslavia.

The Hungarian and the Yugoslav governments soon arrived at an agreement. On December 10 Csáky went to Belgrade to sign the Yugoslav—Hungarian treaty of eternal friendship, the text of which had been endorsed previously by Ribbentrop. Article 1 of the treaty read: "Between the Kingdom of Hungary and the Kingdom of Yugoslavia there will be permanent peace and eternal friendship."

After signing the treaty, however, the Teleki Government was surprised to see that neither in Berlin nor in Rome was the act received with such enthusiasm as could have been expected. Apart from the fact that the German Government did not wish to stand sponsor to the agreement for diplomatic reasons, the main cause for Germany's cool attitude was that by early December 1940, it had become evident that the execution of the 'great transaction' planned by Hitler would not be as smooth as anticipated. The Yugoslav Government, though trying hard to prove its friendship for the Axis Powers, was loath to join the Tripartite Pact. It became obvious that more drastic methods of diplomatic pressure must be employed to break down the stubborn unwillingness of Yugoslavia. Under such circumstances, however, the treaty of eternal friendship might prove to hinder plans to exert pressure upon Yugoslavia through Hungary. What is more, it might bolster up the efforts contrary to German interests not only in Yugoslavia but also in Hungary.

Preparations for the attack on Greece went on at a rapid pace; the deployment of German troops was shortly finished. Hungary also had a share in this, inasmuch as she secured the passage of German forces through Hungarian territory. At Christmas 1940, for example, considerable limitations were introduced in passenger and freight traffic through the Hungarian railways in order to make the main lines freely available for German military transports. Simultaneously with the military preparations the Germans uttered more and more threats against Yugoslavia, demanding her accession to the Tripartite Pact.

Hitler would have been willing, in accordance with the original idea, to guarantee Yugoslavia's frontiers on condition that her accession secured the passage of German troops through Yugoslav territory.

The Teleki Government was now faced with a dilemma which it could no longer solve. At the news of the proposed guarantees, it made vigorous diplomatic representations to Berlin. The new Foreign Minister appointed upon Csáky's death, László Bárdossy, emphasized in his note of March 16: "... a German territorial guarantee would doubtless have an effect upon the shaping of Hungarian–German relations and seriously affect public feeling in Hungary. For this reason we have to request emphatically that the Reich Government should thoroughly think over the matter of guarantees." Ribbentrop finally promised that Germany would declare that she respected the integrity of Yugoslavia only in her own name.

But this did Hungary more harm than good, for Berlin saw clearly that the territorial demands were the weak spot where the reluctance of the Hungarian Government could be subdued once the aggression upon Yugoslavia came into question. And Teleki wanted to avoid this at any price, because he suspected that a Balkan conflict would grow into a Soviet–German war.

From late 1940 onward Hungary's chances of staying out of the war rapidly grew smaller. This was indicated not only by Yugoslavia's reluctance to accede to the Tripartite Pact, and Germany's growing pressure upon Yugoslavia, but also by the accumulation of information about German preparations for an attack on the Soviet Union. Teleki was now sure that, if the Germans launched a military action against Yugoslavia and, if consequently, Hungary were entangled in a war by the side of Germany, this would not only mean a break with the Western Powers but, sooner or later, also confrontation with a coalition of the Western Powers and the Soviet Union.

This was the heaviest blow to the crumbling pillars of Teleki's foreign political conception of 'staying outside'. The fact is that for a long time he rejected the idea of having to reckon with the emergence of an anti-Fascist coalition of the Soviet Union and the Western Powers. Moreover, an innervation of twenty years kept alive the belief of the counter-revolutionary leaders that their anti-Soviet attitude or their inflexibility towards the Soviet Union would always be rewarded by the British. This is why they did not make use of the opportunity offered by the Soviet–German relationship from 1939 to 1941: a rapprochement with the Soviet Union to counterbalance German pressure.

Now Teleki, after accession to the Tripartite Pact (on which occasion he received reliable unofficial information on the preparations for war against the Soviet Union), and before the deterioration of Yugoslav—German relations, began to consider the idea of a non-aggression treaty with the Soviet Union, the improvement of Soviet—Hungarian relations in preparation for the treaty, as such intent had since 1939 been manifest on the part of the Soviet Government. This is how Teleki wanted to avoid being plunged into an anti-Soviet war, because he was aware that an attack on the Soviet Union, as he — back from Vienna — told Count Móric Esterházy, "would mean the end of Germany".

These efforts, however, could yield only partial results, because the plan of a non-aggression treaty was bluntly rejected by Regent Horthy. Teleki had accepted the Soviet offer, and so it came to the return of the Hungarian flags captured by the Czarist army in 1848. As a result of the trade agreement concluded in the autumn of 1940 he consented to the Soviet Union's participating in the Budapest International Fair. (This Fair opened after Teleki's death, in May 1941.)

Tenaciously as Teleki tried to uphold his foreign political conception, he had to see more and more clearly that the hour of decision was drawing near. Amidst the power conditions of the counter-revolutionary system it could not be doubted what that decision would be. This is how the plan of an émigré government was proposed again. In January 1941, Horthy held a conference attended by Bethlen, Eckhardt and others, where they accepted a secret plan which boiled down to this: should the Germans raise demands wholly incompatible with the country's sovereignty, Horthy would appoint a government composed of politicians who would then be staying abroad. Horthy would remain in Hungary but he would withdraw and refuse all co-operation with a quisling régime established by the Germans. On January 26, Horthy made the plan known to British Minister O'Malley, who found out also that the émigré government would be headed by Count Bethlen and headquartered in London, while Eckhardt would go to the United States. Bethlen was promised to obtain a permit to enter England, and O'Malley thought he would be accredited to Bethlen as British Minister.

Early in 1941, Eckhardt indeed left Budapest and, after roving Europe for months, he finally arrived in the United States. At that time Bethlen could also have gone to London if he had wished to leave Hungary. The whole scheme did not make any stir in the Foreign Office. The intention of salvaging the régime was easily seen through. Even O'Malley, who later appropriated the whole idea, wrote in his telegram of January 26 that although Horthy was "very stubborn and personally quite fearless", he would, "if the critical point is reached, exercise a more indulgent view of the German demands than we should wish to see him do."

Eden must have been familiar with the reports of his minister in Budapest when, on February 6, he received Barcza and reiterated the communications made in last November about the conditions of defection and added that the British Government would, when the peace was to be concluded, take into consideration that Hungary had allowed the German troops to cross her territory in the direction of Rumania, had adhered to the Axis Powers, and that her press and radio were in tune with Germany. He then proceeded: "... we hoped that the Hungarian Government realized that our post-war attitude would be influenced by the degree and manner in which the Hungarian Government had endeavoured to withstand Axis pressure and to maintain a genuinely neutral attitude. Recent events had suggested to many people that the Hungarian Government found Axis pressure not unwelcome."

The Foreign Secretary's position was easy to understand if we consider that Horthy and Teleki asked the British Government for guarantees which would have been difficult to make. Notably, that the British Government should accept in advance: it would recognize the émigré government as Hungary's lawful and official government and would continue to do so in the future no matter what would happen in the country. Neither in February nor in March did such a statement come from London, and the preparations for an émigré government were abandoned. Mostly because the holders of power were very much afraid that once they let power slip through their fingers during the war, and if it fell into the hands of the extreme right-wingers, this extreme-right policy could not, later, be replaced by Horthy's policy, not even with British support.

What then did Teleki have left in his hands? To return to the conception of 'staying outside' which was clearly hopeless as it relied on so narrow a basis within the framework of the régime. This was his evaluation of the situation as he wrote in his briefing to the Hungarian Legations in Washington and London on March 3, 1941: "The outcome of the war is uncertain. But, in any case, what is most important to Hungary is that she may stand unruffled in the concluding stage of the European conflict. It is not at all unlikely, especially in the case of Germany's possible defeat, that after the war ... the eastern parts of Europe will be in a state of chaos which will be the greatest danger to those states which, having expended their material resources and their armed force, will stand there defenceless." Among the dangers to Hungary, Teleki mentioned the 'Russian peril' in the first place.

On March 12, Teleki also sent a letter to Barcza with the courier departing for London. He instructed Barcza to explain again to Eden that, although in official statements, in the press and in formal utterances directed to the foreign public, he was compelled to sound pro-Axis because the Germans insisted, still, essentially, he had not yielded to serious German demands related politically and economically to Hungary's independence and sovereignty. In his letter he complained that the struggle against the German exactions was "getting on his nerves", but he could assure the British Government that, as long as he was alive and was at the head of the Government, he would not comply with demands "incompatible with the honour and sovereignty of the country."

Finally, the Cvetković Government gave in to the Germans and signed the Tripartite Pact on March 25, 1941. The next day, however, the protests backed by the Yugoslav bourgeoisie and military officers — the majority of whom were rather disposed towards a Western orientation — overthrew the pro-German Government.

Germany did not view the events with folded arms. The General Staff took prompt measures to extend Operation Marita (cover name for the attack on Greece) to Yugoslavia. Hitler had, from the beginning, counted upon the participation of Hungarian armed forces. On March 27, Sztójay sent Horthy a message urging the participation of Hungarian troops in the action against Yugoslavia and his authorization for the deployment of German armed forces over the territory of Hungary. In return for this, Germany would recognize Hungary's territorial claims on Yugoslavia.

On the next day, on March 28, Horthy already informed Hitler that Hungary was ready to comply with his demands. That same day the Regent presented his decision and the related letter addressed to Hitler to a military conference held with the participation of the Prime Minister and the Foreign Minister, where it was resolved that the final decision should be passed at the meeting of the Supreme Defence Council on April 1. The preliminary decisions were presented to the Council of Ministers, where the related correspondence between Hitler and Horthy was also made known. Although Teleki voiced misgivings and threatened to resign, the Cabinet meeting took note of the communications. On the very same day Colonel Kinzel, head of the Eastern Department of the German General Staff, arrived in Budapest, bringing with him a letter from Chief of Staff Halder addressed to his Hungarian colleague, Colonel-General Henrik Werth, demanding the participation of five Hungarian army corps in the campaign against Yugoslavia.

From that time onward Hungarian foreign policy was desperately trying to avoid disaster by saving what it could. On March 29, the Foreign Minister instructed the Hungarian Minister in Belgrade to unofficially inform the Yugoslav Foreign Minister that a sudden and smashing attack on Yugoslavia was to be expected unless Germany received serious assurances that Yugoslavia would not turn against her during the attack on Greece.

On March 30, Bárdossy sent messages to London and Washington, in an effort to find out their possible reaction to the proposed move. He tried to prove that in case of German attack, Hungary was prompted to intervention only by consideration for the protection of the Hungarian minority living in Yugoslavia, and furthermore that the nationalities' urge for separation was breaking Yugoslavia into various parts, and so Hungary would become free from her treaty obligations towards a non-existent Yugoslavia.

On March 31, however, in order to promote Yugoslavia's disintegration, the Hungarian Government let the Croatian party boss Maček know that it would see with comprehension "the efforts to realize Croatian sovereignty". At the same time the Foreign Ministry desperately tried to collect facts about grievances. It instructed the Legation in Belgrade and the Consulate in Zagreb to report forthwith on any, even minor, atrocities commited against Hungarians in Yugoslavia.

In the meantime, the German and Hungarian General Staffs had begun to map out the plans of a joint action. On March 30, General Paulus arrived in Budapest and had no difficulty in coming to an agreement with the Hungarian General Staff. The agreement was approved at the Supreme Defence Council meeting on April 1. Teleki's stand against the attack on Yugoslavia was still not unambiguous; what he did was to make a few formal proposals to cover up the shame of participation in the aggression. His idea was for Hungary to join in the campaign only a few days after the German attack had started; he wished to ensure that Hungarian units did not operate under German officers, that Horthy was in sovereign command of his armed forces; and, finally, to make the Hungarian attack subject to one of the following three conditions: 1. if the independent Yugoslav state ceased to exist, 2. if the Magyar population was persecuted, or 3. if a vacuum was created in the territories claimed by Hungary. The Supreme Defence Council accepted Teleki's proposals and instructed the General Staff accordingly.

From April 1, there was a steady flow of reports from Belgrade and Zagreb to the effect that no atrocities were being committed on the Magyar population; that, moreover, considering the recently concluded treaty of friendship, many in Yugoslavia believed that Hungary would not allow the German troops to pass through her territory.

The replies from the West came on April 2. Barcza reported by telegram from London that in case of an attack by German troops from Hungarian territory Great Britain would sever the diplomatic relations with Hungary, and went on: "If, however, Hungary should join in the attack under any pretext whatever (the protection of Hungarians in the territory of Yugoslavia), she had to reckon with a declaration of war from Great Britain and her allies (Turkey, and maybe the Soviet Union at a later time)." A telegram from Washington pointed out that the United States of America, which was expected to take sides openly with England, would adopt a similar attitude towards Hungary.

What Teleki had feared came to pass. He was deeply impressed by the reference to the Soviet Union in Barcza's telegram. It was in fact the first time that British Government quarters tried to influence the Hungarian Government by alluding to the possibility of an Anglo–Soviet alliance. The conception of the preservation of armed neutrality, on which he was relying with waning belief, had now collapsed, because the pressure of revisionist ambitions and the influence of the forces behind them were far more powerful than Teleki's conception about Hungary's staying out of the war. He expected neither the leading statesmen nor the army nor the social classes supporting the régime to render him any considerable assistance in turning overtly against the Germans, especially at a time when co-operation with Germany raised expectations of the immediate return of lost territories. Horthy did not listen to his Prime Minister because he had already decided on participation in the attack against Yugoslavia.

At that time the sham advantages of German friendship still made the majority of the population interested in the national question, blind to the danger involved in Axis policy for the country's independence. In April 1941 Hitler's attitude towards Hungary was not that of a leader occupying the country, but he posed as an ally who was helping the twenty-year-old revisionist policy to success. The only way to turn against the Germans would have been by relying to base such a resistance on certain active groups which, keeping out from the régime's circuit deliberately stood to the left of the Government and possessed but a very narrow mass support. To Teleki, however, such a turn seemed a logical and moral absurdity, for it would have required not only open hostility towards the Germans but an open break with the régime, together with all the political and social implications of such an attitude. Teleki was unable and unwilling to take this road. But he was also unable to go on with the régime along the road leading into a catastrophe. The gap widening between him and the counter-revolutionary régime he had so persistently defended was not a result of personal motives, this is why he could not find a solution in his resignation and withdrawal from political life. The only way out left for him was to break completely with all that he, as a politician, had defended for a quarter of a century. It followed from his human conscience that he intended this break as a memento, and this break implied a dramatic and irrevocable step: at dawn on April 3, 1941, he shot himself.

In his suicide note addressed to Horthy he drew his conclusions in impressive terms:
"Your Serene Highness!

"We have become breakers of our word — out of cowardice — in defiance of the Treaty of Eternal Friendship based on the Mohács speech. The nation feels this, and we have thrown away its honour. We have placed ourselves at the side of scoundrels — for there is not a word of truth in the faked stories of atrocities — neither against the Magyars and not even against the Germans! We shall be robbers of corpses! the most abominable nation! I did not keep you back. I am guilty. Pál Teleki."

Those whom he had intended to impress in the first place concealed his farewell note from the public and concocted instead an enduring story of the suspicious circumstances of the Prime Minister's death. The suicide had a greater effect abroad than at home. In Budapest Horthy, the Government, the General Staff reversed nothing. They buried Count Pál Teleki with great pomps and abided by the original decisions, which were carried out by the new Prime Minister, László Bárdossy, appointed upon the motion of Ferenc Keresztes-Fischer on April 3.

That same day, when the British minister called on the Regent to offer his condolences and Horthy told him about the circumstances of Teleki's suicide and about the decision to take part in the aggression on Yugoslavia, Minister O'Malley, disappointed and losing his nerve, declared that if the Regent "... entered into such a corrupt bargain with Germany or in any way acted as a Hungarian jackal to the German lion against a State with which he had just signed a treaty of eternal friendship, his country could expect no indulgence, no sympathy and no mercy from a victorious Britain and United States of America and that he personally ... would be covered with well-deserved contempt and dishonour."

On April 4, the German troops began marching through Hungary. On April 6, the day after the start of the German attack, Great Britain broke diplomatic relations with Hungary. The British move made no impression on the Government headed by Bárdossy. On April 11, on the pretext of an 'independent' Croatia having been proclaimed (by Croatian agents of Germany), Hungarian troops crossed the Yugoslav frontier and took possession of the Bachka, the Baranya triangle and the Muraköz sector. Although meeting with hardly any armed resistance, the march of the Hungarian forces into the southern areas was accompanied by a campaign of terror against the Yugoslav and Jewish population living there and resulted in the killing of 2,300 persons in a few days' time.

The aggression on Yugoslavia increased Hungary's international isolation and thus her dependence on Germany, albeit the British did not yet declare war as they had promised. Churchill, who was deeply impressed by Teleki's suicide, said that, until Hungarian troops came face to face with Allied forces, he would abstain from declaring war, but he condemned the Hungarian conduct.

On April 16, when the Hungarian Minister in London made his parting visit to Eden, the British Foreign Secretary asked him to report to his Government as follows: "His Majesty's Government was until quite lately trying to understand the undoubtedly difficult position your Government has found themselves in both externally and internally. We have shown more than one sign of this understanding. But now you have handed over your country to the opponent of England and have, almost simultaneously, attacked the country with which only a few months ago you concluded a pact of friendship. This will remain an everlasting shame upon the reputation of Hungary. If a country is no longer master of her fate and voluntarily resigns her independence, then at least she should not sign a pact of friendship which she then breaks. Tell it at home that England will remember that when peace will be made.... Teleki was the last man in whom we had confidence. We shall have no more dealing with those who are now in power."

Eden's last utterance was of symbolical significance because it showed that the Foreign Secretary of the British War Cabinet felt little sympathy for Hungary and did not believe that Hungary would ever be able to put up sincere and real resistance to the Germans, but also because it put a stop to a process which had started in 1938, and British foreign policy opened a new trend the essence of which was formulated in the Foreign Office years later, in February 1943, when the new line of British propaganda towards Hungary was elaborated.

Eden's words, even if unintentionally, implied a certain criticism of the past few years' practice of British foreign policy which, although taking for granted that the Horthy régime was irretrievably bound to Germany (and maintaining relations in order to reward only Teleki's efforts — as was put by Frank Roberts, head of the Central Department — "to continue an independent policy"), did nothing to build up contacts with the democratic, anti-Fascist opposition forces in Hungary, to bolster their ambitions and create the foundations of co-operation with those who combined the fight for independence with the programme of Hungary's democratic transformation. Thus the British decision that "we shall have no more dealing with those who are now in power" together with the failure to cultivate the Hungarian opposition led to the awkward situation that when the first peace feelers were made, the British had *nobody* to talk to.

This was not only and not primarily the fault of the British. It primarily followed from Hungary's internal situation and power conditions. None of the *legally* functioning opposition parties had enough influence and power to become the nucleus of a wide national, democratic movement, in opposition to the Government's policy. The two largest opposition parties were the Smallholders' Party and the Social Democratic Party, but their influence was restricted to the agrarian population and the urban working class, respectively, and they could not exercise any considerable influence upon the social basis of each other, let alone the middle classes. The so-called civilian branch of the Smallholders' Party was set up only in 1942; the Social Democratic Party — despite its agrarian programme — was ineffective in the countryside, and it essentially remained an urban party. At the same time the demagogic social programme of the opposition parties of the extreme right was still able to exercise remarkable mass influence. And till 1941, the Government, with its ambitions for neutrality combined with aspirations for territorial revision and even successes, impeded the activity of the opposition parties precisely where they might have been able to mobilize all strata of society.

Throughout the war this problem remained a handicap to the extension of the mass basis of the anti-German struggle. This was especially marked in the case of the professional officers of the army, 45.5 per cent of whom were born in territories annexed by the Trianon peace treaty to neighbouring countries. This is the very reason why the national element in Hungary could not become such motive forces as in other countries of Central Europe in establishing and developing an anti-Fascist independence movement. The Hungarian anti-Fascist democratic and socialist forces could not effectively counterbalance the successes of the revisionist Government — to no small extent due to the fragmentation and weakness of the Left — because it was practically impossible to oppose the revisionist aims in the face of a public brought up in a nationalist-irredentist spirit. What made opposition in this field even more difficult was that in the neighbouring countries, it was precisely the national question that could draw into the anti-German movement, into the fight for independence, forces that did not want social reforms, and were very far from favouring a democratic system or from the idea of social changes.

At that time in Hungary there was not a single oppositionist politician whose voice and authority could have invited a wide response to a programme opposing the existing régime. The leaders of the legal opposition parties were either too closely bound to the social programme of their own parties, or — due to their past and present — they appeared to have too many ties binding them to the established order, which in turn kept alive distrust on the side of the democratic opposition. This situation must certainly have been instrumental in that the British did not see in the democratic opposition a political alternative to Horthyism, to the power élite. True, the British did nothing that could have facilitated their becoming such an alternative.

Finally, the Soviet Union also issued a statement condemning Hungary for violating the treaty of 'eternal friendship' and for participating in the aggression.

5. Hungary's entry into the Second World War

The conclusion of the Balkan campaign made the issue of aggression upon the Soviet Union a question of topical interest. Operation Barbarossa, which was approved on December 18, 1940, scheduled the attack on the Soviet Union for May 15, 1941. But, owing to the Balkan campaign, on March 27 Hitler set a new date — June 22.

Barbarossa and its subsequent variants mentioned only Finland and Rumania whose military participation had to be counted upon. The Germans had not contemplated drawing the Hungarian army into the anti-Soviet campaign. On the one hand, Hitler reckoned that the Hungarian Government would take advantage of participation in the war for making further territorial demands, which would only be of inconvenience to him, especially in the German—Rumanian relations. On the other hand, he was also afraid that Hungary's preliminary engagement might enable the pro-British elements, still prominent in Hungarian political life, to put the Allies wise to the details of Barbarossa. Since the German High Command counted upon the rapid collapse of the Soviet Union and the prompt conclusion of the war, it attached no great significance to the participation of the poorly equipped Hungarian army.

This, of course, did not mean that the Germans did not assign Hungary an important role in the war preparations against the Soviet Union. They counted on Hungary as their base of operations and supplier of economic resources, and the German General Staff did not entirely exclude the possibility of a co-operation with the Hungarian armed forces.

Many of the Hungarian politicians and high-ranking army commanders were dissatisfied with such a restricted role in the coming events. When, in May 1941, the last phase of the deployment of the German forces had begun, Hungarian Chief of Staff Werth, a staunch advocate of Hungary's German orientation, started to ply the Government with a series of memoranda demanding that Hungary should, voluntarily and without delay, offer the participation of Hungarian troops in the war against the Soviet Union.

The Cabinet meeting of June 15 rejected the idea of voluntary engagement on the grounds that the Hungarian army should be left intact for the purposes of further territorial revision. On June 16, Ribbentrop, through the German Minister in Budapest, notified the Hungarian Government that German—Soviet relations were expected to be 'clarified' by the middle of June, and therefore the German Government deemed it necessary to advise Hungary to take certain measures to protect her frontiers. The German communication confirmed the Government's earlier standpoint that it must refrain from volunteering for the campaign but an express German invitation must not be left out of consideration.

At dawn on June 22, 1941, the German troops attacked the Soviet Union without a declaration of war. That same day Erdmannsdorff handed Horthy a letter from the Führer who reiterated his usual phrases in explanation of his act. Hitler only asked Hungary to secure its frontiers and expressed his conviction that the Hungarian

Government subscribed to the attack. And although the Germans did not ask the Hungarian Government to take any definite step, the Government, to demonstrate its assent, nevertheless decided to sever diplomatic relations with the Soviet Union on June 23. This was done inspite of the fact that Article 5 of the Tripartite Pact expressly provided that the agreement did not affect the relations between the Soviet Union and the signatory states.

Practically at the same time with the meeting of the Hungarian Council of Ministers, Foreign Minister Molotov of the Soviet Union summoned Kristóffy, the Hungarian Minister in Moscow, to inquire about the position adopted by the Hungarian Government. He gave him to understand that the German aggression did not necessarily involve a change in the relations between the Soviet Union and Hungary. In recent times the Soviet Government had complied with all requests of Hungary. The requested raw materials had been delivered. A commercial treaty advantageous to Hungary had been concluded. The Soviet Government had never objected, and did not object at the present, to Hungary's revisionist endeavours regarding Transylvania. Hungary could, in the future, count upon Soviet support in the matter of Transylvania in case she remained neutral in the German—Soviet war. The Soviet Union had no territorial claims on Hungary.

Kristóffy's telegram reached Budapest — through Turkey — on the 24th, but Bárdossy failed to present it both to the Council of Ministers and to Regent Horthy.

On June 24, Bárdossy received another message. Werth informed him that the liaison officer delegated to Hungary by the German Supreme Command, General Kurt Himer, had told him on behalf of Colonel-General Halder that Germany would gratefully accept any kind of military co-operation. Bárdossy, being annoyed with the fact that the German demands had been forwarded to the General Staff and not to the Government, did not take Himer's communication as an official message and insisted that the German Government should present an official request to the Hungarian Government.

Presumably the Germans had positively decided to draw Hungary into the war against the Soviet Union in the early days of the attack already. Around noon, on June 22, General Jodl, the Wehrmacht operation chief, telephoned Himer: "We'll accept any Hungarian help at any time. We don't want to raise demands, but we accept any spontaneous offer. There is no question of our opposing Hungary's participation." The next day, Halder himself gave the following instruction by phone: "It is essential now that the Hungarian military authorities should bring the political leaders in motion, that these should volunteer by themselves. Germany does not make demands, for which she would be compelled to pay, but she is grateful for any help, especially if given by means of motorized troops." This was the message which Himer conveyed to the Hungarian Chief of Staff, who in turn forwarded it as an official German request to the Prime Minister.

The instructions from Jodl and Halder give a rather plausible explanation why the German Government refrained from presenting an official invitation, why it wanted a spontaneous offer even after having decided to consider it desirable that Hungary should enter the war.

Hungary's entry into the war against the Soviet Union came to pass before long, without an official invitation from Germany. On June 25, Slovakia, whose military co-operation was not envisaged by the German High Command, announced her entry into war. Horthy and his men feared lest the two antagonists of their revisionist policy, Rumania and Slovakia, should be given a more favourable treatment when it would come to the final sharing of the spoils. Moreover, the Italian Government also criticized Hungary's inaction. Now only a formal pretext had to be found for attacking the Soviet Union. The occasion did not take long to come. On June 26, Kassa, Munkács and Rahó were bombed by unknown airplanes. The official inquiry to identify the nationality of the attackers had not even started when it was simply announced in Budapest that the raid had been made by Soviet bombers.

A few hours after the air raid on Kassa the Council of Ministers met. Prime Minister Bárdossy stated that by decision of the Regent (Horthy had decided to make 'reprisals' on the basis of a report of the Minister of National Defence and the Chief of Staff) Hungary had resolved to enter the war against the Soviet Union. Not long after the Cabinet meeting, Ádám Krúdy, an instructor at the aviation officers' school in Kassa, reported to Bárdossy his findings: Kassa had been bombed by German aircraft. Bárdossy, however, did not mind the facts, he even emphasized: if it was German aircraft, this only confirmed him in his determination to enter the war, since this was what the Germans demanded.

At dawn on June 27, following the German example, the Hungarian air force started raids upon Soviet towns without a previous declaration of war, while land forces, about 40,000 strong, simultaneously crossed the Soviet frontier.

6. The functions of foreign policy in counter-revolutionary Hungary. The road to war

With her attack on the Soviet Union, Hungary was faced with what she had wanted to avoid — entanglement in the war. Her entry into war still cannot be regarded as an accidental event, it was rather a consequence of the contradictions which determined Hungarian foreign policy. This policy had two principal aims: 1. Revision of the peace treaty, recovery of the lost territories. 2. Preserving the rigid political, social and power construction of the counter-revolutionary régime.

It had almost exclusively been revisionism which determined Hungary's relations with the neighbouring countries both in the interwar years and during the Second World War. This policy barred the ways to a rapprochement with the neighbour countries. True, rapprochement would have been extremely difficult, due to the 'let's-keep-everyting' attitude of the Little Entente Governments and because of their oppressing the Magyar minorities — particularly in Rumania and Yugoslavia.

During the establishment and consolidation of the counter-revolutionary régime the revisionist practice, the advocacy of complete revision, did not absolutely determine the country's foreign political orientation, for this was not made possible by the international power relations. It rather represented a means which was intended to secure the internal bearing of the régime in a country which found itself in a state of deep-going social and national upheaval induced by revolutions and the Trianon Treaty of Peace. This was the sole political objective regarding which all groups of the Hungarian ruling classes adopted an identical position; revisionism was accepted by the entire counter-revolutionary public, and which was fit to attract the whole society, except the fairly modest camp of conscious left-wingers.

The practice of foreign policy in those years was tantamount to measures taken to promote the consolidation of the régime. That is, counter-revolutionary foreign policy primarily functioned to 'protect the régime'. This required, first of all, accommodation to the given power relations. The revisionist ambitions first became *decisive* in foreign political orientation when the changes in postwar power relations began to outline, and when the revisionist aspirations found support and partners among the Great Powers. This is what, in the last third of the twenties, laid the foundations of co-operation with Italy and then — parallel to the strengthening of German predominance within the Fascist Axis alliance — established the principal line of foreign political orientation: friendship with Germany. If, however, we took this circumstance for the sole factor motivating the Hungarian foreign policy, we could hardly explain the peculiar pattern of the foreign and domestic policies of the successive Governments headed by Darányi, Imrédy and Teleki. The fact is that every new Government after Gömbös began with a more moderate programme than his predecessor had pursued, but then every new Government soon succeeded its predecessor in co-operating with Germany, which went concomitant with the respective rightist shifts in the country's domestic policy.

This phenomenon cannot fully be accounted for by the fact that, during the office of the above three Governments — that is, from 1936 to 1941 — international power relations changed in favour of Germany, and that first Central Europe, and then the entire Continent, from the English Channel to the Soviet frontiers, became submitted to German hegemony. The growth of German hegemony meant increasing economic, political and ideological pressure from Nazi Germany. This pressure was weighing upon all countries of East Central Europe, which were thus compelled to accept a certain adaptation to the Fascist Powers. But while the Germans were gaining ground in a constant rise from 1936 onwards, the policy of the successive Hungarian governments can rather be described by cyclic spirals.

This peculiarity can neither be exclusively attributed to revisionist policy. What is to be seen clearly here is the how and why of the entire political construction, the meaning of the political credo of the counter-revolutionary system, and this we cannot understand without looking at the antecedents of the counter-revolutionary system, the peculiar circumstances of its establishment. We have to see that the counter-revolution in Hungary did not merely preserve or save the power of the ruling classes against a socialist revolution but that it *regained* — uniquely in the history of our century — power after the actual proclamation and realization of a proletarian dictatorship, and did so with the assistance of an active, internationally sponsored intervention from the outside. This enabled the establishment of a counter-revolutionary régime the like of which existed *nowhere else in East Central Europe:* a rigid political construction, which was completely closed to the left, and which made even the slightest shift towards democracy impossible, but which was neither entirely tolerant towards the extreme right. This system saw the guarantee of its existence, of its survival, not only in the immobile social structure (still overburdened with feudal elements; a social structure built upon the basis of the co-existence and interaction of two hierarchies: the propertied hierarchy and a fossilized, feudal — gentry and non-gentry — hierarchy), but also in a state of *political immobility*. It followed from the logic of things that under the consolidated counter-revolutionary régime, the Hungarian big landowners and big capitalists retained not only the key positions of economic power but kept effective political power too. At the same time a considerable part (a part even growing from the thirties onward) of those political forces which formed the basis of the régime (and on which it exclusively relied), functioned as the *extreme rightist opposition* of the régime.

The power structure established during the twenties seemed solid enough to uphold counter-revolutionary power in its dominion at home. And it functioned well for nearly a quarter of a century. However, the political opposition, not only on the left but also on the right, expected and hoped that it would be through a change in the international circumstances, through *the impact of outside international factors,* that they would be able to achieve their aims, and to rise to power. If to this feature we add that the realization of territorial revisions primarily depended on the international constellation, we can reasonably conclude that during the counter-revolutionary era — especially during the decade from the mid-thirties to the final débâcle — the whole of Hungarian political life was subjected in a large measure to the ups and downs of the international situation.

The changes in the international power relations were also decisive for the rest of the Eastern European countries, particularly before and during the Second World War, but nowhere did they limit the scope of foreign and domestic policy as much as in Hungary.

The strengthening of German orientation in Hungarian foreign policy went parallel to the growth of economic, political and ideological pressure from Nazi Germany. The reason why the German influence was becoming increasingly dangerous was that the forces of the extreme right, growing under the gravitational pull of German hegemony, could only hope support from the Germans, by their external pressure on the country. Their coming into power depended on the effective assistance of Germany. This is why the Hungarian ruling quarters unconditionally supported any German demand concerning economic and both internal and foreign political affairs. And this is why they became advocates of total identification with the foreign policy of Nazi Germany. On April 21, 1941, István Milotay, in an effort to elevate this attitude to the representation of 'national interests', wrote this in the columns of *Új Magyarság:* "A small nation may often get into a situation when it is not especially free to choose its friends or the terms of friendship. It has to give in to the friendship of a party more powerful than itself, and has to pay any price for it." In the shadow of German might the force and influence of the extreme rightist groups grew rapidly, which, in turn, further strengthened the responsivity towards German pressure and encroachment. This responsivity, however, no longer served the interests of those in the highest positions, that is, the interests of the genuine ruling classes which, to secure their power influence, only intended to co-operate with the Germans within certain limits.

In this situation it was the 'régime-protecting' function to which Hungary's foreign policy was subordinated. This meant that foreign policy was shaped to defend the country's peculiarly rigid power structure without any considerable deviation or qualitative change. To keep the power at any price and, from 1939 onward, to salvage the system into postwar Europe despite all unforeseen events of the war — this became the principal programme of foreign policy.

This is why so many governments after Gömbös were turned out of office, and this is why every new head of government was expected to stem the tide by enforcing more moderate foreign and domestic policies. But every succeeding Prime Minister could only build his policy within the rigid, restricted framework of the system, which, under the growing German pressure and with the growth of the domestic extreme right, meant that they had to make concession after concession if only to take the wind out of the sails of the extreme right-wingers. The immanent logic of this policy thus was that it came to concentrate on fulfilling — though not without reserves — the demands of Berlin, or even meeting hypothetical demands, to avoid a situation when the Government's too obstinate unwillingness could have served as a pretext for German intervention coupled with extreme right-wing pressure leading to a Fascist take-over.

This is why Hungarian foreign policy cast its 'watchful eyes' upon London from the moment of the birth of the German–Italian alliance, in which the two Great Powers were not equal partners, but in which Italy had, from the very outset, submitted to the overwhelming superiority of Germany: the Hungarian Government wished to find out how far the British were tolerant of Hitler's aspirations, how far Hungary could go in co-operation with the Germans — which was held to be the guarantee of a successful revision — without having to assume the risk of a general European war, for this would endanger the very survival of the existing régime in Hungary.

The war broke out in the autumn of 1939, and the first years brought German victories. Succeeding to the three Prime Ministers who had all represented groups of the highest bureaucracy, Teleki was a prominent representative of the conservative reactionaries, aristocratic big landowners and finance capitalists. Teleki's only aim thus became to keep the highest power positions during the war at any price, however great an adaptation this policy might require to the interests of Nazi Germany. This is why Teleki's effort to keep Hungary away from the war, which he had so categorically stressed in his messages sent to London and Washington a month before he took his own life, had to fail. This strategy, expected to keep and salvage power into postwar times, was in plain contradiction to the tactical requirements of the same interests. It was Teleki who ultimately openly concluded an alliance with Germany. This move, however, was no more inspired by a hope for further revisions. Neither could it be, for Slovakia and Rumania also acceded to the pact, and a treaty of friendship with Yugoslavia was signed, likewise on German demand. The principal motive, beside gratitude for the Vienna Awards and the desire to secure the new territorial status, was to paralyze the efforts of the extreme-right preparing a take-over, briefly, to protect the existing régime. True, in the autumn of 1940, the open alliance with Germany was instrumental in warding off an extreme right take-over, but the price to be paid for it was entry into the war by the side of Germany barely half a year later, and then the country became more and more deeply involved in the armed conflict. From that time onward the requirement of salvaging the system meant no more for the country's foreign policy than to make Hungary a 'recalcitrant vassal'.

In 1941, the rest of the countries of the Danubian Basin were also plunged into the war as allies of Germany, but they did not have the same rigid power structure that was so much limiting the scope of free foreign policy in Hungary. While these countries, in 1941, were pushed into Hitler's camp by foreign political interests, they were later rescued from Hitler's net precisely by national interests coupled with foreign political interests. The assertion of Hungary's national and foreign political interests, on the other hand, was impeded by the internal power structure mentioned above.

Thus it becomes understandable that in the foreign policy of the counter-revolutionary system it was not only revisionism which had a genuine function, because the protection of the régime was equally important; that these two functions of foreign policy were not independent of each other but acted in conjunction, in interdependence; that the two foreign political objectives acted as specific brakes on each other, hindering one line or the other from becoming predominant, thus making the practice of foreign policy extremely inflexible.

There were periods during which the 'régime-protecting' function was congruous with the foreign political dogma of the régime: revisionism. This latter sometimes brought results. (The first and the second Vienna awards.) And there came a time when these two functions of foreign policy came up against each other. This was in 1941.

For the Horthy régime was beset at home not only by the extreme-right forces, but even more by a fear of the real adversary, fear of the left wing which in times of peace, 'under normal circumstances', was no acute danger to the positions of power, but in extraordinary times it certainly was. And such times were the years of war. Participation in the war by Germany's side promised success both abroad and at home for a short time, but in the long run it threatened with complete failure, considering the likely defeat of Germany, which became more and more obvious from the early days of 1943. Teleki's conception of staying out of the war was appropriate until the war reached Southern Europe. When this came to pass, Hungary could not avoid taking sides, for the geographical location of the country made this impossible. The ruling régime had a choice of two alternatives: act either with, or against, the Germans. But it must also be noted that while the first alternative could — for a limited time — uphold the régime without any substantial change, to choose the second alternative would have required a different kind of system. Alliance with Germany could bring success in revision for a short time, but in the long run, from 1941 onward, a modification of the Trianon frontiers was imaginable only in the anti-German alternative.

All this allows us to state that during the war a turn came about in Hungary's foreign and domestic policy in comparison with the prewar situation. In the course of the war foreign policy was, to a very large extent, subordinated to the interests of domestic policy in a situation when foreign policy ought to have played the principal part. This situation left very small possibilities for a sensible practice of foreign policy even when, in the winter of 1942/1943, the big turn in the Second World War set in, and the Axis Powers' system of alliance began to crumble under the blows of the anti-Fascist coalition. By that time break with Germany had already become a primary requirement.

The wartime foreign policy of the counter-revolutionary régime entailed peculiar internal consequences which must not be left out of account or examined independently if we wish to know and understand Hungary's wartime history as it really was.

A source of the turn to the right in Hungarian domestic policy was the fact that the ruling quarters, which, by the end of the thirties had already been in power for about twenty years, associated themselves with Hitler's Germany. The same fact also brought out specific features of wartime German—Hungarian relations, and this was why no total change-over took place on the power scene in Hungary, either in the economic or in the political field, in favour of the extreme-right forces. Great as Germany was in comparison to Hungary, and however pronounced the swing to the right in the Hungarian official policy was, still until 1944, the forces in power were able to check the pace of a German-type Fascist transformation in domestic policy in order to save their dominant position endangered by the attempts at introducing a Fascist dictatorship.

This is how it was possible that the political construction of the counter-revolutionary régime in Hungary survived practically unchanged; that the parliamentary system continued throughout the war; that a legally existing Social Democratic Party, alone in all East Central Europe, functioned until 1944; that, with limitations though, the Government was facing not only an extreme right but also a legitimate leftist and bourgeois liberal opposition (Independent Smallholders' Party, Citizens' Liberty Party); that trade unions operated somehow or other, and left-wing and democratically inspired dailies appeared *(Népszava, Magyar Nemzet, Szabad Szó);* that the Government, in spite of the anti-Jewish laws, could afford not to comply with the German demands urging, especially from 1942 on, a radical solution of the 'Jewish question' (compulsory wearing of a 'yellow star', deportation); that large numbers of Polish refugees as well as Jewish refugees from neighbouring countries together with escaped French prisoners of war found refuge and means of living in Hungary.

All this, of course, does not at all mean that during the war some process of liberalization took place in Hungary. It was not the state of things in Hungary that had improved; it was rather the situation in Europe, suffering from German occupation and influence, particularly in Central Europe, that went on worsening at a quick pace. In other words, there was a phase lag between the external conditions and the situation in Hungary. Although Hungary became a wartime ally of Germany, and although pressure from the extreme-right wing and the increasingly peremptory demands of the Germans made domestic political conditions more and more insupportable, this phase lag remained the same until the time of Hungary's occupation by German troops. The machinery of oppression and reprisals struck the Communists in the first place. The bourgeois opposition, the populist and even the Social Democratic opposition had lawful means to get their views expressed by their representatives.

Thus, on the eve and in the course of the great world conflagration (until 1944) it was possible to uphold a *relatively* more favourable political and social atmosphere than in the other neighbouring countries under the sway of Germany.

One of the peculiarities of wartime German–Hungarian relations was that, until 1944, the Hitlerite Government had never seriously contemplated the possibility of an extreme-right take-over in Hungary, and did not even urge such developments. The Germans, when urging that the domestic policy of Hungary should be shaped after the Nazi model and supporting the extreme-right wing, did so primarily with a view to having the economic and military demands enforced. But, from the time of Hungary's entry into the war until the spring of 1943, they refrained even from such action. Hungary's given power conditions suited Hitler and his company as long as the Hungarian Government, even though reluctantly, satisfied their economic and military demands. To his trusted men Hitler spoke several times about the socio-political system of Hungary during the war. From the scientific point of view, his expatiations were confused thoughts of a dilettante, but they contained clear notions from the point of view of the German war objectives. Once, in the autumn of 1941, he explained that the system of latifundia was the only guarantee that Hungary should satisfy Germany's agricultural needs, and therefore the system of landed estates in Hungary had to be maintained in spite of the fact that a good part of the landowners were legitimists or belonged to other circles hostile to the National Socialist system. On another occasion, making a comparison between Antonescu's and Horthy's régimes, he expounded that Antonescu's dictatorship had a very narrow political basis, and the system was much too personalized, while parliamentarism in Hungary provided a relatively firm basis for the representatives of power. In Germany such a system would be intolerable, but in Hungary this was rather irrelevant, for in this country the executive power was indeed independent.

From the peculiarities of German–Hungarian relations followed the tragic phenomenon that during the early years of the Second World War, the sham advantages provided by friendship with the Germans could still make a wide section of the people blind to the dangers of the satellite policy towards Nazi Germany, to the instability of national independence. A corollary consequence was that, in spite of the undeniable effect of more than twenty years of anti-Soviet propaganda — entry into the anti-Soviet war met with no great popularity in Hungary, the declaration of war was received more or less passively by the population.

The recovery of lost territories bolstered the nationalism stimulated by two decades of revisionist propaganda. The false notion that close German—Hungarian relationships did not contradict Hungarian national interests was in fact entertained among the bourgeoisie and petty-bourgeoisie and likewise, in the ranks of the working class and the peasantry for a time. For this very reason, nationalism could not become such a stimulus to the anti-Fascist independence movement in Hungary as it was in other countries of Central Europe. Just because in an *allied* country such as Hungary had been, the violation of national sovereignty and independence, the subordination of the national economy to the interests of the German Reich, the humiliation of national feeling, were necessarily less overt and brutal as in Czechoslovakia, Yugoslavia or other *subjugated* countries of Europe, the full monstrosity of the real face of Nazi Germany remained unknown to the population of the country for a long time.

The Hungarian anti-Fascist, democratic and socialist forces — to no small extent due to the fragmentation and weakness of the left wing — could not counterbalance revisionism among the masses. They could not, for example, effectively counterbalance the successes of revisionism, because, for instance, an unbiassed standpoint regarding the question of the frontiers could not attract a public brought up in a nationalist-irredentist spirit.

Moreover, in 1939—1942, people were not very much affected by the real burden and horrors of the war yet. Although, as a result of increased submission to German economic interests, bread-and-butter problems became more and more serious, the full extent of economic subservience was not known to the public. At the same time, unemployment was absorbed by the war boom. Until the middle of 1942, Hungary only took a limited part in the war, so the drafting of men in their working age did not generally affect the population. In the early years of the war these circumstances rather strengthened the moral basis of the Government, and temporarily caused part of the population to cherish illusions about the system. This is why the independence movement was only very slowly growing and, in the critical period of 1943/1944, the holders of power could think they were in a position to make politics the way they used to, enforcing their tactical schemes against the masses and to the exclusion of the masses.

CHAPTER V

HUNGARIAN FOREIGN POLICY IN THE SECOND STAGE OF THE WORLD WAR

1. Hungary's more active participation in the war against the Soviet Union. Declaration of war on Hungary by Great Britain and the United States

Although in the beginning, the German forces advanced at an extremely high speed, the failure of a *Blitzkrieg* against the Soviet Union soon became obvious. In August 1941, after two months of bloody battles causing tremendous losses, the end of the campaign was still far out of sight. In face of the heroic defensive fights of the Red Army it would have been futile to hope for Soviet capitulation. As concerns Hungary this meant the frustration of the hopes of the Hungarian Government to gain the goodwill of Germany by putting minor forces in the field and to come out of the engagement with an almost intact army. It could not be doubted any more that the German High Command would require of Hungary, too, to deploy ever larger forces. From late summer in 1941, this became a most characteristic tendency in German–Hungarian relations. With a view to putting the Hungarian army to the best possible use, direct political and military consultations accompanied by vague promises and drastic threats followed in succession.

These German efforts closely coincided with the aims of the Hungarian military chiefs, notably the General Staff. As early as August 1941, Chief of Staff Henrik Werth proposed a more active participation of the Hungarian armed forces in the war conducted against the Soviet Union. On August 5, sure of what he was after, and unbeknownst to the Government and Horthy, Werth told General Rudolf Toussaint, the German military attaché *ad interim* in Budapest, that he intended to offer Germany the deployment of additional units of the Hungarian army for service in the field and for occupation duties. Two weeks later, he submitted a lengthy memorandum to Prime Minister Bárdossy. In it he denounced the Government that, "despite its traditional anti-Bolshevist attitude", it had joined in the war only "willy-nilly" with small forces, thus causing Hungary "a hardly reparable disadvantage"; that this "wrong" could be repaired by the Government's volunteering as soon as possible about half the Hungarian armed force, at least four or five army corps, without waiting for an appeal to this effect from the German Government. The memorandum stated in conclusion that the offer ought to be made on the political plane, and the ensuing talks ought to make clear what should be done about *(a)* the reconquest of "our thousand-year-old frontiers", *(b)* the relocation of the Slav and Rumanian minorities living within the Hungarian boundaries, *(c)* the deportation of the Jews, and *(d)* the sharing of Hungary in the Soviet raw material resources.

This motion of the Chief of Staff pleased neither the Government nor Regent Horthy. Not that their views regarding further territorial revisions and rivalry with the neighbouring countries were diametrically opposed to Werth's opinion. The difference of views, with less emphasis on the above considerations, partly originated from personal grievances, for Colonel-General Werth's arbitrary action curtailed Horthy's rights as 'supreme warlord' and questioned Bárdossy's loyalty to the Germans. Over and above this, the Government's view was obviously influenced by developments at the Eastern front and in the international situation. The increasingly heavy defensive fights of the Soviet army made their effect felt, and so did, against all expectations of the Hungarian ruling quarters, the news of the emerging anti-Fascist coalition: on July 12, 1941, the Soviet Union and Great Britain signed an agreement on mutual aid and undertook not to conclude a separate peace; early in August 1941, the United States of America pledged itself to give priority to shipments of essential war materials to the Soviet Union; the Atlantic Charter drawn up during the Newfoundland meeting between Roosevelt and Churchill was made public on August 14; on August 25, Soviet and British troops marched into Iran, etc.

Under the effect of these developments, some groups of the Hungarian ruling quarters felt advisable to exercise caution, at least against increasing participation in the war. On August 26, Bárdossy, in a letter to Horthy, stated his opinion of Werth's memorandum: if the Germans wished the Hungarian army to be deployed in greater strength, the demand ought to be considered, but until then "it is by no means to the interest of our country to hurry joining in the war in greater strength, which — for all the expatiations of the Chief of Staff — would evidently react adversely upon the state of our national forces, our domestic conditions and our economy." Finally Bárdossy declared that he saw no possibility of continuing to work together with Werth.

The Germans soon got wise to the uncertainty in Hungary's mood. Early in September 1941, they summoned Horthy to the German General Headquarters. The Regent and Bárdossy left for Germany on September 7, in company with the new Chief of Staff, Ferenc Szombathelyi.

The main topic of discussion was, of course, the participation of the Hungarian army. The Hungarian side suggested withdrawal of the troops deployed at the Eastern front, stressing that 50 to 80 per cent of the equipment of the troops had been wrecked, so it was no good leaving it at the theatre of operations. On the other hand, Hungary would be unable to take part in the fights with other armed services, because this would so much weaken her militarily and economically that "she would no longer be in a position to fulfil the mission of keeping order in South Eastern Europe". But the issue of withdrawal was soon taken off the agenda. The Germans not only argued that the withdrawal of Hungary from the war would be extremely risky 'from the moral point of view', but they promised to supply new equipment to the units fighting at the front. Finally they agreed on the following:

1. The Germans will immediately take care of the re-equipment of the Hungarian motorized brigade fighting at the front, so it will remain at the theatre of war until the conclusion of the operations under way, but at least until October 15; 2. Germany will

make the complete equipment of a motorized division available to the Hungarian army; 3. the Hungarian mountain and infantry brigades doing service outside the battle area will be replaced by units of the same strength and completed by another twelve infantry battalions (four divisions). Thus the Germans succeeded in having more Hungarian troops dispatched, even though not directly to fight on the field, but at least to do occupation duties.

The Hungarian delegation raised a number of territorial problems. Regarding the Banat — which Hitler had promised to let Hungary have at the time of the aggression on Yugoslavia — the Germans only made promises this time, too. They reiterated: that the territory shall belong to Hungary is *res judicata;* but the time when it can be effectively taken possession of "will be determined by extraneous factors". A very important facet of the German–Hungarian negotiations in September 1941 was that the Hungarian Government set up an official claim to territories situated beyond the 'historical' frontiers. On September 10, Chief of Staff Szombathelyi submitted to Colonel-General Jodl a project of 'frontier rectification' proposing that the slopes of the North Eastern Carpathians beyond the frontier running on the mountain ridge, that is, a part of Galicia, should be annexed to Hungary. He supported the idea by geographical considerations and by considerations of defense. The Germans received the proposal rather coolly, although — evidently with the utilization of Hungarian troops in mind — they did not reject it for the time being.

At the talks, the German political and military leaders spoke with self-confidence about the position held by the Axis Powers. Horthy and his retinue returned home, delighted by the promises of German victory. "We make our blood sacrifice in this new crusade on the side of the German armed force and in the spirit of the old brotherhood in arms," Bárdossy said in his radio speech on September 11. But he kept quiet about the real obligations they had assumed.

However, it did not take long to become clear that the Hungarian Government misunderstood the intentions of the Germans if it believed that Hitler would rest content with the contingents agreed upon during the negotiations. In October, the Germans wished to ensure that the new Hungarian troops were thrown into battle, and this possibly — according to the old recipe — through Hungary's voluntary offer. From a certain point of view, this was even facilitated by the conduct of the Hungarian General Staff. Early in October, Szombathelyi told the German military attaché that he knew Hungary would have to gradually stand up for Germany in full strength; to avoid being unprepared for the new problems to be faced in the years to come, it would be good to know what the German High Command expected from Hungary for the next year.

The German Supreme Command instantly made use of the occasion created by Szombathelyi's inquiry and asked for another two brigades to reinforce the troops of occupation and for new, chiefly engineering corps to be deployed. The Hungarian General Staff was, of course, not entitled to decide the issue, so it let the German High Command know that it would have to apply to the Hungarian Government through diplomatic channels. Since the troops were sorely needed, the German Government, to avoid any delays, found it better to comply with this formality. On November 11, Dietrich von Jagow, the German Minister in Budapest appointed in July 1941, called on Bárdossy and officially submitted to him the wishes of the German High Command. The Prime Minister gave a positive answer, so the next day Jagow could announce to the General Headquarters that the Hungarian Government was ready to fulfil the German demands. The Hungarian Chief of Staff had already contacted the German military attaché to clear away the details.

While the Germans sought to obtain fulfilment of their demands usually by a combination of blackmail and promises, by arousing Hungary's jealousy of Rumania and Slovakia, the Hungarian Government always tried to get compensation for services rendered to Germany by making attempts to have its revisionist claims enforced. This time, it wished to use this opportunity for a settlement of the Muraköz issue, which was already half a year overdue, in order to take definitively possession of the disputed area. (Hungarian troops occupied the Muraköz sector in April 1941 and introduced military administration there. The Germans, however, had promised the territory to Croatia, and therefore protested against its annexation by Hungary.) On November 12, Bárdossy informed Sztójay of the fulfilment of the German demands and instructed him to press for the closing of "the question of the Hungarian—German western frontier in this atmosphere most likely favourable to us".

Additional — this time not so much military as rather economic — demands of Germany were discussed during Bárdossy's talks with Hitler and Ribbentrop at the middle of November 1941, when the anniversary of the conclusion of the Anti-Comintern Pact and of Hungary's accession to the Tripartite Pact was celebrated in Berlin.

Having signed, together with representatives of the other satellite states, the document on the prolongation of the Anti-Comintern Pact for another five years, Bárdossy flattered Ribbentrop's notorious vanity by telling him in confidential conversation that he was under the influence of the powerful speech which the German Foreign Minister delivered on the occasion. In this speech, Ribbentrop discoursed upon the theme of 'European solidarity against the Bolshevist peril'. Now, he did not hesitate to give the Hungarian Prime Minister to understand clearly what he understood by 'solidarity'. Germany needed petroleum and grain, he said. Therefore he asked the Hungarian Government to raise the petroleum contingents from 80,000 to 120,000 tons and to secure another 10,000 tons of grain to Germany.

Bárdossy referred to difficulties but promised to meet the demand; then, to get some satisfaction, he began to vituperate savagely against Rumania. "As long as the war goes on," replied Ribbentrop reservedly, "family quarrels must be suspended."

During the festive luncheon the following day, Bárdossy conversed with Hitler. Just as Ribbentrop did earlier, Hitler objected to the U.S. Legation's functioning in Budapest. The Hungarian Prime Minister, on the other hand, complained again about the attitude of the neighbour states which, quoth he, were in no way willing "to adapt themselves to the established principles of the new order, and which do their best to annoy Hungary."

No sooner had Bárdossy returned from Berlin than on November 29, 1941, Herbert C. Pell, the U.S. Minister in Budapest, called at his office and presented an ultimatum from the British Government. In it the Government of Great Britain called upon the Hungarian Government to stop all military operations by December 5, 1941, and to withdraw its forces from the territory of the Soviet Union, or else London would declare the state of war between Great Britain and Hungary.

In April 1941, the severance of diplomatic relations had not been followed by a British declaration of war even after the Hungarian attack on Yugoslavia; Churchill had stated at that time that he condemned Hungary's behaviour, yet England would not declare war on Hungary until Hungarian forces were confronted with British forces in battle. This promise, although it had been made before the German attack on Soviet Russia, could not be left out of account even when the Hungarian Government decided to join in the war against the Soviet Union. Many representatives of the Hungarian ruling classes thought that the war unleashed against the Soviet Union might lead to some kind of conciliation between Germany and the Western Powers. And if this did not come to pass, the Western Powers would not be too much hurt by Hungary's participation in the war if this was limited to fighting at the Soviet front.

Consequently Bárdossy was — or appeared to be — unprepared for the British demarche. But this move was not accidental, it could be expected, and had to be expected, on the basis of a sensible consideration of events.

The anti-Hitler coalition of the Great Powers, despite German phrase-mongering about 'a holy crusade against Bolshevism', grew stronger and stronger. From the point of view of the co-operation of the Powers united in the coalition, in spite of differences of opinion, the dominant interests were determined by the fight waged jointly against the Axis Powers and their vassals, and this could not fail to have an impact upon the relationships between Hungary and the Western Powers. Towards the end of November, upon a repeated request of the Soviet Union, the British Government resolved to declare war on the states participating in the anti-Soviet war: Finland, Rumania and Hungary. This is how it came to the presentation of the British ultimatum.

After reading the note, Bárdossy said that he was extremely surprised by the communication, for he would not have thought that "England wishes to help the Soviets by declaring war on us", for he had thought it impossible that the state of war would set in between Hungary and Great Britain in the absence of armed confrontation. Then, perverting the truth, he insisted that Hungarian troops were no longer fighting against the Soviet Union, and that "the Hungarian Government has no intention of taking part in direct military action."

Pell asked whether the Hungarian Government had something to have conveyed to the British Government. Bárdossy answered 'no'.

On December 3, the Prime Minister informed the Hungarian Legations abroad of the events: "We forthwith take full cognizance of the communication of the British Government because we do not wish to make our attitude dependent on the British Government's decision." The next day, Sztójay showed the text of the telegram to

Ernst Woermann, Under-Secretary in the German Foreign Ministry, who was pleased with Bárdossy's stand and "expressed his gratitude for this understanding support of the Hungarian Government."

Pell, on his own initative, tried to bring the British Government to change its mind. He sent three messages to Washington (one to President Roosevelt in person), in which he explained that he found the British declaration of war meaningless. Prince Primate Justinian Serédi of Hungary also tried, without the Government's knowledge, to intercede through the Vatican. These attempts, however, brought no result. The British Government did not yield.

On the evening of December 6, 1941, the U.S. envoy presented Bárdossy another note from London, informing the Hungarian Government that the state of war between Great Britain and Hungary would set in at 12:01 in the night. The reply of the Ministry of Foreign Affairs was merely an acknowledgement of the note. On December 7 and 8, New Zealand, Canada, Australia and South Africa also declared war on Hungary.

That same day when Great Britain declared war on Hungary the news came that the Japanese air force had carried out a smashing surprise attack on Pearl Harbor and other U.S. military bases. The war had thus spread to the Far East. A few days later, on December 11, Germany and Italy announced that they considered themselves to be at war with the United States. At the same time, Hitler delivered a speech giving publicity to the earlier concluded German—Italo—Japanese military pact which provided that the three states would jointly carry on the war and would conclude neither an armistice nor a separate peace with England or the United States.

Immediately after Hitler's speech Bárdossy, following the old recipe of 'the sooner the better', called a meeting of the Council of Ministers to discuss the situation arising from the German declaration of war and to somehow express Hungary's solidarity before any such wishes would come from Berlin. Bárdossy, in talking about the German declaration of war and the German—Italo—Japanese military pact, declared that there could be no doubt that Hungary was bound by obligation under the Tripartite Pact. As Prime Minister he saw two possibilities for the moment: severance of diplomatic relations with the United States or a declaration of war. He thought it questionable, however, whether the Germans would satisfy themselves with the first alternative.

Several members of the Government showed no enthusiasm for a declaration of war, for it would mean slamming the 'back door', cutting the last thin thread between Hungary and the Western Powers. After a debate, Bárdossy finally proposed that they should choose a formula which was flexible and thus adaptable to any contingency; that they should not make a declaration of war, but the text should imply such a declaration, so that Hungary would not have to declare war explicitly and separately. That the Hungarian Government should express solidarity with the Axis Powers in the spirit of the Tripartite Pact, practically implying only the severance of the diplomatic relations, Bárdossy added: this move, if made quickly and voluntarily, might possibly satisfy Germany. The Council of Ministers accepted the proposal. The statement it adopted read as follows:

"As is well known, the Government of the German Reich and the Royal Italian Government, in their official communiqués issued today, have declared that a state of war exists between, on the one hand, the German Reich and Italy and, on the other, the United States of America.

"The Royal Hungarian Government, in the spirit of the Tripartite Pact, this time also establishes Hungary's solidarity with the Axis Powers.

"Accordingly the Royal Hungarian Prime Minister as Acting Foreign Minister has seen to it that the travel documents are delivered to the Minister in Budapest of the United States of North America.

"At the same time the Royal Hungarian Government has recalled its Minister in Washington."

Still in the evening hours of December 11, Bárdossy made the statement known to the U.S. Minister, to whose question he replied that this did not presently mean a state of war. At the same time, he sent telegrams to the Hungarian envoys in Berlin, Rome and Tokyo, setting forth that the Hungarian Government had also expressed its solidarity by severing the diplomatic relations with the United States. He also instructed his Ministers in Berlin and Rome, in case the Italian or the German Foreign Minister would ask for an explanation, to state that by making a statement of solidarity "... we have fully complied with the provisions of Article 3 of the Tripartite Pact. By declaring our solidarity we have pledged Hungary's full political support. From the start of the war we have exerted ourselves to the utmost to support the Axis Powers economically. Owing to our geographical location military co-operation against the United States is out of the question."

On the night of the 11th, Sztójay phoned Budapest that as far as he was informed Rumania and Bulgaria would declare war on the United States. On the morning of December 12 he announced by express telegram that it was his impression that the German Government, "for high political reasons", anxiously expected Hungary to give evidence of her solidarity by issuing a declaration of war. The Hungarian Minister in Rome sent home a telegram in a similar sense.

Indeed, on December 12, Bárdossy received a call from the German chargé d'affaires and the Italian envoy, who on behalf of their Governments, emphasized that the Axis Powers did not find severance of diplomatic relations satisfactory and demanded the issuance of a declaration of war on the United States. Bárdossy first tried to defend his position, but he stopped arguing further when Werkmeister remarked that he supposed Hungary would not want to hold aloof when the other signatory states wished to express their solidarity by declaring war on the United States.

Bárdossy was always disposed to give up his position with incredible promptitude; he was disposed to 'overbidding', to desultory, inconsiderate steps. As soon as the diplomats left the Prime Minister's Office, he set about burning the bridges without any special consideration. He immediately instructed by telegram the Hungarian Ministers in Berlin and Rome to announce to the German and the Italian Government the following: "If, in the interest of demonstrating a European united front, they wish us to interpret solidarity as involving a declaration of war, we leave it to the Axis Powers to publicize this interpretation, if they mean it ostentatiously to be applicable to all interested sides. In this case we demand to know the set date in order that we may publicize it simultaneously and send the relevant communications to the U.S. Minister here as well as to Washington."

It did not even occur to the Prime Minister to call another meeting of the Council of Ministers. Without the Cabinet's approval he simply phoned the U. S. Minister in Budapest and told him that nevertheless the statement of solidarity made the day before meant the state of war between Hungary and the United States. Pell refused to accept this oral form of a declaration of war. Thereupon Bárdossy informed him by a verbal note that "the Royal Hungarian Government considers the state of war between the United States of America, on the one hand, and the German Reich, Italy and Japan, on the other, to exist also in respect of Hungary".

At the regular meeting of the Council of Ministers in the evening of December 12, Bárdossy presented for approval only a written report on the declaration of war; in the same manner Horthy also was informed afterwards about the step taken by the Prime Minister. The Cabinet acknowledged the report, and Horthy did not even think of protesting against Bárdossy's evidently anticonstitutional act.

The Government of the United States did not take notice of the statement of the Hungarian Government. It adopted the position that this decision was made against the will of the majority of the Hungarian people, as a result only of manifest German pressure. The effective declaration of war by the United States followed a few months later, on June 5, 1942, during the office of the Kállay Government, when a considerable portion of the Hungarian army had already been deployed at the front.

The German defeat below Moscow, at the end of 1941, made it obvious that the Germans would more and more insistently demand a growing amount of raw material and food, and first of all increasing participation of Hungarian troops. On January 1, 1942, Hitler wrote a letter to the Regent of Hungary. He emphasized 'the importance of defeating Bolshevism' and held out to him the hope of final victory. Then he objected that the Hungarian Government intended to withdraw its armoured corps from the front, and finally pressed for a more massive participation of Hungary in the war against the Soviet Union.

A few days later, on January 6, Ribbentrop — who had, barely a month earlier, declined Horthy's invitation with reference to his urgent business elsewhere — arrived in Hungary. By his well-tried methods, the German Foreign Minister, in order to get as much as possible, demanded everything. He began his talks with Horthy and Bárdossy by stressing the German Government's firm belief in the final victory. Bolshevism would be wiped out by 1942. To this end the Axis camp also had to make greater sacrifices, to take part in the war in greater strength. To Hungary, this meant that in the course of that year the entire Hungarian armed force must be deployed on the Soviet front. (This force then consisted of about 28 divisions.)

The Hungarian Government did not reckon with so exorbitant a demand. Bárdossy tried the most diverse arguments to persuade the German Foreign Minister to lower his claims. He referred to the precarious situation in the Balkans, for it was conceivable that Anglo–Saxon forces would land in that area and get the upper hand there. Should this occur, Bárdossy set forth, all the Balkan states, even those which were now siding with the Axis Powers, would at once take the side of the Allies. In this situation, Hungary would be the only dependable support of Germany. Consequently, the Hungarian government had to reckon with attack from the south when deciding on the available armed force to be distributed to the Eastern front. Furthermore, Bárdossy elaborated the Hungarian–Rumanian differences and pointed to the inadequate equipment of the Hungarian troops.

Ribbentrop could of course not be convinced by Bárdossy's arguments. And since — as is written in the German report on the talks — the Hungarian side brought forth all sorts of arguments against the German demands, Ribbentrop decided to take a strong line. He referred to the Rumanian promise to carry out a thorough mobilization if Hungary did the same. Should the Hungarians now refuse the German demands, the Rumanian Government might think they withheld their troops because they intended to start an attack to regain possession of Southern Transylvania. And this would cause the Rumanians to go back on their promise and Hungary would have to take the consequences.

Ribbentrop knew full well that the foreign policy of the Hungarian Government centred on territorial revision. This is why he made it clear enough that the Hungarian reply to the German demands might greatly influence the satisfaction of the still unsatisfied Hungarian territorial claims, for instance, in the case of the Banat. Should the reply of the Hungarian Government be unsatisfactory, there was no way of knowing how it would impress Hitler, whose 'fair but passionate mind' was not familiar to the Hungarians as yet.

Ribbentrop's threats and promises had their effect. On the last day of the talks, after the Government had held a number of meetings with Horthy's participation, Bárdossy informed the German Foreign Minister as follows: Hungary is unable to make her entire army available at the Eastern front, but she is ready to take part in the campaign to the utmost of her capabilities, that is, in a far greater measure than until now. Ribbentrop was satisfied with this reply, for he managed to extort the maximum from the Hungarian Government. The negotiations yielded no concrete result, all they laid down was that the details would be clarified during Keitel's forthcoming visit. Anyway, Ribbentrop told the German envoy in Budapest that he interpreted the promise of the Hungarian Government as meaning two-thirds of the national army.

Ribbentrop left Budapest contentedly, the more so since, in addition to increasing its military participation, the Hungarian Government undertook to augment petroleum shipments to Germany, permitted 20,000 soldiers to be recruited from the German-speaking population in Hungary to the Waffen SS, and made a firm promise, endorsed by Horthy, that Hungary would not engage in any hostile action against Rumania.

Field Marshal Keitel, Chief of the High Command of the Armed Forces, arrived in Budapest on January 20. First he met Bárdossy and then the Minister of National Defence and the Chief of Staff on several occasions to talk over the details. "We were in a very difficult position," wrote Szombathelyi about the negotiations, "because Keitel put his cards on the table. He was perfectly familiar with the condition of the Hungarian army." Keitel demanded 15 infantry divisions, 1 mountain brigade, 1 cavalry brigade, 1 armoured division and 10 divisions of occupation. The Hungarian offer, made after lengthy discussions, included 9 infantry divisions, 1 armoured division and 5 divisions of occupation. Keitel ultimately accepted the offer and promised that Germany would provide the entire equipment of the armoured division. The results of the talks were approved by Horthy and Bárdossy. The Germans found the agreement satisfactory: Hungary's increased participation in the war was guaranteed.

While the German–Hungarian talks went on, the Bachka became the scene of dreadful events which roused world-wide indignation and further worsened Hungary's international reputation. In January 1942, on the pretext of defence against guerrilla attacks and with the connivance of the Government, detachments of the Hungarian army and gendarmerie at Újvidék (now Novi Sad, Yugoslavia) perpetrated indiscriminate massacres of the Serbian, Jewish and Hungarian population. Thousands of men, women and children were killed without trial or verdict.

The coincidence in time of the Bachka massacres and the bargaining with Ribbentrop and Keitel cannot escape our attention. It is quite probable that in this way the Government wanted to prove its arguments that the Hungarian armed forces were needed in the south. With this ruthless carnage, however, those who executed the orders only achieved an effect contrary to what had been expected of the 'guerrilla purges'.

2. The Kállay Government's foreign political ambitions and half-hearted attempts to withdraw from the war

The balance Hungarian foreign policy produced by 1942 was already indicative of a catastrophy. Hungary took an active part in the war against the Soviet Union not only with her divisions fulfilling occupation duties but, from the summer of 1942 onward, with about half of her armed force, the 2nd Hungarian army, in the first line of fire. It was no more possible to enforce the military conception that the formations newly requested by Germany should possibly remain behind the front and be assigned functions of occupation, in order to preserve a combat-worthy army in efficient condition to the end of the war. Although, against the Government's intentions, this conception did more harm than good — as long as it could be maintained — because it brought extremely grave international consequences. The atrocities committed in occupied territory, the so-called partisan hunts, made the Soviet Government deeply indignant, which were expressed at the Soviet–British talks already late in 1941 and was given expression in the views formulated regarding Hungary in 1943.

Hungary found herself at war with Great Britain and the United States, which she would have liked to avoid. She had no Government in exile in the West, although she well knew from the experience of the First World War that such representation was one of the prerequisites of free action in foreign politics. Her relationship with the neighbouring countries was, if possible, worse than ever. And this not only in the sense that even the minimum conditions were missing for approaching the Czechoslovak and Yugoslav émigré Governments. These Governments viewed with suspicion the incipient Hungarian peace-feelers. The second Vienna Award ruled out every possibility of coming to an agreement with the Rumanian bourgeois nationalist opposition. All this questioned the possibilities of the existence of an intact counter-revolutionary régime in a Europe without Hitler, although the primary aim was to salvage this very Régime.

A special problem between England and her small allies in Eastern Europe was created by a regular feature of the BBC Hungarian-language broadcast, namely the commentary by C. A. Macartney, a professor of history, who, in the prewar years, had spent years in Hungary and who, in his high standard radio lectures of a rather subjective tone, tried to persuade his acquaintances among the leading Hungarian politicians to resist the German demands. This displeased a part of the British public and incurred protests, among others, from the Czechoslovak Government on the grounds that British propaganda was addressed to revisionist and antidemocratic circles in Hungary.

What line did British propaganda really follow in connection with Hungary? On February 3, 1942, a proposal was made for 'political warfare' against Hungary. This set as an aim of British propaganda the creation of a political opposition relying on anti-German Catholics, on intellectuals who demanded a land reform, on the Social Democrats and on the progressive aristocracy. This line, held quite possible a year later, still found opponents in 1942. A few months later Bruce Lockhardt, Under-Secretary of State and head of the Political Warfare Executive, explained in a memo that Hungary was the poorest terrain for British propaganda, stating that nothing could be achieved there,, unless it was at the expense of Britain's smaller allies. The memorandum specially demanded that Macartney's radio talks should be discontinued. Indeed, they were suspended for a few months thereafter.

Bruce Lockhardt's position was close to Eden's conception, who at that time did not put much faith in the success of Hungarian resistance. The main line of British propaganda thus held to the opinion that ". . . so long as Hungary continues to fight against our Allies and to help the Axis she can expect neither sympathy nor consideration".

Hungary's relationship with Fascist Slovakia and Croatia as well as with Antonescu's Rumania was the worst possible. A semblance of peace existed between them only under German pressure. Those countries were brought closer together by their territorial interests, and Slovakia proposed a kind of Little Entente under Germany's auspices as early as 1941. The three countries' concerted anti-Hungarian policies made it extremely difficult to carry out an about-face in foreign orientation, because such policies might become an effective instrument in Germany's hands to curb Hungary, to keep her in German bondage. Hitler was well aware of this when he again became warily suspicious about the Hungarian Government's doings in the autumn of 1942.

Hungary's economic situation also grew more and more grave. The German demands were growing at a rapid pace. The exports of agricultural products, chiefly grain crops, amounted to millions of quintals. Hungarian industry, especially war industry, was now geared to the service of the German war machine. A particularly heavy burden was imposed by the outflow of a large part of strategically important raw materials: by 1943, more than half of Hungary's petroleum output and 90 per cent of her bauxite production went to Germany. It only added to the difficulties that the German Government, with reference to the joint conduct of war, was less and less willing to pay its debts due to Hungary. In 1941, Germany's debts already amounted to 326 million pengös, and in later years the sum ran into thousands of millions.

The catastophic deterioration of the international reputation of Hungary undermined Bárdossy's positions. The Prime Minister, owing especially to the Bachka massacres, had to face vehement criticism by the bourgeois liberal opposition and even by opponents from among representatives of finance capital and the aristocracy. His opponents thought it was high time for Bárdossy to be replaced by someone who represented their interests better and was capable of charting more flexible foreign and domestic policies: by someone who, besides speculating upon German victory, would consider also other possibilities on the international plane and, solely because of the foreign political implications, would take steps to check the advancement of the extreme-right wing at home, to simultaneously put down the growing anti-Fascist resistance as well, and who, if the course of the war events made it advisable, would be able to carry out an about-turn in foreign politics without allowing it to lead to a change in domestic power relations, to the advancement of the left-wing forces. In March 1942 — when Bárdossy ran into a personal conflict with Horthy over the election of a vice-regent — Count Bethlen, Count Gyula Károlyi and their associates succeeded in persuading the Regent to dismiss Bárdossy.

The inheritance which the new Prime Minister, Miklós Kállay, took over from his predecessor was a veritable bankrupt's estate in every respect, both morally — in both foreign and domestic policy — and economically. In the first few months of his tenure, however, there was no indication that Kállay would try to seek a way out of this predicament, but he practically confined himself to fulfilling the obligations accepted by Bárdossy. The Germans watched Kállay's appointment with suspicion, because they did not understand why Bárdossy who had perfectly proved his willingness to co-operate with 'the great ally' had to be dismissed. Their suspicion only grew when rumours in Budapest spread about the person of the would-be new Foreign Minister. He was Ullein-Reviczky, head of the press department in the Ministry of Foreign Affairs, whom the Germans considered, with or without reason, entirely unreliable; and Budapest failed even to react to their suggestion that they would be glad if Sztójay, the Hungarian Minister in Berlin, were to head the Ministry of Foreign Affairs. Ultimately, Kállay retained the portfolio himself until July 1943, when Jenő Ghyczy was appointed Foreign Minister.

The first diplomatic step of the new Prime Minister, as was an established custom, would have been to make a visit first to Italy and then to Berlin. To his offer of a visit to Rome he received from Mussolini the surprising answer that he would not be in a position to see him until after a call on Hitler first. This case was a perfect reflection of the character and essence of Italo—Hungarian relations at this stage of the war.

Kállay visited at the German General Headquarters in East Prussia on June 7 and 8, 1942. His talks with Hitler and Ribbentrop covered no major questions and resulted in no new agreement beyond those which had been agreed upon earlier, during Ribbentrop's visit in January. Kállay essentially took over the obligations undertaken by his predecessor. He said that Hungary would live up to her war commitments without reserve and would not deliver less food than in previous years. He consented to another 10,000 (altogether 30,000) Germans' being recruited in Hungary into the Waffen-S. S. This time, Hitler again brought up the necessity of solving the Jewish question in Hungary. On the other hand, Kállay pointed out that the Hungarian Government could not afford to oust suddenly and drastically all persons of Jewish origin without causing serious troubles in economic life.

The talks were for the most part about questions of the Rumanian—Hungarian relations. Hostilities between the two countries took on enormous dimensions that summer. After his return Kállay said that Hitler had told him that he would not object if, at the end of the war, Hungary wished to get even with Rumania by force of arms. When this news spread, the Germans angrily refuted Kállay's assertion, saying that the Hungarian Prime Minister had misconstrued Hitler's words. In this respect the only practical significance of the visit was that the Germans found it necessary to mediate and thereby to temper the hostilities.

The question of the Banat was also broached. Hitler again promised to let Hungary take possession of this region but for the time being he asked for secrecy in this respect. Kállay, on the other hand, spoke as if he made no point of pressing for a solution. At about the same time the German—Hungarian frontier commission concluded consideration of the status of the territory beyond the Carpathians (Galicia), after the Hungarian Government, not without some hesitation, had informed the German authorities that it did not regard the annexation of the said area to Hungary as a topical issue, and that it would possibly return to the matter after the end of the war. In analysing the position adopted by Kállay with regard to the Banat and Galicia, it seems no bold assumption to think that this time — wishing to have a somewhat freer hand than his predecessor had — he did not want, by acquiring additional territories, to turn the German—Hungarian balance still more in favour of Germany and thus to worsen his own freedom of movement which he might well need later on. The turn in the course of war had not yet occurred at that time, and Kállay's steps cannot be interpreted as the first moves made towards deserting the Axis camp. They rather reflect the idea that, while fulfilling the existing obligations but refusing to assume any new burdens, a 'wait-and-see' position was adopted.

This attitude became more firm after the Anglo–American troops landed in North Africa on November 8, 1942, and it was soon coupled with increased attention paid to the Western Powers. The landing in North Africa was the first successful feat of the Western Allies during the war, and its effect on Hungary could not be left out of consideration. In a memorandum dated February 1943, Chief of Staff Szombathelyi wrote that "the Anglo–Saxon troops' landing in Morocco caused very great alarm and excitement in our country". Seen from North Africa, any initiative by the Allies in the Mediterranean or Balkan area did not seem too hopeless. This possibility made a deep impression on those groups of the Hungarian ruling quarters which hardly believed in total German victory. They hoped that with a favourable turn of events it might become possible to revive Teleki's failed conception and, by an about-face in due time, to salvage the system into the postwar period, without any structural changes, maybe by and large within the boundaries of 1942. Already in December 1942, the Germans got wind of the interest Hungarian diplomats showed in the Balkan plans of the Allies. On December 8, they instructed Jagow to intercede with the Hungarian Government because reliable confidential sources had informed them of "Hungarian diplomats' conducting negotiations abroad in which the subject of Anglo–American landings in the Balkans, possibly with Turkish participation, came into question."

Neither did it escape their notice that the Christmas speech by Miklós Horthy, Jr. in the Portuguese-language broadcast of the Hungarian Radio mentioned that "a small nation cannot always be the master of its own destiny". The German Minister in Budapest was given instructions to remark upon this pronouncement at the Ministry of Foreign Affairs.

The British-oriented goups were now able to influence public opinion as well. The events in Africa added to their influence, just as a splendid Soviet victory would have resulted in the strengthening of the reaction of the right-wing forces. This in fact came about, as we shall see, after the battle of Stalingrad and the annihilation of the 2nd Hungarian army, when, under the effect of the Soviet victory and as a consequence of the shaping up of relations between the Allies, the conclusion of a separate peace with the Western Powers became an increasingly improbable possibility.

The landings in North Africa made their effect felt also in the – characteristically very cautious – manifestations of the Hungarian Prime Minister. What was new in Kállay's speeches was only a shift of emphasis. Loyalty to the Axis Powers was invariably the main pillar of Hungarian policy, but now it was strongly interconnected with emphasis and insistence on Hungary's independence, while at the same time, the verbal assaults on the Western Powers were dropped. But it was emphasized more markedly than ever that the war on the Soviet Union was 'a Hungarian war' in which the fighting, "even though at distances of thousands of kilometres away", nevertheless was going on "at the Hungarian frontiers and for the Hungarian frontiers." Serious emphasis was laid upon reference to the Kassa provocation, upon the assertion that Hungary had been attacked, and that Hungary had no territorial claims on the Soviet Union – that is, the anti-Soviet campaign was presented as a defensive war. From this conception it was now easy to derive the thesis that Hungary was fighting in self-defence and at the same time for Europe, for 'Christian civilization'. This time, of course, the matter in question was not any more a 'new Europe', which was an empty phrase to camouflage the war aims of the Axis Powers, but it was merely Europe. This was an old recipe which Kállay now pulled out, and which would not at all be worth speaking about if we did not know that this phrase-mongering had always meant the beginnings of Western orientation in Hungarian foreign policy.

Kállay did not improve on the recipe and had learnt little from the history of past years. Like his predecessors, he saw Hungary in his mind's eye as a leading power in Central Europe, but amidst the newly shaping situation this fancy, addressed now to the Western Powers, took on a stronger anti-Soviet complexion and was coupled with the idea of forming a new bloc. The main political role in this bloc would have been played by Turkey as a neutral Balkan state, its members would have been small states of Central Europe, too, and the spiritual countenance of this whole formation would have been supplied by the Vatican, while Hungary might have had a role as a 'peace-keeping' force, so her military strength had to be spared and preserved till the end of war. Elements of these conceptions are to be found in dozens of speeches, articles and essays from the winter of 1942 onward. And it was not by chance that, when, in the spring of 1943, the plan of such a bloc was being hatched in Turkey, Kállay immediately stood ready to co-operate.

The ground of these plans and conceptions was the lack of comprehension which most Hungarian politicians manifested towards the alliance between the Western Powers and the Soviet Union. They were simply unable to understand which were the motives that, in connection with the war against Nazi Germany, forced the social and ideological differences into the background and what was the binding material that cemented and perpetrated this alliance amidst the conditions of war. They had built upon the differences. In this war, as in the previous one they could only look at the European problems from the aspect of Central Europe. Their view of Hungary's future role was strongly influenced by what commonly characterized the politicians of the régime, no matter which political current they represented: the fact that when the point at issue was Hungary's international position, their mentality was still that of the defunct Monarchy, being imbued with long outdated illusions intended to serve as a kind of historical background to Hungarian nationalism, and this — like a brain tumour which prevents the brain from normally reading the signals coming from outside — made them incapable of judging, at least nearly realistically, the role and possibilities of Hungary in the Danubian basin.

From the autumn of 1942, Hungarian Government quarters began to give greater attention to the Western Powers not only by considering the pros and cons of their chances and the war plans of the Allies, but also by sounding Western public opinion as to the picture it had of Hungary. Obviously this also was instrumental — besides a number of domestic political and economic questions — in that early in December 1942, Kállay rejected in an official note the German demands formulated already in October with regard to the 'solution' of the Jewish question in Hungary. These demands were:

1. By December 31, 1942, the Hungarian Government should either take back the Jews of Hungarian nationality living in territories occupied by Germany, or agree that the measures introduced earlier — confiscation of property, the wearing of a distinguishing sign, deportation — should be applicable also against them. 2. It would be desirable to conclude with Hungary, too, an agreement to the effect that the two states reciprocally dispose of the Jews of foreign nationality living in their respective territories (territorial principle). 3. The German Government would deem it desirable to introduce in Hungary, too, as was done in Slovakia and Rumania, radical measures against the Jewish population: the total elimination of Jews from economic and cultural life, the introduction of the yellow star, the deportation of Jews in co-operation with the German authorities.

In his reply note, Kállay stated that the Hungarian Government was willing to accept the German proposals concerning the regulation of property questions in case all Jews of foreign nationality were to be deported. For this event, however, it set up a claim to the total property of the Hungarian Jews living abroad but wished to obtain previous information on the spot about the state and condition of that property. It could not consent to the application of the territorial principle. The way of solving the Jewish question, in its opinion, should be found by each state itself. As was demonstrated by the great results of the implementation of the anti-Jewish laws, Hungary was paying serious attention to the solution of the Jewish question, but at present the continued elimination of Jews from economic life might take place only at such a rate as not to disturb production, the normal working of the economic apparatus, which was all to the German interest. The introduction of the wearing of a yellow star was out of the question because, in view of the high ratio of Jews in economic life and within the urban population, it would hinder the implementation of the existing government measures and would lead to the unleashing of rude passions. At present, the Hungarian Government was not in a position to bring the deportations into effect, was the concluding statement of Kállay's note.

At the same time, Kállay set about informing his diplomats abroad — except a few prominent pro-Nazi envoys — of his reappraisal of the international situation and his conclusions, and got busy preparing for the establishment of secret contacts with the Western Powers.

To this end, he wished first of all to strengthen the connections that had remained after the break with the Western Powers, especially the relationships with the Hungarian emigration. But the prospects were not so bright, for the left-wing Octobrist emigration was not willing to put its — mainly British — connections at the service of the counter-revolutionary régime, and the Horthyite emigration had hardly any connections in the West. True, after the break with England, an ex-secretary of Legation, Antal Zsilinszky, and a former correspondent of *Pester Lloyd,* András Révai, founded the Society of Free Hungarians. They were on good terms with Tibor Eckhardt who had been living in the United States from the spring of 1941. But since the left-wing emigration made violent attacks on Eckhardt's mission because this was intended to serve the salvation of the counter-revolutionary régime, and since he had declared that he was "unwilling to sit at the same table with Communists" (thus justifying the charges levelled against him), Eckhardt found himself in a difficult position, and even the Zsilinszky group dissociated itself from him. From that time onward Eckhardt staked everything on one card: on the person of Otto of Habsburg, evidently in connection with the Central European federative plans which were much talked about at that time. This, however, did not improve his position either abroad or in Budapest.

The left-wing emigration headed by Mihály Károlyi and headquartered in London only came to agree with Zsilinszky's Society in 1944; the British Foreign Office on the other hand, sympathized neither with the Octobrists nor with the Horthyite emigration. The heaps of applications and memoranda it received from both sides were to no avail, though the democratic emigration exerted some influence through the Labour Party, but this was no good for Kállay's conceptions of salvaging the régime.

The only option Kállay now had to establish contacts was through the Hungarian diplomats and journalists who worked in neutral states and were not pro-German, and who had private contacts with British and American colleagues or with emissaries of other Allied countries.

The first try, in the summer of 1942, was made through Andor Gellért, the Berlin ex-representative of the Revisionist League, who had made friends with a number of British and U.S. diplomats, and who now attempted to resume these contacts at Stockholm, where he had recently been appointed press correspondent. Both the democratic opposition and the Social Democratic Party commissioned Gellért to get in touch with the emigration. In Stockholm Gellért met Vilmos Böhm who was in charge of the Hungarian section of the British information service, Böhm contacted his friends holding leading posts in the Labour Party, who replied to him that they would like to talk over the situation with leaders of the Social Democratic Party. For want of any better expedient, Kállay agreed to Peyer's going to London, but the Germans denied him the transit visa.

In the summer of 1942, another try was made through Ullein-Reviczky, who went to Turkey. The politician spent his holiday with his father-in-law, a retired British diplomat who was living there. Through the Englishman's mediation he contacted emissaries of the British Government. The reply, however, brook no evasion; namely, just as in the case of subsequent peace-feelers, Ullein was given to understand: if Hungary wished to part company with Germany, the Government had to delegate a plenipotentiary to talk over the military issues. So there were no excuses allowed, but the contact through Turkey now existed, and this proved later to be the most practical solution.

By creating connections Kállay only wished to obtain information for the time being; on the one hand, they wanted to make clear at what level and on what conditions the Western Powers were disposed to enter into negotiations; on the other, they wished to lay down certain conditions or rather to receive guarantees for the event of breaking with the Axis Powers.

Upon Ullein's recommendation the Prime Minister intended to send to Turkey András Frey, a diplomatic correspondent of the daily *Magyar Nemzet,* who accepted the commission. At the same time, another initiative was launched. Behind it stood Count István Bethlen or rather groups hallmarked in part by his name and consisting of conservative-reactionary members of the Upper House who were not pro-German, and in part by representatives of the banks and the National Association of Manufacturers (GYOSZ). In the autumn of 1942, a message came from Royall Tyler — the former financial commissioner of the League of Nations in Hungary, who, during the war, was a member of the U. S. diplomatic staff in Switzerland — to the effect that if Bethlen, by himself and independently of the Government, should go abroad, the President of the United States might possibly enter into contact with him as representative of Hungary. Bethlen refused to accept the mission, stressing that he did not want to be an émigré politician, and besides, he thought the time had not yet come to negotiate with the Allies.

After the landings in North Africa, however, Bethlen already found it essential to make use of the given opportunities — even though not through him personally. The choice fell on György Barcza, the ex-envoy in London, who would have made the journey not on behalf of the Government but as a representative of the Bethlen group, of course, after consultation with Kállay.

A group of leading Foreign Ministry officials, headed by Aladár Szegedy-Maszák, wanted to create contacts through the Legation in Stockholm for the purpose of gathering information, first of all, by the good offices of the Social Democratic emigration there.

And finally there was a possibility offered by the Hungarian Minister in Lisbon, Andor Wodianer. He had good connections with Eckhardt and Otto of Habsburg, who were living in the United States, and with the Polish émigré Government. Colonel Kowalewski, the Lisbon emissary of the Polish Government, who had been commissioned to keep touch with the Polish resistance, with the Home Army, had often met Wodianer since 1941. The first line of connection between the émigré Government and the Polish resistance ran through Hungary, for a great many Polish refugees lived in the country, and even a group of Polish counterintelligence secretly settled there after 1939.

Frey and Barcza had confidential talks with Kállay already prior to Christmas 1942, and then, immediately after New Year's Day. The authorization of Barcza was not for concrete negotiations about the possibilities of Hungary's getting out of the war, of her turning against Germany. In fact, Barcza was commissioned only to inform the British of the situation in Hungary as it was in Kállay's judgement, that is, to explain the policy of the Government. Feeling that the diplomatic baggage he was meant to take with him was too small, Barcza made several suggestions during the consultations. First of all, he would have liked Kállay to give him a sort of general promise — to which he might refer in case of need — that the Government would break off relations with Germany at a time it deemed convenient. Kállay was willing to make this promise only on condition that in return he should be promised that only Anglo—American forces, and no Soviet troops, would take part in the occupation of Hungary. The Prime Minister was against any suggestion concerning the need for political changes. He laid down that after the war he would oppose the return of Mihály Károlyi and his emigration, nor would he offer a larger scope for the functioning of the left, because, in his view, Károlyi would make Hungary "a political vassal of Beneš" and, in conjunction with the left, would "throw the country into the arms of the Soviet Union" as he had done in 1919. He added that under Horthy's regency Hungary might remain "a factor of order" in Central Europe. Obviously Kállay himself must have sensed that under these conditions there was hardly any chance to establish contacts with the Western Powers, therefore he authorized Barcza to tell that neither Bethlen nor he, Kállay, had the intention of salvaging the régime intact for the postwar period. Well, the above conditions he stipulated detracted considerably from the value of his promise.

Kállay also rejected another proposal by Barcza as too dangerous a step, namely to set about building up, as a sort of safeguard, the unofficial, so-called shadow representation of Hungary abroad.

The preparation of exploratory activities thus began towards the end of 1942, then nothing was done for a long time to come; or rather, early in December a message was dispatched to Turkey to the effect that, if the Allies were interested in establishing contact, it might be possible to send a Government offical of authority to start negotiations. On December 2, the U. S. Minister in Ankara fowarded this message to his Government as a serious offer and asked for instructions.

The journey of Barcza and Frey was delayed for weeks and months: the reason was, according to Kállay, that the necessary visas could not be obtained. It may well be that, at the time, it was indeed difficult to obtain visas — for this was not for an official diplomatic trip and, besides, the Germans regarded neither of the two passengers as quite reliable from the German point of view — but still, the main reason for the delay was certainly the battle of Stalingrad just unfolding on the Eastern front at that time. At the end of 1942, the battle of Stalingrad was not yet brought to an issue, and Kállay's people must have supposed that a possible turn in favour of Germany might set a new course to developments even in relation to the Western Powers.

In the meantime, the afore-said Foreign Ministry officials tried (likewise through unofficial channels) to inquire what reception would be given to the initiative of the Hungarian Government. At the end of 1942, Andor Gellért again got in touch with Vilmos Böhm. Gellért told Böhm that, with the knowledge of competent persons in the Ministry of Foreign Affairs but not on their behalf, he was seeking contacts with the British because the Government would be ready to enter into unofficial talks with the Western Powers; so he would like to know who were the personalities whom the British would accept as negotiating partners and what plans there were, if at all, with regard to Hungary. Practically, Böhm spoke only in his own name — but evidently on the basis of consultation with representatives of the British Labour Party and cognizant of the official British position — when he replied that the creation of contacts was possible if the Hungarian Government altered its domestic policies, refused to send any more troops to the front, and put a stop to the attacks in the press against Great Britain and the United States. Still in December 1942, the Hungarian Minister in Stockholm, Péter Matuska, officially recommended the Foreign Minister to take Böhm's suggestion into consideration and make positive proposals to the Allies.

In January 1943, the 2nd Hungarian army was annihilated at the Don as a result of the Soviet victory at Stalingrad which was a turning-point in the course of the Second World War.

The Voronezh disaster was a tremendous blow from which the Hungarian army could never recover during the war, and which was, to the Hungarian ruling classes, a grim reminder of the strength of the Soviet army. From that time on, the appearance of the Red Army in the Carpathian Mountains became an immediate possibility. Stalingrad and Voronezh put in motion the diverse parties and groups in Hungary's political life. Groups belonging to the Government party and the extreme right assessed the situation practically unanimously. The fact that the war took a turn was realized by all from Kállay through the General Staff to Imrédy and Szálasi. They were at one in the assumption that as a consequence of Stalingrad, Anglo—American forces could be expected to land in the Balkans in the nearest future.

On February 12, 1943, Colonel-General Szombathelyi, back from a visit with Hitler at the German General Headquarters, presented to the Regent a memorandum stating among other things: "We have to prepare ourselves for the future in every respect. This future projects the picture of dark events before our minds' eyes. We have to reckon that in the course of spring the Anglo—Saxon powers will attempt a landing in the Balkans.... Where and when the Anglo—Saxon forces will land in the Balkans we cannot know. I think that the landing will be feasible from the end of March onward. Führer and Chancellor Hitler is of the opinion that such a landing is very probable..."

The appraisal of the situation was unanimous but the conclusions widely differed. The extreme right sounded the alarm, demanding energetic domestic political and military measures and increased participation in the war. Whereas the Bethlen—Kállay group and the political quarters behind them feverishly began to seek Western contacts.

The ambitions and intentions were characteristically reflected at the meeting of the foreign affairs commission of the House of Representatives on February 19, 1943. Kállay explained (as Szombathelyi did in his memorandum) that the fighting in the East would probably shift to the Balkans, and it was most likely that Anglo—American troops would land there. Hungary had therefore to direct her attention south-eastwards. He emphasized that Hungary's participation in this war was limited to the struggle against the Soviet Union, and she had nothing to do with the other conflicts, she was entirely unconcerned with the West. Kállay's position was endorsed by several M. P. s of the Government Party and, of course, was seconded by members of the leftist opposition, among them Károly Rassay and Zoltán Tildy, who both stressed that it would be most unfortunate if Hungary should get involved in a fight with Anglo—Saxon forces, and that no further troops must be sent to the Soviet front either. On the other hand, Imrédy and his companions pressed in every respect for siding more emphatically with the Germans, inclusive of fighting the Anglo—American forces in case of their landing in the Balkans.

Kállay's analysis, in addition to the search of contacts with the West, dealt with the further tasks of the army in the first place. The problem was practically twofold: (*a*) how to fill the gaps due to the eradication of the 2nd army; (*b*) to what extent and in what manner should the existing and the newly recruited contingents take part in the war in the future? After the Voronezh disaster, the Government and the General Staff soon came to an understanding that the remains of the 2nd army must be brought home, and new units must not be sent instead. Beyond this point of agreement, however, there were sharp differences. Szombathelyi, as already mentioned, went to the German General Headquarters towards the end of January to discuss the fate of the 2nd army. At the talks, he pressed for the return of what was left of that force. On the other hand, the Germans demanded that Hungarian armed forces, if already unable to fight on the front, should at least take a share in the occupation duties, that another six divisions, in addition to the existing ones, should be set up of the remains of the 2nd army for the purposes of occupation. Szombathelyi consented without being authorized to do so.

The Government, with Horthy's approval, first refused the demand by stressing that the 2nd army was so utterly destroyed that it was unable even to perform occupation duties. The German High Command then proposed an alternative: Hungary should dispatch to Serbia two or three divisions of occupation by June 1, 1943, and Germany would aid in providing their equipment. The Chief of Staff accepted this proposal immediately. Participation in the occupation of Yugoslavia had probably been spoken of already during Szombathelyi's visit to Germany; in his memorandum of February 12, the Hungarian Chief of Staff, while making no concrete mention of any such German demand, emphasized, in analysing Hungary's "changed strategic position", that the Hungarian army "should take into consideration intervention in the southern theatre of war". The Germans, when making this proposal, evidently did not intend to serve military purposes but meant first of all to compromise the Kállay Government before the Western Powers, for they had knowledge of Hungary's secret peace-feelers and had resented the Prime Minister's statement made in the foreign affairs commission, too. They thought, and with good reason, that participation in the occupation of the Balkan peninsula would more definitely set Hungary against the Balkan peoples who fought Germany, and would thus turn her also against the Western Powers.

The German and Hungarian General Staffs conducted talks in late February through early March 1943. When Defence Minister Vilmos Nagybaczoni Nagy received word of these talks, he submitted the case to the Council of Ministers. The Cabinet first considered the case on March 10. The Minister of National Defence exposed the stand of the Chief of Staff. According to this it would be most useful to comply with the German demand, for the Germans would equip three Hungarian divisions. And it would be difficult to refuse just at a time when the 2nd army was being withdrawn from the Eastern front. Over and above this, according to Szombathelyi, "the Serbians would rather have us than the Germans occupying their territory, and this fact might win us sympathies among the Serbians" (!). Kállay, Interior Minister Ferenc Keresztes-Fischer and other Members of the Cabinet were for the rejection of the German demand. (The Minister of the Interior threatened to resign in case the German demand was fulfilled.) The Prime Minister strongly objected to Szombathelyi's having entered into negotiations without informing him and the Defence Minister in advance.

The Council of Ministers again took up the question on March 30, and, on the basis of an exhaustive theoretical and practical explanation by the Ministry of Foreign Affairs, rejected the demand of the German General Staff. It was not difficult to see the provocative intent of the Germans, and the Foreign Ministry, in a memorandum based on diplomatic sources, clearly referred to this.

Although their idea of involving Hungary in the occupation of Serbia was refused, the Germans nevertheless scored some results for the time being. Namely the Hungarian Government — changing its earlier position — consented, by way of compensation, to the setting up of two light divisions, composed of the remains of the 2nd army, to discharge occupation duties in addition to the existing contingents.

As we have seen, the Hungarian Government circles regarded an Anglo—Saxon landing in the Balkans as an impending possibility, so Kállay now hurriedly sent off his emissaries. The first wave of peace-feelers went out between late January and early March 1943. András Frey left for Turkey at the end of January with the mission — on behalf of the Prime Minister, the Ministry of Foreign Affairs and the Chief of Staff — to inform the Anglo—American diplomats as follows:

1. Hungary has no intention of offering resistance to the advance of Anglo—American or Polish armed forces when they reach the Hungarian frontier and enter Hungarian territory. But she can make this commitment only towards regular troops of the Allies and not towards guerrilla formations.

2. Hungary is willing in principle to prepare concrete actions against the Germans if the opportunity arises for the interested armies to prepare a practical plan beforehand.

Since Barcza still could not set out on his way, Kállay, early in February, dispatched a message through Baron Albert Radvánszky, an official of the National Bank of Hungary making a business trip to Switzerland. In the presence of Lipót Baranyay (the president of the National Bank) and Jenő Ghyczy he authorized Radvánszky to mention to Allen Dulles, head of the U. S. Office of Strategic Services, and to Royall Tyler — who was at the time counsellor at the U. S. Embassy in Berne — Hungary's intention to negotiate "with the purpose of preparing the foundations of progressive co-operation between the United States and England, on the one hand, and Hungary on the other, co-operation which may eventually lead to Hungary's deserting the Axis Powers" Radvánszky was instructed to stress specially that "for lack of mutual trust" Hungary was not in a position to start negotiations with the Soviet Union. Finally he had to ask the Americans to name the diplomats whom they would accept as permanent negotiating partners at the secret talks.

At the same time, Vilmos Böhm in Stockholm also received a message through Aladár Szegedy-Maszák. The message, which was in fact a reply to Böhm's proposals made late in 1942, was essentially identical with Frey's text but went beyond it by mentioning Hungary's readiness for peaceful co-operation with her neighbours, but only on condition that the latter acknowledged "Hungary's lawful claims".

A young official of the press department in the Foreign Ministry, László Veress, was sent to Lisbon to gather information early in the year. Veress took with him a telegraph apparatus for the Legation there to forward occasional messages. Two university professors, Gyula Mészáros and Albert Szent-Györgyi, left for Turkey at the same time. Finally, on March 22, Barcza also departed for Rome. Mészáros, who was known to be in touch with the Vienna bureau of the Abwehr, the German intelligence service, was asked only to take a look around. Professor Vály as well as András Frey, and for the first time László Veress, were expected to arrive at Istanbul in the first half of March. Except Szent-Györgyi, the other emissaries received from the S. O. E. (Special Operation Executive) men the answer mentioned earlier. "... so long as Hungary continues to fight against our Allies and to help the Axis she can expect neither sympathy nor consideration".

Szent-Györgyi told the British agents that before leaving Budapest he had been in touch with leaders of the Social Democratic Party, the Smallholders' Party, the National Democratic Party and the Legitimists. (He mentioned by name Károly Peyer, Árpád Szakasits, Gyula Kállai, sub-editor of *Népszava*, Imre Kovács, Béla Varga, János Vázsonyi, Antal Sigray.) He had informed Prime Minister Miklós Kállay and Antal Ullein-Reviczky, head of the press department in the Foreign Ministry, of his journey and the Minister of National Defence through General Rudolf Andorka was also notified.

Szent-Györgyi declared that all political parties and other organized bodies in Hungary, with the exception of the Fascists, were willing to accept him as head of a Government to be formed before or during the collapse of the German armies. Even the extreme-right wing would tolerate his leadership as a means for avoiding wholesale reprisals. He stated that the help of the Hungarian General Staff could not be relied upon until the twenty-five superior officers of German origin and pro-German sympathies had been removed. At any case, Minister of Defence Vilmos Nagybaczoni Nagy was preparing two reliable army corps free from German influence, and no Hungarian troops were now being sent to the Soviet front. Finally, he offered his services if it was the intention of the Allies "to re-establish a Hungary capable of taking a worthy part in reconstructing Europe".

He stated that on forming this Cabinet he would be willing to destroy vital bridges and otherwise impede the Axis war effort. He would purify the General Staff in two weeks and he hoped that he would then be able to offer military assistance to the Allies. He suggested that a 'stay-put' warning to all occupied countries before the German collapse would be welcomed and should be strongly worded. He maintained that an Allied occupation was essential to enable Hungary to demobilize the army and to afford time for the establishment of a democratic régime, because he did not believe Hungary to be capable, without outside help, of introducing the necessary social reforms or of freeing herself from the present régime "dominated by the army, the priests and the feudal system".

Szent-Györgyi also managed to convey a message to Steinhardt, the U. S. Minister in Ankara. In it he wrote among other things: "Before leaving my country, I visited the Prime Minister, and told him that I plan to come out this way to try to talk to Mr. Steinhardt and asked him whether I could do any favour to him. He asked me to tell Mr. Steinhardt that (1) he is not giving one soldier or one gun any more to Germany; (2) he has to shout now and then against the Jews but he is doing practically nothing and is hiding 70,000 Jewish refugees in the country; (3) he could not follow a different policy till now because in that case Hungary would have been occupied by the Germans and mobilized totally against the Allies and the Jews exterminated."

In this memorandum he also stressed that he wielded enough influence to get, at a convenient time, the Government's policy to take the desired course. He added that Ullein-Reviczky had outlined to him special conditions regarding a possible armistice.

The programme proposed by Albert Szent-Györgyi at Istanbul was essentially different from the programme of the Hungarian emissaries who had come forth earlier on behalf of the Government or the Foreign Ministry, about which the Secretary of State wrote on February 14, 1943:

"There have been a number of Hungarian attempts to establish contact with British representatives abroad as an insurance against the defeat of Germany."

The basic difference was that Szent-Györgyi — although he was in contact with Kállay and Ullein-Reviczky, and told about it to the Allies — did not act on their behalf but represented the democratic and liberal opposition. He was offering to form a government in the name of the latter. He thought it necessary to overthrow the Horthyite system and to create a democratic Hungary. Another basic difference was that his programme provided for active military co-operation against Germany, too.

One may ask whether such a programme could be realistic in Hungary in those days. Szent-Györgyi's conceptions were obviously built on the general belief that the Stalingrad defeat of the Germans and their allies would shortly be followed by an invasion of the Balkans by Anglo-American armies and that the powerful Soviet onslaught would continue. And in this case Germany's near collapse could be taken for certain.

History did not justify these expectations, but let us not forget that this view was general not only in Hungary. And as to how Germany's collapse would set in, the protagonists of those days had had a sort of 'experience': the First World War. Many thought that the collapse of Hitler's Germany would take place as it had in 1918, and few believed that the fightings would reach as far as the 'Berlin bunker'.

In analysing Szent-Györgyi's programme we may also think that he overestimated the strength of the democratic opposition and had too simple a conception of the transition: break with Germany and break with the counter-revolutionary régime. Certain illusions undoubtedly followed from the general beliefs concerning the end of the war. None the less, those on whose behalf Szent-Györgyi spoke were aware, just like him, that a democratic change-over and social reforms could be effected only with outside help. This is why they regarded Allied occupation as an absolute necessity.

The cross-section of all the various messages, missions and reports clearly shows the main outlines of the conceptions entertained by Kállay and the different political groups which considered the peace-feelers necessary. All plans were built upon the imminent Allied landing in the Balkans.

The possibility of such a landing again brought out the differences with the neighbour countries, especially Rumania, but in a different sense this time. The Hungarian ruling quarters, starting from the conviction that the landing would take place in the area of Turkey—Bulgaria—Rumania, supposed that in this case Rumania would at the first propitious moment take sides with the Allies, and this, if Hungary failed to prevent it, would result in the definitive loss of Transylvania. Kállay seems to have been of this view, and he shared it with Szombathelyi, as can be seen in the afore-mentioned memorandum. Thus the hope of retaining the territories acquired with German help and of establishing internationally guaranteed frontiers favourable to Hungary only added to the weight of the argument for possibly siding with the Allies.

From the early spring of 1943, the Kállay Government made feeble attempts to clarify the relationship with the neighbouring countries for the future. He was especially anxious to settle its relations with the émigré Royal Serbian Government headed by Dušan Simović. Through go-betweens Kállay attempted to make contact with General Draža Mihajlović, the commander of the Chetniks fighting against both the Germans and Tito's partisans, and with an associate of his, Milan Nedić, the Prime Minister of the Serbian Government set up by the German invaders. On other occasions, representatives of the Government emphasized that the settling of relations between the two countries, or rather any action to be taken in favour of the Serbs living in Hungary, was conditional on the recognition of the frontiers of 1942.

Certain feelers reached for Slovakia. But the starting-point, which implied the maximum concession from the Hungarian side, was nothing more than Hungary's willingness to drop any *further* territorial claims on Slovakia.

Late in 1942 and early in 1943, some possibility temporarily presented itself for improving relationships between Hungary and Rumania. The initiative came from Rumania, in a situation when there was, for a short time, a phase lag in favour of Hungary in the balance of power between the two countries. The Rumanian army deployed in the Stalingrad area had been smashed by the Soviet forces in December 1942, and the Voronezh disaster followed only a few weeks later. In this situation, Rumanian Foreign Minister Mihai Antonescu tried to approach Hungary by declaring that he did not insist on the inviolability of the Trianon frontiers and was of the opinion that rectification of the frontiers would be feasible on the basis of population exchange. Some parley started between the two countries in token of 'normalization', but this was not too promising, especially after the Voronezh defat had restored the balance of power. The Hungarian Government insisted that Transylvania, down to the Maros line, should belong to Hungary. This, of course, made it impossible to make any progress. It is worth mentioning that in June 1943, on Bethlen's initiative, a meeting took place between ex-Minister Miklós Bánffy and Iuliu Maniu, a Rumanian oppositionist politician. The talks started from the assumption that the Germans lost the war in all probability, so both countries would find it opportue to co-operate in the interest of breaking away from the Axis Powers and taking sides with the Allies. But the negotiations were soon broken off because Bánffy was firm demanding possesion of Northern Transylvania, while Maniu wanted its reannexation in exchange for Rumanian co-operation.

All things considered, it can hardly be contested that for Kállay, when he began to build up contacts with the Western Powers, the negotiating basis was the position of the 1942 frontiers.

Decisive among Kállay's motives, beside the territorial questions, was the hope that a successful break with Germany might make it possible to salvage the political and social framework of the counter-revolutionary system into the times following the war.

In his memoirs Kállay tried to deny that his aim had been to save the régime, and in proof of his assertion he referred to the text which András Frey had handed to the British emissaries. There it was mentioned that the Hungarian Government asked for nothing in return for its siding with the Allies. Paragraph 3 said that the purpose of this offer was not to save the Hungarian régime but solely to serve the interests of the Hungarian people. However, the message which Frey was supposed to convey did not originally contain the above sentence. In 1967, after Kállay's death, András Frey revealed that this way of offering unconditional surrender had been additionally devised, in his presence, by "an official of the Foreign Ministry and a British agent", who then added it to the original text, because Kállay did not dare or did not want to go thus far. Of course, the one-time Prime Minister in his memoirs readily quoted the definitive text drawn up without him as his own original message.

Nevertheless, it would not be fair to assert that the Kállay—Bethlen group was not aware that, in case the Allies won the war, it would be inevitable to effect certain political and social changes in Hungary, too. These issues were brought up in the Council of Ministers on February 23, 1943, when Kállay declared that "the conclusion of the war will bring with it a social transformation". But they wanted to define or at least to prescribe such changes by themselves in order to be able to check and stop the whole thing. When, in their messages to the Western Powers, they referred to the possibility of a transformation of the régime, the most they thought of was that they might somewhat broaden the framework which Teleki succeeded in saving, and that after the war they might invite a few politicians of the Smallholders' Party and the right wing of the Social Democratic Party to join the Government. Surely they contemplated a limited sort of land reform too, which, however, would not have undermined the economic and political influence of the class of big landowners.

Early in 1943, it seemed that Kállay would have several possibilities of linking Hungary to a new sort of neutral bloc, taking thereby the first step towards the realization of the idea of which there had been so much talk since November 1942, in connection with Hungary's postwar role in a 'Christian' and anti-Soviet combination.

In February 1943, Turkish Foreign Minister Menemencioglu expounded his idea of setting up a Central European and Balkan league which ought to form 'a bloc of order and security' and to prevent the spread of 'the chaotic conditions' to Central Europe and the Balkans which was envisaged for the case of a Soviet advance. The bloc was planned to include Turkey, Greece, Bulgaria, Yugoslavia, Rumania and Hungary. The essentially anti-Soviet aim of the proposed bloc was evident, and the Turkish Foreign Minister, when informing the Governments concerned of his conceptions, did not fail to lay stress on 'solidarity in face of the Soviet peril'. Kállay received the Turkish suggestions with warm sympathy and was pleased to underline Hungary's agreement in principle. At the same time, he pointed out to the Turkish Government that it should consider the existing difficulties in Hungarian—Rumanian relations and accept the need for their solution. Menemencioglu showed readiness to mediate between Hungary and Rumania, but this was of no avail as the bloc-forming attempt failed itself. The British Minister in Ankara protested as early as March against the involvement of Hungary and Rumania in any kind of bloc. After this the whole matter was slowly sinking into oblivion.

The Germans took a dim view of the Turkish experiment, because they thought it concealed some British initiative, and they expressly censured the enthusiasm of the Hungarian Government. In vain did Kállay argue that in this way it might be possible to bring Turkey closer to the Axis, since with the proposal she endorsed the anti-Bolshevist conception of the Axis Powers. The Germans dismissed his arguments and pointed out that Turkey could openly adhere to the Tripartite Pact if she wanted to. The issue, raised again in April 1943, when Horthy was visiting with Hitler, met with Hitler's violent reproaches on Kállay for the positive attitude he took towards the Turkish initiative.

On February 10, 1943, shortly after the Casablanca conference — where the United States and Great Britain enunciated the principle of unconditional surrender — the Spanish Foreign Minister explained to Ferenc Ambró, the Hungarian Minister in Madrid, that his Government believed neither in the applicability of the formula of unconditional surrender at the end of the war nor in the ultimate reality of the German conceptions. Spain and Portugal hoped that there was still some possibility of making 'a reasonable peace' on the principles of Pope Pius XII's message of Christmas 1939. (In that message the Pope designated the terms of peace — beyond a few general principles to the effect that "a nation's will to live can never bring with it the death warrant of another nation" — in the requirement that, besides protection for the national minorities, the possibility of a peaceful revision of treaties should be sought.) Thereupon the Spanish Foreign Minister put the question to Ambró whether Hungary would accept the Pope's speech as a programme of co-operation in principle in the interest of an interchange of ideas and conceptions.

The Spanish suggestion coincided with Kállay's thoughts and his afore-mentioned ideas related to the Vatican. For this reason, he replied on March 3, that he most willingly took note of the idea; that Hungary 'gladly identifies herself' with the Spanish conception and was ready to accept the spirit of the Pope's programme.

Enclosed with Kállay's message was a Foreign Ministry memorandum, which left no doubt as to what this 'glad identification' was for. Hungary feels, the memorandum read, an obligation to her own nation and to European civilization. It is her historic mission to guard over the peace of Central Europe, but she can perform this duty only within the national boundaries "which have enabled her to act for a thousand years now".

Simultaneously, through Prince Primate Justinian Serédi, the Prime Minister sent Pope Pius XII an aide-mémoire as well — in his words: "an entreaty from the eastern frontiers of Catholicism to the Head of the Church" — in which he solicited "protection for Hungary against the Bolshevist peril" and German pressure. This was the time when the Hungarian Government was seeking contacts with the head of the Polish émigré Government, General Sikorski, 'for the sake of joint action against the Soviet peril'. Although the Poles were not averse to establishing contacts, what Kállay gained thereby was nothing more than another warning that Hungary should reduce cooperation with the Axis Powers to a minimum and refrain from enforcing regulations against refugees and Jews, 'if she wants to avoid facing needless reprisals'.

It was also with a view to contemplating a kind of bloc that Kállay set out to visit Italy early in April 1943, at last. Rehashing old conceptions, he suggested to Mussolini that Italy and Hungary should chart a common course of action that would remain loyal to Axis policy, but would not unconditionally be suited to the German conception in every detail. Thus Italy and Hungary would not be exposed to German superiority and to the German policy piling mistake upon mistake. In the given case there might be some opportunity for compromises which were unfeasible under the current state of politics. This might be useful also to the Germans, or at least to a 'more reasonable German policy', for in case of need the Germans could utilize the friendly connections which Italy and Hungary had with other countries. The common policy, Kállay went on explaining, could possibly be joined in by Finland; the bloc could certainly win sympathies from Poland, Turkey and some political quarters of the occupied Balkan countries, and might find support in Spain, Portugal, and perhaps Sweden, namely in those countries which were exposed to the 'Soviet peril' or were afraid of Communism. The spiritual pillar to support the whole edifice might be the Vatican.

As can be seen, Kállay mixed his own ideas with elements of the Spanish and Turkish suggestions to 'square the circle' — to establish, inside the Axis bloc, another bloc which, though associated with it, would slowly become disengaged. In this new bloc he wanted to assemble all forces which he thought could assimilate the idea of anti-Sovietism; beginning from some of the already reluctant vassal states through the émigré governments of the subjugated countries up to the Fascist Iberian bloc which had stayed out of the war. This was, in effect, a somewhat reshaped model of the horizontal axis. But this had been an abortive idea already at its birth in the latter half of the thirties: now, in a radically changed situation, in the fifth year of war, at the time of the decisive superior growth of the anti-Fascist Powers, any such idea was even more doomed to failure. With the idea of such a bloc Kállay turned to Mussolini at a time when the policy of Fascist Italy — even in Kállay's judgement — had long been merely copying and executing German policy, when Mussolini could no more rely on a good part of his own Fascist Party, all in all, when the last hour of his régime was nearing. (Kállay had also a personal experience: his special train arrived in Rome several hours after its due time because it had been held up by a guerrilla action in North Italy.) It seems the Hungarian Prime Minister had no notion of the power wielded by the resistance movements of the subjugated countries, nor of the effective influence of the émigré Government over their peoples, nor of what forces were acting upon those Governments, for it is true that, as far as anti-Sovietism is concerned, Kállay's ideas were not alien to the Governments of either Sikorski or Simović and Mihajlović, but it is also true — and this was what mattered — that these endeavours could not freely and openly prevail owing to the change in the balance of forces between the Powers of the coalition.

In his talks with Mussolini, Kállay was very cautious, he did not say a word about the peace feelers he initiated to the Western Powers. But the suggestions he made let Mussolini suspect that the Hungarian Government was seeking a background for a change of course in foreign policy.

Kállay pressed for a more active Axis policy. The question of a separate peace was touched upon in general, as Kállay took a stand for some arrangement with the Western Powers, while Mussolini expounded that Germany ought to conclude a separate peace with the Soviet Union. But there could be no question of a separate peace for Italy, the Duce insisted.

The Hungarian Prime Minister wished to persuade the Duce to support the Mihajlović group in Yugoslavia, but Mussolini declined. Finally Kállay asked the Italian Government not to apply discrimination against the Jews of Hungarian nationality living in Italy. Beyond an overall emphasis on friendship, this was the only request which Mussolini promised to grant.

Kállay had discussions in Rome with Pius XII as well. The Pope assured him of his sympathy and said he would be ready to mediate between the belligerent parties if the Italian Government asked him to do so. When Kállay, on his farewell visit to the Italian Prime Minister, conveyed the Pope's message, Mussolini refused to discuss the matter, saying that he withheld his decisions until his forthcoming talks with Hitler. The head of the Hungarian Government returned from Rome disappointed, with the conviction that he could no longer rely on Italy for the realization of his foreign policy aspirations.

The emissaries dispatched to neutral countries achieved far less than Kállay had hoped for. Their authorization was too restricted to serve as a basis for successful negotiations. Without concrete commitments and steps towards defection from the Axis Powers, Kállay was bound to fail in his effort to come to a sort of agreement with the Western Powers.

András Frey was able to create appropriate contacts in Turkey, but the only result he achieved was that he could forward the prepared text approximating to the principle of unconditional surrender, and was told that the United States and Great

Britain would be jointly represented during the negotiations and that the message of the Hungarian Government would be answered. But the answer was long in coming. Radvánszky's mission was no more fruitful. He was also promised the dispatch of the message and a reply, but no reply came during his stay in Switzerland. Gellért sent word to Budapest that there was nothing against maintaining the exploratory contacts. But there was no word of any concrete result. László Veress talked with many people in Lisbon, but ultimately he had to conclude that it was hardly possible to build contacts in the Portuguese capital, and, for the time being, the atmosphere was not favourable to such talks. His conclusions proved correct, for when he at last received a reply, it consisted of a single sentence: the Allies would only negotiate on the platform of unconditional surrender.

Barcza was received in audience by the Pope, then he managed to see the British Minister in the Vatican, D'Arcy Osborne, to whom he explained in detail the position of Hungary and presented a memorandum drawn up by himself. Osborne promised to forward the note, then questioned Barcza closely whether Hungary would contemplate entering the Central European bloc after the war which would include South Germany, Austria, Czechoslovakia, Poland and Hungary under Otto of Habsburg's reign. He promised to help Barcza build his connections in Switzerland.

The Allies gave quite a different reception to Szent-Györgyi's mission, on the one hand, because they did not take the professor as a representative of the official Hungarian Government and, on the other hand, because in the spring of 1943, they thought that in Hungary a combination of considerable forces was unfolding against co-operation with the Germans and against the Government's policy.

Prior to Szent-Györgyi's appearance, as we have seen, the British Government was rather non-committal towards the Hungarian peace-feelers. It took the position that Hungary could expect neither sympathy nor consideration as long as she continued the struggle against Great Britain's allies and continued to help the Axis Powers. In the first half of January 1943, when peace-feelers came one after another, and information was accumulating, the British Foreign Office again stated: "The time has not yet come when we have any prospect of detaching Hungary from the Axis. Any advantages we might hope to gain by encouraging anti-Axis Hungarians would therefore be more than balanced by the suspicions caused among our Allies, in particular the Czechs, who are already rather worried about Hungarian peace-feelers." This appears also from the reply given to András Frey early in March 1943, a message which, without reference to the possibility of any kind of political arrangement, requested that two high-ranking army officers should be delegated to talk over the military issues, and stated that the Anglo—American Allies at the forthcoming negotiations would be represented by a former Hungarian journalist, György Pálóczi-Horváth, an agent of the British Intelligence Service.

The first signs of change in the British position regarding Hungary appeared early in February 1943. London had received a lot of information about the situation in Hungary. The insistent Hungarian attempts at creating contacts ultimately prompted the Foreign Office to work out a modified line to be followed in respect of Hungary, a line that might be put to use first of all for the purposes of propaganda. The occasion was given by a telegram from the British Embassy in Lisbon reporting on Gusztáv Kövér's approaches. F. K. Roberts, head of the Central Department in the Foreign Office, wrote in his memo of February 9 as follows: "While we should continue to be sceptical of these approaches in so far as they are clearly inspired by the Hungarian Government, there have recently been some satisfactory developments in the internal situation in Hungary. A relatively strong democratic opposition composed of the Peasant and Socialist Parties and representing workers and intellectuals has grown up." Summing up the actions of this opposition, he referred to the clique behind Bethlen, which he called a right-wing, nationalist, anti-German faction. And while setting no great value on this faction as far as British interests went, he pointed out the great influence it exercised on Horthy and his Government. Finally he mentioned that Jewish organizations in England sympathized with Hungary, due to the strong movement in Hungary to put restraint on the persecution of Jews. He stated that, even if no reply was to be given to the Hungarian feelers, it was well to take note of the satisfactory internal developments.

Permanent Under-Secretary of State Sir Alexander Cadogan voiced his doubt whether the British Government was right in bluntly rejecting the satellite countries' approaches on every occasion. "I only hope our minds are not rigidly closed making trouble our enemies," he wrote, pointing at the same time to the dangers of such an action, to the possibility of accepting obligations which might later cause trouble.

On February 12, Eden added this remark: "There may be a case for modifying our attitude slightly but we can only do it in agreement with the U. S. and Soviet Governments. Maybe we should talk to them of this problem which is largely one of tactics."

These few sentences changed the British attitude towards Hungarian peace-feelers and occasioned the starting of an exchange of views between the Allied Powers about the situation in the satellite states and the conditions of negotiating with them.

When Eden put down this view of his on paper, talks had already begun at Istanbul with Nobel Prize laurate Professor Albert Szent-Györgyi who did not pose as representative of the Kállay Government. It was therefore impossible to assume that the mere purpose of his mission was to secure the position of the régime before the Allies. And this was precisely one of the essential causes which induced the British Government to reconsider the question of Hungary.

Namely, they thought that the democratic opposition in Hungary, that is a government headed by Professor Szent-Györgyi, might be a good *alternative* to the Kállay Government which they would 'have nothing to do with' and whose approaches they had rejected. Now, as there seemed to be a genuine option, it might be necessary to work out a new policy towards Hungary for the purpose of strengthening and encouraging that democratic opposition.

But this was no easy task for the Foreign Office: Hungary was indeed in a state of war with the Western Allies too, but, on the other hand, she only took part in the war against the Soviet Union. Any change in the previous policy line could be made only in agreement with the anti-Fascist Powers. Great Britain and the United States had already enunciated the principle of unconditional surrender, and it was evident that the answer to the peace-feelers and the modification of propaganda could only be in conformity with this principle. Emigrants from Hungary's neighbours, especially the Czechoslovak Émigré Government, felt suspicious of any Hungarian approach and of any attempt made since the outbreak of the war to set up any kind of Hungarian committee in England or the United States, mainly because of the territorial differences. Britain therefore could make no commitment in this respect if she wanted to avoid conflicting with her small allies, if she did not want to get into contradiction with her previous standpoints. At the same time, there was no doubt that the frontier question was the only issue which could influence the whole of Hungarian public opinion. It was also no small problem to make it clear to the Hungarian Government that its future attempts at counter-insurance could not but fail. What was needed were acts, first of all the termination of the war against the Soviet Union.

The real intentions of the Hungarian Government were illuminated, just at the time of Szent-Györgyi's negotiations, by the talks in Stockholm between Andor Gellért and Vilmos Böhm.

On February 8, 1943, London received a report stating that Gellért had asked for Böhm's advice: What could Hungary do to get out of the war? Böhm proposed a four-point programme of action: Hungary should agree to send no new troops to the Eastern front and, at a given time, to make a public statement to this effect. In case the Allies should undertake an invasion of South Eastern Europe, Hungary should put up no resistance and open her frontiers to British, American and, if necessary, Polish troops. She should provide the British Government with any information about actions directed against the Allied Powers. In return for these services, Böhm's advice went on, Hungary might ask to be treated not as a defeated country but in a way "consonant with her future, her vitality and her honour".

Gellért accepted Böhm's advice and explained at length the difficult position Hungary was in, and emphasized that the aim of the negotiations was to fulfil the 'agreed conditions', in which case "the Hungarian people may, without humiliation and without losing their possibilities of existence, devote themselves to re-construction." He stated that Hungary was ready to prove her goodwill by acts which, however, could only take place gradually, and in return she expected that "the United Nations will value these acts accordingly and guarantee Hungary's future."

The report on the talks already interpreted Gellért's words as an indication that Hungary was courting British and American friendship in the hope of escaping the consequences of the inevitable defeat, but she "is still not ready to undertake any action which may be of benefit to Soviet Russia." The Foreign Office agreed with this interpretation and added that Böhm's proposals went far beyond the aims now to be defined in connection with Hungary.

The official position remained one of shunning any approaches by the Hungarian Government. At the same time, it was decided that, until an agreement had been reached with the Soviet Union and the United States, no further step should be taken concerning Hungary. Accordingly, they declined Böhm's request to go to London. And when it became known that Ullein-Reviczky was about to leave for Ankara, the S. O. E. was authorized only to tell him what Szent-Györgyi had already been told: some message may come later. It was decided that propaganda and the press should stop dealing with the peace-feelers, because the Allies might get it wrong and the Axis circles might become confirmed in their opinion that whatever might happen they would always find the way towards a peace built upon some compromise.

Let us see now what was the new policy towards Hungary as it was brought to the notice of the Soviet and U. S. Governments.

On February 24, 1943, Sir Orme Sargent, Deputy Under-Secretary of State, held a conference in the Foreign Office, where it was agreed that the aide-mémoire to be addressed to the Allied Governments should raise the problems concerning all the smaller German satellites; but, since their conditions were different, it was not desirable to work out a common line. From the point of view of both propaganda and the British Government's policy it was found more opportune to adopt a less negative stand towards Hungary (and maybe Bulgaria).

Based on the decisions passed at the conference, the aide-mémoire concerning Hungary (which began by summing up the situation in Hungary and stressed that "Hungary has succeeded in preserving a greater degree of independence than any other satellite in South Eastern Europe", and that "A relatively strong democratic opposition has emerged based mainly on the Peasant and Socialist Parties, upon the Trade Union organizations, which still function in Hungary, and upon the intellectuals") stated the following:

"Although His Majesty's Government do not consider that any early and decisive change in Hungarian policy is likely, the general background seems favourable for some slight modification of the rigid attitude which His Majesty's Government have hitherto adopted towards Hungary. They accordingly propose in response to any serious Hungarian peace-feelers and in their propaganda to Hungary to follow in future the following line. His Majesty's Government cannot enter into any undertakings regarding the future of Hungary nor are they prepared to negotiate with individual Hungarians on the basis that they may in due course be in a position to establish a Hungarian Government. However, instead of confining themselves to saying, as hitherto, that 'so long as Hungary continues to fight against our Allies and to help the Axis she can expect neither sympathy nor consideration,' His Majesty's Government would propose in future to add that they have been glad to note certain developments within Hungary in the right direction, such as those referred to in the preceding paragraph, but that they obviously can have nothing to do with a régime which allied itself with the Axis and, without provocation, attacked in turn Great Britain's Czechoslovak, Yugoslav and Soviet Allies. With a view to disposing of Hungarian fears of a new and more far-reaching Trianon settlement, the line might then be developed that, although Hungary will have to make adequate restitution to our Allies, His Majesty's Government have no desire to see Hungary torn to pieces or to penalize the Hungarian people for the follies of their Governments. Our attitude and that of our Allies will inevitably be influenced by the practical steps taken by the Hungarians themselves to free themselves from Axis domination and to hasten the victory of the United Nations and their own liberation. ... Great care will of course have to be taken in regard to Czechoslovak and Yugoslav susceptibilities, although there have recently been signs of a less rigid attitude towards Hungary from the Czechoslovak side."

This aide-mémoire summarizing the British proposals addressed to the Soviet and U. S. Governments was based on the decisions of February 24. In a special supplement it gave account, in addition to the quoted position regarding the question of Hungary, of the peace-feelers thrown out since December 1942. It dealt in detail with Szent-Györgyi's talks, in connection with which it emphasized that those talks were of a different category: "The earlier approaches had all been clearly instigated by the Hungarian Government in an attempt to reinsure their own position; and His Majesty's Government still see no advantage in adopting a forthcoming attitude towards them. Professor Szent-Györgyi on the other hand appears to enjoy a certain independence and in many respects he seems to be a person with whom discreet contact might usefully be maintained through suitable underground channels."

A supplement to the aide-mémoire contained the records of the House of Commons meeting of December 16, 1942, devoted to questions of the Central European confederation.

The American and Soviet replies to the British suggestions arrived only months later, so the British Government did not enter into negotiations with the new Hungarian emissaries, but obtained, through appropriate channels, exact information on what they intended to convey. Four major approaches were made in the course of March, April and May. They precisely outlined the position and intentions of the Kállay Government and the Bethlen group.

Still early in March, there arrived at Stockholm as a diplomatic courier the deputy director of the political department of the Hungarian Ministry of Foreign Affairs, Aladár Szegedy-Maszák, who, a few months later, was appointed director of the political department. This trip in itself attracted attention, because so high-ranking diplomats hardly ever travelled as couriers. The information which London was to receive soon, confirmed that the courier's trip was only an excuse for him to impart authentic information on the intentions of the Hungarian Government.

Szegedy-Maszák stated the following: "At the present moment when Russia is the only military opponent of Germany on the European Continent, and taking into consideration Russia's future danger, Hungary is temporarily unable to take any concrete steps for her withdrawal from the Axis and the conclusion of a separate peace... until the Anglo—Saxons have arrived on the Continent, Hungary has no choice but to adhere to the Axis, and to endeavour at the same time to preserve her present relative freedom of movement. Hungary ... must preserve herself from total German occupation so as to be able to dispose of her own military forces towards the end of the war. ... There is [in Hungary] much sympathy for the Polish efforts to create a Central European federation. Hungary would be a willing partner of such a federation." Having voiced the opinion that, as a result of the incessant attack of the

Soviet armies, Germany could last for no more than six months, and therefore an Anglo—American invasion of Europe would be urgent, he made it clear that should the Americans, the British or the Poles invade Hungary, her resistance would only be symbolical, but "she would fight obstinately if she were to be invaded by Soviet, Rumanian or Yugoslav troops."

A few weeks thereafter, early in April, György Barcza, the ex-envoy in London, arrived in Switzerland and sought contact with British Ambassador Norton, who had been instructed not to meet him but to find out in some way or other what he intended to tell. It was at about the same time that Károly Schrecker put in an appearance in Turkey and communicated through the Dutch Ambassador in Ankara that "he had been asked by a number of leading Hungarians, from Conservatives to Socialists, to explain to His Majesty's Government Hungary's past and present position and his views as to the future and to obtain information as regards the views of His Majesty's Government". He also stated that he was making this visit with the knowledge and consent of Prime Minister Kállay. The British Ambassador in Ankara had been instructed not to enter into contact with Schrecker either, so the latter landed at Istanbul in mid-April and, reluctantly though, had to talk to György Pálóczi-Horváth and the S. O. E. officers. It is interesting that Schrecker's name has been left unmentioned by all Hungarian recollections. He was probably identical with a person by the same name who had been a member on the board of the National Savings Bank with which Bethlen is known to have had good connections.

In fact Barcza and Schrecker represented the Bethlen group, and what they intended to tell was essentially the same. Since Schrecker's written documents have been discovered among the British Foreign Office papers, we can know about his action from an authentic source. In his letter to the British Ambassador, Schrecker asked, with surprising naivity, for permission and arrangements for him to make a few days' visit in secret to London "to be received there by the competent persons of the British Government and by the Polish Government too". Should this be impossible, he continued writing, he would like to obtain an answer, while in Turkey, to his letter in order to be able to inform his employers upon arrival at home.

Schrecker's memorandum dealt in detail with the history of Hungarian foreign policy and the views regarding Hungary's future. Here it is worth while to quote the passage which describes the concrete proposals for withdrawal from the war and bears the title "The Present":

"Hungary hopes — with so many others — for Anglo—American victory, the only possible protection from German or R u s s i a n hegemony. She must try to help such victory within the modest limits imposed to her by her decision not to risk German occupation, spoliations of her territory, combined with imprisonment or murder of her best people, who were not to the likings of the Germans etc. in the last phase of the war, after she had succeeded in avoiding all this for as long as April 1943. Weakened as she has been by Trianon, she is decided, not to risk life and property of her traditional classes, not to have Jewish pogroms, not to deliver the life of socialists and refugees.

"This decision marks the limits of the aid which she could tender to the Allies, when and if the course of events should offer the opportunity of such aid.

"In the case of an invasion of the Balkans, Hungary is decided not to fight under any circumstances against Anglo—American forces. She is ready to take an obligation in this respect, provided that England shows she understands her position by taking into consideration a few obvious conditions.

"1., If an Anglo—American army gets near the Hungarian frontier, this army should not include any Serb, Croate, Czech or Rumanian soldiers or units. It would be impossible to keep Hungarian public opinion in reason if there would be such formations in an approaching army. If there are such ones, let them be used elsewhere.

"This has nothing to do with future frontier questions.

"2., If Hungary is to abstain from fighting against Anglo—Americans, it is obvious that the Russian army should not, at the same time or a t a l l, attack the Carpathian frontier of Hungary.

"3., No bombing of Budapest, a place of negligible strategic importance. Bombing is bound to foster hatred, incompatible with a policy of proposed character. Besides, the totally inefficient throwing of bombs on Budapest by the Russians last autumn had forced the Hungarian Government to ask for German help or fighters, not possessing any, whereas public opinion was clamouring for them. The Germans came and occupied some Hungarian aerodromes, very much to the dislike of the Hungarian Government.

"It is obvious that a serious bombing of Budapest would immediately fill the Hungarian aerodromes with German 'protection', which would have the opposite effect to that pursued by the proposed policy.

"If England should be prepared to accept these conditions as against Hungarian commitment not to fight against an Anglo—American army, the ways of proceeding should be fixed, a meeting of experts pre-arranged, which would take place as soon as the situation should be ripe for it."

A remark made on Schrecker's proposals in the Foreign Office said: "We are clearly not prepared to enter into any discussion of these proposals with the Hungarians or to give them any reason for believing that we are prepared to accept anything short of unconditional surrender."

On May 11, in Istanbul Schrecker received an answer in this sense. He was told that the British Government rejected the possibility of any kind of discussion with Hungary: the Hungarian Government should give evidence of its fundamentally changed position in advance.

The fourth peace overture was to some extent of a different character from the previous ones, in so far as it sought contact with the Yugoslav émigré Government, yet it was closely related to the above-described proposals and conceptions.

On May 26, 1943, two former Yugoslav officers, in possession of Hungarian service passports, arrived at Istanbul and told the Yugoslav Consul there that General István Újszászy, chief of department II of the Hungarian General Staff, with the knowledge of Prime Minister Kállay, had sent them to Istanbul with the mission to enter into communication with General Mihajlović, the Defence Minister of the Yugoslav émigré Government, who was commander of the so-called Chetnik formations opposed also to Tito's popular army.

Újszászy had intended to inform the Yugoslavs that the Hungarian army was ready, at the decisive moment, to support Mihajlović if he so desired, and then requested that not even on the occasion of an Allied invasion of the Balkans should the Yugoslav troops cross the new Hungarian frontier of 1941, because it would only lead to needless bloodshed. In the message General Újszászy expressed his regrets for the Bachka atrocities and promised to punish the guilty.

The plan of supporting Mihajlović against the Tito-led Yugoslav resistance and of creating contact with him, as we have seen earlier, had already been broached during Kállay's visit to Rome on April 1. In his notes of the negotiations Kállay wrote this: Mussolini "shared my opinion that it would be no good throwing Mihajlović into the arms of the Bolsheviks because now he is vacillating between the Yugoslav Government in London and his own nationalism."

After comparing their views, both the British Foreign Office and the Yugoslav émigré Government declined Újszászy's initiative.

In the early months of 1943 Bethlen contemplated going in person to Stockholm and Lisbon, and even to London through the neutral countries. The British Government was against this latter plan, for as early as 1942 it had opposed the American idea of Bethlen's going to the United States, where he would have been received as a trusted agent of the Government, because the British did not wish to commit themselves to a conservative régime. The reason why Bethlen's journey into neutral countries failed to take place was obviously that there was no way of having concealed it from the Germans.

Having received identical information from several sides, on May 12 Kállay put the question through Istanbul: What change of attitude would be considered in England as sufficient proof to justify starting negotiations?

The reply was then, in the spring of 1943, confined to generalities, inasmuch as the Allies demanded action but did not specify what action. Why? On the one hand, because the formula drawn up by the British Government early in March — a formula which, as mentioned above, while maintaining the principle of unconditional surrender, deemed it possible to pursue a more flexible policy toward Hungary — was still a subject of controversy in Moscow and Washington; on the other hand, because both Washington and London held the view that an early anti-German turn in Hungary was impossible, or rather that the forcing of such a change would lead to a disaster.

The American reply to the British proposals expounded that a genuinely decisive change in Hungarian policy was improbable, and the forcing of an early change would lead to the liquidation of precisely those forces which might be of use when the Allies had the best hopes for success. In London they were of the opinion that a new internal political situation had arisen in Hungary in the three months since the volunteering of Professor Szent-Györgyi, inasmuch as now the forces of opposition had rallied round the Kállay Government for fear that, if this Government fell, something worse would come, and this time it would come under Nazi control. That is, London saw the only alternative to the Kállay Government in Hungary in an extreme-right take-over. This is why they thought that there was nothing to benefit by a reply to the Hungarian peace-feelers.

The British evaluation of the situation was mainly influenced by the German's growing distrust of the Kállay Government, and it was visible that German pressure was growing, partly in form of stimulating the extreme right, to step up its activity against the Government's policy.

In the spring of 1943, the Wilhelmstrasse received news of Kállay's diplomatic moves and of Hungarian Government measures confirming the unpleasant news (e.g., refusal to take part in the occupation of the Balkans, ban on the deployment in battle of Hungarian airmen being trained in France, etc.). Already in March, Ribbentrop sent an expert in Central European affairs, Edmund Veesenmayer, to investigate the situation in Hungary. But before Veesenmayer's report could arrive, Hitler had decided to summon Horthy, who Hitler knew was easy to influence. The invitation of Horthy was a link in the sequence of Hitler's talks with his allies during April. In those weeks, the Führer talked with Mussolini, then with Antonescu, because there were signs of Rumanian peace-feelers put through Western Powers.

The 'Klessheim season' was arranged in the spring of 1943 because the signs of disintegration in the Axis camp were growing out of proportion. So it was necessary for Hitler not only to stimulate his allies to hold out, as had been the case in 1942, but also to threaten them, to deter them from even thinking of an attempt to decamp. The series of talks held at Klessheim, in 1943, can therefore be considered the beginning of a new phase in the history of the diplomacy of the Third Reich.

The invitation arrived in Budapest on April 11. Horthy was summoned to be at Salzburg on the 16th. The original invitation did not specify the questions which the Germans wished to discuss. But it could be surmised that the questions on the agenda would not be restricted to military ones, but would affect Hungary's conduct in general. So the Ministry of Foreign Affairs in Budapest was preparing for the probable accusations. Since the Ministry officials were unaware of the fact that the Germans had detailed information about Hungary's secret talks with the British, the defence was built around the rejection of other German demands. A note by Andor Szentmiklóssy, director of the political department, tried to prove first of all that both economically and militarily, Hungary was taking part in the war to the best of her ability. Owing to the annihilation of the best equipped army, however, she was unable to undertake any further military assignment, especially because, at the current stage of the war, she must concentrate all her attention on the defence of her frontiers. The Hungarian Government was forced to do so by the hostile attitude of the neighbour states, and this course of action was best suited to her 'all-European tasks', for the greatest service Hungary did the Axis was that she maintained peace and order in the heart of the Danubian basin. Therefore the Hungarian Government now considered it a foremost duty to set up again a strong army inside the country.

Thereafter Szentmiklóssy expatiated upon the idea of total territorial revision, stating that Hungary could fulfil her mission only if she was re-established in her 'thousand-year-old rights'. Then he summed up the foreign political aims of the Hungarian Government in the following four points: 1. to fill the role of an orderly state in Central Europe; 2. to secure the historical frontiers 'by peaceful means'; 3. to support the Axis Powers in their struggle against the Soviet Union to the best of its capability, but first of all economically; 4. to display increased diplomatic activity, in harmony with the interests of the Axis Powers, in the defensive fight against Communism and 'in the interest of our historic mission'. In conclusion he dealt in detail with particular economic and military issues; he gave the usual reasons for Hungary's refusal to take part in the occupation of the Balkans, then he explained the position adopted regarding the Jewish question, essentially on the basis of Kállay's note of December 1942.

As can be seen, the note practically tried to make the Kállay Government's policy acceptable to the Germans. That it failed to do so appears from the agenda of the Salzburg negotiations. Before Horthy in company with Chief of Staff Szombathelyi and Szentmiklóssy departed for Germany, the Prime Minister had discussed with him the aide-mémoire point by point. Though it cannot be exactly deduced from the sources, this was the essence of Horthy's argumentation in the course of the negotiations.

The talks began at Klessheim Castle near Salzburg in the afternoon of April 16, 1943, and continued in three rounds until the evening hours of the 17th. Participating in the talks were Horthy, Hitler, Ribbentrop, and interpreter Paul Schmidt.

Hitler did not keep Horthy waiting for the accusations to come. After a short introduction, in which he analysed the military situation and frightened Horthy with 'the spectre of Communism', he started to criticize the performance of the 2nd Hungarian army which had been annihilated in the battle of the Don, arguing that the defeat had been due to the poor morale of the Hungarian soldiers, to their lack of discipline and 'Communist contagion'. This cut Horthy to the quick, and so did Hitler's words of appreciation about the Rumanian army and High Command, which ultimately prompted the Regent to remark that, under the circumstances, Hungary was no longer a 'favourite' of Germany.

Turning to political questions, Hitler said that, according to reports he had been receiving for months, the Kállay Government's conduct gave evidence of a defeatist attitude; that Kállay had visibly lost his belief in an Axis victory and consequently took steps to reduce Hungary's participation in the war to a minimum and to prepare her desertion of the Axis camp. He recounted his information about the missions of Frey, Szent-Györgyi, Mészáros, and the negotiations in Switzerland, made reproaches for the interdiction of the deployment of Hungarian pilots in France, and for the favourable reception given to the Turkish initiative. He quoted Kállay as declaring at the foreign affairs commission on February 19, that Hungary was making war only upon the Soviet Union, that she was wholly indifferent to the war in the West, etc. Finally, he characterized Kállay as a political adventurer whose removal from office was to the interest of German–Hungarian friendship.

Ribbentrop produced documents in support of Hitler's charges, stressing that most of those papers were not reports by agents but intercepted original telegrams deciphered. Ribbentrop even put down in writing the German objections to the policy of the Kállay Government. His note concluded in these terms: "The German Government has received these pieces of information about the Kállay Government's conduct not from the opposition but from circles of the Government party. These point out that with the Hungarian Government, in its current setup, it is impossible to secure increased participation in war production and the intensification of the yield of agriculture. The Government is vacillating and bows to the enemy."

Horthy tried to defend his Prime Minister, he told it was entirely unbelievable that Kállay would have undertaken anything not in harmony with his, Horthy's, political line. He declared that Kállay enjoyed his full confidence, and there was no reason to relieve him of his office, but he would inform him of the complaints. At the same time, he proved to be completely uninformed about many questions. In fact, nothing was agreed upon between the two sides, except one: Horthy consented to further recruitment in Hungary for the Waffen-S. S. from the German minority living in the country, including from the ranks of the Hungarian national army, which earlier the Government had not permitted. All this on condition that those who entered the S. S. lost their Hungarian nationality, and their families would be liable to resettlement in Germany.

As was to be expected, the Jewish question was widely discussed. Hitler violently attacked the Hungarian Government, reproaching it for having failed to comply with the earlier German demands for the deportation of Jews. What was a new element in this respect was the brutal openness which made it clear that for the German leadership the solution of the Jewish question was tantamount to the physical extermination of Jewry. According to Schmidt's records, during the talks in the morning hours of the 17th, to Horthy's question about what he should now do with the Jews — after having deprived them of all means of subsistence, he could not beat them to death after all — Ribbentrop replied: "The Jews must be liquidated or driven into camps of concentration."

The only comic point at the negotiations going on in a gloomy atmosphere might have been the suggestion from Horthy, who, reminiscing about his naval career in connection with effective submarine warfare, broached the idea for the U-boats to take one-man observation kites in tow; in this way, when these subs were simultaneously on the surface, he said, the observers flying the kites at an altitude of 100 metres over the air current produced by the vehicles' motion could survey an immense area. Hitler said a few words about radar — of which the Regent had not the slightest notion — and asked what to do with the kites when an air raid compelled the vehicles to submerge, for this was their only avenue of escape.

At the end of the talks, Hitler requested Horthy to sign a joint communiqué to demonstrate their unity. Horthy agreed. But the last paragraph of the text proposed by Ribbentrop induced misgivings in the foreign service people accompanying the Regent, and its acceptance met with their opposition. The paragraph read as follows:

"The Führer and the Regent have given expression to their firm determination to persevere in the struggle against Bolshevism and its Anglo—American Allies, and to continue it until the final victory." A long wrangling ensued. Horthy first heeded the foreign service experts, but finally — already on the train leaving the station, as some sources say — he yielded to Ribbentrop, who threatened serious consequences of the omission of the communiqué.

No sooner had the Regent's special train left the Salzburg station than the Germans made the communiqué public as originally worded. In Hungary, however, Kállay declared that he would not consent to the communiqué's being published until Horthy arrived home. On his return to Budapest, however, Horthy denied having given his consent. The communiqué appeared in the Hungarian press, a day after time, without the last paragraph; so the original version was published as a German communiqué, not as a joint communiqué. This incident just added to the Germans' distrust of Kállay.

On April 20, 1943, the Council of Ministers considered the reports on the Regent's negotiations and passed a decision that no changes were needed in the Government's policy. Interior Minister Keresztes-Fischer pointed out that "after this visit we have to adopt the same policy and attitude as if nothing had happened. To the German accusations enumerated before His Highness the Regent we have to give a resolute and dignified answer." It was in this sense that the Ministry of Foreign Affairs drafted Horthy's reply letter, which the Regent approved with some softening alterations.

The letter, forwarded to Hitler on May 7, refuted in detail all the German charges. Horthy repeatedly emphasized his confidence in Kállay, at the same time assuring Hitler of Hungary's loyalty. The letter ended in these terms: "In this country nothing can happen against my will, and I will under all circumstances maintain quiet and order."

Denials and assurances were certainly not much help. In his telegram commenting upon Horthy's letter, Ribbentrop stated to the German Minister in Budapest: "Horthy's attitude is no good, and it is evident that he does not want to part with Kállay; but this can only be explained by the Regent's full approval of the Prime Minister's policy of defeatism and detachment from the Axis Powers."

Thus, the Salzburg meeting did not bring much success for the Germans, who of course did not wish to resign to this failure, although the military situation did not for the moment give rise to fear of any major change in Hungary. And if, in the given situation, Germany could not expect any major contribution from the Hungarians, the most essential thing, the placing of Hungary's economic resources at the service of war, proceeded in accordance with the German interests. With regard to the economic aspects of Horthy's letter, Karl Clodius gave Ribbentrop this summary opinion: "...the attitude of the Hungarian Government concerning economic matters — except for stronger control over agricultural production at home — is no cause for serious complaint on the part of Germany." Germany was rather preoccupied with the future prospects of the Hungarian Government's policy. For this reason Hitler temporarily confined himself to influencing Horthy to change his mind, on the one hand, by flattering the Regent's notorious vanity and displaying his own total lack of confidence in Kállay and, on the other hand, by encouraging the Hungarian extreme right, for the first time since the signing of the Tripartite Pact, to start an open attack, with Imrédy in the lead, against the policy of the Government.

Already a few days following the Salzburg talks, Ribbentrop instructed Jagow not to communicate with Kállay and, if the Prime Minister should summon him, to limit himself to simply listening to Kállay's communications. On May 3 he further instructed Jagow not to accept the Prime Minister's invitations and to avoid keeping in touch with him socially, thus giving expression to the German Government's total lack of confidence in the Hungarian Prime Minister. Ribbentrop simultaneously made it known that official personages of Germany would refrain from visiting Hungary "until the situation has been cleared up". The Germans persisted in this position, although the Italian Government, at Kállay's request, tried to mediate.

At the same time, Hitler tried to use his personal influence on Horthy. On the 75th birthday of the Regent he congratulated him in an amiable letter and presented him with a Danube yacht. When the letter and the gift-deed were handed him, Horthy had more than an hour of conversation with Jagow. He strongly stressed his loyalty to the Axis Powers, but again confirmed his total confidence in Kállay; in conclusion, he made a very nasty remark saying that as long as he was alive Imrédy would not come to power again. "The explications of the Regent have convinced me," we can read in Jagow's report, "that he would retain Kállay by all manner of means, so we shall have to reckon with him in the future, too." What must still have captured the attention of the German Foreign Ministry was Horthy's statement that Parliament was of no importance, and the same held true of the Government party, which had the duty to vote for the proposals of the Government. Horthy's words confirmed the Wilhelmstrasse in its increasingly firm belief that it was still possible to influence the situation in Hungary through the person of Horthy, and that at a convenient time they would be able, by having enforced the formation of a Hungarian Government reliable from the German point of view, to consolidate German influence and keep Hungary by the side of Germany.

After the Salzburg negotiations, Kállay became more cautious, and this he found necessary not only because of the Germans' threatening moves, but also because the talks with the Western Powers had brought no kind of political understanding which might have provided even the slightest guarantee in the matter of salvaging the régime and obtaining the revision of frontiers. All this, of course, did not mean that the contacts built up with Anglo—American quarters in the spring and early summer of 1943 were completely broken. Contacts were being sought along several lines (by Baron Gábor Apor in Rome, Ferenc Ambró in Madrid, Andor Gellért in Stockholm, György Barcza in Switzerland), but it was striking how regularly the 'Istanbul line' was neglected. Exploration went on to find out which contact was the 'right one', which led direct to the highest circles of the Allies; whereas the only reply that might have come from all sides was: negotiations can start as soon as the Hungarian Government shows serious willingness to surrender unconditionally. In April 1943 the British

Foreign Office instructed the heads of its diplomatic missions to avoid direct communication with the Hungarian emissaries.

When the British Government seriously began considering the Hungarian peace-feelers and decided to work out a new line of policy and propaganda towards Hungary, the questions related to the future of Hungary necessarily came to the fore. As we have seen, the aide-mémoire of March 10 raised three substantive issues in this respect, and even if it failed to provide the final answers, it gave the outlines of Great Britain's new policy towards South Eastern Europe. The main points were: 1. Hungary's postwar frontiers; 2. the need for political and social reforms in Hungary; 3. the accommodation of Hungary to the new British conception of a postwar Central European settlement, i.e. Hungary's relationship to the proposed confederation.

Of course, these questions were not discussed — in view of the principle of unconditional surrender and for other reasons mentioned earlier — with the Hungarian emissaries, and anyhow, the new conception could not be put in real propaganda until it had been agreed upon among the Allied Powers. In any case, these were basic questions concerning the entire Danubian basin during the Second World War. Thus it was inevitable for those in Hungary who wished to approach the Allied Powers to come out with their opinion on these issues. So, before inquiring into the position taken by the Allies, in 1943, regarding the problems of the future of Hungary, let us see the Hungarian conceptions on the basis of the statements and memoranda which had reached London.

Let us begin with the second question, that of social changes. In this connection, I do not intend to dwell on the ideas entertained by Hungarian democratic and leftist forces about postwar Hungary. (About the first question of the frontiers: the general statement contained in various messages, which made it clear that the Kállay–Bethlen faction, when it started to create contacts with the Western Powers, wished, as was clearly seen in London, to take as a minimum basis for discussion the frontiers of 1942. There are two documents dealing with the frontier problem: the aforementioned Schrecker memorandum and the Szegedy-Maszák memorandum which was drafted in the summer of 1943, with the personal participation of Kállay and which reached London in August. Both documents examined the question of the frontiers in connection with the proposed confederation, so it is better to deal with them at the proper place.)

British sources prove that the peace-feelers coming from Kállay and Bethlen were principally motivated by the hope that successful defection from Germany might enable them to salvage the political and social framework of the counter-revolutionary régime into the times after the war. Notwithstanding, the Kállay–Bethlen group was aware that in case of an Allied victory certain socio-political reforms would become inevitable in Hungary, too.

However, the statements and other documents which had come to England said little, if anything, about these questions. If they did, it was only in a general way and primarily in terms of foreign policy. Early in February 1943, for example, Gellért told Böhm: "The Hungarian nation and people are ready to co-operate with their neighbours with honesty and good-will. .... Hungary will bring about the necessary internal political and social reforms which guarantee a peaceful co-existence with her neighbours."

The Schrecker memorandum had nothing to say about the necessity of political and social reforms. And the Szegedi-Maszák memorandum, which was considered to outline the official position of the Hungarian Government, told just this much: "Hungary knows perfectly well that after the termination of this war a new international order will demand deep changes and modifications in the methods of international life, which have been prevalent hiherto. She knows also that not only will new frontiers be drawn, but also the possibilities of human existence will also be assured in a new way and more effectively than hitherto; that the rights and opportunities of labour, and well-being of humanity, will develop, and new forms of political, economic and social collaboration will come into being, which will enable every human being to live an existence worthy of a human being."

It is this much and nothing more that is to be found in the messages sent to England regarding the transformation of the system. It is clearly seen that the issue was always, if at all, raised in its international context. And this cannot be regarded as a mere chance. The purpose was not only to refuse the charges brought against the social conditions under the counter-revolutionary régime. Kállay and supporters of his policy knew full well that in case they would manage to salvage the Horthy system without essential changes into postwar times, the régime would not be fit to survive in South Eastern Europe if radical socio-political changes, together with liberation, took place in the neighbouring countries.

In other words, for Kállay's aims to be realized, what would have been necessary — in addition to internal political factors — was not only that Anglo—American troops be first to arrive in Hungary. They also had to count upon the victory of the conservative forces in the social struggle simultaneously going on with the anti-Fascist war in South Eastern Europe. This is why the holders of power contemplated entering into contact with the nationalist conservative and anti-German forces of the neighbouring countries. This is why they made a proposal for support to General Mihajlović. But even in this seemingly favourable situation, the aims of the anti-Fascist war and the composition of the anti-Fascist resistance movements in South Eastern Europe and in the Balkans where the Communists took the lead, made it likely that democratic changes would occur everywhere, which meant that these Hungarian politicians had to foresee certain transformations in this line. This is why the social changes are always mentioned in the documents connected to foreign political questions.

In the aide-mémoire addressed to Washington and Moscow on March 10, 1943, Eden dealt with the Hungarian peace-feelers and, in an enclosure, with the issue of the East Central European confederation, quoting an interpellation in Parliament on December 16, 1942, and the reply to it.

Eden was asked whether the intention of the British Government to support the creation of state federations applied to a Danubian confederation uniting Austria, Hungary, Czechoslovakia and Poland. In his reply the Foreign Secretary, with reference to the Polish—Czechoslovak and Yugoslav—Greek pacts, declared: "... so far as we were concerned, we should continue to foster agreements of this kind and to encourage the smaller States to weld themselves into larger, though not exclusive groupings. Whether it will be possible or desirable to include Austria and Hungary within a federation based upon Poland and Czechoslovakia must clearly depend, amongst other things, upon the views of the Polish and Czechoslovak Governments and peoples and upon the future attitude of the Austrians and Hungarians, who are now fighting in the ranks of our enemies."

What did the two pacts provide for and what was Hungary's attitude to the federative plans?

The plan of a Czechoslovak—Polish confederation was first advanced in an agreement signed at London on November 10, 1941. It emphasized that Poland and Czechoslovakia wished to live as independent states in close economic and political association with each other after the war.

At the end of January 1942, a new Czechoslovak—Polish pact was concluded, which now concretely outlined the federative conceptions. The document stated that a confederation (not a federal state) of the two countries would be set up, to which any other state might accede. They would establish a customs union, a common General Staff and a common fiscal system. Their policies were to be co-ordinated in the field of foreign affairs, military matters, with regard to economic and social questions and communication; labour-insurance matters would be handled in common, and there would be co-operation in the field of education and culture.

The pact provided for the citizens' free movement without visas and passports and their right to employment and to settlement in the territory of the confederation, the mutual recognition of diplomas and the execution of court decisions. A separate chapter dealt with the constitutions of the member states with a view to guaranteeing all civil rights and liberties and establishing joint authorities. The parties finally undertook to jointly provide for the common expenses.

On January 15, 1942, a Yugoslav—Greek pact was signed by the Greek Prime Minister and the Yugoslav King in emigration. This was an agreement for the principle of establishing a Balkan Union with common customs areas, common currency and common foreign policies. Any state with free and lawful Government was welcome to accede.

Simultaneously with the conclusion of the Polish—Czechoslovak pact, the two signatories issued a joint communiqué stating that the well-being of the peoples of Central Europe would depend on the two confederations whose foundations had been laid in the Czechoslovak—Polish and Greek—Yugoslav agreements.

These were the conceptions entertained in 1942/1943. (Here we do not discuss the plans proposed at the last stage of the war for the creation of various federations by dismembering Germany.)

The question thus follows: What was Hungary's attitude to these schemes? In 1943, the idea of a Central European or Danubian confederation was no new problem in

Hungary. This question had long preoccupied practically all shades of Hungarian political thinking.

It is known that between the two world wars the leftist foreign political conceptions stressed the interdependence of the peoples of the Danubian basin, the need for their collaboration as the principal condition of the prosperity of the peoples living in that area. The only alternative to nationalism, chauvinism and mutual hatred was the idea of a democratic federation or confederation ensuring the equality of nations. But these conceptions were favoured not only by the left, they were not entirely alien to the conservative-reactionary forces and to the trends inspired by nationalism either. And strange as it is, concrete plans came precisely from this side. Therefore, we can say that the idea of a confederation in itself did not necessarily mean commitment to the right or the left. The difference lay in the socio-political purport of the commitment.

In 1943, the Foreign Office received the afore-mentioned two memoranda dealing with the problem of federation. The two documents backed up two different positions. The Schrecker memorandum represented the views of the Bethlen faction, which was, according to a British definition, a nationalist-inspired, anti-German, right-wing opposition. This document stated, by way of introduction, that in principle Hungary was not against the idea of a confederation but offered her views for consideration. And these were the following:

Hungary would accept close co-operation with Poland without reservations. This union, strong enough in itself, could be joined by all neighbours of Poland (possibly Lithuania), and Hungary would also regard as natural the co-operation of Czechs and Slovaks, though not of a Czechoslovakian state, but separately. The memorandum stated that Hungary was unwilling to adhere to a confederation in which, in addition to the Czechs and Slovaks, the three South Slav peoples also would be members, because this solution would mean Slav preponderance. She would not join this formation even if Rumania should be a member. It added that in principle it would be unwise to set up any confederation uniting the states of Central Europe and the Balkans, because there was no possibility of combining two fundamentally different cultures: the European—Latin culture and the mixed Byzantine—Ottoman culture.

In addition to this most essential reservation, the Schrecker memorandum remarked on three more points. First, the question of Croatia. If Croatia were to be part of Yugoslavia, she would belong to the Balkan confederation, in the opposite case her place, as an independent state, would be within the Central European confederation. Second, the question of Austria. The accession of Austria to the Central European confederation would be a blunder. According to the memorandum, Austria ought to continue as part of Germany (or to be one of several German states), or she should remain a neutral state similar to Switzerland and serve as a dividing zone between Germany, Italy and the Balkans. Finally, it raised the question of a settlement of the Rumanian—Hungarian frontier, because the second Vienna Award did not satisfy Hungary. Either the frontier should be rectified in favour of Hungary, or Transylvania should become an independent state within the historical frontiers.

The Szegedy-Maszák memorandum, which was drawn up a few months later, launched the problem of the confederation as follows: "... Hungary, in spite of her complete sympathy in principle with these plans, has preliminarily observed them only with reserve, as she so far has not been able to discover the clear manifestation of a will to federate among the participants, nor can she see the state which is powerful enough to bring about a federation."

The memorandum did not, on this basis, preclude the solutions pointing beyond the Carpathian basin but it only specified the conceptions regarding this area.

First of all, it took up the question of the Hungarian frontiers. It regarded the western frontiers with some modification (a bridgehead at Bratislava) as ethnically correct but inadequate from the economic and geographical points of view. It accepted the Slovakian–Hungarian frontier defined by the first Vienna Award, but mentioned that the line along the Ostrovsky Vepor and Szepes-Gömör mountain ranges would be more appropriate. This document militated for the preservation of an independent Slovakia, stressing that as such, she should be in close economic and federative association, possibly in personal union, with the rest of the states of the Carpathian basin. The Carpatho-Ukraine ought to be part of Hungary as an autonomous territory, a status which would secure, together with an independent Slovakia, close collaboration with Poland.

For Transylvania, the satisfactory solution would be a frontier along the Maros river, but the genuine solution would be Transylvania's union with Hungary as a dominion, or as an independent state in personal union with her and Rumania. In case of an independent Transylvania, Arad and the Magyar-inhabited areas of the Banat should belong to Hungary. In the south, the Bachka should remain part of Hungary and a minor population exchange would provide for the settlement of relations among the nationalities. Finally, should Croatia wish to remain independent, Hungary would be ready to enter into closer relations with her, but refrained to make any suggestion on this score for the time being. Such a 'Commonwealth of the Carpathian basin' could then co-operate with any general or regional combination, as the memorandum stated.

The conception of Kállay and Szegedy-Maszák thus included every element of Bethlen's conception, yet it was somehow far less realistic than the latter, since it pictured a dream, barely disguised, of historical Hungary in the form of a 'Commonwealth of the Carpathian basin'.

London's attitude towards this conception is clearly shown by the Foreign Office documents dealing with the memorandum. D. Allen, a leading official in the Central European department, wrote this: "Sections VIII and IX are concerned with the more distant future and draw a picture of an enlarged and strengthened Hungary, surrounded by her satellites Slovakia, Croatia and possibly an independent Transylvania, dominating the Carpathian basin and acting in close association with a neighbouring Poland, as the defender of 'Christian democracy'. If these are the ideas upon the basis of which the Hungarian Government hope to enter into discussions with us, they still have a lot to learn."

The first answer to the British aide-mémoire of March 10 came from Washington and was dated May 4. The American reply agreed with the modifications in propaganda to Hungary as a means of psychological warfare, but it deemed it necessary to make the following reservations: "The Department of State . . . believes . . . that neither the friendly elements within the present Hungarian Government nor individuals or groups which, in opposition to the Government, might hope to effect a change of regime, would be able at this state to accomplish the fundamental changes of Hungarian policy, which would be necessary in order to promise a definite advantage to the United Nations. Moreover, it is feared that premature efforts to this end would result only in the liquidation of those elements which would be most useful to the United Nations at the moment when a far-reaching action within Hungary would offer the best prospects of success. The Department is also of the opinion that the individuals now in positions of high authority in the Hungarian Government should be considered as primarily interested in the tenure of the present regime; consequently propositions emanating from them should be regarded in that light with extreme reserve."

As can be seen, the American reply only dealt with the practical aspects of the questions raised in connection with Hungary and found the situation in Hungary far less encouraging than the British had in March. It should be added, however, that not even the British believed that their analysis of March was right, and that, in case of a turn carried out amidst the given circumstances, the democratic opposition might be a realistic alternative to the Kállay Government.

The American reply mentioned only by way of reference the questions related to Hungary's future, stressing that the persons in high positions in the Hungarian Government were most interested in the preservation of the present regime. It was even remarked in the Foreign Office that this reservation ". . . as far as it goes does not suggest that the State Department as a whole want to bolster the classes in power." The question of an armistice and the related problems concerning Hungary's future were taken up by the Department of State as late as the summer of 1944. The project of July 1944 had to take into account the views and decisions formed by the Allies by that time.

The Soviet Government's reply came a month later. Its immediate antecedent was an interview, published by the *Daily Telegraph* of June 4, with George Gibson, a member of the Trades Union Congress. In it, Gibson asserted that, with the knowledge and consent of the British Government, he had established secret contact with democratic elements of Hungary and told them about his views, with which Labourite Ministers allegedly also agreed. These views were: Hungary should withdraw her armies from the Soviet front; she should return the disannexed territories to the Allies; living standards in Hungary should be raised and the land question solved; Hungary should declare her willingness to accede to the confederation envisaged by the Governments of Czechoslovakia, Poland, Yugoslavia and Greece.

Afraid of the response which this interview might elicit in Hungary and in the Soviet Union, the Foreign Office immediately sent to Moscow and Washington a telegram stating that Gibson had falsely asserted that he had conducted secret talks with the knowledge of the British Government; Gibson really had met Vilmos Böhm at the congress of the Swedish trade unions in the autumn of 1941, and in his subsequent correspondence he explained the views of British trades union circles; the British Government did not conduct secret talks with satellite countries through middlemen either; the principle underlying its attitude to those countries was that of unconditional surrender.

Foreign Office documents bear evidence that the Gibson interview had escaped the attention of the censors by mistake. It was nevertheless plausible that the interview was regarded by the Allies as a "ballon d'essai", and this was several times stated in British papers. It is anyway a fact that when the British Government's statement was made known to Molotov by the British Ambassador in Moscow on June 6, the Soviet Foreign Minister, in his reply of the 7th (taking note of the British statement but qualifying Gibson's interview as an unfriendly act), dealt in detail with the aide-mémoire of March 10 as well.

The Soviet reply touched upon all questions raised by the British aide-mémoire of March: responsibility for the war, the question of peace-feelers, the principles of negotiations with the satellite countries, changes in propaganda, the problem of the confederation. Its clear-cut stand and proposals followed from the aims and requirements of the anti-Fascist war and served the obvious effort to eliminate the possibilities of any anti-Soviet combination from the South Eastern European area.

The Soviet Government shared the British Government's view regarding the question of modifying propaganda to Hungary, and found it possible for the Allies to maintain unofficial contacts and enter into negotiations with opposition circles of Hungary. In a few questions, however, it intended to formulate the Soviet position more clearly and unmistakably. Namely Hungary and Germany's other small allies in Central Europe, except Bulgaria, conducted a war against the Soviet Union alone, Hungary was only formally in a state of war with the Western Allies. Let us not forget that Hungarian fighting formations and troops of occupation were deployed in Soviet territory, not in the West. For this very reason, from the point of view of the Soviet Union, the question of responsibility for the war and of the armistice terms might rightly appear in a different light: It has been mentioned already that in elaborating the new line regarding Hungary the British were careful not to confirm an opinion in Axis circles that whatever might happen, there would always be a way towards a peace based on compromise.

It might be the preclusion of this contingency, among other things, which prompted the Soviet Government to state that "... for the help which Hungary has given Germany by means of her armies and also for the murders and violence, pillage and outrages caused in the occupied districts, the responsibility must be borne not only by the Hungarian Government but to a greater or less extent by the Hungarian people." The Molotov letter immediately gave this interpretation when it laid down the principles of contacts to be established with Hungary and other allies of Germany as follows: 1. unconditional surrender; 2. return of the territories occupied by Hungary; 3. an indemnity for the war damage caused by the war; 4. punishment of those responsible for the war. In connection with territorial questions the Soviet position was that the Soviet Government did not consider as fully justified the so-called Vienna Award which had been dictated by Germany and which had given Northern Transylvania to Hungary.

The formulation of the British text is not as precise when it says that "With a view to disposing of Hungarian fears of a new and more far-reaching Trianon settlement ... although Hungary will have to make adequate restitution to our Allies, His Majesty's Government has no desire to see Hungary torn to pieces", but it was evident that the relationships of alliance with Czechoslovakia and Yugoslavia determined the British Government's position regarding territorial issues, and — as has been mentioned above — Britain had rejected the second Vienna Award as early as September 1940.

Since the Soviet Union only entered the war in 1941, there was no Soviet commitment in this respect. It is also a known fact that in June 1941, Moscow still offered Budapest the support of the Soviet Government in the question of Transylvania in case Hungary would remain neutral in the German—Soviet war. So the letter of June 7, 1943, only cross-checked the Soviet position with the position of the other Allies. In the question of Transylvania, however, it also had left some chances open when it said that the Vienna Award was not considered 'as fully justified'.

The most important part of the British aide-mémoire was perhaps where it touched upon the question of federation interrelated with the future of the states of East-Central Europe. It was not without grounds that the Soviet Union was deeply suspicious of these schemings. Not only because it saw behind the plans a British attempt at penetration, but mainly because it suspected a new 'cordon sanitaire'. A perusal of the federative plans makes it clear that the wide gamut of proposals along this line, including the Polish—Chechoslovak federation with the accession of Hungary, were eventually directed against the Soviet Union.

As early as April 1942, in London the Soviet Foreign Minister told Eden: "The Soviet Government had certain information to show that some federations might be directed against the Soviet Union." The Soviet view of the political goals of the project concerning Governments in exile, including the Sikorski Government, was confirmed by a Turkish proposal made for a neutral Balkan bloc early in February 1943. The immediate antecedent of the initiative was that the British proposed an exchange of views on the South Eastern European confederation, obviously with the intention of bringing Turkey to renounce her neutrality. The Turkish Government, however, in the interest of strengthening its own neutral position, interpreted the conception as being intended to set up an anti-Soviet neutral bloc under Turkish direction, with the participation of Greece, Bulgaria, Rumania, Yugoslavia and Hungary. Therefore, without informing the British in advance, Turkish Foreign Minister Menemencioglu immediately laid his conceptions before the Governments allied with Germany, proposing a neutral Central European and Balkan bloc meant to form the pillar of order and security and to set a barrier to the spread of chaos resulting from the Soviet advance to this area, emphasizing solidarity against the Soviet peril. As it turned out the Kállay Government received the Turkish suggestion with warm sympathy and was pleased to voice Hungary's agreement in principle.)

The British tried to hold back the Turkish Government, but it was late, they could only draw the lesson that "it is . . . most deceitful of the Turks to go and discuss these matters without telling us . . . If the Russians get to know . . . their suspicions may be justifiably aroused."

It is no wonder therefore that the Soviet Government, in its note of June 7, pointed out in connection with the terms of armistice that the Soviet Government stands for the preservation of the satellite states and while it harboured no designs against the independence of these states, it opposed the federative plans: "As regards the question of the creation of a federation in Europe of Poland, Czechoslovakia, Yugoslavia and Greece including Hungary and Austria, the Soviet Government are unwilling to pledge themselves as regards the creation of such a federation, and also consider the inclusion of Hungary and Austria within it as unsuitable."

Lots of memoranda and papers had been drafted in the British Foreign Office before the reply to Molotov's letter of June 7 was written, since the British Government had, beyond the general principles, no concrete idea about the issues raised by the Soviet Government. The dispute was mainly about the interpretation of the principle of unconditional surrender and about territorial questions.

In connection with the principle of unconditional surrender, it was pointed out that too rigid an attitude in this matter would only frighten the opposition sympathizing with the Allies, and this would hamper the chances of practical foreign policy in respect of the nearer war aims and the more remote political goals. In connection with Hungary the first proposal expressed two points of view. On the one hand, it was suggested that certain concessions might be made after capitulation. On the basis of Churchill's formula, the Hungarians should "throw themselves upon our justice and mercy". On the other hand, the Soviet reply suggested that the Soviet Government "stand for the preservation of the satellite states and harbour no designs on the independence of these states".

Ultimately the Churchill recipe was omitted from the reply to Moscow dated September 6, 1943. It read: "His Majesty's Government agree that the formula of unconditional surrender should be regarded as applying to all minor European satellite states. It seems desirable that the formula should not be presented in such a way as completely to discourage any groups in the satellite countries who may be working for the reduction of their country's contribution to the Axis war effort and its eventual withdrawal from the Axis camp, and whose activities might prove helpful to the Allies in due course. His Majesty's Government note in this connexion M. Molotov's statement that the Soviet Government stand for the preservation of the satellite states and harbour no designs upon the independence of these states. That statement represents also the attitude of His Majesty's Government."

In the House of Commons, on September 27, Prime Minister Churchill summed up the British position regarding the satellites as follows: "Satellite States suborned or terrorised perhaps, if they can help to shorten the war, may be allowed to work their passage home."

As concerns the return of occupied territories, the British were convinced that in Hungary everybody, including the anti-German forces, were worried by a 'return to Trianon', and so they invariably held the view that it would be a mistake to enunciate categorically that Hungary should retreat within her pre-Munich frontiers. But just because of the afore-mentioned obligations of alliance and the position of principle adopted in connection with the Vienna Award, a position which Eden had reiterated in the Commons on March 17, 1943, it was impossible to propose any concrete solution. True, in the summer of 1943, the Foreign Office still pondered a conception that the Czechoslovak Government would perhaps be ready, of its own will, to concede certain frontier rectifications in favour of Hungary, and in certain memoranda there was the suggestion that it would be better to leave this question open, and the disputed territories should be placed under Anglo–American military control pending final decision.

Against this idea, however, it was objected during discussions that, since Hungary and Rumania were fighting against the Soviet Union, the latter should have the decisive voice in the question of Transylvania; it was doubted therefore that the Soviet Union would accept an Anglo–American occupation of Transylvania. Finally, it was admitted that no established position existed regarding Transylvania. The matter of Transylvania was thus left out of the reply to the Soviet Government. "As regards the return of the territories occupied by the satellite states," the note ran, "while His Majesty's Government have made it clear that they cannot commit themselves to recognize in advance of the general peace settlement any particular European frontiers, they consider that the satellite states should restore to the Allied countries concerned any of their territories which the satellite states have occupied or annexed during or immediately before the war."

During preparations for the Foreign Ministers' Conference in Moscow, the Foreign Office came back to the question of the frontiers. The related paper stated: "As an enemy State, Hungary has no claim to special consideration in regard to her future frontiers, more particularly where our allies – Czechoslovakia and Yugoslavia – are concerned. This presumably, however, does not cover her future frontiers with another enemy State – Rumania."

Furthermore, on the basis of critical comments upon the Trianon peace treaty, it was proposed that the Trianon-created situation might be eased by resettling a considerable number of Magyars within the boundaries of Hungary. This idea, which was proposed by the Czechoslovak Émigré Government, was rejected. The explanation read: "Since Hungary will be faced with the severe internal problems arising out of the major land reform required to raise the status of her large peasant population, she will probably not be able to absorb large numbers of Magyars from abroad within the Trianon frontiers. Therefore, the problem cannot be solved simply by a one-sided transfer of populations." Yet, because of the mixed population, a limited exchange of populations in the case of Transylvania was considered inevitable against the alternative of an autonomous Transylvania.

Finally, in relation to Czechoslovakia and Yugoslavia, the paper proposed a return to the Trianon frontiers immediately after the war on the grounds that the Hungarians, "as regards Yugoslavia and Czechoslovakia, ... hope that sympathetic consideration will be given to some revision of the Trianon frontiers". In the case of Transylvania the British document was for autonomy or for a division into a Hungarian and a Rumanian part.

In the matter of reparations and the punishment of those responsible for the war, the British Government, without insisting on a final solution and with certain reservations, agreed with the Soviet position. But there was one more question which required a decision: that of the confederation. The first records concerning the Molotov letter proposed a separate discussion of the latter. On June 1, Eden submitted to the Cabinet a memorandum on postwar Europe to this effect: "... so far as the Balkans are concerned, we are doing our best to encourage the Greek—Yugoslav confederation, but it is difficult to make much progress ... while the Governments of these countries are exiled and we cannot say what the position will be when the Axis collapses. Much will depend on whether we ourselves are in occupation of that area."

In a marginal note D. Allen wrote on July 11: "There is some reason to suspect that a possible Polish—Hungarian—Yugoslav combination is not without its appeal both to the Hungarians and the Poles. Presumably, however, we should do our best to discourage any such tendency, which would be viewed with the utmost suspicion by the Russians, would have the worst possible effect on Polish—Czechoslovak relations and would finally knock the bottom out of existing confederation plans based on the Polish—Czechoslovak and Greek—Yugoslav agreements." And on July 25, in his draft of a reply to the Soviet note, he proposed that in the given situation it was sufficient to remind the Soviet Government of Eden's stand of December 16, 1942, which had been enclosed to the aide-mémoire of March 10.

Others evaluated this proposal to the effect that in this case it would appear as if they took notice of the differences of opinion in the matter of the confederation. Finally, it was agreed that at a more convenient time a more thorough discussion of this subject should be held with the Soviet Union, and that the reply to the note of July 7 should not touch upon the issue.

The Foreign Office thought the Moscow Conference of Foreign Ministers in October would be an appropriate place to discuss the subject of the confederation within the scope of a draft agreement which would cover Soviet—British co-operation in this area. The preparatory material made for Eden regarding the future of Hungary in this connection contained the following: "In general terms, His Majesty's Government are in favour of the continued existence after the war of an independent Hungary, associated if possible with whatever confederation system may grow up in the Danubian basin. Hungary must, however, first have made suitable restitution to the Allied countries which she has injured." Further on, the reply again quoted Eden's statement made in the Commons on December 16, 1942.

At the Moscow Conference of Foreign Ministers, the British Foreign Secretary could achieve nothing in the question of the confederation. The idea was already dying in consequence of the deterioration of relationships between the Czechoslovak and Polish Governments in exile. Molotov told Eden that it would be an inconsiderate and forced step to align the countries concerned in theoretically designed groups on the basis of decisions made by the émigré Governments. And he added: "Some of the plans for federations remind the Soviet people of the policy of the 'cordon sanitaire' directed, as is known, against the Soviet Union." Thereupon the British conceptions were practically removed from the agenda.

As to the British plans related to Hungary's future, we have so far examined the question of the frontiers and the confederation. Only little was said about what the British thought of what Hungary's internal construction, her political orientation and her government, should be like after the war. Of course, the Foreign Office papers contain nothing about these issues, yet the positions and decisions taken in connection with the peace-feelers point to some kind of British conception in this respect. And this counted on neither Horthy nor Kállay, that is, the ruling set of political figures, nor the right-wing nationalist opposition of the Bethlen type. This means that the efforts of Kállay and company to salvage the system met with no sympathy in London. The way Szent-Györgyi was received, and the new line of policy and propaganda towards Hungary, clearly indicate that, when the British spoke of the need for socio-political changes in Hungary, they had in mind a kind of coalition of the political forces which would include the politicians of the bourgeois opposition, the Smallholders' Party, the Peasant Alliance, the popular intelligentsia they called young intellectuals, and the Social Democratic Party, but which would have excluded the Communists. As F. K. Roberts wrote in a notice: "The general ideas of this opposition are such as we should normally welcome and on which we should desire the countries of Central Europe to base their policies after the war." From the autumn of 1943 onward, when it was certain that the Soviet Union could not be excluded from this area, or at least that the problems of the Danubian basin would have to be settled in conjunction with Moscow, this idea was replaced, under necessity to some extent, by the conception that the coalition should include the Communist Party, too.

Among the émigré politicians, it was Vilmos Böhm alone whom the Allies would have welcomed in a leading position in Hungary after the war. As early as February 1943, Cecil Parrot, director of the Stockholm press office, wrote to the Foreign Office that Böhm "seems to me the type of man we would like to see in the Hungarian Government after the war. He is anti-German by conviction, a great admirer of England, sympathetic towards Russia and, what is perhaps most important and quite unique for a Hungarian, on very good terms with the Czechs. . . . He believes firmly in the establishment of a confederation formed out of Austria, Hungary and Czechoslovakia. If such a confederation ever comes into being he could be one of its most valuable pioneers . . . He is less interested in revisionism than in the question of securing the necessary basis for a thorough social, political and moral regeneration of Hungary."

This opinion on Böhm met with the approval of those who in the Foreign Office dealt with the affairs of Hungary. In a notice of September 1, 1943, F. K. Roberts wrote this: "I had a long talk yesterday with M. Boehm. ... He made a good impression. He is a patriotic Hungarian, who regards it as quite essential that Hungary should modify her social order in a genuinely democratic direction and base her foreign policy on good relations with Czechoslovakia and Austria rather than upon an anti-Soviet alignment with Poland."

As far as the social changes are concerned, we have already quoted, from the British material prepared for the Moscow Conference, that "Hungary will be faced with the severe internal problems arising out of the major land reform required to raise the status of her large peasant population". That is, the British conceptions went as far as the partition of the large estates, the liquidation of pauperism, and first of all the need to improve the situation of the rural population, which had been made known in England through Hungary's literature in rural sociology.

While the Foreign Office waited for the reply from Washington and Moscow to the aide-mémoire of March 10, a change had taken place in the internal situation in Hungary upon which the British built their new line, somewhat overrating the received information. They received a great deal of information that the Germans had found out about the Hungarian peace-feelers; that at the April negotiations at Klessheim Castle, the Führer had demanded Kállay's dismissal; that the extreme right had been getting active in Hungary, so that even Parliament had been dissolved. All this was summed up in a report to the War Cabinet on June 10, with the evaluation that the Kállay Government pursued "the aim of preserving, against the inevitable day of reckoning, as much as possible of Hungary's existing economic resources, social structure, political system and territorial gains".

If, on the one hand, the Foreign Office was again led to the conviction that the aim of the Kállay Government was to save the counter-revolutionary régime, on the other hand it had to arrive at the conclusion that in Hungary the extreme right still represented a political force which might become a possible alternative to the Government if the latter were forced to resign under German pressure. To avoid this contingency, the democratic opposition supported the Government to some extent, and consequently the conception that the democratic opposition could carry out a take-over in Hungary was erroneous.

A notice from July 1943 said: "In the past four months the situation has changed. The opposition parties in Hungary have to some extent lined up behind the Hungarian Government, since they fear that, if M. Kállay's Government were to go, something much worse would be formed under the Nazi control of Imrédy. ..." And since the Germans had found out about Szent-Györgyi's negotiations, the contact created through him with the opposition was broken. The upshots of this were summarized in the notice as follows: "... at the present moment there is no Hungarian emissary to whom we wish to convey any message on the lines originally suggested to Moscow and Washington." The new line of propaganda could not be put into action by agreement of the Allies, but every further approach had to be considered from the point of view whether it should be answered, of course, after consultation with the United States and the Soviet Union.

Practically this appraisal meant acceptance of the American standpoint. The reply of July 18 to Washington (which was made known to the Soviet Government, too) expressed this view when giving information on a new and rather severe situation analysis concerning Hungary: "We share view of State Department reported in paragraph 3. There are still no signs that any section of Hungarian opinion, even the Social Democratic and other opposition groups, are prepared, whatever their attitude towards the Germans, to make amends for Hungary's aggression against her neighbours, two of whom are our Allies. Since Kállay's dissolution of Parliament the opposition has tended to support both his foreign and internal policy as the only defence against the establishment of an Imrédy Government subservient to Germany. Approaches which have come to our knowledge so far seem to have been made with the tacit approval of the Hungarian Government and from a desire to enable Hungary to escape her difficulties with the minimum of sacrifice. There is thus nothing to be gained at the moment by responding to these approaches." The aim of propaganda and the attitude towards Hungary was now defined as follows: "For the present we should concentrate rather on strengthening Hungarian resistance to German pressure and reluctance to co-operate in the Axis war effort, while making it clear that we shall expect Hungary to make restitution to our Alllies and to take active steps to free herself of Axis domination and to hasten our victory." That is, it boiled down to what had already been formulated on several occasions: What was needed were 'deeds, not words'. This was made known to the Hungarian Government from several sides simultaneously with the landing in Sicily and the fall of Mussolini.

The avenues of the search of Western contacts were now far between. In May 1943, Barcza managed to get in touch with a British agent called 'Mr. H.' At that time, Barcza already represented Kállay's post-Klessheim position. The essence of this was an emphatic insistence that, until the Allies came near to Hungary, defection could not be attempted because it would lead to German occupation. The Prime Minister and 'the patriotic, non-compromised Hungarian opposition' (in Barcza's interpretation this meant the Bethlen group) was of the opinion that instead of an ill-fated break-away attempt it was better to opt for the maintenance of order, because order and quiet in Hungary might be of great help 'in the period of reconstruction'. On the other hand, 'Mr. H.' stressed that the Hungarian Government should do more than make declarations of principle and express its Platonic pro-Western sentiments, it should rather contribute deeds to the war effort of the Allies. At the same time, he pointed out that the Allies did not wish to impose a punitive peace after the war and thought it possible for Horthy to keep his seat in the period of 'reconstruction'. Barcza had talks also with Dulles, who adopted a similar position, mentioning that the small Allies had not yet come forth with territorial claims.

In June 1943, obviously in close connection with the military plans of the Allies concerning Italy, the Americans at last replied to Radvánszky's request submitted in February. They named the persons with whom they would be willing to negotiate:

István Bethlen, Móric Esterházy or Lipót Baranyai. In Budapest the choice fell on Baranyai, who, in July, went to Switzerland in company with Radvánszky. As agreed with Bethlen, he took with him a memorandum according to which Hungary would resist the Soviet troops but was ready to open the frontiers to the Western forces if she received a promise that, until a definitive peace treaty, the territories recovered since 1938 would remain under Hungarian administration. Baranyai met Allen Dulles and Royall Tyler, who accepted the memorandum as a basis for discussion. They agreed that in the future the liaison man on the U.S. side would be Tyler and on the Hungarian side Baron Gábor Apor, László Velics or György Bakach-Bessenyey. Kállay decided in favour of Bakach-Bessenyey, who had been seeking contacts already in April, and who, at the end of July, was transferred to Berne from his post as head of the Hungarian Legation in Vichy. Discussions between the two representatives began in the second half of August, in the changed international situation which had been created by the events in Italy.

The Anglo—American landing in Sicily on July 10, 1943, and Mussolini's fall on the 25th signalled that the policy of the Fascist Axis came to the verge of collapse. The fightings were going on not only in the countries subjugated or attacked by the Axis Powers but reached the area of the 'southern flank' of the Axis.

For Hungary, the events in Italy transposed the question of quitting the war from the plane of political considerations to the sphere of political action. Now the Kállay Government had to act provided that it wanted to act according to what was contained in its messages to the Western Powers about a change in foreign policy. The reports coming from the West more and more eagerly urged the Government to act as well. In his reports following Mussolini's fall, Barcza repeatedly stated that, in the opinion of the Allies, Hungary ought to declare her desertion the moment Italy made a similar declaration. England had, thus far, understood that in the given situation Hungary had been unable to take such an initiative, but Italy's example now had to be followed in any case, even if it entailed the greatest risk, the danger of German occupation. The report, coming to the essence of Kállay's tactics, emphasized that it was foolish to hope that Hungary would be capable of manoeuvring by the side of Germany till the end of war while expecting the Allies to be lenient towards her.

After consultation with Böhm, on July 26, Gellért sent to Budapest a cipher telegram pressing for an end to troop transports and the delivery of war materials. The next day, Szegedy-Maszák phoned him asking for an urgent reply from the Allies to the question: what should Hungary do in the present situation? Since Böhm had given as his opinion that unconditional surrender was expected also from the satellite countries, Gellért requested a written statement to this effect. At the same time, Barcza sent home a message pointing out that the Allies insisted that Hungary should declare her withdrawal from the war the very moment Italy would do the same, even if such a step involved the risk of German occupation.

The Western Powers demanded guarantees that Hungary would do as they told her. But Kállay could not bring himself to follow the advice. An agreement of principle was entered into between Kállay, some members of the Government and Horthy to the effect that should the Italian Government act fast and turn against the Germans, resulting in the collapse of the southern front, then Hungary would also take the decisive step, but they did not wish to inform the Allies accordingly beforehand. Though Horthy had then made the reservation that he would inform the Germans in advance of Hungary's withdrawal from the war, because he did not intend 'to stab his ally in the back'. Thus Kállay wrote Barcza on July 31 that Mussolini's fall had only worsened the situation, for now there was nobody to hold back Hitler from using force against Hungary, and Hitler was still strong enough to overrun Hungary. "From our point of view," he proceeded, "the most decisive factor is the German standpoint that is still fully unknown to us, and we have no inkling of it. But the basic fact, our geographical location, has remained unchanged. So our chief object, which we shall ensure to the utmost of our power, is to maintain the Government as the only guarantee of constitutionality and of the preservation of order."

In the early days of August 1943, when the new Italian Government still protested its loyalty to Germany and when German troops departed for Italy, Kállay thought his caution had been justified, the events did not make it possible for him to carry out a turn-about. Therefore, on the 5th, he definitively decided that 'direct action' was impossible.

At the same time, Endre Bajcsy-Zsilinszky submitted to the Prime Minister a memorandum reflecting, among others, the opinion of the left-wing parties. In it he demanded that Hungary should quit the war, withdraw all her military forces from the Eastern front, and declare neutrality; furthermore, to ensure these external steps, he demanded the removal of pro-German elements from the political and military leadership and finally proposed the adoption of domestic political measures promoting the disengagement. The memorandum emphasized that Hungary should even take the risk of incurring German occupation. For this reason preparations should be made for possible resistance to the German armed forces and, accordingly, for the framing of further political action. On August 5, 1943, and the following days Kállay had several talks with leaders of the opposition parties. The talks were also attended by Lipót Baranyay and Móric Esterházy. The Prime Minister tried to convince the negotiating partners — mostly successfully — that direct action would only lead to German occupation. He argued that occupation would entail the coming to power of a quisling government and the extirpation of the opposition, not to mention the Allied air raids; neither were the Western Powers' guarantees reassuring for Hungary's postwar status. Consequently not only an about-turn but even any concrete anti-German move was impossible. Until the Anglo–American troops had reached the Hungarian frontier, the only thing to do might be to gradually draw back from German orientation.

The key sentence in Kállay's argumentation was the reference to Hungary's postwar status, only the formulation was not accurate, for the matter at issue was the survival of the counter-revolutionary régime. It was not the first time in wartime Hungary that the problem was that of keeping power in hand at any price. Kállay was afraid not only that the Allies would judge Hungary after the war by the activities of the quislings helped into power by German occupation, but also that if the leading set of counter-revolutionary politicians should once be stripped of power, there would be no way for them to come back. He well knew that the alternative to the policy of German hirelings could not be that of a Horthyite one after the war. This is why he did not want to risk anything, this is why he did not want to set loose forces which could have barred the way to the restoration of the old régime in the postwar period.

The relations of the Western Powers with Hungary finally made some headway in August 1943, when the announcement of the Italian armistice was imminent, and when under its impact the Kállay Government showed readiness to take a step towards acceptance of the formula of unconditional surrender.

The decision was thus made that peace-feelers should go the official way. It was decided to send László Veress, the young Foreign Ministry official who had kept in touch with the S.O.E. since early spring, to Istanbul in order to establish permanent contacts with the British. Veress was aware, just like his employers, that unconditional surrender was the only formula on the basis of which they could negotiate, but the Government's position was unambiguous to the effect that capitulation was out of the question until Anglo—American troops had reached the Hungarian frontiers, and that all that could be done was retract from German orientation.

The dilemma was solved when Veress, who was complaining about it to the S.O.E. men, was given to understand that the fact of unconditional surrender could be published only when its realization had become possible. It is not clear how Veress informed Budapest of this development, but it was probably thereafter that, in mid-August, a conference was held with Horthy, attended by Kállay, Keresztes-Fischer, Bethlen, Móric Esterházy and Gyula Károlyi. There it was decided that Hungary was willing to conclude a separate peace on the following conditions: 1. The Allies should guarantee that Hungary would not be occupied by Russian troops; 2. they should make a binding declaration in respect to Hungary's future frontiers; 3. they should recognize the current régime, in return for which Hungary would be ready to include Social Democrats in the Government.

At the secret negotiations, it was of course impossible to come forth with such demands, so Kállay authorized Veress to agree to the formula of unconditional surrender. Later Veress related that he had received the authorization in a secret coded telegram which read: "Buy the lost numbers of *The Times*." However it may have been, the fact is that, on August 19, Veress told the British in Istanbul that he represented a group composed of the Prime Minister, the Interior Minister, the Chief of Staff and the director of the political department of the Ministry of Foreign Affairs. This group wished to inform the Allies that Hungary accepted the principle of unconditional surrender and would do her best to carry it out as soon as possible. The Hungarian army was getting ready to defend Hungary's frontiers against the Germans, to make her airfields and other military installations available to the Allies, and would, in every respect, collaborate with them with a view to making it easier for them to occupy the country. He mentioned as references General Náday, then commander of the 1st Hungarian army, Vilmos Nagybaczoni Nagy, the former Defence Minister, and

Gyula Kádár, head of the counter-intelligence department of the Ministry of National Defence.

What Veress had said was officially confirmed by Hungarian Consul Dezső Újváry, and the message was then forwarded to Sir Hughe Knatchbull-Hugessen, the British Ambassador in Ankara, who made it known to the Foreign Office and was then commissioned to send Sterndale Bennett, a high-ranking diplomat of his staff, to Istanbul to negotiate with Veress. The meeting of Veress, Újváry and Bennett took place on August 20. The Hungarian emissaries gave personal assurances that the above-named four persons represented executive power in Hungary, and their plans enjoyed support from the Regent. A letter from Cadogan said this about the talks: Veress's "credentials were not water-tight but it seemed probable that he had authority for his mission. When asked whether the group he represented could implement the decision to accept unconditional surrender he said that this was a technical question which could only be left to a military expert whom the Hungarian Government would send to Istanbul."

The British Embassy in Ankara held the approach to be serious, and the Foreign Office also believed it was worth its while to consider the offer and to keep in touch with Veress. First of all it had to be made clear in military terms what was to be done, if the initiative succeeded. Still on August 20, the deputy of the British Chief of Staff was instructed to work out what should be demanded from Hungary and what specific problems might arise.

The related report was made on August 23 and it stated that Hungarian capitulation would cause great confusion in Germany both militarily and politically, and if the example should be followed by Rumania, Germany would face a critical situation which might compel her to invade Hungary. Since this step would probably require the withdrawal of troops from elsewhere, the report considered this contingency favourable and added: "Hungary will doubtless appreciate that Germans would react to Hungarian capitulation by invasion of her territory and that at present time we are unable to afford any support. Therefore capitulation now is unlikely . . ."

From the Allied viewpoint the most convenient time for Hungary's capitulation would be the time of Italian capitulation, because it would have been advantageous to them in Northern Italy and at the Soviet front and would have had an influence on other satellites, too. The most essential demand was that Hungary should deny the Germans all transport facilities through her territory. Besides, she should stop her deliveries to Germany, particularly the export of petroleum and bauxite, withdraw the troops from the Soviet front and create possibilities for Allied intelligence activities. It was held very probable that the Hungarian Government would reject every demand the fulfilment of which might entail German occupation, so the essence of the proposal was simply this: "We therefore suggest that Hungary should be told to give evidence of her good intention to assist Allies by ceasing all co-operation with Germany and by obstruction, delaying action and even possibly minor sabotage."

The British Foreign Office provided Moscow and Washington with prompt and continuous information about Veress's mission. On August 26 the British Ambassador in Moscow informed Molotov who put to him a number of questions as to whom Veress was representing and what was the position of the British Government. Clark Kerr answered that, in his Government's view, Veress's mission was worthy of attention, and further details would be discussed with the Soviet Government as soon as these became known. Molotov officially replied, on September 1, and said that the Soviet Government did not object to the British Ambassador's listening to what Veress had to say, and expressed doubt about the immediate possibility of Hungary's capitulation.

The Soviet Government — through unofficial channels, according to certain sources — made its opinion known to the Hungarian Government, too. Honorary Consul Ferenc Honti in Geneva, who represented in Switzerland the Smallholders' Party on Bajcsy-Zsilinszky's behalf, contacted a Soviet go-between on August 29, 1943, and inquired about the Soviet position regarding Hungary. A few days later he received a reply which boiled down to the following:

The first and foremost task of the Allies is to smash the military might of Germany. Although there are differences between the Allies in certain questions, these are of secondary importance, and co-operation will continue after the war. At the peace conference, the anti-Fascist Powers would discuss jointly the economic and political problems of the day and will seek a common solution. The standpoint of the Soviet Union in the matter of the peace treaty will be determined by the points of view of its security and by the moral obligations it has under the treaties in force. Although Hungary has committed grave mistakes, her future conduct will considerably influence the verdict. If Hungary backs up Germany to the end, she will have to suffer the consequences which will be given expression in the peace terms as well. The only possibility of avoiding this is by discontinuing all co-operation with the Germans, by withdrawing the troops from the territory of the Soviet Union, and by stopping propaganda against the Allied Powers. This certainly will cause difficulties and would probably result in German occupation, but any delay would be dangerous. Amidst the present conditions the risk may seem tremendous but can considerably lessen when the Anglo—American landing (presumably the imminent landing in Italy) takes place; probably this would be the most appropriate moment for the decisive step.

In connection with territorial problems, the Soviet agent said the Soviet Union rejected the *Lebensraum* theory, was a believer in the ethnic principles concerning the frontiers in general, but wished to show due regard for economic considerations, treaties in force and moral obligations. As concerns the question of Transylvania, in principle it was not against the idea of autonomy but, the Soviet emissary emphasized, since at present both Rumania and Hungary were fighting against the Allies, neither of them had any reason to count upon the goodwill of the Allied Powers at the expense of the other.

Thereupon Honti immediately returned to Budapest where, however, his mediating attempt was given a cool reception.

As we have seen, Kállay, in order to evade taking a resolute step, voiced Hungary's *de facto* neutrality towards the Allies. The Hungarian troops—although most of them were performing occupation duties far from the front—were nevertheless taking part in the war against the Soviet Union. In the summer of 1943, Kállay already had to realize that the phraseology of the struggle against Bolshevism was incomprehensible to the Western Allies. Like the Soviet Government, the Allies demanded the withdrawal of troops from the Soviet Union as a proof of good intentions. Now the Prime Minister would have liked indeed to withdraw the units deployed in Soviet territory, and therefore he commissioned Lajos Csatay — the newly appointed Minister of National Defence, who made his first visit to the German General Headquarters on August 18, 1943 — to put the question to the Germans. Csatay's attempt failed, or rather it seemed feasible in only one way; Field Marshal Keitel did not flatly refuse to agree to the withdrawal of the Hungarian force from Soviet territory but subjected it to the condition that Hungary should make a few divisions available to the Germans for the performance of occupation duties in the Balkans where the Italian units were being replaced by German forces. Obviously the aim of the German proposal was to make the further secret negotiations of the Hungarian Government with the Western Powers impossible.

It was not difficult to win the new Defence Minister over to this scheme. On his return home, he submitted Keitel's request to the Council of Ministers' meeting of August 27 and proposed the following: "With the consent or rather at the request of the Croatian Government, the Hungarian Government accepts the obligation to maintain order in present-day Croatia and, for this purpose, it shall request the return of the 2nd Hungarian army which, after the necessary reliefs and replacements, will be deployed as a force of occupation in Croatia to secure the rear connections of the German troops defending the Adriatic coast and to maintain internal order."

In the Council of Ministers, the proposal was violently opposed by Interior Minister Keresztes-Fischer and Minister of Agriculture Dániel Bánffy. It was objected to also by the Ministry of Foreign Affairs, which laid down in its memorandum: "Anglo—Saxon forces will sooner or later appear in the Balkan area, thus the Hungarian army will find itself face to face with them in foreign territory. A basic principle of the Hungarian Government is that, except in the campaign against Russia, it does not employ the national army outside the frontiers of the country. We cannot even today violate this principle without the gravest consequences; what is more, we have to make every effort to do away with this exception of Russia, too."

The meeting of the Council of Ministers made no final decision, because Kállay himself did not decline certain considerations. During spring, when the idea of participation in the occupation of the Balkans was first raised, he opposed this plan, but now he thought he could make it tally with his conceptions and would not even have to incur the wrath of the Germans by rejecting the request. His conception was to obtain the approval of the Western Powers that he might fulfil the German demand, arguing that in this way it would be possible to withdraw the troops from the Soviet Union; moreover, the Hungarian army — having access to the sea while occupying part of Yugoslavia — could get in touch much earlier with the Allied armed forces and clear the way for them. This was a rather bizarre idea, not to mention that the Hungarian troops could not have gained access to the sea, for the Germans had made it clear that they would guard the coasts and Hungarian occupation would be limited to the internal areas. Kállay talked over his conceptions with Horthy, then instructed Bakach-Bessenyey, who at that time was starting negotiations in Switzerland, to submit to Tyler a proposal to this effect.

At the very first occasion, Tyler positively demanded the withdrawal of Hungarian troops from the territory of the Soviet Union. Then Bessenyey, giving Horthy as a reference, pointed out that he found the withdrawal of Hungarian troops possible only if Hungary undertook to occupy certain Croatian territories down to the sea, a contingency that might mean that her troops could rapidly get in touch with Allied forces. This, however, would require that the Yugoslav émigré Government should, through Washington, take cognizance of the Hungarian occupation, which was worth considering also because it would evidently be less severe than occupation by Germany. Of course the American agent rejected the suggestion as one which would again be helpful to the German war machine. He closed the whole topic by saying that Hungary should by no means take part in the occupation of the Balkans and should positively withdraw her troops from Soviet soil. As a first step, the withdrawal of 5,000 to 10,000 men would certainly be significant enough, since it would demonstrate the goodwill of the Hungarian Government.

On August 28, Bakach-Bessenyey informed Budapest of the position taken by the United States Government. His report did not please Kállay. It appeared that the Americans were not willing to give any assurance or encouragement to the effect that Hungary would not be occupied by Soviet troops and that, after the war, she would belong to the Western sphere of interest. Tyler said, though, that the British Government regarded the Mediterranean area as being in its own zone of influence and did not deem it desirable for the Soviet Union to get into this zone through Hungary. But he also said categorically that the American view was different from the British position; moreover, that none of them wished to make any promise that might arouse the suspicion of the Soviet Union, since it was for years that the Soviet armed forces had been bearing the brunt of the burdens of war.

Tyler clearly pointed to the controversy between Great Britain and the United States in the question of Central and South Eastern Europe. Indeed, Churchill would have liked to secure, in this part of Europe, the influence of Britain against the Soviet Union after the war, so he seriously contemplated landing in the Balkans. The United States was mainly interested in the Far East, and from the point of view of its postwar power aspirations the U.S. showed no special interest in consolidating the British empire in general (for the dollar would have better chances in the new states emerging from colonial status than in the British Empire dominated by the pound sterling) and was not keen on the growth of British power influence in Europe. Roosevelt was of the opinion that he could win a decisive victory over Japan only after Germany had been defeated, and that the struggle might drag on even without the Soviet Union joining in the war in the Far East, which again might take place only after the conclusion of the war in Europe. U.S. interests thus required that Germany should be forced to her knees as early as possible. That is why Roosevelt essentially agreed with Stalin that the war could really be shortened only by means of landings in Western Europe. The difference between the British and the U.S. position was visible as early as 1941, first in the interpretation of the war aims (Atlantic Charter) and later in certain concrete issues as well. Already at the Trident Conference held at Washington in May 1943, the Americans opposed Churchill's proposal for a Balkan landing; they took the same view at the Quebec Conference, and, as we shall see, they did not support the British conceptions at Teheran either.

Tyler did not quibble when he said to Bakach-Bessenyey that Hungary, regardless of her future status, would be in a far better position at the end of war if she broke with Germany in due time than if she stood by Germany to the end, because in the latter case she should be prepared for the worst. Bessenyey reported that according to the Americans the last chance for Hungary to get out of the war would be when Italy capitulated, for this would put an end to the Tripartite Pact to which Hungary was a party. Mere declarations being no more sufficient, Hungary had actually to break with Germany even if this resulted in German occupation.

But Kállay did not want to assume any risk, so he was still of the opinion that any change was possible only when the Western forces reached the frontiers of Hungary. In only one point was he willing to comply with the American demands: he refused to participate in the occupation of the Balkans. On September 4, the Supreme Defence Council considered the German request and in this connection the question of quitting the war, although the Council yet knew nothing about the Allied landing in Calabria and the Italian armistice signed at the same time. Chief of Staff Szombathelyi wrote a long memorandum in support of participation in the occupation of the Balkans and explained that the German army was still strong enough to deal the rebels heavy blows, saying that for this reason it was an extremely dangerous fancy that Hungary should decamp even at the price of German occupation. Besides, he added, the only barrier to Bolshevism today was invariably Germany, so Hungary's interests could be protected only with Germany's assistance. The participants of the meeting were at one in that the break with Germany was ill-timed, but there was bitter dispute over the issue of the occupation of the Balkans. Horthy was leaning rather towards the opinion of the military, while Kállay, Jenő Ghyczy (already Foreign Minister at the time) and a few other members of the Government were against participation.

No final decision was made this time either, but already on September 8, the Minister of Foreign Affairs informed Bakach-Bessenyey that the Government rejected the German request for Hungary's participation in the occupation of the Balkans. He notified him also that they did not take the risk of quitting the war in view of the danger of German occupation, and because German occupation not only would cause terrible suffering to the Jewish population and the Polish refugees but might surely have as a consequence that "Slovaks and Rumanians would seize the opportunity to satisfy their territorial demands"; in this way Hungary's passing over to the Allies would lead to the restoration of the Trianon-established status quo, which Beneš and company would try to maintain under any circumstances. Ghyczy's argumentation went on: "In practice this would mean the repetition of the situation of 1918/1919. ... Hungary would be compelled to accept a boundary line before the peace treaty was, after the example of 1919, formally signed and ratified by the victorious Powers. Therefore the Hungarian Government could assume any risk only if we received guarantees from the Allies, a case which they do not seem to contemplate at present. Furthermore, another danger is involved in the fact that the Germans could still find a few quislings in Hungary who would gladly oblige them, and the other side would interpret this as Hungary's voluntary and enthusiastic collaboration. Thus we would receive 'additional bad marks'."

The memo stated in conclusion that Kállay intended to pursue 'the policy of progressive disentanglement' until he regained freedom of action; but as an expert of the situation he wanted to define the various stages of this process by himself. The message sent to Switzerland left no doubt that the Hungarian Government could not be expected to take the decisive step.

On September 8, 1943, the Allies promulgated the armistice agreement signed with Italy a few days earlier; at the same time Anglo—American forces landed in the vicinity of Naples. Neither the population nor the Government of Hungary were informed of the events that same day. The day of Virgin Mary (Sept. 8) being kept as a holiday in Hungary, the afternoon papers did not come out. Members of the Government, headed by the Prime Minister, were out stag-hunting, so Italian Minister Anfuso found no one in office whom to advise of the happenings. Consequently the Cabinet discussed the situation only on September 9. Kállay declared that the Italian armistice automatically nullified every agreement that bound Hungary to the Axis Powers, but from this he only drew the conclusion that Hungary had regained her moral freedom. To a question from one of his colleagues he replied that this meant that Hungary would act the moment her interests so demanded, but her policy would remain unchanged until then.

The next day, September 10, Horthy summoned his confidential associates as well as all former Prime Ministers and Foreign Ministers except Bárdossy and Imrédy. Kállay, Ghyczy and Keresztes-Fischer attended on behalf of the Government. At the conference, mainly under pressure from Bethlen, Keresztes-Fischer and Móric Esterházy, the following decisions were adopted: 1. In the next few days a delegation composed of high-ranking political and military personages should be sent to Germany to ask for the return of all Hungarian forces stationed in Soviet territory. In case this request would be turned down, the army should be given orders to return home. The related secret preparations must be started forthwith. 2. Every request for participation in the occupation of the Balkans should be rejected. 3. The Germans should be told that German military transports must not pass through Budapest, in the future they should use the side-lines. 4. The policy of the Government should in the future be guided exclusively by the interests of self-defence. 5. The army should fight the partisans and guerrillas, but should be ordered not to resist Anglo—American forces.

The only purpose of the decisions was thus to secure and demonstrate Hungary's *de facto* neutrality and then to keep waiting for the Anglo—American troops. As was decided, Kállay, on September 15, told the Chief of Staff that he would under no circumstances allow Hungarian troops to take part in the occupation of Yugoslavia. (By the way, the Germans had already ceased to demand this.) At the German General Headquarters, on September 17, Szombathelyi again requested the return of the Hungarian armed units stationed in Soviet territory, but the Germans flatly refused this time too. Willy-nilly, the Hungarian Government submitted, and failed to order the troops to return as provided in its previous decision. On September 22 Ghyczy informed Bakach-Bessenyey of the developments. All he could let Tyler know was that the Chief of Staff had received the promise that the Hungarian troops would be transferred nearer to the Hungarian frontiers, and this would, in the given case, make it easier to order them home.

Although, as we have seen, the Allied Powers had not yet agreed on the reply to be given to the Hungarian Government, the Foreign Office and the S.O.E. on September 2, taking account of the position of the General Staff, drafted a four-point text intended to be the answer to the group represented by Veress: "(*a*) H.M.G. would like to see some more authoritative credentials, which could presumably be communicated through any channel which the Hungarian Government thought advisable. (*b*) H.M.G. will expect the Hungarian Government to make a public announcement of their acceptance of unconditional surrender and to take at the earliest possible moment the action originally suggested by the Hungarian Government and summarised in telegram from S.O.E. representative at Istanbul of August 19th. (*c*) If the Hungarian Government feel that the time is not yet ripe for such an announcement, they should as evidence of their good will assist allies by ceasing all co-operation with Germany and by carrying out obstruction, delaying action and even possibly minor sabotage. (*d*) If the Hungarian Government agree to (*c*), H.M.G. would be prepared to discuss ways and means with a Hungarian military representative at Istanbul (Constantinople) as suggested by Veress."

Feverish activity started thereafter. The S.O.E. was instructed to secure contacts with Veress for September 8–9 in order that he might be handed the message. The proposed text of the message was sent to Moscow, Washington and also to Quebec where Churchill was in conference with Roosevelt.

The Soviet reply arrived on September 7. Molotov did not object to the transfer to Veress of the communication based on unconditional surrender, but he suggested that for tactical reasons the answer should be restricted to the first two paragraphs, since Hungary had already expressed her readiness for capitulation. Churchill's urgent and categorical reply was dated the same day. The British Prime Minister thought Hungary's defection from Germany would be a tremendous advantage, provided that it took place at the appropriate moment. ". . . it would be most improvident of us," he wrote, "to squander the Hungarian volte-face and merely produce a premature outbreak followed by a German Gauleiter or super-Quisling installed by force. . . . We should not be impatient in this matter. I should myself like to see the Balkans much riper than they are now, and for this purpose to let impending events in Italy, if they turn out well, play their part."

The Soviet reply and Churchill's telegram somewhat confused London, that is, the Foreign Office thought it difficult to reconcile the two. According to F. K. Roberts: "There is probably a fundamental divergence of view between the Soviet Government and the Prime Minister. The Soviet Government would probably like Hungary to make a desperate gesture at this stage and so force upon the Germans the occupation of Hungary with all the drain upon German man-power which that would imply.

"Incidentally, many friends of Hungary, including Sir O. O'Malley, think that Hungary should make this desperate gesture in her own interests, as the only means of rehabilitating herself." The Foreign Office did not find it possible to soften the text of the message, but it did not insist upon the original formulation.

In accordance with this notice of Roberts, Eden, on the 7th, answered the Prime Minister, stressing more emphatically his consideration for the Soviet opinion and inquiring at the same time after President Roosevelt's position. He wrote: "... Soviet Government would like our message to be restricted to a simple repetition of unconditional surrender. As Hungarian war effort has been entirely directed against U.S.S.R. and not against us, we must, I think, take Soviet views into account so far as we can." The next day, Churchill accepted the text to be handed to Veress with a single but essential modification. He asked that the words "at a suitable moment" be inserted in paragraph (b). The definitive text now read: "His Majesty's Government will expect the Hungarian Government to make at a suitable moment a public announcement of their acceptance of unconditional surrender." Churchill mentioned in his cable also that Roosevelt's only reaction to the communication of the Hungarian emissary was to say: "it was all very interesting." He did not find it necessary to make any further change. He accepted the suggestion that the Soviet Government should be given an explanation of why its offer had not been taken into consideration.

The decision was thus passed. Instructions went to Istanbul for the text to be conveyed to Veress, and for the British Minister to hand it to the Hungarian emissary, which was done aboard a British vessel in the Bosphorus in the night from September 9 to 10.

There is a single debated point among historians, and it is about who presented to Veress the terms of the so-called draft armistice. Historical works and memoirs, after Veress's accounts, give a description of how the British Ambassador, Sir Hughe Knatchbull-Hugessen, passed them on during a dinner aboard ship. On the other hand, British archives papers give evidence that the deliverer of the message was envoy John Cecil Sterndale Bennett, a counsellor of the British Embassy in Ankara. The most recent English work, however, a book by Elisabeth Barker, claiming that Veress must well know to whom he talked, still sticks to the opinion that it was Knatchbull-Hugessen, although she states that this does not clearly appear from the documents. Having studied again and again the available material on the delivery of the message, telegrams, notes, reports and file numbers, which all use the word 'minister' and never the word 'ambassador', and which papers (including even telegrams dispatched by Knatchbull-Hugessen himself) more than once refer to Sterndale Bennett as the one who handed over the message, I myself accept these documents as conclusive until other evidence should come up, and I think that it was Sterndale Bennett who met László Veress on the Sea of Marmara in the night of September 9, 1943.

László Veress noted down the various provisions as read out by the British diplomat. Having memorized the text lest some indiscretion should be committed, on the 14th he left for Budapest, carrying with him two radio transmitters disguised as Corvina codices exhibited at the Izmir fair.

Most members of the Government and the Foreign Ministry officials who were now apprised of the result of the negotiations were surprised, perhaps not so much at the terms — for these could be foreseen on the basis of the earlier talks — as rather at the agreement in accordance with which the peace-feelers now had to be followed by action: they had to accept capitulation and to act even before its implementation. And what had not seemed difficult in August was dangerous now in September, after the Germans had occupied Rome and a great part of Italy and S.S. airborne troops had freed Mussolini. Kállay saw his misgivings justified. But it was up to him to move if he did not want the Western contacts, created through his nearly year-long efforts, to be broken off, for paragraph (a) of the message required confirmation by the Hungarian Government.

The Minister of Foreign Affairs was of the opinion that Veress had promised more than he had been authorized to do, and under this pretext the whole thing might be called off. Kállay, on the other hand, wished to evade the formula of unconditional surrender. Interior Minister Keresztes-Fischer alone demanded positively the confirmation of the deal. As appears from a note by Veress, Horthy who was on vacation at Gödöllő was informed by Foreign Minister Ghyczy personally. The Regent acknowledged the terms and left it to Kállay to decide.

Kállay decided that if the Allies were ready to compromise by accepting a formula without the word 'unconditional', Hungary was willing to give effect to the provisions in advance.

Anthony Eden was somewhat puzzled about how the Soviet Government would react when it came to know that Veress had been given the originally proposed text. Towards noon on September 9, that is still before the delivery of the message, the Foreign Secretary sent the British Ambassador in Moscow a telegram with an explanation that was practically a repetition of Churchill's cable and expressed the hope "that the Soviet Government will not see any grave objection to this", since the divergence of view between them was of only a tactical and not of a political nature.

The Soviet Ministry of Foreign Affairs replied only ten days later but it clung to the opinion that paragraphs (c) and (d) of the text conveyed to Veress were superfluous, because "it would be to the advantage of the Allies to act quickly and resolutely, not allowing either Germans or pro-German Hungarian circles to recover from confusion connected with Italy's surrender. Hungary's unconditional surrender at the present moment, especially in connection with latest events in Italy, would inevitably cause serious difficulties for Germany and more favourable conditions both on the Eastern front and in the Italian theatre of war." The only American comment upon this was: it would be difficult to say how far the Hungarians might go by themselves in implementing paragraph (c) without provoking violent intervention from Germany.

It is now time for us, who know the end of the story and are in a position to compare many sources, to raise the question: Was withdrawal from the German alliance sufficiently grounded in Hungary in the autumn of 1943? We have already pointed out that proponents of such defection were many in England at that time. It is well known, too, that in August 1943, Endre Bajcsy-Zsilinszky submitted to the Prime Minister a memorandum mirroring what was, among others, the view of the left-wing parties, demanding Hungary's denunciation of the Tripartite Pact, the withdrawal of all armed force from the Eastern front, the declaration of neutrality, and furthermore, as guarantees of these outward measures, the elimination of pro-German elements from political and military leadership, and the introduction of internal measures promoting the dénouement. The memorandum emphasized that even the risk of occupation should be accepted so it was necessary to prepare for a possible resistance to the German army and accordingly to make preparations for a change of policy.

On August 5, and the subsequent days Kállay had several talks with leaders of opposition parties. These talks were attended, among others, by Lipót Baranyai and Móric Esterházy, who themselves were of the opinion that even the risk of German occupation must be taken for the sake of Hungary's future.

We wish to state first of all that obviously those who demanded the about-face were morally right. From a certain point of view we may refer to Yugoslavia's example: Who was right, who was a *realpolitiker* there in 1941? Was it Prime Minister Cvetković, who signed the Tripartite Pact, after lengthy wrangling, in the hope of thwarting thereby the occupation of Yugoslavia? Or was it those who expelled the Cvetković Government in anticipation of the inevitable invasion of Yugoslavia by the Nazi war machine? It is evident that the execution of an about-face in Hungary, in the autumn of 1943, would have been of enormous moral significance, and it is incalculable what effect Hungary's defection and resistance might have had on the fighting fronts.

When stating this, however, we have to raise the question whether the forces of the opposition, in the autumn of 1943, would have been capable of effecting a change in the government, or rather whether the 'other Hungary' was strong enough to overrun the given régime, since the official Government did not dare to undertake the break-away.

Before going on seeking the answer, we have to state a few more things. As we have seen, British political leaders did not think that a change-over in Hungary would be either useful or probable before the Allied forces reached the Hungarian frontiers. Nor did the Soviet Government believe in the probability of capitulation, as appears from the first position taken with regard to the Veress action. But Churchill thought the time had not yet come, he was afraid of a fiasco which, together with reprisals against the democratic opposition, would bring with it German occupation and the accession to power of an extreme-right Government as well as the downfall of the group of leading politicians who accepted capitulation, a group which the Allies did not rely upon for the building of Hungary's future, but which would have been compelled to assume responsibility for a far from promising armistice and peace treaty.

The essence of this idea was most clearly illuminated by Vilmos Böhm, as F. K. Roberts wrote, towards the end of August 1943: "M. Boehm feared ... that the present régime was showing favour to the Democratic Parties with a view to handing the Government over to them when things became too difficult, and so saddling them with the responsibility for a peace settlement which would obviously be unwelcome to many Hungarian patriots. It was, therefore, in his view most important that the Demoratic Parties should not be urged by us to enter the Government or to replace the present régime, who should be compelled to accept full responsibility for the consequences of the Hungarian entry into the war on the side of the Axis."

And the British considerations included one more aspect. We read in a notice by George Randall that Professor Namier, an eminent leader of international Jewish organizations, had told him that "... his people were most seriously concerned at the possible consequence to the 800,000 Jews who now enjoy comparative security in Hungary, of any premature desertion of Germany by the Hungarian Government ..." whereupon the German reaction "would be extermination of the last important body of Jewry left in Europe. ... the only hope so far as the Jews were concerned was that the Hungarians would choose not to move until it was practically certain that the Germans would not be able to re-act." In a reference paper D. Allen remarked on October 20: "We have this point very much in mind as one of the arguments against pressing the Hungarians to make an immediate open stand against the German occupation."

We know full well, as we have pointed out several times, that decisive among Kállay's motives were not the above considerations, but the chances of the counter-revolutionary régime's survival after the war. To hold power in hand at any price—this was the key problem of wartime Hungarian foreign policy. Kállay feared not only that the Allies would judge Hungary after the war by the quislings helped into power by German occupation, but also that the leading quarters of the counter-revolutionary régime would never regain power if once they had been ousted from it. This is why they refrained from taking any risk, this is why they were against releasing such forces as might stand in the way of restoring the old régime after the war.

On the other hand, if we examine the conditions of change-over in the countries allied with Germany or the uprisings in the occupied countries, we can see the following: in Italy it was in the summer of 1943, at the time of Anglo–American landings in Sicily and subsequently in Calabria; in Rumania it was in August 1944, when the fighting went on already in Rumanian territory; in France the occasion came with the Paris uprising in August 1944, when the Allied forces were advancing towards the French capital; in Bulgaria it was in September 1944, when the Soviet army was deployed along the Bulgarian frontier; the turn in Finland and the Slovakian insurrection occurred in similar circumstances; and the Prague uprising in May 1945 coincided with Germany's capitulation.

Surely, for Hungary to carry out an about-face in the autumn of 1943 or early in 1944, would have involved a major risk, because at the decisive moment it was impossible to reckon with any possibility of soothing the anxiety of the wavering masses and forcing the Fascist and pro-German elements to draw in their horns and show their true colours — with the possibility that a quick Allied invasion of the country could prevent German occupation or, as we can know today, would limit the inevitable occupation to a short time. In the autumn of 1943, the situation of the front lines did not make it possible for either the Anglo—American forces or the Soviet army to appear at the Hungarian frontiers simultaneously with the accomplishment of an about-face. The break with Germany in the autumn of 1943 would in any case have entailed acceptance of occupation, of active anti-German struggle, with the consequences — even though in far more promising circumstances from the point of view of the outcome of the war — which the peoples of Yugoslavia had accepted in 1941.

The Kállay Government did not dare to choose this road, the only passable one under the given circumstances. The counter-revolutionary system itself, with its closed, rigid political structure, with the upshots of its twenty-five-year development, was incapable of it. The leaders wanted to pull the régime through the war; so they could conceive of defecting only in case Anglo—American forces entered the territory of Hungary, while the political power structure would remain intact preventing both an extreme-right take-over following a German occupation, and a left-wing democratic change-over as well.

In view of this state of affairs we have to answer two questions.

First, the break with Germany—since under the given circumstances the Government did not dare to undertake the volte-face—was conceivable only on condition that simultaneously with, or rather a moment before, the defection from Germany, the Government underwent a change that is, if the current régime were overturned by the forces of the opposition, of the 'other Hungary'. The question is therefore whether in Hungary, in the autumn of 1943, there existed the requisites for the anti-German forces to take this decisive step, to seize power, and this in such a way as to be able to organize resistance to German occupation and to cope with all political and military consequences of their action.

In none of the instances in Europe did the break with Germany take place as an action of those who had dragged the country into the war. This would have been a political absurdity. Everywhere, the turn required a change of government; this was the case in Yugoslavia in March 1941, in Rumania and Bulgaria in August—September 1944. This change still did not necessarily mean an immediate turn to the left in domestic policy, but at least a turn towards liberalism, towards democracy, in solidarity with all anti-Hitler forces.

As regards the conditions of a domestic political change concomitant with Hungary's quitting the war in the autumn of 1943, it is no exaggeration to say that such conditions were non-existent under the circumstances then prevailing in the theatres of war; above all the military conditions for such a change were lacking, the army seemed incapable of the about-face. In the summer of 1944, Veress wrote in his summary report drawn up at Bari that "the Surrender Group ... included no army officers and this proved to be one of the principal sources of its weakness." Kállay and company themselves admitted this in the message which Dezső Újváry took with him in answer to the conditions of September 9: "The Hungarian Government is obliged to point out quite frankly that the Hungarian army has not kept in step with the political evolution of public opinion. The purge of key positions in the army is systematically going on and this is one of the main causes of German suspicion. For the moment, these measures are not yet completed, consequently these are obstacles to the establishment of military contact."

This is how the situation was assessed at the time by the Central Committee of the Peace Party, which clearly saw that the greater part of the masses were not yet ripe for action in favour of a break with Germany and especially not for turning against Kállay. If, under these circumstances, the Bajcsy-Zsilinszky memorandum and leaders of the opposition nevertheless demanded quick action and the break with Germany, this was only due to the general belief that — after the failure of the last big German offensive mounted on the Eastern front, after the splendid victory of the Soviet army at Kursk, and after the Allied landings in Sicily — the defeat of Germany, or at least the end of her domination over the Balkans and South-Eastern Europe, and the appearance there of the Anglo–American armed forces were a reality within reach. Few would have believed at the time that the Allied troops landing in Sicily would not reach Rome until a year later. When they insisted therefore that even the risk of German occupation should be accepted, they certainly did not think of the possibility of a prolonged occupation.

The forces of the Hungarian opposition contemplated the turn with the assistance of the Government, with the representatives of power, they expected action from the latter. Today, however, we already know full well that it was illusory to hope that Horthy and company would be capable of any change without the presence of Western armed forces, or that the change-over with their assistance would be feasible.

Let us then look at the second question. If those among the leftist opposition, who rightly saw that the principal requirement was withdrawal from the war, thought to realize it by co-operating with the politicians belonging to the régime, with the Government in power and the Regent, then the question rightly arises: Where did these illusions come from?

Most conspicuously they came from the fact that it were they, at the summit of power, who, with the consent of the Prime Minister and the Regent, had started negotiations with the Allied Powers. But again it is impossible to understand this without looking into the very nature of the régime. We have to see clearly that in the counter-revolutionary system the conservative-reactionary forces succeeded in retaining the decisive attributes of power up to 1944, the year of German occupation, and, through the person of the Regent, even until later times. It was they who, by dint of their power position, had entangled the country in the war, thereby maintaining a political situation similar to but not identical with that in Finland, namely that the Government of a satellite state had not only a legal and an illegal left-wing opposition but also an extremely strong rightist opposition. This was partly organized within the Government Party and partly in other legally functioning parties. This brought a schizoid political situation in which the most determined followers of Nazi Germany, the domestic Fascists, could busy themselves in opposition to the wartime Governments allied with Germany.

And this is where another problem of Hungarian resistance came up. Namely that at the decisive turning points of the war it would not have been enough, as an internal condition for the break with Germany, to dismiss or to overthrow the wartime Government, but an elementary requirement would have been to smash the extreme-right wing which possessed a broad basis in the ruling classes, mainly in the 'genteel middle classes.' That is, agreement with the anti-German forces would not have sufficed for the creation of an anti-German national unity. The actual holders of power could still be ousted and replaced by the extreme right which constituted a political force. (In connection with the Hungarian extreme right it is not proper to use the notion 'quisling', because quislings nowhere represented any considerable political force. One of the greatest mistakes Horthy and his retinue committed was to be disposed to regard the problem of the extreme right as one of quislingism.) Hitler in fact counted upon this extreme-right force when he prepared for the occupation of Hungary. At his talks with Antonescu, in February 1944, he said he wanted to occupy Hungary in such a way that the German troops of occupation should keep in the background, and the functions of occupation should be performed by a Government formed of extreme-right elements.

That is, in Hungary the question was not merely whether to fight against foreign occupation and pressure or not. An about-face in this country meant fight amidst the given circumstances when support from the Allies could not be expected in the near future. Those fighting ought to have fought against the extreme-right forces aspiring to power, and this would have meant acquiescence to civil war. For this very reason anti-Hitlerism was far from being enough to turn against Germany, and anyone who undertook to join battle against the Germans had to be an adherent of political democratism at the least.

In the thirties, the occasional union and collaboration of those ranging between conservatism and democratic opposition still scored successes against the extreme right to the effect that those Prime Ministers who tried to create an open Fascist dictatorship, or who were willing to let the extreme-right wing have a share in the power, were bound to fall. But hidden behind the common goal were radically different motives. The resistance of the liberal and Social Democratic opposition could coincide with the fears of the landed aristocracy and the big bourgeoisie scared by reform demagogy, because the liberal and Social Democratic opposition found it easier to put up with the Bethlen type of political establishment than with what was in store for them in the case of open Fascist dictatorship.

In the autumn of 1943, however, there were no longer common aims in opposition to the extreme-right wing. By this time the principal aim of the Government's foreign policy was to rescue the régime. The representatives of power were already beset by a double fear — first, the fear of German occupation, which would have entailed the victory of the extreme right with all its political, economic and military implications; and second, an even greater fear of a possible leftist turn brought about by the appearance of the Soviet army. All this confused the self-defence reflexes of those in power. This is what led to the impasse which the political leadership could no longer get over. The slogan of 'not to provoke the Germans' inevitably grew into that of 'not to provoke the extreme right', meaning the postponement of every measure that could have been interpreted as part of political and military preparation for the action of passing over to the Allied Powers.

Kállay felt that he had achieved the most important thing: the Allies "deleted Hungary from the list of enemy countries"; Hungary was granted British protection which, as Kállay himself wrote, applied against the Soviet Union at least as much if not more than against Germany; Hungary thus would not belong to the Soviet sphere of interest, the rest was only a question of time.

Kállay diligently gathered all information which seemed to verify his conclusions, and he rejected those reports which did not tally with his conceptions and tactical moves. Now he saw only one task before him: to evade German occupation by maintaining order inside the country until the arrival of Anglo–American armed forces.

This basic stand also determined his attitude towards the preliminary armistice provisions: to carry out only as much of the agreement as was possible without provoking the Germans and alarming the extreme right. Thus Kállay refrained from complying with the German demand for the severance of diplomatic relations with the Badoglio Government of Italy, but on September 29 he also recognized Mussolini's rival Government. He gave effect to the decision that German troop transports should pass round Budapest, but Hungarian transports to Germany did not decrease at all. He permitted the Allied air force to fly over Hungarian territory, but he allowed the Germans to maintain their air bases in the country. Towards the end of December 1943, those guilty of the Újvidék atrocities were brought to trial in order to exert a favourable influence on Western public opinion, but those really guilty, being able to set up their defence while being at large, took refuge in Germany, so the court-martial verdict could not be carried out.

Instead of effectively organizing resistance, instead of combining forces against the Germans, a so-called 'defection bureau' was set up under the direction (or rather in the person) of Miklós Horthy, Jr. The legitimate task of the bureau was to take care of repatriated Hungarians, but in fact it had the task of securing liaison between the Regent and the forces of resistance. The bureau started to work on January 10, 1944, and resistance to the bureau meant something quite different from what it did to the anti-Fascist forces. In effect, the bureau was intended to keep an eye on, and to build contact with, those paramilitary organizations and associations which were supposed to be free from the influence of the extreme right and were loyal to Horthy.

Traces of Kállay's delaying tactics can also be detected in British documents dealing with developments following September 1943. Through a radio transmitter he had taken with him to Budapest, Veress notified the British that he had informed Horthy,

Kállay and Ghyczy about his talks at Istanbul, and that they 'gave careful consideration to the message from London'. He claimed that Horthy had approved the establishment of radio contact. Two days earlier the S.O.E. had been informed by Consul Dezső Újváry that Budapest regarded Lisbon as the most appropriate place to confirm the offer of capitulation.

The Foreign Office accepted the suggestion and by a letter of October 16, which described the Veress mission in detail, commissioned Campbell, the British Ambassador in Lisbon, to take over the credentials. The surprises came thereafter. Ullein-Reviczky said in Stockholm that he was authorized to continue the negotiations. But the British, for good reasons, stuck to Lisbon where, however, the Hungarian credentials failed to arrive. Nor did a military representative arrive at Istanbul. Újváry informed the S.O.E. that the British military party could not be received in Hungary either, because it was impossible to guarantee their safety. And Veress wrote that the members of the British mission would not be in a position to make contact with the Hungarian General Staff.

These messages certainly did not give London cause for rejoicing. So the answer was not exactly cheerful. It stated, among other things, that "Hungary is an enemy country and will be treated as such by all the United Nations until she reverses her policy and makes a positive contribution to our victory without delay". It demanded presentation of the credentials in Lisbon, reception of the British mission, and detailed information on what of the conditions of September 9 had already been fulfilled.

In the autumn and winter of 1943, the international situation did not conform to Kállay's conceptions and desires. In Italy the Allied forces advanced at a snail's pace. On the Eastern front, on the other hand, the Soviet offensive in December scored big successes. Thus the hope on which Kállay's wait-and-see policy was built — namely that the Anglo—American troops would reach the frontiers of Hungary earlier than the Soviet army — began to fade away. The coalition of the anti-Fascist Great Powers was growing into a kind of co-operation in which the differences of opinion regarding the postwar settlements were eclipsed by the common aim of completely smashing Germany militarily at the earliest possible time. The co-ordination of war aims, of military and diplomatic actions, began to take an organized form in relation not only to Germany but to the vassal states, too.

The Moscow Conference of Foreign Ministers held from October 13 to 19, 1943, decided to set up a European Advisory Council. This body dealt with the armistice agreements to be concluded with the vassal states in addition to drafting the document on Germany's unconditional surrender.

The firm reluctance of the British towards the delaying tactics of the Hungarian Government was obviously stimulated by the Moscow Conference where the issue of the negotiations with Hungary was taken up. And although Eden found no time to hold separate talks in the matter as he had suggested, yet in connection with different drafts prepared in the Foreign Office he laid down that the Soviet Union insisted on unconditional surrender and this had to be communicated to the Hungarians. "We must also remember," he proceeded, "that Russians are fighting Hungarians and we are not. Russians therefore have cause to think that they should have strongest voice deciding allied policy towards Hungary."

The Moscow consultation had prepared the Teheran Conference which took place between November 28 and December 1, 1943, when Roosevelt, Churchill and Stalin met for the first time together. The decisions of the Teheran Conference largely determined the further march of the war events. There it was decided definitively to carry out, in 1944, the Allied landing in Normandy and the diversionary landing in Southern France, to render joint assistance to the Yugoslav partisans led by Tito, and to try to involve Turkey in the war by the side of the Allies. (This latter was only realized the last moment before the end of the war, but the decision put a stop to the conjectures relating to Turkey on whom, as we have seen, Kállay also had built part of his conceptions.)

Kállay and company could not obtain exact information on the secret military arrangements of the Conference, but the diplomatic and military events of the weeks following Teheran — a Soviet mission visiting with Tito, Anglo—American support to the Yugoslav partisans, changes in Turkey — showed clearly enough what kind of agreements must have been adopted by the three Great Powers.

Very important events concerning Central Europe were Beneš's trip to Moscow and the conclusion of a Czechoslovak—Soviet treaty of alliance in the middle of December 1943. Beneš had several talks with Stalin and Molotov between December 14 and 18, and took up the question of Hungary as well. His related demands — in which democratic considerations were mixed with narrow-minded nationalism — touched upon three issues:

1. The overthrow of the 'feudal system' in Hungary and her democratic transformation through revolutionary changes in domestic policy. In connection with this absolutely just requirement Beneš expounded that the British and Americans agreed on this point but were afraid that revolutionary changes would again lead to a Béla Kun type of proletarian dictatorship. Therefore the occupation of Hungary was absolutely necessary. If, however — Beneš argued — Hungary were occupied exclusively by Anglo—American armed forces, the Hungarian aristocrats, during week-ends and at hunting parties, would again impress the British 'with ancient Hungarian parliamentarism and democracy'. So, from the point of view of Czechoslovakia's interests, it would be absolutely necessary for the Soviet Union to take a prime share in the occupation of Hungary. In this connection Molotov remarked that the Soviet army had a shorter way to go to Hungary than the Western armed forces did, although the situation was not yet entirely clear and final. Beneš was in favour of a long-lasting occupation of Germany and Hungary, and wanted to secure to Czechoslovakia a share in it.

2. Territorial questions. Beneš demanded the restoration of the 1937 frontiers between Czechoslovakia and Hungary. But he was a spokesman not only of Czechoslovak territorial demands but also of the Rumanian claims. In respect of Transylvania, he asked the Soviet Union to endorse fully the claims of Rumania. Molotov, though silent about the prewar frontiers, agreed that the Transylvanian question should be

settled in favour of the Rumanians, and — as he said — he had already made this known to the British.

3. Relocation of the Hungarians living in Czechoslovakia. Beneš explained in detail his plan for the removal of the Sudeten Germans, pointing out each time that the Magyar minority of Czechoslovakia should be removed like the Germans, but at least exchanged for Slovaks living in Hungary. To this he asked for Soviet consent.

It appears from the records of the negotiations that in connection with the countries of the Danubian basin Beneš was guided not only by the interests of the anti-Fascist war but also by his purblind Hungarophobia and by his desire to restore the Little Entente. Namely, while he placed Hungary in the same category with Germany and demanded her penalization, he proposed a quite different treatment for Rumania who had also fought on the side of Germany. While he emphasized on behalf of Rumania that the Rumanian people did not like the system, and quoted Maniu as a sincere democrat, he referred to Hungary as a 'feudal, war criminal country' and ignored completely the Hungarian people and the existence of opposition forces in Hungary.

At the turn of the years 1943 and 1944, Kállay also was compelled to draw certain conclusions. First of all, that the Soviet Union would certainly have a voice in the future affairs of Central Europe, but this was slow to take effect in more positive steps.

During November and December, there was little progress if any. Telegrams of Veress came to Istanbul one after another, asserting that the Hungarian Government rejected the German demand for Hungary's participation in the occupation of Yugoslav territories; that the Hungarian armed formations had been withdrawn to Rovno and were allowed only to do occupation duties; that a few Yugoslav partisans had been granted pardon, etc. But no serious steps were reported. Gradually the telegrams confirmed the suspicion that the Kállay Government was only playing for time. Early in November, for example, there came a message that the Hungarian Government had entered into contact with Otto of Habsburg, and this might induce the Government to take back its offer of unconditional surrender because of 'interference and misinformation from Otto Habsburg and Eckhardt'. The fact is that Eckhardt sent word to Budapest that the Americans wanted to have Otto installed on the throne of Austria–Hungary. A quick answer from London went through the S.O.E. to the Hungarian capital that British policy had never given the Habsburgs hope for either Austria or Hungary, and that there was no reason to regard Eckhardt as a spokesman of either British or American policy.

Ultimately it was Veress himself who asked for resolute action against his Government. We read in a letter from the S.O.E. in London: "Veress himself says that he is working under difficulties and suggests that the time is ripe for an ultimatum to the Hungarian Government, asking them to confirm their offer of unconditional surrender. He suggests this might also go in through our Ambassador in Lisbon. We have the impression that he is playing fairly straight with us and does not agree to the prevarication of the group he represents."

This communication from Veress was very significant. In fact the message quoted above was dated December 6, 1943. This means that the offer of capitulation had not been confirmed at Lisbon, which we have so far believed to have been the case, although the question was already the announcement of capitulation. All that happened was that the Hungarian Minister in Lisbon told the local representative of British intelligence that the Hungarian Consul in Istanbul, Dezső Újváry, was authorized to continue the negotiations.

The Foreign Office prepared a number of drafts of an ultimatum to Hungary. Finally Sir Alexander Cadogan, the Permanent Under-Secretary of State, starting from the belief that capitulation was unfeasible until the Allied troops had reached the Hungarian frontiers, made the following proposal:

"The only useful answer would be to the effect that if, after say 2 months, we were satisfied that Hungary had ceased military collaboration with Germany and could prove that she had indulged in useful acts of sabotage, we would consider the case and see whether she could afford us sufficient help to justify our calling off intensive bombardment of Budapest. That seems to us to be more productive than yelling 'unconditional surrender' at people who are not in a position, now, to give it."

In December 1943, the bombardment of Budapest and severance of contacts already came into question. Though bombing did not start until German occupation, the decision to make air raids upon Budapest was made precisely two months later. Radio contact with Veress was broken, because the S.O.E. did not reply to his messages, as he complained later in a letter written after the war. That is, Hungary gradually lost the assets she had accumulated by peace-feelers, by the Veress action in August, by the preliminary armistice terms of September 9.

This is seen very clearly from the controversy within the Foreign Office, early in February 1944, about bombardment of Budapest. On February 3, Professor C. A. Macartney sent F. K. Roberts a long letter contesting the usefulness of bombing Budapest, which the Allied General Staff had already decided upon. He recommended that they should send to the Hungarian capital a new message listing the concrete steps the Kállay Government was expected to take, and warning it that its failure to act would immediately entail the bombardment of Budapest.

No one agreed but there were those who thought that bombardment served political purposes in the first place. "Our main difficulty," F. K. Roberts wrote, "in carrying out a realistic Hungarian policy is that the Russians suspect us of undue tenderness towards Hungary. The best, and indeed the only, practicable way to dispose of such suspicions is to carry out acts of war against Hungary, which could only be air raids against Budapest, where there are important and easily identified industrial targets. Having shown the Russians that we mean business, it will then be very much easier to secure their agreement for any further conversations with the Hungarians aiming at their defection from the Axis." To ensure the political effect of this action, Roberts proposed that information on the time of bombing should be requested in advance in order to contemplate cautioning the Hungarian Government and people, simultaneously with the bombardment, that further air raids would follow if Hungary failed to act demonstrating her turning against the Germans.

Others primarily emphasized the military importance of bombardment. Finally, Cavendish-Bentinck definitely claimed that the bombardment of Budapest was not a function of politics but one of meteorological and strategic factors, and that it would be awkward to inquire beforehand about the date of the attack to be launched by the 15th American airborne division which was assigned to carry out the task.

After the big Soviet offensive in December, the British sent word through Barcza on January 12, 1944, that the Hungarian Government should listen to reason and not wait until the Soviet troops had reached the frontiers of the country, and it should refrain from the incredible blunder, not to say sin, of attempting to mount armed resistance to the Soviet forces, for such an act of foolhardy adventurism might not only lead to the utter annihilation of the Hungarian army but would place the country in the same political category with Germany.

Kállay was shocked to read the British message, so much the more as the British attitude towards the Hungarian plenipotentiaries matched it. The 'Istanbul line' did not react to Veress's radiograms in connection with Kállay's new conceptions elaborated early in 1944. Of course, the British Government and military leaders had not abandoned the efforts to be present in South Eastern Europe after the war. This contingency was not ruled out definitively at Teheran either by the decisions on the opening of a second front in Europe, for the Anglo–American forces were already fighting in Italy, and the effort to involve Turkey in the war likewise presupposed this possibility. Although the Teheran Conference had resolved that, parallel with the landing in the north of France, there would begin an Allied landing in Southern France, this did not mean the discontinuance of the Italian campaign. At Teheran, it was President Roosevelt himself who recalled the plan according to which the Allies would advance up to the northern coasts of the Adriatic and then turn north-east towards the Danube. Churchill described this plan as an alternative of landing in Southern France, and in his work *The Second World War* summed up the result of Teheran as follows: "... I was of course more attracted by the President's alternative suggestion of a right-handed move from Italy by Istria and Trieste, with ultimate designs for reaching Vienna through the Ljubljana gap. All this lay five or six months ahead. There would be plenty of time to make a final choice as the general war shaped itself..."

Late in 1943 and early in 1944, the situation of the fronts did not favour conceptions of this kind. The Western forces got stuck at Monte Cassino, and it took long months to force open the road towards Rome. In the light of the Soviet breakthrough of January 1944, on the other hand, it did not seem impossible for the Soviet army — if it was able to go on at the same pace — to appear soon in the area of the Carpathians. No one could surmise at the time that the Soviet forces would not reach the frontiers of Hungary until September 1944.

British foreign policy again became more active in relation to the countries of South Eastern Europe in the summer of 1944, when the situation at the front, the Moscow and Teheran Conferences, and the British position expressed in the 'draft armistice' of September 1943 (implying that the change in Hungary should not take place until the Allies had reached the Hungarian frontiers) put the Foreign Office into a dilemma: either to tell the Hungarian Government that the preliminary agreement of September was regarded as null and void because Hungary had failed to fulfil her obligations defined in it, or to refrain for the time being from stating its position because politically, there was nothing to say to Hungary. The decision was in favour of the latter alternative, and this was in fact formulated in the views stated before.

American policy towards Hungary — growing more active at the time when the British were backing out — was in a certain sense different.

Late in 1943 and early in 1944, President Roosevelt conferred several times with Otto of Habsburg, who, since 1943, had kept in touch with the Kállay Government through Lisbon, where his emissary was first a Portuguese businessman by the name of Saldanha, and then his own brother, Archduke Charles. Otto of Habsburg claims that after Mussolini's fall, he received word from Budapest that when Hungary would pass over to the Allies, a change would occur also in the supreme leadership of the country: the institution of the regency would be abolished and the monarchy would be restored. Tibor Eckhardt also writes that in the summer of 1943, he received a letter from Kállay: in it the Prime Minister said that he was aware that in case the Allied Powers won the war, Horthy would not be allowed to remain head of state. The Western Powers could stipulate this beforehand as their own condition.

On September 11, 1943, ex-Empress Zita, on behalf of Otto, met President Roosevelt, who explained to her his ideas about the postwar partition of Germany and about the Danubian federation which, by and large, would include the states of the former Monarchy, even though not within the one-time boundaries. At the same time, he left no doubt that the postwar internal development of the Central European countries was not an issue that could set the United States against the Soviet Union.

Towards the middle of October, the Hungarian Government sent Otto a memorandum dealing mainly with problems of the Danubian federation, the status of Hungary among them. Kállay allegedly authorized Otto by letter to act as head of the Hungarian state in case Horthy resigned. The Prime Minister stated again that Hungary would surrender only to the Western Powers, not to the Soviet Union.

After all this, in November 1943, Otto sent to Budapest a memorandum which he had earlier shown to Roosevelt. In it he wrote the following: 1. The Allies can grant favourable peace terms only if Hungary passes over as an active belligerent against Germany. 2. The Allies demand Horthy's resignation, and they want to set up a Government with the participation of all Hungarian anti-Hitler forces, including Social Democrats. 3. The idea of the Danubian federation is popular with U.S. political circles, although Roosevelt had again voiced his friendship for Hungary. 4. The Moscow Conference had not yet decided on the future status of Austria and Hungary. Then Otto explained in detail the conception of the United States, Great Britain and the Soviet Union, and his own information on the postwar status and frontiers of the countries bordering upon Hungary. The memorandum stressed in conclusion that the Western Powers did not yet wish to decide definitively the territorial questions. If

Hungary passed over to the Allies in due time, it might be possible to talk about an independent Transylvania where the Rumanian population would have its rights guaranteed, and if the negotiations brought quick results, it would be possible to recognize Hungary as a belligerent party, or else Hungary would have to share the fate of Hitlerite Germany.

The memorandum reached Budapest towards the middle of December and was given a mixed reception. Keresztes-Fischer, the Foreign Ministry group, Sigray and — with different reserves — Kállay got closer to the left-wing position demanding a change as soon as possible. On the other side, Horthy and Bethlen took the view that in exchange for desertion something more must be obtained than envisaged in Otto's memorandum. According to Bethlen, Otto had concealed that the Allies were preparing for landing in the Balkans and that the foreseeable big German offensive in the East might sap the German and Soviet forces alike. So Hungary could possibly risk less by passing over to the Allies later. The result of the dispute was that on January 12, 1944, Kállay informed Otto that the principles of his memorandum were for the time being unacceptable.

On January 16, 1944, Roosevelt again received Otto, who told him that Horthy was willing, when Hungary withdrew from the war, to transmit power to a Government representing all parties. Prince Primate Serédi might be reckoned with as provisional head of state. Otto described in detail how he imagined the change to take place in Hungary and requested preliminary guarantees that Hungary would be recognized as a belligerent party and that the country would not be occupied by Soviet troops.

Of course Roosevelt could not give such guarantees. He did not dissimulate that he personally would be far from pleased with the Soviet occupation of Hungary, but he emphasized that Hungary's occupation was still an open question, it would depend on the future conduct of the Hungarian Government. He pressed for the military to discuss the details of desertion, with reference to the possibility that, once the change was effected in Hungary, airborne troops of the Allies might arrive in the country before the Germans could pull themselves together. He stressed at the same time that the success of the about-face in Hungary might trigger a chain reaction in the vassal states. The President told Otto that Rumania had offered to surrender unconditionally and that the Western Powers left it to the Soviet Union to decide the matter of Rumanian capitulation. Finally he offered Otto the use of the State Department's Lisbon telephone line for the dispatch and reception of messages. This line was indeed used to exchange the last messages between Budapest and Otto prior to German occupation.

Around the turn of 1943 to 1944, the difference between the British and the American position regarding Hungary was clearly to be seen. London bred a suspicion about Otto's activity, which ultimately prompted the Foreign Office to bring to the notice of the Hungarian plenipotentiaries that England wanted no Habsburg combination and would be much astonished if the Americans were thinking differently. On the other hand, the Americans were invariably for Hungary's defection at the earliest possible time, regardless of how far away the Allied forces were from the Hungarian frontiers, while the British confined themselves to insisting — for lack of anything better — that Hungary should apply to the Soviet Union for an armistice when the Red Army reached the Hungarian frontiers. The Americans could not neglect the Soviet wishes, but they thought they could find another solution which would not rule out the presence of Anglo–American troops in Hungary if the Hungarian Government acted in time. This was clear from what Roosevelt told Otto, and was given a concrete formulation in the offer which an American agent presented to Ullein-Reviczky in Stockholm on January 24, 1944. According to this, the Soviet Union, Great Britain and the United States would jointly discuss the Hungarian capitulation at a neutral place, and — the American agent added — this was better than if the Hungarians stood alone in face of the Soviet Union.

Kállay, however, stubbornly concentrated his foreign policy on the rescue of the régime and thought therefore that any kind of Soviet presence in Hungary was inconceivable. This is why he so brusquely rejected the Stockholm offer. His answer was that Hungary would resist the Soviet Union under all circumstances. She would surrender to the United States and Britain, but not to 'partisan Chetniks or Vlachs'. And on February 2 he wrote Barcza: "If we have to choose — until another factor has presented itself — between an essentially defensive Germany and an expansive Russia, we cannot but stand by Germany."

But something had to be done already if Kállay did not want Hungary to be 'put again on the list of enemy countries'. Time was pressing: the Soviet Army was approaching; the Yugoslav partisans controlled a good part of the territory of their country; the Rumanians offered to capitulate; and the Anglo–American forces were still plodding away at Monte Cassino. To salvage the régime, to avoid German occupation, to keep away the Soviet army, not to allow Rumania to get ahead of Hungary — all this was a requirement for which no realistic plan could be charted.

Kállay's new conception was now to take measures for defence along the line of the Carpathians and, to this end, to bring home the soldiers fighting in Soviet territory and to mobilize the internal military reserves. The Allies should be told that Hungary would only engage in defensive operations on her own frontiers, if necessary, so the Soviet troops should keep off the country. The Hungarian Government would not conclude an armistice and would not formally discontinue its alliance with Germany, but it would forbid German forces to stay in Hungary and would stop all economic aid to Germany.

Preparations were now speeding up. For the conception to be carried out, two things were needed from the international point of view: either to induce the anti-Fascist Powers to accept the conception, or to convince the Germans that the Hungarian forces must be withdrawn. Early in February Kállay expounded his conceptions to Barcza and Bakach-Bessenyey who in Switzerland maintained the Anglo–American connection. On February 16, 'Mr. H.' replied to Barcza that, though the British Government comprehended the Hungarian aspirations, yet it considered resistance in the Carpathians utterly hopeless; therefore it repeatedly advised Hungary that, when the Red Army reached the Carpathians, she should turn against the Germans and ask the Soviet Union for an armistice. This was the last chance for Hungary to avoid being identified with Hitler's Germany after the war.

Dulles and Tyler also explained to Bessenyey that the United States would take a dim view of Hungary's continued participation in the fightings on the Eastern front. After lengthy discussions, they nevertheless offered to request the U.S. Government to ask Moscow whether the Soviet army would stop at the Hungarian frontiers if the Hungarian Government officially undertook (*a*) not to collaborate with the Germans in the defence of those frontiers, (*b*) not to allow German troops to pass through Hungarian territory, and (*c*) in case of need, to resist the Germans by force of arms if they should try to prevent the fulfilment of the provisions under (*a*) and (*b*). On January 31, a memorandum of the Office of Strategic Services arrived at the Department of State, which then replied on February 8: "We don't deal with any of these overtures except on the basis of unconditional surrender."

At the same time, however, they began to consider more concretely the question what they and the British should say to the Hungarian case if Hungary really took serious steps to get out of the war. In March 1944, still before the Germans invaded Hungary, the Department of State prepared a memorandum on this matter stating that any territorial claims on Czechoslovakia and Yugoslavia were ruled out: The Hungarian troops must retreat to the 1938 frontiers, Northern Transylvania must be evacuated, but an attempt might be made at some sort of autonomy for Transylvania.

Still unaware of the position taken by the U.S. Government, Kállay found the terms offered by Dulles and Tyler unacceptable, and although he gave the same reply to the Americans as he had told the British through Barcza, yet the American plenipotentiaries were shocked to hear it. Kállay stuck to his plan. After another attempt by Chief of Staff Szombathelyi with the German General Headquarters – on January 24 in person and afterwards in writing – aiming at the return of the Hungarian troops had failed, Kállay, early in February, wrote Keitel, explaining to him that, if the Hungarian troops were withdrawn from the Eastern front, it might be that the Soviet army would not invade Hungary but would go round her on the north and the south. Finally, on February 12, Horthy wrote Hitler a letter requesting the return home of the Hungarian troops in order to prepare them for defence along the line of the Carpathians.

In the course of the next month, Kállay still made desperate attempts to carry through his conceptions. The most important move he ordered was another journey by László Veress to Istanbul. On February 18, 1944, the S.O.E. London headquarters informed the Foreign Office that, on the 23rd, László Veress would leave for Istanbul as a diplomatic courier to meet the S.O.E. men there. Veress had made it known to them that the 'Surrender Group' intended to enter into communication with the Soviet Union, a step in connection with which it requested the advice and assistance of the British. Major Threlfall asked the Foreign Office whether it had any official or unofficial question to put to Veress which he should convey to the Hungarian emissary.

Starting from the assumption that the Hungarians ought to know the British position, the Foreign Office did not wish to ask any question of a political nature. And since, before Veress's arrival, it could not be known what was hidden behind the plan of communicating with the Soviet Union, no preliminary decision was made. The suspicion arose that Kállay and company wanted to play off the Allies against one another. So, without knowing what the Hungarians would propose concretely, it was decided to wait for what Veress was to tell, and if indeed the Hungarians wished to enter into contact with the Soviet Union, it would be better to help them do it than to let them act alone.

It was towards the end of February, that Veress arrived at Istanbul with the following message: 1. The Hungarian Government wishes, through British intercession or independently, to get into touch with the Soviet Union in order to offer the capitulation of the Hungarian troops stationed at the Eastern front so that "the surrender should appear to be perfectly natural and to result from a hopeless military situation." 2. It wishes to offer to send to Tito's armed forces, with British help, foodstuffs and other supplies through the Muraköz.

In the Foreign Office, a memorandum was made of the offer. Drawing the conclusion that the Kállay Government's intention to approach the Soviet Union was only welcome, F. K. Roberts suggested that the British Government should take steps to start joint Anglo–Soviet negotiations with Hungary, to recommend Tito to accept the Hungarian offer, and finally to clarify with the Soviet Government the matter of sending an S.O.E. mission to Hungary.

Eden approved the suggestions, asked for the General Staff's opinion and instructed the British Ambassador in Moscow to inform the Soviet Government of the Hungarian offer and inquire whether it was willing to discuss it, in the presence of the British representative, with a Hungarian emissary. Finally he approved the sending of a British military party to Hungary during the lunar period in April. (Through radio the Foreign Ministry group had requested several times the dispatch of a British political mission. Once, Veress also asked for the sending to Budapest of Randolph Churchill, the British Prime Minister's son and personal representative at Tito's headquarters, who might possibly exert an influence on Horthy and prompt him to action. The answer was of course a flat refusal.)

Ullein-Reviczky in Stockholm was charged with a mission similar to that of Veress, but he could not establish direct contact with the Soviet Embassy, and talk with Councillor Semonov and Madame Kollontai, until after Hungary's occupation by Germany. According to the telegram of the U.S. Ambassador in Stockholm dated March 26, Ullein had told him earlier that four Hungarian divisions would attempt to return to Hungary from the Soviet front, and if they should fail in this action, 'they would join the Russians'.

At the same time with his diplomatic moves Kállay tried to win domestic public opinion over to his conceptions. On February 22, 1944, the Supreme Defence Council, with the participation of the Privy Councillors, discussed Kállay's new conception. At the discussion Bethlen came forth with the proposal that the Hungarian Government should suggest to Hitler that, simultaneously with the retreat of the Hungarian troops, this force together with the Germans should invade Southern Transylvania and keep it occupied to the end of the war. The whole conception of defence could be effective, argued Bethlen, if the entire line of the Carpathian range was controlled by the Hungarian army; in case of success they could kill two birds with one stone: Hitler would perhaps permit the Hungarian forces to be withdrawn, and the presence of the Hungarian army in Southern Transylvania might be regarded as an accomplished fact at the end of the war.

Bethlen's proposal elicited response from Horthy and others (and, as we shall see, an attempt was even made to carry it out seven months later, in September 1944), but it was proof that Bethlen was also incapable of sizing up the realities of the international situation. In view of the influence he excercised on Horthy, it is no exaggeration to say that Bethlen was one of those who bore a great responsibility for the state of inactivity and unpreparedness in which German occupation found Hungary.

With a view to 'internal mobilization' a large-scale propaganda campaign was launched under the pretext of the 50th anniversary of the death of Lajos Kossuth. (By the way, the celebration scheduled for the anniversary day did not take place because of the German occupation.) The Council of Ministers had laid down in a separate decision that the anniversary should be observed under the slogan of Hungarian independence, resistance, constitutionality and equality in rights, stressing in particular the role of the national army and defence against the pan-Slav menace. Now Kállay — as if it had not been counter-revolutionary Hungary who, in league with Germany, had invaded the Soviet Union — wished to create a sort of defensive patriotic atmosphere in the country. He wanted to launch a vast propaganda campaign addressed to foreign countries, in order to put Hungary in a favourable light before Anglo-Saxon public opinion.

On March 1, 1944, the Prime Minister outlined his conceptions in a letter addressed to the Hungarian diplomatic envoys in neutral states. He began by admitting that he had failed in the supposition that Anglo—American troops would reach this area before the Russians and that the future of Central and Eastern Europe would be determined by Anglo—American policy. "The partner we have counted upon has not put in an appearance." Then he proceeded: "We do not, of course, think in terms of dogmas, and we do not want to make our present attitude overrigid. But it must never be forgotten that, given the situation sketched at the beginning of this letter, a decision favorable to ourselves cannot come at the present moment. I am, however, convinced — although I do not overestimate the present tension between the Anglo-Saxons and Russia, nor expect a split between the Allies — that the Anglo-Saxon powers recognize that Russia constitutes a danger to them, both ideologically and as a power, and that if Russia won, her victory would be followed by collaboration between Russia and a new Germany ... If this were recognized, the East European question might perhaps be judged in a saner and more favorable light." The conclusion Kállay drew from this was the following: "Hungary must, therefore, gain time, for with time things will improve for us." What then, were the practical steps that the

Hungarian Prime Minister regarded as important? He saw the main task of Hungarian diplomacy in trying to make counter-revolutionary Hungary appear blameless in Western public opinion. A "very important aim of ours must be," he wrote, "to desprove the three chief charges leveled against Hungary: that her political and social system is feudal, antidemocratic and antisocial; that Hungary has oppressed the non-Magyars; that she multilated her neighbours' territory." At the end of his letter the Prime Minister stressed his conviction that the Hungarian army was able to defend the Carpathians against the advance of the Soviet army, unless the Soviet troops wanted to break through at any price (!).

What concrete facts did Kállay build his suppositions and hopes upon? None! The big transaction, the salvaging of the counter-revolutionary régime, in early 1944 could be conceived only in illusory plans. And illusory plans could be built only upon illusory premises.

3. The German occupation of Hungary

The 1943 events in Italy caused the Allies to hope, and Hitler to fear, that the Italian example might find followers. The Germans watched the developments in Hungary with particular attention, since through their security service they were quite accurately informed of Kállay's Western connections.

At a discussion on July 26, 1943, Hitler, with reference to the efforts of the Hungarian Government, said angrily: "We have to take care not to let nasty things happen in Hungary." During that summer the German military and political leaders decided to make preparations for the occupation of Hungary. This decision was only precipitated by the fact that, having decoded the cipher, they knew part of what had been discussed between Bakach-Bessenyey and Tyler. In the day following the Italian capitulation, the operations department of the German General Staff received instructions to prepare the plan of operations for the military occupation of Hungary. The draft was finished by September 30, 1943, and was headed 'Operation Margarethe'. (Later when the plan for Rumania's occupation was also ready, the Hungarian scheme was renamed Margarethe I, and the Rumanian version received the name of Margarethe II.)

The framers of the plan, considering the number of the available troops, started from the assumption that the occupation of Hungary and the disarmament of the Hungarian armies required co-operation from the Slovak and Rumanian armed forces, too. For the time being, however, they did not wish to let the interested Governments know about it. For the event of Hungary's occupation they proposed the creation of three independent zones of operations: 1. Western Hungary, including Budapest with the bulk of the Hungarian armed force; 2. Eastern Hungary, south and east of the Tisza river; 3. North Eastern Hungary, north of the Tisza. The task was divided: the occupation of the first zone was the task of the German forces, the second zone was to be occupied by Rumanian and the third by Slovak and German troops. Detailed proposals were worked out only for the first and the third zone, i.e. for the areas where the employment of German troops was envisaged. Eight days were considered necessary for the troop movements by rail and on foot. In addition to a description of the tactical execution of the operation, the proposal laid down as a general principle that the attitude towards the Hungarian army had to conform to the political situation. If disarmament was inevitable, the Hungarian forces of occupation serving at the Eastern front had to be utilized as labour battalions.

No date was set for the execution of the plan, and the reason for it may be found first of all in the overall war situation; the attention of the German High Command had at the time to be concentrated first of all on the growing problems of the Eastern front.

On November 1, 1943, the head of the operations department indicated his general agreement with the proposed plan. Besides demanding slight modifications, he pointed out that the Hungarian army was not to be disarmed but to be won over as it had happened in the case of Austria. The modified plan of occupation was submitted on November 7. An essential new trait was that, from the middle of December 1943, it considered the German army to be capable of carrying out the Margarethe operation by itself, with troops provisionally withdrawn from elsewhere. The draft pointed out that it was impossible to launch an armed action against Hungary and Rumania simultaneously. For this reason the political leadership should either preclude this possibility or ensure that occupation did not come up against organized armed resistance.

No decision was made on the new version of the plan of occupation. In view of the continuous worsening of the military situation, more and more forces had to be made available for the Soviet–German front. Thus the proposal of November soon became out of date.

In the meanwhile, on December 10, 1943, Veesenmayer had finished his report; this agent of Germany whom, in the autumn of 1943, the Wilhelmstrasse had again assigned to Budapest to study the situation in Hungary, stayed in this country as a manager of the Standard Works. "Every Hungarian," he wrote in his report, "either peasant or worker or soldier who reduces our burden through his activity strengthens the Führer's reserves in the Reich. Every Hungarian who bleeds for us reduces our blood sacrifice, strengthens our reserves for the purposes of the further conduct of the war." Veesenmayer deemed it absolutely necessary to solve the situation in Hungary, but gave expression to his conviction that the question called for a political rather than a military solution, because after Italy's capitulation the Hungarian attempts at defection had ceased, so Hungary represented no immediate danger to Germany. For this reason he suggested a solution by which the Hungarian state retained "certain sovereign rights". The main points of the report can be summed up as follows:

Urgent measures are needed against Hungary, but the time must be chosen suitably. Occupation is premature at this hour, it is better to take the necessary steps when the Soviet troops advance further, and when "the greater Bolshevist peril" has made the Hungarian leading circles ripe for negotiations. The most expedient solution would be to concentrate troops at different points of the Hungarian—German frontier and, in the meantime, to summon Horthy to Hitler, or to send to Budapest some Germans who could influence the Regent (Goering or Himmler). Generous treatment of Horthy must be alternated with strong-hand policy, and Horthy must be forced to dismiss the actual Government and to appoint a Prime Minister of Germany's choice. The German Legation in Budapest must be reorganized. A German plenipotentiary with wide powers must be delegated to Hungary. — At the same time, Veesenmayer, on the basis of a co-ordinated plan, proposed immediate measures concerning the Jewish question.

The events at the Eastern front — the crossing of the Dniester and also of the Prut at some places by the Soviet army — brought the possibility that the Soviet armed forces got to the Hungarian frontiers within reach. And in this case, if a turn should take place in Hungary, the collapse of the entire Balkan front would ensue. Late in January and early in February 1944, the German General Staff again revised Operation Margarethe. The execution of occupation was only precipitated by Horthy's letter of February 12 addressed to Hitler.

The German High Command again came to the conclusion that Germany possessed no sufficient reserve for the purpose of occupation, so on February 26—28, 1944, at the time of Antonescu's visit, Hitler informed the Rumanian dictator of the impending occupation of Hungary and of Rumania's possible involvement. Antonescu was pleased with the communication but made his participation subject to the immediate satisfaction of his territorial demands. Hitler therefore deemed it better to dispense with Rumanian participation. Antonescu's visit convinced him that there was no imminent danger of Rumania's desertion in any case. So Margarethe II could be set aside for the time being and all forces could be concentrated on Margarethe I.

On February 28, Hitler issued his instructions to elaborate the final version of Margarethe I in the light of the following considerations: 1. Deployment should take place, as far as possible, in Hungarian territory; 2. troop movements should be camouflaged as if made for other purposes; 3. the assaulting troops should be reinforced with parachute units, motorized and panzer formations, several police detachments and flyers; 4. the most important military and political targets should be marked out.

On February 29, the operations department of the Wehrmacht took the necessary measures. It instructed the Luftwaffe High Command to start preparations and gave the appropriate instruction to the S.S. It made arrangements for the supervision, influencing and, if need be, disarming of the Hungarian forces staying on the Eastern front.

The action was originally scheduled for the end of March, but on March 3, Hitler decided that this would be late, and urged the preparations. The General Staff was of the opinion that the troops could not be deployed before March 12, but the attack could then be started with only limited strength. At least another five days would be needed after the preparations had been made. Hitler approved this plan on March 4, 1944. That same day the concentration of troops began in the environs of Vienna. But the successful offensive of Soviet forces in the Tarnopol area (March 4) made further redeployment necessary. Part of the formations preparing for the invasion of Hungary were again dispatched to the Soviet front. They vere replaced by forces withdrawn from the troops of occupation in the West.

At Hitler's General Headquarters, on March 7, General Foertsch — who had been appointed commander of Operation Margarethe I — proposed the day of March 18, but finally it was decided that *Sunday,* March 19, was a more favourable date for the purpose. On March 8, the headquarters for the operations against Hungary was set up in Vienna. The orders issued on March 12 were for attack upon Budapest from four directions, emphasizing the necessity of disarming the Hungarian troops and breaking down all resistance. The offensive was to be launched by two divisions and various S.S. formations from the direction of the Banat, Újvidék and Osijek, by another two divisions from the West, from the area of Croatia and Slovenia. The main body was to start — unlike in the original plan — not from the south but from the north-west: three divisions including motorized and armoured units. And a few regiments were expected to come from Slovakia.

While the military preparations went on at full speed, a conference was held by Hitler with Ribbentrop and Himmler at Klessheim on the morning of March 15. Their decision considerably influenced the circumstances of occupation both militarily and politically. Namely the S.S. security service (S.D.) and the Wilhelmstrasse had not yet rejected entirely the solution proposed by Veesenmayer, and they submitted to Hitler a memorandum insisting that it would be better for Germany to try to seize power by the assistance of the firmly pro-German elements of Hungarian political quarters. Occupation ought to be used for this purpose. The memorandum, which allowed for Veesenmayer's proposal in all essential details, preferred the 'road of evolution' to military intervention. The latter might possibly entail the emergence of a defensive resistance front in Hungary; it would be impossible to form a Government, except one composed of bribed politicians, for Horthy would immediately resign; a state of military, political and economic chaos would follow, and a partisan struggle might unfold tying up large German military forces. The road of evolution, on the other hand, was expected to bring the following results: a pro-German Hungary would be internally consolidated; the national army and the police force would stand by and be available to the Reich; the total economic exploitation of the country would be secured; it would be possible to spare the deployment of a number of German divisions. According to the memorandum these advantages could be reaped by relatively simple means: Hitler should send a personal message to Horthy, and, "legalized by the Regent, a broad-based Government should be formed of the right wing of the Government party, the Party of Hungarian Revival, the Hungarian National Socialist Party and the Arrow-Cross Party."

At the conference of March 15 Hitler decided for a combination of invasion with the 'road of evolution' in an effort to obtain Horthy's consent to military occupation. Thereafter Ribbentrop immediately instructed Minister Jagow by telegram to call on Horthy that very same evening and tell him that Hitler was staying in the Obersalzberg, discussing military problems with heads of state of the allied countries; that Antonescu and Pavelić had already met Hitler, who now asked Horthy to visit him. Hitler would like to meet the Regent in the evening of the 17th or on the morning of the 18th, and they could discuss the questions mentioned in the Regent's letter of February 12.

On the evening of March 15, the German envoy requested an audience with the Regent, who was spending the evening in the Opera House, and conveyed Hitler's request to him. The next day, the Regent sent for Kállay, Ghyczy, Csatay and Szombathelyi and asked them to decide whether or not he should go to Hitler. They discussed the confidential news of German troop concentration around Vienna and other informations which confirmed the probability of German occupation, and passed a decision that the Regent with his retinue should go by train to Germany on the 17th. Before departure, however, Horthy took some precautions for the event of occupation and of his being detained. He had a telegram sent to the diplomatic envoys stationed in neutral states and instructed them, in case of occupation, to seek contact with the British and American Legations and to be at their service. On April 6, 1944, Otto of Habsburg wrote a memorandum to Roosevelt in which he informed the U.S. President that Horthy had supposedly sent him to Lisbon a document before his departure, investing him with full powers in case of occupation and asking him to take over as legitimate King of Hungary.

At the briefing session at noon on March 16, Hitler's General Headquarters could already divulge that the Regent of Hungary had accepted the invitation. On the evening of the same day Ribbentrop submitted to Hitler the letter of appointment making Veesenmayer the Reich's plenipotentiary in Hungary. This extremely important document, signed by Hitler on March 19, 1944, read as follows:

"1. The Reich's interests in Hungary shall in the future be taken care of by the Great German Reich's Plenipotentiary in Hungary, who will bear the title of minister.

"2. The Reich Plenipotentiary shall be responsible for any developments in Hungarian policy and will receive his instructions from the Foreign Minister of the Reich. His task will be, first of all, to promote the formation of a new Hungarian Government which resolves to retain its loyalty to the alliance under the Tripartite Pact until the final victory. The Reich Plenipotentiary shall provide this Government with authoritative advice and represent in contact with it all interests of the Reich.

"3. The Reich Plenipotentiary shall see to it that the entire administration of the country — including the time of the stationing there of German troops — is conducted by the Government under his direction, with the purpose of putting to maximum use all resources of the country, primarily its economic means, in the interest of the joint conduct of war.

"4. German civilian authorities of any kind functioning in Hungary can be established only in concert with the Reich Plenipotentiary; they shall be subordinated to him and manage their affairs under his direction.

"In order to discharge the tasks of the S.S. and police with the help of German forces in Hungary — primarily as regards the police aspects of the Jewish question — a high-ranking S.S. and police chief, who shall follow the Plenipotentiary's political instructions, shall be assigned to the staff of the Reich Plenipotentiary.

"5. As long as German troops are stationed in Hungary, the commander of these troops shall exercise military sovereignty in Hungary. The commander shall be subordinated to the Commander-in-Chief of the OKW (High Command of the Wehrmacht) and shall receive instructions from him.

"The commander of the troops shall furnish military protection for the interior areas of the country and against surprise attack from outside.

"He shall assist in the political and administrative tasks of the Reich Plenipotentiary, with whom he shall uniformly represent the demands of the Wehrmacht, especially in using the country for supplying provisions to German troops.

"In the civilian sphere the demands of the Wehrmacht shall be satisfied by the Reich Plenipotentiary.

"In case of emergency due to delay the commander of the German troops shall be authorized, also in the civilian sphere, to introduce measures necessary for the solution of military tasks. In respect of these he shall communicate as fast as possible with the Reich Plenipotentiary.

"In matters where their spheres of authority coincide, the Reich Plenipotentiary and the commander of the German troops shall co-operate most closely and co-ordinate the measures they intend to take.

"6. I appoint Party member Dr. Edmund Veesenmeyer to be Plenipotentiary and Envoy of the Great German Reich in Hungary"

The protocol which was to contain the results of the negotiations was drafted before the arrival in Germany of the Hungarian delegation. The draft said that the new Hungarian Government, which would be formed with the consent of the Germans, undertook to stand fast by Germany to the very end. The Government would be headed by Béla Imrédy, with Jenő Rátz as Minister of National Defence. The Germans asserted a right to designate the other members of the Government or to approve of their appointment. In order to assist the Government in and outside the country German troops would come to Hungary; the Government was to manage the affairs "in perfect agreement with the Reich Government," and the Reich Plenipotentiary would be appointed to supervise and assist it. In the future the Hungarian army would be under instructions from the German High Command. The draft protocol finally stated that the Regent would make an appeal to the Hungarian people, soldiers and authorities for a friendly welcome to be extended to the entering German troops.

On March 17, the German General Staff made a list of the military demands to be presented to the newly appointed Hungarian Government: 1. leading posts in the Hungarian army to be filled with pro-German officers; 2. the Hungarian army to be reorganized according to OKW instructions; 3. the Hungarian divisions of occupation stationed at the Eastern front to be subordinated direct to the Wehrmacht; 4. the Hungarian army command at Lemberg (Lvov) to be dissolved; 5. all sorts of military preparation on the Hungarian—Rumanian frontier to be stopped; 6. four or five reliable and combat-worthy divisions to be set up with German help; 7. a census to be taken of the population of military age and able to work, and additional Hungarian fighting and defensive units to be established for dispatch to the Eastern front and occasionally to

France or Istria; 8. war production and accordingly the exports of military equipment, petroleum and agricultural production to be increased; 9. the increased delivery obligations to be fulfilled reliably.

Horthy and his retinue arrived at Klessheim on the morning of March 18, 1944, and the negotiations started immediately in the spirit of the documents described above. Hitler exposed to Horthy his objections in plain words and said that Hungary's attempts at desertion "compelled him to take precautions". Horthy protested against the charge of desertion and asked whether Hitler's measures involved occupation by Germany. Hitler's answer in the affirmative was followed by a bitter altercation, then Horthy indignantly left the room.

When the talks were broken off, his retinue asked Horthy to resume the negotiations with Hitler in the afternoon. After a common lunch consumed in an awkward atmosphere, another two-hour conversation took place. Hitler insisted on occupation, while Horthy refused to consent. The talks were again broken off at 5:25 p.m., but in the meantime, at five o'clock, the orders were conveyed to the German formations to carry out Operation Margarethe I.

Horthy wanted to leave immediately after the afternoon talks, but Szombathelyi asked him not to depart as yet, because he, Szombathelyi, wished to talk once more with Hitler in order to clarify the situation. On the other hand, the Germans said that the Regent's special train could not leave because of an air alarm. Szombathelyi's conversation with Hitler lasted from 5:45 p.m. to 6:40 p.m. Hitler told the Hungarian Chief of Staff, who requested time for Horthy to make up his mind, that occupation was inevitable and he could afford no further delay, so much the more as he had already given the go-ahead signal.

Szombathelyi then met Ribbentrop in conference. The German Foreign Minister said all they requested from Horthy was to sign the joint communiqué according to which the German troops were marching into Hungary 'by mutual agreement'. But Horthy, being told about it, refused to sign the declaration on his consent.

Thereupon Szombathelyi and the Hungarian Minister in Berlin, Sztójay, persuaded Ribbentrop to arrange another meeting between Hitler and Horthy. The next, and at the same time the last, discussion began at 8:10 p.m. This time Hitler, in view of the fact that the German troops were already on their way to Budapest, promised to invite Antonescu immediately to dispatch his troops to the Eastern front, since now the Rumanian politician could no longer parry the German demand with reference to the fact that Hungary wanted to attack Rumania from the rear.

As concerns Horthy's attitude, the picture obtained from various sources is not entirely clear. But that no emphatic protest was made this time is supported by his further behaviour and by his statement made according to the records of the German General Staff: "... now he has completely understood Hitler's intentions and is willing to fulfil his demands." But the details were not precisely cleared away this time either. The General Staff records summarized the case in these terms: "Since the discussions took place in this manner, there was no possibility of presenting the military demands of the General Staff bureau; the prepared protocol could similarly not be signed."

Horthy's special train left for Budapest at 9:30 p.m. In the train Jagow went to see the Regent and let him know that he had just been relieved of his functions of Minister in Budapest, and that his successor, Veesenmayer, travelled by the same train. He then introduced Veesenmayer to Horthy. The newly appointed Minister immediately began to explain the German plans and said that Hitler expected the formation of a new Hungarian Government he could rely upon.

When Horthy and his retinue left Klessheim, the German High Command submitted to Hitler a few proposals concerning occupation. These suggested that the Germans should refrain from carrying out propaganda flights and dropping leaflets as well as taking over Buda Castle and the Citadel (but they deemed it necessary to march a guard of honour up to the Castle). With regard to the Hungarian army they recommended that the military formations should be held in barracks for the time being but should not be disarmed. The supply of weapons should be kept in the arsenals and possibly left intact, for they were already considered common property. It was suggested furthermore that the Regent's special train should not be stopped at the frontier. Hitler accepted the proposals.

The bulk of the German forces of occupation crossed the frontier at four o'clock on the morning of March 19, 1944. Advancing into Hungarian territory were three divisions from the direction of Belgrade, two divisions from Zagreb, two armoured divisions from the Vienna district and finally one motorized division from the area of Cracow. Parachutists were dropped successfully and were joined by the so-called transit land forces according to plan. Nowhere did the Germans come up against any considerable resistance, because the Hungarian Government – although it knew about the preparations of occupation – failed to take countermeasures even when Foreign minister Ghyczy's cipher telegram arrived, making known that occupation was imminent.

On the night of March 18, 1944, Interior Minister Keresztes-Fischer called on the Prime Minister and handed him the frontier police reports saying that at 9 p.m. German troops had crossed the western frontier of Hungary and were advancing in the direction of the capital. Before long another report came saying that German formations were invading the country from the southern and north-eastern frontiers, and military trains were rolling from all directions towards Budapest. Kállay and Keresztes-Fischer summoned the supreme military chiefs for an immediate conference where Count István Bethlen also was present.

The discussion started in the late hours. Kállay raised the idea of resistance, but the soldiers present – including the chief of counterintelligence, Gyula Kádár – found it militarily absolutely impossible.

Still before any plan could be outlined, József Bajnóczy, the deputy of the Chief of Staff, was handed a telegram in which Szombathelyi, while on the special train of the Regent, withdrew the Regent's military instruction issued before his departure and ordered his deputy not to enforce any military precaution until the Regent arrived in

Budapest, and to give the German troops an amicable welcome. This telegram put an end to the conference. The plan of an occasional armed resistance, which was not taken seriously anyway, was rejected definitively. The idea of alarming the population was also dropped. Kállay later, in his memoirs, tried to give as a reason for it that "they did not want to disturb the night's rest of the people."

This is how it happened that on March 19, 1944, the inhabitants of Budapest started up from their sleep listening to the rumbling of German tanks. And when the Regent's special train drew into Kelenföld station at 10 a.m. Kállay, who was waiting for the Regent accompanied by a German guard of honour, already reported to Horthy that all airfields and all points of junction and the most important communication centres were under German control. The only measure he could report having taken as Prime Minister was that he had given instructions to destroy the secret archives of the Prime Minister's Office, the Ministries of Foreign Affairs and National Defence as well as other ministries.

Hungary's occupation by German troops was thus carried out in *less than twelve hours,* so that the Government did not even symbolically attempt to defend the independence of the country, and the advance of the forces of occupation was not hampered by any considerable act of resistance.

The Gestapo units coming along with the occupation forces began making arrests already in the early morning of the 19th, and took over the buildings of the Hungarian public security authorities. They carried off hundreds of opposition leaders, public figures of the left wing, and adherents of pro-English political groups. They encircled the capital and did not let a single Jew slip through the ring. In the provincial towns they took hostages — mainly from among the rich Jews.

After Horthy's return, at noon on March 19 the Crown Council held a meeting where Horthy and the political and military leaders who had taken part in the Salzburg negotiations gave account of the events at Klessheim, and then the Kállay Government tendered its resignation. But the appointment of a new Government did not come at once, because Horthy was firmly against appointing Béla Imrédy, the German choice, Prime Minister. This delay filled the German leaders with alarm. This explains why Hitler, on March 22, gave orders to prepare for the military seizure of Buda Castle. An ultimatum was to be presented to Horthy to the effect that unless a Government to the liking of the Germans was formed before 6 p.m. on the 22nd, and unless a communiqué was issued stating that "... by common agreement German troops have arrived in Hungary", the Castle would be taken by force, the Hungarian army would be disbanded and reorganized under German command, leaving only two minor formations west of the Tisza.

No further armed action took place, however. The Germans accepted the appointment of Döme Sztójay as Prime Minister, so the new Government was formed on March 23, and a communiqué was published legalizing the presence of German troops in Hungary. The members of the Sztójay Cabinet were recruited from the extreme-right elements of the Government Party and from Imrédy's Party of Hungarian Revival. (Imrédy joined the Government, as a sort of 'Chief Minister of Economics', on

May 23.) The National Socialist Party was represented by László Baky as Secretary of State for the Interior. The composition of the Government did not entirely suit the German conceptions, but the Germans were confident that, later on, they would manage to have other trusted men of theirs included in the Government.

In his first telegram addressed to the Hungarian diplomatic envoys abroad, Sztójay described his programme as follows: "The new Government headed by me will follow and effectuate the domestic policy of Gyula Gömbös, and in foreign policy, faithful to the obligations under the Tripartite and Anti-Comintern Pacts, it will most cordially foster Hungarian—German good relations on the basis of our traditional friendly loyalty to the German Reich and relying on our brotherhood in arms. . . . The first task of the Government will be to organize and maintain internal order in the country and to organize, and take part in, the struggle against Bolshevism."

The envoys accredited to neutral states — with the exception of Minister Vörnle in Ankara — refused to subscribe this programme, and although Regent Horthy kept his seat, after March 19, they contacted their British and U.S. counterparts in accordance with earlier instructions and offered them their services. They sought contact with one another with a view to constituting a sort of 'Hungarian Committee' representative of independent Hungary and obtaining for it recognition under international law. On March 25, Andor Wodianer, the Minister in Lisbon, dispatched a circular telegram to his colleagues proposing the formation of a Committee of Liberation and recommending Tibor Eckhardt as chairman, since Otto of Habsburg's person met with great international antipathy. (Otto in his letter of April 6 to Roosevelt suggested the chairmanship of János Pelényi, the ex-Minister in Washington.) In mid-March, Ullein-Reviczky issued a circular telegram, proposing the foundation of an organization to be called National Movement of Free Hungarians which, as he wrote, would not later intend to form an émigré Government but would try to promote the liberation of the country.

The Department of State in Washington and the Foreign Office in London supported the efforts of the diplomatic representatives of Hungary inasmuch as they wanted to launch jointly an effective action of some kind in order to organize resistance, but they were against the idea of setting up an émigré organization. They were especially suspicious of the manoeuvring of Otto and Eckhardt. Instructions in this sense were sent out to the diplomatic missions of the Allied Powers, emphasizing that the Hungarian diplomats should be given to understand that Hungary would be judged in the future exclusively by how far the Hungarian people at home realized the possibility and necessity of resistance.

Weeks went by, and the diplomats were busy organizing the committee instead of organizing effective anti-German actions, and since there was no serious indication of resistance in Hungary either, their initiatives met with growing disillusionment. Finally the dissenting envoys were informed that no kind of committee would be recognized, but it would be well for the Hungarian diplomats openly to stand up against the Germans and their Hungarian lackeys.

German military and political quarters continued to discuss the question of the Hungarian army even after the formation of the Sztójay Government. There were some who insisted on having the army disarmed, while others — Veesenmayer in the first place — were against the idea, arguing on the one hand that it would be difficult in this way to maintain the "semblance of the exercise of sovereignty", and on the other hand that the Hungarian army could be employed on the Eastern front. On March 26, Horthy urged Veesenmayer to lift the Hungarian troops' confinement to the barracks and threatened even to resign but promised to mobilize the available forces "for the beating of Bolshevism" in case "Hungarian troops are treated in the spirit of the traditional brotherhood in arms". The dispute was decided primarily by the further Soviet advance. On March 28, at a conference held at the German General Headquarters — attended by Ribbentrop, Himmler and Keitel, the OKW chief — Hitler decided that the Hungarian army should not be disarmed but the deployment of Hungarian units should proceed only gradually, in order to control them without engaging major German forces. Veesenmayer's position thus prevailed and it was soon justified. The dispatch of Hungarian divisions proceeded rapidly to the Eastern front, where some were used for discharging duties of occupation, while the larger part of them were thrown into battle against the advancing Soviet army. In the meantime the Germans carried out a purge among Hungarian military leaders, forcing Horthy to consent to these changes in the personnel. In higher, responsible positions they tolerated only pro-German officers. Not only was the highest military leadership brought under German control, but German officers and so-called liaison staffs were assigned to the lower military authorities.

After March 19, 1944, the invaders got all the fields of political and economic life under control. The real master of the country was Reich Plenipotentiary Veesenmayer. Already on March 20, leading officials of the German Foreign Ministry, Schmidt, Rühle, Six and Benzler, came to Budapest to assist him. Six and Schmidt prepared the programme of cultural occupation which was then carried out by the competent Hungarian authorities. Cultural regimentation was marked, for example, by an auto-da-fé of banned books and periodicals under the direction of government commissioner Mihály Kolozsvári-Borcsa. Benzler became the chief economic adviser in Veesenmayer's staff, and his personnel included all kinds of liaison officers for aircraft production, arms manufacture, labour supply, etc., whose task was to promote the total exploitation of Hungarian large-scale industry for the purposes of Germany.

On April 1, the Germans appointed a special representative "to guide armament and war production in Hungary". The idea was to expand the common programme of the manufacture of war equipment, ammunition and aircraft, and to extend it to cover other branches, too. It was decided to carry 50,000 labourers for work in Germany as soon as possible and to add to this number a great part of the agricultural labour reserve.

The unbounded claims of various German economic organizations and ministries for the best possible and short-term utilization of the Hungarian economy jeopardized the order of exploitation, so it became necessary to work out uniform directives. A conference on this subject was held by Hitler on April 15, with the participation of Speer, Funk, Ribbentrop and Veesenmayer among others, and they adopted a decision of principle. This was followed by a consultation about the principles of Hungarian economic policy, arranged in the German Foreign Ministry on April 19. Here it was agreed that none of Germany's important war interests should be disregarded because of the threat of Hungarian inflation, and it was to be ensured only that inflation did not become excessively rapid. Hungarian agriculture was to be subordinated fully to the needs of Germany, and everything possible was to be extracted from it. Raw material production was to be increased to the maximum. Hungarian industry was to be changed into a complement of German war production. The German leaders again declared that they would not pay for the Hungarian deliveries, so the overdraft credit was to be raised to 120 million *pengős* a month. In addition, they demanded that manpower should be directed to Germany in large numbers. They contemplated first of all the dispatch of Jewish forced labourers to Germany. On June 2, the German and Hungarian Governments signed two agreements. One was for the establishment of a so-called Hungarian war fund, intended to cover the expenses of occupation and war investments. The other provided for the increase of war material production for the German army at the expense of the Hungarian treasury.

Coming to Budapest along with the Wehrmacht units of occupation was the special detachment of S.S. Oversturmbannführer Adolf Eichmann, authorized to take measures directly, independently of the Hungarian Government, and to issue instructions to the Jewish Council already from the first day of occupation. In charge of handling the 'Jewish affairs' in conjunction with the Eichmann group was Department XII of the Ministry of the Interior under the direction of Secretary of State László Endre. Its decrees were prepared on the basis of advice from a 'specialist' of the S.S. security service (S.D.). Members of the Sztójay Government went along with the German demands without reservation. The torrent of anti-Jewish regulations began with the Cabinet meeting of March 29. Horthy, though disapproving of Jew-baiting, wished the least of all to stand up against the Germans in this question, and allowed the Government a free hand. It was the Hungarian police and gendarmerie who carried off the Jews into ghettoes and concentration camps in accordance with the directives of the S.D. officers. The result of their activity was the deportation of 450,000 Hungarian Jews.

The German occupation of Hungary wholly delivered the country to Nazi Germany. It made possible the total depredation of Hungary. German occupation, the introduction of totalitarian Fascist methods severely tried and further confused the forces of the anti-Fascist resistance movement and its organizations. It became extremely difficult to organize resistance. The leftist parties which had functioned legally until then — the Social Democratic Party, the Smallholders' Party and the Peasant Party — were dissolved according to Interior Minister Jaross's decree of March 29. These parties had been unprepared for the thwarting and even for the eventuality of German occupation. So their organizations and connections ceased to exist; following

German occupation the only organized force of resistance left was the underground Communist Party. The main purpose of the measures of terror was precisely to intimidate the Hungarian people and to make them give up any idea of resistance. The distribution of some Jewish property coupled with social demagogy was aimed at corrupting part of the masses, making them participants in the spreading of vandalism and pogroms. This effort, however, failed to bring the desired result. There were a great many people, especially in the capital, who bravely went to the rescue of the prosecuted, gave them shelter, saving thereby the lives of thousands of innocent people.

Highly instrumental in the absence of an armed uprising, in the weakness of Hungarian resistance, was the circumstance that occupation in Hungary — for the already outlined reasons — took a specific form in which the functions of occupation could be exercised 'indirectly'. Horthy undertook to maintain the semblance of legal continuity, he himself appointed the Sztójay Government and kept his post as Regent, even though he withdrew from any active public role for a time; after a few weeks' hesitation the Hungarian army continued fighting on the side of Germany against the Soviet Union; the older Horthyite state apparatus, except for the change of personnel higher up, functioned uninterruptedly. The terror, the deportations, the total subordination of the national economy were effected by the authorities of occupation mostly with the help and participation of the Hungarian administrative apparatus. The German invaders thus kept relatively in the background. The negative effect of these circumstances upon the resistance movement made itself felt not so much in Budapest and the major towns but rather in the countryside, where the organs of state power and public administration (gendarmerie, magistracies, etc.) remained mostly intact in their composition.

Realizing this, the Allied Powers continued to regard Hungary as a vassal state and not as an occupied country. On May 12, 1944, the Governments of the United States, Great Britain and the Soviet Union issued a declaration in which they categorically condemned the activity of the Hungarian Government, but stated at the same time that Hungary might reduce her own losses, shorten the struggle and contribute to the victory of the United Nations by withdrawing from the war and stopping all cooperation with the Germans. But if she continued fighting further, she would incur disastrous consequences and be faced with the most severe terms of armistice. Therefore, it was stressed in the declaration, Hungary must decide in time whether to continue the war against the United Nations.

Following the German occupation the Hungarian Communists appealed to all strata of the nation, to the leaders of the anti-Fascist parties already forced underground, for national union, for a fight for freedom, for popular resistance. The Party formulated the principal task ahead of the anti-Hitler forces in a single phrase: 'Death to the German invaders!' German occupation, the failure of Kállay's policy, the necessity of saving the nation all acted to convince the leaders of the suppressed political parties still at liberty but driven underground that only a union proposed by the Communists could mobilize the best forces of the nation for the fight against the Germans and their

Hungarian puppets. Thus in May 1944, as a result of many years' tireless activity of the Communists, there came into being the central militant organization of anti-Fascist national resistance: the Hungarian Front. The Hungarian Front addressed to the people of Hungary a manifesto calling for a new fight for independence, a new popular war against the German Fascists and their Hungarian hirelings. The manifesto was signed by the parties assembled in the Hungarian Front: the Communist Party (by the name of Peace Party), the Social Democratic Party, the Independent Smallholders' Party, and an organization called the Blood Association of the Apostolic Cross, which rallied certain pro-Western groups of the bourgeoisie. The Hungarian Front was later joined by the National Peasant Party, and its work was supported by the trade unions and some representatives of the Christian Churches.

The establishment of the Hungarian Front, the effect of its manifesto, and the policy of German Fascists and Hungarian quislings which doomed the country to depredation, to complete annihilation, roused the masses, chiefly the workers and toiling peasants, to resistance.

Resistance was growing among the anti-German wing of the petty bourgeoisie and the bourgeoisie as well. Part of them supported the activity of the Hungarian Front and others brought to life various anti-German underground organizations. Still in May, the Hungarian Front established contact with the Allied Powers through Turkey.

The large-scale Allied landings in Northern France on June 6, 1944, and not much later, the beginning of the great summer offensive of the Red Army made it certain that the total defeat of Germany was only a matter of time. In this situation, Horthy also turned a more attentive ear to the increasingly strong protests against deporting the Jews by the Pope, the International Red Cross, and the King of England. Roosevelt's statement of June 26 also reached Budapest. Roosevelt threatened to start heavy bombing raids on the Hungarian capital unless the persecutions and deportations ceased at once. At the end of June 1944, Horthy received a lengthy memorandum from István Bethlen, who was hiding from the Gestapo in the provinces. Bethlen tried to convince the Regent that he should dismiss the Sztójay Government forthwith, because Hungary's further submission to the Germans, the continued persecution of Jews, the increasing bread-and-butter worries of the population, the growing war losses would "inevitably create a hotbed of Bolshevism in Hungary". Bethlen recommended the nomination of a caretaker Government which should appoint only reliable men to leading posts, and which would continue the war until the fightings could "be honestly liquidated", and in the meanwhile it should restore the sovereignty of the country, restrict its financial and economic subservience to Germany, and put a stop to the persecution of Jews. The memorandum outlined the momentary difficulties and therefore stressed that the new Government should be appointed and the decisive steps should be taken when, on the one hand, the success of the Allied invasion of Western Europe and the crushing attacks of the Soviet army made the military situation of Germany so serious that the Germans would no more be able to launch military counteractions, and, on the other hand, the Hungarian army could still be put in a position to turn against the Germans in case of need. Bethlen made detailed proposals also for the personal composition of the new Government and for the necessary domestic measures to be taken.

Events of the coming weeks showed that Horthy in fact acted upon Bethlen's advice, but in the course of execution he gave clear evidence of so great suggestibility, so poor political abilities, such diplomatic impotence and mediocrity that, even in the eyes of his closest followers, his behaviour smashed to smithereens the slightest elements left of his fast withering reputation built up artificially for the past twenty-five years.

At the Crown Council meeting of June 26, Horthy demanded that Baky and Endre should be dismissed and the deportation of the Jewry of Budapest should be denied. The next day, however, the Council of Ministers decided only to ask the Germans for permission to accept the offer of various foreign agencies to receive a certain number of Hungarian Jews. Early in July, the Regent took military countermeasures to foil the gendarmerie in its attempted coup engineered by Baky and to forestall the carrying off of Budapest Jewry, but he tolerated the deportation of the Jewish population of the outskirts of Budapest. On July 6, he told Veesenmayer that Sztójay had not come up to the expectations; he demanded that Hitler should withdraw the Gestapo from the territory of Hungary with as little delay as possible, but he promised at the same time that, considering the war situation, he was ready to fight with all his might on the side of the Germans against Bolshevism. In the course of the next eight to ten days, he decided even twice to relieve Sztójay of his office and to appoint Colonel-General Géza Lakatos Prime Minister, but he backed down on both occasions. On July 17, he wrote Hitler a letter asking the withdrawal of the German forces of occupation, the S.S. commandos and the Gestapo from the territory of Hungary; at the same time he announced his intention to appoint a new Government. But before he could have dispatched the letter, Veesenmayer handed him Hitler's message trying by most violent threats to stop Horthy from dismissing the Sztójay Government. In any action taken against the Government in office, Hitler wrote, he saw a repudiation of the agreement of March 19. If such a move should be made, he would recall Veesenmayer and put into force much measures which would definitively prevent similar events from taking place again. He threatened to publish "the proofs of betrayal" (the material of Hungary's negotiations with the Anglo-Saxon Powers), which "would act upon the appreciation of the historical role of the Regent". He bandied threats that he would have caught and executed those who stimulated Horthy to form a new Government, and demanded the immediate effectuation of the deportation of Budapest Jewry. The threats scared Horthy. Thus Sztójay remained, and the Regent even left Endre and Baky in their posts.

Although the July 20 attempt on Hitler's life was a clear sign that internal conflicts raged in Germany and part of the General Staff had turned against the Führer, Horthy still did not dare to decide but definitely rejected the plan of a purely military Government. He invited Sztójay to form a 'Government of national unity' but this met with failure owing to the conflicts in the ranks of the extreme right. Early in August Imrédy and company retired from the Government, and the disintegration of the Government party began.

4. Horthy's attempt at defection. The 15th of October, 1944

In the beginning of August 1944, the next great offensive of the Soviet army got as far as the line of the Carpathians. What Horthy and his followers had dreaded for a long time now came to pass: the Soviet army was at the Hungarian frontiers, and the Anglo—American forces were hopelessly far away. While the Regent of Hungary could not do but dream about how to secure the Anglo—American occupation of Hungary, on August 23, at the same time with the Soviet breakthrough at Iași—Kishinev, Antonescu's government was arrested in Bucharest, Rumania asked for an armistice, and her army turned on the Germans.

Rumania's desertion of the camp of Nazi Germany was, both from the political and military points of view, of extremely great consequence to Hungary. The military conception that the Soviet Army might be held up at the Carpathians until 'Hungary's position became more favourable' fell through: the Soviet forces saw the way open for crossing the Southern Carpathian line, so they could advance into Hungarian territory. Of no lesser importance from the political point of view was the fact that Rumania had got ahead of Hungary in withdrawing from the war. The King of Rumania's emissary, Prince Stirbey, arrived at an agreement with a representative of the Soviet Government on April 12, 1944. The terms of armistice presented to Stirbey and drawn up by the Soviet Government in concert with the Western Allies promised Rumania the reannexation of Northern Transylvania. However, the definitive armistice, which representatives of the Allied Powers and Rumania signed in Moscow on September 12, 1944, still left open some possiblity for Hungary in case she would act in due time. Article 19 of the armistice agreement provided that the Allies considered the Vienna Award of 1940 null and void and agreed that Transylvania (or a larger part of it) should be returned to Rumania if this provision was confirmed by the treaty of peace.

On August 24, 1944, under the impact of the events in Rumania, Horthy at last decided to appoint a new Government. First he discussed with Veesenmayer, whom he assured that, in spite of the Rumanian events, Hungary would continue fighting on the side of Germany. At the same time, he requested that, since the Carpathian front line had become longer and it could not be held by the Hungarian troops alone, German formations should take up positions at the Carpathians. Both Horthy and Veesenmayer were satisfied with the discussions, for both felt that they had gained time. Veesenmayer was convinced that no immediate turn was to be expected in Hungary, and Horthy was of the opinion that the Soviet forces might be contained with German help for a while at the Carpathians, and in the meantime he could take steps to resume contact with the Western Powers. In the afternoon of August 24, he compelled Sztójay, who was ill in hospital at the time, to sign his resignation, and soon thereafter he commissioned Géza Lakatos to form a Government. He set the new Government the task of restoring Hungary's sovereignty, putting an end to the persecution of Jews, and preparing Hungary's withdrawal from the war. The Lakatos Government, however, was not definitively formed until August 29. After some bargaining with Veesenmayer the trusted men of the Germans, Reményi-Schneller and Jurcsek, retained their portfolios. The new Foreign Minister was General Gusztáv Hennyey.

In the meantime, on August 25, the Sztójay Government still in office had held a meeting, presided over by Reményi-Schneller, to discuss the military and political situation created by the volte-face in Rumania. At this Cabinet meeting Mihály Jungerth-Arnóthy, the Permanent Deputy Foreign Minister, reported in detail on the messages received from the West, which prompted Hungary to quick action and called attention to "how fatal it would be for Hungary if, after Rumania's defection, she attacked this neighbour in order to take Southern Transylvania". The situation analysis, with reference to Western information, concluded that "the Anglo—Saxons would like the Hungarians to hold up the Russians until the Anglo—Saxons occupied Hungary," but the defences should not be mounted in foreign soil. Finally the Council of Ministers took the position that "if by any chance we still have the necessary military strength, the Germans should march down to defend the frontiers of Southern Transylvania, and we should, with our available forces, defend our eastern frontiers, down to the southernmost corner of the Székely countries". The final decision was to be taken after consultation with the Germans.

The Lakatos Government practically accepted Jungerth-Arnóthy's situation analysis, namely that the Soviet and Rumanian forces must be contained until Anglo—American troops arrived in Hungarian territory, and the armistice should be concluded as far as possible with the Western Powers. It was on these premises that the Government decided on the military issues and made an attempt to open armistice negotiations.

For lack of adequate sources it is difficult to know how far the above situation analysis was based on effective information and how far did it merely reflect pipedreams about Western views regarding Hungary. There is no doubt that, following the landing in Normandy, Churchill wished to carry out, instead of the diversionary landing in Southern France as had been resolved in Teheran, the advance of the Allied troops through Istria and Ljubljana towards Vienna and Budapest. This possibility was indeed brought up at Teheran as an alternative, and now the British Prime Minister found that the time had come to go on with it. At the end of June 1944, Churchill sought to convince Roosevelt by political and military arguments and to obtain his consent. However, the President was not willing to downgrade the landing in Southern France, and he wrote Churchill: "I cannot agree to the employment of United States troops against Istria and into the Balkans. ... For purely political reasons over here, I should never survive even a slight setback in 'Overlord' if it were known that fairly large forces had been diverted to the Balkans."

On July 2, Roosevelt finally decided for landing in the south of France at the earliest possible date. Churchill had to yield, and the landing in Southern France started, though several weeks later than scheduled, on August 15. Barely two weeks later, however, the proposed action against the Ljubljana gap, under the so-called Alexander plan, was brought up again.

Faced with dwindling military chances, in the summer of 1944, Churchill already contemplated the possibility of a political compromise with the Soviet Union. His tactics were based on the admission that Great Britain would sooner or later have to recognize Soviet influence over certain areas in order to get in exchange Soviet recognition for British interests in the Mediterranean countries. Already in April-May 1944, when the Red Army was approaching Rumania's frontiers, Churchill proposed that the Soviet Union should seize the initiative in Rumania, and England in Greece. Shortly afterwards he suggested that Bulgaria should come under Soviet influence, and Yugoslavia under the influence of Great Britain. For the reasons already mentioned, the U. S. Government rejected Churchill's suggestions, therefore Roosevelt informed the British Prime Minister that the United States did not think it desirable to establish exclusive zones of influence in the Balkans and in South Eastern Europe. A few days later, however, he deferred to Churchill's will and accepted his proposal for a trial period of three months: the initiative to bringing about an armistice was, in some countries, to be taken by the Soviet Union and in others by England.

On August 9, 1944, Eden, in his memorandum prepared for his Government concerning the European policy of the Soviet Union and dealing with Central Europe, dwelt on the situation of Hungary, too. He stated that since Soviet–Czechoslovak relations were excellent, and since Austria would be probably occupied by Western troops, Hungary had a key role to play with regard to the consolidation of the Central European positions. "There was some risk of conflict between British and Soviet policy in Hungary," he wrote. The Foreign Secretary saw this contingency in two points: the territorial question (Transylvania) and the question of Hungary's internal development since "there was a danger of revolutionary developments in Hungary similar to the excesses of the Béla Kun régime after the first war. The Soviet Government would not necessarily encourage such developments but might find it difficult not to support them."

To influence the events in Hungary, the British, besides urging the Alexander plan, sought to take the initiative in the matter of the armistice to be concluded with Hungary. On August 11, 1944, the British Government sent a memorandum to Washington and Moscow, proposing that on behalf of the three Allied Powers the European Advisory Council should discuss the armistice terms to be presented to Hungary, because the settlement of the Hungarian question could not be separated from the fate of Rumania.

The United States accepted the proposal on August 15, and instructed its Ambassador in London to sumbit to the Advisory Council the American plan drawn up in July. This plan consisted of two parts. The first, entiled "The problem", exposed the matter on the basis of the earlier commitments of the Allied Powers, the aims of the anti-Fascist war, and the declarations described above. Part two contained the armistice terms, defining in paragraph (*a*) the obligations of Hungary. (Evacuation of the occupied territories, including Transylvania; the Allied Powers' right of occupation and the conditions of occupation; the maintenance of order; prisoners of war; reparations and indemnities; economic reconstruction.) Paragraph (*b*) enumerated the possible concessions in case Hungary would desert Germany in time, set up a democratic Government and fight against the Germans on the side of the Allies. (Independence and international status; total or partial omission of occupation; more equitable Rumanian–Hungarian frontiers to be drawn by the treaty of peace.) This part specially emphasized that if capitulation should take place when the final defeat of Germany was imminent, these possible concessions could not be counted upon.

Barely a few days after the Rumanian about-face of August 23, which entailed a substantial change in the military and political situation of the entire Danubian basin, Field Marshal Alexander's summer offensive started in Italy. This was Churchill's last military hope for getting through the Ljubljana gap towards the Danube. Although he was aware that his armed strength—considering that a good part of the troops he had destined for this section of the front were fighting in Southern France — made this possibility very precarious, yet on August 28, he wrote Roosevelt with great enthusiasm: "I have never forgotten your talks to me at Teheran about Istria, and I am sure that the arrival of a powerful army in Trieste and Istria in four or five weeks would have an effect far outside purely military values. Tito's people will be awaiting us in Istria. What the condition of Hungary will be then I cannot imagine, but we shall at any rate be in a position to take full advantage of any great new situation." Roosevelt wrote in his reply on August 31: "We can renew our Teheran talk about Trieste and Istria at 'Octagon'." (Octagon was the cover term for the Quebec conference held between the 11th and the 19th of September, 1943.)

It is hardly probable that Horthy and company obtained reliable information about the British plans concerning South-Eastern Europe at this stage, but it may be that some details — particularly those which could support Horthy's views — had reached Budapest, indirectly and inaccurately, through various diplomatic channels, first of all through the dissident diplomats. In any case this seems to be verified by the fact that on August 28, 1944, Horthy sent a message to ex-Minister in Berne Bakach-Bessenyey — who, after his resignation, remained in contact with his Western negotiating partners and on August 26 had offered his good offices to the Regent — that he should, as a representative with full powers, start negotiations with the emissaries of the Western Powers; that he should tell them that there were no fighting formations beyond the frontiers, and the forces of occupation were on their way home. (As can be seen, the Regent still clung to his — mildly speaking — strange opinion that the occupation forces were not to be regarded as being engaged in hostilities against the Soviet Union.) Finally Horthy requested Bessenyey not to raise any territorial question, because what mattered now was "independence with democratic guarantees". Barcza was also contacted and given similar instructions; the Lisbon line was resumed in order to enter into communication with Otto of Habsburg and Tibor Eckhardt. The contact was re-established early in September. As appears from British and American sources, similar messages were dispatched to Stockholm and Turkey, too. The real aim of this feverish search for contacts did not escape the attention of the Westerners. The object pursued by Horthy and company was, as we read in a British Foreign Office note, to play off the Anglo–Saxon Powers against Russia.

The British, who hastened to seize the initiative in the question of the Hungarian armistice, immediately informed the Hungarian emissaries that Hungary must surrender to *three* Allied Powers. The U. S. Ambassador in Berne, Leland Harrison, also told Bessenyey that the Allies were willing to negotiate only on the platform of unconditional surrender and that the Soviet Union could by no means be left out of the agreements. The American diplomats accredited to neutral states were instructed to make it known to the Hungarian representatives that if Hungary had seriously resolved to sue the Allies for an armistice, she had to delegate a plenipotentiary or a commission with full powers to sign the protocol. On August 29 Bessenyey wired this to the Government, and the next day he demanded, by telegram again, to be authorized to apply for armistice terms, including the obligation to disarm the German troops in Hungary.

On September 1, the British Government requested the Governments of the Soviet Union and the United States to inform the Hungarians that the three Allied Powers were ready to present the terms of armistice to Horthy's plenipotentiary and the negotiations might take place in Italy. The U. S. Secretary of State on September 2 accepted the British proposal with the modification that, for geographical and other reasons, it would be better to choose Ankara as the venue of negotiations. He informed the Soviet Government accordingly. At the same time, Secretary of State Hull insisted that, on the basis of the above-mentioned American proposals, the European Advisory Council should discuss the terms of a Hungarian armistice as soon as possible. The Soviet reply came on September 20, when Deputy Foreign Minister Vyshinsky informed the Allies of the Soviet Government's agreement that Horthy should be given to know that the Allies were ready to present their terms to his plenipotentiary. He stated at the same time that the place of the talks could be designated later.

When Vyshinsky's letter was handed to the British and U. S. Ambassadors in Moscow, the contact between Horthy's emissaries and the Soviet Union had already been established. In the meanwhile, however, substantial changes had occurred in Hungary and in the Danubian basin.

Although the first Cabinet meeting of the Lakatos Government decided to continue fighting against the Soviet Union, yet the Germans waited with suspicion for what the new Government was up to. Therefore, on August 31, Hitler sent Colonel-General Guderian, the Chief of Staff, to Budapest to find out Hungary's probable intentions and to encourage Horthy to continue the struggle by the side of Germany. Guderian promised the Regent to bring home the Hungarian cavalry division fighting in Poland and to send new German troop reinforcements. Under the effect of the promises Horthy and the Government decided for an attack on Southern Transylvania in order to join battle against the Soviet and Rumanian forces on the line of the Carpathians. They resolved at the same time to appeal to the Western powers to send two or three airborne divisions to Hungary. The Foreign Minister — who knows why — entertained the belief that the Anglo—American armies were just landing in Dalmatia.

That is why on September 1, Horthy, instead of sending an authorization, informed Bessenyey of this change and added that in the question of the armistice he was willing to negotiate only with the Western Powers. In the first days of September, the 2nd Hungarian army was reconstituted from different infantry and motorized divisions, and on September 5, it intruded into Southern Transylvania. But the desperate gamble failed. The poorly equipped army composed mainly of reserve troops advanced at a snail's pace, while the Soviet and Rumanian forces, with a swift move on September 6, began to traverse the passes of the Southern Carpathians and proceeded towards Lugoj, Timişoara and Sibiu.

When Horthy received news of the advance of Soviet and Rumanian forces across the Southern Carpathians and waited in vain for the arrival of the Anglo—Saxon troops, he resolved, with an aching heart, though, to take steps towards the conclusion of an armistice. Therefore, on September 7, he summoned trusted members of the Cabinet and told them that he intended to ask the Allies for an armistice. It had long been anything but a secret to Horthy or to the other participants of this consultation that the basis of an armistice could be nothing else but unconditional surrender, yet they agreed on the following points to be pressed at the armistice negotiations: 1. The Allies to occupy only the main strategic points of the country; 2. Rumanian and Yugoslav troops not to take part in the occupation of Hungary; 3. the Hungarian police and administrative apparatus to be left in their places after the armistice, too; 4. the Allies to allow the German forces to leave Hungary unhindered. Horthy again stressed that at a given time he would inform the Germans of his request for an armistice, because he was under an obligation of loyalty to his ally.

These shocking and entirely unsubstantial decisions did not at all put an end to the tragi-comedy. The participants of the discussion were now seized with constitutional scruples: they wondered whether they were entitled to ask for an armistice and deemed it very essential to obtain either the approval of the National Assembly or at least the consent of the entire Government. Accordingly Horthy convened the Crown Council for the evening hours.

Still before the meeting of the Crown Council, Foreign Minister Hennyey instructed the competent department of his Ministry to prepare the necessary papers, and sent Bessenyey the following telegram: "Very urgent! We shall do our best tomorrow, the 8th, to take steps to conclude an armistice. Appropriate concrete instructions will follow." But nothing followed, because the decision of the Crown Council practically meant the postponement of the armistice. The Council heard Horthy's communications relating to the request for an armistice and accepted his suggestions. At this point, however, Horthy himself began to raise difficulties. What he was brooding over was not what practical steps to take to bring about the armistice, but in what manner to inform the Germans of his resolution, because "he made this a point of honour".

Finally they accepted a formula devised by Defence Minister Csatay, who proposed the dispatch of an ultimatum to the German High Command. In it they stated that unless the Germans sent five armoured divisions within 24 hours to hold up the Soviet advance in Southern Transylvania, Hungary would be compelled to solicit an armistice, for without such assistance she was unable to defend herself.

Prime Minister Lakatos and General János Vörös (who had been appointed Chief of Staff in Szombathelyi's stead on March 22) forwarded the ultimatum to Veesenmayer and Military Attaché Greiffenberg that same night. Vörös wrote a separate memorandum to Guderian as well, giving his military reasons for the request. And Horthy wrote a letter to Hitler, letting the Führer know that unless he was given military assistance, he would conclude an armistice. It could not be doubted that, in this situation the Germans would promise to render assistance until they could find another solution. This is what the large majority of the Ministers attending the Crown Council meeting must have counted upon, and this was obviously what Horthy himself counted upon, or rather he was firmly determined only on one question, namely that he would not surrender to the Soviet army as long as there was a faint glimmer of hope that the German reinforcements would enable him to contain the Soviet advance until the arrival of the requested Anglo—Saxon troops. Indeed, still on the night of the 7th, Veesenmayer promised that Germany would send reinforcements to Hungary, and that the next day he would specify what German forces could be reckoned with.

On September 8, the Council of Ministers met again. Lakatos gave account of the results of his talk with Veesenmayer and called upon the Cabinet members to take a stand on the subject of the armistice. In the lengthy debate the only one who resolutely stood up for the armistice was Minister without Portfolio Béla Teleki, who had been invited to represent Transylvania within the Government. The opinion of the majority may be described by Csatay's summation: "We ask for Anglo—Saxon occupation, even if only a symbolical one, but we are fighting Bolshevism." The meeting was interrupted by a phone call from Horthy, informing the Prime Minister that he had received a threatening message from Ribbentrop just handed over by Veesenmayer. The Nazi Foreign Minister promised to send military aid and even to provide further equipment, but stated at the same time that Germany could by no means give up Hungary because it was to Germany's vital interest to keep her territory. Veesenmayer added on his own that he and members of the Legation's staff had occasion to talk with Hungarian field officers and other high-ranking military personages, who had declared that they would, in any case, stand by the Germans. And as concerns a probable upheaval in Hungary, they, the Germans, would oppose it by all means and would put down any such attempt with the troops arriving from Vienna and with the police force.

Ribbentrop's message and Veesenmayer's statement made their effect felt. Ultimately the Government adopted the following decision: "Differently from the view prevailing in yesterday's Crown Council that we have to receive German assistance within 24 hours or else we have to start negotiations about an armistice, the Council of Ministers today passes a unanimous decision that in case the German promises are kept and German assistance really arrives in a couple of days, and if the Germans guarantee that the promises will be kept, then Hungary is, for the time being, disposed to continue fighting and not to be overhasty in soliciting an armistice from the Allies."

There was really no question of overhaste. Horthy simply took note of the Government's decision. So the next day, September 9, Bakach-Bessenyey received, instead of an authorization to negotiate, a telegraphic explanation that the plan of quitting the war had been postponed, because its execution would be frustrated by the German forces stationed in Hungary, and because German intervention and the advance of the Russian forces as well as the conflict between the left wing and the right wing might lead to a civil war. "It would be of fundamental importance," the telegram went on, "for Hungary to be occupied by Anglo–Saxon forces, therefore we ask for two or three airborne divisions." Lakatos's message was crossed by Bakach-Bessenyey's telegram in which he stated categorically that it was hopeless to wait for Western occupation, because in conformity with an agreement between the Allies the Soviet army alone would occupy Hungary. Somewhat later, in reply to Lakatos's message, Bessenyey stated that unless the Hungarian Government followed his advice, he did not wish to mediate any more.

Not much came of the assistance promised by the German High Command. True, four divisions came to Hungary, only these did not go to the front but encircled Budapest. Neither Hungarian nor German troops were able to contain the advance of the Soviet army. For this reason Horthy summoned the Privy Councillors on September 10, to consult them about the question of the armistice. Participating in the conference were Prime Minister Lakatos, Foreign Minister Hennyey, Defence Minister Csatay, Chief of Staff Vörös, Lieutenant-General Antal Vattay (Horthy's chief adjutant) as well as fifteen Privy Councillors, among them István Bethlen (who had been brought in secret to Budapest from his provincial hiding place), Móric Esterházy, Gyula Károlyi, Kálmán Kánya, Baron Zsigmond Perényi, president of the Upper House, furthermore Generals Vilmos Röder, Hugó Sónyi and István Náday. They invited to the talks Béla Teleki and Dániel Bánffy, who had demanded, on behalf of the Transylvanian Party, that Horthy immediately should ask for an armistice. The meeting of the Privy Councillors decided in favour of soliciting an armistice and adopted the following resolution; 1. To inform the Germans, after the Finnish example, of the decision but to say nothing of the concrete measures, or rather to tell them only as much as would allow them to draw their conclusions; 2. Hungary not to lay down her arms but to stop fighting; 3. the German troops to be granted free departure; 4. "not to insult the Russians and Rumanians", that is, to call off the offensive in Transylvania and to evacuate the territories occupied beyond the frontiers drawn by the Vienna Award. Finally they decided that Lieutenant-General Náday should fly to Rome and make a last attempt to come to an agreement with the Western Powers. (We have no exact information about whether Horthy knew of the British proposal for Italy to be the venue the armistice talks, but the decision makes this very probable.)

On September 11, Lakatos informed the Government of the conference of the Privy Councillors. The majority of the Ministers took a stand against the armistice once more and even those who had agreed to the armistice in principle declared that the action should be carried out by a new Government that was not morally committed to the Germans. When Horthy got to know of the Government's intention to resign, he again yielded, and requested the Government to remain in office. In the following days, the policy of the Government was invariably concentrated on the fight waged by the side of Germany. On September 12, János Vörös went to the German General Headquarters, where Hitler made various promises and thus managed to persuade his guest to continue co-operating. The Führer outlined the plan of a large-scale German offensive, so much so that on September 13 a joint German–Hungarian attack was launched in the direction of Arad and Timişoara. This also proved a hopeless venture. The Soviet forces started a counter-attack and liberated Timişoara on the 16th and Arad on the 19th. At that time, Count Dániel Bánffy again requested an audience with Horthy. He presented a memorandum from the Transylvanian Hungarian Council, demanding most emphatically the immediate conclusion of an armistice and protesting against any act that might turn Transylvania into a theatre of war.

The events ultimately forced Horthy to start considering the idea of negotiating with the Soviet Union. While arranging Náday's mission, he took steps to establish contact with the Soviet Union.

The establishment of Soviet connections was facilitated by the fact that previous to his talk with Horthy the Transylvanian Council had commissioned Count Vladimir Zichy — whose estates were bordering on Slovakia — to enter into communication with Soviet military leaders through the instrumentality of Slovak partisans. Zichy found a connection with Colonel Makarov, commander of the Banská Bystrica brigade of partisans, who, on September 18, gave a favourable reply concerning Soviet readiness to negotiate, listing in writing the terms which were meant to promote the job of the Hungarian armistice delegation and the effective conclusion of an armistice (diplomatic immunity for the delegation, coded radio communication with Budapest, the participation of experts, etc.).

At the same time, other contacts were also established between Soviet and Hungarian emissaries. It was thus that Baron Ede Aczél and his two associates, crossed the front line with Horthy's approval to inquire of the Soviet High Command about the possibility and the terms of an armistice. Although he only returned on September 24, when Horthy had already decided to send off an armistice delegation, Aczél's mission is worth mentioning because the messages he brought from Moscow were essentially identical with those which Zichy received from Colonel Makarov.

The messages covered several points which offered very advantageous terms for a speedy armistice with the Hungarian Government. Should Hungary conclude an armistice and turn against Germany, the three Allied Powers would refrain from interfering in Hungary's domestic affairs; Hungary's independence would be guaranteed; the Hungarian army and police forces would not be disarmed; Hungarian administration would continue in the localities where there lived no Germans, etc. Both messages dealt with the question of Transylvania to the effect that it should be definitively settled by the treaty of peace.

Some authors from among the Hungarian emigration are of the opinion that there is a contradiction between the Rumanian armistice signed on September 12, and the Soviet Russian messages addressed to Horthy, although the study of the facts and documents can convince us that this contradiction was artificially created by the Horthyite emigration, by misrepresenting facts, thus trying to find an exuse for the inactivity and reluctance which led to the fiasco of the attempt at desertion and to the Arrow-Cross rule of terror. The terms presented to the Hungarian emissaries, either in summary or in detail, did not in fact contain anything else than what was described from the opposite angle in the above-mentioned paragraph 19 of the armistice agreement concluded with Rumania. Both from the Rumanian armistice document and from the messages sent to the Regent of Hungary it appears that the definitive settlement of the Transylvanian question was to be a task of the peace conference. These authors also like to emphasize the fact that the Makarov letter was already declared null and void by the Soviet Government at the negotiations with the Faragho delegation, but they prefer to obscure the reasons for it. I shall return to this issue later, but I have to state at this point that the Soviet offers were to be implemented as a *function* of Hungary's behaviour, but their realization could not be a *condition* of the conclusion of the armistice agreement. This was exactly what Horthy had been driving at, although he had exact information of the view of the anti-Fascist Powers regarding unconditional surrender.

When, on September 18, Horthy received the Soviet message from Zichy, he at last decided to send an armistice delegation to Moscow, but, on the pretext of selecting the persons to be appointed to the delegation, he kept delaying its departure for another ten days because he was invariably hopeful of the possibility of Anglo–American occupation.

This hope was also substantiated by one of Otto of Habsburg's last actions. When, early in September, he contacted the Lakatos Government, he drafted in common with Tibor Eckhardt a telegram and a lengthy memorandum urging the Hungarian Government to send a delegation for military negotiations to Rome in order to ensure better conditions for Hungary and to make sure that the country was occupied not by Soviet troops only but at least by mixed forces. Before forwarding these papers to Budapest, Otto took them with him to Quebec where Roosevelt had invited him. During the Second Quebec Conference, on September 15, the President received Otto of Habsburg and told him that the American military authorities had been instructed to receive the Hungarian delegates. He allegedly agreed with Otto's suggestion that, in case the Hungarian armistice was concluded, Anglo–American parachutists should be dropped in Hungary at the moment of her defection.

On September 17, Churchill invited Otto to dinner and allegedly endorsed the text of the cable to be sent to Budapest, agreed with the idea of a parachutist action and proposed that Hungary should send her representatives to the Western Powers, because in this case he would still be able to intercede on Hungary's behalf.

In respect of these conversations we can rely on Otto of Habsburg's letter to Churchill dated September 17, in which he mentions the dinner without quoting what the Prime Minister said there. Enclosed with the letter was a memorandum he had addressed to Roosevelt on the 15th, and in which he linked the question of the Hungarian armistice and Allied military assistance with the question of Transylvania and in general with the postponement of territorial problems until the peace conference. A second enclosure was the copy of a letter dated the 16th and addressed to Roosevelt, in which, with reference to the discussion he had had with Queen Zita the day before, he requested Roosevelt to dispatch to Prince Charles in Lisbon, to Bakach-Bessenyey in Switzerland and to Baron Apor in Rome the following telegram:

"Please communicate urgently to the Hungarian Government by any means that might be available to you the following message: In view of the dangerous development of the Hungarian situation and the imminent Soviet invasion of our national territory I feel it my duty to make a most urgent appeal to the Government in order that it should act before it is too late. I am convinced that if the Hungarian Government now immediately would enter in contact with the Americans and British in order to accept their offer of unconditional surrender and to collaborate with the Allied forces against the Germans Hungary can still escape the Communist domination. By this way only the life, honor and integrity of the Hungarian nation and people can be saved. Our country can obtain today better conditions than it would if it continued the fight alongside with the Germans. I am also convinced that by continuing on the side of the Germans the Hungarian Government will bring Communist domination over Hungary. I say all this in full knowledge of the situation. As a Hungarian patriot and having before my eyes exclusively the interest of the Nation I call on Admiral Horthy and the Government to contact at once, without an hour's delay, the Americans and British with an offer to negotiate surrender on their terms. This could be done as well through Bakach-Bessenyey as through Apor or Wodianer. This is almost certainly the last chance of the Government to save our nation from this dreadful danger. Signed: Otto.

"Identical messages have been sent to Archduke Charles, Bakach-Bessenyey and Apor."

Otto's affirmations are corroborated on several points by official British and American documents relating to the Hungarian armistice and by equally authentic sources concerning the Quebec Conference, although Cadogan, on the British side, closed the whole affair in his memo to the British Prime Minister in these terms: "I am satisfied that the Archduke's interference in these matters can only do harm. The support he enjoys in Austria and Hungary is far too small to counterbalance the certain disadvantage we should incur in Soviet Russia, Czechoslovakia and Yugoslavia (not to mention public reactions in this country) were we to attempt to make use of him. I hope that the Americans will act with discretion."

We have seen that Churchill, in spite of the slowness of the offensive in Italy, still lived in the hope of getting into Istria, and he wanted to revert to the subject as indeed he did at the Quebec Conference. True, he was no longer so confident as a month before. Early in September he wrote in a letter: "The turning over of Rumania to the

Allied cause has given the Russians a great advantage and it may well be that they will enter Belgrade and Budapest and possibly Vienna before the Western Allies succeed in piercing the Siegfried line. . . . However desirable such a Russian incursion may be, its political effect upon Central and Southern Europe may be formidable in the last degree." The Bulgarian about-face of September 9, further shattered Churchill's conceptions, but he still saw certain military and political chances in some places, including Hungary.

At the Second Quebec Conference Churchill and Roosevelt agreed not to withdraw further units from the Italian front until the outcome of the Alexander offensive became known, and not to withdraw landing troops either. On this score Churchill on September 13 cabled home to the British Government: "The Conference has opened in a blaze of friendship. The Staffs are in almost complete agreement already. There is to be no weakening of Alexander's army till Kesselring has bolted beyond the Alps or been destroyed. We are to have all the landing-craft in the Mediterranean to work up in the Northern Adriatic in any amphibious plan which can be made for Istria, Trieste, etc. . . ."

As regards Churchill's political conceptions, these took shape in Moscow about a month later. By the end of September, it had appeared that Alexander's offensive would hardly bring the desired results, so the only practical chance for British foreign policy was to try to agree with the Soviet Union in the matter of the Danubian basin and the Balkan area. Realizing this, Churchill decided to go to Moscow and talk personally with Stalin — of course, not only about the said topic but about all important issues of the war against the Fascist Powers. The talks lasted from October 9 to 17; during the negotiations Churchill and Eden submitted their proposals. In his work, *The Second World War*, Churchill writes that his proposal was the following: the Soviet Union should have predominance in Rumania (90 to 10%) and Bulgaria (75 to 25%), and Great Britain in Greece (90 to 10%). The division of interests in Yugoslavia and Hungary should be fifty-fifty. After several discussions between the Foreign Ministers the ratio was modified with regard to Bulgaria and Hungary in favour of the Soviet Union (80 to 20%).

On October 19, Churchill, in a note prepared for his staff, wrote about the Moscow negotiations among other things: "The system of percentage is not intended to prescribe the numbers sitting on commissions for the different Balkan countries, but rather to express the interest and sentiments with which the British and Soviet Governments approach the problems of these countries, and so that they might reveal their minds to each other in some way that could be comprehended. It is not intended to be more than a guide, and of course in no way commits the United States, nor does it attempt to set up a rigid system of spheres of interest. . . ."

So in the early autumn of 1944, there were still several conceptions extant with regard to Hungary. One thing, however, had long not been disputed — and this is what Horthy and his entourage were unable to understand — namely that any opportunity would open up only if Hungary deserted Germany effectively and turned against her; moreover, that Hungary should not expect the solution from the Allies but must act by herself: ask for an armistice, secure its implementation militarily and politically, and stop bargaining for more favourable armistice terms.

After the Quebec talks Otto of Habsburg dispatched his telegram to Budapest with the addition that his proposal had been accepted for the negotiations to be conducted by the Hungarian Minister in the Vatican.

Now Horthy got moving. On September 18, he requested the Swedish Legation in Budapest to inform the British, U. S. and Soviet Governments that he had decided to cease hostilities and asked where and when he should send his plenipotentiaries. On September 20, on the other hand, he summoned Náday and a South African officer, Colonel Howie (who had come to Hungary after escaping from a German prison camp towards the end of 1943), whom he now appointed to accompany Náday. He instructed Náday to convey to the High Command of the British forces fighting in Italy his intention to sue for an armistice and his request for the sending of Anglo–American troops to Hungary. As a written authorization he gave Náday a letter addressed to the Pope, probably because Otto's telegram had been interpreted as suggesting that the negotiations should take place through the Vatican (that is, he gave no effective credentials to Náday either). He handed him a memorandum for personal use to the effect that as long as the Hungarian troops were out at the front they were not in a position to put an end to German occupation; that the Regent had to know whether the armistice would save the country from the passage of Soviet and Rumanian troops, because, if not, he had to choose to fight further, since thereby, quoth he, Hungary would be spared at least the German attacks and terror raids. It would be desirable for the Allied Powers to prevail upon the Soviet Union that its troops should not cross the Hungarian frontiers, since in this case Hungary could order her armed forces home and take resolute steps with the view of defection. If this could not be done, the Allies should at least land urgently at Rijeka and direct a few divisions to march into Hungary. Otto was notified of Náday's departure.

The technical preparations for the journey were still under way when, on September 21, Bakach-Bessenyey's telegram arrived stating again that there was only one way out for Hungary: "Anything but unconditional surrender is out of the question. It is hopeless to imagine that the Anglo–Saxons will sacrifice their own forces in order that we, who have stood firm against them to the end, should be saved from the Russians and their Allies. The only thing to do was offer to accept an armistice without conditions and thereby avoid the further spilling of Hungarian blood." Although this message allowed of no subterfuge, Náday and Howie nevertheless left on September 22, with the original commission. Their plane landed in Italy that same day.

Náday's arrival at Caserta aroused keen attention among the Anglo–Saxons and sparked off prompt diplomatic actions, although Náday himself could sense very little of this stir. On September 23, he talked with General Wilson and told him that he came to ask for an armistice on behalf of Horthy and his Government. He said he was aware that there could be no question of bargaining, but he would like to receive at least some promise or assurance that British and U. S. forces would take part in the occupation of the country which would thus not be brought entirely under Soviet control. Wilson also had a discussion with Howie who related their mission a little differently from Náday's presentation. Howie said Horthy had told him that he would be disposed to fight against the Germans, but since German occupation and Gestapo control were total, any Hungarian action against the Germans could be 'crystallized' only with the co-operation of the Allies.

The first impression Náday's mission gave the U. S. Department of State was the following: 1. The Hungarian Government did not even contemplate starting any action against the Germans; 2. at this last hour, when the Soviet army was approaching Budapest, Horthy would like to earn some credit by the time he would be able to desert the Germans, and furthermore he wished Anglo—American troops to march into Hungary in order to counteract the Soviet army. From all this the Americans concluded that Náday's mission did not show that Budapest had realized the seriousness of the situation, but that it was evident that the Hungarian Government was ready to consider any offer of an armistice from the Allies.

The British Foreign Office, once it had been informed of Náday's mission, immediately proposed to the U. S. and Soviet Governments that, as soon as possible, Harold MacMillan, Minister Resident in the Mediterranean, should hand Náday the armistice terms of the Allied Powers in the presence of representatives from the Soviet Union and the United States. It requested the European Advisory Council to commission the Soviet and American members to work out the terms of a Hungarian armistice.

The United States agreed to the British proposal, and the Soviet member, F. T. Gusev, applied to his Government for instructions. Although the British felt, too, that the Hungarian attitude was not unambiguous, above all in respect of whether it intended to turn against the Germans or whether it only wished to get out of the war, and although Náday had no written credentials, they recognized his authority to negotiate. They proposed furthermore that the three Allied Powers should inform the Hungarian Government that, as a precondition for the opening of negotiations, Hungary must withdraw her troops and her administrative apparatus from the occupied territories behind the boundaries of December 31, 1937, and make preparations for receiving the Allied military mission.

At the same time, Sir William Strang, the British member on the European Advisory Council, put forward the British draft in 13 point: "(1) Hostilities to cease between Hungary and the United Nations at blank hour blank date. (2) Hungary to sever all relations with Germany and other enemy powers; to disarm and intern enemy forces and nationals and to control enemy property. Enemy war materials and property to be held at the disposal of the Allies. (3) Hungarian forces, officials and nationals to withdraw forthwith within the pre-1938 frontiers of Hungary. (4) The Supreme Allied Commanders to have the right to move their forces freely into or across Hungarian territory if the military situation requires or if the Hungarian Government fail in any respect to fulfil the terms of the armistice. (5) Hungary to carry out such measures of disarmament and demobilization as may be required. Hungarian war material to be held at the disposal of the Allies. (6) Hungary to release and take all necessary steps for the protection, maintenance and welfare of Allied prisoners of war and internees until repatriated. Lists of all such persons indicating their places of detention to be furnished. Hungary to supply information on United Nations displaced persons, to accept financial responsibility for them and to take such measures for maintenance, welfare and control as may be required by the Allies. Hungary to be responsible for the control of enemy refugees and displaced persons under the direction of the Allies. (7) Hungary to comply with Allied requirements for the use and control of shipping and transport including Danubian navigation and transport facilities. (8) Hungary to release all persons detained for political or racial reasons or as a result of discriminatory legislation. Such legislation to be repealed and the effect of such legislation to be reversed. (9) Hungary to cooperate in the apprehension and trial of persons accused of war crimes. (10) Hungary to protect and restore all United Nations property; to make reparation for war loss and damage; and to dispose of any of her assets without the consent of the Allies. (11) Hungary to furnish free of cost supplies, services and facilities as the Allies may require for the use of their forces, missions or agencies and such local currency as they may require for expenditure within Hungary. Hungary to redeem and hand over to the Allies free of charge any currency issued by them in Hungary. (12) Hungary to furnish such further supplies (including foodstuffs), services or facilities as the Allies may require. (13) Hungary to comply with any further Allied instructions for giving effect to the armistice and to the Allied interpretation thereof: to give all facilities to such missions as the Allies may send; and to meet Allied requirements for the reestablishment of peace and security. These instructions and requirements will be communicated to the Hungarian Government by an Allied Control Commission which will be appointed to Hungary for that purpose."

On September 28, the United States, having repeatedly asked for the final draft of the Hungarian armistice terms, moved some modifications. First of all, it disagreed with the provision that, as a prerequisite of armistice negotiations, Hungary should be obliged to retreat to the pre-1938 frontiers; it opposed this on the assumption that this provision could hinder Hungary from speedily withdrawing from the war. It found it sufficient to stipulate such provisions only in the armistice agreement to be concluded. It proposed that the term 'nationals' should be deleted from paragraph (3) because this word could be interpreted in different ways, and this might cause difficulties. After a number of insignificant comments it proposed finally that the prohibition of Fascist and semi-Fascist organizations should be included in the armistice terms.

The Americans mentioned that the British draft did not touch upon about Hungary's entry into war against Germany. Since in the case of the Bulgarian and the Rumanian armistice it was held advisable for the satellite armies to take part in the war against Germany, they thought it would be proper to oblige Hungary to declare war on Germany, with the proviso that the use of Hungarian troops on the territory of Allied countries should depend on the consent of the countries concerned. Finally it was interesting that, in respect of signing the armistice agreement, the Americans would have found it useful if the Soviet Commander-in-Chief and the British Supreme Commander for the Mediterranean also signed it, but they thought it necessary for

Wilson to sign it only in case the Mediterranean forces took part in the operations in Hungarian territory, or in case U.S. forces occupied part of the country.

While these events took place the British did not enter into talks with Náday at Caserta, because on September 4, Wilson received instructions not to take any step until the three Allies had come to an agreement in the matter of the Hungarian armistice. The Soviet reply to the Anglo–American proposal arrived as late as October 6, when the Hungarian armistice delegation was already engaged in negotiations at Moscow.

In the meantime in Budapest, where nothing was known of the developments concerning the Náday mission, the list of the armistice delegates had at last been compiled with much difficulty. The head of the delegation was Colonel-General Gábor Faragho, inspector general of the gendarmerie, an ex-military attaché in Moscow. Members were University Professor Count Géza Teleki and Secretary of State Domokos Szent-Iványi, who at this time was appointed Envoy Extraordinary and Minister Plenipotentiary, but his letter of appointment contained no special authorization to sign the armistice. Since Horthy waited in vain for a message from Náday, on September 27, he received Faragho and the members of the delegation. He handed them his letter to Stalin in English asking for an armistice. The letter read as follows:

"Field Marshal!

"In the name and for the sake of the Hungarian people in their extreme danger, I address myself to you. – Doing so in the name of the Hungarian people, who has no responsibility for this war. For thousand years and particularly during the last decade, the fate of our people has been influenced by the neighbouring German Colossus. – It was again under this influence that we were carried to this unfortunate war with the Soviet Union.

"I have to lay a particular stress on the fact that my poor country has been practically filled with the German 'Fifth Column'. This penetration has started in a large scale at the same moment when German forces marched into Rumania and Bulgaria. As a result, every movement and every step in Hungary have been closely watched by German agents and the most important news and reports have never reached me. I have now come to the knowledge, that after the air attack upon Kassa and Munkács, Foreign Minister Molotov – during a conversation with the Hungarian Minister – emphasised the peaceful aims of the Soviet Union towards Hungary. If this was really so, it is fatal, for it did not reach me at the time.

"For the sake of justice, I would like to inform you that we have never ever wanted to take but a single inch from anybody that was not ours by right. On the contrary, the Rumanians took Bessarabia from their own Russian ally after the first world war and wished to take an important part of South Russia during the second world war with German help. Furthermore, when in 1940 we intended to make an end to the monstrous treatment of the Hungarian people in Transylvania, it was again the Rumanians who asked help from Germany in asking Hitler to help them to retain at least a part of this land by the Vienna Award.

"When sending with full authorization my delegates to the negotiation of armistice I beg you to spare this unfortunate country which has its own historic merits and the people of which has so many affinities with the Russian people. Kindly exercise your great influence upon your allies, that you may make conditions compatible with our people's interests and honour, who would really deserve peaceful life and a safe future.

"I avail myself of this opportunity to express to you, Field Marshal Stalin, my highest consideration.

Yours truly
Horthy m.p.

"P. S. As our troops are still on the borders and we are invaded by strong German units, I am asking to treat my letter with discretion, until we are able to manage the situation."

Besides, Horthy gave Faragho oral instructions to try, during his negotiations, to obtain the immediate cessation of hostilities, the participation of Anglo–American troops in the occupation of Hungary, and the free withdrawal of the German troops.

The delegation left on September 28, 1944, and proceeded towards the Slovak frontier, on the other side of which the Soviet emissaries already waited for the Hungarians. Faragho and company spent two days in Zólyom (Zvolen) held by Slovak insurgents, and continued their way by a special plane, which arrived at Moscow on October 1. Immediately after arrival they were received by Colonel-General Kuznetsov, Deputy Chief of Staff of the Soviet army. Right at the start of negotiations, it became clear that even now, practically in the very last minute, the task of the Hungarian delegation was not to sign Hungary's capitulation but only to obtain a political arrangement preparatory to the armistice. Starting from the principle of unconditional surrender, Kuznetsov wanted first of all to discuss the modalities of the Hungarian army's desertion and entry into war against Germany. But Faragho could not even think of talking about it before the signing of an armistice agreement that would ensure to Hungary favourable political and territorial conditions. Thus he declared that he asked for a plenipotentiary of higher rank to whom he might present Horthy's letter addressed to Stalin. In such circumstances the discussions were resumed as late as October 5, this time with a personal representative of Stalin's, Army General Antonov, the Chief of Staff. Antonov also emphasized that the most essential thing was to discuss military co-operation, for if the defection of the Hungarian army was successful, the Soviet forces could pass quickly through Hungary's territory without the country becoming a theatre of war. Antonov inquired whether Horthy's letter contained a detailed description of the modalities of desertion. Faragho replied in the negative, declaring that this was precisely what the delegation had come to work out. Then he related his conceptions in detail with the request that Stalin and the Soviet Government should be informed of the following:

1. Hungary is making preparations for stopping the fight against the Soviet Union and for fighting against Germany on the side of the Soviet army. 2. The Soviet armed forces will be granted freedom of movement in the territory of Hungary. 3. The Soviet army is requested to take Budapest speedily. 4. It is requested that the Rumanian

army should not cross the frontiers of 1940. 5. The bombing of Hungary should be stopped. 6. Coded radio communication with Budapest should be permitted.

Antonov remarked that these questions could not be settled immediately. Then Szent-Iványi spoke up and broached the subject of the Makarov letter. Finally Antonov promised to secure radio communication with Budapest and adjourned the meeting.

That same night, Colonel-General Kuznetsov called on Faragho at his quarters and told him that without an authorization to sign the armistice the Soviet Government saw no reason to negotiate.

The next day, Faragho sent a radio telegram to Budapest stating: "Without authorization to sign they refuse to negotiate about details. Please send immediately personal authorization to sign armistice with three Allies or to conclude any other agreement." In the telegram he named Major József Nemes, a former school-mate of his, who might take with him the written authorization to confirm the one given by radio. Since they in Budapest were unable to decipher the telegram, Faragho repeated it on the 7th, adding that the atmosphere was not bad, the Allies wanted prompt agreement, they were mainly interested in military co-operation. Horthy's reply arrived at Moscow on the 8th. In it he confirmed that his intention to conclude an armistice was serious and Faragho's commission was valid, but he stated that he could give the requested authorization only when he knew the terms. Finally, with reference to German troop concentrations around Budapest, he asked for time.

In the meanwhile, on October 6, Molotov had informed the British and U. S. Ambassadors in Moscow that, although preparations were under way for the presentation of the armistice terms to a Hungarian plenipotentiary, the Soviet Government supposed that Náday possessed no such authorization, so it requested the Allies not to communicate to him anything. Then he presented to the two Ambassadors an aide-mémoire describing the arrival in Moscow of the Hungarian armistice delegation and told them about Horthy's letter and the requests of the Hungarians. Molotov, finding these requests unacceptable, made the following proposition: 1. Plenipotentiaries of the three Allies should immediately set about working out the armistice terms for Hungary. 2. The three Allied Governments should make a joint statement to the effect that Horthy and the Hungarian Government must accept the preliminary terms and comply with them before starting negotiations on the armistice. Molotov read out the text of the preliminary terms, stating that when formulating them he had done his best to allow for the related British proposals. Finally he suggested that, in case the Hungarians accepted the preliminary terms, the armistice negotiations should be conducted in Moscow.

On October 7, the British and U. S. Governments, taking note of the Faragho delegation's arrival at Moscow, and admitting that they could not direct the armistice negotiations through Náday, consented to the preliminary terms and to negotiations being held in Moscow and gave their Ambassadors in Moscow the necessary authorization on the basis of the earlier elaborated American and British armistice proposals.

After Faragho related the content of Horthy's telegram, Foreign Minister Molotov on the night of October 8, received the Hungarian armistice delegation in the Kremlin on behalf of the three Allied Powers and put forth the preliminary terms proposed by the anti-Fascist Powers:

"Hungary shall evacuate all Hungarian forces and officials from the territories of Czechoslovakia, Yugoslavia, and Rumania occupied by her to the confines of Hungary's frontiers as they existed on December 31st 1937. This evacuation shall begin immediately and shall be completed within ten (repeat ten) days from the date of receipt by the Hungarian Government of the present statement. For the purpose of verification and control of this evacuation the three Allied Governments will send control representatives to Hungary who will act as a United Allied Military Mission under the chairmanship of the Soviet representative.

Hungary shall be obliged to break off all relations with Germany and immediately to declare war on Germany, the Soviet Government being willing to give Hungary assistance with their troops."

The Soviet Foreign Minister told Faragho that in case Hungary accepted these terms, the Allies would be ready to discuss in Moscow the terms of a definitive armistice — which would be by and large identical with those applied to Rumania — and to sign the armistice agreement, which must be signed on behalf of Hungary by a plenipotentiary having the necessary written authorization. Should Hungary refuse the preliminary terms, there was nothing to discuss any more.

The position of the Allied Powers was plain and clear, and on the basis of the principle of unconditional surrender it suggested the only solution possible that could serve not only the anti-Fascist war but also the immediate interests of Hungary: the earliest possible break with Germany, the rapid liquidation of the consequences of German occupation, and even favourable peace terms in case Hungary, turning against Germany, contributed to the speedy conclusion of the war. Szent-Iványi nevertheless took issue on this score. Complying with the mission he had received from Horthy, he tried to extract concessions, chiefly with reference to the Makarov letter. In vain did the Soviet Foreign Minister tell him repeatedly that the Allied Powers were disposed to negotiate only on the platform of unconditional surrender, and the Hungarian plenipotentiaries must not set any conditions — the Hungarian delegation did not give in and provoked a long debate. It had become plainly obvious that Horthy and his clique wished to make use of the armistice negotiations in order to secure favourable political and territorial conditions without accepting any obligation. To break the deadlock, the Soviet Foreign Minister permitted Faragho to inform Horthy that the Soviet Government considered the Makarov letter to be void. It seemed necessary and inevitable to state this position because engaging in discussion about final terms instead of prompt action would have resulted in an endless temporization which again might have been useful to German interests. At 12:03 a.m. on October 9, the head of the Hungarian delegation was at last disposed to take note of the preliminary terms and to forward them to Budapest.

Although Faragho's telegram containing the preliminary terms must have reached Buda Castle on October 9, instead of answering right away Horthy continued manoeuvring. In the evening hours he sent to Moscow only a laconic telegram indicating the dispatch of an important communication. Then at 12:20 a.m. on October 10 the following message was sent out: "Conclusion of armistice is desirable. Authorization to sign is granted. Readiness for stipulated co-operation is given. Major Nemes with written authorization leaves via Kőrösmező. . . . Please state conditions urgently before signing." The text of the telegram indicates as if Horthy had had no knowledge of the preliminary terms. Or does it mean that the Regent, again delaying his final decision, had granted authorization to sign the armistice but intended the last sentence to demonstrate that he had not yet accepted the preliminary terms?

In the morning of October 10, Horthy conferred with Prime Minister Lakatos, Foreign Minister Hennyey, Defence Minister Csatay, Chief of Staff Vörös, as well as with General Vattay and Gyula Ambrózy, chief of the Regent's cabinet bureau, about how to respond to the terms of the draft armistice. After a long debate, Lakatos, stressing that there was no alternative, proposed acceptance of the terms and suggested that they should ask the Soviet Union to halt the advance of its forces for a couple of days in order to enable the Hungarian troops to retreat and to attack the Germans. Lakatos's proposal was accepted, but the armistice delegation in Moscow was not informed until 12:30 a.m. on October 11. "Hungary accepts preliminary terms of armistice," the telegram read. "She asks for earliest possible opening of armistice talks and strict secrecy until we can concentrate forces withdrawn from the front against the German troops outnumbering ours in Budapest, in order to prevent a German putsch and an ensuing bloodbath, especially a Jewish pogrom. To be able to carry this out and secure the fulfilment of conditions, we ask for a halt of the advancing Russian troops."

Upon receipt of the telegram in Moscow, Faragho immediately called on Molotov, who received him in the early hours of the 11th. In a telegram two hours later he gave account of the meeting as follows: "At 4 a.m. today we informed the Foreign Minister of the content of the telegram on Hungary's acceptance of preliminary armistice terms. The atmosphere became warm and friendly. British Prime Minister and Foreign Secretary are here, their presence secures solemnity and prompt action in our case. This was stressed by the Foreign Secretary. They demand repetition of authorization to sign with simultaneous recapitulation of the stated preliminary terms. Please grasp the importance of the situation and take the necessary measures to enable us to fulfil our obligations."

In the afternoon of the 11th, Molotov conferred on the Hungarian armistice issue with Foreign Secretary Eden, British Ambassador Clark Kerr, and U. S. Ambassador Averell Harriman. He showed them Horthy's telegram on his acceptance of the preliminary terms, and told them that the Soviet High Command granted the Hungarian request and authorized its representatives at the same time to negotiate with representatives of the Hungarian army in order to expedite the retreat of the Hungarian troops. Eden and the U. S. Ambassador agreed with the Soviet suggestions.

Thereupon the Soviet Foreign Minister asked them to consider, as a first step related to the armistice terms, the dispatch to Hungary of an Inter-Allied military mission with the task of supervising the evacuation of the occupied territories; then he let them know that the Soviet armistice proposal was on the model of the armistice with Rumania. (Molotov presented this draft to the Allies on October 13.)

Still in the afternoon of the 11th Faragho sent home another message which already referred to the practical implementation of the agreement and indicated that the Soviet Government wished to come to Hungary's help with prompt action in order to prevent the Germans' launching an assault on Budapest.

In a telegram sent off at 10:30 p.m. Horthy reiterated his having given the authorization to sign the armistice agreement. He announced that Major Nemes with the written authorization would leave on the 12th and recapitulated the armistice terms with his confirmation. Finally he stated that he, Horthy, would not leave Budapest. (By the way, Horthy still pinned his hopes on the Anglo–American occupation of part of the country; in another telegram he instructed Faragho to try to communicate with Náday through Moscow: Náday should at once enter into contact with Horthy on the stated radio frequency and with the agreed call signal.)

Still before Horthy's telegram reached Moscow, Molotov had summoned the Hungarian delegation and said that it was neddless to wait for Nemes to bring with him the written authorization to sign the preliminary armistice. Thus, at 7:57 p.m. on October 11 in the Kremlin, Molotov and Faragho signed the preliminary armistice agreement drawn up in duplicates in French and Russian. The act of signature was attended by the members of the Hungarian delegation as well as by Deputy Foreign Minister Dekhanazov and Colonel-General Kuznetsov. Thereafter Molotov stated that the Soviet High Command, in compliance with Horthy's request, would stop the advance of its troops for one or two days from midnight that day. Géza Teleki recommended the Soviet Foreign Minister not to do so because it would give the Germans time for an offensive. Dekhanazov then hurried into the neighbouring room where Foreign Secretary Eden was staying. Returning from there, he told something to Molotov, who then confirmed that Horthy's wishes as well as Faragho's request for stopping the bombing of Budapest were granted.

At half past nine in the evening, Faragho dispatched a telegram saying that the armistice agreement had been signed: "At eight o'clock this evening we signed the preliminary terms; Regent Horthy's request has been acceded to, the advance of Russian troops will be stopped tonight for a couple of days. Return of Hungarian troops has been granted. I shall be told which Hungarian commanders should go over to which Russian commanders through the front line for a detailed discussion. An Inter-Allied Mission is to leave as soon as possible. Nemes has not yet come across the frontier, final authorization to sign is essential. Please grant it by telegram at the same time. Asked whether troops will be faithful to the Regent, we firmly answered yes. To complement the delegation please accommodate experts in a safe place now, possibly in Debrecen. Are Government and Regent still in Budapest? Please take care of communication, radio signals remain."

When the preliminary armistice agreement had been signed, it was time for action. First of all, military measures ought to have been taken with all internal forces which might have secured the about-face. At that time the Hungarian Front uniting the forces of national resistance concentrated on accomplishing the break of Hungary with Germany in order to carry out, if possible together with Horthy, an armed uprising, to turn against Germany. Therefore, already at the end of September, and then early in October, the Hungarian Front forwarded to the Regent a memorandum proposing joint action in the interest of the armistice. It stated the conditions of co-operation as follows: Armistice with the Allied Powers and declaration of war on Germany; the formation of a coalition Government constituted by the Hungarian Front parties and military chiefs; the arming of the workers; the release of political prisoners. Even a personal talk took place between Horthy and representatives of the Hungarian Front — Zoltán Tildy and Árpád Szakasits — on October 11. Horthy told them about the conclusion of the preliminary armistice agreement and announced that it would be made public in about eight to ten days, but he refrained from making any concrete arrangement. Tildy and Szakasits proposed the calling of a general strike for October 17. Following these talks, the Hungarian Front set about preparing the strike.

Although having commissioned János Vörös to keep in touch with the Hungarian Front, Horthy in fact wished to carry out the armistice without assistance from the left-wing forces, by relying on the army alone. However, even this remained only wishful thinking. True, he instructed Béla Miklós Dálnoki and Lajos Veress, commanders of the 1st and 2nd armies, to establish contact, the moment he would give orders, with the Soviet army and stop fighting, but he took no further steps to fulfil the obligations assumed under the preliminary armistice agreement, to promote Hungary's withdrawal from the war, to foil any possible counteraction on the part of the Germans. He did not make use of the halt of the Soviet troops to bring back the Hungarian armed formations to Budapest.

In a telegram of October 12, Faragho urged military measures: "A senior staff officer as truce-bearer should go from Kistelek to Szeged. There he should call on the commander of the Russian task force to discuss the details with him. The Russian troops along the Tisza south of Szolnok will not attack. We may immediately bring all troops from this front line back to Budapest." At ten in the evening, he repeated this telegram and added: "Send urgent reply concerning implementation. Russians can't understand why it has failed. They recommended us to take away our armoured forces, too."

Under the impact of this telegram Horthy, on the 13th, at last gave orders for a corps of the 2nd army to retreat in the direction of Budapest and sent to Szeged Colonel Loránd Utassy, head of the P.O.W. department of the Ministry of National Defence. Owing to his complete ignorance of questions of military operations, Utassy's mission was a failure.

While Horthy remained passive, the Germans made energetic preparations in order to clear the situation in Hungary by adopting military measures, to arrange a coup by raising Arrow-Cross people to power. They had no exact information about the armistice agreement, but they guessed that Horthy would soon make up his mind to take a decisive step. This is what they wished to prevent by an action which was to be carried out by General Bach-Zelewski and Ambassador Rudolf Rahn, whom Hitler sent to Budapest on the 13th and 14th respectively. Major Otto Skorzeny, Mussolini's rescuer, also came to Budapest with the task of taking Buda Castle by force. When preparing the military plans the Germans decided to make a last attempt to bring pressure to bear upon Horthy. With this end in view Veesenmayer requested an audience with the Regent for Rahn and himself for October 15.

In the morning of October 14, Horthy definitively decided to announce the armistice the next day, Sunday, October 15. What convinced him of the necessity to act was the actual military situation, as well as information about Arrow-Cross preparations for a take-over, and the insistence of Faragho. (Originally he had scheduled the execution of defection for the 20th, but he did not inform the Soviet Government of this date either, he told about it only to Major Nemes, who arrived at Moscow on the 15th, ignorant of the change of date.) The Regent had the idea that at twelve noon on the 15th he would summon Veesenmayer and announce to him his decision; at 12:30 p.m. his armistice proclamation would be read out over the radio, and simultaneously he was to send the command of the 1st and 2nd armies a coded telegram containing the general order. On October 14, Horthy conferred with General Lázár, commander of the Guards, met Generals Vattay, Aggteleky and Ferenc Farkas, and agreed with them on the military precautions to be taken for the defence of Budapest. His intentions are clearly shown in what he said to General Farkas: "By virtue of the armistice terms we ought to retreat to the Trianon frontiers and to join the Russians in the offensive against the Germans, but I will find a means to dodge this provision."

In the afternoon cabinet bureau chief Ambrózy told the Prime Minister that the Regent wished to convene the Crown Council for the next morning, because he saw the time had come to proclaim the armistice. Although Lakatos declared that he did not find this step expedient because the situation was not yet ripe for it, he undertook to inform the Government and to represent Horthy's position. Soon the Prime Minister announced Horthy's decision to members of the Government — with the exception of the two out-and-out pro-German henchmen, Reményi-Schneller and Jurcsek. The Ministers heard the announcement, and in the belief that they had to decide on the conclusion of the armistice, they started a debate about constitutional law and worked out the terms of the acceptance of an armistice. (The Cabinet members did not know that the preliminary armistice had been signed on the 11th.) Finally they agreed that Horthy had the constitutional powers to ask for an armistice without consulting the National Assembly, and summed up their conditions in three points: 1. The German army shall evacuate the territory of Hungary as it did in Finland. 2. All three Allied armies shall occupy the country simultaneously. 3. The Hungarian police shall take part in the maintenance of order. The Government also decided to permit the publication of left-wing papers, to ban the extreme-right press and to release the political prisoners. Justice Minister Gábor Vladár issued the related decrees still on the evening of the 14th.

When the Ministers had left, Lakatos told Horthy about his objections to the text of the proclamation; on his demand the Regent changed the term 'armistice' in the original text to 'preliminary armistice' and deleted this sentence: "From this day Hungary considers herself to be at war with Germany."

Still in the late hours Horthy met the Chief of Staff just back in Budapest from the front line. Vörös was instructed to dispatch the secret order the next day. He recommended Horthy to travel urgently to Huszt, in the sector of the 1st army, but the Regent declined the offer. Then, taking leave of his Chief of Staff, he retired to rest, and it did not even occur to him to inform the Soviet High Command of the events scheduled for the next day.

On the other hand, the Soviet High Command was impatient to receive some signal on the implementation of the preliminary armistice agreement. Utassy's miserable performance at Szeged also demonstrated that the master of Buda Castle was playing for time. Therefore Army General Antonov, on the evening of the 14th, presented an energetic note to Faragho, who forwarded it by telegram at 11:45 p.m. The telegram read as follows:

"At 8 p.m. we received a note from the Chief of Staff: Colonel Utassy is an entirely ignorant man, so he cannot conduct negotiations. The Hungarian state, in order to be able to withdraw its own troops and direct them towards Budapest, asked the Soviet Government to halt the offensive in the direction of Budapest. However, Hungary has not withdrawn her troops, but instead she displays strong activity in the environs of Szolnok. The above is proof that the Hungarian Government probably does not wish to observe the armistice provisions. Therefore the Soviet High Command demands that Hungary should fulfil her obligations within 48 hours, and especially:

"1. Break off every connection with Germany and start active military operations against her troops.

"2. Begin to withdraw her forces from Rumanian, Yugoslav and Czechoslovak territories.

"3. Send The Russian army command at Szeged, by 8 a.m. on the 18th, complete information on the positions taken up by the German and Hungarian armed forces and on how the armistice provisions have been implemented.

"Please comply strictly with the above and inform me in detail. A prominent general and Colonel Nádas should go to Szeged."

Still on the evening of the 14th Stalin showed the text of this note to Churchill, then negotiating in Moscow, and to the U. S. Ambassador.

The telegram was deciphered in the Castle after midnight. Horthy's war council (members of his family, Generals Vattay and Lázár, as well as Ambrózy) decided, however, that it was needless to wake up the Regent on this account, because there was nothing more to do. In the early hours they simply wired to Moscow that, until the Hungarian reinforcements had arrived, it was impossible to take any military action against the Germans because these had the advantage in numbers; it was probable that, as soon as the request for an armistice was made public, the Germans, who already guessed a lot about what was going on, would attack; the attack would be resisted, and until Budapest had been liberated through an urgent action by Soviet and Hungarian troops, the Castle, the headquarters of the Government, would be firmly held; the plenipotentiary would arrive in Szeged at the appointed time.

Antonov's ultimatum and the reply sent to Faragho were shown to Horthy in the morning of the 15th. The Regent, who did not tell anybody about those documents until the evening hours, mentioned them neither in the Crown Council nor at the ensuing conference.

The Crown Council meeting scheduled for 11 a.m. on October 15, 1944, opened with delay, because at about 10 o'clock the news came that the Germans, as a result of provocation, had apprehended the Regent's son, Miklós Horthy, Jr.. The meeting was opened by Horthy who — without making mention of the Moscow negotiations, the signing of the preliminary armistice agreement, or the Antonov ultimatum, and with reference to the serious military situation and the hostile attitude of the Germans manifested also in the abduction of his son — announced that Hungary had no other choice than to sue for an armistice. He said that there were real hopes for acceptable armistice terms, and asked who among the members of the Government was willing to co-operate in implementing the armistice. Thereafter Vörös described the military situation. He declared that — since, owing to the defeat at Debrecen and to the openness of the Danube—Tisza interfluve area, the danger existed of the 1st and 2nd armies being cut off — he had given orders for retreat. He said also that hardly half an hour before he had received an ultimatum from Guderian declaring the entire territory of Hungary to be a theatre of operations, where only the German High Command was entitled to issue orders, and demanding that the Hungarian Chief of Staff should rescind his own orders.

Vörös's situation analysis and the Regent's announcement was followed by a lively debate, again about questions of constitutional law. Lakatos announced his intention to resign, for which he gave formal reasons. Horthy then called upon the Prime Minister and the Ministers present to undertake to form a new Government. All members of the Cabinet, including the trusted men of the Germans, complied. The constitutional dispute was also closed with the earlier adopted view that Horthy as supreme warlord had the powers to ask for an armistice.

At twelve noon, the Crown Council meeting was interrupted because Reich Plenipotentiary Veesenmayer put in an appearance. Horthy received him in the presence of the Prime Minister and the Foreign Minister. In the course of a sharp dispute lasting for about half an hour, Horthy made reproaches for the behaviour of the Germans and the harassment by the Gestapo. He said that Germany had not fulfilled any promise she had made and thus put the Hungarian army in an impossible position. Therefore he decided to ask for an armistice with the Allied Powers. Then he demanded an explanation of his son's abduction. Veesenmayer apologized and protested, and finally asked Horthy, before doing anything, to receive Hitler's personal emissary, Ambassador Rahn, who had brought with him a message from the Führer; this was intended to resolve the conflicts between the two countries. After some altercation Horthy gave in, remarking that it would not alter the case after all.

After Veesenmayer's audience, Ambrózy and Horthy's daughter-in-law, who were staying in the next room, issued orders for the broadcasting of the proclamation. After some wrangling — because Prime Minister Lakatos wanted to wait for the results of the parley with Rahn and therefore had not countersigned the document — Endre Hlatky, the Government commissioner for the Radio, read out Horthy's proclamation specifying the serious consequences of German occupation, the tyrannies of German military and police authorities, the breach of promises. The Regent's address concluded in these terms:

"I have resolved to protect the honour of the Hungarian nation even from our ex-ally, when, instead of rendering the promised military assistance, this ally wants to deprive definitively the Hungarian nation of its greatest treasure, its freedom and independence. Therefore I have told the representative of the German Reich that we conclude a preliminary armistice with our adversaries and cease all hostilities against them. In concert with them and trusting in their sense of justice, I wish to ensure the continuity of the nation's future life and the realization of its peaceful aims. I have instructed the leaders of the national army accordingly, so the troops, faithful to their oath and in accordance with my simultaneously issued general order, shall obey the commanders appointed by me.

"And I invite every honest Hungarian to follow me on the arduous road of saving the Hungarian nation."

While most of the members of the Government were listening to the proclamation in astonishment, Horthy received Hitler's personal emissary. The Regent repeated all that he had told Veesenmayer, and Rahn tried to use more delicate methods to impress Horthy. He inquired about the armistice terms, then began cursing how Horthy could submit himself to Russian occupation by which he was digging the grave of his own régime. He argued that the situation would be different if Western troops should also come to occupy Hungary. Horthy then asked whether there would be a way, as it happened in Finland, to withdraw the German troops from the territory of the country. Rahn feigned to consider the question but said that he could not give any definitive answer until Hitler had decided, therefore he asked Horthy that, until he could give an answer, the Hungarian troops should refuse to open the front before the Soviet formations. Horthy, although having already given the instruction to dispatch his general order, promised to talk about Rahn's request with members of the Government and to inform him of their decision that same day.

Then followed the most tragi-comical event of October 15. Foreign Minister Hennyey, who knew nothing about the Moscow negotiations, received the Swedish and Turkish Ministers in a separate room of the Castle. He told them about Horthy's decision concerning the armistice and requested them to forward to the Great Powers Hungary's application for an armistice and ask them where and when the Hungarian representatives should appear to start negotiations. Later Hennyey wrote in his memoirs with satisfaction: "Without dealing with the matter on its merits, the impression I gained from the attitude of both diplomats was that they approved of the decision of the Regent and the Government." The diplomats did their duty, and the

Swedish and Turkish notes to the British, American and Soviet Governments caused a considerable consternation everywhere.

When Veesenmayer's audience began, the Crown Council practically finished with its business. The Cabinet members only waited for the reconstitution of the Government and for being sworn in. After the oath the Ministers left the Castle without having agreed on any concrete measure.

In the general order to be dispatched to the armed formations simultaneously with the proclamation, Horthy announced the armistice and called upon the members of the army to scrupulously obey the orders issued by their superiors. This general order was an instruction for the 1st and 2nd armies to stop fighting and to contact the Soviet troops. After Veesenmayer's audience, Horthy issued the instruction to forward the general order. The officers of the General Staff, however, failed to follow the instruction. They did not know exactly what practical steps were involved in the general order, but its connection with the proclamation was obvious. When, towards three o'clock in the afternoon, Vörös arrived at the Ministry of National Defence, the staff officers and Veesenmayer, who came there shortly after, demanded an explanation of Horthy's general order and prevailed upon the Chief of Staff to issue an order differing from the original text. Vörös gave in and drafted another general order: "Nobody must interpret the Regent's radio proclamation as meaning that the Hungarian army has laid down its arms. Up to the present the question is only about armistice negotiations. The outcome is still rather precarious, so every Hungarian soldier and every unit should continue resisting any attack from whatever direction it may come."

His subordinates, however, falsified this text further. They deleted the phrase "from whatever direction it may come" and thus made the order quite explicit: continued resistance could mean only fighting the Soviet troops. This instruction was forwarded to all military formations at about 5 p.m. The text was read over the radio at 5:20 p.m. This instruction and the attitude of the Arrow-Cross-inclined officers prevented the 1st and 2nd armies from acting in accordance with the armistice agreement, and made it impossible for the troops stationed in Budapest to turn against the Germans. The staff of the 1st army headed by Colonel-General Béla Miklós passed over to the Soviet army and thus sparked off a process as a result of which about 20,000 Hungarian troops went over to the Soviet army in the course of the next few weeks, but the Arrow-Cross officers frustrated the contemplated organized desertion of the Hungarian forces and their turning against the Germans. In the afternoon, the commander of the 3rd army, József Heszlényi, already spoke up in favour of Szálasi. The 1st army corps staying at Budapest also refused to obey Horthy.

General Lázár alone took steps to defend Buda Castle. He had all roads leading up to the Castle undermined in the early evening hours.

The bulk of the officers of Horthy's army remained true to themselves, to the counter-revolutionary spirit in which they had been trained and had lived throughout twenty-five years. And when they refused to follow even the 'supreme warlord', Horthy, who was wholly relying on this army, turned out to be a mere puppet without it. But he also remained true to himself, and completed his 'oeuvre' with his last deeds, securing legal continuity to the Arrow-Cross riff-raff.

The armistice proclamation came as a surprise to the Germans and the Arrow-Cross men, but wrangling, inactivity, political impotence and the officers' revolt gave them an opportunity to seize the initiative promptly. In the afternoon hours the Arrow-Cross leadership headed by Szálasi showed up at the German Legation. The Germans distributed arms to the Arrow-Cross commandos, and Arrow-Cross leaflets were given out in the streets of Budapest.

In the meantime, at about 6 p.m., Lakatos and Hennyey made their appearance at the German Legation in order to negotiate, in pursuance of the arrangement between Horthy and Rahn, for the withdrawal of the German armed forces. In exchange for German withdrawal and for the release of Lieutenant-General Szilárd Bakay and Miklós Horthy, Jr., they offered that, until the Germans had finished withdrawing, the Hungarian army would not lay down its arms. This discussion, however, was intended only to gain time, and the Germans made really good use of it. For example, they demanded the offer in writing in order to 'forward it to Hitler'. When Lakatos, to comply with this demand, wanted to leave, the Germans — with reference to the fresh news of a mine blockade — declared that they would not negotiate as prisoners. At about 7 p.m. Bach-Zelewski handed Csatay an ultimatum stating that, unless the mine blockade was removed by 10 p.m. they would make an assault on the Castle. A little later he changed the ultimatum to the effect that the storm would start unless the negotiations with Veesenmayer came off well by 6 a.m.

While these events were taking place, confusion reigned in the Castle. Desultory measures followed one another. Horthy was no longer master of his own entourage either, and he left practically everything to his councillors. This time already he would have liked to do something to comply with Antonov's ultimatum. He summoned Chief of Staff Vörös together with Colonel Nádas. He wanted to send the latter to Szeged in accordance with the request of Moscow. But Nádas did not accept the mission and recommended General István Szentmiklóssy in his stead. Horthy left the decision to the Chief of Staff who, however, now declined responsibility for the general order that was just read over the radio. They tried to find General Szentmiklóssy, but by the time he arrived they had given up the plan.

After 8 p.m., Lakatos submitted to Horthy the draft text of the note to be presented to Veesenmayer. The Regent approved it with the remark that he had the impression that everything had been lost by now. In the evening hours it appeared that the Germans controlled all Budapest except Buda Castle, and they or the Arrow-Cross people had taken possession of all important objects in the capital. It was about that time that Ribbentrop angrily called Rahn by phone and demanded that all bargaining should be stopped and an assault should be made on the Castle. But Veesenmayer still thought to himself that Horthy could be persuaded into anything, so he started a double game. He gave the green light to the Arrow-Cross take-over but tried to obtain Horthy's consent to it. The aim of negotiations with the Government now was only to find the proper form of raising Szálasi to power.

Meanwhile, at 8:20 p.m., a short telegram describing the events of the day was sent to Moscow: "Regent's son abducted by Germans and Arrow-Cross this morning. Building he was in was bombarded. No further news available. City is surrounded by large Reich forces. We received ultimatum from Germans." At the same time three more telegrams were drawn up to be sent to Moscow, asking for help, but they were dispatched as late as 5 a.m. on the 16th.

Szálasi's order of the day was broadcast at 9:20 p.m., followed by János Vörös's general order to continue fighting. A few minutes to 10 p.m. a proclamation of the Arrow-Cross Party came on the air. A couple of minutes later Horthy summoned Prime Minister Lakatos, Minister Hennyey and Rakovszky, and told them about the Antonov ultimatum which, in accordance with the preliminary terms, demanded that the German troops should be attacked. The Ministers were for rejecting the ultimatum. They argued that no answer should be given to the Soviet ultimatum, because the request for an armistice had been addressed to three Great Powers. (It is worth mentioning here that the ultimatum was known to, and even approved by, the British and U. S. Governments.) Chief of Staff Vörös had also been invited to attend the conference but, for fear of the consequences of his general order broadcast just before, did not dare to appear before Horthy. (A few days later Vörös crossed the front line at Szeged, but the Hungarian army was already controlled entirely by Arrow-Cross officers.)

In the late hours, in the Prime Minister's Office, Lieutenant-General Vattay proposed that Horthy ask for German protection for himself and his family, since in this way he might relinquish the exercise of power without appointing a new Prime Minister. The Government should then resign, so it might be left to the Germans to form a new government without Horthy's approval. Lakatos and the Ministers present accepted the proposal and instructed Vattay and Ambrózy to obtain the consent of the Regent. The emissaries returned to the Prime Minister's Office after midnight, asserting that Horthy had accepted the recommendation. In reality the Regent, whom they called on in his bedroom towards midnight, refused to accept it and, at repeated requests, replied: "We shall discuss it in the morning." (After the war Vattay, in excuse of his conduct, affirmed that it was for the sake of the Regent's safety that, before the Ministers, he had given a clear form to Horthy's uncertain answer.) At 3 a.m. on the 16th, Lakatos phoned German Councillor of Legation Feine and read out the following letter addressed to Hitler: "On behalf of the Royal Hungarian Government I have the honour to inform Your Excellency that in view of the situation, and in order to avoid a civil war and the ensuing bloodshed, the Government has decided to resign, the more so since it had been informed of things of which it had had no knowledge before. Likewise His Highness the Regent has decided to resign from the regency and to retreat to private life. It is the wish of His Highness to be placed, together with his family, under the protection of the Reich Government, and he has commissioned me to forward to the Reich Government his request for asylum in Germany."

At about 4 a.m., Feine showed up at the Prime Minister's Office to take over the letter and to agree on what was to be done. At the German Legation, Lakatos's letter was received with relief, for it made it possible to raise the Arrow-Cross people to power with the semblance of legality, without removing Horthy by force. Therefore Veesenmayer asked right away for Hitler's permission to accept the offer. Hitler granted protection to Horthy and his retinue.

In the meantime, the German units instructed to take the Castle had made the necessary preparations for the action. At first Horthy gave instruction to resist. At 5 a.m., the three telegrams drawn up earlier were dispatched to Moscow. They read as follows:

1. "Dead-line of German ultimatum expires at 10 p.m. German assault is expected. Request help by airborne units and advance towards Budapest."

2. "All our communication is cut off. Questionable whether truce-bearer arrives tomorrow in matter of armistice. Please enter into contact with the command of the 1st and 2nd armies at the front line. If contact proves impossible please inform Soviet Government that Colonel-General Veress is appointed to be Prime Minister, to conduct negotiations. He is empowered to issue orders, but Hungarian Radio has fallen into German hands."

3. "Chief of Staff's general order was falsified in the broadcast of German-controlled Hungarian Radio."

There is no explanation why these telegrams were delayed for eight hours — but they were. The first telegram might indeed make it appear in Moscow as if they had nearly a whole day up to the expiry of the German ultimatum, although only one hour was left even according to the modified ultimatum. Was Horthy really hoping that Soviet troops might possibly arrive in Budapest already on the 16th, and that the Hungarian army's desertion also could be carried out in a situation when the soldiers did no longer obey the Chief of Staff either? Let us suppose that he wanted to give a free hand to the two army commanders to act, but why then did he waste decisive hours? Isn't it more probable that he wanted to decline responsibility in both directions: towards the Germans by ensuring that, should the army's desertion succeed, he was not blamed for it, he had kept his 'gentlemen's word of honour'; towards the Allies by trying to make the last-minute telegram prove that he wanted to observe the agreements but the events prevented him?

After he succeeded in dispatching the telegrams, Horthy sent his family to the Papal Nunciature, then at 5:30 a.m., after repeated talks with Vattay, he decided to withdraw the order to resist the Germans. A few minutes later Horthy was called on by Veesenmayer in company with Prime Minister Lakatos. They met in the courtyard of Buda Castle. Veesenmayer requested the Regent to go with him to the Hatvany palace, because the assault on Castle Hill would start in ten minutes, and Horthy, being given assurances that his wife might join him, followed Hitler's plenipotentiary. Before getting into the car, Horthy instructed General Lázár to stop resisting. At 6 a.m. Skorzeny's units got moving and, after a minor skirmish, took Buda Castle.

The Germans wanted to obtain Horthy's formal consent to the appointment of Szálasi as well. In the late morning hours, they sent Szálasi to Horthy in the Hatvany palace to discuss in person the formalities of the take-over. Horthy was not yet willing to give his agreement to Szálasi's appointment in writing, but Veesenmayer and Rahn insisted. Therefore in the afternoon, they invited Prime Minister Lakatos to submit to Horthy their written demand of three points: 1. the Regent's formal resignation in writing; 2. Szálasi's appointment to the post of Prime Minister; 3. disavowal of the proclamation of October 15. Lakatos undertook to submit only point 3, to which Horthy consented, and thus at 4 p.m., after the Germans had promised to set free the Regent's son and allow him to take some personal effects with him, Horthy signed his proclamation of October 16, in which he said: "I hereby declare my proclamation to the Hungarian nation, made on the 15th October, null and void and repeat the order to troops issued by the Chief of the Hungarian General Staff, calling for the devoted continuation of the fight. The serious military situation demands that the Hungarian Army should defend its country in a manner worthy of its galant reputation. May God guide our Army and Hungary on the road towards a better future. Dated October 16, 1944".

At 6 p.m., Veesenmayer called on Horthy (who at that time was again in the Castle packing) to have him sign a declaration on his resignation and Szálasi's appointment. Veesenmayer found the Regent in the bathroom. After a short quarrel Horthy — having been promised that his son would be released — signed the declaration, which was then broadcast in the evening hours reading: "My greetings to the Honourable Presidents of the two Houses of the Hungarian Parliament! In a heavy (and difficult) hour of Hungarian history I make known this as my decision: in the interest of the successful prosecution of the war and of inner unity and coherence of the nation, to abdicate from my office of Regent and to renounce all legal rights occurring from my power as Regent. At the same time, I entrust Ferenc Szálasi with the formation of the Cabinet of national contrenration. Horthy."

The events of the Arrow-Cross take-over thus ended. On October 17, Horthy, under German escort, left Hungary to live through the last months of the war at Hirschberg Castle near Wilheim in Bavaria, while the Arrow-Cross terror was reigning in the still unliberated part of the country. Having come into power, the Arrow-Cross men did their utmost to put all remaining military and material forces of the country at the service of the war waged on the side of Germany. The German High Command wanted by all means to delay the advance of the Soviet troops, therefore it demanded from Szálasi total mobilization. The Arrow-Cross 'national leader' promised Hitler 1,500,000 Hungarian soldiers. He wanted to use every man and every woman between 12 and 60 years for armed or labour service. The Arrow-Cross Government signed an agreement with the Germans for the delivery to Germany of all factory equipment, livestock and rolling stock of the country, and the gold reserve of the National Bank. Evacuation was ordered in the operational areas. In November 1944 the political prisoners were delivered to the Germans. Before the Soviet army closed the ring around Budapest, Jews by tens of thousands were carried off into concentration camps. Tens of thousands of innocent victims were tormented to death by 'Hungarist' terror commandos in the Arrow-Cross houses or shot dead on the Danube embankments.

A great part of the population, however, refused to obey the order of evacuation and to comply with the Arrow-Cross decrees. Workers of Csepel and Diósgyőr unanimously refused to dismantle the factories and to leave their homes. From the autumn of 1944, the most varied forms of passive resistance were developed while active resistance also strengthened as a result of the efforts of the Hungarian Front. Although the coming of the Arrow-Cross to power and the concentration of two German armies upon the military operations going on in Hungarian territory were serious impediments, the preparations for the outbreak of an armed rising of Hungarians were intensifed in the new situation. The camp of the resistance movement considerably broadened because every anti-German element, from the various bourgeois and petty-bourgeois groups to certain Horthyite circles, saw in the Hungarian Front the only forces capable of opposing the German invaders and their Hungarian hirelings.

5. Formation of the Provisional Government at Debrecen. Signing of the armistice

In the autumn of 1944, the Hungarian Front took steps to co-ordinate with the Soviet army the plan of an armed rising and to contact the Allied Powers. Early in November 1944, it resolved to send a delegation, composed of representatives of the parties assembled in the Front and of military personalities, to Moscow with a memorandum outlining the aims and plans of the Hungarian Front. It was the task of the delegation, furthermore, to inform the Soviet army leaders of the military situation in Budapest. On November 13, the Military members of the delegation — Ernő Simonffy-Tóth and János Vörös's son — managed to fly across the front line and arrived at Moscow a few days later. (The political members of the delegation, owing to a car accident, failed to arrive at the meeting place in time.) The parties of the Hungarian Front, the military committee headed by Endre Bajcsy-Zsilinszky and other underground organizations set up, on November 19, a Liberation Committee of the Hungarian National Uprising and appointed its military staff. President of the Committee was Endre Bajcsy-Zsilinszky, among the members of the military staff were Lieutenant-General János Kiss, Staff Colonel Jenő Nagy and Staff Captain Vilmos Tarcsay.

The foremost task of the Liberation Committee was to prepare the plan of an armed uprising, to mobilize the available generals, officers and military units, to carry out the rising. The insurrectionists were supposed to break through across a thoroughfare of the capital to pass over to the Soviet army and open the way for Soviet troops to get to the Danube and to attack from the rear the Germans and the Arrow-Cross formations stuck in Budapest, thereby averting the destruction of the capital city. The armed rising was scheduled for December 1, 1944. The Liberation Committee, for want of information from Simonffy-Tóth, decided to send another delegation to the Soviet High Command. The delegation was to take with it two letters signed by Endre Bajcsy-Zsilinszky on behalf of the Hungarian Front. In them

Bajcsy-Zsilinszky stated that the Hungarian Front undertook to give effect to the proclamation of October 15 and asked for the establishment of contacts and co-operation. He requested Marshal Malinovsky to secure the route of the delegation and to provide assistance in its journey.

But the uprising did not take place because, on November 23, as a result of treachery, the Gestapo arrested the military staff of the Liberation Committee and another thirty officers participating in its work. (The non-military members of the Committee arrived at the secret meeting-place later, and most of them thus evaded being arrested.) But resistance continued. The Communist Party and groups of the left-wing Social Democrats oraganized guerrilla actions first of all in Budapest and environs, as well as in provincial industrial centres. Irregular troups recruited from Hungarian prisoners of war were active in the Carpatho-Ukraine, the Borsod industrial district and the Bakony Mountains. The advance of the Soviet army was helped by guerrilla fights, varied active and passive forms of resistance and the rapid disintegration of the Hungarian armed forces, disobedience of orders and mass desertions. But the lion's share of Hungary's liberation fell to the Soviet army. By November–December 1944, two-thirds of the territory of Hungary had been liberated. In the liberated parts of the country a democratic transformation began as a result of which a Provisional National Assembly and a Provisional National Government were formed at Debrecen in December 1944.

Preparations for the formation of a Provisional Government had started earlier, in October 1944. A particular part in this was played by members of the armistice delegation staying in Moscow and by Horthyite generals who had gone over to the Soviet troops after the abortive desertion. Already on October 16, the armistice delegation in Moscow requested the Allied Powers by note to issue to the Hungarian people the following address:

"The Hungarian Radio has been seized by the Germans who use it to spread false rumours. On October 15 they falsified the appeal of the Hungarian Chief of Staff. [Here followed the text of the appeal.]

"The Germans have most hideously betrayed the Hungarian people. They have pillaged the country.

"The Red Army does not menace the peaceful life of the Hungarian people. The Red Army continues advancing not in order to fight against the Hungarian army but, as a friend, to liberate Hungary from under the German yoke."

At the same time, the delegation requested the Soviet Government that Soviet and Hungarian forces should rapidly occupy Budapest so as to hinder the bridges from being blown up and a massacre from taking place. For this reason, it found it desirable to deploy paratroops. It requested also the dispatch of liaison officers to bid the commanders of the 1st and 2nd armies to get in touch by radio with the armistice delegation. It asked the Allied Powers to co-operate in preventing the German bombing of Budapest, to expedite rapid advance towards Budapest, and to prepare the dropping of parachutists for an assault on the fortified points held by the Germans and on the Citadel where the Fascists intended to hold out to the end.

The Soviet Foreign Minister immediately informed the British and U.S. Ambassadors of this note, and on the night of the 16th, the armistice delegation was asked to appear in the building of the Soviet General Staff. Kuznetsov spoke of Béla Miklós's defection and inquired whether the army would obey Miklós's orders. The Hungarians having answered in the affirmative, Kuznetsov said that Béla Miklós must be told about the tasks, because he had deserted in an effort to stop all operations against the Soviet forces and start fighting the Germans. The decision was up to the Hungarians. But the members of the delegation said that they could not decide without Veress, who was the designated Prime Minister. (Veress had been arrested by the Germans at 5 a.m. on the 16th, but Moscow did not yet know about this development.)

After Kuznetsov had informed them that Béla Miklós waited for instructions from the delegation in Moscow, this latter asked for telephone connection with Miklós. Faragho and Miklós conferred by phone, in the afternoon of the 17th, and agreed that Szent-Iványi would fly to Béla Miklós, who will fulfil the orders of the Soviet General Staff.

On the 18th, Szent-Iványi flew to Lisko, where he was received by L. Z. Mekhlis, a member of the war council of the 4th Ukrainian Front and then met Béla Miklós. They agreed that, in case Veress had been arrested by the Germans, a new Government should be formed of politicians staying in liberated parts, including Dániel Bánffy.

On October 20, Antonov and Kuznetsov held further discussions with the armistice delegation about the establishment of a government. Antonov expounded that the Soviet Government found it necessary to set up as soon as possible, a government centre to counteract the Arrow-Cross Government. The new government was to rally all forces which were against the war and wished to fight Germans. This was when Debrecen was first proposed as seat of the new government, and the idea was broached that the nucleus of the new government should include members of the armistice delegation, which, before long, was to change its name to 'Moscow Hungarian Committee'.

On October 23, after repeated consultations with the Soviet General Staff, the Hungarian Committee sent the Allied Powers a note stressing that — since Horthy had been apprehended by the Germans and his appointed successor, Lajos Veress, commander of the 2nd army, had disappeared — the armistice delegation was the only depository of Horthy's constitutional will and of constitutional legal continuity. It requested the Allies to entrust the delegation with the establishment of a new Government at Debrecen, which would be the constitutional successor to the Lakatos Government and would co-operate with the Allies in the spirit of the negotiations in progress.

In the meantime, by Stalin's order of October 28 — stating to Malinovsky that it was extremely important to take the Hungarian capital at the earliest date possible — an attack was launched in order to liberate Budapest. The entire front got moving, but the capital city could not be liberated on the march, because Hitler, intent on holding it for strategic and political reasons, had concentrated great forces in its defence.

When Béla Miklós, commander of the 1st army, arrived at Moscow on November 8, the rivalry for precedence started at once. Miklós pointed out that he was, after Lajos Veress's disappearance, the lawful successor to Horthy, because in order of rank the commander of the 1st army followed the commander of the 2nd army. When the dispute was closed by co-opting Béla Miklós to the armistice delegation, there arrived János Vörös who, with reference to the assignment he had received from Horthy, arrogated the leading role to himself. The dispute continued even after the Allies had expressed their agreement in principle with the formation of the new government, although the contestants had been given to understand — notably after Simonffy-Tóth's arrival — that representatives of the Hungarian Front should also be included in the government.

Meanwhile the democratic mass movement was energetically unfolding in the liberated parts of Hungary. At Szeged on December 2, 1944, on the initiative of the Communist Party, a body to succeed the Hungarian Front was established — the Hungarian National Independence Front, with the participation of the Communist Party, the Social Democratic Party, the Independent Smallholders' Party, the National Peasant Party, the Bourgeois Democratic Party and the trade unions. In the villages and provincial towns representatives of the parties of the Independence Front formed national committees which prepared the convening of a Provisional National Assembly and elected the M.P.s at mass meetings.

In Debrecen on December 21, 1944, the Provisional National Assembly met in the oratory of the Calvinist College, and the next day it elected the National Government with Béla Dálnoki Miklós as Prime Minister. Delegated to the Government were three members of the Communist Party, two from the Smallholders' Party, two from the Social Democratic Party, one from the Peasant Party and four members, including the Prime Minister, from the Horthyite armistice commission. The participation of the latter four in the democratic Government, in a situation when Germans and Arrow-Cross bands were ravaging in the western parts of Hungary and in Budapest, was certainly a necessary and positive phenomenon, because it exerted a disruptive effect upon the army units still fighting on the side of the Germans, and contributed to the strength of the resistance movement in the German-occupied areas of the country.

Upon its formation the Government issued a declaration emphasizing the following: "The Provisional National Government breaks once and for all with the German oppressors who have for centuries been subjugating the country and with the German alliance which has twice in the course of two generations plunged our fatherland into war, into a national disaster. The Provisional National Government undertakes to compensate for the material damage which Hungary has caused by her war waged against the Soviet Union and the neighbouring peoples. The Provisional National Government makes every effort to establish good neighbourly relations and co-operation with all the surrounding democratic countries as well as with the United States and Great Britain, and sincere friendship with the powerful Soviet Union which assists our people in shaking off the German yoke." The declaration stated that the nation was vitally interested in contributing by force of arms to the annihilation of Hitlerism, so the Government regarded it as its foremost duty to mobilize all forces for this purpose. In the interest of Hungary's democratic transformation it would repeal all antidemocratic laws and regulations, dissolve the Fascist parties and organizations, purge the state authorities and call the traitors to account. It took a stand in favour of the prompt realization of a land reform, adding that it first intended to seize for this purpose the estates of traitors, Volksbund members and those who had served in the German army. It proclaimed the restoration of the democratic liberties and the rights of the working class. At the same time, it stated that the Provisional Government, by dint of its composition, function and the circumstances, "regards private property as the basis of the economic and social order of the country and will secure its inviolability. It will effectively promote private initiatives and private undertakings", but "will introduce, with the view of equitable taxation, a substantially progressive fiscal system". Finally it called upon the population of the country to support the Provisional Government in its work aimed at saving the country.

On December 23, the Provisional Government requested the Soviet Union to make known the armistice terms, and at the same time gave expression to its firm intention to declare war on Germany. Accordingly, at its meeting of December 28 it passed a unanimous decision invalidating the treaties concluded with Germany and declared war on her. In January 1945 a Government delegation went to Moscow to sign the armistice agreement. Members of the delegation were Defence Minister János Vörös, Foreign Minister János Gyöngyösi, and István Balogh, Secretary of State in the Prime Minister's Office.

The text of the armistice agreement had been drafted jointly by representatives of the Soviet, British and U. S. Governments, in the course of negotiations held in several stages, on the basis of Soviet proposals. At the negotiations, disputes mainly arose about the amount of the reparations. On January 15, 1945, the representatives of the three Great Powers rejected the request of the Czechoslovak Government for the relocation of Hungarians from Czechoslovakia to be included as a principle in article 2, and for the Hungarian Government to be obliged to take in the relocated population for resettlement. This day witnessed the finalization of the text after slight modifications.

The armistice agreement was signed on January 20, 1945. The document drawn up in twenty articles laid down that Hungary had ceased hostilities against the Allied Powers and had declared war on Germany. It obliged the Hungarian Government to disarm all German armed forces left in Hungarian territory and to surrender them as prisoners of war; to intern the German nationals (except the Jews of German nationality); to set up eight Hungarian infantry divisions equipped with heavy armament and to place them at the disposal of the Allied (Soviet) Army Command and, after the conclusion of the operations against Germany, to demobilize them and reduce the armed force to peace-time strength.

The agreement obliged Hungary to withdraw all military and administrative authorities from the occupied Czechoslovak, Yugoslav and Rumanian territories behind the frontiers of December 31, 1937; to guarantee freedom of movement to the Soviet and other Allied forces and to assist in their transports at her own expense; to release all the Allied prisoners of war and internees as well as the political prisoners of Hungarian nationality, and to set free all those who were in detention because of their political conviction, religious views or national extraction. The Provisional National Government undertook to restitute in full, until the date set by the Allied Control Commission, to the Soviet Union, Czechoslovakia and all members of the United Nations, those material goods which had been public, social or private property, namely factory equipment, railway engines, railway carriages, historic relics, museum treasures and all other assets which had, in the course of the war, been transported to Hungary from territories of the United Nations; to surrender as booty to the Allies all German military property in the territory of Hungary, and to deliver all other German property to the Allied Control Commission; to make available, in cash, goods and services, to the Allies everything the Allied (Soviet) Army Command might need when discharging its functions.

The armistice agreement obliged Hungary to pay reparations in the form of consignments of goods worth $300 million in six years. Of the $300 million $200 million was due to the Soviet Union ($65.7 million was later cancelled by the Soviet Government), the remaining $100 million went to Czechoslovakia and Yugoslavia.

The agreement made it a duty of Hungary to disband all Fascist parties and organizations. It provided for the establishment of an Allied Control Commission which was to remain under the direction of the Allied (Soviet) Army Command until the end of the military operations against Germany. An appendix to the armistice agreement contained the modalities of implementation. The agreement came into force upon its signing.

The provisions of the armistice agreement, which were consequences of Hungary's participation in the war by the side of Nazi Germany, although imposing certainly heavy burdens on the population of the country, were on the whole equitable terms. The prompt signing of the agreement contributed to the consolidation of the position of the new, democratic Government, for it was the first step towards breaking the international isolation into which the country had been thrown by the foreign and domestic policy of the counter-revolutionary régime, and the agreement thereby opened the way towards the restoration of Hungary's sovereignty, in a situation when in Budapest and in the western parts of the country the fighting was still going on against the German invaders and their Arrow-Cross hirelings.

Owing to the stubborn and mad resistance of the Germans, the complete liberation of the country took another three months. As a result of the Soviet military operations in Hungary, Budapest was liberated on February 13, 1945, and the liberation of Hungary was completed on April 4. Barely a month later Nazi Germany capitulated. The Second World War ended in Europe.

The war demanded enormous sacrifices from the people of Hungary. It took the lives of nearly half a million Hungarians at the fronts, in concentration and extermination camps. And those who managed to survive the ordeals of war had to suffer the economic consequences of the war ravages. The retreating German and

Arrow-Cross troops plundered the country and laid most of it in ruins. They carried to Germany the most valuable machines and raw materials of the factories. They blew up each and every one of the bridges across the Danube and the Tisza; as many as 1,704 bridges were demolished. Altogether 48,000 of the 68,000 vehicles of the State Railways were carried off. The number of totally ruined or partially damaged dwelling houses amounted to 120,000. There was hardly any factory or mine in the country to have its productive capacity left. A great part of the public utility installations in Budapest were destroyed, 98 per cent of the electric cables were wrecked. Agriculture also suffered enormous damage. The stock of cattle decreased by 1.5 million head, the pig population by 2 million, the horse-stock by half a million, and the poultry stock by 18 million. The Second World War destroyed *40 per cent of the national wealth of the country.* This was the state to which the foreign policy of twenty-five years of counter-revolutionary régime reduced Hungary, a policy which led to complete bankruptcy even as far as its own aims were concerned: this foreign policy, which, only to secure the territories acquired with the help of Nazi Germany and to maintain the counter-revolutionary system at any price, dragged the country into a war which resulted in the collapse of the régime, in the loss of the acquired territories.

With regard to the frontiers the armistice agreement concluded with Hungary stated that the Allied Powers refused to recognize the territorial changes effected by Axis arbitration and by participation in aggression on Czechoslovakia and Yugoslavia, and provided for retreat to the frontiers of 1937. The position adopted by the Allies followed from the requirements of the anti-Fascist struggle and Hungary's part in the war. The territorial consequences of aggression had to be rendered ineffective and eliminated as a natural result of victory over Fascism. And this included Hungary's responsibility for the war. The Allies declared on many occasions during the war that it was part of their war aims to restore the sovereignty of Czechoslovakia and Yugoslavia, that they refused to recognize any territorial change resulting from the dictates and aggression of the Axis Powers, and that their view regarding territorial questions was influenced, in addition to by the above principles, by their obligations of alliance.

During the war, the question of Transylvania was, to a certain degree, an open question because Hungary and Rumania had both been members of the Axis camp from the beginning of the war. This was no secret for either the Hungarian ot the Rumanian Government. As mentioned earlier, the armistice with Rumania did not rule out the possibility of the peace treaty's making some territorial concessions to Hungary as against the frontiers of 1937. But this was also subjected to the requirements of the anti-Fascist war. The different functions which the two countries performed during the last stage of the war essentially precluded even this possibility. In the last eight months of the war, Rumania fought in arms on the side of the Allies, while Hungary failed to break with Nazi Germany. This is why it could hardly be doubted at that time that the treaty of peace would not render decisions in favour of Hungary. And indeed, the Paris Treaty of Peace signed on February 10, 1947, restored the Hungarian frontiers of 1937 with the modification that it adjudged three more localities near the Bratislava bridgehead to Czechoslovakia.

The purpose of the Paris peace treaties of 1947 was to close the anti-Fascist war, so in territorial questions, the treaty concluded with Hungary left out of consideration even those social changes which took place in this country after the liberation. Hungary, just like the neighbouring countries, embarked on the road of development into a people's democracy. What was decisive from the point of view of the people's happiness and future was not the issue of the frontiers but the possibility created by the liberation for the building of a new society. The liberation of the country resulted in the collapse of the structures obstructing social progress, in the eradication of the capitalist social conditions encumbered with feudal vestiges, conditions in whose overlong survival, as we have seen, no small part was played by the almost one-hundred-year-old efforts to maintain the illusion of a historical Hungary. The way traversed since the liberation has convincingly demonstrated to the Hungarian people that the flourishing of a nation, its social and economic advancement, is not dependent on the size of its territory.

The victory over Fascism, the creation of new social conditions in Hungary and the neighbouring countries, has made it possible for the peoples of the Danubian basin to develop — by overcoming the heritage of the past, i.e., the mutual grievances stemming from the oppression of nationalities, and conflicting territorial claims—new forms of co-operation on the basis of their social transformation and common socialist future.

SOURCES AND REFERENCES

Archival sources

A valuable source for the study of the foreign policy of the counter-revolutionary period is the *National Archives Foreign Ministry Material*. I have used first of all the diplomatic documentary material of the Ministry of Foreign Affairs. I have studied in particular detail the documents from the years 1933 to 1944. Some difficulties have arisen from the fact that the Foreign Ministry material is incomplete. Very few documents are extant from the period of the creation of the counter-revolutionary régime. Barely a few cipher telegrams can be found from the 1920's. Important reports and minutes of negotiations from the whole of the Bethlen era have been destroyed or disappeared. In 1944, in the days of the German occupation, nearly all documents that might have been compromising were destroyed. A great many materials perished during the siege of Budapest. The Foreign Ministry material available to us contains very few documents from the time of the German occupation and almost none from the period of Arrow-Cross rule. Part of the deficiency could be supplied from the stock of other archives or from collections. The first to be mentioned here is the *Szent-Iványi Manuscript* kept in the National Archives. It was upon instructions from Count Pál Teleki that the Secretary of State in the Prime Minister's Office, Domokos Szent-Iványi, set about collecting Foreign Ministry documents which might be used in justification of Hungarian foreign policy at the peace conference. Those were mainly papers on German–Hungarian relations. On the basis of these papers Szent-Iványi wrote his work "The Foreign Policy of Trianon Hungary" which has remained in manuscript form. In point of fact, this work contains textual copies of the collected Foreign Ministry documents. It is valuable as a source because the originals of a considerable part of the published papers have perished. The reliability of the manuscript can be authenticated on the basis of extant original documents.

The collection entitled *Papers of László Szabó* may be used with due source criticism, especially in respect of Italo–Hungarian relations. László Szabó, who was the Hungarian military attaché in Rome for about a decade and was a friend of the Italian dictator, made and kept many valuable records of his talks with Mussolini and of his special missions in Italy.

From the National Archives material, other than Foreign Ministry documents, the *Records of the Council of Ministers* are indispensable. Unfortunately this is not complete either; moreover, the records of the Cabinet meetings, especially those from the war years, are of little documentary value. It is known that, during the tenure of Prime

Minister Bárdossy, many important records and minutes were falsified. And, under the Kállay Government, essential questions of foreign policy were discussed by a restricted Cabinet or in absolute privacy. Decisions were passed at confidential conferences between Horthy, Kállay and the Privy Councillors. Of specially good use are the *Bethlen papers,* furthermore the *Kozma papers* kept also in the National Archives, as well as the collected documents dealing with the trials of war criminals, such as *The Szálasi trial* and *The Bárdossy trial.*

To reconstruct the foreign policy of a small country, it is absolutely necessary to study, in addition to domestic archival materials, the diplomatic papers of certain great Powers with which it entertained close diplomatic relations, or which considerably influenced the aims of its foreign policy and often determined its tactical moves. Today, the scholar is in the fortunate position to make himself familiar with the *British, German, French and Italian diplomatic documents* relating to Hungary in original or in the form of collected papers. In recent years, the British Government has reduced the 50-year interdiction on archival materials to 30 years, so it is now possible to delve for information into the Foreign Office papers relating to Hungary up to 1945 (*Public Record Office. Foreign Office 371, Hungary 1918—1945*). I was in a position to peruse these papers. The British documents contain very important data, first of all, concerning the history of the rise to power and consolidation of the counter-revolutionary régime in Hungary. The papers dealing with the period of the world economic crisis are of great value. The documentary material of the British Foreign Office is of unique value for the study of foreign politics during the Second World War. The principal sources I have used for my book bear the following file numbers: 20.395; 20.396; 22.373; 22.376; 24.422; 24.890; 24.958; 25.034; 26.602; 30.965; 30.966; 32.882; 34.447; 34.449; 34.450; 34.451; 34.452; 34.453; 34.498; 34.502; 34.504; 34.505; 34.506; 37.031; 37.179; 39.252; 39.253; 39.254; 39.264.

The documents of the German Foreign Ministry, as is known, were captured by the Allied Powers in 1945. A stock of about three million microfilm copies made of the papers is available to researchers in U. S. and British archives, and the originals can be studied in the archives at Bonn. In London, I studied the smaller part of the German diplomatic documents relating to Hungary (*Public Record Office. German Foreign Ministry*), while the larger part of those papers were made available to me from the microfilm strips made on the basis of György Ránki's collection and kept by the National Archives as well as by the Institute of History of the Hungarian Academy of Sciences in Budapest. The German diplomatic documents, in particular those dating from after 1933, are indispensable sources not only for the study of German—Hungarian relations but also for the understanding of the entire Hungarian foreign policy of the Second World War period. With the German material, not only the original copies of the minutes of negotiations, exchanges of notes and ambassadorial reports have been preserved, but, thanks to the conscientious attention of the Nazi foreign service and its intelligence bureau organized with German thoroughness, notes of almost all decisions of the Hungarian Government, memoranda made of the assessment of the international political situation, etc. are also available. The German diplomatic material is practically our only source concerning the year 1944.

It would be equally very important to have access to diplomatic documents of the neighbouring countries. But, except the papers of the Czechoslovak Foreign Ministry, they are not open to the public. As to the Czechoslovak documents relating to Hungary (1937—1939), I have perused them in the archives of the Foreign Ministry of Czechoslovakia (*Archiv ministerstva zahraničnich věcí*).

Background materials

In this place I will mention only those publications which survey longer periods of the foreign policy of the various countries and serve as bases for the study of the history of international relations between the two world wars and during the Second World War. The publication, in four series, of the papers of the German Foreign Ministry was begun in 1948, by a committee composed of English, American and French historians. The series is entitled *Documents of German Foreign Policy 1918—1945*. I used with good results the six volumes of Series C (1935—1937) already published, and thirteen volumes of Series D (1937—1945). The excellently edited series contain very many documents on Hungary, too, but since the primary aim of these volumes is to throw light upon the entire German foreign policy, they contain only part of those papers that deal with Hungary, that is, those which are related to some international event. So these volumes are mainly important to us because they present an overall picture of Germany's policy in Central Europe and make up, at least in part, for the deficiency caused by the inaccessibility of diplomatic documents of the neighbouring countries. In connection with the series, it is to be noted that this background material, like every such publication, is a selection of documents.

Important German documents are published in the volumes containing the material of the Nuremberg trial of war criminals: *Procès des Grands Criminels de Guerre devant le Tribunal Militaire International* (Nuremberg, 1946—1949); *Trials of War Criminals before the Nuremberg Military Tribunals* (Washington, 1946—1949); *Nazi Conspiracy and Aggression* (Office of United States Chief of Counsel for the Prosecution of Axis Criminality, Washington, 1946). Part of the German documents which had been captured by the Soviet army have been published by the Ministry of Foreign Affairs of the Soviet Union (Hungarian edition: *Okmányok és adatok a második világháború előzményeihez* [Documents and Data on the Antecedents of the Second World War] Budapest, 1949). The most important German documents relating to Hungary have been collected in one volume by historians working at the Hungarian Institute for Historiography. Thus, a volume, unique of its kind, is the collection of papers concerning a single country from the entire Nazi era: *A Wilhelmstrasse és Magyarország 1933—1944* [The Wilhelmstrasse and Hungary 1933—1944] (Compiled, edited and the preface written by György Ránki, Ervin Pamlényi, Loránd Tilkovszky and Gyula Juhász, Kossuth Publishers, Budapest, 1968).

Important aid is provided for the study of Hungarian foreign policy by the series of background materials in which documents of the Italian Foreign Ministry from the interwar years have been published, the more so since there is no way of studying Italian documents in archives and since the documents from the decade following the First World War have already been published: *I documenti diplomatici italiani* (6th to 9th series: 1917–1943; Rome, 1956–1965). The British Foreign Office has also published its diplomatic papers: *Documents on British Foreign Policy 1919–1939* (London, 1947–1966). Since the time of interdiction on research in England has been reduced, it is mainly the third series (1938–1939) that is of great value to the historian. All three series contain documents of interest to Hungary, but these papers are few in number. The French Foreign Ministry published its papers in a series entitled *Documents Diplomatiques Français 1932–1939* (Paris, 1963–1966). Its papers relating to Hungary are insignificant in number and are of no particular interest. Important are, on the other hand, the documents relating to Hungary which are contained in the background material series dealing with the international relations of the United States: *Foreign Relations of the United States* (Diplomatic Papers, Washington). The volumes presenting the documents of the Second World War are particularly useful.

Hungary was the first among the socialist countries to publish diplomatic papers shedding light on the antecedents of the Second World War. The Institute of History of the Hungarian Academy of Sciences set about this job in 1958. The title of the series is *Diplomáciai iratok Magyarország külpolitikájához 1936–1945* [Diplomatic Papers on Hungary's Foreign Policy 1936–1945] (Editor of the series is László Zsigmond). Four volumes have appeared so far. Vol. I: "A Berlin–Róma tengely kialakulása és Ausztria annexiója, 1936–1938" [Formation of the Berlin–Rome Axis and the Annexation of Austria, 1936–1938] (Compiled and edited by Lajos Kerekes; Akadémiai Kiadó, Budapest, 1962). Vol. II: "A müncheni egyezmény létrejötte és Magyarország külpolitikája, 1936–1938" [The Making of the Munich Pact and Hungary's Foreign Policy, 1936–1938] (Compiled and edited by Magda Ádám; Akadémiai Kiadó, Budapest, 1970). Vol. III: "Magyarország külpolitikája 1938–1939" [Hungary's Foreign Policy 1938–1939] (Compiled and edited by Magda Ádám; Akadémiai Kiadó, Budapest, 1970), Vol. IV: "Magyarország külpolitikája a második világháború kitörésének időszakában, 1939–1940" [Hungary's Foreign Policy at the Time of the Outbreak of the Second World War, 1939–1940] (Compiled and edited by Gyula Juhász; Akadémiai Kiadó, Budapest, 1962). The fifth volume of the series is now in print. Finally, there is the collection of documents edited by Dénes Halmosy, *Nemzetközi szerződések 1918–1945* [International Treaties 1918–1945] (Közgazdasági és Jogi Könyvkiadó, Budapest, 1966), which contains the most important international treaties and conventions concluded between 1918 and 1945.

Compendia

The first modern synthesis of Hungary's history from 1919 to 1945 is to be found in Volume II of *Magyarország története* [History of Hungary] (Gondolat Publishers, Budapest, 1964) by Iván T. Berend and György Ránki. The same authors have written the economic history of the Horthy era: *Magyarország gazdasága az első világháború után, 1919–1929* [Hungary's Economy after the First World War, 1919–1929] (Akadémiai Kiadó, Budapest, 1966); *Magyarország a fasiszta Németország "életterében", 1933–1939* [Hungary in the 'Lebensraum' of Nazi Germany, 1933–1939] (Közgadasági és Jogi Könykiadó, Budapest, 1960); *Magyarország gyáripara a második világháború előtt és a háború időszakában, 1933–1944* [Hungary's Manufacturing Industry before the Second World War and during the War, 1933–1944] (Akadémiai Kiadó, Budapest, 1958).

The modern economic history of the entire region is summed up in their *Közép-Kelet-Európa gazdasági fejlődése a 19–20. században* [Economic Development in East Central Europe in the 19th and 20th Centuries] (Közgazdasági és Jogi Könyvkiadó, Budapest 1969). To the works of these authors I owe a debt of gratitude for the economic aspects of my book.

C. A. Macartney's two-volume work *October Fifteenth, a History of Modern Hungary: 1929–1945* (Edinburgh, 1956, 1961) excels with its immense material of facts concerning foreign politics in the first place. The renowned scholar wrote this work in the most crucial years of the Cold War the traces of which did not escape the pages of his book either. It is, however, incontestable that the work betrays a deep knowledge of Hungary's political life between the two world wars. The author's great collection of materials composed mainly of memoirs is to be found in the library of *St. Anthony's College* at Oxford. I had occasion to study the collection on the site.

Literature by chapters

CHAPTER I

Collected papers: A selection of documents on the rise and consolidation of the counter-revolutionary system is contained in three volumes of *Iratok az ellenforradalom történetéhez 1919–1945* [Documents on the History of the Counter-revolution 1919–1945] edited and prefaced by Dezső Nemes. The background material of these volumes was compiled by co-editor Elek Karsai (I: "Az Ellenforradalom hatalomra jutása és rémuralma Magyarországon 1919–1921" [The Rise to Power of the Counter-revolution and Its Reign of Terror in Hungary 1919–1921], Szikra, Budapest, 1956; II: "A fasiszta rendszer kiépítése és a népnyomor Magyarországon 1921–1924" [Mass Poverty and the Establishment of the Fascist Régime in Hungary 1921–1924], Szikra, Budapest, 1956; III: "Az ellenforradalmi rendszer gazdasági helyzete és politikája Magyarországon 1924–1926" [The Counter-revolutionary System in Hungary: Its Economic Situation and Policy 1924–1926], Kossuth Publishers, Budapest, 1959).

Useful contributions to the study of the antecedents of the Peace Conference and the Trianon treaty of peace have been provided by the following sources: *A History of the Peace Conference of Paris* (Vols. I–III. Ed. H. W. V. Templerly, London, 1920); *Papers and Documents relating to the Foreign Relations of Hungary* (Vols. I–II. Ed. Francis Deák, Dezső Ujváry. Budapest, 1939, 1946). The redaction of this latter, excellently edited publication began on the eve of the Second World War. The work was written in justification of Hungarian revisionist claims. Yet, researchers of the period cannot do without it, because most of these Hungarian Foreign Ministry documents are to be found nowhere else. Useful sources for Chapter I are the diary of the white terrorist Pál Prónai (*A határban a halál kaszál... Fejezetek Prónay Pál feljegyzéseiből* [Death Is Reaping in the Fields... Chapters from the notes of Pál Prónay] edited and prefaced by Ágnes Szabó and Ervin Pamlényi; Kossuth Publishers, Budapest, 1963), as well as *Páter Zadrawetz titkos naplója* [Father Zadrawetz's Secret Diary] (edited and prefaced by György Borsányi, Kossuth Publishers, Budapest, 1967).

Monographs: A fundamental source for the foreign politics of 1918/1919 is the book by Zsuzsa L. Nagy, *A párizsi békekonferencia és Magyarország 1918–1919* [The Paris Conference of Peace and Hungary 1918–1919] (Kossuth Publishers, Budapest, 1965), which, relying on a vast background material, is a dependable guide for the reader amidst the complicated international relations and diplomatic problems of the revolutions of 1918/1919. Very substantial features of the policy of the French Government are described, on the basis of recent French sources, in the following essays: "Vix és Károlyi" [Vix and Károlyi] by Sándor Vadász (*Hadtörténeti Közlemények*, 2/1969); "The Vix Mission in Hungary" by Peter Pastor (*Slavic Review*, Sept. 1970); "Az első világháború és az 1918–1919-es forradalmak időszakának magyar vonatkozású anyagai a francia levéltárakban" [Materials in French Archives Relating to Hungary from the Period of the First World War and the 1918–1919 Revolutions] by György Litván (*Történelmi Szemle*, 2/1967). Until the publication of György Ránki's essay "A Clerk-misszsió történetéhez" [On the History of the Clerk Mission] (*Történelmi Szemle*, 2/1967), little was known about the history of the rise to power of the counter-revolution in Hungary, especially about its international aspects, whereas works on its domestic political interconnections are in plenty. Starting from the exact realization that the years 1918–1919 constituted the period when international relations exerted a direct influence upon the domestic policy of Hungary, the author, in his essay bearing a modest title, wrote the authentic history of the birth of the counter-revolutionary system. To clear up the background of the origin of revisionist foreign policy, to explain why revisionist propaganda could make such a deep impact on broad strata of Hungarian society, remarkable thoughts are conveyed by the treatise of Péter Hanák "A magyar nacionalizmus néhány problémája a századforduló idején" [Some Problems of Hungarian Nationalism around the Turn of the Century] (*Történelmi Szemle*, 2–3/1960) and by the essays of István Bibó, *A kelet-európai kisállamok nyomorúsága* [The Misery of the Small States of Eastern Europe] (Budapest, 1946) and "Eltorzult magyar alkat, zsákutcás magyar történelem" [Hungarian Mentality Deformed, Hungarian History Deadlocked] (*Válasz*, 1948). The history of Hungarian nationalism and the influence of the nationalist ideology in the Horthy era are thoroughly elucidated by the volume of essays entitled *A magyar nacionalizmus kialakulása és története* [The Birth and History of Hungarian Nationalism] (Kossuth Publishers, Budapest, 1964). Different foreign policy problems are being investigated by Katalin G. Sós's booklet under the title *A nyugat-magyarországi kérdés* [The Question of Western Hungary] (Akadémiai Kiadó, Budapest, 1962) as well as by Mária Sz. Ormos's two essays, "Magyarország belépése a Nemzetek Szövetségébe" [Hungary's Entry into the League of Nations] (Századok, 1–4/1957) and *Az 1924. évi magyar államkölcsönök megszerzése* [Acquisition of the Hungarian Public Loans of 1924] (Akadémiai Kiadó, Budapest, 1964).

CHAPTER II

Collected papers: The Foreign Ministry documents of 1927–1931 are to be found in the book by Elek Karsai, *A magyar ellenforradalmi rendszer külpolitikája: 1927. január 1. – 1931. augusztus 24.* [The Foreign Policy of the Hungarian Counter-revolutionary Régime: January 1, 1927–August 24, 1931] (Kossuth Publishers, Budapest, 1967).

Monographs: The first comprehensive work on the so-called 'active' foreign policy of the Bethlen era is the monograph by Dezső Nemes, *A Bethlen-kormány külpolitikája 1927–1931-ben* [The Foreign Policy of the Bethlen Government in 1927–1931] (Kossuth Publishers, Budapest, 1964). The situation in Hungary during the world economic crisis is excellently discussed in the volume of essays edited by Miklós Incze, *Az 1929–1933. évi gazdasági világválság hatása Magyarországon* [The Effect of the World Economic Crisis of 1929–1931 upon Hungary] (Budapest, 1955).

A recent survey of the questions of Italo–Hungarian relations is the essay by Mária Ormos, "Bethlen koncepciója az olasz–magyar szövetségről" [The Bethlen Conception of the Italo–Hungarian Alliance] (*Történelmi Szemle*, 1–2/1971). The political history of 1931/1932, which has, until recently, been practically a blank spot in our historiography, is explored by the monograph of László Márkus, *A Károlyi Gyula-kormány bel- és külpolitikája* [The Domestic and Foreign Policy of the Government of Gyula Károlyi] (Akadémiai Kiadó, Budapest, 1968). The book by Márkus analyses the international causes of the fall of Bethlen's Government and gives a reliable sketch of the Károlyi Government's foreign policy without going into details. These details are discussed, on the other hand, in the dissertation by Mária Ormos "Franciaország és a keleti biztonság 1931–1936" [France and Eastern Security 1931–1936]. This outstanding monograph deserves attention also because it examines the problems of Central Europe in the context of world history, and this has led to new results in respect to Hungarian foreign policy. Interesting details about Austro–Hungarian relations are to be found in a remarkable essay of Lajos Kerekes revealing the Italian and Hungarian connections of the Heimwehr movement "Olaszország, Magyarország és az osztrák Heimwehr mozgalom, 1920–1930" [Italy, Hungary and the Austrian Heimwehr Movement, 1920–1930] (*Történelmi Szemle*, 2/1961).

CHAPTER III

Collected papers: Most of the background materials relating to the history of 1933–1939 have already been mentioned. Many things relevant to Hungarian affairs are contained in the diary and diplomatic papers of Italian Foreign Minister Galeazzo Ciano: *Diary* (1937–1943: Vols. I–II, London, 1952); *Ciano's Diplomatic Papers* (London, 1948). Important Hungarian documents have been published in the volume by Elek Karsai, *Iratok a Gömbös–Hitler találkozó történetéhez* [Documents on the History of the Meeting of Gömbös and Hitler] (Akadémiai Kiadó, 1962).

Monographs: There is no comprehensive monograph of foreign politics concerning the entire period under review here. But excellent books and essays are available dealing with some related problems. Treating of a whole range of problems concerning the Darányi and Imrédy governments and the effect of internal political conditions upon Hungarian foreign policy are, for example, the book by Sándor Kónya *Gömbös kísérlete totális fasiszta diktatúra megteremtésére* [Gömbös's Attempt to Establish a Totalitarian Fascist Dictatorship] (Akadémiai Kiadó, Budapest, 1968), a pioneer work by Miklós Lackó, *Nyilasok, nemzetiszocialisták 1935–1944* [Arrow-Cross and National Socialists 1935–1944] (Kossuth Publishers, Budapest, 1966), dealing with the Hungarian extreme-right movements, as well as the dissertation by Péter Sipos entitled "Imrédy Béla miniszterelnöksége és a Magyar Megújulás Pártja létrejötte" [Béla Imrédy's Premiership and the Formation of the Party of Hungarian Revival]. The history of the Rome Tripartite Pact is dealt with in György Ránki's study "A római hármas egyezmény és a német külpolitika" [The Rome Tripartite Pact and German Foreign Policy] (*Századok*, 4–5/1961). The Hungarian aspects of the assassination at Marseilles are revealed by Mária Sz. Ormos's book *Merénylet Marseilleben* [Regicide at Marseilles] (Kossuth Publishers, Budapest, 1968). A fine monograph on Austria's annexation by Germany is a work by Lajos Kerekes, *Anschluss 1938* (Akadémiai Kiadó, Budapest, 1963).

The foreign policy of the Darányi and Imrédy Governments with its broad international implications is dealt with by T. L. Sakmyster, *Hungary and the Coming of the European Crisis 1937–1938* (Indiana University, 1971). Hungarian foreign policy towards the Little Entente states and her participation in aggression on Czechoslovakia are discussed in detail by Magda Ádám in her *Magyarország és a kisantant a harmincas években* [Hungary and the Little Entente in the Thirties] (Akadémiai Kiadó, Budapest, 1968). Important aspects of Hungary's behaviour at the time of the aggression on Czechoslovakia are elucidated by the essay of György Ránki "Adatok a magyar külpolitikához a Csehszlovákia elleni agresszió idején" [Some remarks about Hungarian Foreign Policy at the Time of Aggression on Czechoslovakia] (*Századok*, 1–2/1959) and by the book of Aladár Kis, *Magyarország külpolitikája a második világháború előestéjén* [Hungary's Foreign Policy on the Eve of the Second World War] (Kossuth Publishers, Budapest, 1963). The Polish–Hungarian relations in the interwar years are surveyed in Endre Kovács's monograph *Lengyel–magyar kapcsolatok a két világháború között* [Polish–Hungarian Contacts between the Two World Wars] (Akadémiai Kiadó, Budapest, 1972).

CHAPTERS IV AND V

Among the collected documents, memoirs and monographs on the history of the Second World War, which amount to a whole library, I mention only the most important or most recent works relating to Hungary.

Collected papers: The most important works in addition to the volumes mentioned above: *Sztálin üzenetváltása az Egyesült Államok és Nagy-Britannia kormányfőivel 1941–1945* [Exchange of Messages by Stalin with the Heads of Government of the United States and Great Britain] (Vols. I–II, Kossuth Publishers, Budapest, 1958); *The Conferences at Malta and Yalta 1945* (U. S. Department of State, Washington, 1955). Rich in data about Hungary are *Kriegstagebuch des Oberkommandos der Wehrmacht 1940–1945* (Vols. 1–4, Frankfurt am Main, 1965); Franz Halder, *Kriegstagebuch* (Vols. 1–2, Stuttgart, 1962–1963). Minutes of Hitler's negotiations with leaders of countries allied with Germany are contained in Andreas Hillgruber, *Staatsmänner und Diplomaten bei Hitler* [Vol. I (1939–1941), Vol. II. (1942–1944)] (Frankfurt am Main, 1970). Important documents on wartime Czechoslovak–Hungarian relations are published in V. Mastný, "The Beneš–Stalin–Molotov Conversations in December 1943" (*Jahrbücher für die Geschichte Europas,* Vol. 20 [1972], pp. 367–402). Interesting documents on Hungary's role in the Second World War are to be found in the publication *Horthy Miklós titkos iratai* [Miklós Horthy's Secret Papers] (Kossuth Publishers, Budapest, 1963), which made public 88 papers from the Regent's cabinet archives captured by the Soviet army (ed. Miklós Szinai and László Szűcs). The original file sent back from the Soviet Union contained a valuable document on the court-martial trial of the persons guilty of the Újvidék massacre. This paper is missing from the volume, but it is contained in the collection entitled *Magyarország és a második világháború* [Hungary and the Second World War] (comp. by Magda Ádám, Gyula Juhász, Lajos Kerekes; Kossuth Publishers, Budapest, 1959). Photocopies of the German documents relating to the Jewish question in Hungary are published in a two-volume collection of documents by Randolph Braham, *The Destruction of Hungarian Jewry* (New York, 1964). The related Hungarian papers are contained in the two volumes of *Fegyvertelenül álltak az aknamezőkön* [They Stood Unarmed on the Mine Fields] (ed. Elek Karsai, Budapest, 1962) and in the three volumes of *Vádirat a nácizmus ellen* [Indictment of Nazism] (ed. Elek Karsai and Ilona Benesovszki, Budapest, 1960–1967). A chronicle of the birth of the Debrecen Provisional National Assembly and Government is the publication *Debreceni Feltámadás* [Resurgence at Debrecen] (ed. Antal Radó, Budapest, 1967). In this place I mention two interesting books of a different character. One is a compilation by Dezső Saly, *Szigorúan bizalmas* [Strictly Confidential] (Budapest, 1945), which contains the articles and news items left out of the press owing to wartime censorship, and the other, a book by Dezső Szirmai, Fasiszta lelkek [Fascist Souls] (Budapest, 1946), which contains a psychologist's notes of talks with war criminals in prison.

Memoirs: From the rich material of wartime memoirs I mention only those which were written by one-time Hungarian politicians or are of direct interest to

Hungary. N. Horthy, *Ein Leben für Ungarn* (Bonn, 1964); Nicholas Kállay, *Hungarian Premier: A Personal Account of a Nation's Struggle in the Second World War* (New York, 1954); Antal Ullein-Reviczky, *Guerre allemande, paix russe* (Neuchâtel, 1947); Stephen D. Kertész, *Diplomacy in a Whirlpool* (Notre Dame, 1953); Ferenc Adonyi, *A magyar katona a második világháborúban 1941–1945* [The Hungarian Soldier in the Second World War 1941–1945] (Klagenfurt, 1954); Ferenc Kisbarnaki Farkas, *A Tatárhágó visszanéz* [The Tatar Pass Looks Back] (Buenos Aires, 1955).

In the book by György Ránki, *Emlékiratok és valóság Magyarország második világháborús szerepéről* [Memoirs and Reality about Hungary's Role in the Second World War] (Kossuth Publishers, Budapest, 1964) we find a Marxist criticism of the émigré literature. Gusztáv Hennyey, *Magyar erőfeszítések a második világháború befejezésére* [Hungarian Efforts to End the Second World War] (Cologne, 1965) is a recollection of the Foreign Minister of the Lakatos Government. There is only one point Hennyey finds necessary to prove, namely that by the armistice negotiations of October 1944 Hungary did not violate the requirement of loyalty to Germany. A work written with a quite different approach from among the afore-mentioned memoirs is the recollection of a one-time Defence Minister, Vilmos Nagybaczoni Nagy, *Végzetes esztendők* [Fatal Years] (Budapest, 1945), which contains important political and military documents. I mention here György Pálóczi-Horváth's memoirs *The Undefeated* (London, 1959), which gives insight into the mechanism of secret British–Hungarian negotiations during the war. Finally, I refer to the memoirs of John Flournoy Montgomery, *Hungary, the Unwilling Satellite* (New York, 1947). Montgomery, who was the U. S. Minister in Hungary in 1940–1941, relates interesting things about U. S.–Hungarian relations. A work falling under this category, though a biography, is the book by Emil Csonka, *Habsburg Ottó* [Otto of Habsburg] (Munich, 1972), which contributes data on the peace-feelers of 1943 and primarily the conceptions of legitimism.

Monographs: The first Hungarian-language monograph on the entire history of the Second World War is the work by György Ránki, *A második világháború története* [History of the Second World War] (Budapest, 1973). I wrote Chapter IV on the basis of my Teleki monograph (Gyula Juhász, *A Teleki-kormány külpolitikája 1939–1941* [The Foreign Policy of the Teleki Government 1939–1941] (Akadémiai Kiadó, 1964). The initial stage of the Teleki Government's foreign policy is dealt with also by the above-mentioned work of Aladár Kis, but my views are, in several respects, different from his. Hungary's history during the Second World War is discussed by Soviet historian A. N. Pushkash in his book *Hungary in the Years of the Second World War* (Moscow, 1966, in Russian) containing very many new data collected from Soviet archives. Many new facts about Hungarian foreign policy during the Second World War are revealed in the monograph by Mario D. Fenyő, *Hitler–Horthy–Mussolini* (Yale University Press, 1972), based mainly on sources to be found in the United States. The policy towards the national minorities in the territories annexed to Hungary in 1938–1940 is dealt with by the monograph of Loránd Tilkovszky, *Revizió és nemzetiségpolitika Magyarországon 1938–1941* [Revision and Nationality Policy in Hungary

1938—1941] (Akadémiai Kiadó, Budapest, 1967), written on the basis of a vast source material. A fine analysis of Rumanian—Hungarian relations is the book by Dániel Csatári, *Forgószélben* [In the Whirlwind] (Akadémiai Kiadó, Budapest, 1968). Important data about Polish—Hungarian relations between 1939 and 1941 are published in the essay by István Lagzi "Adatok az 1939 őszén Magyarországra menekült lengyel katonák evakuációjának történetéhez, 1939—1941" [Data on the History of the Evacuation of Polish Soldiers Who in the Autumn of 1939 Escaped to Hungary: 1939—1941] (*Hadtörténelmi Közlemények,* 4/1973).

Fresh data are contributed to the Teleki Government's plan of emigration in Gyula Borbándi's essay with documents "A Teleki—Pelényi terv nyugati magyar ellenkormány létesítésére" [The Teleki—Pelényi Plan for the Establishment of a Government-in-exile in the West] (*Új Látóhatár,* 2/1966, Munich). Interesting details about Hungary's entry into war against the Soviet Union are published in the paper of József Kun "Magyarország második világháborúba lépésének katonai vonatkozásai" [Military Aspects of Hungary's Entry into the Second World War] (*Hadtörténelmi Közlemények,* 1/1962). A detailed analysis of the Anglo—American declaration of war is to be found in the essay by Gyula Juhász "Magyarország hadbalépése Nagy-Britannia és az Amerikai Egyesült Államok ellen" [Hungary's Entry into War against Great Britain and the United States of America] (*Történelmi Szemle,* 1/1965).

British foreign policy during the Second World War, including Anglo—Hungarian relations, is discussed on the basis of British Foreign Office papers by E. Llewellyn Woodward, *British Foreign Policy in the Second World War* (Vols. I—III, London, 1970). The most recent book treating these questions is that of Elisabeth Barker, *British Policy in South-East Europe in the Second World War* (London, 1976). A vast material was contributed to the history of Central Europe during the Second World War by an international conference held in Budapest at the end of September 1973, the lectures of which appeared in *Történelmi Szemle,* 3—4/1973 ("Kelet-Közép-Európa a második világháborúban" [East Central Europe in the Second World War]).

The birth and growth of the Hungarian anti-fascist resistance movement is related, with valuable contributions to the foreign policy of the Kállay Government, in the book by István Pintér, *Magyar kommunisták harca a Hitler-ellenes nemzeti egységért* [The Struggle of Hungarian Communists for Anti-Hitler National Unity] (Kossuth Publishers, Budapest, 1968). An earlier monograph on largely the same subject is the work by Mihály Korom, *A fasizmus bukása Magyarországon* [The Fall of Fascism in Hungary] (Kossuth Publishers, Budapest, 1961). It is a pity that this book containing valuable data is inspired by a misconception. The first elaborate and high-standard monograph on the antecedents and the story of German occupation is the book by György Ránki, *1944. március 19.* [March 19, 1944] (Kossuth Publishers, Budapest, 1968). Important features of the armistice negotiations of October 1944 are illuminated in the article with bibliography by C. A. Macartney "Ungarns Weg aus dem zweiten Weltkrieg" (*Vierteljahrshefte für Zeitgeschichte,* 1/1966). In it, the author publishes the telegrams sent from Moscow by the Hungarian armistice delegation and the replies to them. Further data are contributed to this subject by two essays of Péter Gosztonyi,

"A magyar-szovjet fegyverszüneti tárgyalások 1944 októberében" [Hungarian—Soviet Armistice Talks in October 1944] and "A Moszkvai Magyar Bizottság történetéből" [From the History of the Moscow Hungarian Committee] (*Új Látóhatár*, 5/1969, 5—6/1970).

The story of the Arrow-Cross take-over has been written by Ágnes Rozsnyói in her book *A Szálasi puccs* [The Szálasi Putsch] (Kossuth Publishers, Budapest, 1962). A comprehensive monograph on Arrow-Cross rule in Hungary is to be found in the work by Éva Teleki, *Nyilas uralom Magyarországon* [Arrow-Cross Rule in Hungary] (Kossuth Publishers, Budapest, 1974).

In writing the story of the formation of the Debrecen Provisional Government and the liberation of Hungary, I have made use of the book by Gyula Kállai, *A magyar függetlenségi mozgalom* [The Hungarian Independence Movement] (5th ed., Kossuth Publishers, Budapest, 1965) and of the monograph by Dezső Nemes, *Magyarország felszabadítása* [The Liberation of Hungary] (Kossuth Publishers, Budapest, 1965).

INDEX OF NAMES*

Aczél, Ede, Baron 307
Adonyi, Ferenc 248
Aggteleki, Béla, General 321
Alexander, Sir Harold, General 301, 302, 310
Alexander, King of Yugoslavia 177, 178
Allen, Denis William 245, 251, 268
Altenburg, Günther 154
Ambró, Ferenc 225, 240
Ambróczy, Gyula 318, 321, 322, 327
Andorka, Rudolf 221
Andrássy, Gyula, Count 63
Anfuso, Filippo 263
Antonescu, Ion 177, 196, 271, 286, 287, 290, 299
Antonescu, Mihai 223
Antonov, Alexei Innokhentievitch 315, 316, 322, 323, 326, 327, 332
Apor, Gábor, Baron 240, 255, 309
Apponyi, Albert, Count 35, 36, 44, 60

Ádám, Magda 342, 346, 347
Ábrahám, Dezső 23

Bach-Zelewski, Erich 321, 326
Badoglio, Pietro 372
Bajcsy-Zsilinszky, Endre 256, 259, 267, 331
Bajnóczy, József 291
Bakach-Bessenyey, György 178, 255, 261, 262, 264, 280, 281, 284, 302, 304, 306, 309, 311
Bakay, Szilárd, General 326
Baky, László 293, 298
Baldwin, Stanley 76
Balfour, Arthur, Lord 31
Balogh, István 334
Baranyai, Lipót 171, 220, 255, 256, 267
Barcza, György 157, 167, 171, 181, 182, 184, 216, 217, 228, 233, 240, 254–256, 272, 280, 281, 302
Barker, Elisabeth 265, 349
Barthou, Louis 116, 117

Bánffy, Dániel 260, 306, 307, 332
Bánffy, Miklós, Count 60–64, 66, 74, 223, 224
Bárdossy, László 131, 180, 183, 185, 189, 190, 200–208, 210, 263, 340
Beck, Josef 133
Beck, Ludwig, General 140
Beneš, Eduard 11, 57, 58, 61, 62, 64, 66, 101, 139, 217, 262, 274, 275
Benesovszky, Ilona 347
Benzler, Felix 294
Berend, T. Iván 343
Berinkey, Dénes 18
Bethlen, István, Count 23, 29, 30, 40, 46, 59, 60, 62, 64, 67, 71, 73, 74, 77–92, 95–102, 108, 112, 125–127, 135, 171, 181, 210, 216–218, 223, 224, 232, 233, 235, 241, 244, 245, 252, 257, 263, 271, 279, 282, 283, 291, 297, 298, 306, 339, 340, 345
Bédy-Schwimmer, Róza 16
Bibó, István 344
Blomberg, Werner von 110, 120
Borbándi, Gyula 349
Borghese, Livio, Duke 20
Böhm, Vilmos 26, 215, 217, 218, 220, 230, 231, 241, 247, 252, 253, 255, 268
Braham, Randolph 347
Briand, Aristide 129, 130
Brocchi, Iuginio 98, 101
Bruce, Hamilton 137
Bruce-Lockhardt, Sir Robert 209
Brüning, Heinrich 88

Cadogan, Sir Alexander 138, 229, 258, 276, 309
Campbell, Sir Ronald Hugh 273
Carol, King of Rumania 173
Cavendich Bentinck, Victor Frederick William 277
Chamberlain, Sir Joseph Austen 76, 85, 87

*The names in italics refer to items in the bibliography.

Chamberlain, Neville 131, 137, 141, 149, 157, 167, 170
Charles Louis, Archduke 278, 309
Chicherin, Georg Vasilyevich 74
Churchill, Randolph 282
Churchill, Sir Winston Spencer 170, 186, 200, 203, 249, 261, 264, 267, 274, 277, 300–302, 308–310, 322
Ciano, Galaezzo, Count 124, 125, 144, 146, 149, 163, 164, 166, 174, 175, 179, 346
Clemenceau, Georges 14, 15, 20, 22, 24, 26, 34
Clerk, Sir George Russel 31–34, 36, 41
Clodius, Carl 165, 173, 239
Codreanu, Cornelius Zelea 148
Coolidge, Archibald Cary 17, 18
Csatay, Lajos 260, 288, 305–306, 318, 326
Csatári, Dániel 349
Csáky, Imre, Count 46, 55
Csáky, István, Count 142, 144, 148–152, 160, 163, 164, 170, 173, 175, 178–180
Csonka, Emil 348
Curtius, Julius 88
Curzon, George, Lord 45, 55
Cvetković, Dragiša 182
Cziráky, József Count 63

Darányi, Kálmán 125, 127, 131, 132, 135, 136, 143, 144, 146–148, 191, 346
Daruváry, Géza 71, 74, 75
Dawes, Charles Gates 72
Deak, Francis 344
Dekhanazov, Vladimir G. 319
Dollfuss, Engelbert 110, 114, 116
Dulles, Alan 220, 254, 255, 281

Eckhardt, Tibor 126, 181, 214–216, 275, 278, 293, 302, 308
Eden, Antony 177, 181, 182, 186, 209, 229, 242, 248, 250, 252, 265, 266, 273, 282, 301, 310, 318, 319
Edward VIII 122
Eichmann, Adolf 295
Endre, László 295, 298
Erdmannsdorff, Otto von 143, 146, 163, 164, 176, 188, 204
d'Esperey, Franchet, General 14, 15, 22
Esterházy, Móric, Count 181, 256, 257, 263, 267, 306

Faraghó, Gábor, General 308, 314–323, 332
Farkas, Ferenc, General 321, 348
Feine, Gerhardt 327
Fenyő, Mario D. 348
Foch, Ferdinand, Marshal 18, 20, 26
Foertsch, G., General 287
Fouchet, Maurice 47, 48, 55
Franco, Francisco 124
Frey, András 216, 220, 221, 224, 227, 228, 237
Friedrich, István 27–31, 34, 35, 37
Funk, Walter 295

Garami, Ernő 31, 32
Gellért, Andor 215, 217, 228, 230, 240, 241, 255
George V 122
Ghyczy, Jenő 210, 220, 262, 263, 266, 273, 288, 291
Gibson, George 246, 247
Gigliucci, Vinci 149
Goering, Hermann 118, 120, 129, 132, 136, 141, 142, 286
Gorton, Reginald, General 35, 45
Gosztonyi, Péter 349
Gömbös, Gyula 23, 64, 79, 103–105, 107–116, 118, 119, 121, 124–128, 133, 135, 191, 193, 293, 346
Grandi, Dino, Count 77, 81
Gratz, Gusztáv 55, 58, 59, 63
Greiffenberg, Hans, General 305
Guderian, Heinz Wilhelm 303, 305, 323
Gusev, Fedor Tarasovich 312
Gyöngyösi, János 334

Hainisch, Michael 66
Halder, Franz von 183, 189, 347
Halifax, Viscount Lord 131, 132, 162, 168
Halmos, Károly 46
Halmosy, Dénes 342
Hanák, Péter 344
Harriman, Averell 318
Harrison, Leland 303
Hácha, Emil 154
Hennyey, Gusztáv, General 300, 306, 318, 324, 326, 327, 348
Herczeg, Ferenc 86
Heszlényi, József, General 325
Héjjas, Iván 62
Hillgruber, Andreas 347
Himer, Kurt 189, 190
Himmler, Heinrich 286, 187, 294

Hindenburg, Paul von 88
Hitler, Adolf 79, 105, 106, 108–111, 114, 116, 121, 122, 124, 127, 131, 132, 134, 136, 137–144, 146, 150, 151, 153, 154, 157, 160, 161, 165, 171–176, 178, 179, 180, 183, 184, 188, 189, 193, 195, 196 201–204, 206, 207, 209, 211, 218, 222, 225, 227, 236–240, 271, 278, 281, 283, 284, 286–288, 290–292, 294–296, 298, 303, 305, 307, 314, 321, 323, 324, 326–329, 332, 333, 346
Hlatky, Endre 324
Hlinka, Andrej 43
Hodža, Milan 123
Hohler, Thomas 35, 36, 45, 61
Honti, Ferenc 259
Horthy, Miklós 24, 29, 31–37, 40–45, 48, 52, 55–57, 59, 63, 72, 75, 77, 100, 115–116, 120, 122, 124, 132–134, 137, 140, 141, 143, 144, 148, 152, 154, 165, 171, 175, 177, 181–185, 188, 189, 190, 194, 196, 199–201, 206–208, 210, 214, 215, 217, 219, 222, 225, 229, 236–240, 252, 254–256, 257, 261–263, 266, 270–273, 278, 279, 281–283, 286–288, 290–299, 302–312, 314–329, 331–333, 340, 348
Horthy, Miklós Jr. 212, 272, 323, 326
Howie, Charles T., Colonel 311, 322
Hull, Cordell 303
Huszár, Károly 34, 35

Imrédy, Béla 135–137, 140, 141, 143, 145, 148, 149, 152, 158, 191, 218, 240, 253, 254, 263, 289, 292, 299, 346
Incze, Miklós 345

Jagow, Dietrich von 202, 212, 240, 287, 291
Jankovich, Arisztid 79
Jaross, Andor 295
Jánky, Béla, General 92
Jászi, Oszkár 16
Jodl, Alfred 189, 189, 201
Joseph of Habsburg, Archduke 28, 32, 35, 36
Juhász, Gyula, 341, 342, 347–349
Jungerth-Arnothy, Mihály 74, 75, 300
Jurcsek, Béla 300, 321

Kahr, Gustav Ritter 43
Kalinin, Jakov Ivanovich 166
Karsai, Elek 343, 345–347
Kádár, Gyula 258, 291

Kállai, Gyula 221, 350
Kállay, Miklós 206, 208, 210–229, 233–235, 237, 239–242, 245, 246, 249, 252–257, 259–264. 267–270, 272–276, 278, 280–284, 288, 291, 292, 295, 340, 348, 349
Kállay, Tibor 70
Kánya, Kálmán 74, 75, 88, 112, 114, 119, 120, 128–134, 136, 139, 140, 144, 148, 306
Károlyi, Gyula, Count 23, 98, 99–101, 103, 171, 210, 257, 306, 345
Károlyi, Mihály, Count 8, 14–17, 19, 215, 217
Keitel, Wilhelm, Field Marshal 143, 207, 208, 294
Kellog, Frank Billings 129, 130
Kemal, Mustafa 90
Kerekes, Lajos 342, 345–347
Keresztes-Fischer, Ferenc 169, 171, 185, 220, 239, 257, 260, 263, 266, 279, 291
Kerr, Sir Archibald Clark 259, 318
Kertész, D. Stephen 348
Kesselring, Albert, General 310
Khuen-Héderváry, Sándor 89, 149, 171
Kinzel, Eberhard, Colonel 183
Kis, Aladár 346
Kiss, János, General 330
Klebesberg, Kunó, Count 82
Knatchbull-Hugessen, Sir Hughe 258, 265, 265
Kollontai, Alexandra Mihailovna 282
Kolozsváry-Borcsa, Mihály 294
Kónya, Sándor 346
Korom, Mihály 349
Kossuth, Lajos 283
Kovács, Endre 346
Kovács, Imre 221
Kozma, Miklós 99, 127, 142, 145, 340
Kowalski, J. 216
Kövér, Gusztáv 229
Krestinsky, Nikolai 74–76
Kristóffy, József 166, 189
Krudy, Ádám 190
Kun, Béla 24, 26, 274
Kun, József 349
Kuznetsov, Nikolai Gerasimovitch 315, 316, 319, 332

Lackó, Miklós 346
Lagzi, István 349
Lakatos, Géza, General 298, 300, 303, 305, 306, 308, 318, 321–324, 326–329, 334

Laval, Pierre 119
Lázár, Károly, General 321, 322, 325, 328
Lehár, Antal, Baron 63
Lenin, Vladimir Ilyich 53
Lindley 55
Litván, György 344
Litvinov, Maxim Maximovitch 74, 136, 150
Lloyd George, David 17, 21, 25, 30
Ludendorff, Erich von, General 43, 79

Macartney, C. Aylmer 209, 276, 343, 349
MacDonald, James Ramsay 76
Maček, Vladimir 183
Mackensen, Hans Georg von 116, 129
MacMillan, Harold 312
Makarov, Colonel 307, 308, 316, 317
Malcomes, Béla, Baron 134
Malinovsky, Rodin Yakovlevitch, Marshal 331, 332
Maniu, Iuliu 223, 224, 275
Mary of Savoy, Duchess 99
Masaryk, Thomas G. 11
Masirevich, Szilárd 120
Mastny, Vojtech 347
Matuska, Péter 218
Márkus, László 345
Mecsér, András 117, 134
Mekhlis, L. Z. 332
Menemencioglu, Numan Rifaat 225, 248
Mészáros, Gyula 221, 237
Mihajlović, Draža 223, 227, 235, 242
Mikes, János, Count Bishop 59
Miklós, Béla, General 320, 325, 332, 333
Millerand, Alexandre 46–48, 56, 62
Milotay, István 192
Molotov, Vyacheslav Mikhailovitch 189, 247, 249, 251, 252, 259, 264, 274, 314, 316–319
Montgomery, John Flournoy 348
Mussolini, Benito 69, 81–88, 90–92, 95, 97, 99, 101, 104, 111–114, 116–123, 142, 144, 160–162, 170, 173, 177, 211, 226, 227, 235, 236, 254–256, 266, 272, 278, 321
Müller, Hermann 88

Nagy, Jenő, Colonel 330
Nagy, Zsuzsa 344
Nagyatády Szabó, István 29
Nagybaczoni Nagy, Vilmos 257
Namier, Professor 268
Nádas, Lajos 322, 326

Náday, István, General 257, 306, 311, 312, 314, 316, 319
Nádosy, Imre 79
Nedić, Milan 223
Nemes, Albert, Count 82
Nemes, Dezső 343, 345, 350
Nemes, József 316, 318, 319, 321
Neurath, Konstantin Freiherr von 110, 132
Ninčić, Momčilo 77, 78, 81
Norton, Clifford John 233

O'Malley, Sir Owen St. Clair 138, 181, 185,
Orlando, Vittorio Emanuele 21
Ormos, Mária 345, 346
Osborne, D'Arcy 228
Osuský, Stefan 66
Otto of Habsburg, Archduke 99, 215, 216, 228, 275, 278–280, 288, 293, 302, 308, 309, 311, 348

Paléologue, Maurice 46, 56
Pamlényi, Ervin 341, 344
Papen, Franz von 110
Parmour, Lord 78
Parrot, Cecil 252
Pastor, Peter 344
Paulus, Friedrich von, General 183
Pavelić, Ante 288
Páloczi-Horváth, György 228, 233, 348
Peidl, Gyula 26, 27
Pelényi, János 171, 172, 293, 349
Pell, Helbert C. 203, 206
Perényi, Zsigmond, Baron 306
Peyer, Károly 40, 215, 221
Piłsudski, Josef 89, 118
Pintér, István 349
Pius XII 225–228
Poincaré, Raymond 14
Prónay, Pál 62, 344
Pushkas, Andrei N. 348

Radvánszky, Albert, Baron 220, 228, 254, 255
Rahn, Rudolf 321, 323, 324, 326, 329
Rakovszky, István 63
Rakovszky, Iván 327
Randell, A. Walter George 268
Rassay, Károly 218
Ránki, György 340, 341, 343, 344, 346, 348
Rátz, Jenő, General 140, 289

Reményi-Schneller, Lajos 300, 321
Ribbentrop, Joachim von 140, 144, 147–151, 163, 164, 174, 175, 179, 180, 188, 202, 206–208, 211, 236–240, 287, 288, 290, 294, 295, 297, 305, 326
Roberts, Frank Kenyon 186, 229, 252, 253, 265, 268, 276, 282
Romanelli, Guido 27
Roosevelt, Franklin Delano 200, 261, 264, 265, 274, 277–280, 288, 293, 297, 300, 301, 302, 308, 309, 310
Rosenberg, Alfred 128, 129
Rozsnyói, Ágnes 350
Rothermere, Lord 85, 86
Rothschild, Lionel N. 96, 97, 100
Röder, Vilmos, General 306

Sakmyster, T. L. 346
Saldanha, Dom Jose 278
Saly, Dezső 347
Sargent, Sir Orme 138, 169, 170, 231
Schmidt, Paul 237, 238
Schmidt, Paul Karl 294
Schober, Johann 62, 92
Schrecker, Károly 233, 234, 241, 242, 244
Schulze, Arthur 79
Schuschnigg, Kurt 118, 123, 128
Semonov, Vladimir Semionovich 282
Serédi, Justinian, Primat 204, 226, 279
Sforza, Carlo, Count 56
Siegler, Géza 78
Sigray, Antal, Count 59, 221
Sikorski, Władisław, General 226, 227, 248
Simonffy-Tóth, Ernő 330, 333
Simonyi-Semadám, Sándor 46
Simović, Dušan 223, 227

Sipos, Péter 346
Six, Karl 294
Skorzeny, Otto 321, 328
Smuts, Jan C., General 21, 22
Sónyi, Hugó, General 306
Sós, Katalin 345
Speer, Albert 295
Stalin, Joseph 262, 274, 310, 314, 315, 322, 332, 347
Steidle, Richard 92
Steinhardt, Laurence A. 222
Sterndale Benett, John Cecil 258, 265, 266
Stirbey, Prince of Rumania 299

Stojadinović, Milan 130
Strang, Sir William 312
Stresemann, Gustav 72, 87, 89

Szabó, Ágnes 344
Szabó, László 339
Szakasits, Árpád 221, 320
Szálasi, Ferenc 175, 218, 325–329, 340
Szegedy-Maszák, Aladár 216, 220, 232, 241, 245, 255
Szent-Györgyi, Albert 221–223, 228–232, 235, 237, 252, 253
Szent-Iványi, Domonkos 314, 316, 317, 332, 339
Szentmiklóssy, Andor 236, 237
Szentmiklóssy, István, General 326
Szinai, Miklós 347
Szirmai, Dezső 347
Szombathelyi, Ferenc 200, 201, 208, 212, 218, 219, 223, 237, 262, 264, 281, 288, 290, 291
Sztójay, Döme 121, 129, 136, 141, 142, 147, 148, 154, 163, 165, 168, 175, 176, 180, 202, 203, 205, 210, 290, 292–300
Szücs, László 347

Tarcsay, Vilmos, Captain 330
Tardieu, André 101
Taylor, Alonso 17, 18
Teleki, Béla, Count 305, 306
Teleki, Éva 350
Teleki, Géza, Count 314, 319
Teleki, Pál, Count 23, 24, 29, 46, 47, 55, 57–59, 61, 79, 150, 152–155, 157–164, 167–173, 175, 177, 179–182, 184–186, 193, 194, 212, 339, 349
Templerly, H. W. V. 343
Tevfik, Rüstü 90
Threlfall, H. M., Major 281
Tildy, Zoltán 218, 320
Tilkovszky, Loránd 341, 348
Tiso, Stefan 143, 153
Tito, Josip Broz 223, 235, 282
Titulescu, Nikolae 123
Tolnay, Kornél 46
Toretta, Pietro Paulo Tomasi 62, 63
Toussaint, Rudolf 199
Troubridge, Sir Ernest, Admiral 29, 30
Tyler, Royall 137, 171, 216, 220, 255, 261, 262, 264, 281, 284

Újszászy, István, General 234, 235
Újváry, Dezső 258, 270, 273, 276, 344
Ullein-Reviczky, Antal 210, 215, 216, 221, 222, 231, 273, 280, 282, 293, 340
Utassy, Lóránd 320, 322

Vadász, Sándor 344
Vansittart, Sir Robert 122
Varga, Béla 221
Vass, József 59
Vattay, Antal, General 306, 318, 322, 327, 328
Vály, Ferenc 221
Vázsonyi, János 221
Veesenmayer, Edmund 236, 285–289, 291, 294, 295, 298–300, 305, 321, 323–326, 328, 329
Velics, László 255
Veress, Lajos, General 320, 328, 332, 333
Veress, László 221, 228, 257–259, 264–266, 269, 272, 273, 275, 276, 281, 282
Vix, Fernand 16, 17, 19–21
Vladár, Gábor 321
Voloshin, Augustin 154

Vörnle, János 293
Vörös, János 306, 307, 318, 320, 322, 323, 325–327, 330, 333, 334
Vyshinsky, Andrei 303

Walkó, Lajos 76, 78, 81, 84, 86, 89, 90, 101, 102
Weizsäcker, Ernst 134
Werkmeister, Karl 127
Werth, Henrik 169, 183, 188, 189, 199, 200
Wilson, Henry Maitland, Field Marshal 311, 313, 314
Wilson, Woodrow 14, 15, 17, 22, 24, 25, 51, 53
Windischgraetz, Lajos, Prince 79
Wodianer, Andor 216, 293, 309
Woermann, Ernst 163
Woodward, Sir Llewellyn 349

Young, Owen 94

Zalenski, August 89
Zichy, Vladimir, Count 307, 308
Zita, ex-Queen of Hungary 64, 278, 309
Zsilinszky, Antal 214, 215